HOUSE OF SNOW

An Anthology of the Greatest Writing
About Nepal

HOUSE OF SNOW

An Anthology of the Greatest Writing
About Nepal

FOREWORD *by*

SIR RANULPH FIENNES

INTRODUCTION *by*

ED DOUGLAS

First published in the UK in 2016 by Head of Zeus Ltd

9 7 5 3 2 4 6 8

A CIP catalogue record for this book is available from the British Library.

ISBN (HB): 9781784974589
ISBN (E): 9781784974572

Typeset by Adrian McLaughlin

Printed and bound by CPI Group (UK) Ltd,
Croydon, CR0 4YY

Head of Zeus Ltd
Clerkenwell House
45–47, Clerkenwell Green
London EC1R 0HT

WWW.HEADOFZEUS.COM

CONTENTS

FOREWORD

Sir Ranulph Fiennes

House of Snow is the literal translation of the Sanskrit word "himalaya"; a combination of the word "hima" meaning snow and the word "alaya", meaning "dwelling" or "abode". Home to nine of the world's highest peaks including Mount Everest, the Himalaya is a vast mountain range that spans India, Nepal, China (Tibet) and Pakistan.

The lofty heights of these dramatic landscapes were raised as a result of a collision of the Indian tectonic plate with the Eurasian plate. These plates are constantly moving, so it is an area of outstanding beauty, but it is also very geologically vulnerable.

My expeditions have taken me to many such stunning vistas, formed by forces of the natural world. The Earth's surface is constantly changing as a result of phenomena such as earthquakes and volcanoes.

Nepal is particularly vulnerable to such threats as is situated completely within the two plates' collision zone. Geophysicists and other experts had warned for decades that the country should expect a deadly earthquake, particularly because of its geology, urbanization, and architecture, and in 2015, it happened.

The April 2015 earthquake in Nepal killed over 8,000 people and injured more than twice as many. The epicentre was east of the district of Lamjung in the Gandaki region, however, the majority of the casualties occurred in the nearby capital Kathmandu.

The aftershocks continued for days afterwards, causing further devastation. Villages were flattened and hundreds of thousands were made homeless, UNESCO world heritage sites and centuries-old buildings were destroyed. It was the worst natural disaster to strike Nepal since the earthquake in Bihar in 1934.

Despite its geological vulnerability, Nepal is a country with a rich culture and a fascinating history. There is far more to this nation than its mountains, though this is where the focus of outside onlookers often lies.

Neolithic tools found in the Kathmandu Valley indicate the area has been inhabited for at least eleven thousand years. It has seen great dynasties rise and fall and witnessed wars and empires. It is the birthplace of the Buddha. And in recent years, the location of a royal massacre, lengthy civil war and establishment of democracy. Its diverse terrain ranges from the loftiest of peaks to hills, plains and lowlands.

Home to those accurately famed for being some of the strongest people on Earth, the instinct and capacity for survival and evolution is undeniably powerful. In this volume you will find not only the voices of explorers and mountaineers, but of authors from the length and breadth of this fascinating nation that have been chosen to represent it as fully as possible.

INTRODUCTION

How do we Discover New Countries?

Ed Douglas

How do we discover new countries? In 1950, after two centuries when the kingdom of Nepal kept tight rein on who could and mostly could not cross its border, the doors opened a crack and the world rushed in. Geographers, explorers, aid workers, anthropologists, filmmakers, mountaineers, hippies and art dealers rummaged through the valleys and up the mountainsides as though some vast emporium of the exotic had just announced a fire sale. Toni Hagen was among them, arriving 1950 as part of a sustained Swiss development aid project; he walked the length of the country, filming the people he met and wrestling Nepal's complex geography into some kind of order. A blank on the map was rapidly filled in.

The opportunity to get to grips with the greatest mountains on earth was equally irresistible. In the following decade all the mountains of Nepal over eight thousand metres were climbed. In the same year as Toni Hagen arrived, the wry and self-deprecating Bill Tilman, whose writing features in this book, joined a team of Americans to become the first Westerners to visit Khumbu and the southern base of Everest. Within three years the mountain was climbed. Nepal became one of the most desirable destinations for the world's adventurers, a country apparently lost in time, full of arcane spiritual wisdom, near-continuous religious festivals and a people who seemed endlessly hospitable and wholly lacking, it seemed, the cynicism and materialism of the modern world. It was a similar impulse that sent me to Nepal for the first time more than twenty years ago, following on the coat-trains of earlier generations of climbers and explorers.

That rush of discovery was invigorating and transformative but it didn't come close to unravelling the dense and complex tapestry of Nepali culture and society – or finding out where decades of political oppression and cultural stagnation had left ordinary people. For this kind of work, poets make better explorers. In 1959, the Bombay-born poet Dom Moraes arrived in Kathmandu, still only twenty but already a published poet and the winner of the Hawthornden Prize. He later wrote a book about it, *Gone Away*. Moraes, drunk half the time and excited by the louche sensuality of the recently deposed Ranas, was not complimentary of the poetry he heard, but on his last day in Kathmandu he took the chance to sit with Nepal's great poet Lakshmi Prasad Devkota, who was dying of cancer, aged only forty-nine, near his own funeral pyre at the temple of Pashupatinath. I came across Moraes' book by chance and left it with a desire to read Devkota and much more – and so a fascination with Nepali literature began. Overshadowed by its colossal neighbours, Nepal's voice often struggles to be heard, but it is a voice that is distinct, often playful, long-suffering, proud, resigned but undoubtedly of its own making.

Devkota was a great liberalising force in Nepali literature, which had previously cleaved between the formal, highly metrical Sanskritised poetry of the elite and that of the oral, folk tradition. Despite his disdain for the colonialising weight of the British Raj, Devkoṭā was an admirer of English Romantic poetry, translating Wordsworth and Coleridge into Nepali and drawing on their guiding spirit for his most popular poem, *Muna Madan*, written not in an arcane, highly stylised form, but in the *jhaure* metre and more colloquial lexicon of the Nepali folk tradition. It is a story of separation and loss, of true love and human worth beyond caste or ethnicity, and consequently popular – and still is – with a wider public despite Nepal's woeful literacy rate in the 1930s. For myself, his later work, *Pagal*, about his experience of mental illness, is even better and certainly more experimental and challenging.

My discovery of Moraes led to Devkota, Devkota to the work of the English academic Michael Hutt and his book *Modern Literary Nepali*, which included many of the best Nepali writers from the late twentieth century, particularly Gopal Prasad Rimal and Bhupi Sherchan. The sardonic sense of fun in Sherchan's work, blended with the tragic, seems to me essentially Nepali. 'This is a land of uproar and rumour / Where

deaf men who must wear hearing-aids / Are judges at musical contests,'
he wrote in the 1960s, 'and those whose souls are full of stones / are
connoisseurs of poetry.' It's easy to see why, given Nepal's protracted
political and social agonies, his poetry still resonates today.

Modern readers are doubly blessed, with access not just to translations of famous Nepali works but also to new generations of Nepalis
writing in English. Manjushree Thapa's novel *The Tutor of History* is a
moving exploration of thwarted lives and cynical exploitation of democratic ideals. She is also a formidable journalist and traveller and her
non-fiction works are also an essential part of modern literary Nepal.
In the last couple of years I've been introduced to new Nepali writers,
particularly Rabi Thapa and Prawin Adhikari, who have published
vital and revealing collections of short stories. They capture seismic
social upheavals that were only reinforced by the actual seismic upheavals that captured headlines around the world in April 2015.

It is rewarding also to know that while the literature of exploration
and adventure that drew me to Nepal may not have penetrated deeply
into the fabric of Nepali culture, the awareness and appreciation of
Nepal's complexity and richness among foreign writers is also there,
particularly Thomas Bell's exploration of his adopted city *Kathmandu*.
I haven't read anything by an outsider that captures this most exceptional of cities better.

Ultimately, ironically, and I think Bhupi Sherchan would appreciate the
joke, discovering another country, one that starts off seeming foreign and
exotic to a European sensibility but ends up, in the Nepali phrase, as *man-
pareko jhutta* – a favourite pair of shoes, reveals only how little we know
of our own country, or else how unfamiliar it can become when we shift
perspective a little and look afresh. Dom Moraes, like Devkota, died prematurely, having lost his way after an electrifying start, but finding it again,
to some extent, towards the end. One of his later projects was a biography
of the Elizabethan traveller Thomas Caryate, who walked to India and
whose first-hand knowledge of Indian customs had a deep impact in his
native England. Caryate lived in the Somerset village of Odcombe, and it
was there that Moraes requested that some of the soil from his grave be
sent, the East mulching the west. In the churchyard, carved on a block of
Rajasthani stone, is a small memorial – the end of all our exploring.

NEPAL HIMALAYA

H.W. Tilman

Major Harold William "Bill" Tilman (1898–1977) was an English mountaineer and explorer, renowned for his Himalayan climbs and sailing voyages. He was involved in two of the early Everest expeditions in the 1930s.

THE LANGTANG

The upper Langtang is a fine, open valley, rich in flowers and grass, and flanked by great mountains. It is a grazier's paradise. At 11,000 ft. one might expect to find a few rough shelters occupied only in the summer, but at Langtang there is a settlement of some thirty families rich in cows, yaks and sheep. These are, besides, like young Osric, spacious in the possession of dirt; for their fields are no mere pocket-handkerchief terraces clinging to the hillside but flat stone-walled fields of an acre or more growing wheat, buckwheat, potatoes, turnips, and a tall, strong-growing beardless barley called "kuru".

The grazing extends from the valley bottom to the slopes above and far up the moraines and ablation valleys of both the main and the tributary glaciers; and dotted about are rich alps with stone shelters, called "kharka", where the herdsmen live and make the butter. Considerable quantities of this are exported to Tibet. In the Langtang gompa I saw 25 man-loads of butter sewn up in skins which a lama had bought for his monastery at Kyerong, and which, he told me, represented a year's supply. Besides being drunk in innumerable cups of tea, butter plays an important part in religious ceremony. In well-run monasteries butter lamps burn continually before the images and at certain festivals pounds of butter are moulded into elaborate decorations for the altars. I noticed the Langtang lama placing a dab of it on people's heads as a blessing, while a little is always placed on the edge of the cup or plate offered to a guest.

The valley has religious traditions. Like many out-of-the-way places it was originally the home of the gods, those happy beings, to whom, with their ready means of locomotion, remoteness was of little account. But at a more recent date the beauties of the valley were revealed to mortals in a way reminiscent of that other story – "Saul he went to look for donkeys, and, by God, he found a kingdom". In this case the missing animal was, of course, a yak which its owner, a very holy man, tracked up the Langtang. The spoor was not difficult to follow, for at the Syabrubensi and at Syarpagaon the beast left on a rock the imprint of a foot which is visible to this day. The lama caught his yak at a place called Langsisa, seven or eight miles above Langtang village where, having fulfilled its appointed task, it promptly died. The lama, with less regard for sentiment than for money's worth unfeelingly skinned it and spread the skin on a rock to dry; but the yak had the last laugh; for the skin stuck and remains there to this day, as a big reddish coloured rock at Langsisa plainly testifies.

Near Langsisa there are two other rocks of greater note. A couple of miles up a valley to the east, standing some hundreds of feet above the glacier, are two big rock gendarmes which are said to represent two Buddhist saints, Shakya Muni and Guru Rumbruche. Tibetan lamas come as far as Langsisa to worship them. Since the etymology of many English placenames is still, as it were, anybody's guess, I have little hesitation in offering the following derivations. "Lang" is Tibetan for cow or yak, "tang", or more correctly "dhang", means to follow. Langsisa means the place where the yak died.

A valley with such traditions is, of course, a sanctuary; within it no animal may be slaughtered. According to the lieutenant, the observance of this ban on slaughter, which dated back for hundreds of years, had been neglected and the present headman, Nima Lama, took it upon himself to visit Katmandu to have the matter put right. The original decree, having been looked up and verified, was formally confirmed, and the fine for any breach of the rule was fixed at Rs. 100. Our wish to shoot small birds for specimens had to be met by the issue of a special licence; but apart from two sheep thoughtfully slaughtered for us by a bear of non-Buddhist tendencies, we had no meat while in the valley.

The people of Langtang are very like Tibetans, engagingly cheery, tough and dirty; but they have sufficient regard for appearances to wash their faces occasionally and were scrupulous to remove those lice which strayed to the *outside* of their garments. They themselves say their ancestry was a mixture of Tibetans from around Kyerong and Tamangs from Helmu – the district to the south of the valley. They now call themselves Lama-Tamang. (It should be noted that "lama" is the name for a class of Gurungs, one of the Nepal tribes from which many of the so-called Gurkhas are drawn.) They conversed very readily with our Sherpas in what was presumably some sort of Tibetan dialect. According to Tensing their speech is like that of the people of Lachen in north Sikkim.

We had arrived on 5 June, and since the monsoon might be expected to break at any time we immediately began the survey of the middle valley so that we could have fixed points to work from when we reached the frontier ridge at the head of the valley. The triangulated peak of Langtang Lirung, only two miles to the north, could not be seen from the village, and a tiny triangle of white, sometimes visible over the rock wall behind our camp, might or might not have been the tip of a 21,500 ft. peak to the west of it. Accordingly we started next day with six Langtang men carrying three weeks' food, leaving behind Polunin and the escort. With him we also left a Sherpa, a lad called Phutarkay who had been with me on Rakaposhi two years before, who as well as looking after his master had already learnt to press and handle specimens. On the march few strange plants escaped his keen eyes.

Tensing, who combined the roles of sirdar and cook, was widely travelled and an experienced mountaineer whom I had last met on Everest in 1938 when he carried a load to Camp VI. Having spent the war years with an officer of the Chitral Scouts he had further enlarged his mountaineering and ski-ing experience. Since then he had been to Lhasa with an Italian Tibetan scholar, for whom he had purchased whole libraries – he told me they had brought away forty maunds of books. Tensing, who gets on with everyone and handles the local people well, has a charming smile, great steadiness on a mountain, and a deft hand for omlettes which he turns out nicely sloppy but firm. With paragons such as this one can afford to be blind to minor faults.

Neither of the others, Da Namgyal and Angtharkay, had had any experience, but the former soon learnt what was expected of him either in camp or on a mountain. Angtharkay, who is not to be confused with his wellknown namesake, who is probably the best Sherpa porter ever known, was a little old for the job and a little "dumb". In fact I suspected that he had not long come down from his tree. He came to us with a pigtail which I was sorry to see him remove, but it had to make way for the heavy Balaclava helmet which he wore even in the hottest valleys. I have a liking for men with pigtails because the first three Sherpas with whom I ever travelled all wore their hair long and were all first-rate men. Nowadays, among the Sherpas, long hair and pigtails are outmoded, but not long ago they indicated a good type of unsophisticated man who had not been spoilt by long residence outside Nepal. Angtharkay, unsophisticated enough for anyone, unfortunately lacked mother-wit. He had the air of an earnest buffoon which neither the striped heliotrope pyjama trousers he wore one day, nor the long woollen pants he affected the next, did anything to diminish.

Half a mile above Langtang was another hamlet with large fields of wheat and kuru, still very green, a big chorten, and the longest mani wall I have ever seen – nearly three hundred yards of it. These walls or "mendongs", which are seven or eight feet high, must be passed on the left. On each side are flat stones with carved Buddhas or religious texts for the benefit of passers-by on either hand; and the equally well-worn paths on both sides of the wall show that the rule is observed. In the main Trisuli valley Buddhism, or at any rate the observance of this particular tenet, seemed to be weakening, for one of the paths round each mani wall tended to fall into disuse. In Timure village, only a day's march from the Tibetan border, some abandoned scoffer had had the hardihood to carry his miserable maize field right up to a mendong, thus abolishing the path on one side.

Having crossed a stream issuing from the snout of the Lirung glacier we camped a short four miles up from Langtang village. The grass flat, white with anemones, where we camped, lay tucked under the juniper-covered moraine of the glacier. Hard by were the gompa of Kyangjin Ghyang, some stone huts and turnip fields, and beyond a wide meadow stretched for a mile or more up the north side of the valley. The Lirung peak, from which the glacier came, and several others, overlooked it, but across the river the south containing wall was comparatively low. It can be crossed by the Gangja La (19,000 ft.) over which lies a direct route to the Helmu district and thence to Katmandu. On that side, the north-facing slope, birch trees and rhododendrons maintained a gallant struggle against the height, which, by altimeter, was 13,500 ft.

Naturally, for two of us the Lirung peak had a powerful appeal. At Katmandu we had admired its graceful lines with longing eyes. It had looked eminently climbable then, as indeed most mountains do when looked at from far off, but now we were forced to admit that its south side, defended by a great cirque, was quite impregnable. However, at the moment, climbing took second place. Neither of us was ready for serious work. Indeed, as the result of some months spent in Australia, Lloyd had become a little gross, a fault which an insufficiently arduous approach march had done nothing to rectify. Moreover, in our cautious eyes, not one of the few Langtang peaks we had seen invited imme-diate assault, and in new country the urge to explore is hardly to be withstood. Around a corner of the valley a few miles up, the whole Langtang glacier system waited to be unravelled, and at its head lay the untrodden frontier ridge and the unknown country beyond. During the monsoon, we hoped, we might still climb, but the survey work must be done now or never. Our first three weeks, which were moderately fine, proved to be the only fine weeks we were to have.

We spent nearly a week at this gompa camp. Lloyd wished to occupy stations on both sides of the valley before moving up, while I had made the exciting discovery of a way on to what we took to be the frontier ridge to the north. Having walked up the left moraine of the Lirung gla-cier, Tensing and I turned right-handed up steep grass and gravel slopes until we came to a sort of glacier shelf lying along the foot of the ridge upon which Lirung and its neighbouring 22,000 ft. peak stood. We judged the lowest point to be under 20,000 ft. A little tarn at the foot of the ice offered a convenient and tempting camp site at about 17,000 ft. Going back we made a wide detour over a bleak upland valley of more gravel than grass, where we found a scented cream and mauve primula (*P. macrophylla*) already in flower though old snow still lay about. On the way we took in a great rounded bump of over 17,000 ft., its grass summit incongruously crowded with long bamboo poles and tattered prayer flags.

On the assumption that this ridge would prove to be the frontier ridge upon which we should have a most valuable station, we stocked the tarn camp and occupied it, intending to spend a full week. Early next morning, having gained the glacier shelf, we plodded eastwards on good hard snow to a point below the most accessible part of the ridge. Warned by gathering clouds, Lloyd decided to get busy while he could, so at about 19,000 ft. he put up the machine, as he called the theodolite, and began taking rounds of angles and photographing the fine confusion of peaks and valleys spreading eastward. Meanwhile Tensing and I pushed on up good snow to the ridge and traversed along it to a small summit. Having expected to see much from here, we were proportionately cast down at seeing so little. Another ridge, the frontier and the watershed, intervened to the north, and between the two lay a high glacier bay from which the ice curled over like a breaking wave before falling abruptly to some hidden arm of the Langtang glacier below. To the north-east, behind a tangle of peaks, rose a lump of a mountain with a long, flattish summit and a western face of more rock than snow. We thought it neither high nor distant enough to be Gosainthan which, according to the map, was over twelve miles away. It so happened that we never saw this mountain again, but Lloyd's survey data show that it was, in fact, Gosainthan.

Under a threatening sky we trudged back to camp through snow which was already soft and wet. A night of rain fulfilled the threat of morning and when we turned out at 4 a.m. it was still falling. Since the frontier ridge could not be reached there was no point in staying, but before going down we wanted to put the theodolite on the small summit reached the day before. What with the drizzle and the waterlogged snow Lloyd soon turned back, leaving Tensing and me to struggle obstinately and rather aimlessly towards a notch in the ridge. Although the snow was too wet for them, a pair of snowshoes I had with me seemed to make for easier progress. Later I wore them a lot and tried to convince myself that those behind, who had no such aids, benefited from the huge steps I made. Having reached the rocks below the notch and found them very loose, we contented ourselves with collecting a few inexpensive rock presents for Scott and a couple of hibernating moths for myself. As a lepidopterous insect a moth has something in common with beetles, and I thought that anything that contrived to live at 19,000 ft. deserved an honorable place in any insect museum.

On returning from this damp excursion I went on to Langtang to check the food, where I was astonished by the swift growth resulting from the recent rain – by the many new flowers, the masses of white erica which had suddenly blossomed, and the dwarf rhododendron whose resinous fragrance filled the air. Kyangjin, too, had suddenly come to life. The long bamboo poles of the gompa and the roofs of the now occupied stone huts carried small flags of red and yellow, and the long, grass flat was thick with yaks and horses. Kyangjin is the first stage on the summer grazing itinerary which the yaks graze down before moving successively higher with the advance of summer, the sheep following humbly in their wake eating what is left. The horses roamed at will. They, we were told, were the property of the Government – the reason, perhaps, for their moderate condition.

Our friend Nima Lama had come up, bringing with him an adequate supply of beer, the better to fumigate the gompa and to confront and exorcise any evilly disposed spirits which might have occupied it during the winter months. Tensing had a private chat with Nima Lama, obtaining from him some confidential information which he unhesitatingly passed on to me. Having warned him on no account to let the sahibs know of it, Nima had told him that there was a pass into Tibet at the head of the valley. Neither he nor any living man had seen it, much less used it, for it had been closed at the time of the second Nepal–Tibet war (1854) – whether by man's edict or by some natural cataclysm was not made clear. It is difficult to imagine any shorter or easier way to Tibet than that by the Trisuli valley, but the oldest inhabitant well remembered people coming by the pass, bringing their yaks with them. Now I admire the yak, but his reputation for crossing passes, like that of Himalayan climbers, is apt to be enhanced by time and distance. Still, some weight must be accorded to tradition, and we resumed our journey to the valley head much encouraged by the story of this ancient pass.

We started with a scratch team, two men, three women and a boy, on a fine sunny day. The Langtang has not only the austere beauty of ice mountains accentuated by the friendly smile of flowery meadows alive with cattle – but it has the charm of reticence and the witchery of the unexpected – a quality which Mr Milestone considered more desirable in a garden landscape than the beautiful or the picturesque. A gentle but continuous bend tantalizes its admirers, draws them on impatiently to see beyond the next corner, maintaining for them the thrill of discovery almost to the end. So far we had seen no more than two miles up the valley where the bend began, a place marked by a magnificent peak which we soon acknowledged to be the loveliest gem of the valley. On account of the snow fluting traced like the ribs of a fan upon its western face we called it the Fluted Peak. It is a few feet under 21,000 ft., but it stands alone, smiling down upon the valley with a face of glistening purity framed between clean-cut snow ridges of slender symmetry.

As we drew past, fresh vistas of higher but less graceful mountains opened before us. But close at hand, stretching across the floor of the valley – still wide and green – lay a vast moraine, some 500 ft. high, the piled debris of a great glacier descending from the west. The narrowest of gorges, cut by the river draining the main Langtang glacier beyond, alone separated the toe of the moraine from the eastern wall of the valley. Beyond this barrier lay Langsisa, which we should easily have reached the first day. In our haste to see round corners we outran the porters, missed the path which went by the gorge, and charged straight at the giant moraine. While we were scurrying about on top of this eyesore looking vainly for water and a camp site, the porters sat calmly below in a pleasant meadow where presently we were obliged to join them.

Next day Lloyd explored this west glacier, while Tensing and I went to Langsisa and straight on up the main valley. Neither of us got anywhere near the heads of our respective glaciers, both of which seemed to terminate without undue abruptness at the frontier ridge. On returning I found the lieutenant had brought up our Sherpa corn merchant, with whom we did some hard bargaining. In the end I advanced Rs. 100, receiving as security his necklace of large corals. I would not have given 6d. for it, but Tensing assured me it was worth Rs. 200. Anyhow the owner evidently set considerable store by it and not very much on my honesty. He wanted to have it sealed up so that there could be no juggling with the corals.

Three of us, three Sherpas, and two Langtang men, carrying 400 lb. (twelve days' supplies), now moved up the main valley. In an hour we reached Langsisa, a rich meadow on the river bank where there is a stone shelter. Hard by are three inscribed stones set in the ground whence pilgrims make their obeisance to the two saints. The ice of the big east glacier flows down almost to the river on the opposite side, and a couple of miles up the two rock gendarmes or saints stand out prominently. To these our Langtang men at once paid their respects by going down on their knees, along with two Tibetan lamas who had come for the same purpose. Beyond Langsisa the track grew rougher and steeper. We walked for five hours up the right bank, sometimes on moraine and sometimes in the ablation valley below, the tumbled stone and ice of the main Langtang glacier lying on our right. Polunin came part of the way to collect a very lovely primula we had noticed the previous day – a pale blue, scented, bell-shaped flower, five, seven or even nine on one stem. It was *P. Wollastonii* which Wollaston had first found when, as members of the Everest reconnaissance party of 1921, he and Morshead were travelling in the vicinity of Nyenam. This village lies over the Tibet border about twenty miles east of where we were.

On leaving this camp we were forced on to the glacier up which, in a sort of trough, we made a short but very rough march to a little tarn tucked away behind the moraine of a side glacier. We were still not within striking distance of the frontier ridge but the two local men would go no farther. Up to and a little beyond the last camp we had followed a track which might well be accounted for as a grazing track; but down in the glacier trough I found traces of what might have been its continuation, indicated by stones placed on top of boulders. As there was no grass farther on, this ancient track, if track it was, may have led to a pass. The existence of a pass at the head of the Langtang is thus supported by a track as well as tradition – the keys, or rather the only clues we have, to another Himalayan enigma, the Abominable Snowman.

For the next day we had a full programme. While the Sherpas moved the camp to the head of the glacier, Lloyd and I, carrying the machine, attempted to reach the most westerly of three cols. This precision instrument which, by the way, used plates and had no shutter, made an awkward load. As it was essential to beat the clouds, which usually came over between 9 and 10 a.m., by seven o'clock we had covered the remaining mile or so of level glacier and had begun to climb. From an upper snow shelf which we reached at 10 o'clock, the low rock ridge marking the col looked close enough. But it was noon before I got there, while Lloyd, who was still carrying too much weight, sank by the way. Excited though I was, my plodding steps could not be hurried, and when at last I looked over the top to the glacier below, its surface seemed to wrinkle in a derisive smile. The col was not on the frontier ridge and the glacier below was none other than the west Langtang whose high, ugly snout we had rounded on the way to Langsisa. The altimeter registered 20,700 ft., a height which I could easily credit. Unhappily that was the instrument's last coherent message. A knock which it got on the way back, besides shattering the glass, must have affected it internally. Never again did it speak a true word. Instead, with little or no provocation, it would often shoot to heights undreamt of in our philosophy, heights which we could only have attained by means of a balloon.

This was not the only misfortune. When, after a long and fruitless day, we reached the appointed camp – a shelf above the glacier – there were no tents. To save themselves trouble the Sherpas had camped on the glacier, thereby compelling us to lie on devilish knobbly stones with ice underneath instead of on warm, soft gravel. Scott's altimeter, which had not yet met the inevitable fate of all such instruments, made our height 18,000 ft. Rather surprisingly, rice cooked well, and we slept warm in only one sleeping bag.

There were yet two cols to visit. Unless the curling west glacier was longer than the main trunk, which was unlikely, the easternmost col must be on the frontier ridge. In order to ensure reaching it in good time we took a light camp to some rocks at the foot of the snow slope, the height being about 19,000 ft. We spent a poor night and overslept ourselves, for it was warm even in only one sleeping bag and we were both excited. The view from any col, a mountain window opening upon a fresh scene, holds an expectant thrill; how much keener is expectancy if that view promises to reveal unsurveyed country and perhaps a 26,000 ft. mountain.

Aided by this flying start of a thousand feet, on better snow, and with Tensing making light of the 30 lb. theodolite, we reached the col by 7.30 of a fine morning. It proved to be a false col. Nearly a mile away and at the same height lay the true col, and in between was a snow hollow which drained by a sort of backdoor into a tiny branch of the Langtang glacier. On each side of the true col rose high peaks of the order of 22,000 ft. Lloyd remained with the machine on the false col to get a fix from known peaks, while Tensing and I sped on across the still hard snow. Now was our big moment, the moment for which I had been, as Pepys says, in child ever since leaving Katmandu. Our survey plans depended on what we saw and to our disgust we did not see very much. Below us a big glacier flowed westwards, across it lay a knot of mountains, part of a range which stretched north-west into Tibet, effectually blocking our view to the east. We could not even see the junction of this range with the Himalayan crest-line a mile or so to the east of our col, but since there was no hint of the great mountain elsewhere, we surmised that Gosainthan lay just about the point of junction. The key move for the solution of the problem was a descent to the glacier on the Tibetan side, thus violating the frontier. We had no scruples on that score, having persuaded ourselves, with commonsense rather than logic, that no trespass would be committed provided we remained within the uninhabited glacier region.

> He that is robbed, not wanting what is stol'n,
> Let him not know't and he's not robb'd at all.

But it was too steep. Even had we had with us that earlier and better strain of yak, habitual crossers of traditional passes, I do not think we could have taken a camp over that col.

After collecting some spiders and rock fragments we returned to the high camp. We had still to visit the third col which lay between the other two and looked slightly higher. With perhaps as much luck as skill we climbed in dense mist by an intricate corridor, reaching the foot of the final pitch as the mist dissolved. We knew pretty well what to expect this time, and sure enough we looked once more upon the west glacier and beyond it to a mass of undistinguished-looking Tibetan peaks.

We had now done our duty. Certainly, for Lloyd, our visits to the three cols held little pleasure, taken up, as they were, with the twiddling of screws, booking of angles, changing plates, all of it having to be done against time. I, on the other hand, once I had recovered from the successive disappointments, had merely to sit munching biscuits while Tensing scrabbled in rock crevices for victims for my Belsen chambers.

Since there was no reaching the unsurveyed territory on the Tibetan side, our survey work had to be confined to the Langtang itself. Nor was this merely painting the lily; for the existing ¼-in. maps published by the Survey of India in 1931 are good only so far as they go. Good enough, that is, to destroy any illusions one might have of being an explorer, all the main peaks having been triangulated and the general run of the main valleys indicated. But the detailed topography of the mountain regions is either not shown or is largely guesswork, thus the glaciers often provided charming surprises and the cols unexpected and puzzling vistas.

The station on this col was the last for some time. Next day, 22 June, when we began moving down, expecting to complete several stations on the way, the weather broke. Monsoon conditions of mist, rain, with rarely any sunshine, established themselves and prevailed almost unbroken for the rest of our stay.

On the way down Tensing and I crossed the main glacier to take a one-night camp up a tributary glacier to the east. The eastern side of the Langtang glacier is a very high wall of mountains unbroken except by this one glacier. Having crossed a high pass at its head, and having gone some way down the other side, we recognized below us the east branch of the Langtang which, after making an abrupt bend close to the two rock images, follows a course almost parallel to the main glacier. Beyond it we noticed yet another col leading southeast, a discovery of which we made good use later when we tried to reach the Jugal Himal. In a sanctuary one would expect to see game, but in this valley alone did we see any – three wary tahr, the rufous, shaggy Himalayan goat. At much lower altitudes we had occasionally seen a small deer which we took to be a musk deer, and on one occasion we had assumed without any strict enquiry the presence of some kindly disposed bears. Apart from that we saw no game, not even a marmot.

Twice, once at sunset and again at dawn, we carried the theodolite to the top of the 500 ft. moraine which in better weather would have made an excellent station, and then in disgust we went straight down to Langtang village. On this stroll, the more pleasant because it was all downhill, we met with a fresh crop of flowers, most of them, like Mr Pyecroft's lilac, 'stinkin' their blossomin' little hearts out'. Besides the tall ream primulas, nearly 2 ft. high, there were little ground orchids of a delicate pink, bronze bell-shaped fritillaries, copper-coloured lilies, and great hairy yellow poppies. Lurking behind a bush of white briar, clutching a catapult, was a dark, hungry-looking figure, wearing, by way of dazzle camouflage, an American shirt. It was bird-skinner Toni who, with more zeal than sense, had left Bombay without waiting for the release of either stick-gun or ammunition.

MAD (PĀGAL)

Laxmīprasād Devkoṭā

Lakshmīprasād Devkoṭā (1909–1959) was a prolific Nepali author, poet and playwright. Devkoṭā is honoured by the title of Maha Kavi "The Great Poet" in Nepali literature. He wrote more than 40 books and his works also include short stories, essays, translations, a novel and many poems. His notable works include *Muna Madan, Kunjini, Sakuntal.*

Surely, **my** friend, I am mad,
that's exactly what I am!

I see sounds,
hear sights,
taste smells,
I touch things thinner than air,
things whose existence the world denies,
things whose shapes the world does not know.
Stones I see as flowers,
pebbles have soft shapes,
water-smoothed at the water's edge
in the moonlight;
as heaven's sorceress smiles at me,
they put out leaves, they soften, they glimmer
and pulse, rising up like mute maniacs,
like flowers – a kind of moonbird flower.
I speak to them just as they speak to me,
in a language, my friend,
unwritten, unprinted, unspoken,
uncomprehended, unheard.
Their speech comes in ripples, my friend,

to the moonlit, Gangā's shore.
Surely, **my** friend, I am mad,
that's exactly what I am!

You are clever, and wordy,
your calculations exact and correct forever,
but take one from one in my arithmetic,
and you are still left with one.
You use five senses, but I have six,
you have a brain, my friend,
but I have a heart.
To you a rose is a rose, and nothing more,
but I see Helen and Padmiṇī
you are forceful prose,
I am liquid poetry;
you freeze as I am melting,
you clear as I cloud over,
and then it's the other way around;
your world is solid, mine vapour,
your world is gross, mine subtle,
you consider a stone an object,
material hardness is your reality
but I try to grasp hold of dreams,
just as you try to catch the rounded truths
of cold, sweet, graven coins.
My passion is that of a thorn, my friend,
yours is for gold and diamonds,
you say that the hills are deaf and dumb,
I say that they are eloquent.
Surely, my friend,
mine is a loose inebriation,
that's exactly how I am.

In the cold of the month of Māgh I sat,
enjoying the first white warmth of the star:
the world called me a drifter.

When they saw me staring blankly for seven days
after my return from the cremation ghāṭs,[1]
they said I was possessed.
When I saw the first frosts of Time
on the hair of a beautiful woman,
I wept for three days:
the Buddha was touching my soul,
but they said that I was raving!
When they saw me dance
on hearing the first cuckoo of Spring,
they called me a madman.
A silent, moonless night once made me breathless,
the agony of destruction made me jump,
and on that day the fools put me in the stocks!
One day I began to sing with the storm,
the wise old men sent me off to Rānchī.[2]
One day I thought I was dead,
I lay down flat, a friend pinched me hard,
and said, "Hey, madman, you're not dead yet!"
These things went on, year upon year,
I am mad, my friend,
that's exactly what I am!

I have called the ruler's wine blood,
the local whore a corpse,
and the king a pauper.
I have abused Alexander the Great,
poured scorn on so-called great souls,
but the lowly I have raised
to the seventh heaven on a bridge of praise.
Your great scholar is my great fool,
your heaven my hell,
your gold my iron, my friend,

---

[1] A *ghāṭ* is a stepped platform beside a river where Hindus take their daily baths and
    where the bodies of the dead are cremated.
[2] Rānchī is the mental asylum in Bihār, northern India.

your righteousness my crime.
Where you see yourself as clever,
I see you to be an absolute dolt,
your progress, my friend, is my decline,
that's how our values contradict.
Your universe is as a single hair to me,
certainly, my friend, I'm moonstruck,
completely moonstruck, that's what I am!

I think the blind man is the leader of the world,
the ascetic in his cave is a back-sliding deserter;
those who walk the stage of falsehood
I see as dark buffoons,
those who fail I consider successful,
progress for me is stagnation:
I must be either cockeyed or mad –
I am mad, my friend, I am mad.

Look at the whorish dance
of shameless leadership's tasteless tongues,
watch them break the back of the people's rights.
When the black lies of sparrow-headed newsprint
challenge Reason, the hero within me,
with their webs of falsehood,
then my cheeks grow red, my friend,
as red as glowing charcoal.
When voiceless people drink black poison,
right before my eyes,
and drink it through their ears,
thinking that it's nectar,
then every hair on my body stands up,
like the Gorgon's serpent hair.
When I see the tiger resolve to eat the deer,
or the big fish the little one,
then into even my rotten bones there comes

the fearsome strength of Dadhīchī's soul,[3]
and it tries to speak out, my friend,
like a stormy day which falls with a crash from Heaven.
When Man does not regard his fellow as human,
all my teeth grind together like Bhīmsen's,[4]
red with fury, my eyeballs roll round
like a half-penny coin, and I stare
at this inhuman world of Man
with a look of lashing flame.
My organs leap from their frame,
there is tumult, tumult!
My breath is a storm, my face is distorted,
my brain burns, my friend, like a submarine fire,
a submarine fire! I'm insane like a forest ablaze,
a lunatic, my friend,
I would swallow the whole universe raw.
I am a moonbird for the beautiful,
a destroyer of the ugly,
tender and cruel,
the bird that steals the fire of Heaven,
a son of the storm thrown up
by an insane volcano, terror incarnate,
surely, my friend, my brain is whirling, whirling,
that's exactly how I am!

---

[3] According to the Mahābhārata, the magical "diamond-weapon" of Indra, the god of war, was made from a bone of the legendary sage Dadhīchī. Dowson [1879] 1968, 191.

[4] Bhīmsen "the terrible" was the second of the five Pāṇḍava princes and was described in the Mahābhārata as an enormous man of fierce and wrathful disposition.

MOUNTAINS PAINTED WITH TURMERIC

Lil Bahadur Chettri

Lil Bahadur Chettri is a Nepali writer from Assam, India. He is a recipient of the Sahitya Academy Award for his book *Brahmaputrako Chheu Chhau*. He is one of the most successful novelists in Nepali language.

1

This night was not as cold as it usually is in the high hills during the month of Phagun.[1] The sky was overcast, and the cold breeze did not blow from the peaks, so the night was still. Although it was the bright half of the month, all the moon's light could not reach the earth, and there was only just enough light to see by.

From a distance, Dhané Basnet looked as if he were asleep, bundled up from his feet to his head in a dirty quilt that was torn in places. But he was not sleeping. He was trying to set aside the flood of emotion that was tumbling down on him, so that he could welcome the goddess of sleep. But his efforts were all to no avail. One moment he would shut off the flow of thoughts and try to sleep, but the next second those feelings would revive and come back to surround his brain. So Dhané got up, went to the fireplace, plucked out a glowing ember from the ashes, and lit a stub of tobacco wrapped in an *angeri* leaf. As he blew the tobacco smoke out into the room, he sank back into his thoughts. Questions, objections, answers; and then more questions arose one after the other in each corner of his heart.

"The old *baidar*[2] is prepared to give me a buffalo, but he's asking a

---

[1] Phagun: mid-February to mid-March.

[2] *Baidar* is probably a corruption of the word *bahidar* and is defined by Turner as "clerk, writer" (1930:459). The baidars fulfilled an important role in village com-

terribly sharp price – and then of course I have to pledge my plowing oxen as security. If I don't pay off the interest each and every month I'll get no peace at all. 'Four-legged is my wealth; do not ever count it,' they say.[3] If anything goes wrong I'll lose the oxen and everything else as well. But what *could* go wrong? The buffalo's pregnant, and she's already got a sturdy calf. And she gives plenty of milk, too. In a year or two the calf will grow up. And if we get another female calf the next time she gives birth, that will be better still. My little boy will get some milk to wet his throat as well. If we put a little aside for a few days we'll have ghee, and we'll surely make a few annas.[4] That would be enough to pay the interest, and we'll keep the buttermilk. If the maize is good this year I'll use it to pay off half the debt, and we'll just live on millet." His thoughts raced by like a powerful torrent. When the tobacco was all gone, Dhané, "the wealthy one,"[5] wrapped himself in his quilt again. Half the night had passed already, and he yawned.

2

Dhan Bahadur Basnet is a young man: he has just turned twenty-five. His frame attests to the mountain air and the nutritious food of his homeland, but his handsome face is always darkened by clouds of worry, like black clouds sullying a clear night. He has just one life companion: his wife, Maina, who supports him through his times of sorrow and rejoices when he is happy. In Maina's lap there plays the star of Dhané's future, a three-year-old boy. The family also includes a girl of fourteen or fifteen, Dhané's youngest sister, Jhumavati, whose marriage Dhané has not yet arranged because of his financial difficulties. The boat of Dhané's household bobs along bearing its little family of four, facing many storms on the unfathomed seas of the world.

Dhané's crisis may be likened to the black clouds and moon of this night. The moon wants to cut through the net of clouds and spread

---

munities in eastern Nepal, acting as advisers to village headmen on legal issues and drafting documents for them.

[3] A proverb meaning that livestock can never be a sound or permanent investment because of its vulnerability to disease, old age, natural calamities, and so on.

[4] In the old currency system, an anna was one-sixteenth of a rupee.

[5] Dhané is the diminutive form of Dhan Bahadur's name, and the name is chosen ironically: *dhan* means "wealth" and *dhané* means "wealthy one".

light throughout the world, making it blissful in the cool soft joy it provides. But it is unable to do so: the clouds have reduced its light to nothing. Dhané wants to burst through the net of his money problems and bring his little family happiness and the cool shade of peace. He longs to restore the foundations of the roofpoles and posts that the termites of his debts to the moneylenders have made rickety. For that he has relied on his industry and labor. He works hard, he is industrious. For every four cowries[6] he is willing to lay down a bet on the last breath of his life. But his hardships do not change.

The rotting posts of his house just go on rotting. Like mist rising up to join the clouds, the land owners and moneylenders of the village add to his problems. The sharp interest rates they charge, the way they snatch the security pledged if a promise is broken: in Dhané's life these are like the blows of staves on a man who is already unconscious. But despite all this he has not admitted defeat. He hides his sorrows and goes on treading the path of labor.[7]

3

"Hariram! The price of the buffalo is 120 rupees, the interest must be delivered to Hariram's house at the end of every month. And listen! If you are late by even a day during the months that you owe money to Hariram, I tell you I'll remove the oxen and the buffalo from your shed! There, what do you say? Make a mark with your thumb on the agreement." So said the baidar, who wore a fresh mark of white sandalwood paste on his brow.

The baidar was an old man, a firm traditionalist who paid great attention to matters of purity and touchability. He ate nothing that had

---

[6] Cowrie shells were a common form of currency in rural areas of Nepal before the economy became centralized and monetized.

[7] Nepali prose narratives such as this switch between present and past tenses more frequently than an English translation can reflect. The present tense is often used to depict physical settings or to analyze psychological or emotional conditions, producing a period of reflective stillness in the text, while the events of the story are usually recounted in the past tense. In this text, the present tense is also sometimes used to recount the unfolding of events, and this is reflected in the translation as far as possible. There are a few instances, however, where a paragraph begins to describe events in one tense and then switches to another for no apparent reason: the translation departs from the original in such instances so that this switching between tenses (which can be confusing in English prose) does not occur within the body of a single paragraph.

not been prepared by his own Bahun cook. So that the name of Ram might always be on his lips, he sprinkled everything he said with his pet word, "Hariram." His mornings passed in ritual and scripture, and he considered the giving of alms and feasts to Bahuns to be the highest duty. But he was always on his guard when the poor and suffering of the neighborhood came to borrow something petty. He did not forget to crank up the interest when someone borrowed a rupee or two, and the wages for all his hard work were earned by extracting high rates of interest from his creditors. Dhané knew the baidar well. Even though he knew that dealing with him was like setting his own house alight, he held his peace and made his mark on the paper.

It was time to let the livestock out to graze. The farm workers were making their way down to the fields, carrying baskets and *ghums*.[8] Dhané came back to his yard, dragging the little calf behind him. The buffalo brought up the rear, bellowing as it came. Maina hurriedly scattered a handful of hay to one side of the yard, and the buffalo sampled it casually.

4

Dhané expected to profit from the buffalo in every way. "After a year or two my bad days will be over and my good days will begin," he thought. But if things always worked out as they were envisaged, no one in the world would ever have blamed fate for anything. It was only about two weeks since Dhané had bought the buffalo. He came out that morning to milk it, carrying a milk pail with a little butter smeared on its rim. He went over to untie the calf, but then he saw that it was lying with its legs spread out and that one of its legs was quivering. He had tethered the calf in a hurry the previous evening, and when he saw it like this he nearly lost his senses. He told Maina and then went up the hill to call Kahila Dhami from the big house.[9] The *dhami* came quickly,

---

[8] The baskets (*doko*) are carried on the back and shoulders and secured by a strap (*namlo*) around the forehead. The *ghum* is a boat-shaped covering made of interlaced bamboo strips that protect its carrier from the rain.

[9] Kahila means "Fourth Eldest Son." Very few characters in this novel are addressed by their given names, and this reflects colloquial speech, in which kinship terms and birth-order names are used much more commonly. The birth-order names that occur in this novel are Kancha (m), Kanchi (f): "Youngest"; Kahila (m): "Fourth Eldest"; Sahinla (m): "Third Eldest"; and Jetha (m), Jethi (f): "Eldest." A *dhami* is a shaman or diviner.

and when he had fingered the grains of rice in the tray for a long time he said, "It seems that Bankalé has got it.[10] You just light incense for the deities of the house, and I'll conduct an exorcism."

It was just time to light the lamps in the village houses. The cowherds were busy laying out feed and spreading litter for their livestock. Over by the stream the crickets made the air resound with the music of their ensemble, as if some musicians from the city were playing their *tanpuras*. Down below, Telu Magar's dog barked monotonously. Dhané was standing beside the calf, his eyes brimming with tears. The calf turned its eyes toward him and gave a cry of utter misery, as if it wanted to tell him in its mute infant's language that this was the last hour of its life. Dhané wiped his tear-filled eyes with the hem of his shirt and sat down beside the calf. "Go now, mother, go happily. May your soul find joy in the other place." The calf gave one strong kick and then gave up its breath, as if it were obeying his command. At milking time, the buffalo kicked out, brandished its horns, and jumped around, and Dhané was unable to touch it.

It was Phagun, and the fields were empty and bare. Several farmers had just begun their plowing. Dhané had let his buffalo out onto his dry field, and at midday he lay sunning himself on some straw on the open roof of his lean-to. Just then, Leuté Damai arrived in a foul temper.[11] Leuté was very wealthy. He reaped a profit from sewing for the whole village, and he also had plenty of fields of his own, so he did not need to defer to anyone. Dhané climbed down from the roof, and Leuté saluted him, lifting one hand to his brow: "*Jadau*, Saheb," he said[12] "Have you let your buffalo loose? It's been through my field, and it hasn't left a single stem of my buckwheat standing. If my patrons let their stock wander out like this as if they were bulls,[13] what

---

[10] *Bankalé*: a malevolent forest spirit.

[11] The Damai are an artisanal case who traditionally work as tailors. They occupy a low position in the caste hierarchy.

[12] "*Jadau*" is a deferential greeting used by lower castes when addressing a member of a higher caste (Turner 1930:207). Leute's use of this form of greeting would appear to contradict the author's claim that he "did not need to defer to anyone": the inference is perhaps that the status acquired by birth remains a more powerful factor than any status acquired through wealth. Alternatively, in view of the ensuing tirade, it could also be construed as sarcasm.

[13] Bulls are not generally confined but permitted to wander at will and are often held up as symbols of lustfulness and irresponsibility.

will be left of me? Come with me and see the damage your buffalo has done!"

"It can't have been in there for long; it was in my own field just now!" said Dhané.

"I don't know anything more about it, but I'm going to get the *mukhiya* to fine you for this. You'll have to pay whatever he decides."

"All right, all right, there's no need to get so excited, Damai! If it's destroyed your crop I'll repay you!"

"Do you think you can still talk down to me like that when your buffalo has ruined me? I'm going to the mukhiya right now!" Leuté strode off. Very soon he returned with the mukhiya and several other men, and they went over to Leuté's buckwheat field, taking Dhané with them.

There was a ravine between Dhané's and Leuté's fields. The far wall of the ravine, on Leuté's side, was very high, and cattle and buffaloes were unable to climb into Leuté's field. But Dhané's buffalo had followed the ravine right down to the main path and had then gone around to get into Leuté's large terraced field, where it had destroyed roughly half the buckwheat. It was resolved that Dhané should pay a fine of three *mohars*.[14] He was made to promise to pay within ten days, and a written record was made of this. When they had secured Dhané's mark on the paper, the mukhiya and the other men returned to their homes.

Haay, the ways of fate are strange! One afternoon in the burning sun of Chait[15] the buffalo came staggering into the cowshed. Dhané came down from the yard and was about to pat it when he noticed that it bore some bruises, which he guessed had been caused by some blows from a stick. He was speechless. But what could a poor man like Dhané do? Slowly he muttered, "Who hit you like this? You must have got into someone's crops. That's just how it is." The buffalo's womb had been injured, and four days later its calf was stillborn.

---

[14] A *mohar* is half of one rupee.
[15] Chait: mid-March to mid-April.

SCHOOLHOUSE IN THE CLOUDS

Sir Edmund Hillary

Sir Edmund Percival Hillary (1919–2008) was a mountaineer, explorer and philanthropist from New Zealand. On 29 May 1953, Hillary and Sherpa mountaineer Tenzing Norgay became the first climbers to reach the summit of Mount Everest. They were part of the ninth British expedition to Everest, led by John Hunt. Hillary was named by *Time* as one of the 100 most influential people of the 20th century.

PANGBOCHE-SCHOOLHOUSE IN THE CLOUDS

Pangboche was one of the first villages to petition me for a school. It is the closest village to Everest and sprawls over a scanty terrace high above the Imja River. The people are mostly poorer than in the neighboring villages, and they have locally the reputation of being unreliable and dishonest. But on several expeditions I have known a number of the better Pangboche Sherpas, and they have proved just as hardy and loyal as the rest of them. Life in Pangboche is even more rigorous than in the ordinary Sherpa village, and perhaps this has made the people more suspicious and less demonstrative. No words of praise have been written by expeditions about Pangboche – only complaints about the pilfering, and hard words about the local insistence on being paid for everything and paid in more than full. This seemed a place that badly needed a school.

On April 1 Desmond Doig, Murray Ellis and I left Khumjung, bound for Pangboche. In heavily falling snow we strolled along the spectacular rocky path above the Dudh Kosi River and then plunged down the abrupt two thousand feet to the river itself. Above us the long, rising track clung to the side of the steep spur leading to the Monastery of Thyangboche; we puffed our way up this slope, which never seems to get any shorter or any easier. We reached the crest in fast fading light. Through the whirling snow we could see tall, distinguished figures waiting for us at the ornately decorated entrance arch of the monastery grounds. It was the head lama himself, some of his senior lamas, and old friend Dawa Tenzing, veteran of a score of tough expeditions.

Doing us much honor, the head lama led us across the grassy crest of the spur to the new monastery rest house. Largely donated to the monastery by Dawa Tenzing, this rest house filled an urgent need in supplying accommodation for distinguished visitors – religious dignitaries, village headmen and expedition members. Much of the timber had been salvaged from the "Green Hut" my expedition had built at 17,000 feet in the Mingbo Valley some two and a half years before, and it was satisfying to see it being put to such good use. The head lama showed us around with great pride and then beckoned us over to a table spread with food. We sat down in jovial mood and had placed before us delicate china cups resting on exquisitely carved silver-and-gold stands. After drinking ceremonial tea, the head lama gave a few formal words of welcome and then departed, having invited us to dinner on the following day.

We awoke to a brilliant morning. The monastery, the trees, the peaks around, were all dressed in a layer of new snow, sparkling and gleaming in the early sun. At the head of the valley, only ten miles away, the summit of Everest, crowned with a long plume of wind-blown snow, thrust up into the blue Tibetan sky. Our walk up the valley to Pangboche was a delight. The landscape was incredibly beautiful under its new snow and reinforced my belief that this is surely one of the loveliest places on the surface of the earth. Even Pangboche itself looked clean and peaceful.

Our first visit was to the gompa, where we paid our respects to the lamas and laid an offering of Rs 100 ($13) on the altar. Slowly the village elders gathered while I waited with an outward show of patience I certainly didn't feel. When a quorum was present we moved off leisurely up rapidly drying paths to the ridge above the village. Here on a piece of communal land the village had chosen the site for the school, and nearby was a huge pile of rocks gathered for the school building.

In Pangboche flat land is at a premium and I had no desire to use the best arable land, which is urgently needed for food. But this site had many limitations. A building could be constructed on it but there was no room for a playground, and my eyes kept straying to the dry wash funneling down from the slopes above. I strolled over to a group of rocks piled in the form of an open fireplace and noticed ashes and half-burned remnants of many fires.

"What is this fireplace doing out here?" I queried.

"It is the burning ghat for cremating the dead," was the reply, "and it will be necessary for the lamas to have many prayers and ceremonies before it can be moved elsewhere." The thought of the delays and expense of such a proceeding was rather daunting, and we all sat around in the sun in a glum silence.

Finally someone made a suggestion. Farther up the ridge was an old house for sale – the house wasn't very good and the land was very poor so the total price was only Rs 600 ($80). Were we interested? We were. Anything was better than the religious problem of moving a burning ghat. En masse we drifted up the hill, surmounted a little crest and then came suddenly on an old rock house surrounded by two small potato fields enclosed in dry-rock walls. We stopped, enchanted. It was the most glorious position. A hundred feet below us the gompa and houses of Pangboche lay spread-eagled in the warm sun. On every side were tremendous mountain vistas – Everest to the north Ama Dablam and Kangtega to the east, Numbur to the south and Taweche directly above to the west.

Protected by a rock wall from the sharp wind, we sat in the sun and discussed the matter. After careful deliberation the headman agreed that the village would try to raise the money for the land by levying a charge on each house – "but we must have time, sahib." This was a worthy suggestion but time was now more important to us than money. Desmond, Murray and I had our own little conference. Murray felt we should start clearing operations on the site immediately, and Desmond and I agreed. I put to the village another proposition. I would purchase the land and donate it to the village for the school. The village in return must reaffirm its intention of giving free labor for the clearing of the land, the assembling of rocks, and the carrying of timber from the forest. The foresters, carpenters and stonemasons would be employed by us. The elders accepted this offer with enthusiasm and assured us that villagers would start demolition work on the site next day. We agreed that the necessary documents would be drawn up and brought to Thyangboche in the morning for signing in the presence of the head lama. Everything had gone amazingly well and we were in high spirits as we strode back down the valley to Thyangboche.

"TEA"

At 5 P.M. we went to the monastery to have tea with the head lama. First we made our bows in the great temple and I placed an offering on the altar. Then we were conducted by a young lama along a narrow alley and through a heavy door into a paved courtyard. Here we were greeted by a ferocious Tibetan mastiff, who threw himself against his chain in frantic efforts to get at us. The young lama took hold of the brute's collar and pulled him back out of the way, but we were glad to slip past the snapping jaws onto dark, winding stairs and up into the head lama's private room. This was small but beautifully decorated, and the window framed the most stupendous view of Kangtega. Sitting cross-legged on a carpeted bench in the window alcove was the head lama, dressed in gorgeous brocades. We each in turn presented him with scarves and presents and received his blessing. For the next hour we sipped Tibetan tea – a horrifying mixture of black tea, salt and rancid yak butter. The head lama was in fine form and most vivacious. He and Desmond and I were old friends, so formalities went by the board. The Nepali interchange of gossip became too quick for me to hope to follow.

Finally food appeared. First a greasy soup made from venerable yak – and with the full flavor that only year-old meat can give. Despite my long experience of this dish I had difficulty in getting it down, but my discomfort was relieved a little by observing the suffering of Murray Ellis, a conservative New Zealand eater, tackling his first traditional Tibetan meal. Next course was rice, fried yak, fried potato chips and a thicker soup from the same old yak. We all managed to do better with this. Dessert was a large bowl of dahi (curds) with sugar added and we devoured this with enthusiasm. Yak dahi is excellent food, and with the addition of sugar and tsampa (cooked ground barley) is popular with all expeditions.

The head lama's room had no heating, and a vigorous breeze came through the partly open window. Outside I could see Kangtega outlined against the cold night sky; there were signs of a hard frost. Sitting on a cushion in the unaccustomed cross-legged position, I was rapidly becoming stiff with cold despite my down jacket. But the lightly clad lama seemed unaffected by the temperature and chatted gaily on. At 7:30 P.M. I'd had all I could stand and politely suggested that we had taken too much of the lama's time and must now leave him in peace. But no he said, we must have our final ceremonial cup of tea. Fortunately someone took pity on us and the tea was hot and sweetened, the milk fresh. We left the head lama with mutual expressions of affection and esteem and scurried across the frosty sward to our warm sleeping bags in the rest house.

It was with reluctance that we crawled out of bed next morning, for it was cold although the sun was shining on the peaks above. We were immediately advised that we had been commanded to breakfast with the abbot of Thyangboche – the second in seniority in the monastery. A combined groan went up from the three of us. Dried, matured yak is hard enough to take in the evening – but for *breakfast*? No, we couldn't do it! Despite our obvious distress Sirdar Mingmatsering was adamant – go we must or insult our hosts. We staggered outside and watched clouds writhing around the summit of Everest. Then we marched off to the execution. The abbot is a wonderfully genial old man whom I remembered from as far back as 1951. He welcomed us with glasses of raw rakshi. Then breakfast was placed before us. It was as bad as we had feared – Tibetan tea with rice and yak stew. The day was saved by the final dish – hot fresh yak's milk with tsampa and sugar – and this helped quiet our queasy stomachs.

At the appointed time we gathered at the rest house for the meeting with the Pangboche villagers and the signing of documents, and were there joined by the head lama attended by two of his junior lamas. After an hour's delay the only people who had turned up from Pangboche were the old mother of the owner (who himself lived in Katmandu) and the man who was acting as agent for the land – no headman, no elders, no Pangboche lamas. It was becoming clear that things had gone far too easily the previous day – the village had taken it all as a game not to be played too seriously.

"How is work going on the school site?"

"No one turned up."

'Where is everyone?'

"Digging their potato fields and upvalley, grazing their yaks."

The head lama advised us not to complete the deal for the land. It was agreed that Dawa Tenzing and the head lama's secretary would go to Pangboche the next day and find out definitely whether a school was wanted or not. A diary entry illustrates my feelings at the time. "Pangboche is so backward in every way that it badly needs a school. But there seems some doubt in our Sherpas' minds whether the parents will take their children away from work and send them to school. In general the village is terribly poor and the inhabitants notoriously moronic. Would it be better to transfer the school to the smaller village of Phorche, where the people are a more cheerful and robust type?"

"You must be patient with Pangboche," said the head lama. "My people at times behave like children and must be treated as such. You must be patient!" Dawa Tenzing drew us into his house as we departed and thrust into our hands large bowls of excellent chang. "Drink it," he said; "it will be a horse for your road." Ten minutes later we were striding through a heavy snowstorm on our way back to Khumjung.

We didn't have long to wait for a reply from Pangboche. Next day it was still snowing when a group of men appeared, led by the head lama's secretary. It was all a mistake, they explained. They hadn't realized there was a meeting at Thyangboche. Already thirty-five children were signed up and these would definitely not go up to the Dingboche fields for the potato planting. As soon as the word was given they'd dash madly down to Khumjung and carry the building material back up to Pangboche. Finally, they'd already started to demolish the old house. I was a little skeptical of this enthusiasm but the head lama's secretary assured me there had been a misunderstanding and recommended we go ahead with the deal. I paid over the Rs 600 and we received the signed documents. Then I asked Dawa Tenzing to represent our interests in Pangboche and the villagers promised to give him every support in preparing the site for the school.

By April 10 we were ready to move to Pangboche and start our construction program. The majority of the party carried the building equipment over the shorter route via Thyangboche and vaccinated everyone as they went. Desmond, Murray and I went the long way around via the village of Phorche, for we wanted to meet the panchyat and assess the interest and enthusiasm of the village for a school in the future. The route to Phorche is a spectacular one. The track climbs through the vast rock bluffs above Khumjung on wooden staircases and delicately perched rock platforms. Then you plunge steeply down into a narrow gorge enclosing the Dudh Kosi River. With knees quivering from the solid pounding of your descent, you cross the cantilever bridge and then climb steeply up the other side through twisted rhododendrons draped with long fingers of silver moss. Cupped in a smiling hollow on the flanks of Taweche, Phorche has a charm all its own. Mountains are all around, but you are hardly conscious of them. The village lies in the warm sun and your eyes instinctively follow the river to the south, over the foothills of Nepal towards the throbbing plains of India. Phorche has no easy approach – it is frequently cut off even from the other Sherpa villages – and yet its warmth and aspect make you forget at times that you are living high on a grim Himalayan peak.

There are fifty to sixty houses in the village, and we seemed to visit most of them to be plied with chang, rakshi and hospitality. The elders conducted us to the site they had chosen for a school – a gorgeous position amongst spidery trees on the edge of a huge bluff – but one careless kick of a ball and its next stop would be 2000 feet down in the Dudh Kosi River. I told the village elders they should plan to send their children to Pangboche School for the next few years and we would then try and get them a school of their own. But the elders shook their heads. "It is too far for our children to go to Pangboche each day, sahib, and the track is too narrow and dangerous."

In a haze of bonhomie, we carried on to Pangboche, following the tiny twisting track high above the valley floor. Slips and bluffs, loose traverses and falling rocks made it an adventurous trip and we could easily understand the reluctance of Phorche to send their children over it. But the villagers' enthusiasm for education had been so encouraging that I was determined to think up some way of helping them.

Camp at Pangboche was set up on a terrace above the village in a pleasant grove of stunted pine trees. A tinkling stream was near at hand and there was a tremendous sweep of valley and mountains in front of the tent doors. I wasted no time in camp – I wanted to see what progress had been made on the school site and rumor had it that the village had been slothful and disinterested. I climbed up to the ridge to find women and children swarming over the place like ants, carrying rocks and timber and I leveling out the rough spots (as I found later, there had been a sudden increase of workers on the day of our arrival). Progress had not been as rapid as we had hoped but at least *some* progress had been made.

Dawa Tenzing, the masons and carpenters, Murray Ellis, Desmond and I gathered on the site to lay out the foundations of the school building. The back and side walls were to be of rock and would be constructed by the Sherpa masons.

"How many inches wide are the rock walls, Dawa Tenzing?" we asked.

"Inches, sahib? We don't measure in inches. The width of the wall is the distance from the mason's elbow to the tips of his fingers."

With a broad grin the chief mason presented his arm for measurement – about eighteen inches more or less. Under Murray's watchful eye we laid out the positions for the walls and took the necessary levels. Then we were brushed aside as the masons rolled big rocks into position for the cornerstones. It soon became apparent that Dawa Tenzing and the masons regarded us as hindrances when rock walls were being built, so we slunk off to camp. Later in the afternoon I returned unannounced to the school site to inspect progress on the foundations. To Dawa Tenzing's chagrin I arrived just at the wrong moment – they had discovered that one of their walls was ten inches out of line and were laboriously shifting the stones. I refrained from comment but resolved that a quiet check on distances and angles wouldn't be a bad idea.

The weather in Khumbu had been unstable for some time and as the Pangboche School was at 13,500 feet, we were getting daily falls of snow – rarely more than a couple of inches but enough to make work on the building a cold and arduous business. For the next week I left Bhanu Bannerjee in charge at Pangboche with instructions to harry the masons unmercifully and get the rock walls finished as soon as possible.

Over small radio transceivers we kept in touch with Bhanu and he told us of his many problems. One morning he reported 3 inches of fresh snow and a dense fog; another time it was shortage of labor to carry rocks; then one day nobody turned up. Religious festival.

On April 21 we moved back to Pangboche in force with the intention of getting on with the main building program. I found all sorts of troubles in the village. The stonemasons and carpenters were doing a good job but they were constantly hampered by lack of labor to collect stones, as had been promised. Little of the timber had been earned from the forests, and worst of all, none of the children had turned up for enrollment at the announced time. About the enrollment we received a variety of comments:

"They'll be enrolled in seven days."

"The lamas have to give their blessings."

"They're too busy digging the potato fields at the moment."

I summoned the headmen to a meeting on the school site. After much delay they all appeared. This time there was a new addition – the senior headman, who had been away previously on a trading trip.

He was a much more sophisticated character than his compatriots and seemed determined to be obstructive. Why hadn't the village supplied the labor they had promised? we asked. It was all our fault, the headman advised. We had vaccinated the village for smallpox and as a result everyone had been prostrate and unable to work. We pointed out that Khumjung and Thami had also been vaccinated but they had still managed to turn out in force. But he only scowled and muttered about "when the village was good and ready!"

In a fine old fury I gave an ultimatum – tomorrow there'd be a man from each house carrying timber and the children would all enroll or we'd pick up our building material and put a school at Phorche instead. I stamped off, leaving them in a stunned silence, and Desmond, Tom and Phil only waited to deliver a few more well-chosen words before departing as well.

As we sat around camp, sipping tea and simmering over the injustices of the world, another crisis was rapidly developing.

HORROR STORY

One of our young Sherpas, Purbu Chundu, was a favorite nephew of the famous sirdar, Passang Dawa Lama. He now appeared before us in the grip of fierce emotion and asked permission to tell his story.

He explained that in 1962 he had been a member of a German expedition of which his uncle was sirdar. This expedition had tackled the formidable peak, Pumori, a mountain which had rebuffed a number of previous expeditions. The German party was not to be denied and they forced a difficult and spectacular route to the summit. On the descent of the mountain the assault team was very late and the weather had become cold and thick. On one rope were two men, the only Swiss climber in the party and an experienced Sherpa. Tired from their climb and baffled by the bad visibility, the two men strayed too close to the edge of a bluff and when the snow underneath gave way they plunged thousands of feet to their deaths.

On the other rope were three men – two Germans and the renowned Sherpa, Annullu, who had first made his name with us on Everest in 1953. Only after a terrible struggle were these men able to make their escape. At one stage the two Germans slid off in an avalanche and only a superhuman effort by Annullu was able to prevent them all from being swept away. The cold powder snow and the bitter weather took their toll and the men's extremities were white and frostbitten before they reached safety in their assault camp.

Purbu explained how next day they had started the search for the bodies of the two men and had found them on the glacier at the foot of the mountain. Two graves were made for the men in a deep crevasse. The expedition leader placed in the Sherpa's grave his down jacket as a bed and in the grave of the Swiss his colorful wool sweater. Then the bodies were lowered gently into place and after a short ceremony rocks were piled high above them. Over the Swiss a cross was erected and over the Sherpa a Buddhist chorten.

Quite a number of high-altitude Sherpas and ordinary porters were present at the funeral, said Purbu including a man from Pangboche – the village elder we called the Nike, who was now helping build the school. Purbu quickly came to the heart of the matter. Yesterday he had seen the Nike wearing a jersey that was far too big for him. "Even the sahibs noticed the jersey and made jokes about it," said Purbu. He had recognized it as the jersey from the grave.

I sent Mingmatsering to see if he could get the Nike to come to our camp, but he proved hard to find. It wasn't until we were crowded around the campfire after tea that he was led up to us. Desmond started to question him quietly.

"Yes," he admitted quite freely, "I was wearing the pullover that belonged to the dead sahib."

After further prompting he conceded that he also had the down jacket belonging to the Sherpa.

"How did you get them?" asked Desmond. The response was glib and well prepared. "I was given them by Sirdar Passang Dawa Lama."

At this accusation against his uncle, Purbu Chundu sprang to his feet and with eyes full of fire asserted that this was an outright lie. "I was with my uncle all the time after the accident," he said, "and at no time did he go near the graves. In fact he warned everyone (including the Nike) that if the graves were disturbed he would come back and kill them with his own hands. Already in Darjeeling the wife of the dead Sherpa has heard rumors that a man has been seen in Pangboche wearing the ring she had given her husband on their wedding day!"

At this fierce denunciation the Nike hastily withdrew his story and replaced it with another. Some time after the accident, he said, he happened to be strolling up on this lonely glacier and he'd come upon the opened graves. To his astonishment he'd found the pullover and down jacket stuffed carelessly under a rock. They were too good to waste and he'd brought them home.

I had been listening to this tale with growing horror. The man was so obviously lying and was so confident that nothing could be done about it anyway that my gorge rose. When he cracked a hearty joke with the silent ring of Sherpas round about I could stand it no longer. I leaped up and thumped him vigorously around the ears and knocked him down. He scrambled about on his hands and knees, trying to escape, and presented the seat of his pants to my irate gaze. Next moment I had delivered a mighty kick to send him tumbling down the hill into the darkness.

Whether it was my ultimatum to the village or harsh treatment of the Nike I don't know, but early next morning we heard signs of action in the village and saw loads of timber starting to come up the long climb from the river. At breakfast time the headman and Dawa Tenzing arrived in conciliatory vein and assured us that all the timber would be brought up by the end of the day.

At 10 A.M. we gathered on the school site for the enrollment of children. Nobody had yet appeared but first one little family group and then another – all spick and span in their best clothes – left their homes and climbed slowly up towards us. Everyone gathered around as teacher Tem Dorje took particulars and then instructed the parents to sign the register with their thumb marks. Each parent had to agree to leave his children at the school at all times and not take them away for yak tending or potato planting. By the end of the day we had thirty-five children enrolled. I had been surprised at their caliber. I suppose I had expected a group of morons but this red-cheeked and sparkling-eyed group didn't look much different from any group of children anywhere.

Half a day's walk up the valley from us was the encampment of a small German scientific expedition. I had sent them a message about the Nike's activities and two of them arrived the same afternoon. They considered it their duty to visit the sites of the graves and re-establish them if necessary. I agreed to make Purbu Chundu available for this. When weather permitted, the Germans trekked up to the foot of Pumori. The mountain had done the job for them. A huge avalanche had swept down over the graves, covering everything in millions of tons of ice and leaving the dead men to sleep peacefully and undisturbed.

Desmond and I were determined that the Nike should he punished by the authorities for his crime. Our liaison officer, "K.C.," had authority to represent the government and marched off to place the Nike under arrest. He found him lying in bed, groaning and holding onto his head and claiming he was about to die – whether from shame or from my blows wasn't quite clear. K.C. warned him not to try to escape and placed a guard outside his door.

By now my wrath had subsided considerably and although I still regarded the Nike as a nasty piece of work, I couldn't help feeling that in a way he was a product of his village. The other headmen were now freely admitting that they'd known about the Nike's activities all along and though they hadn't approved of his actions, they'd never raised their voices in censure in the village council. This attitude is common indeed amongst the Sherpas and is a direct consequence of their religious beliefs. They accept the existence of cause and effect and are all too ready to explain away any misdeed by saying that it wouldn't have happened to the victim if his karma hadn't attracted it to him. The Sherpas will rarely combine together against a bully or even put in a complaint to the police. They prefer to accept the bully and criminal as an ordinary member of society who will receive his punishment in due course – but they don't want to be the ones giving the punishment, as by so doing their soul may be linked by cause and effect with that of the transgressor for many reincarnations. Perhaps this basic trait is at the back of many of their more charming qualities as well, but when an emergency arises one can't help wishing for a little more materialism.

When K. C. and the senior headman suggested that the Nike should not be handed over to the police but should be subjected to the village "disgracing" ceremony, I was only too happy to agree. The Nike had been given a considerable scare and his disgrace in front of his neighbors would serve as a salutary lesson to the village.

In the middle of the afternoon we gathered in the courtyard of the gompa and a miserable Nike was brought stumbling in with a bandage around his head, completely crushed by the whole proceeding. He seated himself in the gloom of a corner with his head between his hands. Desmond refused to allow this – the man must face his punishment in the open – and he instructed the headman to have the Nike brought out in front of the people. He sat on the bottom step of the gompa with a weeping sister on one side and his stalwart and dry-eyed wife on the other.

The tension built up to a high pitch as the proceedings commenced. First a document was read to the assembled gathering, a confession from the Nike in which he admitted his guilt but pleaded for mercy and forgiveness. Then another, longer document, signed by all the senior men of the village, in which they condemned the Nike's action and guaranteed that such a thing would not happen in the village again. I was then called on to say a few words to be translated into Nepali by Desmond, and into Sherpa by Mingmatsering. By now I was feeling

rather sorry for the Nike, who must have been undergoing mental torture, and my words were brief: a suggestion that he had been punished
in the sight of his equals and it was now up to him to rehabilitate
himself by his actions over the next few years. Desmond, too, had few
words to say but they were telling ones.

"We can forgive your crime," he declaimed to the crouching man.
"But you will have to make your own peace with God!"

There was a deathly hush after this statement, broken only by the
sobs of the Nike's sister, and there was no doubt that these last words
had made a strong impression.

The Nike and his family were asked if they had anything to say,
but the man was glad to be silent. Only his wife, a tall, handsome woman, wanted to speak. Still dry-eyed, with a hard set to her jaw, she
repeated the story of the discovery of the clothes – how her husband
had found them under a rock. When questioned by the headman, she
admitted that this was the story her husband had told her. The headman shrugged his shoulders and passed on.

We admired the way this woman had supported her husband, although there seemed little emotion in her reactions. Later we discovered that her background had given her some training in such crises:
she was a "fallen" nun, a category accepted but not really approved by
this non-critical Buddhist community. And her brother was the biggest
racketeer and strong-arm man in the Khumbu area.

I was glad when the proceedings were over and we could see the
shattered Nike being led off to his house. Undoubtedly this function
had been good for the village. Not only the Nike had been under judgment. We knew that in a week's time the Nike would be drinking chang
with his fellows as though nothing had happened, but suspected that
the village might still remember the original cause.

A few days later the Nike's wife made a pilgrimage to Thyangboche.
Her husband had been sorely shaken by Desmond's comment on making his peace with God, and she was bearing gifts and a request that
the head lama intercede. Three times she saw the head lama and stated
her husband's plea and three times she was turned away. "This man has
committed a great crime," said the head lama. "He must work out his
own salvation."

SKYLIGHT TO THE CLOUDS

Our firm stand in the village had produced immediate improvement in the support we received for the school construction, and real progress was made over the next few days. The daily bad weather was making climbing conditions on the mountains both difficult and dangerous, and I recalled a reluctant group off Taweche to come and help us with the building program. The school site had become a hive of industry. In one corner two men with an 8-foot saw were pitsawing balks of timber into rafters, beams and planks; the masons were putting the final touches to the rock walls; the carpenters were completing the joinery for the windows and the decorative frieze, called *langdy pangdy*, which was to come under the overhanging roof; the school children were gathering rocks for the enclosing walls of the playground; most of the sahibs were sawing and hammering at the floor and framework; and Desmond Doig was building a seesaw and swing. Already the building was taking shape and our pride in it was growing accordingly.

The weather was still harassing us. Fresh snow on the rafters made them slippery and dangerous and a stiff wind whistled around our ears, making down clothing a necessity. During the worst spells we'd come off the building and crowd around a blazing fire with our umbrellas up and the snow weighing them down. In the few moments when the clouds lifted we could see the mountains heavily plastered with snow, and sounds of frequent avalanches rumbled across the valley.

"This is the worst winter we have known for a generation," said the Sherpas, "and still the summer refuses to come. When can we plant the rest of our potatoes?"

Under our determined onslaught the building grew rapidly. The floor joists were placed in position and the flooring timbers securely nailed down. The heavy central beam was raised with much grunting and groaning, and the rafters were cut and then hammered into position. To combat the vigorous winds that could be expected here, we threaded wires through the rock walls a foot from the top and nailed these securely onto the roof structure. It was quite an exciting moment when we were ready to put the corrugated aluminum onto the roof. Dave Dornan and I started this and made haste with such enthusiasm that we didn't notice we were lining up the sheets a little out of plumb.

Perfectionist Murray Ellis came to supervise our work and to our chagrin made us pull off a dozen sheets and put them back square. Despite such setbacks we completed the covering of the roof in a day. Our particular pride was the sheets of corrugated Fiberglas we had set into the roof as skylights. It was already apparent how effective they were going to be.

To our delight, the next two days were fine. The snow rapidly disappeared from the ground around us and black rock could be seen again on the peaks above. We reveled in the warm sun and hurried on to the last jobs, perhaps the most difficult ones – the fitting of windows into the front and side walls, the hanging of the door, and the cutting and nailing of planking onto the front wall. These would not have been problems with square-cut timber, but with the irregular product of pit-sawing it was difficult to produce a good flush finish. There were many grumbles and complaints before all the holes were blocked and our sliding aluminum-frame windows from Chicago were safely in place and causing gasps of admiration from the local experts.

Desmond and I were still worrying about how to arrange schooling for the children of Phorche. The only solution to their isolation seemed for them to stay in Pangboche for the week and return home on weekends. On investigation we found that it would be prohibitively expensive for the children to be boarded out with individual families. The practical answer was to have them all living together. After much negotiation we managed to lease one of the biggest and newest houses in the village. The rent was Rs 200 ($27) per annum, so I signed the lease for three years and paid the money in advance. The lease was then presented to the village of Phorche. We worked on the house, transforming one end of the upper story into a comfortable room for Mr. Phutenzi, the schoolteacher. The elders of Phorche came in force to examine the house and were happy with it. They advised us that seventeen of their children were coming to the Pangboche School. Various adults would take turns living in the house to maintain discipline.

Opening day for the school was April 29. It was a patchy morning with sun at first, but by midday we were enveloped in a warm drizzle. We had hoped for brilliant sunshine. Our Sherpas were far from despondent. "This weather is most propitious, sahib," they said. "We need the warm rain for our potatoes. The gods must be looking with high favor on our new school."

At 12:30 the head lama of Thyangboche entered the village, and at 1 P.M. approached the school with a long procession. Despite the rain it was a colorful and cheerful scene. People had come from far and near. All the Pangboche children and parents were there in their best finery – even the Nike with his pretty daughter – and there was a strong contingent from Phorche. As a special treat for this occasion, we had brought eighteen bright-faced children from the Khumjung School. We crowded into the new school for the ceremony, with the patter of rain on the roof adding to the din of cheerful voices. The many who couldn't get inside crowded at the windows, oblivious of the rain and we were afraid that the walls would burst under the pressure. But the speeches, the exchanging of scarves, the ceremonial drinks, the blessings by the head lama all went off without a hitch in an atmosphere of warmth and goodwill.

After the ceremony we had Tibetan dancing by the people of Pangboche and, as a crowning event, a series of songs by the Khumjung school children. Their Nepalese songs were quite delightful but we had to hide our smiles a little when we heard English nursery rhymes rendered with vim, vigor and very little accuracy.

The Pangboche School started with a roll of fifty-four pupils, ranging in age from five years to twenty-six. Two of the men in the village were determined to learn to read and write and had signed themselves on as pupils at the same time they had enrolled their little daughters of six and seven. For the two months the school was in operation before I left the area they attended classes regularly. As all the pupils were starting completely from scratch irrespective of age, I asked Phutenzi how the progress of the fathers was comparing with that of their little daughters. "There is no comparison, sahib. The daughters are already far in advance of their parents. Their little minds remember things so much more easily."

It is our hope that the school in Pangboche will transform it. No longer will the village be regarded as a den of thieves by Sherpa and expedition alike. We are confident that the basic material is the same as in any village, and by education and guidance it can learn to follow more closely the pattern of cheerful tolerance and natural dignity which is so much a part of the Sherpas we love. And we have learned, too, from Pangboche – learned not to judge a village by the grubbiness of its faces or the poverty of its homes. Where opportunity has been completely lacking, how can we expect people to meet standards we accept as routine – but too often flout ourselves? We are expecting much from Pangboche's schoolhouse in the clouds!

TIGER FOR BREAKFAST

Michel Peissel

Michel Peissel (1937–2011) was a French ethnologist, explorer and author. He was an emeritus member of the Explorers Club and a Fellow of the Royal Geographical Society. He has produced, directed, or initiated 22 documentary films on his various expeditions.

A strange land, Nepal . . . its existence is due more to the work of surveyors than to any very definite modern administrative unity. Mountains are the only common denominator, mountains and mountain people from east to west, north to south, from the damp pestilential terai jungle up through the rice-terraced foothills on to the mighty snow-covered peaks of the Everest Range, the Annapurna Range, and the Dhaulagiri Range, which separate Nepal from the invisible but ever present psychological mass of Chinese-occupied Tibet. From the bar I could see the snow-capped mountains beyond which looms the specter of communism and mysticism combined, representatives of which occasionally come down to the sunny Valley of Kathmandu, where Tibetan monks brush elbows with silent employees of the Chinese Embassy.

As always, the hotel was buzzing with projects and intrigues, millionaires and princes. Boris had just returned from Hong Kong, barely in time to cater successively the banquets given on successive nights by King Mahendra of Nepal in honor of Nehru and to Nehru in honor of the King. Sir Edmund Hillary of Everest fame, now engaged in building schools for the Sherpas, was scheduled to arrive the following day. And Boris told me of his pleasure that Russia's space couple, Valentina Tereshkova and her husband, Andrian J. Nikolayev, were due in on their honeymoon the day after, accompanied by another cosmonaut and his wife. The depressed, bearded members of the ill-fated Italian expedition still haunted the corridors of the hotel, wearing blue jeans and smelling of Tibetan butter, amid American tourists complaining that in Nepal conditions were not up to pay, having forgotten that the country, to use Boris's expression, "was still in the seventeenth century, having already in ten years moved up from the Middle Ages."

How I was to get to know Boris in such a whirlwind was a question that no one could answer. Being around Boris was like touring the world in a capsule. One unusual character after another appeared, seemingly with each round of whisky, ranging from the Russian cosmonauts on their honeymoon to the newly arrived German ambassador, whose room adjoined that of the Pakistan ambassador. Both were waiting for their new legations to be built.

"How do you think you can catch him alone?" remarked Inger, Boris's beautiful young Danish wife. "In the fifteen years we have been married, I have spent only two evenings alone with him." Upon which Inger hurried off to have the tea ready for the Tibetan refugee committee that would meet in their private flat before the king's brother, Prince Basundhara, arrived with his American fiancée.

Just how, I wondered, would I find out about Boris in Russia, Boris and the ballet, Boris in World War II, Boris and the Maharaja of Cooch Behar, Boris and Hollywood, Calcutta, politics, Saigon, tigers, elephants, and Nepal?

The day after our arrival a slight noise awoke me at dawn. The room servant was bringing my "morning cup of tea," a detestable colonial custom of British India that requires that the white "sahib" have a cup of tea left by his bed at five in the morning. Needless to say, the only advantage of this custom is that when you get up three hours later the tea is cold and you have to order more.

That morning I could not fall asleep again. I therefore rose and strolled out of my room into the park. There I was surprised to see rows and rows of maidens coming in through the gate. Girls of marriageable age, they were covered with heavy gold and silver trinkets that dangled upon their black, tight blouses, which were tucked into the broad belts that held up their long pleated skirts. They laughed and joked as, bent in two, they carried in heavy loads of pink wood cut from the rhododendron forests that cover the summits of the green hills that enclose the valley on all sides. In Kathmandu there is no modern fuel. Cow dung is the most common source of heat, and as Boris could hardly use cow dung, he has had to resort to the services of the Tamang tribe, a mysterious people notable for their jewelry and the way they put their young women to use. It is the privilege of the members of this tribe to bring each morning to the hotel the wood necessary for the clients' daily baths. The isolation of Kathmandu and the primitiveness of services in Nepal have resulted in the slightest convenience becoming a complicated ritual. A good example is the preparation of a hot bath.

The wood carried in each morning is stacked in neat bundles in a corner of the gardens, and while the Tamang girls await their pay (given in silver coins, as paper money is still regarded with suspicion by the peasants), a lowly caste of half-naked coolies, wielding primitive axes about their bare feet, go about smashing it up. Once this operation has been performed, the hotel room servants, known as "bearers," come and collect the wood and bring some to each room. As central heating would be unthinkable in a land where lead pipe is unknown, every room has a small, archaic oven, along with its own boiler and water supply. Such a complicated system, through careful synchronization at the expense of the hurried guests, can occasionally provide a tepid bath at about ten A.M. This is the time when Boris himself gets up and grabs a book to retire for an hour in his bath, a morning ritual that he misses only when in the jungle.

Immediately after the Tamang girls have disappeared, the hotel sees its grounds invaded by the goldsmiths and other merchants who come in to take up their positions by the small showcases that cluster the ground floor gallery of the hotel. Ever since Boris first proved that Nepalese handicrafts were beyond doubt one of the greatest attractions of the country, the artisans of the valley have been busily at work. Most of them speak Tibetan, as their best clients before the arrival of American tourists were the monks and wealthy nobles of Lhasa, where thousands of Nepalese craftsmen used to resort to carry on their trades before the takeover of the Tibetan capital by the Communist Chinese.

The Nepalese seem to excel in filigree copper work encasing thousands of semi-precious stones, and their wares vary from bejeweled miniature birds to great representations of Kathmandu's pagodas executed with a refinement worthy of the most precise scale model.

Kathmandu, which has no regular modern industry whatsoever, is still a medieval hive of goldsmiths, wood-carvers and engravers, and remains the greatest market town of all the Himalayas.

Strolling out of the hotel gate, I stepped out into the road. A few hundred yards away from the hotel is the end of what seems like a small footpath. This is in fact one of the twenty or so trails that lead into the city from the hinterland. Unimpressive to see, these paths nevertheless lead on for hundreds of miles over hills and down valleys, winding a network of communications all over Nepal.

Here I could watch the porters and coolies jogging to the sway of the bamboo poles balanced on their shoulders. From before sunrise till after sunset a constant flow of humanity brings to the capital the varied fragrances of all the districts of the nation of Nepal. Here can be seen every dress, every costume, every cargo, and every type of man from the innumerable different regions of the country: wool coming in in large bales carried by red-dressed, sweaty and often smelly Tibetans; small steel ingots brought in by the *kami*, or steelworkers, from Those, where mines thousands of years old are still worked. Here also come the wealthy merchants with their leather bags containing gold and precious stones: turquoises from the high Himalayan plateau, coralline and other semiprecious stones from the hills. Over these paths also travels rice, the great commodity of the country, which pours in incessantly to feed the thousands of city dwellers. Along these same tracks come peasants with great baskets loaded with chickens, or driving herds of thousands of goats to be either killed in sacrifice or simply shorn of their wool in the main squares of the capital.

Food is a great problem for the inhabitants of Kathmandu, who are forever menaced by a rice shortage. It is almost as great a problem, however, for Boris. In Kathmandu the only meat available is buffalo meat. Practically everything else has to be imported. This forces Boris to spend much of his time fighting the customs officers; not those of Nepal but those of India. The primitive postal service further complicates transactions for Boris. Until recently all mail had to be sent through the Indian Embassy, as Nepal had not yet joined the International Postal Union. Boris has now finally helped set up a customs office in Nepal, explaining to rice-eating clerks the origin and ingredients of such things as caviar and salami. In fact there is not a single dish served at the Royal Hotel that could not tell of an incredible journey. And between Copenhagen and Calcutta more than one precious cargo has been lost. Usually this happens in Calcutta, where goods are frequently mislaid, and very often are found only when the smell of their putrefaction finally succeeds in attracting the attention of negligent customs officials.

His towel wrapped around him after his one-hour bath, Boris then begins his daily fight to keep the hotel supplied with necessities, sending endless messages to customs offices in India to the border towns of Nepal.

In 1954, when Boris started the Royal, he had had no experience in hotel operations. Even in his former activities as executive secretary of the famous 300 Club, which he had founded in Calcutta, his functions had been primarily social. It came as something of a shock to discover that in Nepal almost everything, even providing the guests with baths, had to be arranged from scratch.

It was only as the years went by that it grew somewhat easier for the most urgent necessities to find their way into the valley. The newly built road from the Indian border to Kathmandu was the first great leap forward. Although it looked at first as though this masterpiece of engineering would revolutionize the valley overnight, much patience was needed before it came into full use. The lack of vehicles was the first problem. Then the Indian government delayed in building a linking road between the Nepalese border and any Indian town of significance. The nearest large Indian town was more than 200 miles from the border. All this led Boris greatly to enlarge and develop his own vegetable gardens on part of the hotel grounds. In these gardens a variety of vegetables new to the country now grow in abundance under the influence of Kathmandu's exceptional climate.

I have always marveled at what has drawn foreigners away from the peaceful countrysides of Europe and America to establish themselves in outposts of civilization. In that respect Boris was to me a mystery. Why would such a man as he have chosen the strange hardships of Nepal, when all Europe and the West were open to him?

Though I had at first regarded Boris as a sort of efficiency expert, I was soon to discover other facets of his personality when, upon climbing a rattling, spiral steel staircase, I was first introduced into his private apartments. Situated above the hotel in a studio-type loft, Boris's flat, the inner sanctum of the hotel, is lighted by the great windows rising to the ceiling and looking out over the rooftops of Kathmandu. Here, tucked away and aloof, Boris directs his small world.

To know Boris it is essential to know his wife Inger. Twenty years younger than Boris, she has now been sharing his life for fifteen years. Inasmuch as Boris is an exuberant extrovert it is she who protects the privacy of their personal lives. In her flat she attempts to bring up their three sons, Mikhail (nicknamed Mishka), Alexander and Nicolas, out of reach of the slightly mad atmosphere of the valley.

Boris's flat reflects clearly the varied aspects of his personality. Beside a huge fireplace, welcome in the cool Nepalese evenings, stands a grand piano on which rest the photographs of famous ballet stars with whom Boris has danced on the stages of Europe and South America. Beside golden Buddhas from Tibet stand the autographed portraits of Queen Elizabeth II of England and King Mahendra of Nepal, reminders of Boris's important role in the nation.

A huge cabinet stretching around the room harbors Boris's incredible record collection, ranging from the music of Stravinsky, which Boris knows so well, to the folk dances of his Ukrainian homeland. Here in these surroundings Boris is the artist and musician of his youth; here are collected the souvenirs of a life so varied and full that at first I was at a loss to grasp its scope.

So unusual is life in Kathmandu that the business affairs that fill a large part of Boris's days are a strange combination of the modern and the medieval. Tourists arriving daily from the airport, with their minds still vividly impressed by the luxury of the great hotels of Hong Kong and Calcutta, naturally expect the same conveniences in Nepal. In this they are in for a disappointment, and they have to learn to adjust to such peculiar requirements as ordering a bath two hours in advance. On the other hand, Boris has laid out for them sight-seeing trips that would send not only the most blasé tourist into ecstasies, but even the most sophisticated and best heeled travelers.

One of the marvels of Nepal is Patan, the sister town of Kathmandu, which up to the present has entirely escaped the encroachments of

Western ways. Patan is a dream city in the same sense that Venice is: not a single structure is out of place, its narrow, brick-paved streets separate large blocks of pink brick houses whose wooden frames are covered with the most delicate representations of dragons, goddesses, and other carvings. The imperial city of Peking cannot have been more beautiful. But there is nothing imperial about Patan, nor is it, like so many of the great historical sights of today, a dead city. You do not have to close your eyes and imagine how the city was four hundred years ago, for nothing has changed. In each little workshop craftsmen perpetuate their trades and one encounters goldsmiths with their minute anvils and small hammers, bell founders with their antiquated blast furnaces, and every sort of artisan imaginable. High in the attics of the houses can be seen those who spend their lives setting jewels into the delicate work of the coppersmith.

In the city each block of houses, surrounded by its streets, encloses a vast stone-paved courtyard where rise the shrines of the district's gods and goddesses. Once a year the thousands of copper divinities are taken out of the surrounding pagodas and exposed in these courtyards. The Newars are Buddhists of a primitive sect that has survived nowhere in India or in the rest of Asia. Distinct both from Tibetan Buddhism and from that of Southeast Asian, the Buddhism of the Valley of Nepal is descended from religion as it was practiced in India two thousand years ago, shortly after the death of Buddha. Hinduism has now gained much ground in Nepal; the fact that the local population practices both religions has simply resulted in every other day being a religious festival.

These festivals, if they are the delight of travelers, are one of Boris's main headaches. There is no written calendar, and often it is only after one of these holy days has arrived that Boris realizes that there are no cooks or servants to run the hotel.

All these problems soon have the head bearers running up the small, rattling spiral staircase to see Boris, who, before he has finished his bath, suffers at least ten interruptions. Then comes the moment for the accounts, methodically kept in a great ledger by a medieval clerk who spends most of his day squatting by the kitchens keeping an incessant eye on all that goes on. The paying off of cooks, room boys and coolies goes on all day long. If there are no unions or syndicates in Nepal,

Boris still has to tackle similar problems when he runs into the incompatibility of various castes and religious groups. Sweepers will not do beds, bed doers will not sweep, servers will not cook, and cooks will not associate with anyone of lowlier occupation.

Once he is dressed Boris immediately makes for the kitchens, which offer the casual visitor a vision of Dante's Inferno . . . a dozen vast, smoke, dark rooms whose walls are blackened darker than coal. Boris cruises about through the kitchens like some sort of steamship caught up in fog. Years ago in India he learned that everything must be supervised and watched, and not the slightest thing is done without his advice or orders.

The other side of the kitchen partition shows a different picture that does not let the tourist suspect what goes on behind the stage. Here white-dressed servants flutter around, barefooted or in slippers, with their usual smiles. Practically none speak English, Nepal never having been a British colony – a source of frustration for the guests, who are rarely understood. The servants smile wider and wider as certain guests grow angrier and angrier, all this ending in a confrontation of all involved with Boris. So the day moves on, and Boris shifts constantly between the two strange worlds of the valley – the modern one he has helped to create and the ancient world with all its picturesque ways and customs.

Outside the hotel gates the valley continues in its leisurely, centuries-old tempo. The introduction of bicycles, today the most popular means of transport among both local people and foreigners, is the only widespread concession to Western manners. One rapidly learns the art of weaving in and out among coolies and porters, over and around stray dogs, and through and in the midst of swarms of flies and rats. The streets of Kathmandu are alive with a great variety of fauna. One might assume the animal life of the town ended with pigs, sacred cows and bulls (the fierce bulls seem to keep to certain well-defined districts where none of the inhabitants dare to go out of their homes except in sprints and dashes). This is not so; the valley is alive with animals, insects, and various birds. Giant flying foxes share the sky with countless flocks of crows whose chorus is the most characteristic background music of the entire valley. More picturesque are the hundreds of white cranes that majestically pace about the rice paddies, treading slowly above their hazy reflections, when not clustering in hundreds like great blooms upon the tentacular branches of the bodhi trees, the sacred trees of Nepal, which grow out of many wayside shrines.

Behind all the activity of the streets, and floating like a mist above the valley, is the mystery of Nepal. Although intangible as such, it can be felt in everything. It has something to do with the thin air and the lofty mountains, ever present at the end of the slightest alley or behind each monument, that remind one that Nepal and Kathmandu are truly the lost paradise of the Himalayas. There is a sense of intimacy in the valley derived from the great peaks that cut this small part of the world off from the rest of our planet.

KATHMANDU YOUR KATHMANDU

Kamal P. Malla

Kamal P. Malla is a writer and retired professor of linguistics. His collection of essays, *The Road to Nowhere*, was originally published by Sajha Prakashan in 1979. *Kathmandu Your Kathmandu* first appeared in *The Rising Nepal* in 1967. Malla lives in the United States.

THE TWO LANDSCAPES

Kathmandu is an absurd city. The absurdity of Kathmandu, the capital of the world's only Hindu kingdom, is both physical and metaphysical. The physical absurdity of the capital is in the deep incongruity between the beauty of its natural landscape and the ugliness of its human habitations. The metaphysical absurdity of Kathmandu is in the wide incongruity between the primitive, animistic and elemental simplicities of the rest of the kingdom and, the pseudo-civilisation of the capital. Perhaps in the whole kingdom nature has been nowhere more generous than in the Valley of Kathmandu. The climate of the Valley is nearly perfect: high up from the blazing malarious plains, but fairly below the snow line. Except winter and a little rough weather Kathmandu has no other meteorological obsessions. Nobody dies of the sunstroke and no human habitations are washed away by ferocious rivers. Above all, the Kathmandu sky is never dull and flat. When there is nothing to engage you right and left, the sky holds out a prospect of a dramatic gradation of the Mediterranean blue converging on the liquid horizon of the folding layers of the mountains. Receding in the background are the peaks of gold, silver and ruby, depending upon the time of the day and the angle of the light in which the peaks are bathed. There is nothing so much as dull and grey in the Kathmandu landscape if only one could step up some hundred feet above the human habitations to look around. If the pervasive colour washing the whole landscape is not liquid blue, it is bright silver, and if it is not silver it is deep gold. The opulence of Nature, refulgent in light and shade, in green and gold, becomes more and more pronounced as we move away further and further from the city centres. In every centrifugal direction from the municipal area lies an outskirt not yet overrun by civilisation. Somewhere between the municipal area of Kathmandu and its adjoining outskirts lie the fatal borders between the purity of man before the fall and his depravity since he ate the forbidden fruit. Not only that the outskirts are more neat and healthy, but these places are also in a closer harmony with the surrounding natural landscape. These places have subtle and meaningful touches of the deep interior of the country.

On all six days a week the adjoining areas of Kathmandu are safe. They are safe so long as the weekend picnic parties do not wish to open another Pandora's Box, letting all the civilised beasts out of their plastic bags, and desert the place with ripples of transistorised music. Kathmandu, among other things, is a sprawling city, bursting at all the suburban seams accessible to the asphalt roads of one sort or another. More and more green fields are mowed down, more and more open spaces are overrun. Even the secretive walls of the Rana compounds are coming down. In their places buildings of one sort or another are coming up at the rate of one a day. The affluence of Kathmandu is manifest. It is manifest, not only in the window-shopping and cement pavements – all refulgent in phosphorescent illuminations, but also in the suburbia where pseudo-smart bungalows are cropping up – many of them in the form of brick edifices plastered with cement and painted with garish colours of all shades. In fact, for nearly a century Kathmandu has been encircled by numerous pockets of civilisation which flourished behind the lofty walls of the Rana mansions. The truth, however, was that before the deluge of the 1950s the people on either side of the brick curtain communicated very little. Now that we have survived the deluge, the walls are coming down, the mansions stand exposed, the plasters are peeling off, and the roofs are thick with weeds. At least such are the ravages of time wherever the foreign saviours, embassies, missions, hospitals and hotels are not housed. The patriarchal Ranas have receded; their descendants are more keen and indifferent to see glib bungalows rising around their ancestral mansions than to maintain an unprofitable compound enclosed by a groaning wall.

THE CIVILISATION BEHIND THE BRICK CURTAIN

Civilisation started to encroach upon the heart of the selfcontained, primitive, insular and agricultural life of Kathmandu much earlier than the deluge. In many ways the Ranas were the first civilised rulers of Kathmandu. Jung Bahadur was the first Hindu maharaja to sail the high seas and pay a state visit to Her Britannic Majesty. When the first Rana Prime Minister sat with Queen Victoria in the Royal Box to hear an Italian *prima donna* singing lustily, the power elite of Kathmandu took a decisive step towards the Forbidden Tree. In June, 1850 the Hindu maharaja was already eating the first fruit of civilisation.

For the next hundred years the Ranas remained religiously loyal to Jung Bahadur's symbolic gesture. The first thing they apparently succeeded in accomplishing was a cheap transplantation of the West. By the twilight hours of the Rana regime the architects of the dynasty had succeeded in erecting monumental day-dreams of mimicry – each a monstrous monument to the idea of mimicry. Today each Rana mansion stands as a museum without character. All their walls are covered with sinister life-size portraits of the Rana ancestors, standing either by a dead tiger or a dimpled wife. Presumably, the helpless painter in the narcissistic Rana court failed to discover a third subject to smear the tall imported canvas with gaudy paints. The Ranas imported everything except probably boiled rice. Of all things, they imported Western architecture and built brick and mortar labyrinths to house their harems and prodigious households. With a redeeming touch of taste, generosity and sensibility each of these Rana mansions would have been founded in an entirely different tradition. For instance, in England "the great houses" that punctuate the English landscape were built by the nobility and the gentry who were in organic touch with the rest of English society. In Kathmandu the Ranas, on the contrary, refused even to communicate with the rest of society except for money and cheap labour.

They turned their backs upon the traditional Nepalese arts, crafts and architecture. There is not a single building which shows the regime's patronage of the homespun style. A Rana palace is not only a depressive monument to the Western mimicry: it is also convincing evidence of a collective schizophrenia. After all, the Ranas were the rulers; they ought to feel different from the ruled; they must live differently in dream-castles inaccessible to the vulgar herd. But is not all mimicry vulgar, particularly the mimicry of a culture only imperfectly understood? It was wise of the Ranas to have lived within the colossal compounds of their own, encircled by the walls, tall and thick enough to perpetuate this vulgarity among their own family tree. Mr Kingsley Martin visited Kathmandu once and unthoughtfully remarked that he did not like the tall walls of the Rana castles. The Ranas felt otherwise, and were rather wiser. Mr Martin would not probably like to guess what Kathmandu would have looked like with completely exposed and nude Rana castles. In all likelihood the capital might not have looked different from a medley of *Hohenschwangau*, a dream-castle of the Mad King Ludwig II of Bavaria. The architectural prodigality of the Ranas impoverished rather than enriched the capital precisely because within the closed walls it created a dream-fantasy for the rulers who were never in fruitful contact with the ruled inhabiting the world without.

THE TWO BUILDINGS: THE TWO WORLDS

The Ranas did not, however, confine their fantasies within the four walls of their compounds. The mimicry was also imposed upon the city of Kathmandu at large. Here the Ranas built a number of squares converging on the traffic islands where the chivalric Ranas rode upon bronze horses. They also built a large number of edifices with rhetorical Gothic colonnades or pseudo Greco-Roman motifs, like the Gaddi Baithak, Military Hospital, Bir Hospital, TriChandra College, Durbar High School; to these were later added glib structures like Saraswati Sadan and the Police Station. Of all these public buildings the most pretentious one is the Gaddi Baithak. This was where the few state visitors to the Rana Court were ceremonially received during the last fifteen years of the regime. The architectural affectations of the regime are eloquent in the very location of this building: it is imposed upon the heart of a unique square in the whole city, the Durbar Square. With its tall colonnade fronts the Gaddi Baithak appears completely out of place, standing out as a freakish lapse in a chain of buildings with a distinct and indigenous character. One can come across buildings like the Gaddi Baithak in any part of the world, from say Calcutta to Timbuctoo. But the ancestral buildings like the House of Kumari, the south western front of the Hanuman Dhoka Durbar can be found only in the Valley of Kathmandu. The Ranas also contributed their share of vandalism to the Durbar Square by plastering the fine polished brick buildings with lime and mortar. In the whole Square only one building stands now in its original exterior. It is the nine-storied palace of Pratap Malla, also called the Basantpur Palace. The Gaddi Baithak and the Basantpur Palace stand side by side in the heart of Kathmandu, not only representing the two styles of architecture, but also symbolising the two incongruous worlds of values.

THE DISDAINING REPOSE

In an excursion to a city, to begin with architecture is to begin with the most obvious. Architecture is not just a style of building. Architecture or the style of the buildings where the people live, is often an index, as in the case of the Ranas, to what they live by. In Kathmandu the lyrical and dramatic qualities of the natural landscape surrounding the city, throw the city's architectural incongruities into painful contrast. Here the generosity of Nature is oppressive, because the city falls apart at all seams in the face of the more meticulous and discriminating harmony of Nature. It is as if the human affectations appear less real and human than the solid walls of green and gold, the dramatic canopy of blue and orange. Kathmandu does not hold together as a symbol or a metaphor. Only the ugliness of the city acquires a sharp definition because here Nature is in a better form than elsewhere; here men are more pretentious than elsewhere in the kingdom. As we lose our ways in the old parts of the city, struggling through a maze of dark, slimy and narrow lanes, jammed with vehicular traffic of all sorts – the Stone Age cart coexists here with the space age limousines – we forget all the oppressiveness of Nature. Except a narrow strip of sky Nature ceases to matter thereafter. What compel our attention are the details and didacticism of the man-made town. Here the incongruity is not so much between the beauty of nature and the ugliness of the human habitations as between the disdaining repose of art and the bewildering details of the surrounding material squalor. It is in this labyrinth that one realises that Kathmandu was never built; it just grew up like weeds. That is why the city takes the knowledgeable tourist perpetually by surprise. He can never tell what next he may bump into after drifting along for a five-minute distance from a golden pagoda. The old city abounds in the deposits of time-groaning buildings with beautifully carved but rotting verandas, temples and pagodas in disrepair, cracking door frames with exquisite details, places of worship with obscene terracotta. It is the art in ruins and disarray, the islands of symmetry in the thick of fuming slums and green gutters, the harmony in bronze and stone thick with pious scum that unnerve every outsider in Kathmandu. Amidst such a mighty confusion of holy cows and mangy dogs, elusive men and markets, suffocating traffic and pedestrians, stubborn street-vendors and obscure holes suddenly there is an island of calm and order, repose and harmony – the work of an unknown artist or artists who betrayed their disdain everywhere in stone, wood and metals. Their disdain is eloquent in every inch of the exterior detail which is subjected to the most exacting concern for texture and symbolism. Each building or pagoda is a triumphant solution of the problems of space and scale, mass and proportion, details and perspective, parts and the whole. The windows, the doors, the beams, the posts, the capitals, the balconies announce not only the artist's triumph over stone, metal and wood, but also his triumph over the chaos of teeming symbols and details. Yet today each classical Nepalese abode is merely an island disdaining its own environment, neither enriching nor enriched. In Kathmandu the golden pagodas float upon the entrails of the fuming city like Noah's Ark. Each ancient pagoda in the heart of Kathmandu appears as a sad imposition upon the teeming labyrinth of mercantile slums: the golden pagoda in the heart of obscure holes displaying toothpastes and cabbages with equal religiosity.

A XANADU IN THE MAKING

Evidently, the most distinctive feature of Kathmandu is its architecture both in its chief glories and pious follies. While the chief glories like the

Basantpur Palace and the Durbar Square are in steady ruins, the architectural follies of the city are multiplying. Most unlikely state buildings and monuments are rising in Kathmandu: the Martyrs' Memorial, the Town Hall, the Central Telegraphic Office, the General Post Office, the Academy, the Mint, the Bureau of Mines, the Supreme Court, the National Archives; the NIDC Office, the Police Club, the Warehouse and so on. But the bemused tourist is bewildered at his inability to distinguish one from the other. Except the Cottage Industries Emporium, these buildings are in no way different from the public utility buildings like the Saraswati Sadan or the Police Station built by the Ranas before the 1950s. At this steady pace soon Kathmandu will be an unenviable wilderness of reinforced concrete buildings, a lesser Xanadu where the descendants of Changhis Khan might have hunted for a roof over their heads. Because by now the city plebeians too have cultivated the cheap taste for plastering their aging mansions with cement. The engineers, draughtsmen and architects are also showing a soft corner for architectural patriotism by curving the roof-corners of otherwise unearthly structures. While this craze for humourless reinforced concrete buildings rages in the Nepalese capital a great many of the *locus classicus* of Nepalese architecture, including the Basantpur Palace and the Durbar Square, are steeped in the slimy public urinals. The ancient Nepalese propensity to fuse the sublime and the sordid is irresistible. While our ancestors built the temples of delicate symmetry supported by the beams teeming with erotic details, we fulfill our animal urges by pissing at their foot. It is not shocking if the ancient royal palace in Patan is used to house the city police. In these matters Kathmandu has always been ahead of Patan: Kathmandu is only a step further in its *avant garde* vandalism.

A TRAGIC INSTITUTION OF BABYLON

The Nepalese have not gone much further since the deluge, except in the glossy brochures of the Department of Tourism and the Publicity Department documentaries. In the meantime, tired of the computerised wisdom of the West, tourists of one sort or another are pouring down at the Gaucher Airport. But as soon as they drive down to the city office of the Royal Nepal Airlines Corporation they are disenchanted.

The mythic Shangrila, the Forbidden City which a great many tourists obstinately hope to find in Kathmandu, is being swallowed by the woolly cosmopolitan replica of Baudelaire's Paris and Eliot's London. Today Kathmandu holds out the prospect of a muddle where one loses one's identity in a maze of dark alleys enticing one to a confused destiny. The narrow alleys of the city have no logic; the tall new buildings have no character; the old city is in steady ruins; the new city centres are breeding cosmopolitan philistines. No one can stop for a quarter of an hour in the New Road without being suffocated, both mentally and physically, by the muddle that is Kathmandu. Here are the exposed nerves of the kingdom; here is the cream of the nation's confused elite. Evening is the time to stand and stare, a time to stand on your inch of the pavement. In Kathmandu the cement pavement is a tragic institution from where men rise and whither they fall. So the elite stick to it with grim determination. Many of them stand in a kind of mystic trance in collusion with the sagacious cattle and cold machinery. The motley crowd that assembles every evening on either pavement of the New Road does not have a place to go, anybody to see or anything to do. For a few chosen hours here is a perfect Georgian dream kingdom of Walter de la Mare – each man a pair of legs and eyes. (Oh, what is this life so full of care/ If there is no time to stand and stare?) Where does this crowd come from? Presumably, the crowd that gathers every evening at the pavements is the same crowd of urban robots who run the efficient ten-o'-clock rat race to their desks and destinations. Having played its part the crowd steps out and stands apart on the pavements to watch the perfection of the spectacle it has collectively conjured up. The crowded pavements reveal that evening pursues Kathmandu's private life with void and loneliness. It is from this prospect of a gnawing mental and physical void that the lonely crowd flies to the cement pavements. After all, there is no fancy dress show or fireworks display all 365 nights a year at the New Road.

Kathmandu has no articulate intelligentsia other than those who stand every evening on the New Road pavements. The intellectualism of Kathmandu is confined to the machine-cast columns of the local dailies. There is no third avenue of articulation, no societies, no clubs, no fruitful gatherings, no place to get together except the pavements and the movie theatre. A great many take a fancy to the literature of anxiety in vogue in the West. Kathmandu's precocious literary nerves are more and more exposed to Camus and Kafka, Sartre and Gide, Eliot and Yevtushenko. But to what gross consequences? Speaking of the contemporary culture, literary or otherwise, Nepal's sudden exposure to the Western culture has ended up either in an insular recoil or in an exhibitionistic fiasco. The only two tribes who seem to have profited creatively from the exposure are the young poets and the young painters. Here, as elsewhere, the borders between the prodigy and the charlatan are constantly overlapping. Out of its assimilative spasms the new poetry or the new painting has yet to produce a Devkota or a Bala Krishna Sama. Elsewhere there never was a preparedness for a creative assimilation of the intellectual inroads from the West. The young men who strike Byronic postures in front of the shop windows, are a monument to Kathmandu's cultural failures. Today if they stand culturally indifferent, it is because yesterday the generation of young men looked at the world with pious eyes. The worldliness of the present generation of Kathmandu's virile youth is a vengeance upon the idealism of the lost generation of their predecessors. If a sample sociological survey of the present youth is undertaken the data may be shockingly Babylonish: a white collar job, a sleek transport, a reinforced concrete bungalow, the stainless steel wares and the plastic bric-à-brac, a fulfilled wife, and a steady bank-balance. Today in this city of shopkeepers and clerks the endemic daemon that haunts the intelligent youth is the petty-bourgeoisie ideal of breeding a fulfilled family. In its consummate perfection Kathmandu will groom a trinity of casualties, intelligence, sensibility and articulateness, to be crucified on the shop windows displaying all the new-fangled wares from Hong Kong to Helsinki.

THE UNLIKELY OFFSPRING OF THE HINDU SOCIETY

In the meantime, the shopkeepers display their wares; the clerks stick to their desks, the elite to their pavements. While the impious go to the Hindi movies the pious continue to pray at the Hindu temples. From the sanitation point of view every Kathmandu street is a nightmare, but there is invariably a chorus of radios blaring in full blast round the clock, no matter whether it is the Hindu hymn or the sentimental Hindi film songs. There is invariably a wide stretch of public wall displaying the natural history of Hindi movies in ugly, loud and gaudy posters. In a sense, Kathmandu is metaphysically steeped in Hindu lore. The city priests and patricians are spiritually enchanted by the higher mythology of the *Vedas*, the *Upanishads*, the *Puranas*, the *Gita* and the epics; the plebeians are mentally addicted to the lower mythology of the appetising Hindi filmdom. In this confused anatomy of Kathmandu's Hindu society run arteries of alien blood which provoke the prodigal Hindu youth to dress tighter and tighter, wear shorter and shorter skirts, dance to wilder and wilder beats of the brass, and drink more and more exotic cocktails. The transistor-carrying, picnic-minded, twist-obsessed, Hollywood-sinister gangs of Kathmandu's youth eat a crazy salad in expensive restaurants and every midnight fly past the dark alleys of Kathmandu at a record speed. This unlikely offspring of a Hindu society is on the tide, and its hedonist delinquency is an insidious commentary upon the inadequacies of the Hindu upbringing. The *mlecchha*-detesting xenophobia of the Hindu parents is visiting upon their children with a vengeance. In such a context, the Hindu piety of the *Gorkhapatra* editorials reads as a verbal utopia, particularly when every two patrician and priestly Hindu families breed a dozen hippies who swing to the twang of the beat melody. Yet Hinduism is eloquent in the most unlikely niches of Kathmandu's clerical and mercantile society. It is eloquent in Kathmandu's mass-addiction to the trendsetting Hindi movies. In this hippie capital of the world it is eloquent in the civilised clichés of the Radio Nepal, in the opaque journalese of the *Gorkhapatra*. It is eloquent in the strangled cry of *the* Nepali language which is groaning under the dead-weight of unpalatable Sanskritised Hindi. Above all, it is eloquent in all the pious social and religious processions in Kathmandu. For in Kathmandu all processions – except the funerals, march to the hit tunes of the trendsetting Hindi movies.

RHETORIC AND REALITY

If Kathmandu were the junkyard where time deposits all the relics of the receding civilisations, including the latest of the homo sapiens – the hippies, the most incongruous heap of the deposits is the Hindu ideologue. The Hindu ideologue is a romantic creature. He has just crept out of the Vedic caves, and is obstinately looking at the world with blinkered eyes. To him the world has not changed much since the Hindus fought at Kurukshetra. His romanticism is betrayed in his rhapsodic over-simplification of the complex ethnic, linguistic and sociological realities of Nepalese life. The Hindu journalists of Kathmandu parade mythic clichés to mask their ignorance of the Nepalese sociological realities. The first tribe who should go to the villages – the teeming villages of the Sherpas, Limbus, Rais, Tamangs, Gurungs, Dolpos, is the tribe of Hindu doctrinaires who formulate Nepalese values in terms of Vedic jargons. Let them see for themselves that the Nepalese societies are not monolithic and that no societies are further from the Vedic-Aryan or the Hindu-Brahmanical society of the Indo-Gangetic plains than the societies which characterise the interior of Nepal. The research works like Dor Bahadur Bista's *People of Nepal*, Iman Singh Chemjong's *History and Culture of the Kirat People*, Gopal Singh Nepali's *The Newars*, S.K. Shrivastav's *The Tharus*, Furer-Haimendorf's *The Sherpas of Nepal*, John T. Hitchcock's *The Magars of Banyan Hill*, or the relevant works of Brian H. Hodgson, Dr David Snellgrove and others are never read by Kathmandu's insular Hindu journalists, partly because some of these are written by the *mlecchhas,* but mainly because they speak a barbarous tongue and speak of all unpalatable sociological realities. Kathmandu is not the whole Nepal. Its metaphysical absurdity lies pre-cisely in its pretensions that it is. The primitive, animistic and elemental society of the Sherpas, for example, compels the sociologist to conclude that Hindu piety in Nepal is a rich fantasy largely anchored in Kath-mandu – a child of the creative Indophile nostalgia of the Nepalese Hindus who wistfully trace their ancestry to one of the *gotras* of the Indian *rishis*. Kathmandu houses a great many of their descendants. As ancestor-worshippers they tell us that the Hindus are the most civ-ilised and the purest of the Aryans, and that the Hindus had, once, excelled in every conceivable mode of human activity – from aircraft engineering and guided missiles to yoga, mysticism and metaphysics. Ask them and they will tell you that the roots of the Nepalese societies, both ethnic and cultural, are somewhere in the Indus Valley. Yet the irony of Nepalese history is that it was the Hindu priestly and patrician conspiracy of the Rana regime which had left the Nepalese people in a century of stagnation, breeding parasites at the top and all ignorance, superstition and poverty settling at the bottom. Today Hindu mysticism and metaphysics have little relevance in Kathmandu, the home of shop-keepers and clerks; Hindu rhetoric has much less relevance in the rest of the kingdom, the home of indigenous folklores and folk cultures, of animism and primeval rites. In Kathmandu Hinduism has survived, not as a creative force, but as a fabric of fossilised rites and rituals, feasts and festivals to which both the believers and the non-believers subscribe, not as an act of conscious faith, but as a matter of inherited habits.

In fact, even in India the rhetoric of Hindu spiritualism, like the rhetoric of the Old Testament prophets, was a product of the exile mind, perpetually at the mercy of the tyrannical tropical environment. Hindu spirituality was a metaphysical hill-station of the world-weary exiles. It was not for nothing that the ancient Hindu exiles came to the cooler foots of the Himalayas seeking a metaphysical asylum. The epic heroes of the *Mahabharata*, after gaining victory at Kurukshetra, had nowhere to go but the Hindu heaven, and significantly they chose the Himalayan passes as a way out to their Garden of Hesperides.

Today in India Hindu rhetoric has a pragmatic value as a political ideology or a party programme. But in Kathmandu vocal Hindu journalism sounds a little out of place, not only because the natural landscape is softer, the Himalayas closer, but also because the disguised sycophancy of the orthodox doctrinaires sounds frightfully out of touch with the country's socio-cultural realities. The sociocultural realities of Nepal are not what these stargazing doctrinaires have made out of them. They never see Nepal for themselves with the detachment or involvement of the social scientist. Scanning the country's dust is a much more salutary occupation than gazing at the stars through the Indophile lenses. The discrepancy between Kathmandu's Hindu journalism and the country's rich, indigenous and variegated folk traditions is not just the classical antithesis between the town and the country: it is also the fatal inconsistency between rhetoric and reality.

WAITING FOR THE BEAST

Everything conspires to make Kathmandu a muddle, an absurd city, a city without walls, a city without a symbol. The muddle is both physical and metaphysical; the incongruities are both material and cultural. To-day at the heart of Kathmandu, from Jung Bahadur to Juddha Shum-shere, all the Rana Prime Ministers stand in an undisturbed bronze repose and shed dark tears of satisfaction at the consummate perfection of their fantasy. Not that like Lazarus they rose from the dead. They had never been buried. Kathmandu does not bury its dead. Meanwhile, Kathmandu is flooded with the tourists who come to see this last stretch of Orient, hoping to find it still bathed in the mystique of the Forbidden City. But they go back to write books of disenchantment, telling the world that Kathmandu is waiting not for tourists, nor for Messiahs, but for comedians, satirists and cartoonists. Of course, the Second Coming is not at hand; if it were the Beast slouching to be born in Kathmandu must be a Yahoo – a Cervantes, a Swift or a Hogarth.

Meanwhile, the streets of Kathmandu are thick with forebodings. The omniscient eyes of the Buddha are transfixed in a searching gaze upon Kathmandu your Kathmandu.

POEMS

Bhūpi Sherchan

Bhūpi Sherchan (1936–1989) was a Nepali poet. He was awarded the Sajha Puraskar for his 1969 poem collection *Blind Man on a Revolving Chair*. His other collected works are entitled *Waterfall* and *New Songs*.

THIS IS A LAND OF UPROAR AND RUMOR (*YO HALLAI-HALLAKO DESH HO*)

This is a land of uproar and rumour,
where deaf men wearing hearing aids[1]
are judges at musical contests;
and those whose souls are full of stones
are connoisseurs of poetry;
where wooden legs win races, and bayonets of defense
are held by plastered hands;
where, basket upon basket,
truckload after truckload,
souls are offered for sale
along the roads, in front of doors;
where the leaders are those who can trade in souls
like shares on a stock exchange;
where the men who presume to lead our youth on
have faces wrinkled like roofing steel;
where the "wash and wear" creases of honor
are never spoiled by any malpractice,
and even the prostitute's terylene skin

---

[1] The English words "ear phone" are used in the Nepali original.

cannot crease, whatever her crime;
where seeds which double production
are displayed at farmers' fairs
which fill with news of drought and famine;
where beer and whisky flow instead of sacred rivers[2]
and people come to our holiest shrines
less to receive the food of the gods,
more to consume the forbidden fruits
of Adam and Eve in the gardens behind;
where the sugar factory makes booze, not sugar,
and mothers of freedom give birth to soldiers instead of sons;
where the great poet must die an early death to pay his debts
and a poet, driven mad by the pain of his land,
must take refuge in a foreign hospice;
where Saraswati's lonely daughter
must live her whole life shriveled
by a sickness untreated in her youth[3]
where a guide describes to a tourist
Nepal's contributions to other lands
then departs, demanding his camera,
where young men sing the songs
of forts and foreign conquests,
marching in parades . . .

In this land I am forced to say,
clipping a *kukuri* to my tie and lapel,[4]
tearing open my heart:
compatriots, nation-poets of this land
who sing the songs of my country's awakening,
respected leader of my people:

---

[2] The original Nepali poem refers to the Bishnumati and the Bagmati, the two sacred rivers of the Kathmandu Valley. Similarly, the following line names the temples of Swyambhu and Pashupati.

[3] The "great poet" referred to here is Lakshmiprasad Devkot, the poet who is driven mad is Gopalprasad Rimal, and "Saraswati's lonely daughter" is Parijat.

[4] The khukuri is the ubiquitous Nepali knife that has become a military emblem and almost a national symbol. Sherchan perhaps intends to show that he does not lack patriotic feeling.

if you wish, you may call me a slanderer, a traitor,
but this land is mine as well as yours,
my hut will stand on a piece of this land,
my pyre will burn beside one of our rivers;
I am forced to say, made bold by this feeling,
this is a land of uproar and rumour.
dig deep, and you find hearsay
heaped up beneath every home,
so this is a land of tumult and gossip,
a country supported by rumours.
a country standing on uproar:
this is a land of uproar and rumour.

I THINK MY COUNTRY'S HISTORY IS A LIE (GALAT LAGCHA MALAI MERO DESHKO ITHAS)

When I pause for a few days
to look at these squares steeped in hunger,
these streets like withered flowers,
I think my country's history is a lie.

These gods, dug in all down the street,
these knowing men who are deaf and dumb,
these temples ravaged by earthquakes,
these leaning pinnacles,
these statues of great men at the crossroads:
when I see all these ever present,
never changing, all alike,
then I think it is a lie,
the history of these men who share my table.

When I constantly see young Sītās[5]
in the streets, the alleys, the markets,

---

[5] Sītā is a consort of Lord Rāina, the princely incarnation of Vishnu, and the epitome of female chastity and fidelity.

in my country and in foreign lands,
stripped bare like eucalyptus trees,
when I see countless Bhīmsen Thāpās,[6]
standing still and silent,
shedding the songs of their souls,
like *kalkī* trees[7] with their hands hanging down,
I really feel like mocking my blood.

I hear that Amarsingh[8] extended the kingdom to Kangra,
l hear that Tenzing climbed Sagarmāthā,[9]
I hear that the Buddha[10] sowed the seeds of peace,
I hear that Arniko's[11] art astounded the world;
I hear, but I do not believe it.

For when I pause for a few days
to look at these squares steeped in hunger,
these streets like withered flowers,
l know that this is the truth of my past,
and I think our history is a lie.

---

[6] Bhīmsen Thāpā dominated Nepalese politics from about 1804 until 1837 and is given especial credit for building up the military strength and prestige of Nepal. See M. S. Jain (1972, 4–13).

[7] A *kulkī* is a flower or the plume on the Rāṇās ceremonial helmet. The ambiguity is almost certainly intentional.

[8] Amarsingh Thāpā was the commander in chief of the Nepalese army who pushed the borders of the kingdom westward as far as Kangra, in modern Himachal Pradesh, during the early nineteenth century.

[9] Sagarmāthā is the Nepali name for Mount Everest.

[10] Because Lumbinī, the birthplace of Shākyamuni, is now within the borders of modern Nepal, the Buddha is sometimes claimed to have been a Nepali.

[11] Arniko (1244–1306), a Newār craftsman, was taken to the court of Kubilai Khan by a powerful Tibetan lama in 1265. The khan was overwhelmed by Arniko's skills and assigned him a number of major projects, including the building of several famous temples.

THE WAITING LAND

Dervla Murphy

Dervla Murphy is an Irish touring cyclist and author of adventure travel books. She is best known for her 1965 book *Full Tilt: Ireland to India With a Bicycle*, about an overland cycling trip through Europe, Iran, Afghanistan, Pakistan and India. She followed this with volunteer work helping Tibetan refugees in India and Nepal and trekking with a mule through Ethiopia. Murphy took a break from travel writing following the birth of her daughter, and then wrote about their travels in India, Pakistan, South America, Madagascar and Cameroon. She later wrote about her solo trips through Romania, Africa, Laos, and the states of the former Yugoslavia and Siberia.

On Foot to Langtang

9 NOVEMBER – KATHMANDU

I have spent the past few days trying to forget the Pokhara Tibetans and organising a fortnight's exploratory trek to the Langtang area due north of Kathmandu – though perhaps 'organising' is too strong a word for my sort of pre-trek arrangements.

Trekking parties here vary enormously according to the status, pernicketiness and physical fitness (or unfitness) of their members. The most elaborate are the comical Royal Progress of Ambassadors, who travel accompanied by scores of porters, a team manager to control them, a cook, a kitchen-boy, a guide, an interpreter, personal servants, quantities of imported food, cases of alcohol and every conceivable piece of equipment from a mobile lavatory to a folding wardrobe. The next and largest group are the lesser Embassy officials and Foreign Aid men, who travel in moderately luxurious parties numbering their porters by the dozen and forgoing lavatories and wardrobes – but bringing tents, tables, chairs, beds, larders and cellars; and then there are the hoi-polloi, who are too poor – or too sensible – to do anything but rough it.

I had planned to go alone on my own short trek, but Rudi Weissmuller, a Swiss friend who is familiar with the area, told me that this would be unfair on the locals because during winter they have no surplus food to sell to travellers; he also pointed out that I would be permanently lost without a guide, and advised me to go to the notorious Globe Restaurant to look for a Sherpa who would be willing to act as both porter and guide.

Had I not by now been semi-integrated in the Nepal province of Tibland it would have been difficult to find such a combination; the Sherpas are being a little spoiled by the Big Time Expeditions and are no longer very enthusiastic about ambling in the foothills with ordinary mortals. However, through Tibetan friends I contacted Mingmar, a twenty-four-year-old native of Namche Bazaar who agreed to come with me for eight shillings a day – by Sherpa standards a sensationally low wage.

A month ago I applied to the Singha Durbar for a trekking permit, but inevitably I have spent most of my time during the past few days prising it out of the relevant Government Department. In addition to losing my application form these caricatures of bureaucrats had also lost my passport, so I just hung around the office waiting . . . and waiting . . . and waiting . . . until at last I became a Public Nuisance. Then someone bestirred himself to excavate a mound of documents (doubtless losing several other passports in the process), and a battered green booklet inscribed EIRE eventually appeared. This was at once seized on by me – to the great distress of the clerk, who insisted that it belonged to a Czech stocking-manufacturer – and in due course the permit was grudgingly issued by a more senior clerk, who reprimanded me for not having made my application until the last moment.

This morning I again met Mingmar and gave him money to buy rice, salt, tea and a saucepan. He seemed considerably agitated by the scantiness of these provisions – not on his own behalf, but on mine – nor was he much consoled to hear that I myself was bringing twelve tins of sardines, twelve packets of dried soup, a tin of coffee, two mugs, two spoons and a knife. This was still not the sort of provisioning and equipment he expected of even the humblest Western trekker, and despite my assurance that I perversely enjoy hardship he remained convinced that I would fold up en route for lack of comfort.

Yesterday I spent an unforgettable afternoon wandering around Patan – beyond a doubt my favourite part of the valley. To me there is by now something very special about this disintegrating yet still lovely city; familiarity with the most obscure of its filthy little alleys and a positive sense of friendship towards its time-worn, grotesquely carved animal-gods has changed my original excited admiration to a warm affection.

The rice harvesting is at its height week and as I strolled around the narrow street, feeling the local magic rising like a tide to engulf me, the air was hazily golden with threshing dust. Now Patan is to be seen in the role of a big farming-village and even in the Durbar Square, where a prim group of guided tourists was pretending not to notice the temple-god's penis, I had to pick my way carefully between mounds of glowing grain and stacks of straw. Most people quit all other work at harvest-time and return home to help – a delightfully sane arrangement of priorities which does nothing to speed the modernisation of Nepal. While the men cut the crop in the field the women attend to the threshing, and outside every house along every street the family's rice supply for the next year was being heaped. Normally the surplus is sold to bazaar merchants, but unhappily there will be little surplus this year, for Kathmandu has also had vile weather during the last fortnight.

Perhaps there won't be time for me to visit Patan again, but I could have no lovelier a final memory than yesterday's, when the streets were one vast sun-burnished granary, with crimson skirts swirling above golden grain, and sheaves of shining straw being balanced on raven heads, and the untidy music of swinging jewellery sounding faintly as lithe bodies displayed a timeless art.

10 NOVEMBER – TRISULI

A typical Nepalese day, with lots more waiting. Mingmar and I had arranged to meet at 6 a.m., on a certain bridge; but we each went to a wrong one – unfortunately not the same wrong one – and by the time we had got ourselves sorted out it was 9 a.m.

Trisuli is a valley north-west of Kathmandu where the Indian Aid Mission is now working on a colossal hydro-electric project. A rough forty-mile track has been hacked out across the mountain and every day an incredible number of heavy, battered trucks carry machinery, piping and cement to the work-site. To my annoyance Mingmar decided that we would do the first stage of our trek – in what he most misleadingly described as 'comfort' – by taking a truck to Trisuli. I argued that my conception of a Himalayan trek did not include rides in motor vehicles; but it is against modern Sherpa principles to walk one yard further than is absolutely necessary, so I soon gave in and we set out for Balaju, the suburb of Kathmandu from which the Trisuli track begins.

This is the industrial area of the valley, where foreign aid has already done its worst and produced incongruous little factories, schools and blocks of 'workers' flats – not to mention a deep-freeze plant with a notice advising foreigners to book space for storing their PERCIABLE goods; even in the context it took me a few moments to decipher that one.

We waited here by the roadside for over an hour, during which I became more and more restive. It is easy to wait patiently when a situation is beyond one's control, but to sit around pointlessly when one could be happily walking into the hills is very galling indeed. Yet Sherpas are as obstinate as Tibetans, and it would have been impossible to convince Mingmar that some people do enjoy walking.

When a cement truck finally appeared we joined the twenty other passengers after a prolonged haggle about fares; obviously, though his own purse was not affected, it was a point of honour with Mingmar to secure the lowest possible rate from the Sikh driver. We then drove a few hundred yards up the village street, which is being newly paved, but soon our way was blocked by an ancient steamroller that looked as though it had been abducted from some Museum of Early Machinery. This fascinating object, having expired on the narrowest section of the embryonic road, was now resisting all attempts to push, tow or otherwise move it out of the way. Occasionally a scowling young Indian with set jaw appeared from somewhere, shinned up to the driver's seat and struggled violently with whatever it is that makes ancient steam-rollers roll; but nothing ever happened.

Meanwhile our driver was having trouble with the police, who could not make up their minds whether we should proceed to Trisuli (steamrollers permitting) immediately or at 5 o'clock this afternoon. (It was not clear to me why the police were in control of our apparently innocent movements: but I have long since ceased to be surprised by the quirks of Nepalese officialdom.) No less than three times all twenty-two passengers and their luggage were moved out of the truck, and back into the truck, as the police vacillated. One feels that Lewis Carroll must have secretly visited Nepal; a strong 'Alice' atmosphere now enveloped the whole scene, and to Mingmar's alarm I succumbed to an uncontrollable giggling fit when, for the third time, we were ordered back into the truck.

At this point an Indian Senior Engineer arrived at the scene of the breakdown and did something so drastic that the steamroller gave a scream of terror, emitted unbelievable clouds of steam and moved at terrifying speed down the steep hill, grazing the side of our truck as it passed. Fortunately this development coincided with a police mood favouring our immediate departure, so off we went at full speed – 10 m.p.h. – up the hill over the half-made road.

One suspects Sikh drivers of fiddling their loads so that they can make a good profit on carrying passengers and our covered truck was only one quarter full of cement sacks; but, as these constitute a most unpleasant cargo with which to travel, I soon climbed out on to the roof of the cab and hung on there, obtaining splendid though terrifying views for most of the forty-six mile, six-hour journey.

This track makes the Rajpath look like the M1 and, as we crawled along, I reflected yet again on the unlikelihood of Nepal ever having a conventional network of roads, or of China ever wanting to annex a country that could be of no possible use, either agriculturally or industrially, to anyone. There is only one Himalayan range in the world, much of which happens to be right here in Nepal, and even the ingenuity of mid-twentieth-century technologists can do very little about it. The Chinese have just spent four million pounds on building their sixty-five-mile dirt track 'strategic highway' from Kathmandu to Kodari – on the Tibetan frontier – and no doubt they regard this final link in the Lhasa–India road as being worth every penny of these four millions; but the building, and even more the maintaining of commercial roads throughout landsliding Nepal is never likely to be considered economic by any government.

As we left Balaju I was brooding morbidly on yesterday's American jet crash, in relation to our flight home; but before we had travelled far on this track I could only think how very slim my chances were of ever again boarding an aeroplane. The snag is that when sitting in a corner of the box on a cab-roof one's seat is projecting beyond the wheels – which are only a matter of inches from the often crumbling verge – so at hairpin bends one imagines repeatedly that the lumbering vehicle is about to go over the edge. Recently I have been congratulating myself on having an improved head for heights but, though it is true that I no longer even notice 1,000-foot drops, and am only mildly impressed by 2,000-foot drops, I do still take fright on finding myself poised over 4,000-foot abysses while being driven by a slightly inebriated Sikh. Yet when I had adjusted to the singularity of this road – which is not to be compared with anything I have ever seen elsewhere – it became para-doxically soothing to go swinging around mountain after mountain, hour after hour; but the jolting was hellish, and tonight my whole body feels as though it had been put through a mangle. Such journeys are not the best sort of preparation for strenuous treks.

The soil in this area appears to be much poorer than around Pokhara. The main crops are millet and maize, but three-quarters of the land is an uncultivable – though gloriously beautiful – mixture of rock and forest.

During the day several trucks and two jeepfuls of Indian engineers came towards us en route for Kathmandu, and during the complicated manoeuvrings that have to be executed before vehicles can pass each other here our lorry went axle-deep into soft mud at the cliff-side of the track. Obviously there was going to be a long delay, while the more able-bodied passengers freed the vehicle with spades borrowed from local peasants, so I suggested to Mingmar that we should walk the remaining ten miles to Trisuli Bazaar: but the idea was spurned. I then briefly considered going on alone; however, Nepal being Nepal, the truck could suddenly take a fancy to return to Kathmandu with Ming-mar and most of my kit on board – or some other inconceivable cata-strophe might occur to prevent us from ever meeting again in this life.

I noticed that the four Tibetans among the passengers were the most willing and energetic helpers; they showed no resentment of the Sikh's peremptory instructions, which so antagonised the local farmers that they were understandably reluctant to lend their spades and finally charged for the loan.

Within the past decade there has been some deterioration in Indo-Nepalese relations, and by now, having studied at close quarters quite a number of individual Nepalese-Indian relationships, I feel that India must accept rather more than half the blame for this. Admittedly the Nepalese have the usual excessive – though attractive – pride of mountain peoples and are very quick to resent, or even imagine, minor slights; but it is unnecessary for them to over-exercise their imagination in this context for the Indians usually treat them with breathtaking tactlessness. As citizens of a country to which the British introduced railways, hospitals, electricity and postal services the Indians now affect extreme contempt for a city like Kathmandu – forgetting that Delhi might be similarly undeveloped had foreigners never meddled with Indian affairs. In a place like Pokhara the condescension of the resident Indians is beyond my endurance, let alone that of the Nepalese. Were it not so infuriating it would be funny to see how expertly these men reproduce the attitudes of the worst type of British sahib in India; and frequently too there is venom in their voice, for they seem to be compulsively avenging themselves on the Nepalese for the unforgotten hoard of trivial insults directed at their own countrymen in the past.

However, it is probable that in any case the Nepalese would have been hostile to India at this present point in history, because of our common human inability to accept assistance graciously. During the past six months a number of Nepalese have sulkily told me that had India not been given so many dollars by America she could not possibly have given so many rupees to Nepal – which make one wonder just how much furtive animosity is provoked in materially poor countries by the lavishness of Western financial aid.

Our truck mishap had occurred when we were almost down to river level, and now long streams of late sunshine were making the savage clefts in the hills – relics of monsoon landslides – glow redly amidst the dark green of the forests and the pale golden-green of ripening millet. At this season there is no great urgency here about work in the fields, and as time passed a small crowd gathered around the truck to enjoy our little crisis. One woman was accompanied by her self-possessed five-year-old son who, feeling a bit peckish, had a long drink from his mother's breast – and then stood up, wiped his mouth, took a cigarette from the pocket of his tattered shift and strolled over to me to request a match. One hears that mothers should not smoke while breastfeeding their children: but apparently it is quite in order for Nepalese children to smoke while being breast-fed.

After seventy minutes of hard work the truck was at last liberated and we drove down to the valley floor where, at 1,700 feet, the air seemed thickly warm. Then, having crossed the river by a startlingly posh new bridge, we arrived at Trisuli Bazaar just as darkness fell and are spending the night in a ramshackle eating-house that calls itself an hotel – having evidently 'got notions', as we say in Ireland, since so many Indians came to work here. This small town is built on a steep slope directly above the river, and all the streets are smelly flights of steps. As usual in Nepal the men seem to spend most of their evening hours gambling intently, and it was difficult to get the hotel-keeper away from his cards for long enough to lead us to the top of a dark, narrow stairway. We have a most luxuriously furnished room to ourselves – with no less than three straw mattresses on the floor; but these are probably the headquarters of an army of bed-bugs so I have urged Mingmar to sleep on all three and am hoping that the army will concentrate on his impervious body. My own sleeping-bag has been laid in the centre of the mud floor, as far away as possible from the presumably infested walls.

11 NOVEMBER – IN A SHACK ON A RIDGE

After an undisturbed nine-hour sleep we woke at six o'clock, and fifteen minutes later were on the track, Mingmar carrying sixty pounds (a light load for a Sherpa) and I myself carrying thirty pounds (a heavy load for an effete Westerner). Mingmar's load could be much lighter were his standards not modelled absurdly on those of the expeditions he has worked for; in addition to his flea-bag he is carrying an inflatable rubber mattress and a thick blanket, which together must weigh at least twenty-five pounds.

The Trisuli Valley would be very lovely had the Indian Aid project not already desecrated it with the roar of machinery, and with hillocks of cement and stacks of piping. Now monstrous bulldozers and angular cranes are bullying the river into submission, and one is frightened by the speed with which men can despoil beauty. I was glad when after two hours' brisk walking we had passed those scenes and recrossed the river to where our track began its climb. Here a hamlet of wooden houses stood just above the river and, though it was a little early for trekkers' brunch, Mingmar decided that we should eat now as we would come to no other settlement before dusk.

By the time we had finished our meal and set off up the first mountain (alias ridge) the sun was quite fierce and Mingmar was muttering impolite things about the heat. On being questioned he admitted that he was wearing woollen ankle-length underpants and nylon skiing pants under his denim jeans, plus a woolly vest, a flannel shirt and a sweater under his down-padded wind-cheater. As I was too hot in a thin cotton shirt and shorts the mere thought of this apparel weakened me and eventually I talked him out of two-thirds of his garments – leaving him still grossly over-dressed and considerably increasing his load. This Sherpa predilection for excessive clothing amounts to a mania; having acquired these status symbols from various expeditions they cannot bear not to wear them everywhere and all the time.

Today we were climbing most of the way, going north above the Kyirung River. Our track was never forced right down to river-level, though it often descended a few thousand feet to avoid the more intractable precipices and then climbed steeply again to its average level of about 5,000 feet; but at no stage was it as gruelling as the Pokhara–Siglis route.

Yet simply to say that we were going up and down hills all day gives a misleading impression of monotony; around every corner of the winding track one saw a new loveliness, or an already familiar and striking vista from a completely different angle. Sheer mountains rose beyond the narrow Kyirung gorge and we passed from thick forests to barren stretches of rock-littered moor, and from sunny, grassy glades half-encircled by high grey cliffs, to cool, dim tunnels overhung by giant shrubs and filled with the tumult of waterfalls – while everywhere were patches of pungent herbs, and a glory of wild flowers splashing the mountainside with oranges, blues, reds, yellows, whites and pinks.

This region is virtually a no-man's-land between the Hindu dominated area to the south and the almost exclusively Buddhist area to
the north, and I felt ridiculously moved on coming to my first ancient
wayside chorten – a sight which indicated that now I'm as close to
Tibet, spiritually and geographically, as any ordinary traveller can be
in this sad decade. These stone chortens, usually built in the middle of
paths, are symbols of Nirvana; when walking around them Buddhists
always keep them on their right and it is one of the signs of a Bon-po
that he keeps them on his left. This was a very old chorten, with grass
and weeds flourishing in the crevices between the stones; one could almost have passed by without noticing it, yet its very inconspicuousness
seemed to symbolise most fittingly the often imperfectly understood
but ever present Buddhist influence that guides all Tibetan peoples.

I arrived at this solitary hovel on the crest of a ridge forty minutes
ahead of Mingmar, who is in rather poor shape today because of a nasty
boil on his right cheek. Western travellers do not often trek around here,
yet the seven members of the household accepted my arrival without
showing a trace of curiosity, disapproval or welcome: their apathy took
me back to that appalling train-journey through Bihar.

This hut is built of rock-slabs, with a plank roof anchored by stones,
and the squalor makes it seem more like a nineteenth-century convict's
cell than a home. I am not easily shaken by Asian standards of living,
which frequently are not nearly as low, within their own climatic and
cultural context, as affluent Western travellers imagine them to be; yet
this degree of poverty is devastating by any standards. These people
grow a little millet on the unsympathetic mountainside, but it is pitifully inadequate for their annual needs and tonight they had a supper
of stewed nettles (known to them as stinging-grass), flavoured with
chillies and washed down with rakshi. Seeing this fare Mingmar and
I simultaneously suggested to each other that we should cook a double
ration of rice, and on being offered the extra food they seized fistfuls of
it from our saucepan and ate it ravenously.

There are two rooms here – an outer one leading on to the verandah
and containing two plank beds, and an inner one with a fire in the
middle of the floor, around which everyone crowds when darkness has
fallen. Mercifully fuel is no problem and cheerfully-leaping flames do

something to alleviate the general misery. When any object is being sought beyond the radius of the firelight a blazing brand is used as a candle, and crimson embers replace tobacco in the family hookah, which is passed silently from person to person; but the acrid woods-smoke (one of the causes of glaucoma) is very hard on the eyes and I can hardly see to write this.

In the darkness of the outer room a youngish woman is lying alone beneath a filthy blanket, moaning and coughing. Obviously she is in the last stages of TB, yet the rest of the family seem dully indifferent to her distress. A little while ago I gave her some aspirin, just to show an interest; she was pathetically grateful and now says she feels a little better, but the moaning and the rasping cough continue.

I've tried to find out which tribe these people belong to, but they don't seem to know themselves; Mingmar says that their dialect is almost incomprehensible to him, though definitely derived from the Tibeto-Burmese rather than the Sanskrit language-group. Their features are more Mongolian than Aryan and, as none of the universal signs of Hinduism are apparent in the hovel, I assume them to be nominally Buddhist – though at this stage of dehumanisation it is unlikely that religion plays much part in their life.

As I write the complicated shutters that serve instead of a door are being lifted into place and securely barred with long wooden poles; so now I must spread my flea-bag on the second plank-bed before the firelight has entirely faded.

12 NOVEMBER – THANGJET

We were on our way by 6 a.m., having slept from 8.30 p.m. – if you can call it sleeping, between the biting of bugs and what sounded like the death-throes of that unfortunate woman.

From outside the hovel, before we continued down the ridge, we caught our last glimpse of the broad Trisuli Valley, far away beyond all the hills we crossed yesterday; and now the valley was so covered in cloud that it seemed like a sea of milk, whose motionless waves were clinging to the bases of many mountains.

Five hours later we stopped for brunch at a tiny hamlet of filthy stone farmhouses. Here was the same absence of food – too acute to be called a mere shortage – and at least every second person, including the children, had goitre. The skin diseases were not as bad as one would expect them to be but significant coughs were prevalent, and eye infections very common. The shattering poverty of this region almost counteracts the splendour of the surroundings; yet Langtang has always been among the most backward areas of Nepal, so it would be unfair to generalise from what one observes here. The people are mainly Tamangs, who speak a dialect of Tibetan, and Dr David Snellgrove estimates that they moved across the main Himalayan range before the sixth century AD.

Like all Nepal's hill-people they have suffered from consistent governmental neglect, and even now, when some feeble effort towards responsible government is being made in other areas, as despised 'Bhotias' they are not receiving their fair share of attention. Also few Gurkha soldiers are recruited from this district, so army pay-packets don't help the economy.

My Swiss relief-map of Nepal puts Thangjet west of the Kyirung River but, with all due respect to Messrs Kummerly and Frey, it happens to be east of it – or else I'm too addled to know where the sun is setting. (However, even such distinguished geographical publishers can readily be forgiven for losing their grip when producing a map of Nepal.) At first I thought it probable that a more prepossessing Thangjet existed beyond the Kyirung and that this was merely Little-Thangjet-Across-The-River: but the locals deny that any other similarly named place exists nearer than Tange in Thakkholi.

This is my first Tibetan-style village and on seeing the neglected *mani*-wall and the decrepit arched gateway I again experienced the bitter-sweet thrill of nearness to the unattainable. Today we passed several more chorten and a few very tall prayer-flag poles – suddenly recalling the existence of gods and men in the midst of the mountains' isolation. And now, when I look up from my writing, I can see a large, tumbledown chorten in the middle of the village 'street', with white prayer flags fluttering beside it in the cold evening wind. It gives me a special pleasure to see these flags flying against their natural background, instead of merely indicating refugee settlements; yet here one has the sad feeling that a long separation from the mainstream of

Tibetan Buddhism has reduced local religion to a rather perfunctory following of superstitious customs.

We arrived at Thangjet just before 3 p.m. after a much tougher walk than yesterday's, and when Mingmar decided to call a halt, though the next village was only three hours away, I mutinously suggested that we should go on. In reply he pointed to a mountain north of another river and said, 'Look at our track.' Obediently I looked – and stopped feeling mutinous. Thangjet is at 8,000 feet and to get to the next village we must descend 5,000 feet to river-level, before climbing to 9,000 feet, at which point the track rounds the flank of the opposite mountain – and for all I know continues to climb.

Thangjet consists of about a hundred and fifty slate-roofed houses, and, being one of the main halts on the Langtang–Kathmandu route, it sports an astonishingly clean doss-house, run by a cheerful Thakkholi woman. The place is a lean-to rather than a building, with an inner wall of stones, loosely piled together as in Connemara, an outer wall and roof of bamboo-matting and no gable-walls. The result, at this height in mid-November, adds up to a Cold Night; but luckily Rudi Weissmuller insisted on lending me a windcheater, which I will wear with my slacks as pyjamas.

There was a treat for supper – boiled buffalo-milk poured over my rice instead of the usual soup. This establishment is also a tea-house, the hallmark of Thangjet's sophistication! – and when darkness had fallen some half-dozen men, wrapped in ragged blankets, came to sit around the fire and drink glasses of tea. As they spoke in Tibetan I could follow some of the conversation, which was all about yetis. Our hostess and Mingmar denied that any such things exist, but the locals and our fellow lodger (a Tibetan trader) believed in them very firmly and only disagreed about the yeti's nature: some maintained that it was an animal, while others insisted that it was an evil Spirit incarnate. Two of the villagers claimed to have seen small yetis, about the size of a five-year-old child, and at this stage I offered, through Mingmar, my own opinion that the yeti is indeed an animal, unknown to zoologists, which lives at exceptionally high altitudes and very sensibly declines to be captured.

At present I am sitting in unparalleled comfort on the Tibetan trader's wool-sack, which measures five feet by three – though the significance of this statistic cannot be appreciated by anyone without first-hand knowledge of these Nepalese tracks. John Morris has written '. . . but I must emphasise that the paths in the hills of Nepal cannot in any way be compared with even the roughest tracks in the more remote parts of Europe: they are merely the result of people having walked over the same route for many generations.' Indeed they are – and 'path' would be too flowery a description for much of the route we covered today. I now see that quite apart from carrying food Mingmar is essential as a guide. No doubt one could find the way eventually, but this afternoon we were climbing over fantastic wastes of colossal, wobbling, jagged rocks, through which my eyes could detect no vestige of a track; and the most disconcerting thing about this terrain is that when one is heading for a northern destination the *right* path often goes south and the *wrong* path north.

I am being fascinated this evening by the passers-by, who walk up and down the rocky, steep street carrying long branches of blazing wood at arm's length – street lighting, Thangjet style!

13 NOVEMBER–SHABLUNG

The gods were against us today, and an individual who calls himself 'The Police' has forbidden us to go north-east from here into the Langtang Valley. It's another of these Nepalese muddles – or is it? According to this unsavoury bit of humanity – whose uniform consists of cotton underpants and a torn Western shirt and who is the only Brahmin in the village – my permit says that we can go to Gosainkund Lekh, but not any further north. The document, being written in Nepali, is of course unintelligible to Mingmar and me – so we can't argue. Admittedly it is very possible that within the Singha Durbar a request for a Langtang permit would elicit a Gosainkund Lekh permit, either through stupidity or for political reasons, and 'The Police' may now be luxuriating quite justifiably in this rare opportunity to exercise his authority against a Westerner; but it is equally possible that he sees here a glorious chance to land a fat bribe. However, unfortunately for him I am quite happy to turn south-east in the morning instead of north-east: the real frustration is not being able to go due north, where Tibet lies less than five hours' walk away.

Among the more dramatic contrasts of this trek are the frequent swift transitions from season to season. When we left Thangjet at dawn it was winter: sharp air stung our faces, the early light was metallic and the fields were colourless and quiescent. Yet by three o'clock it was high summer in Shablung and we sat arguing with 'The Police' under a deep blue sky, among blossom-laden almond-trees which seemed like pink clouds that had drifted to the cliff edge. Here long grass grew lush beneath flowering shrubs, above a flashing green river, and the air was soft with warm content. We had enjoyed an autumn zone too, during our long descent, seeing shining red, black and brown berries and nuts, and walking through the crispness of crimson, orange and russet leaves.

After our very tough climb on leaving Thangjet we had been glad to stop for an early brunch at a four-shack Tamang hamlet half-way down a mountainside. Here the poverty was grim enough, yet the people seemed alert – indeed, almost gay – and they showed both a normal curiosity and a shy friendliness.

The population of these stone-walled, grass – or plank-roofed shacks was thirty-six and there was a prodigious number of charming children who seemed surprisingly fit, apart from the inevitable eye infections. I asked if coughs were common here but apparently they are not. The health of these settlements is largely controlled by chance; if one tubercular trader spends a night in a house he can infect the whole community.

While Mingmar was cooking I watched part of the millet harvest being threshed. On a level, hard-earth terrace in front of one of the shacks an elderly man was rhythmically pounding the grain with a thick six-foot pole; beside him fluttered tall prayer-flags, beyond him was an abrupt drop of 3,000 feet and in the background shone the snow-peaks of Tibet. When the grain had been sufficiently pounded the womenfolk collected it in large, oval wicker baskets and, having taken it to another terrace, spread it out on round wicker trays and tossed it so adroitly that all the chaff quickly flew off. This looked easy, yet when I tried to do it half the grain fell to the ground and half the chaff remained on the tray – to the delight of the onlookers.

While we were eating Mingmar added to my cartographical confusion by declaring that the east-west river which we had just crossed is the Kyirung. Logically the Kyirung should be the north-south river which this torrent joins below Thangjet, which we have been following up from Trisuli and which rises some thirty miles north of the Tibetan frontier town of Kyirung. I note that Messrs Kummerly and Frey have cautiously refrained from naming this river above its confluence (where we stopped for brunch the first day) with what I had perhaps mistakenly assumed to be the young Trisuli, which rises a few miles northwest of Helmu. The whole thing is rather intriguing – and personally I like vague maps that leave one free to speculate.

No less intriguing in its way is the amount of rice consumed daily by Mingmar. Though lean, and hardly five foot tall, he gets through three-quarters of a pound of the stodge at each meal. Two ounces go to make the average rice pudding so you can imagine what twelve ounces looks like when cooked and heaped on a big brass platter. I myself would be immobilised for a week after one such repast – but Mingmar cannot understand how I walk so far and so fast on a mere ladleful of rice and a small tin of sardines. Neither can he understand my impulse to leap into glacial torrents whenever possible. Admittedly these waters are cold, but it is a supremely satisfying sensation to immerse one's sweaty, weary body beneath a white rush of iciness and then to emerge, tingling, into warm sunshine.

Shablung is only about 3,000 feet high, yet it has an even stronger Tibetan flavour than Thangjet. It is not marked on my map, nor is the considerable torrent that flows from the north-east and here joins the Kyirung – or the Trisuli, as the case may be. The village stands on a little plateau just north of this tributary, which is spanned by a wood and rope suspension bridge, and it is in the shadow of the next high ridge. The Kyirung is crossed by a rope pulley-bridge, on which men hang by the arm high above the water, and beyond it there is a long strip of cultivable land along the lower slopes of the opposite ridge; so the people are relatively prosperous, though the inherent Tibetan filthiness keeps the appearance of squalor well up to local standards. Millet and maize are the main crops, and herds of cattle, goats and sheep graze on the higher pastures. Shablung also has a school house, of which the villagers are inordinately proud; but naturally it is not now staffed, nor likely to be in the foreseeable future.

To outsiders there is an exhilarating atmosphere of siege about all these isolated settlements. They are at the furthest possible remove from the industrial areas of Europe where scraps of countryside, disfigured by pylons and wire-fencing, are only grudgingly tolerated by those to whom financial profit comes first. Here in the Himalayas it is Man who is just tolerated, in meagre communities at infrequent intervals, where the mountains relent enough for him to survive by the exercise of heroic labours – and also by the exercise of much more intelligence than is recognised by those theorising agricultural advisers who come East in droves, laden with university degrees, and who would be dead within a month if left to fend for themselves on a potentially fertile Himalayan mountainside.

Tonight we are staying with a delightful family whose home like all the others in Shablung, is roughly constructed of stone, with a plank roof. Animals are housed on the ground floor and from the street one ascends a shaky step-ladder to a five-foot high doorway which leads to a single room, some twenty-five feet by twenty, with a large stone fireplace sunk into the uneven wooden floor at one end. Over this projects from the wall a smoke-blackened canopy of bamboo-matting laid over wooden slats – something I have never seen elsewhere; it is about five feet above the fire and appears to be used as a hot-press-cum-larder. These houses all have decorated wooden facades which vary considerably in artistry, though even the best of them are more crudely executed than the famous Newari carvings.

At the moment I am sitting in the little window-embrasure making the most of the fast-fading daylight and being attacked by a vanguard of bed-bugs who are too greedy to wait for darkness. From the rafters above hang three bows and a quiverful of arrows, and my unashamedly romantic soul rejoices at the idea of staying with people who still regularly use bows and arrows to shoot wild goat. This household consists of parents – Dawa and Tashi – who are in their early forties, and nine children; the eldest is aged eighteen and the youngest six months, which seems to indicate careful if not restrictive family planning. All have survived, which must be rather unusual in these parts, but at present the three eldest are away tending flocks on the high pastures, from which they will soon be descending for the winter.

Now Mingmar has lit one of our candles and I have moved to sit on the floor. Beyond the fire Tashi is lying on a pile of piebald dzo-skins, naked from the waist up, feeding the baby. Her muscular torso is copper coloured in the flame-light and shoulder-length, lousy black hair draggles round her face as she beams at the infant while it happily sucks. Meanwhile the other children are tumbling in the shadowy background, like a litter of exuberant puppies, and Dawa is chopping with his kukri at a hunk of fresh mutton – making my mouth water at the prospect of *meat* for supper.

The manifold uses of the kukri fascinate me. One can do anything with it, from beheading an ox or felling a tree to sharpening a pencil or peeling a potato – not to mention killing men on all the battlefields of the world. The nonchalance with which these heavy, razor-sharp weapons are handled by small children is quite terrifying; if they made the slightest miscalculation they could very easily slice off one of their own limbs.

This evening I myself found use for the kukri as a surgical instrument. Mingmar has been unwell all day, the boil on his face having grown to carbuncle proportions, so I lanced it with the sterilised tip of Dawa's kukri and squeezed out an awe-inspiring amount of pus. It must have been causing him agony and making him feel as weak as a kitten – but like a good Sherpa he never complained. When the operation was over we were each given a mug of thick brown *chang*, made from millet instead of the more usual rice or barley. It tasted sour and was full of vaguely alarming foreign bodies; but the alcohol content was gratifyingly high and I did not say 'no' to either the second or third rounds.

Earlier this evening the Nyingmapa village lama came to greet me. He is a tall and very handsome man of about thirty-five, whose swinging maroon robes well become him; but he seemed a good deal more interested in trade than in theology and I doubt if he contributes much to the spiritual life of the community.

14 NOVEMBER – A GOMPA ON A MOUNTAIN

This is the first evening that we have arrived at our destination exhausted rather than pleasantly tired; we left Shablung at 6 a.m. and by 5 p.m. had climbed more than 10,000 feet.

On recrossing the suspension bridge outside Shablung we went back towards Thangjet, and in my innocence this slightly puzzled me, as I couldn't remember seeing any track branching off to the east. Here flat, narrow, maize fields lay on our left and I was enchanted to see a troop of giant silver langurs having their breakfast among the crop. These monkeys do a lot of damage and are always stoned on sight by non-Hindu farmers, so they fled when we appeared, moving most gracefully with long, loping. strides.

Leaving the maize fields behind, the track curved around an almost sheer mountain until Shablung could no longer be seen, and as I was walking ahead a whistle from Mingmar recalled me. I found him pointing towards one particular section of the mountain for no apparent reason, and he said 'Here we go up'; which we did, for the next ten hours.

Before long I realised that the rough track from Trisuli in fact represents a Nepalese main road. This hardly discernible path, which Mingmar had never used before, was so steep that for the first hour we were not really walking, but pulling ourselves up through long thick grass (there were no trees and few shrubs), using our hands as much as our feet. Soon Mingmar had been left far behind and I was alone, feeling like a lizard on a pyramid and rather proud of my newly acquired ability to follow the illogic of an almost non-existent track.

Often I stopped to rest and look round, and unhopefully I took a few photographs, knowing full well that my unique incompatibility with cameras made the effort a waste of money. Moreover, this incompatibility was now being aggravated by an aversion to the falsification of mountain photography. In such surroundings even the most expertly wielded camera cannot help but lie, and once the reality has been seen the preservation of fragments seems futile. Also it distresses me to break up visually the wholeness of a Himalayan landscape in an effort to see it as a series of 'good pictures'. So I soon freed myself from my camera and surrendered to the purity of the light, the foaming strength of the already distant river, the heaving complex of mountains on every side and the tantalising cleft that leads to Tibet, drawing one's eye to that ultimate glory of snow-peaks blazing coldly along the near horizon.

Soon I began to wonder why any path existed here, since it seemed unlikely that even Nepalese humans would settle on such a slope; but then suddenly I found myself scrambling on to a wide, level ledge, where a crop of unripe barley was overlooked by two solid stone farmhouses.

As I walked across this ledge – luxuriating in a movement that was not upward – I fancied something fairy-tale-like about these austere, improbable, grey dwellings. It seemed as if they must be inhabited by witches, whose broomsticks could provide a helicopter service to Shablung; but in reality the settlement consisted of twelve delightful Tamangs, including a young monk from the Gosainkund Lekh Monastery who was visiting the home which he had left at the age of nine. Only this youth had ever seen a Westerner; yet even before Mingmar arrived, to give a lucid explanation of my presence, everyone had welcomed me warmly, though wonderingly.

The origins and patterns of such settlements fascinate me – where the people came from, why they chose to live in so remote a region, where their sons find wives and their daughters husbands, and how far afield they go on trading trips. I asked all these questions, through Mingmar, but got no satisfactory answers to the first two. Questions about why people had settled on this plateau they clearly regarded as absurd; there was land to be cultivated, and water and fuel near by, so it was an obvious place for humans to live – and apparently it was not as isolated as passers-by might imagine. During the summer people from Langtang go to and fro to the yak pastures higher up, and both Thangjet and Shablung are, after all, quite near. In reply to my other questions I was told that marriages are not arranged, the young people choosing their own mates from these neighbouring villages or from the summer settlements of herds-people. Barley is their only saleable commodity and most of this goes to the Langtang folk, who are glad to have an easily accessible supply to supplement the potatoes and radishes that they grow for themselves beside the yak pastures. In exchange they give yak-butter, tea and salt, and for the rest this little community is self-supporting, producing its own tsampa, chang, potatoes, radishes, chillies and goat cheese, and weaving its own blankets and garments from goats' wool.

These people clearly felt no allegiance to any government, north or south. The surrounding mountains were their nation and their world, and no outside event could be said to affect them much; yet the Dalai Lama's flight to India and the subsequent Communist persecution of religion in Tibet had undoubtedly made some faint impression on their minds. I tried to find out – without implanting any disturbing ideas – if they feared a Chinese take-over of Nepal, but obviously the possibility did not worry them; either they had never considered it or they felt – probably rightly – that such a development would not make the slightest difference to them on their remote little ledge.

While Mingmar was cooking I sat smoking in the sun, and when I threw away the butt four waiting children dived for this precious prize which was won by a little girl who somehow coaxed two more puffs out of it. The adults then gathered to look wistfully at my packet of 'Panama' – a luxury Indian brand costing 8d for twenty. No one actually asked for a cigarette, but when I handed the packet round every face glowed with delight.

After our meal Mingmar and the monk held a long discussion about the track, and as we set off Mingmar informed me that from here onwards there was only a yak-path. I said that this sounded satisfactory, since yak presumably create a more distinct trail than humans; but according to Mingmar such infrequently used paths soon fade away, especially among dead leaves.

An easy twenty-minute climb brought us to the edge of a forest, where all signs of our path vanished, and after a moment's hesitation Mingmar admitted that he had no idea whether we should now continue upwards or go around the mountain. He only knew that our destination was on the other side of the ridge – and as the ridge in question stretched away vastly to north and south this degree of knowledge was not very helpful. Eventually he decided that we should try rounding the south flank and for the next half-hour we wandered along on the level, sometimes imagining that we had found the yak path, but soon realising that all these faint trails had been made by wood-gatherers from the settlement. Then suddenly we came to a sheer 5,000-foot drop into a side valley and at the sight of this abyss Mingmar shrewdly remarked that we were going in the wrong direction – so we promptly turned back.

Personally I was not at all averse to these haphazard wanderings. Here the trees were wide spaced – many had been felled – and in the brilliant midday sunshine the shrubs and ferns of the undergrowth filled this high silent world with rich autumn glows. We passed several open glades where amidst tawny, tangled grasses I saw the gleam of wild raspberries, strawberries, cranberries and blackberries – and stopped to eat them in fistfuls, with a view to stocking up on Vitamin C.

There was a strange familiarity about this scene 10,000 feet up in the Himalayan foothills. If one did not look beyond the immediate cosiness of the warm, mellow woodland one could imagine oneself in an Irish wood on a sunny October day – though however sunny that October day might be one would still need to wear more than the shirt and shorts that were adequate here in mid-November.

When we got back to where our path had vanished Mingmar took off his rucksack, announcing that he was going to look quickly in various directions for some trace of a yak-trail – and soon he came trotting triumphantly back, having found unmistakable signs of the creatures' progress. This path climbed very steeply, around the northern flank of the ridge, and in general it was visible only to Mingmar's eyes; had I been alone I would have denied its existence.

Here the forest was a twilit cavern of immensely tall and very ancient trees which repelled the sun and created an atmosphere of chill gloom. Many of these monsters had been blasted by lightning or uprooted by gales and we were slowed by having to scramble under or climb over the rotting, giant trunks that so often lay across our route. Soon my faith in this track was wavering and I suspiciously asked Mingmar how yaks were supposed to negotiate such obstacles. He replied that they jumped over them and, never having seen a yak in action, I felt in no position to argue; but it seemed to me that for this purpose a Grand National winner would be more appropriate than a yak.

The ground here was thickly covered with soft, slippery, black leaf-mould, and before long there was crackling ice underfoot, for we were climbing steadily. Now it was growing colder every moment and I staged the reverse of a strip-tease show, stopping repeatedly to put on socks, slacks, a vest, a sweater, a windcheater, a balaclava and gloves.

At about 12,000 feet the forest began to thin and then the path levelled out and became plain for all to see, curving past a herdsman's wooden hut and leading to a windswept, sunlit yak pasture.

Now freshly covered snow-peaks were visible directly ahead – no more than a mile away as eagles fly – and I rejoiced at our emergence into this brilliant world of blue, gold and white.

Already I was feeling the lack of oxygen (no doubt because I smoke too much) and was finding it difficult, when climbing, to keep pace with Mingmar. After a ten-minute walk across the plateau we came to a fork in the track, where one branch continued around the mountain and another climbed steeply towards the summit. Some instinct (or perhaps it was only my hammering heart) told me that the gompa path went around, not up; but Mingmar, pointing to three chortens on the summit path, said 'up!'. So up we went, to the 13,400-foot summit, where there was no sign of any gompa and the icy wind almost stripped the skin off our faces. Moving a little way down I sat in the shelter of a yak-house and said rather breathlessly, 'I suppose we may call this a mountain-top?' – but Mingmar replied firmly that it was no more than a high hill-top; apparently in these parts only permanently snow covered peaks qualify as mountains.

By now the sun was about to disappear behind the ridge beyond the Kyirung and we still didn't know where the gompa was: but I was too exhilarated by the magnificence of the scene to worry. Apart from the snow-peaks our hill-top was the highest point in the area and, despite its relative insignificance, I felt a surge of triumph while surveying the countless lower ridges that surrounded us on every side like the immobile breakers of some fantastic ocean.

Then, wandering over to the eastern edge of the plateau, I saw the shining roof of the little gompa some 1,000 feet below us – approached by that track which went around instead of up. Now I was glad that we had taken the wrong fork, but poor Mingmar almost wept on realizing that our final climb had been unnecessary. No track led directly down, and were we to follow our original path darkness would fall long before we reached shelter – so we decided to attempt a descent in as straight a line as possible.

The gompa had looked quite close from the summit but it took us over an hour to reach it, and that descent was almost as exhausting as the upward climb. At first the slope was densely covered with an odd sort of bushy undergrowth, about five feet high, which had extraordinarily springy and progress-resistant branches; yet without these the way would have been even more difficult – they provided something secure to clutch at when we were in danger of hurtling to eternity on the steepest stretches.

When the gradient eased we entered a weird forest of dead trees, some very tall, some mere broken stumps. All the branches had been lopped off, and at first I assumed that a half hearted forest-fire had recently swept the hillside; but a closer scrutiny revealed no trace of burning so I can only suppose that some obscure disease attacked this forest long ago. Whatever the cause, the effect was extraordinarily sinister in the twilight, and it would not have greatly surprised me had we come upon Dante and Virgil standing on the brink of an abyss watching souls being tortured.

The young monk had told us that the five Nyingmapa lamas who spent each summer in the gompa had recently left, so we expected to find the place deserted – but to my astonished horror we discovered three small children in a stone hut beside the temple. They are aged about eight, six and three and they haven't seen their mother for over a fortnight; nor do they expect her back until next week. Yet this strange, solitary existence, in a region to which very few travellers come between October and April, doesn't seem to disturb them in the least. They know nothing of the world beyond their mountainside and would probably be more frightened by a street-scene in Kathmandu than they are by these long, cold, dark nights spent huddled together in a heap of dried bracken. Named Tsiring Droma, Dorje and Tashi Droma they are typical little Tiblets, black with dirt and full of the joys of life – though understandably a little in awe as yet of their Western visitor.

However, despite the apparent contentment of these diminutive waifs I can't help feeling that their mother must be unnatural by any standards. When alone they have nothing to eat but raw white turnips, which grow on a small patch of fertile soil near the gompa, and in this region hungry snow leopard have been known to kill children during the winter. (As I write the Babes-on-the-Mountain are ravenously devouring some of our rice and Knorr's tomato soup.)

This hut measures about 20' x 8' and the low ceiling-beams don't allow me to stand upright. Both they and the thick stone walls have been so tarred by many years of wood-smoke that they now look as though newly painted with shiny black varnish. Since I sat down here in a corner by the huge mud stove – on which the lamas' cooking is done – a faint, steady, dripping noise has been puzzling me and I have just now realised that it is coming from a huge earthenware jar in which arak (the Tibetan poteen) is being distilled for the edification of Their Reverences next summer.

Normally, while their mother is away, these children sleep in a little empty yak-house at the edge of this level shelf of ground, where the rats are less troublesome than in the hut. When alone they are unable to light a fire, having neither matches nor flint (which deprivation seems the only vestige of commonsense shown by the missing mother), and now they are delightedly spreading malodorous dzo-skins on the floor in front of the stove. Already it's freezing hard, and the sky is trembling beautifully with the brilliance of the stars.

15 NOVEMBER – THE GOMPA

Yesterday evening I suspected that diarrhoea was on the way and by this morning my prognosis had been proved correct. I would have attributed this to mountain-sickness were Mingmar not similarly afflicted, which indicates a dysentery bacillus acquired en route – probably in the course of our potations at Shablung. I was out four times during the night, which in this weather is enough to give one chilblains on the behind, and by dawn I had got to the stage of scarcely being able to lift my head. Poor Mingmar was no better and we both had massive doses of sulphaguanidine tablets for breakfast, and at three-hourly intervals during the day; as a result we are now rapidly recovering, though neither of us could look at food this evening. (Not that there's much to look at.) We spent all day lying in hot sun – sheltered from the wind by three chortens that stand beside the yak-house – overlooking a tremendously deep valley that lies between our mountain and the dazzling snow-peaks opposite. Occasionally we stirred to help each other to our feet for the next instalment, and every few hours Mingmar staggered to the hut to brew the tea which our dehydrated bodies craved.

Last night it froze so hard that our water was solid ice this morning, the gompa's water supply comes from a stream some miles away and is cleverly brought here through a line of hollow tree-trunks, finally trickling from the last of these "pipes" into a large brass jar.

The Babes-on-the-Mountain really are adorable – I'd love to kidnap them. Tsiring Droma, the elder girl, today spent hours sitting near us slicing white turnips, which she then spread out on a bamboo mat so that the sun would dry and preserve them for use later in the winter. The rest of her time was spent with Dorje, the boy, practising the writing of Tibetan – a startlingly erudite pastime explained by the fact that these are the offspring of the lamas, who share one wife or concubine between them and who evidently take quite seriously the educational – if not the material – welfare of their family. Both children show great reverence for their tattered school books, which are pages from the ancient tomes of Buddhist scripture stored in the gompa. A deep respect for every object connected with their religion is ingrained in all Tibetans, however illiterate or uncouth they may be, and this respect is also extended to the religious objects of other faiths – an example of true civilisation which adherents of other faiths could profitably emulate.

On the last lap of our trek to the summit yesterday we saw – to my surprise – innumerable pheasants, but around here the only birds visible are a pair of ravens, who spent much of the day perched on top of the prayer-flag poles, croaking companionably.

There was a most dramatic sunset this evening – ribbons of scarlet above distant, deep blue mountains, and higher a width of clear pale green, and higher still tenuous sheets of orange vapour swiftly spreading across half the sky. But Mingmar did not share my enthusiasm for this display, saying it presaged a blizzard tomorrow.

16 NOVEMBER – THE GOMPA

How right Mingmar was in his weather forecast! We reckon we're lucky to have got back here safely this evening.

Both of us were in good form on awakening and we breakfasted then, having eaten nothing yesterday. When we left here at half-past seven the sky was cloudless and the snow-keen air intoxicating; but already Mingmar was studying the wind and being gloomy in consequence.

About a mile from the gompa I saw my first leopard-trap – a crude contrivance of wooden stakes built around a deep pit and looking as though it would delude none but the most seriously retarded leopard. Yet Mingmar assured me that this model is very successful.

We were now on the main Thangjet-Gosainkund Lekh track, beside which the gompa is built, and for about an hour we walked around the mountain just below the tree line, passing many herdsmen's huts and yak-houses. Then we came to a wide expanse of moorland, sloping up to a minor glacier, and here began an easy hour's climb towards the 15,800-foot pass. Today I found myself well adjusted to the altitude, and I irritated Mingmar by frequently taking off my knapsack and scampering up the low ridge on our left to revel in an unimpeded view of the Langtang range, now thrillingly close. Because of these detours it was almost eleven o'clock as we approached the steep, final lap of the upward path, which here was barely distinguishable beneath new snow. And now we had our initial warning – a grey veil suddenly wisping around the snow-peaks to the south-east. At once Mingmar hesitated, looking rather uneasy; but then – to my surprise – he decided that we should at least cross the pass and survey the weather-scene on the far side, where it might possibly be clearer. However, his optimism was not justified. As we reached the top so did the blizzard and we were almost lifted off the ground by an icy blast. Five minutes earlier the sun had been shining, yet now we were deep in that odd, muffled gloom which seems to belong neither to night nor day, and the thick flurry of flakes was reducing visibility to a few yards. When we quickly turned back our fresh footprints had already been obliterated, and within fifteen minutes we were very thoroughly lost. There seemed no real cause for alarm, with five hours of daylight remaining and the tree line quite close; yet to be blundering around so unsurely in this sort of terrain does put one slightly on edge, and I was relieved when we suddenly emerged into sunshine on an unfamiliar plateau.

Hereabouts a hill is not simply a hill, but a succession of similar looking ridges, and it's only too easy to go half-way down the wrong ridge before realising one's mistake. This we did twice, while searching for the main track, and by the time we had found it both of us were feeling the weakening effect of yesterday's intestinal contretemps; so I then produced my emergency ration of raisins, which we chewed while ambling leisurely downwards, our chilled bodies luxuriating in the warm sunshine.

The children were delighted to see us again and their pleasure quite made up for the disappointment of not being able to continue towards Gosainkund Lekh. Less than half-an-hour after our return the sky again clouded over and as I write it is snowing heavily outside – a cosy sight, as the five of us crouch around a blazing pyramid of logs, eagerly awaiting our rice and soup and boiled turnips; but it would have been pretty grim for the Babes-on-the-Mountain had they been alone this evening.

Mingmar has decided that our best plan for tomorrow is a return along the main track to Thangjet, where we will rejoin our original route. Having followed it about half-way back to Trisuli we can then branch off to the east and explore that high pocket of Sherpa settlements which lies towards Helmu, returning to Kathmandu down the valley of the Indramati River.

17 NOVEMBER – BACK AT THE SHACK ON THE RIDGE

The woman who was so ill here last week died a few days ago, leaving four little children motherless; but as they all look and sound tubercular they may not be long following her.

Today's nine-hour walk provided superb contrasts. When we left the gompa at 7.30 a.m., having given the children a final hot meal, snow lay a foot deep on the track – yet three hours later we were walking through groves of bamboo and banana-trees. I long to give some not entirely inadequate description of the glory and variety of that 8,000-foot descent, during which we saw many deer and pheasants but not one other human being; yet perhaps it's best to know when you're beaten.

Such a continuous descent on a very rough path is much more exhausting than any but the steepest climbs. This morning the nimble Mingmar was always far ahead of me, and he remarked that the majority of Westerners do find these descents very difficult, since we lack that inherent sure-footedness which enables the locals to skim so efficiently down stairways of insecure boulders.

From river-level a 4,000-foot climb took us to Thangjet, where we stopped for brunch. Since our last visit the tea-house has been enriched by a sack of sugar, but as it cost sixpence per teaspoonful we did not indulge.

This afternoon we saw a group of about twenty men and boys transporting newly-cut bamboo poles from the forest to their village – a distance of some five miles. Each load consisted of thirty eight-foot poles, divided into two bundles which were harnessed to the shoulders with long strands of tough jungle-grass. I could hardly believe my eyes when the first four men came racing at top speed down the precipice above our track dragging these unwieldy loads – which made an oddly musical clatter as the ends swept swiftly over the rough ground. At the junction with the main track the men had to do a sharp turn but even then they never slackened speed; and on approaching one of the many shaky, narrow, plank bridges that here span racing torrents they accelerated even more, so that their loads would have no time to slip over the edge and pull them into the water. Rarely have I seen a more impressive display of nerve, skill and strength; these men aroused the sort of admiration that one feels when watching a good toreador in action against a brave bull. Among the last to cross the bridge was a boy who looked about twelve but was probably at least sixteen. Perhaps this was his first bamboo expedition and he did not quite make it, one side of his load slipping off the planks. For a horrible moment it seemed that he must topple into the water; but he had kept his balance by some miracle and now he stood still, straining against the weight of the bamboo, while the man behind him struggled out of his own harness and rushed to pick up the hanging load. He then helped the boy to get safely over by walking behind him, holding both sides of the load clear of the bridge.

We followed the bamboo team for an hour, and their endurance, as they hauled these loads uphill, was even more impressive – if less spectacular – than their downhill sprints. Repeatedly one wonders just how these seemingly undernourished bodies manage to achieve physical feats that would be far beyond the powers of most well-fed Westerners.

18 NOVEMBER – SERANG THOLI

What a day! If we are not getting anywhere in particular we are certainly getting off the beaten track – and very nearly off every other track too! By now Mingmar has given up pretending to know exactly where we are, or where we will be by tomorrow night. He says that this whole expedition is "a bad trek"; yet our erratic wanderings suit me very well indeed – I feel blissfully happy all day and every day.

We set off this morning at six o'clock and for the first two hours were following the main track back towards Trisuli. Then we turned east and, having twice lost the faint path, eventually came to a small Tamang village where we stopped for a badly-needed brunch; the morning's climb had been tough, and by now I am beginning to suffer slightly from protein-deficiency.

This village, of some fifty houses, was almost deserted because the millet harvest has just begun. After brunch Mingmar tried to get some idea of where we should go next, but the only available informant was a deaf nonagenarian who insisted on directing us back to Trisuli; so we were left to the sluggish inspiration of our own senses of direction.

By 3 p.m. we had descended to river-level, where we were confronted by one of those nightmare tree-trunk "bridges" which demand the skill of a trapeze-walker. Admittedly this specimen was only twenty feet long – but it did look terrifyingly insecure, being casually held in place at either side by little piles of loose rocks, while its width could barely accommodate a single human foot. After one glance I funked it completely. Forty feet below the water was churning violently through a boulder-filled channel and even my trick of crossing such bridges a cheval seemed inadvisable. Merely to see Mingmar tripping lightly over almost made me ill and when he returned to take my knapsack I also handed him my shirt, shorts and shoes, informing him that I was going upstream to find some point at which I could either wade or swim across. Then it was his turn to feel ill; he went quite pale and said "You'll drown!" "Very likely," I agreed. Yet somehow I prefer drowning to falling off that unspeakable contraption you call a bridge.

It was easier than I had expected to find a fording point. Some quarter-of-a-mile upstream – where the river was about 100 yards wide and ten feet deep – a little dam had been built, and though the current was still strong here it seemed that by swimming diagonally above the dam I could just about make it to the other side. Fortunately my self-confidence when in water equals my lack of self-confidence when over water; I always enjoy a challenge from this element and poor Mingmar, who had anxiously followed me upstream on the opposite bank, was suffering most from tension as I dived into the icy, clear green pool. By the half-way stage I had the measure of the current and knew that there was not the slightest danger; yet I didn't dare ease off for long enough to yell reassuringly to Mingmar and until I stepped onto the rock beside him he remained convinced that I must drown.

After this refreshment by immersion I was in excellent form for the next lap – a long, long climb up the steepest cultivated slope we have yet seen, where there was no path and we simply pulled ourselves somehow from one narrow terrace of ripening millet to another.

Tonight we are staying in a Tamang hamlet at 7,500 feet, where the slate-roofed houses are built of ochre mud and stone as in the Hindu villages around Pokhara. At the moment the populace are almost pushing each other over a precipice in their efforts to see me; and Mingmar is hardly less of a curiosity, for we are now far from the main tracks and few of these people have ever before seen either a Western female or a Sherpa porter in all his sartorial glory.

The filth of this house is extreme and the stable seemed so much less filthy that I chose it as my bedroom and am now leaning against the warm flank of a reclining buffalo. One hopes that bed-bugs will be fewer here than indoors: and the cow-bugs that must inevitably frequent Nepalese cattle are not so likely to be interested in me.

19 NOVEMBER – SENTHONG

Leaving Serang Tholi at dawn we climbed steadily to the summit of a 9,000-foot hill. Ordinarily the sun comes over the mountains to us, but today we went over a mountain to the sun and it was wonderful to step from cold early shadows into warm golden air, and to see the new, gentle light lying on a wild tumble of deserted mountains.

By ten o'clock we had negotiated two of these mountains, following a faint path that frequently vanished. Then we came to a tiny settlement, on the verge of another cultivated hillside, where we ran into caste trouble for the first time on this trek. When Mingmar inquired where he might cook our brunch we discovered that this was a very orthodox Chetri village in which we, as untouchable non-Hindus, would not be admitted to any house; but eventually we found a woman who consented to cook for us, provided we remained outside her compound.

The conscientious Mingmar was frantically worried at the idea of anyone but himself cooking for me, and he swore that after this meal I would get every disease in the book. However, I consolingly pointed out that my immunities are abnormally well-developed, by Western standards – and also that Chetris are cleaner, as well as more intolerant, than Tamangs. Yet I must admit that this village was loathsomely smelly, and our rice did look and taste as though cooked in a pretty sordid pot. None of the people we have stayed with (apart from the Thakkholi woman at Thangjet) ever practises the art of washing up – unless one counts the licking of platters at the end of a meal, which happens to be the labour-saving device that I too employ when living alone in my own home.

From half-past eleven we walked almost continuously for six hours – first down to river-level, next up and over an 8,800-footer, then two thirds of the way down this "hill" until we came to Senthong, where there are a few Tamang households among many Chetris. It is an odd sensation, when looking for lodgings, to go from door to door asking what the family religion is and receiving cold stares from the Hindus. The Tamangs here are very much poorer than the Chetris and are unmistakably the outcasts of the village; but equally unmistakably they are a far nicer group of people than their Hindu neighbours. I don't resent being shunned by orthodox Hindus, who can't reasonably be expected to fraternise with the likes of me, yet it is sad that Hinduism, despite the breadth of its basic philosophy, has in practice the effect of blighting many potentially valuable human contacts – whereas Tibetan Buddhism, however imperfectly understood by the masses, has the precisely opposite effect.

Tonight I have again chosen the cattle-shed as there simply isn't space for me inside this tiny house, which shelters a complex family of eighteen children and six adults. I discovered last night that cattle are noisy creatures with which to sleep because of their extraordinarily tumultuous digestive processes, which seem to go on all night like a thunderstorm.

20 NOVEMBER – LIKARKA

This morning I was awakened at half-past four by the ancient, soothing rhythm of millet being ground between the stones of a hand-mill. It was still dark and quite cold, and for the next hour I lay drowsily warm in my flea-bag, looking up at the golden throb of the stars and listening to the little stirrings of the village. The rice harvest had everyone on the move early, and as Mingmar and I made our way down to river-level soon after dawn we passed families already threshing grain on the wider terraces of the paddy fields. Here bullocks are used for the thresh-ing, but at Serang Tholi – where the people also have cattle – we had seen the operation done by hand, each separate sheaf being beaten vig-orously on the ground until every grain was shaken loose.

Were I only allowed a single adjective to describe Nepal I would have to use "varied". No two villages are quite alike in language, dress, customs, attitudes, architecture or surroundings, and one could not possibly refer to "a typical village" of this region. Doubtless the isola-tion imposed by the terrain on each settlement is responsible for this most pleasing diversity, which makes one realise anew how horribly our Western uniformity impoverishes life. And an equally rich variety is found in the landscape; at every turn one is confronted by new, tre-mendous vistas of unimaginable beauty as though Nature, when creat-ing these mountains, had been exercising the subtle imaginative power of a great musician elaborating on a simple basic theme.

Today has been the most strenuous of the entire trek. This morn-ing's river was a wide seething torrent, spanned some 80 feet above the water by a swaying, decrepit suspension bridge; but luckily the hand-rails were sufficiently intact for me to feel no fear of the crossing, and at 7.15 a.m. we began the upward climb. From river-level – 3,400 feet – until we had crossed an 11,800-foot pass there was no respite on level ground, and even Mingmar had to admit that he felt "very tired" at the top – a sensational confession.

We had stopped soon after nine o'clock for an hour's brunch-break at a three-house Tamang settlement, and these were the last dwellings seen until we crossed the pass at midday and descended some 1,500 feet to this region of scattered Sherpa houses.

After the savagely steep climb up it was a relief to find ourselves looking down from the top of the pass over an easy green slope. Here huge grey boulders were strewn on the grass, patches of unmelted snow gleamed in shady spots, and flocks of long-haired, sturdy goats grazed in the care of a little boy who lay alone on a slab of rock, thoughtfully playing a flute. From this point the circular valley – some fifteen miles in circumference – appeared to be quite shallow, though later we saw the ravine in the centre through which a river flows away to the south. Immediately above us, to the north, a jagged mountain was only thinly wooded with giant pines, but about a mile beyond the sunny expanse of pasture dense forests darkened the sides of the valley. And here I felt more than usually aware of that special tranquillity always experienced at these heights – a depth of peace impossible to describe or explain, but reaching to every fibre of one's being.

Our destination was a little settlement already visible on the far side of the valley and it looked so deceptively close that now we dawdled along, relishing our walk down the easy incline. Half-an-hour's ambling brought us to a sheltered hollow where we saw two Sherpa dwellings, with freshly-printed prayer-flags flying between them. There was a well here, beside the path, and pausing to drink from it I noticed something that almost paralysed me with astonishment – wrapping paper off a bar of Lifebuoy soap. I beckoned to Mingmar, and we stood staring at this baffling manifestation of "civilisation" as though we were the first men on the moon and had found an empty matchbox there before us. Then, continuing towards the houses, we came upon two gorgeous silk saris spread on the grass to dry – and next we saw a most beautiful young creature, wearing a pink sari and golden slippers, with attractive bazaar jewellery in her glossy hair and on her slender neck and arms. This vision was leaning against a low stone wall, talking to an older woman with a weather-roughened face whose muscular body was clad in the filthiest of rags and who obviously had never washed in her life.

Mingmar and I did not even attempt to conceal our curiosity; having greeted the women we too sat on the wall, and in reply to questions were told that three years ago the girl had gone to Bombay to be trained as a nurse and was now home on a month's leave. "Careers for Girls" are of course unheard of in these parts and it was inexplicable to me that this youngster should have had sufficient education to undergo a nurse's training. Evidently there was a story here, but neither mother nor daughter was very communicative and we could find out nothing more.

I wondered how the girl's relatives were reacting to the appearance in their midst of such unprecedented elegance and sophistication. Would they feel proud of her, or uneasy, or a little scornful of her fussiness and daintiness? Certainly the girl herself, by so scrupulously maintaining 'Bombay standards' against the heaviest of odds, was affirming her belief in the superiority of her new mode of life. She was most affectionate towards her mother, yet she did look rather strained, and it seemed likely that the immediate impact of the return had been disquieting and that she was secretly and guiltily looking forward to her departure.

Meeting this girl helped me to understand why Asian villagers who have had a medical training are so reluctant to return to those areas where help is most needed. For them the sheer novelty of both the material and mental opportunities of urban life is overwhelming, and in such a totally new world they become new people, continually discovering unsuspected potentialities within themselves. Some people accuse them of allowing improved conditions to "go to their heads"; yet this seems an unfair description of the natural excitement caused by widening horizons. The comparative values of what is lost and what gained by migration to a city is not relevant to this argument. These young people are usually conscious only of gaining, and at this stage of individual development are as self-centred as babies, reaching out with both hands for all the advantages of education and unaware that their own good fortune imposes on them a responsibility to help their fellows. It seems unrealistic to demand, from this generation of newly-educated Asians, the self-discipline that would enable them willingly to relinquish their brave new world. Such a sacrifice would require a much riper fruit of education than any that they can be expected to bear; and this is one of the main obstacles that for years to come will hinder Health Programmes in Asia – however generously the West may finance them.

Before leaving this curiously pathetic mother and daughter we had asked about the path through the forest; yet within an hour of entering the twilight beneath the trees we were more lost than one could believe possible. I had expected quite a clear track between the two settlements, but if any such exists we never found it. For over two hours we went scrambling up and down precipitous slopes, through thick, thorny undergrowth, and repeatedly we were thwarted by impassable ravines. At half-past four we knew that less than ninety minutes of day-light remained and now Mingmar was getting really frightened; he had begun to pray non-stop, using that odd Buddhist hum which sounds rather comical until one has become familiar with it. Neither of us had any idea of the way back, so we decided to continue the struggle forward – and then suddenly we came on something that had once been a track, though now it is in a dangerous state of disrepair. Having nervously followed it through two deep dark ravines – even Mingmar was nervous, to my immense gratification – we emerged at last on to another wide stretch of level turf; and twenty minutes later, after cross-ing several fields of buck-wheat, barley and potatoes, we were relaxing with this charming Sherpa family.

Their house is similar to the one we stayed in at Shablung, though the living-room is twice as big and very much cleaner. Dry maize-cobs hang from the rafters and handsomely carved cupboards line the wall that faces the low door and two tiny windows. If one can judge by the array of silver votive bowls, and silver-bound wooden tea-cups, the family must be quite rich by local standards. Against the wall in one corner leans a four-foot-high copper-banded bamboo churn for making buttered tea, and in a little room leading off this is the family chapel, where eleven tiny butter-lamps flicker cosily beneath a grimy but very lovely thanka representing the Compassionate Aspect of the Lord Buddha.

This family consists of a grandmother, her son, his wife and five ad-orable children who stopped being shy of me in record time. As I write, sitting on the floor near the fire, the two younger ones are standing beside me, leaning on my shoulders and intently watching that strange procedure which covers clean paper with a nasty mess of squiggles.

As soon as we arrived here I sat in the window-embrasure to enjoy one of the most beautiful sunsets I have ever seen. This house – at 10,400 feet – faces due west, and I was overlooking range after range of dusk-blue mountains, beyond which the ghostly snows of the distant Dhauligiri Massif were just visible against a crimson horizon. Above this sunset flare was a blue-green ocean of space, in which the golden boat of Venus sailed alone; and higher still the zenith was tinged pink-ish brown. Truly this was a most noble scene, so still with peace and so vital with beauty in the ebbing of the day.

On a more mundane level the evening was scarcely less memorable, because we had potatoes and milk for supper. Perhaps only a compatriot could appreciate the gastronomic ecstasy into which an Irishwoman can fall when served with potatoes after living on rice for a fortnight. Yet Mingmar seemed equally thrilled; though he can eat rice in such abundance, potatoes are the staple food of the Sherpas in their home district. He successfully consumed thirty-three large specimens and was quite concerned when, after twelve monsters, I reluctantly declined a third helping for sheer lack of space. Indeed this fourhouse settlement is a veritable food-paradise; we have been able to buy five eggs, which we will hard-boil and take with us tomorrow as both our rice and sardine supplies are getting low.

21 NOVEMBER – A FARM ON A HILLTOP

I am willing to concede that this is only a hill-top, since we are now down to 6,000 feet. The hill in question is a spur of one of the giant mountains that overshadow this valley on both sides, and after the silence of the heights it's quite disconcerting this evening to hear the roar of the nearby river.

Oddly enough it was Mingmar who felt poorly today, after yesterday's marathon. This morning's easy ten-mile walk was mainly downhill and we stopped frequently; yet he made heavy weather of the few inevitable climbs, and when we arrived here at half-past two he suggested that an early halt might be good for me! Perhaps he overindulged in *chang* last night, forgetting our dire experience after the Shablung binge.

Soon after leaving Likarka at 6.30 a.m. we crossed the steep wooded ridge that rises sharply behind the settlement and that loveliest of valleys was out of sight. About an hour later I saw my first herd of dzo – and was vaguely disappointed to find they look exactly like cows with very bushy tails. They were being guarded by a pair of enormous, ferocious-looking Tibetan mastiffs who almost foamed at the mouth as I wandered through the herd taking photographs. Mingmar says that these dogs are trained to kill intruding humans; during the day they are usually tied to wooden stakes with short, heavy chains and they wear large, clangorous iron bells around their necks. But at night they roam free and are far more dangerous than wild animals;

I know several Tibetans whose faces have been horribly disfigured by their attacks. Today I felt decidedly apprehensive when we had to pass a herd in charge of an untied dog; but the enraged creature was restrained by two tiny children who flung their arms around his neck and told him to be quiet. I didn't really expect him to obey – yet immediately he subsided and began to wag his tail at the children, ignoring us as we sidled past.

Soon afterwards we met a youth returning to Likarka from his first trading expedition to Kathmandu. He had received a Rs. 100 note in payment for wool, but being illiterate and having never before handled big money he was not at all sure what this signified. When he stopped us to ask for a definition Mingmar said that such a large note would be useless in this area, so I changed it for twenty Rs. 5/- notes, to the boy's delight; he evidently imagined that his father would be much better pleased by twenty notes than by one! He then showed us what had once been a very good Swiss watch; it had been sold him in Kathmandu for – he thought! – Rs. 50/- and was still ticking, but the minute-hand had come off the day before – doubtless because he had been playing too vigorously with the winder. (He had of course no notion how to read the time.) I advised him to leave it alone until he next visited Kathmandu; but then there ensued a lengthy discussion between him and Mingmar on the advisability of exchanging watches. Mingmar's would have been the better of the two even had the boy's been perfect; yet the Sherpa trading urge is so strong that apparently a losing deal is preferable to no deal at all and finally Mingmar accepted the broken watch, plus Rs. 25/-, in exchange for his own Omega.

Half-an-hour later we stopped again at one of those "dairies" fairly common in this area, where small herds of dzo are looked after by cheerful shepherdesses who make Tibetan-type cheese and butter. I intend bringing home a piece of the cheese, which has to be seen to be believed. It is harder than any rock except granite and is said to be still edible three centuries after it has been made – if one knows the technique required for eating granite-hard substances. This "dairy" was a little bamboo-matting hut on a grassy slope encircled by the forest and here we each enjoyed a long drink of buttermilk, and a platter of whey fried in butter and pleasantly tainted by the smoke of the wood-fire.

Several very young dzo calves stood near by and completely captivated me. At this age they have their father's thick coat and are bundles of furry huggableness, with huge melting eyes and affectionate licks for all and sundry.

Several other brief delays were caused by Mingmar stopping at every farmhouse en route to enquire if there was any butter for sale; his mother died a year ago and now he wants to make tormas and burn lamps in honour of the anniversary. His trader father had two wives, one living in Namche Bazaar and the other in Lhasa. When he died Mingmar was only four and was brought up by both his mother and his step-mother, who themselves traded extensively between Tibet and India. Lhamo, his twenty-two-year-old sister, now looks after the family trading concerns and Pemba, his elder half-brother, runs one of the Tibetan hotels in Kathmandu – assisted by his own mother. This morning Mingmar bought two pounds of Tibetan cheese for her, as he always brings back a present of her favourite delicacy when he has been away on trek. So between butter for his dead mother and cheese for his live step-mother our progress was considerably slowed.

Obviously his sister Lhamo is Mingmar's favourite; he repeatedly refers to her with affection and pride, saying what a clever business-woman she is and how much he is looking forward to seeing her, after a year's separation, when she comes from Lhasa to Kathmandu next month, en route for Calcutta. These Sherpas certainly get around – and they seem to need no passport for all their travels between Tibet, Nepal and India. Of course, Lhamo now flies from Kathmandu to Calcutta, and for all I know travels by truck in Tibet. She has two husbands, so far one who looks after the family farm near Namche Bazaar and one in Kathmandu, who also has another wife permanent-ly resident there to comfort him while the tycoon Lhamo attends to her International Business. No wonder Sherpa relationships are not easy to sort out!

Our last and longest delay came soon after midday, when we paused to watch a religious ceremony being conducted outside a stone hut on a ledge. For some time before reaching this ledge we could hear the wonderful melody of drum, bell, cymbals and conch-shell – music that made me feel very homesick for the Pokhara camp, and that sounded even more stirring against its natural background. I tried to find out what the ceremony was all about, but even if Mingmar knew he clearly did not want to discuss it with an outsider; so I stopped probing and contented myself with imprudently drinking four wooden bowlfuls of the best *chang* I have ever tasted.

The elderly lama conducting the ceremony was dressed in black instead of the usual maroon robes, and his young monk assistant wore layman's clothes. Both sat cross-legged on the ground, with their backs to the hut wall, and the Scriptures were laid before the lama on a low wooden table. His Reverence held a bell in his right hand and a dorje in his left – the dorje being frequently abandoned when he needed another swig of chang, which he favoured instead of the buttered-tea consumed endlessly during ceremonies by the more orthodox lamas. At right angles to the wall stood a painting of the Lord Buddha with the usual tormas and butter-lamps laid before it, and in front of this was a hanging drum, some three feet in circumference, which a tall, slim youth, clad in the local kilt, beat regularly in time to the chanting. About thirty people sat nearby in a semi-circle, laughing, chatting, drinking chang and eating cold sliced potatoes. The atmosphere was gay and friendly, and we were made to feel so welcome that we remained with the little group for over half-an-hour, each of us giving an offering to the lama before we left.

The young mother of the Sherpa family with whom we are staying tonight recently spent three years as a coolie on the roads in Assam, and Mingmar told me that it is common for the people of this area to emigrate temporarily to India and work in road gangs with the Tibetan refugees. Then, having saved up more money than they could ever earn in Nepal – and increased it on the way home by astute trading in Kalimpong – they return to settle down here. I attempted to discover whether they are officially accepted into the road gangs as Nepalese citizens, or whether they masquerade as Tibetan refugees; but my questions on this subject were plainly regarded as indelicate so I did not pursue the enquiry.

Tonight Mingmar at last knows where we are and says we will be back at base by midday on 24 November. The track from here to Kathmandu is familiar to him, which seems sad; it has been sheer bliss wandering lost-like from mountain to mountain.

22 NOVEMBER – A HOVEL ON A MOUNTAIN-TOP

This is the most squalid lodging we have encountered on the whole trek; it is even filthier than the children's hut beside the gompa. The small room is windowless and now that darkness has fallen a bullock, four goats, seven hens and a cock are sharing the apartment with a family of six, plus Mingmar and me. Here we are again above 9,000 feet and the night-air is so cold that the door has been shut fast, allowing no outlet for the billowing wood smoke, which is making me cough incessantly and having the usual excruciating effect on my eyes; but as compensation these gentle, cheerful Tamangs are exceptionally likeable, and their anxiety to make me comfortable is all the more touching because of the irredeemable discomfort of their home.

Today's walk was another marathon, and by brunch-time I knew why Mingmar had not been keen on going further yesterday afternoon. We started the day's adventures at 7 a.m. with quite a hazardous fording of a fiercely-fast, waist-deep, icy river. Here Mingmar was the terrified one – for a change – and as we waded across together he clung to me so frantically that he very nearly unbalanced us both. We needed every ounce of our strength to keep upright against the force of the water and it was so extremely difficult to retain a foothold on the large, constantly shifting stones that I didn't really think we could make it without a ducking.

At times the water had been up to our armpits and now we were painfully cold; but that was soon cured by a ninety-minute climb up a precipitous, slippery and very narrow path through dense scrub. Here it was my turn to be terrified; the snag was that I couldn't see the crumbling path through the thick grass and undergrowth – but I could see very plainly the drop on the right, though I didn't dare look down for long enough to estimate its depth.

By about half-past nine we had left this unwholesome path behind and gone downhill again towards the river. We stopped for brunch at a stinking, fly-infested hovel near the junction with the main Kathmandu–Gosainkund Lekh track; and an hour later we were on this highway, sharing it with groups of heavily-laden Tibetans, Tamangs and Chetris and feeling already halfway back to the bustle of metropolitan life.

For the next four hours we continued gradually but steadily downhill, following the river. At times the path led over stretches of colossal boulders, or through bright widths of fine silver sand, and once we crossed a dilapidated suspension bridge that swayed uncertainly 150 feet above the water. One feels slightly impatient about the neglect of these plank bridges; with so much forest on every side there can be no shortage of raw material for their repair.

At three o'clock we reached a village which boasted the first shop seen since our departure from Trisuli. Here we asked for tea, since our own supply expired a few days ago, but the shop stocked only ancient, flyblown, Indian sweets and unsmokable cigarettes and mildewed biscuits – of which we bought two packets for consumption on the spot.

Next we again climbed steeply for three hours – up and up and up, with the shining snow-peaks to the north becoming lovelier every moment. Here the lower, richer slopes are cultivated by Chetris or Newaris and the upper, more barren slopes by Tamangs. The whole region seems very densely populated – and smelly in proportion – when compared with the lonely mountains now behind us. One of the incidental joys of lonely mountains is the absence of that overpowering stench of human excrement which is always present in the more populous parts of Nepal.

These insect-plagued lodgings are beginning to prey slightly on my nerves – and it's not difficult to foresee that tonight is going to be a bug-classic. Since leaving Trisuli I've not had one unbroken night's rest and, though the locals do not suffer to the same extent, I hear them scratching and muttering in their sleep every night. So the bugs must do real damage to health by making sound sleep impossible.

23 NOVEMBER – KATHMANDU

We achieved yet another marathon today, which got us here ahead of schedule – and what a welcome I received from Tashi! Like most Tibetans she is very soft-spoken so she didn't bark or yelp, the only audible sign of rejoicing being that peculiar, rapid sniffling noise with which she always greets my returns; but for the first few moments it seemed that she would wriggle out of her skin with joy, or that her over-wagged tail would come adrift – it's nice to be so important to somebody.

This morning I saw my first total eclipse of the sun, which lasted from about 8.15 until 9.30 – and in honour of which today is yet another public holiday throughout Nepal.

We left our hovel before dawn, since last night even Mingmar was unable to sleep for bugs, and by eight o'clock we had reached the top of a 9,000-foot hill, after an easy climb through crisp, early air. From here we were overlooking a long, deep, narrow valley, and our path now continued almost level for some two miles, before plunging abruptly down to a small village by the river.

As we were scrambling down from the ridge-top to join this path I noticed something very odd about the quality of the light, and simultaneously I registered an unnatural drop in the temperature. Overtaking Mingmar I said, "What on earth is happening? The light's gone funny, and it's so cold!" To this obtuse question a native English-speaker might have been forgiven for replying that nothing was happening on earth; but Mingmar merely said, "The moon is having a meal." I stared at him for a moment, wondering if he were going dotty – and then I realised that the dottiness was on my side, for when he pointed to the sun I saw that about a quarter of its surface had already been obscured by the "hungry" moon.

What an appropriate place this was for experiencing the eeriness of a solar eclipse! As we walked along that path, so high above the valley, we could hear conches being blown wildly and cymbals and drums being beaten frenziedly, while all the lamas and priests of the little villages far below shouted and wailed and screamed in their contest with those evil spirits who, by attacking the sun, were threatening the whole of human existence. This extraordinary panic of sounds, combined with the "evening" twitter of bewildered birds and the unique, greenish half-light, evidently aroused within me some deep racial memory, and for an instant, at the precise moment of total eclipse and estrangement from our whole source of life, I felt as my own that primitive fear which was then dominating the whole of Nepal.

NARENDRA DAI

Bishweshwar Prasad Koirala

Bishweshwar Prasad Koirala, (1914–1982) known as B. P. Koirala, was a Nepali politician and a prolific writer. He was the Prime Minister of Nepal from 1959 to 1960. He led the Nepali Congress, a social democratic political party.

As the past fades away and the days fall by, they burrow deep into me, leaving behind tunnels of varying shapes and sizes, some deep and others shallow. When I look back, I see – like images flickering on a screen – a black and blue mountain range standing tall, blocking the past from view; but I can see holes riddled across its entire chest. My past has been burrowing tunnels for longer than I can remember. I spend my days digging. Sometimes, when I am alone, I escape the present and find myself walking down one of these tunnels. Some of them are so dark that I am unable to see or find anything in them. Others retain a faint light, but I can barely make out a thing. But then, there are those tunnels that no matter how deep they go, when I walk into them, they are illuminated with a light that escaped a memorable moment. I can pull back the curtains of time and once again embody the emotions, colors and sounds of that moment. It's almost like in grandmother's tales of kind fairies who rub soothing balm on tired children's eyes, through some mystical trick, the years fall off like clothes from a naked body. I become a child and I relive those days as I once did. And then I call out – "Sannani, Phaguni, Narendra dai . . . !!!"

So, is this not a fable? Is this story a fabrication, merely an imaginary palace of dreams, a fantastical tale that never happened? Let me tell you, no fable is ever untrue. Imagination never lies. A palace of dreams can never be built on nothing – Never. Dreams are built upon the foundations of reality. No matter how much I twist and exaggerate an event or story, or use imagination to polish or shape it, I would only make the truth more obvious and the story itself would take on a more and more realistic form. Man cannot shield himself from his own past. Even a story written as fiction is but a small incident – a singular truth – picked from the reserves of memory. What a writer writes is but a fragment of his memoirs. A story is perhaps nothing more than an attempt to reawaken and relive an experience from the past. I remember those times clearly, I recall those people like they are right here, and with a trusting voice I call them close to my heart – "Gauri Bhauju, Munariya, Narendra dai . . . !!!"

Narendra dai was an attractive person. Tall, wearing a clean white kurta and dhoti, with a carefully folded four-layered dupatta wrapped around his neck, curls of meticulously groomed dark, long hair settling gently upon his dupatta – Narendra had won the hearts of all the men and women in our village. Mind you, he wasn't fair and beautiful, neither was his countenance really exemplary – where his nose should have stood tall it flattened slightly, his ears were as wide as leaves of the flame tree growing from the sides of his face, his eyes were ordinary but obscured by thick eyebrows that made them look small and sunken, his raised cheek bones made his well-nourished face take on a famished look, and, on top of this, his dry skin gave his face a look of slight depravation. But, he did have a rugged attractiveness. Not like the beauty of sculpted alabaster, but more abundant in the hardness of rough carvings on ordinary stones that reveal its inner strength and wild nature – like the beauty of a wild mountain cliff, saturated in a feeling of dread. We, the children, would experience fear, anxiety and terror in front of him and, for no reason at all, we would try to avoid him.

I did call out above – "Narendra dai!" But, as children, we were never so close to him to call him with such boldness. It's not that he treated us badly. Rather, he always tried to be friendly with us – he would even make arrangements for and join in our sports. He'd tell us, "Boys! Play hard! If you build your bodies now, you won't have to worry about anything later!"

It is only in the world of memories that Narendra appears so close. When we were children, our group would wander around the village, without a care for whether Narendra was home or not. Besides, Sannani and I had a small world of our own – one that was unique to us.

We lived in a small and ordinary village in the Madhesh by the banks of the River Koshi, but even in that small place, the two of us could find and invent unending treasure troves of fun as we wandered over farms, fields and canals.

Picking out a rosary pea seed from the vines entangled below the monkey fruit tree, Sannani placed the seed into the corner of her eyes with great care and made it disappear, and then, dusting her hands, said – "Look! The seed has vanished!"

I was looking at her in amazement when the rosary seed fell out from the corner of her eye.

"I'm going to pick some rosary seeds too," I said as I jumped up and started yanking at the vines. But Sannani shouted – "Wait! Wait! You might pull a velvet bean vine instead."

Pointing out a vine with shimmering rotund pods that was wrapped around the lowest branch of the monkey fruit tree, Sannani said, "Look! See – that sparkling pod, that's velvet bean. You can tell them apart from a rosary pea vine. See – that one!"

Since that day, I've been able tell a rosary pea vine from a velvet bean vine. Not only that, on that I day, I also learnt how to carefully place a rosary pea into the corner of my eyes and make it disappear.

Around then, on the trail that skirted around the mango groves we saw some Madheshi girls from our village heading south to cut grass. I called out, "Phaguni! I know how to put rosary pea seeds in my eyes! Look, if you don't believe me!"

Phaguni didn't respond, but Rampiyari gave a response that eluded my comprehension, "Don't pick up such habits at such a young age, dear!"

The girls continued walking, laughing, jostling each other, stamping their feet on the trail, hitting each other on the back with their bamboo baskets. And, one of them said, "This one is such a brat, how could she say such a thing . . ."

Sannani called to them, "Phaguni! Please cut down the velvet bean vine with your sickle. The monkey fruits are ripe, but we can't pick them . . ."

Dinanath, the owner of the garden must have been on a machan close by. He suddenly appeared, angry – "Get out of my garden – these imps won't leave anything standing in this garden!"

We tore across the garden fence and ran until we found ourselves standing upon Lakhan Madar's threshing floor. Catching her breath, Sannani wheezed, "Dinanath is an angry one . . ."

"I dropped all my rosary seeds," I said.

"We'll go there again tomorrow," Sannani said. "Those ripe monkey fruits too . . ."

We then started watching the drama around the threshing. Occasionally, just for fun, we would twist the ox's tail – "Ha, ha, ha, ha, ha . . . Piyari."

"This isn't Piyari," Lakhan Madar's son pointed out.

"Our ox is Piyari," I explained.

Then, suddenly deciding that the fun there was over, we left and meandered our way down to the banks of the pond by the shrine of Gosaisthan. On the southern bank was a large cluster of jujube shrubs. We ate some jujube berries, went down to the pond, got naked, and started bathing.

After a while, we came up to the embankment and were drying ourselves when Sannani's eyes fell upon an oxcart coming our way from the west. She worriedly exclaimed, "Hide, Hide! Narendra dai! Hide, Hide!"

This is how, every now and then, we would remember Narendra as he abruptly appeared before us, and we would invariably hide from him, wishing that he wouldn't see us.

We entered the pond again. The embankment hid us. The road lay in a dip below the northern embankment of the pond.

"Narendra dai is returning from Calcutta today," Sannani explained.

"He would have killed us if he had seen us," I said. "Because we ate unripe jujube, and on top of that, we walked in the sun and bathed in the pond."

The rumbling and creaking of the ox cart came from across the embankment and then gradually faded into the distance. The sounds of the driver urging the oxen on – *Ha, ha, ha, ha . . . La, ha, ha, ha, ha*! – also came close before gradually fading away, while the swirling cloud of dust kicked up from the road resettled upon the embankment.

By the time we overcame our fears and climbed upon the embankment, Narendra dai's ox cart had left the main road and was heading south towards home. After a while it vanished behind a cluster of Sissoo trees. We, too, went home as soon as our bodies dried.

Narendra dai's arrival had moved the house into frenzy. By the outer door of the house, beyond the courtyard, the two oxen that had been pulling the cart were free of the yoke, and now had their snouts buried in a wooden trough as they feed on a mush of lentil husks, pressed mustard seeds, water with rice starch and salt. Sannani put her hand on the rump of an ox. The ox's skin quivered in response, sending playful ripples across its body. The cart driver spoke, "There is no ox comparable to this one in the entire district. The master bought him in Kushesorethan, understand? They glided like an airplane on the Distibot road."

Patting the oxen for their good work, he continued, "Eat well, Bhadesara." Then, patting the other ox, he said, "And you, too, Jogendara!"

Confused and lost, we stood in the courtyard, in front of Narendra's room. I prodded, "Sannani, let's go inside."

"I'm scared," she said.

"But you're his own sister. What are you scared of?" I asked.

"Why don't you go in, if you're so brave!" she snapped.

Narendra saw us outside and called, "Look – I've brought you all a football! Come in!"

I ran into the kitchen. Sannani stood in the courtyard, but did not go into Narendra's room. She seemed as if transfixed by fear.

That day, Narendra gathered all the boys and girls from the village to form a football team. It was a memorable day, we had a lot of fun. We were on our knees next to Narendra, excitedly waiting as he pumped the football with air.

"Sannani! Go and fetch the pump from my bicycle," Narendra asked. Sannani ran off.

Narendra asked me, "Know how to play football?"

I was petrified to suddenly find myself all alone with him in his room. I didn't say anything. He went on, "Try pressing the football – see if it's hard enough. After I fill it with the pump, it will get very hard."

I touched the football with trepidation. But, the discomfort of being all alone with Narendra dai in his room was unbearable, so I made calling Sannani my excuse and ran out.

Sannani was standing outside in the courtyard. She whimpered, "I broke this nail when I took out the pump from the cycle. He will kill me. What should we do?" She was perplexed.

Narendra yelled from his room, "Sannani! What is taking you so long?"

We entered Narendra's room in fear. Narendra took the pump off Sannani and started to attentively fill the football with air. Sannani did not mention the broken nail and I was scared until the moment he finished pumping air into the ball and said, "Now – press the ball and see if it is tight or not." Sannani and I touched the ball together.

Narendra himself picked an abandoned ground for us to play on. The barren field that lay towards the southeast of our village, spread abundantly from the eastern banks of the Koshi and far towards the south. Further east, there spread a big camp of the gentlefolk of Fulkaha – a large mango grove, and beyond that elephant stables and horse stables, a small, quaint looking Ram temple by a pond, with zemindary offices just south of the pond beyond the main gate. Other villagers called that space the *Agana* and called the residences of the landlords *Deudi*. From the ground that Narendra had picked, we could see their residences and a small section of the verandah shining in the sun. The ground itself was completely abandoned. We could see pieces of bones belonging to cattle and other animals scattered across the field, some simal and sami trees and below them, bushes of thatch grass and jujube.

"This is a haunted field, isn't it, Bhatana?" whispered Sannani.

Bhatana's eyes widened in response.

"Of course! Look around, if you don't believe it," added the other children of the untouchable castes.

Narendra, who was walking ahead of us, then said, "Okay, play. I'll watch." Then, he kicked the ball high into the air.

"Look! See how high into the sky the ball has gone," the girls who had come to cut grass there exclaimed in surprise.

Phaguni spoke slowly, "Babu has come as well. He hit it."

The girls who had come to cut grass shyly turned their back to the field, squatted down and hurriedly started cutting grass with their sickles.

"Hey, Munariya!" Narendra called out, "Give us your basket. We don't have goal posts. I'll set it down on one side. Come on! Give it to us!"

By then, we had already started running around breathlessly, kicking the ball willy-nilly, not really caring whether we had a goal post or not. Perhaps I couldn't run very well, because I felt that the ball never really got under my feet. It was as if Sannani and the untouchable children had taken possession of the ball. Nevertheless, there was no shortage of enthusiasm among us; we kept chasing after the football. At times, Sannani would kick the ball towards me and say, "Here! Here! Kick it! Kick it now!" But by then one of the untouchable children would pick it up and kick it in another direction. Sannani would get angry with them. Sometimes, Sannani would grab the ball with her hands and place it on the ground in front of me, and I would kick it with all my might.

We tired quickly. There was still some light left in the day. Drenched in sweat, I said, "Enough for now. Let's play tomorrow." Sannani picked up the ball and pressed it in the nook of her right arm and her chest.

The girls who had been cutting grass stopped their work and surrounded her. "Sannani, let us see what a football looks like," they said.

They each took the ball one by one and played with it, pressed it and said, "Wow! It's so light. Air! It's filled with air." Phaguni put the ball on the floor and with one hand pulled her dhoti above her calves, swung her leg and kicked the ball. Everyone laughed in delight.

"Where did Narendra dai go?" I asked, remembering him.

"He left a while back," Phaguni responded. She smiled and continued, "Munariya said she wouldn't give him her basket. She said, 'Don't I have to cut grass today?' Babu said 'The better grass is over on the southern side, green grass.' And she asked, 'Where?' The girl doesn't know her place. Babu responded – 'Over there, beyond that cottonwood forest. Come with me, I'll show you.'"

Rampiyari turned her head towards the south and yelled, "Hey Munariya! We're going home! If you want to go, hurry up!"

Munariya didn't answer from any direction.

As the sun set, we all went back home. The grass-cutters also headed back to their own homes, as did the others, the untouchable children, Bhatana, Parema, everybody.

"Today was a lot of fun," Sannani said.

"Sannani, can I keep the football in my room?" I asked.

That was how our village got a football team out of Narendra dai's efforts. He would make us bows and arrows, slingshots and mud pellets; and during the months of September and October, he would head over to the dam with his kites, telling us, "Come along! Watch me fly kites. In Lucknow they hold this in high esteem."

But we could never get close to Narendra dai. We were scared, felt something akin to dread.

That day, Narendra dai had come out ready to go somewhere. He was wearing a long white kurta whose arched neckline didn't button on his chest, but instead was fastened with a knot on his shoulder. His hair falling on his neck in curly locks, the lower tip of his Shantipuri dhoti tucked into the right pocket of his kurta, his well-folded dupatta falling from his shoulders to his thighs, and his freshly polished pump shoes. There was no one else in our village, even the district, who had such a clean and refined look. That's why the babu sahibs from Brindakatti and Fulkahi considered him their equal and invited him during festivals. Mother and Gauri Bhauju were sitting on a rug on the porch by the kitchen and cutting vegetables for the evening meal. Gauri Bhauju was the only constant help mother had with her daily chores. Maharani was after all a daughter who had come home; Junthu Nani would be too busy laughing and socializing with the men in the living room; my aunts would mostly be too busy with their own domestic chores, and even if they found some free time, they would sit with Kaptanni Ama and draw wicks in one of the corners of the balcony where Kaptanni Ama would sit and recite the *Mahabharata* or *Ramayana* or some scripture or the other. Gauri Bhauju was the only one who didn't have any household chores of her own, and therefore she could help mother all day long. She and mother would continuously talk whether they were making leaf platters or cutting vegetables. Mother was the only one who could confidently command her to do something – "Gauri, do this, do that . . ." Gauri would set forth wordlessly and, after finishing her chore, would return and sit next to mother to help her with whatever she was doing.

That day, with nothing to do, I found myself next to mother and Gauri. Kaptanni Ama had just dragged Sannani up to the balcony. This would happen occasionally when Kaptanni Ama would find her daughter's rustic ways unbearable. She would drag her away, smooth her tangled and matted hair with oil, and rake her hair with a thick comb – with something of an angry demeanor. Sannani would start protesting in her nasal tone, "Ouch . . . Don't pull my hair Kaptanni Ama!" In response, she would get a whack on her back. Sannani would start crying while Kaptanni Ama would scold and reprimand her, and continue muttering to herself. It would take a long time to comb Sannani's hair – after a long battle of complaints, fights, crying and scolding, perhaps Kaptanni Ama's anger would gradually dissipate and the severity of Sannani's protests would also cool. By then, Sannani would look nice and clean – her hair, combed and oiled, would be smooth and slick, it would get tied in the back with a thin red ribbon. Her face, hands and legs would also get washed. Kaptanni Ama would collect the hair that Sannani had shed, spit into it and roll it up into a ball and, getting up, she would then throw it off the balcony. Sannani would take that opportunity to make her escape; I would be waiting at the bottom of the stairs.

Whenever Kaptanni Ama grabbed Sannani's arms with purpose, I would run away in fear. I felt like I was an accomplice in all her crimes because I was always invariably involved in all the things that Kaptanni Ama would scold her for – wandering around the gardens and fields, picking and eating raw fruits in the sun, bathing in the Koshi, stealing produce from other people's gardens and fields (in other words, doing everything you possibly could at that age). Once Sannani was pulled away, I would walk around with nothing to do. That was how I had ended up where mother and Gauri were cutting vegetables. I wasn't really having any fun there. At that very moment, Narendra came out of his room looking very well put together. He bent down to save his head from hitting the roof and came down from the porch. The moment Gauri saw him in the courtyard, she abruptly got up and went into her room by the kitchen. Narendra looked happy. He casually asked mother, "Sani Ama, what you cutting?"

Even before mother answered him, he was already asking me, "You play a lot of football no?"

Feeling uncomfortable, I got up and ran behind the kitchen, towards the waste pit. There, I stood next to the wooden partition and waited for Sannani.

Around then, Narendra asked again, "Sani Ama, why don't the kids like me? Why do they stay away from me?"

Mother answered while cutting vegetables, "Narendra, you couldn't become a family man."

I peeked at them through the fence.

"Why? Am I not a part of the family?" Narendra asked. He had one of his feet resting on the edge of the porch.

Mother responded, "You are a member of this family, but not a part of it. Your relationship with your father . . . Let us leave that aside. Your relationship with you wife . . . With such a relationship, do you think you will be able to find the warmth of the family hearth? A neglected wife keeps her husband outside the boundaries of family life."

Mother was about to say something else, but Narendra spoke with some anger, "Stop scratching at the same thing all the time. I don't like hearing any talk about her. She does not exist for me – you all need to comprehend this truth. Let us not raise this issue again."

It became awkward for mother. Narendra was not her son; he was only five or six years younger to her. Perhaps because she didn't have the authority to get angry with him, she spoke softly. "Then you, too, should not talk about love and affection, Narendra. Don't say that you can't understand the way that children perceive you and don't flock to you. Don't you see, the humanity inside of you has dried up?"

"Why?" Narendra asked thoughtfully, "Can one's humanity only be judged through the relationship one maintains between husband and wife? Don't presume that the husband-wife relationship is a natural relationship."

Mother smirked and retorted, "Well, is it natural to wander around acting like Krishna among the village girls?"

"Who said I . . ."

Cutting him off, mother continued, "Please, Narendra, don't try to trick me. Who doesn't know in this house about Munariya and you . . ."

Narendra yelled, "Sani Ama, if you can't understand something, you shouldn't waste your breath by going around and giving your opinion everywhere."

Dusting himself off and adjusting his dupatta by gently tugging at its frills, as he habitually did, he got up and spoke to end the discussion,

"Sani Ama, you can only see the world as a wife, because of which you can only see a small portion of it. There are many things that you have not seen, many things that you don't understand."

Mother had some very strong thoughts about this. It would be difficult to find another person who was so staunchly on the side of wives in our society. She was ready to speak her mind. But, Narendra had clearly ended the argument and was already walking away.

TIME, YOU ARE ALWAYS THE WINNER (*SAMAY TIMI SADHAIMKO VIJETA*)

Bānīrā Giri

Dr Bānīrā Giri is a Nepali poet, author and scholar. She has published three volumes of poetry and two novels: *The Prison* and *Unbound*. Giri was the first woman to be awarded a PhD by Tribhuvan University for her thesis on the poetry of Gopal-prasad Rimal. She teaches at Padma Kanya Campus, a women's college in Kathmandu and participates regularly in literary conferences in Nepal and internationally. Her work has been translated into English and Hindi.

Snatch me up like an eagle
swooping down on a chicken,
wash me away like a flood destroying the fields,
fling me from the door
like my daughter carelessly sweeping out dirt.

In infinite wilds I lead
a solitary life.
just a naming ceremony,
set aside, forgotten;
even in the Rāmāyaṇa, Lakshmaṇ's line
had first to be drawn
before Sītā could cross it.[1]

---

[1] This is a reference to an event in the Rāmāyaṇa epic.

Time, you are always the winner,
I bent my knee before you
like Bārbarik faced by compulsion,[2]
like King Yāyati faced by old age,[3]
I fell prostrate like grandfather Bhīshma
before the arrows from your arms.[4]

Touch my defeated existence just once
with your hands of ironwood;
how numb I am,
how hard to grasp, how lifeless
in the presence of your strength and power.

You spread out forever like the seas,
I rippled like the foaming waves,
you blazed up fiercely like a volcano,
I smouldered, slow as a forest fire.
You are power, wholly embodied,
ready to drink even poison,
we follow – my fellows and I at a party,
we descend on a wheel of birth and death,
bearing bags full of gifts,
gifts of alcohol and oxygen,
blood and cancer,
tumors and polio.

---

[2] Bārbarik is mentioned in Hindu scriptures such as the Skanda Purāṇa. He lived his whole life under a curse, inherited from a previous life, that he would be killed by Vishṇu. He was therefore compelled to worship various deities to preserve his life (Vettam Mani 1975, 107).

[3] Different versions of the story of King Yāyati are told in the Padma Purāṇa and the Vishṇu Purāṇa. Both, however, agree that his amorous disposition and infidelity to his first wife brought upon him the curse of eternal old age and infirmity from his father-in-law. Dowson [1879] 1968, 376.

[4] In the Mahābhārata wars, Bhīshma took the side of the Kauravas on the condition that he should not be called upon to fight against the warrior Arjuṇ. Goaded on by another warrior, however, Bhīshma attacked Arjuṇ and wa pierced by innumerable arrows. When he fell, mortally wounded, from his chariot, the arrows that filled his body held him above the ground. Dowson [1879] 1968, 52–53.

My grandson will be born
with sleeping pill in his eyes,
his potency already dead,
needing no vasectomy.

Perhaps he will be born as a war,
embracing every cripple,
perhaps he will be born as a void,
to replace the meaningless babble
of revolt, lack of faith, and being.
Perhaps he will even refuse to be born
from a natural mother's womb;
Time, you are always the winner:
revealed like a crazy Bhairava,[5]
keep burning like the sun,
keep flowing like a river,
keep rustling like the bamboo leaves.

Upon your victory,
I will let loose the calves from the tethering post,
fling open the doors of grain stores and barns,
hand over my jewels to my daughter-in-law,
and lay out green dung, neatly,
around the *tulsī* shrine.[6]

So snatch me up like an eagle
swooping down on a chicken,
wash me away like a flood destroying the fields,
and, like my daughter carelessly sweeping out dirt,
sweep me from the threshold with a single stroke,
sweep me from the threshold with a single stroke.

---

[5] The Bhairava is a fearsome emanation of the god Shiva who figures prominently in the religious iconography of the Kathmandu Valley.

[6] The *tulsī*, or sacred basil tree, is often grown in special shrines in front of Hindu homes or in domestic courtyards.

AGAINST A PEACOCK SKY

Monica Connell

Monica Connell is an Irish author and photographer. She studied Sociology at London University followed by Social Anthropology at Oxford. Her first book, *Against a Peacock Sky* was shortlisted for the *Yorkshire Post* Best First Work award and has been translated into German and Dutch. Her latest book, *Gathering Carrageen*, is about her return to live in a Donegal village she knew as a child.

With the permission and orders of the
king of heaven, Indra, I have crossed
mountains and rivers and hills and
other strange and lonely places and
have come to this world of the mortals.

It's the time of the *karāti*, the nights leading up to the full-moon festival, when the gods enter the *dhāmis* and use their bodies to dance among the villagers. Somewhere people are drumming – it must be at the far end of the village, because at times the rhythm is distinct but when the wind takes it it becomes muffled, merging with the roar of the full monsoon river.

Later, well into the night, Mina and Kāli wrap blankets round their shoulders and walk out through the village. Dogs mark their progress, a different one barking from each rooftop they pass. They sound anxious tonight and fierce, troubled by the full moon and the drums. When they reach the source of the drumming they climb up one ladder and then another on to the top roof of the house.

Already there's a crowd – men, women, boys and girls, toddlers and babies. The door of the shrine at the back of the roof is open. Inside there's a group of men sitting round the fire, their faces striped with flames and shadows. Outside young girls in pairs hold hands facing each other and, leaning back, they pirouette so fast that their shawls flare out from the tops of their heads. One young boy streaks through the darkness, like a small fish, in and out of the groups, stinging ankles with a handful of cut nettles, then melting into the shadows before the inevitable angry rebukes.

> I have plucked flowers from twenty-two
> pastures and twenty-two mountains and
> from plateaux and green lowland meadows.
> There are flowers of nine different
> colours, and I gathered them and put
> them into my hair out of sheer joy, and
> they have become part of me.

The drum-beat intensifies. The musicians are sitting in a row on the edge of the roof, facing inwards. Their drums, half spheres of hand-worked copper, are laid out in a line in front of them. They're pounding them with bent drumsticks, hard and fast, with all the strength of their hands and wrists. The roof is vibrating. Inside the shrine the bells start ringing, rhythmically clanging as they swing up and down, round in an arc as the cord is pulled and released. Close by the doorway two boys clash cymbals, hard so they hit together squarely, hollow full against cupped hollow. Next to them a baby shrieks in its mother's arms.

> For twelve years I have wandered through
> different places. I have walked in the
> truth and spoken in strength. I have
> shaken twenty-two regions with my power.
> And I have done much that is good as
> well. I have made places of pilgrimage,
> and cared for their pilgrims. I have
> built temples. On the banks of a lake,

in a place called Garagāli, there was a
temple inlaid with gold and silver, and
when you saw that temple, even if you
had never wept in your life, tears would
fill your eyes and you would weep.

A man sitting in a group, leaning against the wall of the shrine, starts
shaking and stands up, throwing aside the woollen blanket he wears as
a shawl and kicking off his shoes. His body still convulsing, he fumbles
to untie his turban and release the long twisted tuft of hair, the *dhāmi*'s
insignia, that's always covered from sight except when he's possessed
– when he becomes the god. The crowd clears back and he moves into
the middle of the roof.

Standing alone in this pool of moonlight, he puts his thumb and
forefinger into the corners of his mouth and, staring out across the
houses and the fields and the river valley to the stark moonlit mountains, whistles long and loud into the night.

For an instant the moon disappears. The sky is still bright and the
roof illuminated, but where the moon had been there are now heavy
black storm-clouds brightly outlined in white light. Then it slides back,
perfect in its pale roundness.

The *dhāmi* stands motionless before it. It seems for a moment as
if the world is peopled only by this god and this moon, facing each
other through the aeons of the night. His face is unearthly – eyes glazed
in concentration, cheekbones and jaw protruding floodlit from heavy
black shadows.

He disappears for a minute into the shrine and returns with two
pairs of bells and with a yellow *ṭikā* marked between his eyes. He begins to dance, holding the bells – a pair in each hand – rigid by his
groin. He dances to the rhythm of the bells and the drums and the
cymbals, moving fast, careening about from one end of the roof to
the other. His arms hardly move at all – just the legs move, and his bare
feet on the ground as he jumps up and down, and the long tuft of hair
that bounces back and forth over his shoulder. He's wearing white,
the only white on the roof, a symbol of his purity. He wears white for the
same reason that he never drinks *raksi*, and that he's eaten no food

since morning. It's a mark of reverence that the vehicle provided for the god to come to his people is pure and empty and won't pollute.

> One place especially was beautiful.
> The mist would blow off the top of the
> mountains and there were always a few
> fine clouds and a light rain. It gave
> me so much pleasure. And near that
> plateau was a forest of larch and
> evergreen oak. And below it the wide
> open grassland. There I took twenty-two
> stakes and in twenty-two hours I
> pegged them into the ground and marked
> out twenty-two boundaries.

Another *dhāmi* has joined him and they link arms for a while and then move closer together, stretching their arms across each other's shoulders so they dance as one, their bodies tilting first forwards and then back as they bounce across the roof. They're brothers, two of the Bāra Bhāi, the twelve *Maṣṭā* gods. They're smiling, eyes ablaze, lost in each other's presence, in the dance.

They embrace, then separate, and one goes over to a woman in the crowd with a child cradled in her arms. She talks to him, anxiously tilting her face upwards so it's exposed and openly imploring, a look designed to tap compassion. He answers without looking at her, his eyes focused on space, on the moonlight. His voice is high-pitched and breathless, floating in the back of the mouth, instead of pushing up from the throat and chest. It's a voice that doesn't belong to one of the villagers and she seems not to understand: maybe she can't even hear, above the bellow of the drums.

Still twitching and shuddering, as if to the beat of the wrong pulse, the *dhāmi* looks at the child, willing his eyes to focus, be still. Standing close above it, he presses the rim of a bell hard against its skull and, leaning forward, blows a blast of air into each ear, one after the other. Then he stands back and, from a distance, sprays the child's face with a fistful of rice grains, and dances away.

There are three of them dancing now, sometimes together, sometimes separately, all in white. Without warning one falls out of step and drops back to his place in the crowd. Panting and breathless, but no longer shaking, he takes hold of his tuft of hair, winds it into a coil on top of his head and reties his turban. His god has left him.

The other dhāmis carry on dancing for a while and then their gods go too. The bells in the shrine have stopped ringing and gradually the drumming abates and the vibrations are stilled.

People spill back across the empty space of moonlight, and the dancers' faces merge with the crowd. Someone is closing the double doors of the shrine, fastening the chain latch, and firelight flickers out dimly between the slats.

> There were rocks and boulders that made
> it difficult to walk to and from that
> place. Those rocks and boulders were
> like mountains. And I took my stick
> and swung it round, and my power was so
> great and so terrible that the hills
> and mountains shook. And I split that
> place in two and made a path for people
> to come and go, and for their sheep and goats.
> And there was little water in that place.
> So when I saw that, I dug my knee into
> the ground and water welled up beneath
> and flowed out around it. And I dug
> wells of milk and wells of oil. And I
> sowed seeds and grew plants and trees so
> that that place would be still more beautiful.

Ekādaśi, duadaśi, tetradaśi, chaturdaśi: the days of the *karāti*, when the gods dance at night. Then follows the day of the full moon, *purnimā*, and the full-moon festival, called the *paiṭh*. It dawns sunny and clear, with a strong wind blowing, and storms of chaff from the barley-threshing on the roof rain down yellow against a peacock sky.

No work is done in the fields today and Kalchu is sitting in the sun, making a necklace of marigolds by sinking a needle into the yellow hearts and sliding them together along coarse black thread. Chola is replastering the floor with fresh mud and cow-dung in deference to the gods' visit. Since early morning there has been intermittent drumming in different parts of the village and the echo rolls round the valley like the stifled rumblings of a caged lion.

> There was a demon called Banba, and
> he was king of all the demons. There
> was a great battle between Banba and
> myself. We fought for seven days and
> seven nights. Then I chained him to
> the four corners of the earth, and I
> danced on his chest and sat on his
> back. There was blood streaming from
> his mouth and nose, and he was
> frightened and said that he would
> leave that place and would go to the
> underworld. I made him take an oath
> that he would never frighten anyone or
> cause them any harm – only then did I
> let him go. He even licked my feet.
> First he wanted to fight, then he
> licked my feet. That made me laugh.

Mina and Kāli are taking their offering for the festival to the house where the *dhāmis* have been dancing at night. Mina is carrying the wheat flour in a bronze plate and the oil in a smaller bronze bowl bedded inside it. They pass a group of boys, a jangling procession, on their way to wash the temple bells in the stream their annual cleansing and consecration. They wait in turn while the *ḍāṅgri*, dressed in white, measures other households' offerings.

Two *mānās* of flour is the quota, plus one ladle of oil that's poured into a wide-mouthed container so that the yellow mustard oil, the greener walnut and hemp-seed oils and the cloudy melted ghee combine.

Later in the afternoon, while most people are still washing and dressing and getting ready, the preparations begin at the shrine high above the village, on a plateau under the shade of two juniper trees. The wind is even stronger at this height. It carries the scent of pine and tosses the juniper branches back and forth across the sun, so the ground and the roof of the shrine are slashed with creeping shadows.

The *ḍāṅgri* is there, plastering the floor with a wash of red mudand cow-dung, filling and lighting the oil lamps, burning some sprigs of juniper as incense. That's in the darkness of the inner room, with its raised seat for the *dhāmi* when he's possessed, and its rows of bells and strips of red and white cotton cloth strung in a jumble from the rafters.

Outside on the veranda, where the eaves are supported by pillars crowned with carved wooden rams' heads and the real skulls and horns of sacrificed rams and he-goats, two men are kneading the dough for *puris*, pummelling the flour of every household in the village. They're talking and laughing as they work. Beside them, tethered to the corner post, are six lambs. One is alert and quietly bleating; the others are lying crumpled in a heap of fluffy whiteness in the sunshine.

It's almost evening when Kalchu climbs up the hill carrying Hārkini on his back with Kāli, Nara and Lāla Bahādur following behind. The shrine is packed with people. Children cram themselves into the doorway and cling to the window, like moths to light, hoping to catch a glimpse of the possessed *dhāmi*. Inside, the god is reciting his *paṛeli*, the story of his wanderings through the earth before he settled in the village. And people are asking for advice and blessings, telling him about the problems they trust him to solve.

Outside the shrine the crowd is waiting. Almost everyone is there – the whole village dressed in its festival finery. The musicians, six or seven of them, are crouched in a row behind their drums, playing abstractedly until the dancing begins. One of the juniper trees is enlaced with the spreadeagled bodies of children, fighting for the highest branches and the best view of the dancers below.

At last the bells start to ring in the shrine and the drummers respond, picking up the strength and intensity of the previous nights' rhythm, pounding again so the earth shakes. The *dhāmi* bursts out through the crowded doorway, carrying his bells and a bronze bowl of turmeric-stained rice grains in one hand. He dances about among the crowd, greeting people here and there by stamping yellow rice marks on their foreheads with the thumb of his other hand.

The evening sun is low in the sky with its rays almost horizontal, piercing the *dhāmi*'s eyes as he turns back to face it. It tints his white tunic orange and projects his dancing shadow right back across the ground until it rises up with the juniper trunks.

He doesn't dance on his own for long. Soon two more *dhāmis* emerge from the shrine with their bells, and their heads bare and shaved bald except for their waist-length black tufts, braided at points with silver bands – gifts to the gods from their devotees. Then other *dhāmis*, immersed in the crowd, stand up shaking, jostling their neighbours and struggling to take off their jackets and their *topis* or turbans, and shoes if they have them. Two boys and a woman, who aren't even *dhāmis*, leap to their feet, possessed, their bodies spinning-tops set turning by the strength of the gods' will to dance.

A man from the audience is walking out among the dancers. He's wearing a garland of marigolds and carrying a bowl of yellow rice grains. He stops in the path of one of the dancing *dhāmis* and drapes the garland round his neck and plants a yellow *tikā* between his eyes, greeting the god. The *dhāmi* stoops his head for the garland's embrace.

Other people follow suit and surge out into the space enclosed by the crowd. And as the *dhāmis* dance in the sunshine, the tiers of yellow garlands collide with their hair and bounce up and down against their white tunics. And there are flowers in their hair and loose yellow flowers strewn about under their bare feet on the ground.

> To test me the Bārakote king made me
> knead sand into a ball and made me carry
> a load with rope made of stones. He
> told me that if I had the power then I
> could carry water to him in a basket.
> And this I did. And then the king said,
> 'Now that you have shown me all that is
> good, I wish to see all that is evil as
> well.' I told him that I could do
> anything, but that he would have to

suffer. Still he insisted that he
wanted to see all that is evil and he
forced me to prove my power.
So I brought about twenty-two earthquakes
and I caused that kingdom to tremble.
And when it had trembled for twenty-two
hours I told him that this glimpse
should be enough. I reasoned with him
in all manner of ways, but still he
wouldn't listen. So I shook the houses
and the palace and destroyed them and
caused the black-and-white snake demon to
fall from the skies, and stones and rocks
to fall from the skies. There was no
chance of survival. And then, when the
houses and palace were destroyed, the
floods came and washed everything away so
that you couldn't tell that this was this
place and that was that. Nothing could be recognised.

Ten or twelve different gods are embodied now, and they are all amusing themselves in different ways. Some are dancing on their own, or in twos or threes, as they did in the moonlight. One is dancing his way round the outside of the shrine, carrying another sitting upright on his shoulder. It's the Bāhan, one of the demons the gods defeated in the past, who then reformed and became a lesser deity. Now he's restating his submission to the Bāra Bhāi and the forces of good.

There are others who aren't even dancing: one who has just gone over to the veranda and plunged his hand into the vat of boiling oil so he could offer a hot *puri* to a child in tears: another who is standing in the midst of the dancers being continually buffeted as they come and go, and hungrily eating a plateful of raw rice grains. When he's finished someone takes him some water and he drinks it, spilling it over his face and down his chest and bare legs and feet.

The crowd is delighted by the gods' high spirits and pleasure in the dance. People laugh and point as they recognise a particular god by his mannerisms, by the way he contorts the dhāmi's body to dance, or smile, or leap high into the air. They've all come today: Bijulī Maṣṭā, Thārpā Bāhan, Ukhāṛi Maṣṭā, and Bhawāni the goddess, younger sister of the twelve Maṣṭā brothers. Even Yangre has come, standing on his own with his back to the dancers, chewing marigold heads and squirting a jet of yellow pulp into a child's face. It cries out, horrified by the affront.

> There was a widow who came to me
> saying, 'There is no water in my land,
> so I have no rice to eat. My urine is
> like blood. I have come to ask for
> the gift of water.'
> And when she said this I struck the
> ground with my fist and water sprang out.
> I told that woman that if she offered me
> rice on the day of the transplanting
> there would always be water to flood her
> paddy fields.
> But because the woman was a widow and
> contemptible to other people, they
> rechannelled her water and she came to
> me weeping.
> So I destroyed that place to which the
> water had been taken and I cursed those
> people. I cursed those people and said
> that if ever they did scrape together
> some little wealth, then it would vanish
> like ice in water. I cursed those people
> and said that there would never be a
> single day when there wasn't someone ill
> in their house.

The sun sets and the harsh lines of sun and shadow dissolve into blurred shapes and muted colours. The *dhāmis* look almost human – as vulnerable as actors when the stagelights fail.

They carry on dancing, but they're only holding the attention of a small part of the audience. Most faces have come to watch the *ḍāṅgri* who's just come out of the shrine and is standing in the doorway. He's wearing only a new white *dhoti* and his body looks old, its loose flesh striated with veins and sinews. In his right hand he's holding a curved knife with a short wooden handle.

He walks out of the shrine without looking at the crowd, picks up one of the lambs, frightened and bleating, and carries its almost weightless body round to the side of the shrine. He puts it down at the base of the new *liṅga* – the stripped pine trunk that all the men brought back from the forest and erected early this morning – and pours some water over the lamb's head and in a stripe down its back to the base of the tail. The lamb shrugs it off – nodding, they say, the god's acceptance and its own acquiescence – and the *ḍāṅgri* stoops down and saws through its throat. There's no resistance; it seems that the neck has no muscle, no bone, no leather hide, that it's just a blood-filled tube of white fur.

The *ḍāṅgri* holds the body while the young red blood squirts out and slashes the base of the *liṅga* in criss-cross patterns. When it has stopped coming, he drops the body and goes back for another lamb and another, creeping down the earthen steps with his bloodstained knife and his feet and ankles splashed with red.

He sacrifices four lambs at the base of the *liṅga*, then takes two inside and kills them by slitting open the throat and the chest and cutting off one of the forelegs at the shoulder, so the heart can be taken out, still pumping, and offered to the god on a plate on the *dhāmi*'s raised seat.

The dancing has stopped now. All eyes have turned to the killing. And when the *ḍāṅgri* goes inside they remain fixed for an instant on the *liṅga* and the ground around it, with the four white bodies, and the separate wide-eyed heads, and the stains of blood going brown already in the trampled grass.

> In those days I brought about stability
> and made laws. If there was anyone who
> was suffering then I did whatever there
> was to be done and wiped away that
> person's tears. And if there was anyone
> who was causing suffering to others,

then I would build a trap of poisoned
bamboo, and I would ensnare and kill
that person. I told them that I could
do whatever I wanted – if I wished to
do good, then it would be good and if I
wished to do evil, then it would be evil.

Suddenly the crowd rearranges itself, like the changing pattern in a kaleidoscope; one twist and the border of any empty space dissolves into small agitating clusters spread throughout. There's a hiss of people talking and laughing, and the explosive shrieks of children playing, shaking off the intensity of the afternoon. A man is passing round some morsels of raw heart and liver. It's the *prasād*, food offered to the gods, eaten in essence and then passed back, blessed, for the people to eat.

The crowd lingers for a long time, until it's almost dark. There's a sense of release after the excitement, of fulfilment. The gods came; they ate and danced and then left contented. Now they're honour-bound to watch over the crops and the livestock and ward off ghosts and evil forces.

A group of men are standing on the veranda. They're calling out, one by one, the names of all the households in the village. Shapes move forward in the fading light to collect their pile of *puris*, the due from their offerings of flour and oil, and a few small pieces of meat, *prasād*.

That place with its sweeping cedar trees
and juniper. That place where I could be
blessed by Kaskā Sundari Devī in the
mornings and the evenings. There I built
a shrine and sacrificed a he-goat in the
name of the truth.
If a bell is tied round the neck of a crow
then, as it flies about, everyone will hear
the ringing – so there was no one who did
not know about the powers of this god. But
mostly his influence was barely perceptible,
like the blowing of a breeze, like the
sound of a butterfly wafting through the air.

DUKHA DURING THE WORLD WAR

Pratyoush Onta

Pratyoush Onta has a PhD in history from the University of Pennsylvania. He has written about Nepali nationalism, Gurkha history, institutions, area studies, the politics of knowledge production, and media. He has written, co-written, edited or co-edited several books including *Nepal Studies in the UK, Social History of Radio Nepal, Social Scientific Thinking in the Context of Nepal, Radio Journalism: News and Talk Programs in FM Radio, Growing up with Radio, Mass Media in Post-1990 Nepal, Ten Years of Independent Radio: Development, Debates and the Public Interest, Autocratic Monarchy: Politics in Panchayat Nepal, 25 Years of Nepali Magazines, The State of History Education and Research in Nepal* and *Political Change and Public Culture in Post-1990 Nepal* (forthcoming). He is also the founding editor of the journals *Studies in Nepali History and Society* and *Media Adhyayan*. He has been associated with the research institute and public forum Martin Chautari in Kathmandu since 1995 and is currently one of its directors of research.

Laxuman Gurung was awarded the Victoria Cross for his performance in the Burma Front in 1945. He lost his right arm and much of his hearing during the medal-winning action. Last year, he was asked by *Gorkha Sainik Awaj*, a magazine representing the interests of former and serving soldiers, how many people he had recommended for the army. The pensioner replied: "I joined a foreign army; was involved in a war and lost my arm. I could have died but with luck I lived. Many of my friends died in the war, some froze to death, many were blinded when engaged in war in the high Himalaya.

Anybody who sends an able young person to the army to experience all that dukha is guilty of paap. I cannot do such paap. I cannot recommend anybody to join the army."

Dukha – bodily pain, mental suffering, extreme hardship and death – has been real in the life of Laxuman Gurung. And yet, as a subject of reportage and scholarship, the Gurkha's dukha has remained virtually unexplored. Celebratory accounts over the course of the century have glorified the dogged courage and loyalty of the men from Nepal's hills, and the vicarious honour they bring their country while fighting the Empire's war. Gurkhas emerged from the two World Wars as icons of superhuman bravery, who were in a class apart when it came to enduring the pain and suffering of battle.

The genre of celebratory writing is exemplified by B.M. Niven's 1987 coffee-table book, *The Mountain Kingdom: Portraits of Nepal and the Gurkhas*. Niven, himself a Gurkha officer, wrote: "Even terribly wounded [Gurkhas] cling on and their tough bodies and harsh upbringing enable them to endure. The job in hand and the name of the regiment are everything . . . Death and the threat of it, they are used to by their very upbringing and so they do not hold back at the prospect of death or of danger that may precede death. Discomfort, they are inured to from childhood and so at war the prospect of being out in, and at the mercy of, the elements, does not in any way inhibit them."

The Gurkha's stoicism, accounted for by "harsh upbringing", is invariably linked to his proverbial loyalty to the sahib commanding officer. There is, for example, the lore reported by the writer Edmund Candler in his 1919 book, *The Sepoy*. In France, a British officer is knocked out by shell-shock. He opens his eyes to find his orderly kneeling over him fanning the flies off his face, tears streaming down his cheeks.

"Why are you crying, Tegh Bahadur?" he said; "I am not badly hit." "I am crying, Sahib," he said, "because my arm is gone, and I am no more able to fight." With a nod, Tegh Bahadur indicates the wound. The shell that had stunned the sahib had carried off the orderly's forearm at the elbow.

More than 60 years later, Byron Farwell wrote in his popular book, *The Gurkhas* (1984), "The stoicism of wounded Gurkhas impressed all who witnessed their sufferings. Often enough their first question on reaching the field dressing station was, 'How soon can I get back?'"

Professional historians have been equally adept at ignoring the suffering of the Gurkha, focusing as they have on matters of high diplomacy, geopolitics and Gurkha romance. Most historians have relied on written sources of British India (now housed in various archives in India and the United Kingdom) which were created in the process of acquiring information on the localities from which the "raw materials" that could be turned into the "Gurkhas" could be found. Diplomatic negotiations between the British and Nepali rulers regarding the recruitment of Gurkhas also gave birth to voluminous writings. Gurkha historians who have thus side stepped the entire question of dukha include Asad Husain, Kanchanmoy Mojumdar, and Sushila Tyagi.

Among Nepali historians, the recent book *The Gurkha Connection* by historian Purushottam Banskota (1994) recognises the heavy casualties suffered by the Gurkha regiments during the two World Wars. But even he prefers to analyse the impact of Gurkha recruitment more in terms of Nepal's prestige in the world, modernisation of her army, enlightenment of Nepalis through experience abroad, and benefit to the economy.

Only Prem Uprety's *Nepal: A Small Nation in the Vortex of International Conflicts 1900–1950* (1984) contains a brief but useful discussion of the "physical impact of war". The faces of many Gurkhas who had been wounded in World War I, he writes, were disfigured due to the loss of noses and eyeballs; in one case the forehead had been damaged so badly that both the eyeballs "were protruding out like that of an unearthly creature". General Babar Shumsher, son of Rana Prime Minister Chandra Shumsher, after an inspection tour of the wounded wrote "how could life linger on in such desperate souls?" According to Uprety, arrangements were made so that fresh recruits did not come across the demobilised soldiers, who bore the scars of the battlefield.

MEMORIALISING MASS DEATH

The Gurkhas who arrived at the recruitment centres of the Raj mainly came from four ethnic groups of Nepal: Magar, Gurung, Rai and Limbu. During the early years of the twentieth century, none of these groups were represented in Kathmandu's intellectual class that sustained itself by chakari – sycophantic attendance to the Rana court. This class, with Bahuns and Chhetris dominant, seem to have been vaguely aware that huge numbers of Nepali hillmen had been sucked into British Gurkha regiments. It would have been too much to expect them to show concern for the recruits' war-induced hardships.

In an account that describes Nepal's participation in World War I, mahila guruju Hemraj Pandey, who headed the Rana office of military supplies during the war years, fully supports his master Chandra's decision to help the British. Without understanding the apocalyptic nature of WW I, he wrote, it was not possible to understand the crisis that had beset the British Empire and the world, nor appreciate the importance of Nepal's help to her British friend. In risking their lives in the battlefield, soldiers from Nepal had enhanced the country's and the jaati's glory.

In Purano Samjhana (1972), a selected compilation of journal entries of Rammani A.D., a member of Chandra Shumsher's court, we find out that he was aware that many "sons of Nepal" had "sacrificed themselves" during the First World War. The Tribhuvan-Chandra Military Hospital in the capital was apparently made to honour these brave sons who gave up their lives to increase, in the words of Chandra Shumsher, "the glory of their motherland and to ameliorate the pain of their (wounded) colleague-soldiers."

Kedarmani A.D., Rammani's son, recalls in his autobiography *Aaphnai Kura* how as a student in Calcutta he read news about the war in English newspapers but he does not mention Nepal's connection to it. The versatile litterateur Balkrishna Sama, who was in his early teens when the war began, remembers the war years in his autobiography, *Mem Kabitako Aaradhan*, writing that, "After reading the English newspaper, *Statesman*, my grandfather used to describe the war to my grandmother and say 'in the end, the English will win, will win.' The Nepalis serving in the Gurkha regiments had already reached Europe for the war. . . . The photograph (in *The Illustrated London News*) of Nepali Gurkhas crossing a river with their khukuris held in their mouths boosted my morale. Thereafter, whenever we played, I felt like playing war games. I kept thinking that I too should participate in a war and die fighting."

Kathmandu's intellectual class thus responded to the Gurkha participation in the First World War by cheering from a distance, memorialising mass death as if it were blood sacrifice to add glory to the motherland. They sanitised the suffering and death of the Gurkha soldier as a moment of national celebration. The soldier's pain in the battlefield was legitimised as part of one's necessarily sacred duty to the Nepali nation. Of course, no one asked why it was always other Nepalis who had to die to enhance the name of their motherland.

THE MOTHER'S INSTINCT

Before World War I, there was hardly any administrative structure for Gurkha recruitment within Nepal. The approximately 2,000 Gurkha recruits a year that were necessary to keep the 20 Gurkha Rifle battalions at full strength were rounded up by labour contractors in Central and East Nepal and taken to Gorakhpur, India. But when the British required larger numbers of recruits in the fall of 1914, Rana Prime Minister Chandra Shumsher of Nepal put to work a whole new internal mobilisation scheme. Chandra ordered his district governors to ensure that the supply of "raw materials" was up. Although it was emphasised that only volunteers were to be taken, there seems to have been considerable forced recruitment. Incentives of various kind were given both to recruiters and those being recruited. Chandra also allowed the opening of several recruitment centres on the Nepal frontier and recruiting agents were allowed into previously prohibited areas in the hinterland. Between 1914 and 1919, over 60,000 Gurkhas were recruited into the combat regiments, and about twice that number were taken into supporting non-combative roles in units like the Army Bearer Corps and Labour Battalions.

It has been long estimated that over 20,000 Gurkha soldiers were killed during the course of the war. However, even until today we have very little knowledge of those who perished, and we do not know the names of the families, villages and communities that suffered the most losses.

When anthropologist Mary Des Chene was researching Gurkha recruitment in Kota, a village in central Nepal, one Gurung woman, born in 1898, recalled the First World War in the following words: "Now it is different, but in my time everyone who left was lost. They walked out of our Gurung country and got lost. They died there or they got lost. My father, I never knew him. He was coming home, we heard, but then he died, too. My elder brother, my younger brother, my father's sister's son. All died. Many, many others too. So many!"

The number of soldiers that were seriously wounded and disabled for life is not known but it certainly ran into tens of thousands. And we can only guess the number of soldiers shell-shocked or mentally affected for life after seeing and experiencing the hardships of the First World War. Many of the disabled were returned to Nepal during the war itself. They were met by Nepali frontier officials and occasionally assisted to their individual homes in the hills.

There is nothing to be said for the dead, but the wounded and disabled retired as unreported and isolated individuals who returned to the hinterland villages from where they emerged to be recruited. Other than the odd mountain minstrel who would sing ballads of the trauma, there were no Nepali reporters, writers and chroniclers in the early decades of the century to bring the suffering to notice. Besides, it was hardly in the wartime interest of the British or Chandra to highlight the dukha.

In terms of casualties, the Second World War is thought to have been a repeat performance of the earlier conflagration. The devastation of the First World War was still fresh in the memory of families across the Nepali hills when the Second began. In her 1991 Stanford University dissertation, Des Chene writes that when the gatlawata (recruiter) arrived at Kota at the start of World War II, mothers who were teenagers or young wives during 1914–18 uniformly resisted the enlistment of their sons, "going to great lengths to hide them from recruiters and pleading with them not to go."

These women, a few of whom were still alive in the mid-1980s, feared "that their own sons were being 'grabbed' in the same way that their fathers, brothers and sometimes their husbands had been." For these mothers and grandmothers, the lands beyond the Modi valley were, in the main, "a source of sorrow" – lands where their fathers, husbands, brothers and sons had died or disappeared.

THE DUKHA THEME

Gurkha dukha, of course, does not begin in this century and is not limited only to the battlefield. The cases of desertion sporadically re-ported in the nineteenth century sources indicate that Gurkha soldiers were prepared to go to considerable personal risk in abandoning the army. Separation of families, additional burdens imposed on wives whose husbands are away in service, anxieties caused by broken lines of communication and forced recruitment during the two World Wars are some other examples of hardships induced by this long-distance form of labour. But it is the dukha of the battlefield that is most phys-ical, most obvious, and the least recorded and reported.

During the course of the First World War, the Gurkha soldiers saw action in various fronts in Europe, the Middle East and Africa. A war time censor's office was located at Boulogne, France to keep track of mail to and from troops from the Subcontinent in France and Eng-land. It was the responsibility of this office to seize letters containing 'sensitive' information about the war fronts and conditions back at home. The censor officers prepared frequent reports which sometimes included lengthy extracts from letters they read.

Letters written by Gurkha soldiers during World War I provide the most direct written evidence found thus far for an examination of the psychology, if you will, of Nepal's soldiers on the battlefield. The letters which are excerpted below are from the stacks at the India Office Collection of the British Library in London. In the more than 20 volumes of censors' reports, each consisting of more than 200 folios, one can find only about 50 letters from Gurkha soldiers.

More often than not, the exact names of the sender and receiver were deleted from these reports, and the identification went something like "from a Gurkha wounded in France to his friend in India". The language in which the letters were written is identified as "Gurkhali" or Hindi and the extracts given are in English translation.

It is obvious that in a war participated in by thousands of Gurkha sol-diers, these letters come from but a very small percentage of them. Those who could write, like the writers of these letters, must have learnt to do so in the army. It also seems reasonable to assume that most of the soldiers did not know how to read and write and their experiences are lost forever.

No other written evidence originating from the common Gurkha soldiers from World War I have been found, although it is likely that letters and diaries do exist, undiscovered in archives or attics. Even though these are translated and extracted versions of the original letters they remain useful in weaving the dukha theme into the Gurkha history of the First World War. It is sobering to note that these letters, and their messages of dukha never got through to their addressees and have only now been discovered for historical analysis.

These censored letters give us some preliminary insights into the consciousness of the Gurkha warriors, as they tried to make sense of the unbelievable horrors experienced on the front. They also provide a glimpse of the disastrous early phase of the World War from the point of view of the Gurkha soldiers. We hear about the deaths of friends and fellow fighters, of amputations, personal regrets, and the terror of earthshaking explosions. We learn that the hospitals in England are full of the wounded. We read about prisoners of war begging for a few rupees' worth of supplies.

THE CENSOR'S TROVE

After the British Expeditionary Force sustained severe losses (in the magnitude of 15,000 men in five days) in the early phases of the war in France, a decision to reinforce it with Indian Army troops was made in August 1914. Corps of the Indian Army, with Gurkhas as part, had reached France by early October and seen action by the end of the month.

All accounts suggest that the Indian Army soldiers were poorly equipped and ill-prepared for the war in Europe. By early November, the Indian battalions had seen heavy fighting and sustained severe losses, resulting in the serious reduction of average battalion troop strengths. As has been reported by the military historian Jeffrey Greenhut, on 30 October alone the 2nd Battalion of the 8th Gurkhas lost more than 600 men in an assault by the Germans. Those who survived "straggled to the rear in confusion."

The morale plummeted in these battalions which bore the first shocks and, as Greenhut has reported, many men seemed to be "shooting themselves in order to be taken out of the line" – there was an unusually high incidence of wounds in the left hand. There were court-martials to improve troop discipline, and a much needed rest was given to the soldiers of the Indian Corps in early January, which seems to have boosted morale a bit. Yet in February, E. M. Howell, a mail censor officer, reported that "a breaking strain was near."

A letter written in January 1915 by a wounded Gurkha in England to his friend in a regiment serving in India: "Be anxious for me. For the war is like a huge mutiny. The Indian troops have suffered terrible losses. In my double company, the 4th, five men have been killed; and in the 2nd, one-third of the total have been killed . . . Our Gurkha regiments have suffered great losses . . . for the remainder to survive is difficult." A letter written in March 1915: "And the firing of bullets goes on, and sister, I would like to see it. Several hundreds of thousand of men have been killed and there is no hope of survival. The water (in the trenches) is up to the knees. Ishwar (God) is ruler. What can one do? Do not worry about me." Another letter written during the same month from a hospital: "It is not a war but the divine wrath of God (Parmeshwar). In a few days hundreds of men have been destroyed. The shells of the cannon have been flying about like rain in the rainy season. . . . The men who survive and go back to India should consider it as a new life. The whole world is being destroyed."

"Perhaps the Germans will be beaten. They attacked in three lines. Two lines were blown away . . . When the Brigade attacks, the Gurkhas and Sikhs go first and the white troops are put in the second line. No one asks about the dead," wrote one soldier. A Gurkha convalescing in England to another Gurkha also in England: "At first the fire of the cannon was just like an earthquake . . . The piles of the killed on both sides were like heaps of slaughtered goats. I am sorry that my company lost so much." In other letters we come across lines like "it is said that all (regiments) are being finished. Here wounded men come sometimes 200, sometimes 300, and all the hospitals in England are full." A man being treated in a hospital in Brighton wrote in May 1915: "I am wounded. What can I do. Just as on parade we used to practice the position for musketry firing, so in the war we lie down. O God, O God, when can I see my elder brother?" Another letter from hospital: "I am in the Milford Depot and am now ready for the firing line. The people who are returned to India are those whose heads, eyes, feet or hands have been rendered useless."

Death seemed impossible to escape, hence there is repeated reference to those who have returned to India as lucky ones who have been given a new life. A soldier at the front wrote to his brother in Dehra Dun, "About the state of affairs here I tell you that both sides are using machine guns and cannon. Rifles are not much used. Consider yourself very lucky that you have returned to India."

Some of the correspondents were dearly aware that the letters were checked, and there is often guarded reference to "I will tell you later". Wrote one Gurkha: "You asked me about the state of affairs here. It is like being between the devil and deep sea. When I come back to India then I will sit beside you and tell you everything, but I do not know when that will be." Another wrote: "I would write fully about the affairs here but I am sorry that the order is not to do so. Several of our letters are opened in the Post, and if anything is found written contrary to what is ordered the writer is punished. Brother, without doubt you also have a lot of hardships and work to do. But we also have more. Brother, here rain falls a lot, and it is very cold and there is lots of mud."

THE WESTERN FRONT

The reference to rain, water and mud in the trenches draws attention to the kind of warfare that these Gurkhas were engaged in, a mentally and physically excruciating variety of fighting known as trench warfare that was new even to the soldiers of Europe. Many western historians have long argued that trench warfare determined not only the perception of the First World War of the soldiers who participated in it, but also how it was remembered and understood by future generations. That certainly could be said to apply to the Gurkhas as well.

By early 1915, a system of multiple trenches – roughly 475 miles long – that stretched from the North Sea through Belgium, Flanders, France to Switzerland had already been dug. In this so-called Western Front, the armies were in a stalemate, and movement was measured in yards, not miles. The trench criss-crossed landscape, in the words of historian George L. Mosse, "was more suggestive of the moon than the earth, as heavy shelling destroyed not only men but nature, a devastation that would haunt the imagination of those forced to live in the trenches."

In the trenches and hospital beds, the soldiers' mind travelled homewards. One Gurkha wrote; "Subedar Bahadurji . . . do not let my wife have any difficulty about living." A letter from a Brighton hospital bed dated 23 October 1915: "My mother used to tell me that if I did not give up my job and come and earn my living at home I should be sorry for it I laughed at this and now I am repenting at my leisure. When I think of my mother I say to myself 'What can I do?' What was fated to happen has come to pass. We have been caught just as fish are caught in a net . . . My wound is paining me a good deal just now, but I hope that in a few days, it will be much better."

Some desperately hope for a return to the village: "If there is any arrangement for making peace do . . . find out the true news and let me know." Another one put it in the following manner: "Up to date there (has) not been the slightest indication of the end of the war . . . The spring is now on and the buds appearing but we think of our own hot country." Another letter "Since we are attached to our country when will that day appear when we will see our native land?"

There is also thanksgiving: "Now in my regiment all the sepoys are finished and I am left alive with a little to eat and drink, but Panneshwar showed me great favour, on the day on which I was wounded my fellow bandsman was killed."

Naturally, the Gurkhas thought a lot about the enemy. One put it this way, "On 9th day of May 1915 our Division was ordered to take German trenches at 5 a.m. Enemy trenches were 400 yards off from us. This trenches is near new Chaple (sic) we went with fix swords and khukries in mouths, this was the famous charge I have been through. We lost many men but we captured the enemies line, I could not follow my company owing to sharpnel bits struck on my right forearm but it missed the bone, by mercy of Almighty God. Now I am in England and getting much better and shortly I will be back to France again and kill some more bastered (bastard) German because they are not men because they use poisness (sic) gas."

*

FOKKERS AND ZEPPELINS

The major participation of the Indian Army Corps in the Western Front was limited to the first year of the war, after which they were transferred to more fighting in the Middle East.

Among those who were left in Europe was one soldier with keen eye and lucid pen. In May 1916, he wrote: "There is no official news about peace, but how long can the enemy continue such violence? The enemy are shut in all four sides, and nothing from outside can reach them. From this it appears likely that the war will end this year, but whatever seems best to God will happen. I have petitioned to be sent back to India, and I hope for favourable reply . . . This war is very terrible. There is no safety for a man on the earth, or under the earth, in the air, or on the sea. Strong fortresses are overturned like dust, what chance then has anything else? When the artillery fires continuously, hills are converted into dust heaps, and the same thing happens to ships on the sea. Under the sea, submarines go and fight.

On land poisonous gases and liquid fire are used. Under the earth, mines are dug and exploded 200 or 300 yards away. In the air 'Aeroplane,' 'Zeppelin' 'Fokker,' 'Aircraft,' etc make war amongst themselves. All these things are employed for the destruction of men. Is this true warfare? All these means are not employed on one side only. No, no, the other side is equally pugnacious. The fighting is not confined to one locality. It is spread all over the world . . . From all this it would seem that God is displeased with the peoples of the world."

A soldier in an English hospital who had a limb amputated writes in February 1916 to a friend in Egypt with a matter-of-fact directness: "On the 25th of Asoj [mid-October] I was in the attack against the German trenches. I was wounded and left in the trench. I was taken prisoner into Germany and there they cut my foot off. I was two months in hospital there and was then sent to England, and I am now under orders to be sent back to India." And a request from a prisoner-of-war adds an entirely different perspective: "Your brother Bahadur Pun sends his blessing. If you have three or four rupees about you please send them, also things to eat and drink, and clothes should be put up in a parcel and sent. Dhani Ram Pun and I are prisoners of war in Germany."

Without doubt, some of the fighting men thought of the World War I fronts as occasions to "prove the Gurkha name" – there is some evidence of this in a handful of the letters at the British Library. However, the more thoughtful among the letters indicate more of an effort by these men of Nepal to understand the scale of destruction around them. While some describe the war's great losses in a seemingly matter-of-fact way ("The land was so full of the slain that it was difficult to set foot on the ground . . ."), others resorted to metaphors to convey what seemed beyond description. Thus, the reference to divine wrath and the destruction of the whole world.

What these letters offer is an image of the Gurkha soldier entirely different from the standard battlefield image which pervades the public consciousness in the world and in Nepal, of the Gurkha, khukuri raised, charging the enemy with the battle cry, "Ayo Gorkhali!" This congealed image of the battle-hungry Gurkha – true to his salt, loyal to his commanding officer, (mfadaar to his country – is the product of the sahib's imagination, later identified by sycophantic Nepali intellectuals as the embodiment of the most special quality – bravery – of all Nepalis.

The soldier from the hills of Nepal as he comes across in these letters is a different kind of Gurkha. He is a hero, but because he is sensitive, intelligent and human. He feels pain and does mourn the loss of a friend in the battlefield. He is afraid of death and is thankful when it spares him.

Dukha has been central to the lives of Gurkha soldiers throughout their history. It is time, many decades late, that we begin to listen to the soldier's cry from the battlefield.

SO CLOSE TO HEAVEN

Barbara Crossette

Barbara Crossette is an American journalist and author. She served as editor and chief correspondent in Southeast Asia and South Asia for *The New York Times*, and was their United Nations bureau chief from 1994 to 2001. She has been awarded the 1992 George Polk award, a 2008 Fulbright prize, and the 2010 Shorenstein prize for her writings on and coverage of Asia. She is currently United Nations correspondent for *The Nation*.

BUDDHIST NEPAL

Lakpa Nuru Sherpa was happy to be back in his two-room house in Chaurikarka, a hamlet deep in a sheltered valley a couple of thousand feet below the village of Lukla, a starting point for treks into the Mount Everest region of Nepal. The Himalayan kingdom of Nepal, nearly the size of Florida, must support a population of almost twenty million people scattered over difficult topography; life is hard for most. Lakpa Nuru, a mountain guide like many of his fellow Sherpas, was lucky. Fit and healthy in middle age, when many other Nepali men are dead or spent beyond their years, he was able to retire from the trail and come home to tend a small plot of land. He sent his children to school. And then, with what money was left from his years of trekking and climbing, he went off to India, several hundred miles away, to buy books.

The Sherpas are Buddhists, descendants of migrants from eastern Tibet who settled centuries ago in the Solu-Khumbu region of northeastern Nepal, the region best known to foreign trekkers. Before he died, Lakpa Nuru said, he wanted to own the most precious thing he could think of: a set of Lord Buddha's teachings, produced in all their authenticity by Tibetan monks in the northern Indian hill town of Dharamsala, the headquarters of the Dalai Lama's government in exile. Like all traditional Tibetan Buddhist books, these volumes are assemblages of narrow loose-leaf pages inserted between boards, wrapped in colorful cloth and secured by a bright ribbon. The script, read horizontally, is in a classical Tibetan language unknown to Lakpa Nuru. He spent his life savings knowingly on a set of books he will never read. That didn't matter. "Maybe my children and grandchildren will read them one day, because they are more educated," he said, as he asked to be photographed with his treasured library. When I told the story later to His Holiness Ngawang Tenzing Zangbo, abbot of Tengboche monastery, in the shadow of Mount Everest, he was not surprised. "Every Sherpa home is a cultural center," he said. "How much so depends on each family's means."

"The government may call us a Hindu kingdom and His Majesty may be an avatar of Vishnu," a businessman once told me in Kathmandu, "but if you scratch the surface of Nepal almost anywhere, you'll see how Buddhist we really are." Buddhism came to Nepal early, as might be expected, given the religion's origins in nearby northern India, and was soon adopted by the people called Newars, who are as close to an indigenous population in the Kathmandu Valley as anyone will probably ever find in the darkness of barely explored Nepali history and legend. The Newars were not alone in their faith. All over Nepal there were other Buddhist minorities, particularly along the Tibetan border. All or most of Nepal apparently fell under Tibetan dominance in the seventh and eighth centuries, but with or without conquest, Tibetans and Newaris cross-fertilized each other's highly developed Buddhist cultures for hundreds of years.

Much of this history can be politically inconvenient not only in Nepal, where most of the kings and all the hereditary Rana prime ministers of the nineteenth and twentieth centuries were Hindus, but also in India, where upper-caste Hindus have dominated politics since independence and Buddhism is more coopted as part of history than honored as a living religion. Not a few Indians argue that Buddhism is no more than an offshoot of Hinduism; Hindu priests have control over some of Buddhism's holiest places, including the temple at Bodhgaya, where Buddha reached enlightenment.

Back in Chaurikarka, Lakpa Nuru had invited me to visit his *lheng*, or prayer room – in effect, half his house – where he had constructed a traditional bookcase of deep cubbyholes beside the family altar to house his new library. He was wearing a trekker's abandoned T-shirt that read "Enjoy Victoria B.C." and a woolen stocking cap that said "Aspire" as he sat down behind a rough reading desk to unwrap a sacred volume. His altar was a wondrous thing, covered in part with aluminum foil and festooned with paper chains, gauzy white *khata* scarves, a peacock feather, more than a dozen Buddha images, statues of the much-traveled Guru Rinpoche and the goddess Tara, incense burners, butter lamps, and offering bowls. A photograph of the Dalai Lama shared a large picture frame (its glass cracked) with various postcards of people and places important to his faith. Though his small house, built of stone and wood, was roughly finished elsewhere, the prayer room had religious paintings on two walls; these were inherited from his father and grandfather, who had lived in the house before him and employed an itinerant artist to do the work. The room next door, where his family lived, ate, and slept, was a much more spartan place, except for a collection of Chinese ceramic rice bowls and copper plates displayed (along with two Chinese thermos flasks and two glass tumblers) on shelves along one wall. The family cooked on a stove made of stone and fueled by a wood fire. There was no running water.

Chaurikarka is a small hamlet with a few dozen houses, almost all built of stone, their roofs of loose wooden shingles held down by more rocks. In simple villages like this, Himalayan Buddhism is lived in its most down-to-earth form around countless family altars by people who speak Tibetan dialects, far away from the great lamas of their faith, who disdain their rustic ignorance and superstition. There are compensations, though, in a setting that is both physically magnificent and spiritually alive. In the center of Chaurikarka, a solid chorten sat astride the path leading away in the general direction of Khumbila, the Khumbu Sherpas' sacred mountain, whose distant presence bestowed blessings on those within its view.

This path toward the distant holy landmark is also Chaurikarka's main street, a porters' highway from the last market town – several days' walk back down the trail – into vast alpine regions without roads or airstrips. In a patch of open space near the chorten and a cubbyhole general store with very little for sale, about a dozen porters, Tamang people from farther west, plodded into town and paused to rest along a stone wall just high enough to serve as a shelf for the huge woven back-pack baskets of consumer goods they were hauling to the scoreless interior. The porters backed wearily toward the stone ledge and eased the weight of their burdens onto it without having to unstrap from their shoulders the cargo of blankets, small jute rugs, at least one bolt of cloth, tins of oil, boxes of crackers, sacks of rice, instant noodles, and a few plastic utensils and toys. The loads, most of them extremely heavy, were borne by young men, some still in their teens, and by one or two white-haired porters in faded, shredded clothes, too old to be doing this job but too poor to stop. Tamangs from north-central Nepal, who are also Buddhists, are a cut below Sherpas in the world of mountain people. Sherpas are the guides and mountaineers, talents they have developed to an art in recent decades of climbing Mount Everest – called Chomolungma by the Sherpas and Sagarmatha by other Nepalis – and the Tamangs are the heavy lifters.

Later, on another trail leading to Namche Bazaar from Lukla, a Tamang porter passed by carrying a thick plate-glass window four or five feet square roped to his back in a wooden frame; he had to turn sideways to let others on the route go by. His face was a portrait of strain as he shouldered this piece of air freight, yet he was barely out of Lukla, with its crazy little grass-and-gravel ski-slope airstrip, and had at least another day to march, most of it uphill. Porters have delivered all kinds of cargo to Namche, including a whole dental clinic, disassembled. They also serve in emergencies as human ambulances, rushing trekkers stricken with altitude sickness to lower levels or ferrying their own lame or elderly up steep and rocky tracks.

The porters pausing in Chaurikarka had thin, sinewy legs from years of walking. Some didn't own shoes, but maneuvered along the stony trail in rubber sandals or the remains of flimsy Chinese sneakers. They spoke little as they paused to stretch and relieve the weight they bore, except to exchange a few pleasantries with Sherpa women bent over their short hoes planting potatoes in a small walled field beside the trail. Each porter carried a walking stick with a T-shaped top, which could be used (when there wasn't a handy wall) to rest the large basket long enough for a breather. They were dressed in tatters, the shoulder seams of their thin cotton shirts lacerated by the straps of their baskets despite the thicker sleeveless vests most of them wore to protect their skin. These men are the human trucks and freight cars of Nepal. They are not the porters who work for trekkers and have the down vests, baseball caps, satin team jackets, and English, Italian, German, French, or Japanese phrases to show for it. These are the long-distance haulers, passing through a landscape hardly changed since ancient times – instant noodles notwithstanding. Chaurikarka is like that: no bicycles or other wheeled vehicles make movement easier (the mountainsides are too steep for bikes or carts), no electricity lights the houses, no cooking gas or kerosene eases the burden of gathering firewood.

On the climb out of the hamlet toward Lukla on the ridge above, the hiker is struck by the deathly silence of the forest. It is forbidden to cut most trees in Nepal – a desperate measure, patchily enforced, intended to hold back rampant deforestation – so people unwilling or afraid to break the law scavenge for anything else that will burn. The wooded slope I climbed exuded a strange unreality: there were no leaves or twigs on the ground, no small animals or birds to be seen or heard. The trees stood alone, as if constructed for a natural history museum diorama; a stuffed squirrel would not have been out of place. The contrast to the teeming woodlands of Bhutan or Sikkim could not have been more stark. Nepal is one of the world's most densely populated countries, and even here, in the shadow of holy mountains, life illustrates the statistics. A lack of environmental consciousness has no religious connection when people need fuel to cook their meals or warm their houses. It would have been lunatic to run around Chaurikarka pressing people to explain how Buddhists, protectors of nature, could allow this vacuuming of the woodlands to take place.

Not too long ago, Lakpa Nuru's devotion to Buddhism, and moreover his hope that his offspring would follow his example, might have seemed pitiable, given the headlong rush of young Nepalis, including Sherpas, into urbanization and a taste for the material goods foreigners tote casually into Himalayan villages for all to admire. Before the Chinese suppression of a Tibetan uprising closed the Nepali-Tibetan border in 1959, Sherpas had been the Solu-Khumbu region's commodity traders, bringing salt and wool from Tibet to barter for manufactured goods from Kathmandu and India. Nowadays they run teahouses, trail lodges, trekking and mountaineering services, and shops where trekkers' castoffs may be sold along with a variety of unexpected imported goods shopkeepers have been quick to realize there is profit in stocking: toilet paper, track suits, canned beer, scented soap, and trail mix. Rustic cafés in Lukla serve French toast and muesli.

Some Sherpas who don't succeed turn to job-hunting in Kathmandu (where richer Sherpas are investing in hotels) and run into competition with other Nepali Buddhists from the hills also searching for an income. Over the course of not very many years, Kathmandu has turned from a dozy, slightly ethereal town left over from a distant century into a warren of exhaust-choked, garbage-strewn streets and byways where thousands of shops tumble over one another, pouring out into the patchily paved lanes the cheap clothes, sweaters, and jewelry (almost none of it Nepali) bought by bargain-hunting backpackers, the descendants of the hippies who once made this town the narcotics nirvana of the Eastern world. More than a million residents scramble for space in hives and warrens above stinking gutter-sewers which foster the spread of epidemic diseases; the warnings were out for cholera and encephalitis on my last visit. Low-budget tourists, charmed by small lodges where a few dollars will still buy room and board, succumb with increasing frequency to gut-wrenching maladies. Japanese tourists and some international aid workers ride or pedal around wearing masks to filter the particle-heavy air. Oddly, a lot of us still love the place, though affection is tested a little more each year.

The mountain people are a particularly sad sight as they hang around the capital looking for work or for a foreign woman with a hankering to try some exotic Eastern sex. On a winter evening over dinner in a guesthouse in the capital, the French Tibetologist Françoise Pommaret pointed out several of her compatriots who had stayed behind to marry porters or trail guides, only to discover they didn't quite belong in Nepal. They drift into budget restaurants to drink a good deal and find European company. On their laps they hold the tiny children who have given them a stake in trying to make life work here despite disappointments. At night, during one of the frequent power cuts, they stumble out into the potholed streets or the few treacherous patchwork sidewalks to bump into knots of young men lurking around some of the better-known nightspots – usually small restaurants of indifferent upkeep but reasonably safe and tasty food. All of this teeming world, it should be noted, exists outside the cocoons of the major hotels that shelter the higher-priced crowd. It is possible to spend days in Kathmandu and never have to walk its noisome streets; the sellers of wares and services will come to your gate, and air-conditioned vans do the rest.

The prosperous Sherpas – more than other Buddhists from the mountainous north who still struggle for a livelihood – are one of the engines pushing a Buddhist revival in Nepal, though Buddhism itself took root here long before the Sherpas were a significant presence. The Kathmandu Valley's creation myth (or at least the most popular one) tells of a turquoise sea where the capital now stands. Out of the water grew a magnificent phosphorescent lotus recognized as a manifestation of Swayambhu, yet another form of Buddha. The Boddhisattva Manjushri, wishing to reach the flower, which radiated an entrancing light, grabbed his sword and sliced through the valley wall to drain the lake. When the water had receded, he built a stupa on the hill where Swayambhunath's cluster of shrines now stands, capped by a golden spire with an eye on all four sides of its base to watch over the valley. No one knows exactly how old the first buildings at Swayambhunath are, but an ethnic Gurung Buddhist happily and ecumenically named Krishna Lama assured me as we walked around the main stupa that it had been there at least three thousand years.

Though the borders of Nepal encompass the birthplace of the historical Buddha, this is a nation where Buddhism and Hinduism – much of the worship of Shiva and his omnipresent phallus, the *shivalinga* – co-exist to an often confusing degree. Bodhnath seems to nurture a rigorously Buddhist milieu, yet Hindus come to worship and leave offerings there as well as at Swayambhunath, where it is not uncommon to find a nearly naked sadhu daubed in vermilion sitting cross-legged in front of a side altar. In the Durbar squares of Kathmandu, Patan, and Bhaktapur, Buddhist and Hindu shrines and iconography mingle in endlessly fascinating ways and places.

In a Kathmandu neighborhood where I once stayed for a month, every morning began with Buddhists igniting fires in bowls of incense on their rooftops and the Hindus pausing at a small crossroads shrine to pray, light a candle, or leave an offering. Then Buddhists and Hindus (and their Muslim neighbors) merged and mingled on the dusty lanes on the way to work, school, or the daily shopping. The scholar David Snellgrove, whose *Indo-Tibetan Buddhism* provides the most exhaustive and lucid early history of this region, thinks that Nepal's Buddhist-Hindu symbiosis provides the last living example of what religious life in northern India must have been like before aggressive Hindu Brahminism and the Muslim conquests changed the landscape forever. "One realizes," he wrote, "how much has been lost in India, and how fortunate we are to have a small surviving replica in Nepal."

With the arrival of many Tibetan exiles in the 1950s, especially after 1959, Buddhism got a critical if unexpected boost in the valley, where new religious centers sprang up, existing communities expanded, and monasteries proliferated. Tibetans, successful in a variety of businesses, most of all carpet-weaving, give generously to monks and shrines. An articulate and cosmopolitan Tibetan middle class, larger than that of any other Himalayan Buddhist community, has been successful at explaining and promoting Tibetan Buddhism internationally. So apparent was the resurgence by the 1980s that some influential Nepali Hindus sought to curb the growth of Buddhism. In the royal government of King Birendra Bir Bikram Shah Dev, the call resonated among those who saw the high profile of Tibetan Buddhists in Nepal as a potential irritant to China. Many Tibetans vow openly to see their homeland liberated from Chinese rule, a thorn if not the hoped-for dagger in Beijing's side. Consequently, in deference to China, the Dalai Lama has never been able to make an official visit to Nepal, except for Lumbini, and public celebrations of his birthday are banned or severely restricted. For Nepal, good relations with the Chinese are a necessary balance against pressures from India, which is forever seeking a dominant role in Nepali affairs.

Not long ago, Tibetan refugees in Nepal worried that their welcome was wearing thin. Searching for information on events in Lhasa, where an anti-Chinese movement is always rumbling beneath the surface, exploding now and then in demonstrations, I met new émigrés from Tibet nearly surreptitiously in the late 1980s, so great was the concern of host Tibetans who had established themselves in Nepal and did not want their livelihoods jeopardized. But in 1990, a Nepali democracy movement forced a change in the country's constitution to reduce the power of the monarchy. New elections brought secular parties into office, and threats to Buddhism seemed to dissipate, just as they did when Nepal first tried democracy in the 1950s.

The Buddhist renaissance has probably had the least effect on the Newars, despite long years of good relations with the Tibetans, says Purna Harsha Bajracharya, a Newar from a family of Buddhist scholars. Bajracharya was instrumental in beginning the Nepali Archaeology Department's first excavations of Lord Buddha's birthplace in Lumbini in the 1960s. His name, *vajra-acarya* in its Sanskrit form, literally means a Tantric master. I went to see him at his small home above a busy bazaar near the center of Kathmandu. The high-pitched product advertising of the street vendors and loud arguments of barter combined with bicycle bells and the horns of motorized rickshaws were so pervasive that Purna Harsha's soft voice was hard to hear when I played back my tapes of our first talk that evening.

But this cacophony was probably appropriate, for the Newars have always been Nepal's most committed urbanites, thriving at the heart of commerce. For more than a thousand years, they dominated trade routes between India and China from their family bases in the Kathmandu Valley and their trading houses and mercantile associations in Lhasa. Wool, silk, tea, rice, precious corals, works of art, silver, and finally manufactured goods moved along Himalayan trails on pack animals. Along the same routes, Tibetan Buddhists came south to visit the great shrines of Nepal. Newar lamas, including Purna Harsha's forebears, went to Lhasa to exchange learned opinions. The Newar trade monopoly was not broken until early in the twentieth century when the British encouraged the opening of new routes to Tibet from the northeastern Indian hill town of Kalimpong through Sikkim.

Purna Harsha's house backed onto a much quieter zone built around a Newari Buddhist *vihara*, a small temple-monastery marking the home of an important family. This vihara was in a state of decline, its owner having died some years ago "without issue," in Purna Harsha's words. He has informally taken over responsibility for the small enclosed square with delicately carved wooden doors and lintels that enclosed the shrine to a god now gone. A tailor has moved in on one side; other families fill the rest of the space, using the pump that Purna Harsha's family installed over a centuries-old well that still produces good water. In front of the shrine stands a *chaitya*, the Newar equivalent of a chorten or stupa. Purna Harsha, a man of great dignity and generosity, says that his duties amount to little more than "putting a few flowers there from time to time." In truth, he seems to take pains to salvage this corner of history, abused as it is by newcomers without an appreciation of its value.

Many other Newar compounds have suffered amid the general decay of old Kathmandu, where buildings collapse and mounds of fly-covered garbage fill once-sacred pools and pile up at many an intersection, repelling tourists. Newars, with their considerable intellectual and design skills, were responsible for the architecturally remarkable cores of the valley's three magnificent medieval cities – Bhaktapur, Patan, and Kathmandu – and were sought after across the Himalayas and in Tibet as craftsmen for both Buddhist and Hindu buildings.

Newars believe that one of their own, the young Princess Bhrikuti, carried a civilized form of Buddhism with her to Tibet when she became one of two wives of the Tibetan king-emperor Songsten Gampo in the seventh century. Indeed, Newars say that she took with her to Lhasa a statue of the Lord Buddha so valuable and exceptional in its execution that the famous Jokhang temple was built (by Newar craftsmen) to house it. Purna Harsha says that Newari women have always taken important parts in religious ceremonies and family affairs. They were traditionally free to move around the town and sometimes took lessons from monks – at least until the Rana period, when they became the targets of licentious officials whose militant Hindu upbringing conveyed little understanding of the Buddhist social order. A kind of self-imposed purdah set in, and is only now being broken down.

That the Newars' Tibeto-Burman language became Sanskritized, and that the Newars were apparently forced beginning in the fourteenth century under the Malla dynasty to adopt a Hindu caste system completely alien to Buddhist teaching, did not diminish their firm commitment to Buddhism, even after the Gorkhas, Hindus of Indian origin from the Terai, took over the Nepali monarchy in the eighteenth century. Purna Harsha Bajracharya argues that the caste system was forced on Newars out of necessity by the Malla kings, some of them Buddhists or sympathetic to Buddhism, who feared Newari solidarity. "When the rulers found everyone united among us, they were angry. The caste system became useful to divide us." It was enforced more rigorously after the end of Malla rule by Gorkha rulers, who also imposed caste on the Tibetan-speaking people of the north and assigned most of them a low status.

Purna Harsha says again and again that the Newars never had a quarrel with Hinduism, which some of them adopted. The problems were political. He adds that in any case the term "Hindu" is too broad to apply to most Nepalis, who concentrate their devotion on one god in the Hindu pantheon, Shiva, and should rightly be called Shivaites. "In the histories of Nepal you won't even find the word 'Hinduism,'" he said. "Buddhism and Shivaism grew side by side here. Both hold each other in great respect. We speak of the *Shiva-dharma* and the *Buddha-dharma.*"

Purna Harsha Bajracharya, now retired, talked about how the persecution of Newar Buddhists during the century dominated by the Rana dynasty of hereditary prime ministers had inevitably led to a lack of self-assertion and a paucity of research into their own history and culture. He tells of scholars unable to publish or forced into exile because they did. Newar Buddhist culture can never really be obscured, however, because of the extraordinary public architecture and religious institutions it contributed to Nepali life. The child goddess Kumari, whose temple in Kathmandu's Durbar Square draws sightseers hoping to catch a glimpse of the living deity, is a Newari ingredient in the Nepali cultural mix. The prepubescent Kumari, to whom by legend the valley belongs and to whom, therefore, everyone, including the king, must pay tribute once a year, is one of several such goddesses; Newar temples once had many more.

News of the vigor of Buddhism in Nepal is fast spreading beyond the Himalayas. Because Nepal, once closed to outsiders, has in recent decades become one of South Asia's most open societies, easily accessible by air from both Western nations and East Asia, Kathmandu is attracting more international scholars and new believers from several continents. Go to prayers at almost any gompa around Kathmandu and there is likely to be, in addition to a few American or European voices, a handful of respectful Japanese, Thai, Malaysian, or Singaporean worshippers. The Westerners are no longer the stock characters who once drifted in from the fringes of the drug-taking, hippie Freak Street culture that was prepared to get high on just about anything the Nepalis could offer in the 1960s and '70s, including the erotic Tantric Buddhist art whose proliferation a nineteenth-century Englishman had labeled a "filthy custom." That carefree scene bottomed out sometime in the 1980s after the overland route from Europe was closed by war in Afghanistan and by a Nepali decision to raise the costs of travel in Nepal and to reorient tourism toward more affluent visitors and serious trekkers. The casual age has not entirely passed, of course. In a Kathmandu garden café I heard two backpacking Americans discuss what to do with their day. "Let's go to Swayambhunath," one said. "A lot of really cool things go on there."

At the well-heeled Orgyen Tolku Gompa at Bodhnath, Chokyi Nyima Rinpoche said he had noticed a continuing evolution of tourism in recent years. "Before, tourists came to look at the mountains. Then some started coming to see the monasteries. They see Kathmandu is a special place. Very holy. Tourists changed. Some began wanting to hear some teaching, to study with us," he said. With new interest obviously came money. The rinpoche's private quarters include a private chapel of evident affluence, decorated in the brilliant colors traditionally favored by Tibetans. The high ceiling was painted a bright aquamarine, with rafters lacquered red. Stylized paintings of religious motifs covered the walls, along which six brass and crystal sconces had been installed for light. From the rafters hung two large crystal chandeliers. At the altar, dominated by a larger-than-life image of Buddha, there was a collection of gold statues and fine ceramic temple guardian lions. The floor was carpeted in Tibetan rugs. The one unharmonious note was the hideous three-tiered plastic waterfall with a trick faucet and plastic flowers installed on a corner table. The faucet seemed to be suspended miraculously in midair, producing a stream of water from no visible source. (The water was being pumped up to the shiny golden tap from the bottom collection dish, through an unseen clear tube obscured by the stream flowing back down around it.) Incongruous kitsch though it was, it certainly caught the attention of disciples. Two boys sat riveted in front of it.

One of the most powerful and beloved of contemporary Tibetan Buddhist lamas, the late Dilgo Khyentse Rinpoche, established his base in Kathmandu, where he and his followers built the impressive Shechen temple and monastery. His Holiness, who had at one time instructed and inspired the Dalai Lama and served as a personal guru to members of Bhutan's royal family, was the internationally recognized ranking lama of the Nyingmapa school and one of the last – if not *the* last – of the great Tibetan-born teacher-saints and *tertons*, discoverers or revealers of holy treasures. Twenty-two years of his life were spent in meditation, some of them in isolated caves in the manner of the great lamas of the past. He established and consecrated temples in Bhutan, India, and the West as well as in Nepal and set up a school of classical studies at Bhutan's Simtokha Dzong. (His daughter Chhimi Wangmo is assistant director of Bhutan's National Museum.) Though rooted in the Nyingmapa school, the rinpoche devoted much of his later life – he fled Tibet for Bhutan in 1959 – to preaching a nonsectarian Buddhism, drawing on the holy writings and philosophies of all schools.

I had often heard in Bhutan about the blurring of sectarian divisions. I remember in particular what the abbot of Tashigang Dzong told me as we stood by a huge, complicated, multifaceted sculpture in one of his temples that looked at first sight like a confusing jumble of images piled on a giant plant. "This is the holy tree," he said. "Here is the lotus grown from the lake. On the leaves the different Buddha scholars are. We have different sects. Here is the leader of Nyingma and how he achieved enlightenment. And next is another sect called Karmapa, and this is its lineage. And this is Guru, and this is the sect that was followed by Shabdrung. Up there at the top is Buddha himself. So you see no matter what denomination or what sect, the root is same, the body same, and ultimate truth is one. Root is same, ultimate goal is same. Only approach is different."

In poems, essays, and talks in Asia and the West, Dilgo Khyentse Rinpoche went beyond mere nonsectarianism. He gave the religion that recognized him as a leader in 1910, while he was still in his mother's womb, a true sense of universality. After he died in September 1991, Bhutan spent more than a year praying and preparing for his final funeral rites. Present at the *purjang* or cremation ceremony in November 1992 – during which, Bhutan's weekly newspaper said, "the last mortal remains of His Holiness dissolved into the state of luminosity" – were the Bhutanese royal family, more than fifty thousand monks and tulkus, and thousands of other followers and admirers from around the world. Many more would have come if Bhutan could have handled them. The cremation took place on a meadow in Paro, in view of the Taktsang monastery, where the Guru Rinpoche was believed to have descended on a flying tiger in the eighth century bearing the Nyingma Tantric teachings. The cremation pyre of Dilgo Khyentse Rinpoche was a work of Bhutanese artisanship at its best: a carved, roofed pavilion bedecked in silk, with altars around the clay coffin overflowing with the finest offerings of food and religious objects. Tibetan Buddhism may never again see this exalted ceremony performed with such purity of ritual and in such an unspoiled cultural and natural environment. While Himalayan Buddhists await the rinpoche's reincarnation, his legacy lives on in Kathmandu in the shadow of Bodhnath.

"Kathmandu is developing into an important center for Buddhist study," another Tibetan lama, Khenpo Rigzin, said during one of our conversations at the Nyingma Institute of Nepal, a new monastic school just outside Kathmandu memorable for its quiet, superserious atmosphere. The institute has a Tibetan-American patron, Tarthang Tulku, a publisher of Buddhist texts in Berkeley, California, Khenpo Rigzin said. Novice monks – still all boys, no girls – from across the Himalayan region and India come here to take a nine-year course that is heavy on Buddhist philosophy. So far, no Westerners had enrolled as students, Khenpo Rigzin said, though they are admitted for research. He added politely, even sweetly, that Western students might pose a problem, given the very different intellectual and spiritual environment that produced them. In his experience, he said, he found it took them a little longer to grasp things. A concept he could teach a Bhutanese,

Sikkimese, or Sherpa in a week would take two or three weeks to pen-etrate the mind of an American, he thought.

Khenpo Rigzin has turned down many offers to teach in the West, because he believes the Himalayan milieu is important to him. "I know that the standard of life is very good in America. But we need something different. According to our philosophy, we must realize the dharma. The way of living must be there. It is good for monks to stay in a group, to practice prayer together. Here I feel sure, secure. It's easier to live as lama in Nepal."

If anything, Nepal is already becoming spoiled by success, Khenpo Rigzin said, reflecting the burgeoning sense among some leading Buddhist lamas that too much luxury is creeping into monastic life. In some cases, that is already an understatement. A Kathmandu busi-nessman told me how when he tried to sell a Mercedes-Benz, he got no takers in the royal family or among wealthy houses, but found a Tibetan rinpoche ready and willing to pay cash for the car. One day, leaving a Kathmandu restaurant after lunch, I saw two monks head toward a new Hyundai parked out front. The older one got into the back; the younger one (wearing a cowboy hat) folded his robes, slid into the driver's seat, and sped away. The ideal life of a monk, Khenpo Rigzin said, is to fol-low the Lord Buddha's own advice to avoid cities, corrupting influences, distraction. He said that only the greatest of lamas would be able to concentrate in the busy atmosphere of some gompas these days.

His Holiness Ngawang Tenzing Zangbo, the Sherpas' Tengboche abbot and overseer of all Buddhist gompas in Nepal when I met him, said pithily that these days too many monks "prefer electricity to butter lamps." He expanded on this to say that there was nothing inherently bad about new inventions and modern life in general. The problem came when these things became preoccupations. "Good clothing, for instance," he said. "In other times, lamas never wanted the best gar-ments. They could go barefoot and possess nothing. Now they are ask-ing for better robes. At Tengboche, I am trying my level best to keep things as traditional as possible. I want to improve life a little bit, make it more comfortable, but stay always within tradition. I believe that when you learn the harder way, when you experience hardship, this means more and is closer to our teaching."

He said that he is not surprised to see Westerners flocking to Tibetan monasteries in Nepal. "In the West, there are too many distractions," he said. "People long to come to these mountains. Here you can learn things through your heart." He noted that Kathmandu also drew many Himalayan people because of its proximity to sacred places, but was confident that many lamas among them would return to remote areas and practice a wholesome religion, free of urban temptations. He hopes that the spiritual boom will result in higher levels of religious life all around the region and not the further degradation of monastic life through materialism. He sounded as if it might be touch-and-go in some places.

Almost all Buddhists in the Himalayas, not just lamas, are coming into frequent contact with wealthier Buddhists, both Mahayana and Theravada, from Southeast Asia, Hong Kong, and farther east. A glimpse of their obvious affluence has a powerful effect. Bhikku Nirmala Nanda, one of a small number of impoverished Theravada monks in Nepal and the abbot of a temple in Lumbini, is grateful for the gifts brought by Thai pilgrims, but alarmed at their materialism. "They come with so many baggages full of things," he told me as we shared tea, he in his chair of honor near the altar and I on the steps nearby that led to his mango grove in the sunny courtyard. "I have to tell them, 'If you carry so much heavy baggage, it will be very difficult to get to Nirvana. Reaching enlightenment will take a longer time than if you are free of this weight.'" I told him the biblical story in which Jesus declared that it would be easier for a camel to pass through the eye of a needle than for the rich man to enter heaven. He said he hadn't heard that one, and chuckled at the symmetry.

CHOMOLUNGMA SINGS THE BLUES

Ed Douglas

Ed Douglas is a journalist author and climber. He is the editor of the *Alpine Journal*, the world's oldest mountaineering publication, and has written regularly for the *Guardian* for 25 years. His ten books include a biography of Tenzing Norgay, with Sir Edmund Hillary, the first man to climb Everest.

REBEL WITHOUT A YAK

Another steep climb brought us to the entrance of the Sagarmatha National Park. Gaps among the trees just before the park boundary were strong evidence of how development of the Khumbu had damaged the area's ecology. This was the worst example of deforestation I would see while trekking in the Khumbu, although further south in Solu on the trek back from Lukla to Jiri the damage was much more extensive and little was being done to correct it. The determining factor is the park authority which regulates the management of the Khumbu's forests. People building lodges had come outside the boundary to cut trees for construction which was why the damage was so bad just here above the village of Monjo. There has historically been considerable friction between Sherpas and the park's managers who were heavily prescriptive in their early attempts to control deforestation. Since then the authorities have learned to work more closely with established local forestry practices. The whole subject of forestry is highly complex and controversial and evidence can and has been used to suggest that tourists are wicked, national government is wicked or that "ancient" Sherpa forestry management practices – known as *shinggi nawa* – are not so ancient and were probably introduced by the Rana regime in the nineteenth century. Anyone who has an urge to understand the maintenance of this crucial resource has no shortage of material to go to. No environment or culture in the world has been picked over like the Khumbu.

It is clear that the nationalisation of the forests after the Rana regime fell had some negative effect on the Khumbu, but that this effect has been exaggerated. It is also clear that the Sherpas themselves started using a lot more wood in the 1960s and 1970s, before large numbers of tourists arrived, because their trading habits which took them away from the Khumbu for as much as five months during the coldest time of the year were disrupted when the Chinese invasion of Tibet closed the border. Ironically, news of the decision to establish a national park prompted many Sherpas to cut trees in large numbers because they feared access would be severely restricted in future years. Their fears were realised when in the early 1980s, soon after the establishment of the park, new regulations that banned all tree-felling, even lopping of branches, were enforced by a Nepalese army unit. There were those in the park's administration who understood that such draconian measures would alienate local people and the New Zealand advisors who helped in the park's establishment tried hard to include Sherpas in its management, consulting widely at village meetings and training Khumbu Sherpas in conservation and park management.

Part of the problem has been that the term "national park" means different things to different people. In Nepal, to the Sherpas, it meant parks like Chitwan in the Terai or Rara in the far west of the country where people had been cleared from their homes. People establishing the parks had in mind such models as the Yellowstone in the United States where natural preservation is paramount. This may work in wilderness areas with no or very few local inhabitants but could not possibly in a region as settled and developed as the Khumbu where every scrap of land that can be used has been for the benefit of people. This concept of conservation and development is something more commonly understood in England and Wales since national parks there have had to wrestle with these problems since their inception.

The revolution in 1990 gave fresh impetus to Sherpas who wanted to re-establish their rights to managing land and forestry. The local panchayats were dissolved and two development committees, each covering several villages, were established to replace them. These changes also coincided with the appointment of a new chief warden for the park, Surya Bahadur Pandey, who proved sympathetic to established Sherpa ways of land management. He oversaw a range of changes which in effect created a two-tier system of control which reinstated shinggi nawa at a local level but left final authorisation with the park. The Himalayan Trust has established nurseries in the Khumbu and the Worldwide Fund for Nature has started work on improving those areas like Monjo that have suffered because they are just outside the boundary. These changes have improved the outlook greatly. What has become clear, however, is that nothing can be done for the long term without the co-operation of local people. At the same time, the importance of the environment to their economic future has to be stressed. Trekkers come to the Khumbu because it is beautiful and the income they provide is very sensitive to its maintenance. I was reminded of the continuing tensions between national and local opinion as I handed over the few hundred rupees permit fee to the park official. Where this money goes and what it is used for I still don't fully understand but I felt sure that it wasn't all going to the maintenance of the park.

From outside the office there was a burst of shouting and a German in his late forties appeared in the doorway, closely followed by a strutting, moustachioed soldier carrying a sten gun that looked like it was last fired in Burma in 1945.

"These idiots!" the German said to me. I saw his hands had been tied behind his back with red string. "I know what all this is about. It was the pictures I took in Kathmandu, wasn't it? You're out to get me." The German had been arrested coming out of the park with a video camera for which he lacked a permit. He would now be returned to Namche Bazar where there was a small garrison and the headquarters of the park.

His girlfriend, blond and severely beautiful, came into the office and stood a little behind him. There was blood on her hand and I asked if the soldier had injured her. She shook her head and turned her hand over and I saw that one of her fingers was notched, as though a wedge had been cut from it, almost to the bone. She had a voice that bled indifference. "You know, it doesn't hurt me," she said, looking at her finger as though it were a specimen.

Dachhiri, who looked at me and shrugged at this further illustration of European strangeness, led the way down the hill, back to the mint green waters of the Dudh Kosi and the flowering pink rhododendrons. Even relatively minor changes in altitude brought a change in the density and type of forest. It was as though you could move through place and time, from summer to spring, simply by walking up hills.

Ahead of us was the long climb to Namche Bazar, 700 metres in gain to an altitude of more than 3,400 metres, and with my heavy sack it was hard work. There was a dramatic suspension bridge to begin with, whose boards had rotted badly. I could see the river rushing beneath where the wood had gone completely and the whole structure swayed alarmingly. Suddenly it began to bounce as well and I grabbed the thick wire that supported it to steady myself. Looking behind me I saw Dachhiri jumping up and down.

"Bridge not so good," he shouted over the roar of the water. Dachhiri's English may have been limited, although not nearly as much as my Nepali, but he used what he had with considerable ingenuity. Things that were good – lodges, food, bridges – were "'s okay". Things that were adequate were "not so good, not so bad". Things that were truly desperate and threatened disease – or catastrophe were "not so good". His assessments were almost always correct. My biggest problem was keeping up with him. Dachhiri was formidably strong and loved to be on the move. On the long climb to Namche he would wait at a bend in the track as I gasped after him to greet me with a comment like "I love to walk," or "Not so far now." At the apex of a bend he pointed to a small subsidiary track and said "Everesh" I followed him for twenty yards and sure enough beyond a wooded ridge the black triangle of the mountain appeared, a long streak of snow blowing from its distant summit like spittle in the wind.

Finally, just as my weakened body seemed on the verge of calling it a day, we came over a rise and I found myself on the fringes of Namche Bazar, a town I had visited second-hand dozens of times before. I felt I knew it already. Bill Tilman was one of the first people from the West to see it and with his precise intelligence offered this impression of the town in *Nepal Himalaya:*

Namche Bazar lies at about eleven thousand feet on the ridge between the Dudh Kosi and the Bhote Kosi, facing westwards across the valley to the peak of Kwangde. The houses are detached as if the owners were men of substance. There are about thirty of these whitewashed, two-storeyed houses, with low-pitched shingle roofs. The ground floor serves as stables and stores, while above is the one long living room, with an open fire and clay stove against one wall, wooden shelves for fine copper ware and cheap china on another, and large trellised window frames set with five or six small panes of glass.

In several interviews I had read with Ed Hillary, he described the town as having been changed utterly by tourism and I was expecting to be disappointed. But the town's position, set in a huge natural amphitheatre with a stupa where the stage would be, gives a dramatic appeal which no amount of development could alter. There are more houses now than when Tilman came but not many more and they are constructed in similar fashion, although most now have metal roofs in place of the old wooden shingles. Some of the new lodges are three storeys, but there are plenty of old three-storey houses in Solu, two or three days' walk to the south. Few if any in the centre of town have a lower storey used as a barn any more but that is not to say that their owners don't have animals elsewhere. There was some garbage on the streets, but not a great deal and certainly less than I'd seen in towns of comparable size in other mountainous areas of Nepal.

Dachhiri led the way down a narrow, flag-stoned street, to the Kala Pattar Lodge – "'s okay" – and ducked through the low doorway. The Kala Pattar is a substantial building with three floors, granite walls, and rough pine beams and window frames. There was a fluorescent tube lighting the dining room and a tape machine blasting out Hindi music. Rugs on the walls and benches softened the room's appearance. Out of the window I could see other houses spreading round the hillside, the prayer flags and white trimming on the windows giving the village the appearance of a ship at sea, straining under the constant breeze.

In the mud enclosure at the back of the hotel a dozen men were hard at work building an extension, dressing stones and planing wood without ever seeming to stop. Until darkness fell, the sound of hammer on chisel on rock tapped away like a noisy clock. On the other side of the village, another lodge was nearing completion at a cost of some $25,000 for land and construction. I cannot imagine what the cost will be even in twenty years' time.

The only other guest was an Israeli who had alarmingly bucked teeth and the type of sunglasses which clip onto spectacles and can be levered up. This is how he always wore them. His guide was a Magar from Jiri called Rudra and he and Dachhiri compared notes in the way all Nepalis do, not just Sherpas: "Where have you come from? Where are you going?" Always the talk was of movement in a nation that still walks pretty much everywhere.

The lodge was owned by one of the wealthier Sherpa families, people who had benefited most from the influx of tourists. Only a few hundred visited Namche in the early 1970s. Now more than ten thousand come through each year. In the kitchen, a young Sherpani was making tea and I asked her name. Dachhiri and the Magar looked at me, then at her and collapsed in laughter. "Her name is Mayar," said Dachhiri. "That means love. Heesh-heesh-heesh." She blushed, tutted loudly and spoke rapidly to Dachhiri in the Sherpa's own language before disappearing back into her kitchen. I decided to go for a walk.

Out on the street, two men were playing dice, smacking the tumbler down on a round leather pallet before an engrossed crowd of a dozen men. Another two picked up badminton rackets and batted a shuttlecock over the heads of chickens scratching in dirt. A sign outside the café next door to the Kala Pattar read Hermann Helmers Bäckerei und Konditorei. Inside two Japanese drank cappuccinos and ate fresh doughnuts. A horse grazed on hay spread over a mud bank opposite. Men in baseball caps, often wearing clothes with labels like Levi's and Patagonia, drifted through the streets. Sherpas are better off than the Rai and other tribes who fill the streets on Saturdays during the weekly market. Few Sherpas from the Khumbu earn their living carrying loads for trekkers, although this is what most in the West believe them to do. Sherpas still act as porters for climbing expeditions, something which is comparatively well paid, but portering along the trails is left to Tamangs and other tribes.

The fame of their association with early Everest expeditions and their proximity to the mountains are not the only reasons for the success of the Sherpas. They have an inherent ability to trade and much of their income came from this activity when they were still allowed to travel freely over the Nangpa La into Tibet, before the Chinese occupation. Tourism has filled the gap in trade left by the closure of the old trading routes. Now the Sherpas sell surplus expedition equipment back to the Europeans who brought it to Nepal, everything from camping gas and chocolate to novels and ice axes; Namche is the centre for this trade. Providing hospitality is also a long-standing tradition. The first expeditions found lodgings with villagers as other travellers would and this has simply been formalised with the construction of lodges.

I looked into a pool hall below the Daphne Lodge. A dozen young Sherpas with baseball caps on, their hair swept back into pony tails, were shuffling round the tables. There were pictures of James Dean and Elvis on the wall and bottles of Tuborg on the shelves. Some people find this kind of development corrupting, a dilution of a culture that might threaten its integrity. I found it rather groovy and a little hypocritical of those who visited Namche in the 1950s and 1960s to complain if local people absorbed some of their habits. Adverts round the village inviting me to a video evening and the few satellite dishes confirmed my view. Rupert Murdoch beaming down Star TV onto the heads of communities like that in the Khumbu was going to have a far greater influence on the expectations and attitudes of Sherpas than trekkers ever would.

Cultural influence and change were hardly new to the Sherpas. They had lived in the Khumbu after migrating from Kham in eastern Tibet – Sherpa, pronounced Shar-wa by the people themselves, means "east people" – for roughly as long as the Spanish had been in South America. During that time there had been all kinds of upheaval from the introduction of the potato in the nineteenth century to the collapse of trade with Tibet. Sherpas once travelled regularly from Lhasa to the plains of India while trading, so I doubted whether James Dean would bring them to their cultural knees on his own.

Western culture is so pervasive in South Asia and elsewhere because it is delivered so efficiently through satellite television or fashion and Sherpas are open to these changes. Tenzing Norgay, who followed the exodus of Sherpas to Darjeeling in search of work with expeditions, once said that the Sherpas "do not, like people with older cultures, cling to ancient traditions, but adapt themselves easily to new thoughts and habits". But that doesn't mean that Sherpas will throw away the things they've got right. Wearing a baseball cap or wanting a tape recorder doesn't necessarily make you rude to your mother. The elders of Namche can also take comfort from the knowledge that their sons are truly awful at pool I can beat these people, I thought. Then I saw the angle of the floor and decided against it.

Back at the Kala Pattar, Dachhiri and Rudra were drinking tea in Mayar's smoky, narrow kitchen, the wood stove roaring against a blackened wall. The completion of a substantial hydro-electric scheme at nearby Thamo hadn't yet resulted in a clean electric cooker at the Kala Pattar. Mayar was stirring a big pot of stew with a ladle. "These are two very good boys," she said. Rudra made another joke about Mayar's name and then they both looked at me again. Mayar waggled the ladle at them. I changed the subject, asking whether the showers were electric or not. Several in Namche are. Mayar said no, but that the water was already hot. I pondered the difficulties of explaining the environmental consequences of burning wood so that pampered westerners can wash their bodies and be clean for five minutes but accepted the offer anyway. She probably knew all that stuff and no one else was likely to use the water now it was dark. Why let it cool overnight? There was no light in the shower-room bar a candle.

In the evening I walked round to the Khumbu Lodge to say hello to Audrey Salkeld who was part of David Breashears' Everest expedition. Audrey knows more about the early attempts to climb Everest than anyone else alive and was offering his team the benefit of her historical perspective. I found her hunched over a portable computer, typing a letter to the park authority asking permission to establish a weather station on the South Col. There seemed to be no one else to go and have a drink with, so I looked round the lodge which was an altogether grander affair than the Kala Pattar. On the wall was a photograph of the well-known Sherpa Pasang Kami with President Jimmy Carter and Sir Edmund Hillary, each with a stack of white scarves – kathas – round their necks, given on greeting as a mark of respect. (I assume

Hillary recycles his, otherwise he would have a collection of several hundred thousand.) The kitchen at the Khumbu was spotless and, more importantly, smokeless, creating an atmosphere of clean efficiency. Posters from mountaineering expeditions lined the walls, attesting to the lodge's long-standing reputation. I was glad I'd showered.

Dachhiri had already gone when I woke next morning, so I settled in for a long breakfast. The number of guests had increased by two. A middle-aged Japanese couple had put up a tent in the lodge's backyard and were drinking tea in the dining room. They smiled and nodded when I pushed through the curtain and sat down but otherwise remained silent, even with each other. I felt, and indeed was, large and smelly in comparison but they remained polite and circumspect, without giving the remotest indication of whether they were enjoying their holiday, a discretion which was rare during my time in the Khumbu where trekkers seemed desperate to report on their condition and attitudes. The woman wore an expensive cardigan draped across her shoulders, her coiffure incongruous in the basic surroundings. They didn't look like typical trekkers and in fact they weren't, although I wouldn't discover that for several days. In contrast to the Japanese, the Israeli kept up a constant monologue of complaint. He changed his plans every fifteen minutes, driving his guide Rudra to silent despair because he was much too polite to respond in kind.

When Dachhiri returned we walked up the steep hill to the police station to register my trekking permit with them and to help in my acclimatisation. My body would require a fortnight to adapt fully to the reduction in oxygen but the extra day in Namche would help in the process. On the wall of the police station was a map of the Sagarmatha National Park. I was confused by the origin of the word Sagarmatha, which is Sanskrit for "Brow of the Ocean" and has been used by the Nepali authorities as an indigenous name for Mount Everest. One reference to the name has been found in a half-forgotten collection of essays held in a library in Kathmandu but this seems fairly lightweight evidence to base a name-change on, not least because a perfectly good local name that was recognised on both sides of the mountain already existed.

"Where does the name Sagarmatha come from, Dachhiri?" I asked him.

"Sagarmatha is Kathmandu name," he said. "Chomolungma is Sherpa name."

In truth, using the name Sagarmatha is another way for the Kathmandu authorities to illustrate their control of the Khumbu. Chomolungma, which is most often translated "Goddess Mother of the World", seems an appropriate name and I for one regret that most of the world will continue to call it Everest. When the Survey of India calculated that the mountain was the highest in the world in 1852 it already had an official number – Peak XV. Clearly this wouldn't do and the Surveyor General of India, Sir Andrew Waugh, was determined to honour his predecessor Sir George Everest. Everest was the central force in the success of the Survey of India whose contribution to human knowledge was considerable but he was not that keen on his name being preserved in this way. He pointed out that local people wouldn't be able to pronounce the name and judging by the number of Sherpas and other Nepalis I met who call it "Everesh" this judgement has proved correct. Brian Hodgson, by then retired as Resident in Kathmandu, told the Royal Geographical Society that it was called Devadhunga. Douglas Freshfield preferred Gaurisankar, which exists but is a mountain entirely separate from Everest. When both these names, supported by such notable experts, were shown to be without foundation, the Waugh faction claimed victory. There was, however, already evidence that the local name was Chomolungma – transcribed as Tschoumou-Lancma – as long ago as 1733, published in a map drawn from information supplied by French Capuchin friars who had established a mission in Lhasa. Other travellers later confirmed this, although the controversy continued well into this century. It is all too late now.

It may seem like an over-indulgence in political correctness to prefer the local name but I am in good company. Douglas Freshfield argued that "it is impossible to acquiesce in the attempt permanently to attach to the highest mountain in the world a personal and inappropriate name in place of its own." There are unpleasant colonial undertones to the name Everest, but I suppose it is better named after a geographer than a politician. Mount Gladstone or Disraeli would have been ghastly.

Everest himself died in 1866, too early to be sure that his name would go down in history in quite such a memorable fashion but the Chinese were infuriated that the mountain should be known around the world as an illustration of the range of the British Empire. The current regime has resolutely stuck to its version of the Tibetan name Chomolungma, a situation which is pregnant with irony. In 1951 *The Times* published a leader on the subject following another attack from the Chinese on the use of the word Everest, although political correctness was yet to be invented, *The Times* preferring the term "appeasement". "The whole question," *The Times* concluded, "is one which it may take a considerable time to decide; and meanwhile the individual in this country, faced with the choice of talking about Chu-mu-lang-ma [sic] and being execrated as an appeaser or calling it Everest and being reviled as a provocative war-monger with no consideration for Asiatic susceptibilities, had better shun the Himalayas as a topic for general conversation." Perhaps the final word on the issue of Everest's name should rest with Tenzing Norgay and his mum:

Usually Chomolungma is said to mean "Goddess Mother of the World." Sometimes "Goddess Mother of the Wind." But it did not mean either of these when I was a boy in Solu Khumbu. Then it meant "The Mountain So High No Bird Can Fly Over It." That is what all Sherpa mothers used to tell their children – what my own mother told me – and it is the name I still like the best for this mountain that I love.

INTO THIN AIR

Jon Krakauer

Jon Krakauer is an American writer and mountaineer. He was a member of an ill-fated expedition to summit Mount Everest in 1996, which became known as the 1996 Mount Everest disaster, one of the deadliest disasters in the history of climbing Everest. Krakauer is the author of best-selling non-fiction books *Into the Wild* and *Into Thin Air*, both of which have been made into feature films, as well as *Under the Banner of Heaven*, *Where Men Win Glory* and *Eiger Dreams*. His magazine articles have appeared in *Outside*, *GQ*, *National Geographic*, *Rolling Stone*, *Architectural Digest*, *Playboy*, *The New Yorker* and *The New York Times*. In 1999 he received an Academy Award in Literature from the American Academy of Arts and Letters. *Into Thin Air*, became a #1 *New York Times* bestseller and was translated into more than twenty-five languages. It was also *Time* magazine's Book of the Year, and was one of three finalists for the Pulitzer Prize.

O ur route to the summit would follow the Khumbu Glacier up the lower half of the mountain. From the *bergschrund*[1] at 23,000 feet that marked its upper end, this great river of ice flowed two and a half miles down a relatively gentle valley called the Western Cwm. As the glacier inched over humps and dips in the Cwm's underlying strata, it fractured into countless vertical fissures – crevasses. Some of these crevasses were narrow enough to step across; others were eighty feet wide, several hundred feet deep, and ran half a mile from end to end. The big ones were apt to be vexing obstacles to our ascent, and when hidden beneath a crust of snow

---

1 A *bergschrund* is a deep slit that delineates a glacier's upper terminus; it forms as the body of ice slides away from the steeper wall immediately above, leaving a gap between glacier and rock.

they would pose a serious hazard, but the challenges presented by the crevasses in the Cwm had proven over the years to be predictable and manageable.

The Icefall was a different story. No part of the South Col route was feared more by climbers. At around 20,000 feet, where the glacier emerged from the lower end of the Cwm, it pitched abruptly over a precipitous drop. This was the infamous Khumbu Icefall, the most technically demanding section on the entire route.

The movement of the glacier in the Icefall has been measured at between three and four feet a day. As it skids down the steep, irregular terrain in fits and starts, the mass of ice splinters into a jumble of huge, tottering blocks called *seracs*, some as large as office buildings. Because the climbing route wove under, around, and between hundreds of these unstable towers, each trip through the Icefall was a little like playing a round of Russian roulette: sooner or later any given serac was going to fall over without warning, and you could only hope you weren't beneath it when it toppled. Since 1963, when a teammate of Hornbein and Unsoeld's named Jake Breitenbach was crushed by an avalanching serac to become the Icefall's first victim, eighteen other climbers had died here.

The previous winter, as he had done in winters past, Hall had consulted with the leaders of all the expeditions planning to climb Everest in the spring, and together they'd agreed on one team among them who would be responsible for establishing and maintaining a route through the Icefall. For its trouble, the designated team was to be paid $2,200 from each of the other expeditions on the mountain. In recent years this cooperative approach had been met with wide, if not universal, acceptance, but it wasn't always so.

The first time one expedition thought to charge another to travel through the ice was in 1988, when a lavishly funded American team announced that any expedition that intended to follow the route they'd engineered up the Icefall would have to fork over $2,000. Some of the other teams on the mountain that year, failing to understand that Everest was no longer merely a mountain but a commodity as well, were incensed. And the greatest hue and cry came from Rob Hall, who was leading a small, impecunious New Zealand team.

Hall carped that the Americans were "violating the spirit of the hills" and practicing a shameful form of alpine extortion, but Jim Frush, the unsentimental attorney who was the leader of the American group, remained unmoved. Hall eventually agreed through clenched teeth to send Frush a check and was granted passage through the Icefall. (Frush later reported that Hall never made good on his IOU.)

Within two years, however, Hall did an about-face and came to see the logic of treating the Icefall as a toll road. Indeed, from 1993 through '95 he volunteered to put in the route and collect the toll himself. In the spring of 1996 he elected not to assume responsibility for the Icefall, but he was happy to pay the leader of a rival commercial expedition – a Scottish Everest veteran named Mal Duff – to take over the job. Long before we'd even arrived at Base Camp, a team of Sherpas employed by Duff had blazed a zigzag path through the seracs, stringing out more than a mile of rope and installing some sixty aluminum ladders over the broken surface of the glacier. The ladders belonged to an enterprising Sherpa from the village of Gorak Shep who turned a nice profit by renting them out each season.

So it came to pass that at 4:45 a.m. on Saturday, April 13, I found myself at the foot of the fabled Icefall, strapping on my crampons in the frigid predawn gloom.

Crusty old alpinists who've survived a lifetime of close scrapes like to counsel young protégés that staying alive hinges on listening carefully to one's "inner voice." Tales abound of one or another climber who decided to remain in his or her sleeping bag after detecting some inauspicious vibe in the ether and thereby survived a catastrophe that wiped out others who failed to heed the portents.

I didn't doubt the potential value of paying attention to subconscious cues. As I waited for Rob to lead the way, the ice underfoot emitted a series of loud cracking noises, like small trees being snapped in two, and I felt myself wince with each pop and rumble from the glacier's shifting depths. Problem was, my inner voice resembled Chicken Little: it was screaming that I was about to die, but it did that almost every time I laced up my climbing boots. I therefore did my damnedest to ignore my histrionic imagination and grimly followed Rob into the eerie blue labyrinth.

Although I'd never been in an icefall as frightening as the Khumbu, I'd climbed many other icefalls. They typically have vertical or even overhanging passages that demand considerable expertise with ice ax and crampons. There was certainly no lack of steep ice in the Khumbu Icefall, but all of it had been rigged with ladders or ropes or both, rendering the conventional tools and techniques of ice climbing largely superfluous.

I soon learned that on Everest not even the rope – the quintessential climber's accoutrement – was to be utilized in the time-honored manner. Ordinarily, one climber is tied to one or two partners with a 150-foot length of rope, making each person directly responsible for the life of the others; roping up in this fashion is a serious and very intimate act. In the Icefall, though, expediency dictated that each of us climb independently, without being physically connected to one another in any way.

Mal Duff's Sherpas had anchored a static line of rope that extended from the bottom of the Icefall to its top. Attached to my waist was a three-foot-long safety tether with a carabiner, or snap-link, at the distal end. Security was achieved not by roping myself to a teammate but rather by clipping my safety tether to the fixed line and sliding it up the rope as I ascended. Climbing in this fashion, we would be able to move as quickly as possible through the most dangerous parts of the Icefall, and we wouldn't have to entrust our lives to teammates whose skill and experience were unknown. As it turned out, not once during the entire expedition would I ever have reason to rope myself to another climber.

If the Icefall required few orthodox climbing techniques, it demanded a whole new repertoire of skills in their stead – for instance, the ability to tiptoe in mountaineering boots and crampons across three wobbly ladders lashed end to end, bridging a sphincter-clenching chasm. There were many such crossings, and I never got used to them.

At one point I was balanced on an unsteady ladder in the predawn gloaming, stepping tenuously from one bent rung to the next, when the ice supporting the ladder on either end began to quiver as if an earthquake had struck. A moment later came an explosive roar as a large serac somewhere close above came crashing down. I froze, my heart in my throat, but the avalanching ice passed fifty yards to the left, out of sight, without doing any damage. After waiting a few minutes to regain my composure I resumed my herky-jerky passage to the far side of the ladder.

The glacier's continual and often violent state of flux added an element of uncertainty to every ladder crossing. As the glacier moved, crevasses would sometimes compress, buckling ladders like toothpicks; other times a crevasse might expand, leaving a ladder dangling in the air, only tenuously supported, with neither end mounted on solid ice. Anchors securing the ladders and lines routinely melted out when the afternoon sun warmed the surrounding ice and snow. Despite daily maintenance, there was a very real danger that any given rope might pull loose under body weight.

But if the Icefall was strenuous and terrifying, it had a surprising allure as well. As dawn washed the darkness from the sky, the shattered glacier was revealed to be a three-dimensional landscape of phantasmal beauty. The temperature was six degrees Fahrenheit. My crampons crunched reassuringly into the glacier's rind. Following the fixed line, I meandered through a vertical maze of crystalline blue stalagmites. Sheer rock buttresses seamed with ice pressed in from both edges of the glacier, rising like the shoulders of a malevolent god. Absorbed by my surroundings and the gravity of the labor, I lost myself in the unfettered pleasures of ascent, and for an hour or two actually forgot to be afraid.

Three-quarters of the way to Camp One, Hall remarked at a rest stop that the Icefall was in better shape than he'd ever seen it: "The route's a bloody freeway this season." But only slightly higher, at 19,000 feet, the ropes brought us to the base of a gargantuan, perilously balanced serac. As massive as a twelve-story building, it loomed over our heads, leaning 30 degrees past vertical. The route followed a natural catwalk that angled sharply up the overhanging face: we would have to climb up and over the entire off-kilter tower to escape its threatening tonnage.

Safety, I understood, hinged on speed. I huffed toward the relative security of the serac's crest with all the haste I could muster, but since I wasn't acclimatized my fastest pace was no better than a crawl. Every four or five steps I'd have to stop, lean against the rope, and suck desperately at the thin, bitter air, searing my lungs in the process.

I reached the top of the serac without it collapsing and flopped breathless onto its flat summit, my heart pounding like a jackhammer. A little later, around 8:30 a.m., I arrived at the top of the Icefall itself, just beyond the last of the seracs. The safety of Camp One didn't supply much peace of mind, however: I couldn't stop thinking about the ominously tilted slab a short distance below, and the fact that I would have to pass beneath its faltering bulk at least seven more times if I was going to make it to the summit of Everest. Climbers who snidely denigrate this as the Yak Route, I decided, had obviously never been through the Khumbu Icefall.

MUSIC OF THE FIREFLIES (*JUNKIRI KO SANGEET*)

Khagendra Sangroula

Khagendra Sangroula is a Nepali author who is famous for his unique style of satire.

It was the first day of lessons. It had been appointed a name: the Adult Literacy Class. Three new, clear and bright kerosene lanterns dazzled brilliantly in the room. A few people gradually arrived as the dusk deepened. The first to arrive leaning on his cane and swaying in his kachhad wrap was the arrogant Somey. Close at heels came Katwal, who held a low opinion of the filching Somey. By eight o'clock a small crowd had gathered under the shed. Not a woman was among them. A few young men were there, with a lot more men of middle age and a few elders. To the right of the door was a large board hanging on the wall. A thin layer of straw had been spread on the floor and over it were arranged some straw mats.

The natives sat on the mats. Kapil and Sheshkant, their beards dense as jungles, stood on either side of the board. A stranger stood near Kapil – gaunt, tall, skinny like a new stalk of bamboo.

Kapil began the lesson. "Should I put out this lantern?" These were his first words addressed to the class. The natives who had congregated to listen to something new and learn something were astonished. It is a pitch-black night near a new moon. But, the bearded man asks if he should put out the lantern!

"No, sir! No! Would be disastrous!" Katwal protested to rid the itch on his eager tongue.

"But, why do we need these lanterns lit?" Sheshkant added to the elder beard's threat.

"The night is thick, sir. We'll become lost," Somey, squatting in the front row and leaning against the wall with his crooked cane still in hand, replied in a subdued voice.

"How many in Simring village have the light in their eyes?" Kapil asked again, along with hand gestures. Those in the classroom looked at each other, some seemingly with a vague notion of understanding, and others without any comprehension.

"You could say there isn't a single pair," Katwal said, the wheels of his mind turning as he tried to understand the meaning of the question. "Maybe I am the man with the dimmest light in him. And, after me, may be Younger Uncle has some in him."

"Katwal – what are you saying about understanding something or other?" Somey raised his voice a bit.

"I understand a little, Younger Uncle."

"Tell us then – what do you understand?"

"The thing is, Uncle, sirs here are asking who among the villagers has the light of education in their eyes."

"Oho! The boy seems to have some sense, after all. Or, isn't that so, sir?"

"He is right, Somey," Sheshkant affirmed.

"Even without the light of education in their eyes, the people of Simring have never stubbed their toes on the ups and downs of life and fallen on their faces. Nobody has had their knees knocked out by stumbling onto rocks. None has fallen into pits. No man has tumbled off a cliff. Nobody has drowned in the river. Or, have they?" Sheshkant staked out his argument.

A line of answers jostled for attention.

"Because our eyes are shut we stumble daily, sir, and fall on your faces."

"As we feel our way forward in the dark we have fallen down pits, sir."

"When our people have gone about without light in their eyes they have drowned in the river and died."

Somey turned his head to every voice and listened attentively. Then he said, "What have you understood, and what are you talking about?"

"We have understood the talk about eyes, and now we talk about life. Younger Uncle – you are kin in name, and I don't want to tell you off, but sometimes you are thick as a plank!"

"Katwal – if you understand half of what's being said, why do you make as if you understand everything?"

"I have understood it all, Younger Uncle."

"Of course, you have, you dunce!"

The two bobcats of the nettle bushes of Simring began snarling at each other. And, with the intention of sweeping aside their arrogance, Kapil appealed to Somey, "Brother Somey, regardless of anything, you have seen quite a few more winters than us. If we could please hear some things from your mouth . . ."

"If you, sir, command and say – Somey, tell us a thing or two! – it may be so that I could tell you a thing or two."

"Please do, Somey, please," Sheshkant moved to appease.

"What I reckon, sir, is that by light of the eyes you mean reading and writing. How well placed is my guess?"

"Very well placed, Somey."

"You sirs have been talking in a roundabout manner. Stumbling, knees getting knocked out, falling into pits, tumbling down cliffs, and drowning in the river – my guess is that by this you mean to talk about how the rich folks and the upper castes have been tricking and cheating and wringing and draining dry the poor folks of the lower castes. Well, sir – how well placed is my guess?"

"Very well placed, Somey."

Kapil addressed his question to Mangaley, who sat in the middle of the group, craning to follow the conversation, "Mangaley, what are your thoughts on this?"

"I support Uncle Somey on this, sir. No matter how long a rope is drawn, the ends always look the same. Now that I have lent it my ears and listened carefully, I think we are talking about receiving an education in order to light up our eyes.'

"What does the rest think?"

"That's just what it is, sir," Kaude Kanchha, sitting behind Mangale, watching with the one good eye he was born with, said in agreement, "The issue is resolved."

Sheshkant scribbled three large letters on the board in Devnagari. And, with a pen in one hand, he scanned the room man by man, as if hesitating to pick someone to ask the question. A middle-aged man sat in the back row, near the wall. He decided that the man was illiterate, and so Seshkant showed the man the pen in his hand and asked, "Brother at the back – what is this?"

"It is a pen, sir," the man in the corner answered innocently.

Sheshkant then pointed to the letters on the board and asked, "And what are those, brother?"

"All dark blobs of ink are as beasts to me. I call this a buffalo!"

"Katwal, tell us what this is."

"That, too, is a pen, sir."

"It was a buffalo to the brother sitting in the corner. How did it become a pen for you?"

"It may be a dim one, sir, but there is a light in my eyes."

"May I say something?" Somey sought permission.

"Please, do."

"A thought just came to my mind, sir – the truth is, the blind man sitting in the corner just now knocked his knee into a rock. But, Katwal, with his sight – he leapt across the rock and has reached the other side."

"What does the brother sitting in the corner have to say about this?"

"They speak the truth, sir. I walked blindly, knocked my knee and fell on this side of the rock. Katwal had his eyes open, so he leapt across to the other side. The blind stumbled and fell, the sighted crossed over."

"What does a pen do?" Kapil began, twirling the pen.

"A pen's job is to write, I think."

"What does a pen write in the setting of Simring?"

After a protracted discussion a conclusion was reached: a pen in Simring either writes letters to those who have traveled to India to work as servants, or it writes promissory notes to money lenders.

"Alright – let us write a promissory note," Sheshkant proposed as he paced about the room. "Let us assume for a moment that I am the village chief. I have lent both Somey and the brother in the corner a hundred rupees each in their hours of need. We need to write promissory notes, don't we? Should we write them?"

"Immediately," Katwal said, trying to quell the excitement of his tongue.

In no time Sheshkant finished writing a promissory note on the board. After finishing it, he turned towards Somey first. "Somey – is this note correct according to the amount of loan you took out and the interest rate you promised to repay?"

Somey scrutinized every word with squinted eyes and said, "I find it alright, sir."

"What was the amount borrowed, and what amount is written down?"

"Hundred rupees were borrowed, and the amount written down is also a hundred."

"And, the interest?"

"Five percent per month."

"Is that the amount promised?"

"That is, after all, how much the lenders charge us."

"The promissory note is accurate, then, according to the terms agreed upon?"

Before the question was articulated, Katuwal, who thought of the arrogant Somey a pilferer, barged in to answer. "Absolutely alright, sir."

Now Sheshkant's eyes turned to the corner of the room. To begin with, he casually edited the wording of the note, and then asked, "Brother Kaudey, sitting in the corner – is this note right about the money borrowed and spent and what payment was promised in return?"

Kaudey stared at the promissory note on the board with bewildered incomprehension. Then he spoke, "Sir – I am but a blind man. How does a blind man tell apart what is honey and what is poison? Since my eyes lack any light, I am forced to accept the note as it is, sir."

"So, you agree that the note is alright, don't you?"

Kaudey took a long, defeated breath. The pupils of his anxious eyes trembled. He tried to say something but his lips didn't move. He now vividly recalled the deception played on him through the game of promissory notes when Gopilal relieved him of his remaining two strips of paddy-rich land. He didn't speak – he didn't speak at all!

"You approve of the note, don't you?"

"I have no other choice. To misfortunate ones like us all blobs of ink are like dark beasts . . ."

"Mangaley – your eyes have the light in them, don't they?" Kapil called the attention of Mangaley, who had been watching the proceedings with the utmost attention and bated breath.

"No, sir," Mangaley spoke in defeat.

"So – is this note correct?"

"But the blind don't have the choice of saying no. We nod and grunt and agree, no matter what the moneylenders say."

"Somey," Sheshkant drew the conversation towards Somey.

"Just as I watched, sir, Kaudey walked into the snare laid for him by the moneylenders."

"How is that?"

"How can you even ask that, sir? Because the loan amount on the note has already changed from a hundred to two hundred rupees. The interest rate has jumped from five to ten percent."

"Kaudey – seems to me that we've lost grasp of the issue!"

Kaudey, didn't speak. His face appeared pocked with the marks of hardship and calamities.

"What can a blind man like me say, sir!" said Kaudey from his corner and hid his face behind his hands. And, in the quiet air of the classroom spread the cold sighs from numerous men whose chests had been rent apart by the saws of deception and cunning of other, better-off men.

Now began the game of alphabet. Slate boards and pieces of chalk were distributed to the aged students. Then Kapil and Sheshkant held each person's hand and guided them in drawing lines and curves and tails and necks, encouraging their wards to write the letters *Ka, La* and *Ma* to spell 'pen'. The skinny man, who had been quietly observing with folded hands, also came forth to assist the teachers. Once the mature students had learned to write the assigned letters, the two bearded tutors started the game of moving the letters around.

Kapil spelled out *Ma, La* and *Ma*, the letters for "balm". Then he thrust his eyes towards Mangaley and asked, "What might this be?"

Mangaley craned his neck and tussled with the letters on the board. It was torturous for him to recognize the letters. He counted one by one the three letters that had until just now been spelling "pen" and grappled with the new word with his gaze and with great difficulty tore apart each letter – *"Ma, La, Ma"*.

"What word does it spell?"

"I reckon it spells the word for balm, sir."

"Mangaley seems to get the drift," Katuwal said, not without a hint of jealousy.

"The boy has found his footing," Somey said in agreement.

"How has something that was a pen just a moment ago become a balm now, Mangaley?"

Mangaley was astonished. Truly – how did a pen wriggle away from its meaning and within moments become a balm? To the aged students the letters on the board – which, until a moment ago were but dumb, lifeless beasts devoid of meaning – now seemed speak and shift, gain vitality and meaning. Momentarily, a list was created of the novel and unfamiliar. By moving up, down and sideways the three letters *Ka, La* and *Ma*, and by exchanging one letter for another, words like *Kalama, Malama, Makala, Mala, Malamala, Lamak-lamak, Kal, Kalkal*; words for a pen, a balm, a brazier, dung, muslin, a loping gait, a machine, the onomatopoeic sound of running water. To the aged students it was as if a strange light had entered their eyes and, as if through sorcery, the light flickered there. There are scrawls on the board. Study them intently and the scrawls begin to move and speak. The scrawls say one thing now and in a few moments say something else. Incredible miracle!

"Do you see anything, Mangaley?"

"How can I say anything, sir?" Mangaley struggled in his attempt to string together his sensations of bewilderment and joy. And, with some effort, he said, "Sir, these eyes were blind until now. But I sense in them a dim light, like that coming from a sooty lantern."

"And you, Kaudey?"

"I'm stunned by your magic tricks, sir."

Thus ended the game of letters. It was now the stranger's turn. Sheshkant drew the conversation towards the corner and said, "Our new guest who arrived today would like to tell you a few things."

"Would be good if we could be acquainted first," Katuwal said with curiosity, looking at the reedy stranger and Kapil.

"He is a raconteur," Sheshkant offered.

"What sort of a name is that?"

"It is not a name, Mangaley. A raconteur spins tales."

"If we could know his name, home, trade and creed . . ." Somey, who had kept silent for some time, showed an interest in learning everything about the storyteller.

"I am a wayfarer. My trade is to collect and relate life's tales." The storyteller revealed his strange identity with a grave and pensive attitude.

"And your caste?"

"I am a Nepali."

"Nepali of the leather-working caste?"

"No – I have no caste. I am a Nepali from Nepal."

The students in the Adult Literacy Class found the storyteller's introduction very strange. This beanpole hides his true name, the villagers thought. When asked about his native home the tall man answered, "I don't have a home. Wherever I am given refuge, there is my home. Wherever I am loved, there are my kin."

This was indeed a strange man!

"Now our storyteller will relate a story to you. Tell us – what sort of a story do you want to hear?"

What sort of a story, really? Students in the shed hesitated. The stories familiar to them spoke of demons and wizards, witches and ghosts, spirits and warlock. And occasionally there were stories of love and lust, the matters of the heart. And the scriptural tales from *Satya Narayan*.

"What sorts of tales do you know," it was again Katuwal who spoke.

"Our friend knows all sorts of stories. He even knows the creation story."

"Alright, sir – let us hear the creation story at this opportunity."

The storyteller stared into the thick darkness outside the door and seemed momentarily lost in thoughts. Then, scanning the faces of the new students, he said in a soft voice, "Let us ponder this – how might have man been created?"

"May I say something here?" How could Katuwal ever resist seizing any opportunity?

With a nod and a gesture of his eyes the storyteller signaled, "Yes, do."

Katuwal puffed up like a know-it-all and began, "The scriptures say this, sir. Man was created by the four-faced Lord Brahma. From his mouth he created the Brahmins, from his arms he created the Chhet-riyas, from his thighs he created the Vaishyas, and from the soles of his feet he created the Shudras. They say he mixed cow dung and clay and ashes and what not and created man. Brahmins, created from his mouth, became the purest. Chhetriyas, created from the arms, became a little less pure. Vaishyas, created from the thighs, came even lower. And we the people of the lowest castes were created from the soles of the Lord Brahma. They say it is because we come from the soles of feet that step on shit that people of upper castes call us turds, sir."

A razor-like tongue, a clear voice, speech fluent as a stream rushing downhill, and a tireless zeal – Katuwal recounted the creation story su-perbly. It wasn't as if they hadn't already heard the creation story many times before. But when Katuwal so skillfully told the same story, the mature students in the Adult Literacy Class became spellbound. Yes, Katuwal is immensely clever. That is why he is in the good graces of the higher castes in the village and enjoys their favor.

"Sir, is your story of a similar sort?" Somey opened his mouth wide to yawn and show toothless gums and asked without enthusiasm.

"My story is a bit different, Somey."

"The creation story can't differ from the one I just told, sir," Katuwal insisted eagerly. "Can there be two versions of something written by the gods into the scriptures?"

The men in the class thought – Katuwal has caught tight the bean-pole's tongue in a vice of words. The beanpole is in trouble, for sure!

"We just now discussed the issue of promissory notes, didn't we?" the storyteller laid the four cornerstones for building the plot of his story. "And you faced some troubles regarding the issue of promissory notes, didn't you?"

A few men clamoured, each adding to the voice of another, "Yes, sir, great many troubles." Here, too, Katuwal's voice clambered above the other voices, galloping roughshod over everyone else.

"Do you remember who wrote the promissory note in the story about it?"

Answers jostled to come to the fore.

"Well-off and clever ones."

"Village chief and upper castes."

"Village conmen and scoundrels."

"Backstabbers."

"Ever in your life, have notes written by such people been true and without deceit?"

"What are you saying!" Katuwal drew out the phrase. "Never! Not once!"

"Tell me, then – if those very men write the creation story, for whose profit will they write it?" Now the storyteller attempted to strongly grasp at the heart of the matter. "For poor folks like you and I, or for cunning liars themselves?"

"They will write for their own profit, sir. If they would ever write with our benefit in mind . . ." said Mangal, who had been listening intently.

"Just like the promissory note earlier?"

"Yes, sir. Exactly like that."

"The creation story must be similar, don't you think?" the storyteller laid his snare; the people in the classroom became ensnared. But Katuwal wasn't going to be moved by a hair's breadth from his stubborn beliefs. On the one hand is the creation story written by the gods, and on the other hand a promissory note! On the one hand is Gopilal the moneylender, and on the other hand Kaudey the tailor! Tsk! What a thing to say! Katuwal nearly jumped up and screamed as he muttered these thoughts.

"Didn't the gods write the creation story?" Katuwal asked, vigorously sharpening each word.

"Aren't the money lenders and village chiefs gods too?" The storyteller firmly drew the strands of his logic. "Do we not fall prostrate before them as we do before the gods? We sing their praises like we sing hymns, don't we? Don't we hold them high in our esteem and worship them as gods? We think of them as the most pure and mark our foreheads with the dirt beneath their feet, don't we?"

"This much is true, sir."

"And that is all I understand," the storyteller, too, sharpened each of his words. "Today's gods write false promissory notes, just as the gods of the past wrote a false creation story. Isn't it so." The storyteller's words fell like heavy hammers upon the minds of the listeners. Now, isn't this beanpole a shrewd one! He calls the creation story a forged promissory note! And, the four-faced creator Brahma he calls a trickster and a forger! A quick anger stirred through the men in the classroom. How dare he talk as if he knows more than the four-faced Brahma!

"We don't quite understand you, sir," Katuwal said, puckering his mouth, as if ready to attack.

"And you are right, Katuwal," the storyteller said quietly and politely. "For thousands of years our heads have been stuffed with this story. The frauds of today stuff the same nonsense into our heads. Their fathers had stuffed the same falsehood into the heads of our fathers. And, similarly, their fathers' fathers had filled the heads of our fathers' fathers with the same lies. For generations upon generations, their kind has been battering and stomping on and dragging through the mud the minds of our kind and rendered us dumb, as senseless as a corpse. And we run blindly after them, accepting their every command, don't we? Tell me – haven't we been doing that?"

The mature students in the Adult Literacy Class at Simring, a village of the tailor-caste, found themselves mired in hesitation. If they agree, the creator Brahma joins ranks with frauds like Gopilal. If they disagree, the clever beanpole leaves them no space to talk back. The mature students searched each other's faces; helpless pairs of eyes met other helpless pairs of eyes. The two bearded men sat under the board, scratching their beards, observing the classroom.

"We still don't understand what you are saying, sir," Katuwal scratched his temple and showed his dissatisfaction in a bewildered voice.

"Sir – I have seen fifty winters, and worn through many, many a shirt. But here you speak of things nobody had ever spoken of before this. It feels as if you have struck an axe-blow upon all of my beliefs. I feel lost, like a crow in a fog."

"Mangaley – did you have anything to add?"

"I am also struggling to understand, sir"

"And Kaudey?"

"Let me not pretend to be clever and talk about this, sir."

"Is the issue settled?" The storyteller interrogated each face, moving slowly through the classroom.

Drat! This beanpole, who volunteered to recount the creation story, now asks if his story is finished even before he begins to tell it! What kind of a man does that? What is he trying to do? Is he trying to show everybody how dull they are, so that only he seems sharp? He has no name, no home or caste to speak of – but just listen to him! What is he getting at? The dalit men were stupefied. Neither a branch to hang from, nor the ground beneath to stand on. The beanpole seemed intent on hanging them like gourds suspended over a cliff!

And, even as he hesitated between speech and silence, these words escaped Mangaley's lips: "You did promise us the creation story."

"Yes, I did."

"If we could hear it, just the once . . ."

The storyteller glanced at his watch and turned towards the two bearded tutors, who signaled to him to continue. The storyteller thought about where he should begin. And, clearing his throat with a cough, he started: "I have listened to the creation story with which you are familiar. Should I now tell you the creation story that I know?"

"Tell us, sir," said a chorus of curious voices.

The storyteller continued, "As far as I know, the creation story you told me is a forgery, just like the promissory notes nowadays. It is a fraudulent tale told by defrauding forefathers of the frauds around today, created to serve their line."

"Sir," Katuwal protested with irritation, "How can we call fraudulent a story created by God himself?"

"If you don't mind, Katuwal, may I ask you a little question?"

"Yes, sir."

"From where did Brahma create you?"

"The soles of his feet."

"You are a turd, created from the soles of feet that tread upon shit, aren't you?"

"That is what the upper caste folks tell us, sir."

"And, according to your scriptures, the story of creation by the four-faced Brahma is unassailable, isn't it? Undeniable and unchangeable?"

"Yes, sir. That is what they have told us."

"And therefore you'll forever remain a turd? Never changeable, incapable of changing. Isn't that so?"

"The upper castes say just that, sir."

"And haven't you have followed them, agreeing with everything they have said?"

Here, Katuwal found himself in a bit of a fix. And so he bowed his head and scratched his forelock.

"You are the dirt beneath the feet, and you are a turd. You were born a turd, with the purpose of dying a turd. An immutable piece of turd, aren't you?" The storyteller paused. When Katuwal bowed his head further, he continued speaking, "Why do you keep up your worthless complaints about how the upper caste folks give you one kind or another kind of trouble, or how they keep you in serfdom, how they cheat you and how they walk all over you? A piece of turd belongs on the ground, does it not? If feet that walk on the ground don't step on pieces of turds littered over the ground, what else is the fate of turds? To be picked from the ground and smeared on the head as blessing? According to the scriptures you are a piece of turd in an alley. Why shouldn't those who claim to be from the upper castes step all over you?"

The confounded and slack-jawed men in the class stared at Katuwal, whose head, bending ever to the ground, found his knees for support.

"That is why, brother Katuwal," the storyteller added in a soft voice, "I say that the creation story you told me is a forgery no different from the forged promissory notes written by your moneylenders. That deceitful document puts us on par with turds, piles of dung. If we really want to rise from the status of dung to the ranks of men we must seek out the true story of creation. What are your thoughts on this, Katuwal?"

Katuwal hid his face between his knees and said in a dull voice, "Let it be, sir! I have nothing to say to this."

"If that is so, sir," Mangaley's curiosity tumbled forth, "let us hear the true account of creation!"

"It might astonish you to hear it," the storyteller walked through the class in a slow and deliberate pace, "but man is descended from the monkey."

Man came from the monkey! Oh, my lord! Man was created from the monkey? The listeners turned to each other in amazement. Suddenly, they felt a surge of discomfort; chill shivers ran down their backs. The hair stood on ends all over their bodies. On the surface of their minds they saw monkeys approach them, scratching their armpits, picking and eating lice.

"Of course!" said the storyteller, pacing about the room. "It is a tale from millions of years ago. A tribe of monkeys encountered insuperable distress in an impenetrable forest. They were surrounded on all sides by devilish beasts and other predators with sharp claws and fangs, poisonous tongues and enormous horns. The lives of the monkeys were in grave peril. They had two options before them: get killed, or adapt to a new idea and save their lives. After all, who doesn't love life?"

"Everybody does, sir! A lot!" Katuwal agreed excitedly.

"Therefore, to save their skins, the tribe of monkeys invented a new course of action."

"What new idea did the worthless monkey invent?"

"Brother Somey, the monkeys picked stones with their fore-paws and pelted them at the enemy. Found sticks to hurl. When it pelted stones and hurled sticks, it was forced to stand on its hind-legs and raise its head high. As they practiced picking and pelting stones and hurling sticks, their fingers became more flexible, more energetic. As they stood on their hind-legs frequently, the spine became straighter. As they confronted and fought off their enemies, and as they foraged for food, they were forced to learn to use their various limbs and appendages in new manners. Gradually their bodies morphed and took new forms. Eventually, over thousands of years, that tribe of monkeys stood upright on hind-legs and walked, head raised and the spine erect. It was no longer sufficient to employ the fore-paws as hands when confronting enemies. And so, as they encountered new needs, the minds of the monkeys also sharpened, became keener. Thus, the hands helped make the mind keener, and the mind that had become sharpened taught truer aim to the hand. Over time, the monkey became the wild-man ape of the jungles. An ape is half human and half monkey. Over thousands of years the same apes transformed and improved into full humans."

A stunned quiet hung over the men in the shed. It was so quiet that their breathing sounded like bellows being worked.

"Calamities!" Katuwal opened wide his mouth in amazement. "The boys tried very hard, didn't they?"

"Yes, Katuwal, they tried very hard."

"What happened after that, sir?"

"After that, Somey, in the process of changing, the monkey-man learned to fashion weapons out of bones, and learned to tame wild animals like dogs and horses and put them to work. Gradually, the ape-man who lived in caves learned to build and live in huts and till the land. The ape-man found fire, which must have come either from an exploding volcano or from dry trees rubbing together in a storm. Fire became a reliable and favoured friend to man. Food tastes superior when cooked over a fire. Good to taste, and easy to digest. And – whenever the enemy saw fire it ran away cowering. Of course, it gives warmth in the cold. Man learned to wear the barks of trees, the pelts of beasts. And gradually he shed the fur on his body. After thousands of years man discovered metals like copper and bronze. He had fire – now he could smelt ores and forge metals in different shapes to make weapons and tools. With the beasts he had tamed and the tools he had forged, man began a new method of tilling and sowing the land. When there wasn't much work to accomplish utterances and gestures had been enough to tell and listen. But, as the business of work increased utterances and gestures became insufficient. And so man took another epoch of thousands of years to learn the language of words. Thus, through the relation forged between the hand and the mind the monkey of the wilderness became the man of the household. That is why I said – Man is created from the monkey."

"How do you find this story?" The storyteller asked with a faint smile playing on his face. The mature students flitted their dull, dumb eyes to other pairs of dumbfounded eyes. They were still feeling discomfort and disgust. Goosebumps that had grown on their bodies stood unabated. Some even felt nauseous. Are we – Men – created from monkeys? We are descendents of the monkeys? Oh God!

"Sir – you bring brimstones here today!" Mangaley hesitatingly opened his mouth. "I am stumped by this tale you have raised today, and which nobody has ever heard before."

"Sir," Katuwal raised his bowed head and asked with the intention of locking horns, "You spoke as if you saw it with your own eyes. Who told you that this is exactly how it happened all those years ago?"

The storyteller realized that Katuwal had found the crux of the matter. He began thoughtfully unfurling the issue, "Brother Katuwal

– hundreds of learned people have spent hundreds of years to search and study these matters to come to this conclusion."

"And that too I don't grasp, sir. A man who lives the longest perhaps lives for eighty or a hundred years. As you told us – this story is hundreds of thousands of years old. How do men from our time see events from so long ago?"

"You ask the right question, Katuwal." The storyteller tried to politely explain what he knew. "Of course, people from so long ago couldn't have lived to our time. And, of course, people from our age can't see into the past. But, the thing is, Katuwal, in the new scriptures there are schemes for determining matters of this nature."

"What is that scheme?" Kaudey, who has been sitting still as an owl in a corner, asked.

"When animals walking the world die their bones and skeletons remain on earth. Sometimes there are earthquakes, and sometimes there are landslides. Sometimes glowing flames of lava erupt from inside the earth and are called volcanoes. When that happens, there are innumerable disturbances on earth. Skeletons and bones on the surface get buried. Some of them become like rocks, remain exactly the same and at exactly the same place. Learned people search for them, dig them out, and minutely examine them. Then they make guesses – they talk among each other and ask if something really happened one way or another, and then they determine what must have really happened. Katuwal, this is not the sort of silly talk that goes with "Brahma did this, Brahma did that." This requires searching for evidence, examining the evidence, showing it to others, convincing them of the truth and then finally settling the matter. This, Katuwal, is the irrefutable."

"All of this seems like a dream to me, sir," Somey, who had remained quiet so long, showed his perplexity. "If this tale were true, why don't the monkeys of today turn into men? I am stuck on that point, sir."

"Like I said, Somey – the kind of monkey that turned into man was different from the kind of monkey we see today. This is a long time ago. That one tribe of monkey found itself in grave peril. It had to either confront the perils and overcome them or die and disappear. It acted out of a love for life. I told you what it did, Somey. This is the second thing. The third thing is that the monkeys of today are not in the peril of dying and being destroyed. And so these worthless idiots haven't had to utilize their hands or employ their minds. They raid people's crops in gangs, eat what they can and raze what they won't eat – they have enough to get by. Why would they change then, these miscreants?"

"This is something I can agree with," Katuwal scratched his ears in agreement.

"When I listen and ponder it," Somey started with hesitation, "I feel as if this will drive us to madness. What I have listened to and believed in all of my life is one thing. But I am now hearing this in my dying hours."

"Age is no barrier to hearing and learning about new things, Somey."

"This is beyond my abilities," Somey sighed and let his limbs go slack. "Let the younger boys put their strength to it. It is beyond me. If I had only heard these stories when I still had time . . ."

"I agree with Younger Uncle," Katuwal, who felt the millstone of uncertainty burden his head, buckled under and fell to his knees.

"You are a coward!" The arrogant Somey growled at Katuwal, who thought Somey was a pilferer. "As long as you have days, you have to put your strength to these matters."

"I have already said I can't do it, Younger Uncle."

The bearded Kapil looked at his watch. It was already eleven o'clock. After signaling something to the storyteller he turned to the men in the classroom, "Brothers! Should we end our talks for today?"

When everybody stood to get on their way, Katuwal raised his voice to ask, "Sir, the other creation story had come from the four-faced god Brahma. What is the name of the Brahma behind this creation story?"

"The name of the man who found the roots of the true creation story of humankind is Charles Darwin. He was a learned man from England, which is a nation of white people."

"Everybody! Listen carefully!" Katuwal ordered his peers in the manner of the village crier that he was. Then he slapped his own head and asked again, "What was the name again, sir?"

"Charles Darwin."

"Yes. Charles Darlin." Katuwal repeated the name a few times, trying to commit it to memory, "Charles Darlin, Charles Darlin, Charles Darlin, Charles . . ."

And so ended the first day of classes in the shed in Simring. When the mature students of Simring walked home they felt as if they carried on their shoulders the foul forms of monkeys. In their disturbed ears echoed the words of the storyteller: We are created from monkeys. When they dwelled upon the significance of those words it disgusted them, as if a large lemur perched on their shoulders, with its belly splayed over their heads, and with one hand scratching under its armpits while the other shaped itself into a spoon of dead, dry digits trying to dig out the eyes. And the echo of the beanpole's voice ringing – It's from the monkey that man is descended!

Damn it! Damn it all!

THE TUTOR OF HISTORY

Manjushree Thapa

Manjushree Thapa is a Nepali author, translator and editor. She grew up in Nepal, Canada and the United States and began writing after completing a BFA at the Rhode Island School of Design. She later graduated with a Masters in English from the University of Washington. Manjushree's essays and editorials have appeared in the *New York Times*, *London Review of Books*, *Newsweek* and other publications in the US, UK, Canada, India and Nepal. She has written several non-fiction titles including *Forget Kathmandu*, which was a finalist in the Lettre Ulysses award in 2006, *The Lives We Have Lost* and *A Boy from Siklis*. Her novels include *The Tutor of History*, *Seasons of Flight* and *All of Us in Our Own Lives*. She lives in Toronto.

Kathmandu. One day after another in a lifetime of rambling. One day after another, as though they had some order. Rishi followed a set routine, but it was a routine that lacked purpose. Every day he walked the city's tortuous alleys to the house of a student. There he reviewed the student's homework, made corrections and assigned the boy textbook pages to study more carefully. The student's mother brought him tea. Sometimes she also brought two slices of bread. Most days she didn't. Biding his hunger, Rishi watched the boy struggle to understand simple facts. In the background he could hear family members in the inner rooms, which he had never been let into. A scrape. Creaks. Footsteps sliding on the linoleum floor. The easy rhythmic sounds of bodies at home.

From there Rishi headed to the house of another student, who was richer, and to another. At both houses he was fed snacks. He stopped at evening time to read papers at a pavement stall, and then at the end of the day he made his way through the halogen-lit city to Hotel Tanahun. That was his day. That was his drift.

Hotel Tanahun was a street-side diner owned by a couple who had migrated from Rishi's home district. Many of their clients were also from the district, but Rishi didn't know them. He sat apart in a corner, watching everyone through the steam that rose from his tea: men holding out plates for second helpings of sour rice and vegetables oversalted to hide their staleness. He eavesdropped on the exchanges that took place around him.

"I Work as a peon at a factory." "I'm a driver at a hotel." Entire lives compressed into short sentences. "I arrange visas for boys to go to Korea." "I have a farm in the district." Some sentences were longer: "I didn't weigh enough to qualify for the army, but I'll try again next year." All these people who thought they knew who they were.

He was, himself, unwilling to respond to queries about what he was doing in the city. He no longer felt he needed to know. When anyone asked he said he was a tutor of history. "A teacher?" No, a private tutor. "Eh." People assumed he was in between jobs on the way to a more stable position. The truth made them uneasy: he was cut off from his family and he had no friends in the city. He had no connections and couldn't find a job. Since he left the UML party's student wing, he had no political patrons to look out for him. He'd been working five years as a tutor, and this life wasn't leading him anywhere.

Sometimes Rishi would lie. "I teach at a local school," he would say. When people asked why he was still unmarried, he would say, "I'm already engaged." And he had been, once. But now he couldn't imagine starting a family with the pittance he earned. When he was pushed for more detail, he extended the lie. "My family adopted a Bahun name, but we're actually from the lower castes," he would say, deriving a sharp pleasure when people shrank from him. Casually, he steered himself into the bare jutting walls and cold corners of his pariah's place. "Actually, my father died in a landslide," he would say. "My mother took up with another man whose name is Parajuli." Why not? In the city he could shrug off identities or wear them like a shawl to cloak himself. This was the mobility he'd sought when he had decided, years ago, to leave home.

Heading back at night to his boarding house on New Road, Rishi was all eyes. A man with ropes strapped to his back: a porter waiting for work. A child washing dishes in a restaurant. Three men talking in Gurung tongue. He stopped and watched an auto-rickshaw driver arguing with a customer. He watched a man come out of a house reading an air-mail letter. He mimicked the hand gestures of a teenage girl and adopted the rolling gait of a foreigner. This was what it meant to live unnoticed in the gaps of Nepal's history: to grow unrecognizable, unknowable to others and to himself.

Yet every now and then Rishi felt overwhelmed by the hardness of his life, its objection and lack of charity. On such days he felt tugged by untenable desires. Unlike his college friends he didn't want to go to Osaka to wash dishes, or to Kuwait to tend gardens. He didn't want to earn vast sums of money. What he wanted was a modest life which would let him live with his mind in flight. At times he thought he might return to Khaireni Tar and work as a teacher there. But for what? Home. The accusation of his father and reproach of his mother. The tenacious orthodoxy of village society –. He couldn't return. He could neither move backward nor could he spring forward. All he could do was lose himself.

To commit himself to his straying, Rishi had hewn a map onto the city of Kathmandu, with one constant path leading from his boarding house to Hotel Tanahun. The shifting community of the diner's customers – villagers coming to Kathmandu on errands – was his only link to home. Sometimes he even recognized people there – family acquaintances, friends from childhood, shopkeepers he had bought grains from, long ago, in Khaireni Tar bazaar. He kept his distance from them. One evening he spied his old schoolmaster from Khaireni Tar, and he turned away to avoid him. The next night the schoolmaster was in the diner again, surrounded by other men. The following evening, Rishi stayed away from the diner. When he came back the day after, he found the schoolmaster there, sitting with someone. It was as though the man had never left.

Rishi took his place in the corner of the diner, facing his old high school teacher. The schoolmaster was probably in his sixties now, and he looked hard, whittled with age. His silver hair was unkempt and his eyes were narrowed onto the man he was talking to. He exuded the same aura of heedlessness that had impressed Rishi as a boy, with his steeled look of someone who'd survived disaster intact. It was he who had recruited Rishi into the UML party. The schoolmaster glanced up, scanned the room, seemed not to recognize Rishi, and looked back at the man he was with.

Rishi lowered his head and listened to the clatter of steel plates and spoons, and the distant moaning of radio songs. A mosquito whined near a light bulb. The man with the schoolmaster was talking about the elections. The UML must win a majority this time. The woman who ran the diner put a plate of rice and daal in front of Rishi. Some men sitting by the door guffawed. The schoolmaster mentioned Tanahun district's third electorate. Rishi leaned in to hear what he was saying. "The People's Party will make it a three-way race."

"They'll cut votes from the Congress."

"We need sixteen thousand."

"If they were to cut three, four thousand . . ."

The schoolmaster's words rustled beneath the din of the city, and Rishi remembered late meetings in a dark room in Khaireni Tar, lectures on Bolshevism in this voice at once forceful and hushed. He remembered a distant blue moon, crickets rapping at night and the schoolmaster's steps pattering behind him.

The schoolmaster looked up several times during that evening, but his eyes always swept past Rishi, who puzzled at his own taut spine, at his disappointment in not being recognized. When he finished eating, he left feeling empty. It was raining outside. The city flickered behind a sheen of reflected halogen. It didn't look real. Rishi submitted to the nostalgia welling up inside him. He was a boy caressed by the warm rains of the hills. He was running barefoot with pebbles grinding into his toes. Swallows flitted above. Marigolds grew thick along the path. He came to a hillside. He was stumbling on rock steps, his pants were torn. Steep slopes. He was sliding home.

The next evening, Rishi walked up to the schoolmaster and introduced himself. Almost as soon as the schoolmaster's eyes steadied in recognition, another man joined them. Before turning away, the school-master said to Rishi, 'I thought it was you.' He slid aside to make place for him on the bench, then turned to the other man. They seemed to be resuming a conversation they were holding earlier, about the Minister of Agriculture.

Rishi settled into his seat. The bench was warm with the schoolmas-ter's heat. Even though the conversation had nothing to do with him, he felt included in it by the way the schoolmaster sat, their shoulders touching. There was allowance in that contact. The older man's voice vibrated against Rishi's arm. The Minister of Agriculture was to be watched, the schoolmaster was saying. Who came from and went to his house: it could be useful to know.

The other man glanced uncomfortably at Rishi.

"We can talk freely," the schoolmaster assured him. "This comrade is my former student. He was with us during the protests. He was – weren't you? – one of those jailed during the democracy movement."

"I was."

Rishi settled in and listened to the two of them plotting for scandal. The woman who ran the diner brought three plates of food and they ate in silence. Afterwards, when the other man left, the schoolmaster turned to Rishi, casually. He didn't inquire about Rishi's present life but asked instead after his parents, as though he didn't know that Rishi hadn't been back to his village or even to Khaireni Tar in all these years. Rishi responded to his queries as best he could: "They're probably in good health."

TRAP

Maya Thakuri

Maya Thakuri was born in 1938 in Assam, India. She is the author of four short story collections: *Najureko Jodhi*, *Gamalako Phool*, *Sanghu Tarepachhi*, and *Maya Thakurika Kathaharu*. She teaches in Pokhara, in west Nepal.

That day, too, Bam Bahadur left home early in the morning. With Bhagate by his side, he was looking for a goat to purchase.

The price of goats was increasing day by day, but Bam Bahadur didn't care; no matter what price he had to pay, it was always Vijay Bahadur who footed the bill. Bam Bahadur was content in knowing that, in the eyes of his neighbors, his wealth appeared to increase with the price of goats.

This Vijay Bahadur was an astonishing man. He'd come to the village four or five times already this year, and each time he'd slaughtered a goat and feasted all of Bam Bahadur's companions on large quantities of meat and liquor. The drinking and gambling went on all night during these feasts, held at Bam Bahadur's house. Naturally, the villagers praised Vijay Bahadur, saying, "No matter how hard you look, you can't find a man as generous as Bam Bahadur's nephew. Vijay Bahadur has so much money! He spends as he pleases, but never runs out."

Before meeting Vijay Bahadur, Bam Bahadur had had an utterly shabby life. His house had needed a new roof, but he could hardly even afford the morning and evening meals for his wife and three children. To pay off his gambling debts, he had sold his wife's nose ring and her earrings. He'd fallen so low that he'd even sold off the family's few pots and pans to support his vices.

Bam Bahadur had worked nearly nineteen years for the Indian army. By the time he'd retired and returned to his village, he appeared to have left all his youthfulness and vigor in that foreign land. He blindly threw

himself into drinking and gambling. It was only thanks to the industri-
ousness of his wife, Him Maya, that they made ends meet.

Once a year, Bam Bahadur traveled to the town of Gorakhpur,
India, to collect his pension. But by the time he had returned, his pockets would already be empty. With tears streaming from her eyes, Him
Maya would plead with her husband, "Drinking and gambling have
never helped anyone improve his lot. Stop these vile habits." Bam Bahadur paid no attention. Before long, he had even managed to gamble
away the fields that he'd taken over from his brother.

Everyone knew about Bam Bahadur's older brother, Hum Bahadur.
When he was a young man, Hum Bahadur had run off with the wife of
another villager, Santa Bir. Years passed, but Hum Bahadur never came
back; nor did anyone hear again of Santa Bir's wife, who had taken
with her all her jewelry and gold coins. Apparently, Santa Bir wandered
for quite some time with a *khukuri* knife tucked into his waistband,
saying, "If I find them, I won't let them get away; I'll slit their throats."
But even though he hungered mightily for revenge, Santa Bir entered
death's mouth before he could satisfy his hunger.

A year ago, Bam Bahadur went to Gorakhpur to collect his pension.
Two or three other villagers who were also pensioners went with him.
Those villagers returned before the winter month of Magh was over,
but there was no sign of Bam Bahadur. When Him Maya asked the
other villagers about her husband, they said, "We didn't see him after
he got his pension. We don't know where he went."

A few days later, Him Maya was working in the fields. All manner of
worries were playing with her heart when her eleven-year-old daughter, Kamali, came running to her, shouting, "Aamai, Aamai, Ba's come
home! There's someone with Ba. There's also a porter."

"Eh, is that so?" Him Maya followed her daughter home.

As soon as he saw his wife, Bam Bahadur said, "Here, look. I've
returned with our nephew. Poor thing – he was living abroad like an orphan, thinking he had no living relatives." Bam Bahadur turned to the
young man. Pointing to Him Maya, he said, "This is your aunt." Then,
pointing at the three wide-eyed children, he said, "And these are your
cousin-brother and your cousin-sisters." Gesturing once again toward

the young man, he said, "This is Vijay Bahadur, the son of my older brother, Hum Bahadur."

Vijay Bahadur bowed to Him Maya.

Then Bam Bahadur opened his bags and placed in Him Maya's hands all the clothes he'd brought for her and the children. "Our nephew bought all of this," he said. "He wouldn't listen when I told him it wasn't needed."

When the other villagers heard that the son of Hum Bahadur had come, they crowded into Bam Bahadur's front yard. Offering everyone cigarettes, Bam Bahadur said, "What can one do? It seems my brother earned a lot of money after leaving this village. At the end of his life, he talked of returning home, but what can people do when faced with death? My brother and his wife passed away within a year of each other. Afterwards, Hum Bahadur's only son lived a lonely existence, despite his wealth. My brother had told him the names of his father and grandfathers and the name of his village, but my nephew gave up hope, thinking that the village and his relatives were too far away. After all, he'd never been to this village in the hills. Thankfully, we were fated to meet. Otherwise . . . !"

Taking a drag from his cigarette, Chandra Bir asked, "So, how did uncle and nephew come together? Where did you meet the boy?"

"After getting my pension," Bam Bahadur said, "I was wandering through the bazaar to buy the children some clothes. Because it was so hot, I went into a hotel and bought a glass of curd to drink. This young man was also there, sipping curd. For some reason, as soon as our eyes met, I immediately recalled my brother Hum Bahadur. I couldn't stop myself; I went right up to the young man and asked him his father's name and surname. He said, 'My father's name was Hum Bahadur. I'm the grandson of so-and-so, and this is the name of my father's home in the hills.' And then I responded, with great pride, 'I am your father's younger brother, Bam Bahadur!'"

Vijay Bahadur was an attractive youth of about twenty-five or twenty-six, quite plump and healthy. Within a few days of arriving in the village, he had established warm relations with the villagers, who said among themselves, "Bam Bahadur's nephew seems quite nice. He doesn't act big no matter how many *rupees* he's got. Now that's what people should be like!"

One day, Bam Bahadur extended an invitation to his neighbors Chandra Bir, Bhagate, Lal Bahadur, and Ritte, saying, "Tomorrow my nephew's offering a goat in the shrine. All of you must attend the feast."

The next day, Chandra Bir chewed heartily on goat's meat, swallowed, and asked, "So, I hear that your nephew hasn't married yet. Is he really single?"

Bam Bahadur refilled Chandra Bir's glass. "What can one do? Once the father and mother had passed away, who was there to look for a girl for the son? Now that he's with us, I'm thinking of looking around here for a girl for him to marry – the kind of girl who'd serve her husband's home well. All of you must also give the matter some thought."

Chandra Bir emptied his glass. "So, would your nephew agree to marry a girl born and bred in a village like this?"

Bam Bahadur placed a stitched-leaf plate filled with fried meat in front of Chandra Bir and replied, "Well, now, what can I say? The day before yesterday my nephew went to the spring to bathe. There he saw your daughter Jamuni. Since then, he's been after me, saying, 'Uncle, I'm going to marry that girl.' Now you've seen the boy for yourself. Since he's my nephew, my home is his home. If it's the case that one day or another you'll send your daughter away in marriage, you might as well marry her to my nephew."

Chandra Bir reached for the fried meat. "You've spoken well, but I just married off my eldest daughter last year. Right now I don't even have a broken coin for another daughter's wedding. So how could I dare –"

Bam Bahadur laughed. "No, you needn't worry about that. We're neighbors after all. I'll get my nephew to pay the bride's expenses as well as his own. All you have to do is say yes."

Jamuni and Vijay Bahadur were married a week later.

Shortly afterward, Vijay Bahadur left the village with Jamuni by his side. Jamuni's friends said, "Jamuni's the luckiest girl. She got herself a good, rich husband." Chandra Bir and his wife were giddy with joy at having gotten a son-in-law like Vijay Bahadur.

Not even two months had passed when news of their daughter's untimely death came, shaking the hearts of Chandra Bir and his wife. The villagers said, "What a pity! They say Jamuni had a high fever for over a week. Poor thing! How ruthlessly death snatches away even those who enjoy the luxury of dressing well and dining lavishly."

It wasn't long before Vijay Bahadur came back to the village. In a melancholy voice he said to Chandra Bir, "What can be done, Father-in-law? My fortunes seem to be cursed. I spent money like water, but in the end couldn't save your daughter."

Wiping tears from his own eyes, Chandra Bir consoled Vijay Bahadur. "Nothing can be done now, Son-in-law. She was fated to have only so many days in her life. No matter how much we cry and shout, she's not coming back."

One evening, Bam Bahadur placed liquor and chicken meat in front of Bhagate and Lal Bahadur. "My heart is torn apart when I see my nephew's face. He seems to have forgotten how to sleep, how to eat. He'll go mad if he keeps this up. I've told him so many times that living and dying are in the hands of the gods, that he mustn't neglect his health by grieving day and night. If only he'd listen to my words! You must advise me what to do."

Bhagate gulped his drink. "In my opinion, it would be right to get the boy married again, because the first wife's memory will fade away only after another marriage. Isn't that so, brother Lal Bahadur?"

Bam Bahadur added meat to Lal Bahadur's plate. "I too have had this thought. But who'd offer a girl so soon? The villagers might talk, saying it hasn't been two months since his wife's death and yet he's already marrying a second time."

Lal Bahadur put on a grave expression. "Eh, given a chance to talk, people will say anything. Should one heed such talk? One should heed one's own mind. Bhagate spoke well you should arrange a second marriage for your nephew."

Bam Bahadur refilled Lal Bahadur's glass. "Then why go elsewhere to find a girl? You must marry your older daughter, Laxmi, to my nephew." He added, "My nephew probably wouldn't agree to a showy wedding since his wife just died, but it will still be necessary to slaughter a goat for a feast."

Lal Bahadur said, "Nothing of the sort should be done at this time. If he's going to marry my daughter, it should be done with utmost discretion."

After Vijay Bahadur quietly married Laxmi and took her away with him, Bam Bahadur said to Chandra Bir and the other villagers, "My nephew refused to agree to a second marriage, but I insisted. I said, 'If you don't marry again, you will have to sever your relations with me.' So, he finally agreed."

About three months after marrying Laxmi, Vijay Bahadur returned to the village and, bearing gifts, went to see his wife's parents. Lal Bahadur said to him, "You might have also brought our daughter with you, Son-in-law."

"I'd wanted to bring Laxmi along, but the doctor said it wouldn't be good for her to walk uphill and down while her body's heavy with child," Vijay Bahadur replied. "I'll bring her when her body's light again."

Laxmi's mother asked, "When will you go back to your wife, Son-in-law?"

"I just came to fulfill a promise I'd made to the deity in gratitude for answering my prayers," Vijay Bahadur said. "I'll offer a goat at the shrine tomorrow, we'll all feast, and I'll leave the day after." Looking at Laxmi's younger sister, Saraswati, he added, "Oh, yes. Your daughter asked me to inquire whether her younger sister would agree to come along. If you send Saraswati with me, she can return with her sister the next time Laxmi visits."

Saraswati and her aunt's daughter, Maina, both departed with Vijay Bahadur.

It was soon after this that Vijay Bahadur unexpectedly arrived late one evening at Bam Bahadur's house. Surprised, Bam Bahadur said, "Oho, not even fifteen days have passed and you've come back?"

Vijay Bahadur took several hundred *rupees* from his pocket and placed them in Bam Bahadur's hands. "I had to come, Uncle. Do go and find a good goat for me early tomorrow morning."

Bam Bahadur laughed. "It looks like you're in quite a hurry to leave."

It was the next morning that Bam Bahadur and Bhagate went to the neighboring village to look for a goat. After they'd spent the whole day looking for just the right one and were leading it back, Bhagate said, "You must ask your nephew if it's possible to find any kind of small job out there where he lives. I'm suffering greatly staying here. With three children and a wife to support, how can I live off my meager fields?"

Bam Bahadur muttered something to himself, then replied, "I was just thinking the same thing: you should go back with my nephew and take your entire family. Your wife can open a shop and earn a little money. Even if it's just a little, it will be better than what you would earn here. Your children will be able to go to school. You'll also find work. You could ask one of your neighbors to look after your house and fields while you're gone, then come back home after earning as much as you need." He paused a moment and then added, "If you like, I'll talk to my nephew today. If everything is agreeable, you could go with him right away, along with your wife and children."

Bhagate was thrilled. "If you can arrange that, I'll sing your praises till the day I die!"

To himself, Bam Bahadur thought, What fools I've made of these villagers! I've introduced as my nephew a man I don't even know. Who knows who he might be? And that greedy con artist acts as if he really were my nephew. Is Vijay Bahadur even his name? He's managed to gobble up the tastiest fruits of this village and now he's after the leftovers. Sometimes I worry that someone might find out – but he acts as cool as ever. He does everything slowly and methodically, keeping his wits about him. The greedy bastard says, "You mustn't eat quickly when the food is hot or you'll die of indigestion; you must proceed calmly and use your brain." If he hadn't used that cunning brain of his, where would he be getting all his money? My fortunes have turned around since he's entered my life. Money is the most important thing in this world, it seems. What can't be done provided you have enough money? Yes, and now if I can send Bhagate and his wife and two daughters away with him . . .

As he walked along the trail, Bam Bahadur recalled the first day he'd met Vijay Bahadur, about a year ago in Gorakhpur. After picking up his pension and heading home, Bam Bahadur had spent three days in a hotel in the border town of Butwal. By the fourth day, he had spent all his money. With empty pockets, he'd slumped against the big bridge of Butwal when a young man in his twenties approached and started talking to him.

Bam Bahadur was impressed by the youth's speech and manners. After introducing himself as Vijay Bahadur, he invited Bam Bahadur to a tavern and bought him meat and liquor. After chatting for a long time, Vijay Bahadur proposed his scheme to Bam Bahadur. "If you agree to what I say, we can rake in the money. Understand?"

Five days later, Bam Bahadur returned to his village with his "long-lost nephew."

Bhagate, walking silently all this while with the goat in tow, suddenly turned to Bam Bahadur. "Your nephew will stay two or three days longer, won't he?"

Startled from his thoughts, Bam Bahadur asked, "Hunh? What did you say?"

"Won't your nephew stay here a few days more?"

"If all of you are going with him, he'll have to stay longer."

When Bam Bahadur and Bhagate reached Bam Bahadur's house, dusk had fallen. As soon as he saw his father, Bam Bahadur's seven-year-old son cried gleefully, "Ba's come! Ba's come, and he's brought a goat!"

Bam Bahadur's younger daughter rushed to him. Eyeing the goat greedily, she said, "Ba, I'll eat a lot of seared meat tomorrow – all right, Ba?"

Bam Bahadur turned to Bhagate and aid, "Take this goat and lock it up in the shed." Then, spreading a straw mat on the front porch, he told his daughter, "Go and ask for three small jugs from your mother. Ask her, too, if there are any relishes." Bam Bahadur sat down and took four bottles of liquor from his bag. When Bhagate returned from locking up the goat, Bam Bahadur invited him to sit down, too.

Him Maya brought a plate covered with turnip relish and placed it in front of her husband. Bam Bahadur said to her, "Well, now, what's my nephew doing? Send him out here."

"But they left this morning, after their meal," Him Maya said.

At first Bam Bahadur looked confused. "What's this you're babbling about?"

Him Maya continued, "He took Kamali with him, saying that you and he had talked it over. He said he'd bring our daughter back in ten to fifteen days, when he returns with his wife –"

She had barely finished speaking when Bam Bahadur jumped to his feet and began kicking her. "Eh, whore!" he bellowed. "What reason did you have to send my daughter with that stranger?!"

Hurt and confused, Him Maya said, "What do you mean by 'stranger'? He's your own nephew. Why vent such anger on me?"

"That's not my nephew! That's a cheat who lives off selling girls! Oh, God! He's taking my daughter to sell her right now! Bring me my knife! I'll go after him and slit his throat!"

Bam Bahadur ran to his bed, pulled his *khukuri* knife from its sheath, and dashed into the darkness, brandishing the naked blade.

It's been about seven years since Bam Bahadur went insane. These days he mostly sits, staring straight ahead. Sometimes when a stranger enters the village, he rushes over and grabs the person by the collar, shouting, "Do you have a goat, a nice fat goat?! I've got to set a trap!"

THE SCREAM

Dhruba Sapkota

Dhruba Sapkota is a Nepali author based in Kathmandu. Recipient of the Udanyananda prize, he has published four collections of short stories and a novel entitled *Broken into Pieces*.

They're seated around the fire pit – from the grandmother *badeni* down to the granddaughter *badeni* – three generations of flowers threaded onto one necklace. Flowers for the picking, for the plucking. To be slung around anyone's neck. The grandmother flower was plucked ages ago, and today the granddaughter will be plucked. It's natural. A flower is a flower. But the grandmother no longer has any fragrance; old flowers wither away. Someone plucks the new ones. Before they have a chance to come into full bloom, someone is in a hurry to pluck them, to twist them from the vine. Such a hurry, such a hurry!

The women live with the waiting and the hardships. In one day there may be as many as twenty hardships. No one can say for sure. And as for the wait! They have been waiting for generations. Their lives are spent waiting.

There is a fire in the fire pit. The wet wood is hissing and steaming. Tears are streaming from their eyes. The fourteen-year-old granddaughter says, "Grandmother, my eyes are stinging. I'm going to bed."

She cannot leave the fire pit without her grandmother's permission. She knows her grandmother controls the household. The old woman is sixty years old. The girl's mother and aunts do what her grandmother says, so how can she not?

The old *badeni* understands her granddaughter's problem. She had been that age, too. She would like to give her permission to go to bed, but all at once she changes her mind and says, "Go ahead, if you want to die of hunger tomorrow."

This explains a lot. We can guess the meaning of this. To fight hunger, they need rice, vegetables, salt, and oil. But it's not enough just to fill their stomachs; they can't walk around naked. They need *saris*. They need blouses and flashy jewelry to wear. Red lipstick is essential; otherwise, how will people recognize them? They need wood for the fire pit. At night mere embraces are not sufficient. They need quilts as well.

The granddaughter says nothing. She takes out a leaf-rolled cigarette, lights it in the fire, and takes a long pull on it. She looks at her grandmother's wrinkled cheeks. She certainly has not told her to stay without a reason. Someone must be coming. Someone will come. Her hairs stand on end just imagining it. She takes a strong pull on the cigarette. It glows brightly.

"Let her go if she wants to. We're here; after all," suggests the girl's mother. She cannot give orders to her own mother. Not her mother, who brought her up, taught her how to behave, and in whose footsteps she is following. But she loves her daughter no less than her mother. This is the age for her daughter to eat treats and play, not be played with. And if she were to talk the language of the city bazaars, she would say that at this age her daughter ought to be learning, clutching books under her arm on the way to school. It isn't the age to be clutching a man in her arms. She has learned of the great gulf between books and men.

"I wouldn't bother you if I could still work – let alone your daughter." It is impossible to disagree with the old woman. She is one hundred percent right. A sixty-year-old *badeni*, she has a nagging cough. It's been many years since she wore nice clothes, and more since she slept in a comfortable bed. This is our old *badeni*. She believes in her work. She has accepted the body as a means of making a living. She is a strict follower of tradition. She believes in the divine, our old *badeni*.

One day a young man appeared; they were sitting around the fire pit just as they are now. He asked her, "How many men have you had in your life, Mother? Could you say?"

At such a question, the rest of them burst out laughing. They hadn't had the courage to ask the old woman themselves. A shameless question like that should be asked in private. But the young man had never imagined that *badenis* might have their own private moments. It had never occurred to him that they might have their joys and sorrows. The old *badeni* said, "I'll burn you with a brand, bastard!"

That was a stab at their laughter and a sharp blow to the youth. They hadn't expected such a bold answer from the old woman. Her reply energized the women. The oldest daughter said, "If you want to talk dirty, you can go away and stay away."

It was the youth's turn to be surprised. The women didn't want to name their profession. To name it was to call it "dirty." The women know that their work is dirty work. But tradition lies so comfortably at their feet. It pushes them into this mudhole. They even try to make it more convenient. Their house is right by the side of the road. Very few passersby will look openly at it. They glance furtively this way and that. If no one is about, they slip inside – from the village's high-caste *brahmin* sons down to whomever the women can get, even the sons of the low-caste *shudras*. What do they care; anybody can come in. Sometimes the women make alluring gestures. It amuses them to make lewd gestures at boys just coming into their youth.

The old *badeni*'s wealth consists of the four of them. She is a glimpse into their future. The old woman has prepared them to drink all the bitter poisons she herself has had to drink.

Her life has been spent within the limits of this house and yard for many, many years now. The days when she danced and sang in the big cities for money are just a memory. Now, whatever has to be done, these daughters and this granddaughter are the ones who will do it. The old woman's hopes rest with them. She is nothing but their guardian. She wishes them well. It was in their best interests that she didn't send her granddaughter to bed a moment ago. Suddenly, the old *badeni* is seized by a coughing fit; she coughs until she is faint. Finally, she stops. She is panting. She says quietly, "It's gotten quite late, hasn't it?"

Although she is old, her ears are sharper now than ever. She can hear very soft noises. She can even hear the mice. Now she hears a footfall near the house. She hears the murmur of voices in the dark.

"I didn't tell you to wait for nothing!" She gets excited. She thinks of hot rice. She smacks her lips and thinks of the tomato chutney they will eat. She imagines the family happily eating and talking together. She strokes her granddaughter's head and says, "If they don't choose you, you can go straight to bed. My sweet girl. My obedient little girl – just like a little bird."

The granddaughter wriggles happily under her grandmother's affectionate touch. The touch of the old woman's hand has love in it. Many hands have caressed her head and body, but she has felt love only from her grandmother's hands. The hands of others are not like hands at all, but rather like pincers. She knows the old woman's hands won't twist her, pin her down. They have no element of that in them. She wishes that her grandmother's hands would caress her forever, that she would always be showered with affection.

"Mother! Can we warm ourselves by the fire here?" call two youths from the doorway.

"Of course, of course. Come inside." A space is made for them inside the circle. The youths have come to be threaded onto the necklace.

They look at the thirty-year-old daughter. They look at the twenty-five-year-old daughter. They look at the twenty-six-year-old daughter. They look at the fourteen-year-old granddaughter. At last they look at the old woman who runs this trade in human beings.

"Old mother! Are all these your descendants? Are they keeping up the family tradition?"

"Yes, Babu! They honor family tradition."

Now the women start a competition, looking at the youths. Whenever a youth glances at one of them, the woman smiles. But none of them can guess whom the youths will prefer. The fourteen-year-old granddaughter has other thoughts, though. She is hoping they will not choose her and that she can go to bed.

"Give me a cigarette," says the boldest *badeni*, making the first move.

A youth gives her a cigarette. A Surya cigarette, an expensive one. As he gives her the cigarette, the other three women hold out their hands. They know that at this moment they can get whatever they ask for. Later no one will care. After handing out cigarettes to the four of them, the youth lights one himself. Having gotten her cigarette, the boldest *badeni* says, "What a cruel man. Won't you leave one for our mother, who's lying down?"

"I see Mother's descendants are all very well spoken." Now the youth is starting to flatter them. He'd found them cheap when they asked for the cigarettes.

"Yes, Babu, they are good." The old woman is quite accustomed to hearing such talk. She tries to say as little as possible. She hopes they will talk little, finish their business, and go.

"And where are their fathers?" asks the youth, seeing no men in the house at such an hour of the night.

"They've gone drinking in the village," the old woman answers curtly.

"All of them went drinking?" asks the youth, acting surprised. "We would've liked to drink, too," he suggests.

"It's late, Babu; otherwise we could get some," the old woman says, trying to avoid a problem.

At last the youth stares at the fourteen-year-old granddaughter. The one who, at her age, should be playing and going to school. She is sitting by the fire pit, smoking a cigarette. She wears red lipstick, as if she were trying to force her way into maturity.

The youth pinches her cheek – in front of everyone. In front of her mother and grandmother. The youth pinches her tender cheek so hard with his strong hand that he leaves a red mark on her face. The granddaughter doesn't enjoy this. It hurts. She pushes his hand away and expresses her pain in words. "Don't you have any shame? Doing whatever you please in front of my mother!"

Now the old *badeni* is certain that the youth will choose the girl. She cannot watch this happening in front of her own eyes and remain still like a corpse! She covers her face with her stained and ragged shawl and says to herself, If only they will get it over with and leave the money.

It is dark outside. All that can be heard are dogs barking and laughter in a house nearby. People are eating and working there. She has seen drivers pull up there even in the middle of the day. She has to sleep by the fire pit, where she has slept for many years, so she is forced to listen no matter how long the youths sit in vulgar talk with her daughters and granddaughter. She has one alternative: she can pretend to be asleep and cover her face.

The youth puts a hand on the granddaughter's shoulder. "How long have you been working?" he asks.

The granddaughter throws back his question, mocking him. "How long have you been working?"

Seeing the situation, the daughter reacts. "If you're going to stay, do it quickly. It's getting late. Go to the room upstairs."

His eyes roam the room, looking for the stairs. He doesn't see any and asks, "How do you go up?"

The granddaughter takes an oil lamp in her hand. There is a hole in the mud wall. She goes through it. He is right behind her. He supports himself with his hands to get through. The room is tiny. Leading up are stairs made from a notched log. The steps are very narrow. He holds on with his hands to climb up. Upstairs is a larger room. She puts the lamp on the windowsill and stands in an attitude of surrender. She waits to see how the game will begin.

He sits down on the clean mattress. He feels very comfortable here. There is no smoke, no old woman nagging. Here he is free to say or do anything.

"You're so big and tall." The granddaughter starts the game with words.

He stretches out his huge body and replies, "What sort of girl are you, to start this work at your age? Isn't there any other kind of work to do?"

"How could any work be more important than this? It is traditional for us to do this work."

Downstairs, his friend at the fire pit awaits his turn. He just waits. To pass the time, he forces himself to joke with them.

"Which one of you will go with me?" He gives them a choice.

The daughter thinks that if the first youth had asked this, her own daughter would already be in bed, dreaming sweet dreams. Now she is seized with worry over the state in which her daughter will return. The old *badeni* is snoring.

All they have to call their own is this two-story house. After a few minutes, the room upstairs begins to tremble and pieces of dirt from the ceiling begin to fall where they are sitting. They all feel very strange, but no one expresses it. The daughter's face goes white. A moment later, they hear a scream. A human scream. A scream full of pain. The scream descends to the place where they are sitting. It doesn't stay long. It exits the house. It scatters into the sky, where it turns into thunder and lightning. It's moving back and forth, looking for a place to strike. It resounds throughout the landscape and strikes the most important building. The villagers say, "There was thunder and lightning like this once before, many years ago. A man was making young children plow in the place of bullocks. That day both children died." Since then, the tale has been repeated around the village: this is what the height of inhumanity is like. But no one knows whether this story is true or made up.

The old woman wakes up in fear. The scream has pierced her ear like a needle. She jumps up and cries, "Has the bastard killed my dear granddaughter or what?!" The other women have seldom seen the old woman cry. Today they see it. The old woman is agitated and shouts, "Why don't you go and see?! Has the bastard killed her or what?!"

The lightning had burned the most important building down. All that the helpless villagers could see were flames from the fire. The old woman's eyes were wet. Slowly, that wetness spread to the eyes of the others.

CHHINAR

Sanat Regmi

Sanat Regmi is a Nepali author and editor. He has published six short story collections and is the recipient of the prestigious Mainali Katha Puraskar award.

On the plains of our Tarai, in virtually every village settlement exist one or two women of loose morals. Although treated in a civil way in public, these women are scorned behind their backs. The men in the villages refer to them as *bhauji*, or sister-in-law. But when a woman like this is called *bhauji* even by very young boys and old people, she is then referred to as a *jagat bhauji*, or sister-in-law of the world. In her absence, she is usually referred to as a *chhinar* – a whore.

In our village there was a *jagat bhauji* named Sabitari. Around thirty or thirty-two years old, she wore a shameless smile on her face, a red *tika* on her fair forehead, and *sindur* in her hair. On her body she wore a *dhoti* with a tight shirt; around her neck a copper amulet; and on her wrists bangles. Dressed this way, she roamed the village and helped people with various jobs. Someone was getting married or giving birth to a baby, Sabitari was present; someone needed help planting rice, Sabitari went to the fields; someone was ill, Sabitari became a nurse. If no one needed anything special, Sabitari wandered around the village and helped the women with their small, daily chores.

While Sabitari's conduct was good in many regard, she had one very bad behavior: she flirted and joked in a vulgar way with the menfolk of the village, even though she was married. That's why the villagers called her a *chhinar*. It was said that she had illicit relations not only with the older men, but also with boys who had just reached puberty.

Whenever Sabitari *bhauji* entered our home, my mother kept a cautious eye on me. If she tried to flirt with me, my mother said, "Look, Sabitari, you can hustle the whole world, but don't touch my son."

"Auntie, you're scared for no reason," Sabitari *bhauji* would say, laughing lewdly. "This son of yours is of no use to me. I need a man's man, not a shy boy like him."

Faced with her brazen dismissal of me, I was filled with a sense of inferiority. At the same time, I felt sharp anger and hatred toward her. Following Mother's advice, I kept my distance from Sabitari, but she toyed with me like a cat plays with a mouse.

"O Ramesh brother, when are you going to be a man? Chanda Auntie is afraid of me for no reason. My Ramesh brother's manhood has yet to rise." She pinched my cheek with her tough hand while I glared at her. She looked back coquettishly and said, "Wow, brother-in-law. *Now* you're gaining some manhood. I feel like crushing you in my arms, squeezing your whole body, but what can I do? I'm afraid of Chanda Auntie." Laughing, she left.

"Whore bitch!" I spat, hatred boiling inside me.

Sabitari's husband, Sukai Ahir, was a bone-thin, ill man with a limp, who did not have many friends. He had about an acre of land on which he grazed a buffalo and two cows. Before Sabitari came into his life, he had not been married for a long time. While single, he had suffered from all the difficulties that beset a man who has no wife to take care of the household, so he looked much older than his fifty years.

The villagers would always tease him. "Sukai, shouldn't you get married? No house is a home without a wife. They say a house without a housewife is like a ghost's dwelling."

"What to do? Who's going to give a daughter to a fifty-year-old like me?"

"You *have* to marry, Sukai. Someone dark, someone with only one eye, someone with a limp – anyone will do. All you need is someone to take care of the house. Why don't you bring in that madwoman from Rampurwa?"

Listening to such talk, Sukai would become irate. "You rascals! You're making fun of me? May God give *you* dark, blind, and lame wives!"

So when the same Sukai who had been the target of mockery suddenly ushered in a pretty, young wife, the whole village was stunned.

"How did this crippled old man capture this angel?"

"She's just reached puberty – the fresh bud of an orchid."

"How fair she is, Sukai's wife, sparkling with such glitter. The cripple turned out to be very lucky. Where did he find this gem?"

The gem had been brought from Parwanpur. Her father had married her off at an early age to a man who died soon after the wedding. She blossomed into a teenager, but no one wanted to marry her because of her previous marriage. Around this time, Sukai entered her village asking for a girl, and he returned to his own village with Sabitari.

"This cripple can't take care of a girl like that."

"What beauty, what youth. An angel, yes, an angel she is."

"This angel will surely fly away one day. She's not going to remain shackled to the cripple."

The speculations of the villagers remained just talk. Sabitari soon became a good wife and began managing Sukai's household. In the morning, Sukai would milk his buffalo and cows and take the milk to sell at the market. Sabitari would feed grain and hay to the animals and refill their water, then cook food for her husband. Sukai would return from the market and go to work in the field. Sabitari would bring water and food to him. Both worked hard to manage their home life.

The rowdies of the village were very impressed with Sabitari's beauty. Given the slightest excuse, they slithered up next to her, saying, "Sister, here I'll help you. Sister, I'll do this for you." But Sabitari didn't look at anyone with impure glances, and the villagers became jealous of Sukai's luck.

Meanwhile, Sukai had become very contented with his married life. A new motivation and excitement were kindled inside him. Soon, he demolished his thatched hut and built a bigger house with a tiled roof. He then bought another buffalo and hired a servant to help in the field and the house.

After five years of married life, Sukai said, "Sabitari, you've come into my house a Laxmi, the goddess of wealth. Since you've arrived, my luck has been shining. I am completely, satisfied in almost every way. Only one lack remains. I wish we had a son."

Sukrai's talk made Sabitari shrink. For a moment she stared at the ground, then said in a sad voice, "When you go to the bazaar, get a pack of peanuts. I'll grind it in milk, then you drink it. You've become very weak these days."

Over time, Sukai's desire for a son grew, but his strength did not. One morning, I was lying in the mango grove near their house. I had just returned from school in the city and was enjoying my summer holiday. The cool morning breeze had lulled me into a nice sleep when I was suddenly awakened by Sabitari's screams and cries.

"Oh, Lord, the bastard butcher is killing me! Oh, father, I am dying!"

"You whore, you harlot, you're bent on cutting my nose! Take this! Isn't this what you want?! You slut, let's see you whore some more!" Sukai's thick stick landed heavily on Sabitari. I quickly got up and rushed over to them. Several people were already there. Sabitari had fallen to the ground, her body spotted with darkening bruises.

"What are you doing, Sukai *dada*?" someone asked. "How can you beat your wife like this?"

"She tells me that I am becoming impotent. But this *chhinar* is philandering with Lakhpat!"

The villagers understood. They counseled and calmed Sukai. Two women helped the severely beaten Sabitari to her feet and escorted her inside to a bed. One woman cooked onions and turmeric and applied the ointment to Sabitari's bruises and wounds. "What havoc you have created, Sabitari. The whole village is spitting."

"What should I have done, sister? That eunuch can't satisfy my body, but he's always pining for a child, saying his lineage won't continue. The bastard's wish prompted me to become involved with Lakhpat. I was hoping that I'd have a son, but the bastard found out. His own body is so weak, and my burning youth – he should have understood and kept quiet. He wants my skin to play with, he wants a son, and he also wants honor. I have served him very well, and even when I was squirming with frustration, I let him play with me. He himself doesn't have the strength to beget a son, so how can I give the bastard a son without sleeping with someone else? He cut his own nose today, and then made the whole village spit at me."

After that incident, Sabitari became known as *chhinar*. Her shame had been put on public display, but she refused to be cowed. She turned aggressive and unpredictable toward Sukai. Mindful of the burden of household chores, the drudgery of farm work, and his own health, Sukai couldn't kick her out. With the strength and determination of a man, Sabitari took over Sukai's entire affairs.

Sukai began to shrink. He appeared saddened by both Sabitari and his married life. He went to the field in the morning, worked all day, and in the evening went to a hut near the village and became intoxicated with *ganja* and opium. Returning home at night, he ate whatever Sabitari offered him, then collapsed in a corner.

Sabitari's repressed sexual needs began to burn like dry wood. Now she feared neither Sukai nor the opinion of the villagers. She started distributing her lust evenly, and everyone became ravenous for Sabitari *bhauji*'s unabashed generosity.

Sometimes, Sukai said in a very pitiful voice, "Sabitari, why do you insist on defiling your name? And why, along with yourself, do you want to push me into hell? It's better you go somewhere else and find a husband. Free me from this."

"You're not going to get off so easily." Sabitari's voice trembled with rage. "I want you to burn every day, do you understand? I have turned into a harlot. Why? I wanted to give you a son to continue your lineage. But you exposed me in front of the whole village. You stripped me naked, so you watch and burn. The more you burn the more you squirm, the more my soul will be at peace." Faced with such fierceness, Sukai withered.

Sabitari became a common well, where anyone who was thirsty could quench himself. Sabitari discriminated against no one, gave everyone equal satisfaction. The amorous old men of the village said, "Sabitari *bhauji*, we too are thirsty." She would banter with them for their amusement, saying, "Brother-in-law, Sabitari is water from a gushing stream. You don't have a throat muscular enough to contain this stream."

Wherever Sabitari went, men's voices called to her, and, smiling seductively, she showered pleasure upon them. The honorable men of the community said, "That woman is a complete whore." The village wives said "Why does she hustle everyone so much? Is she going to seduce our men?" They told Sabitari, "Don't come to our house with your bawdy ways."

But totally unperturbed by such talk, Sabitari went to each house, helped people in their daily errands and participated in their joys and sadness. She was kind and generous. If she learned that a neighbor's stove was cold and there wasn't enough to eat, she immediately went to help her. If someone fell ill in the village and there was no one to nurse him, Sabitari did not hesitate to reach his bedside, fetch medicine from the village health post, give him his medicine, and attend to him until he got better.

Nanakau Pathak, for example, was forever indebted to Sabitari. One day he and his only son were at the garden east of the village. Nanakau Pathak had climbed a tree to pick some leaves for the goats, and his son was playing on the edge of a nearby pond. The child became attracted to the white lotuses growing in the pond. He reached out to pick them, and suddenly lost his balance and fell into the water. The pond was deep, so he started to drown. At that very moment, Sabitari was approaching the pond to wash her pitcher after relieving herself in a nearby field. She saw the boy and, tossing the pitcher to one side, tightened her *dhoti* at the waist, plunged in, and quickly brought him on land. He had swallowed a lot of water, so she pressed his stomach as Nanakau Pathak slid down from the tree and came running. The boy opened his eyes, and Sabitari smiled.

"Sabitari *bhauji*, I will never forget this kindness," Nanakau Pathak said. "If you hadn't saved him, my only son would be dead. The village might curse you, but I give you blessings: may you bathe in milk, may you produce numerous children." Sabitari became serious and stared at Nanakau Pathak's face.

On the one hand, Sabitari *bhauji*'s amorousness terrified the village wives. They feared her presence, never invited her to their homes. On the other hand, when their household chores became overwhelming or when someone became sick, they hoped she would appear. Without an invitation, and despite being shunned by everyone, Sabitari managed to help every needy home.

At that time, Ramdev Kurmi was considered one of the big men in the village. Because he was a landlord, be had become known as Big House Baba. But Ramdev's wealth was matched only by his stinginess.

He kept his family at arm's length, depriving them of good clothes and good food. His son and daughter-in-law were forced to live by his strict rules; as a result, they came to resent him. Eventually, when Ramdev became old and weak, his son and daughter-in-law took over his household and started to neglect him. Even in this helpless state, Ramdev cursed his family, so they stopped caring for him completely. When Sabitari heard that the old man had become incapacitated, she went to see him. Entering his room, she had to cover her nose with the edge of her *dhoti* because of the stench. The old man was mired in his own urine and feces, and Sabitari felt like vomiting. But she suppressed her nausea, carried him outside, and washed and cleaned him. She then washed his bed in the pond and put it in the yard to dry out. After that, she nursed the old man every day.

When the villagers saw her caring for him in this way, they gossiped. "It's not for nothing that Sabitari is nursing that Ramdev. She's after the wealth he's hidden." But they were wrong.

Pleased with her care of him, old Ramdev one day took out his bag of jewelry and gave it to Sabitari. "Daughter," he said, "my son and daughter-in-law turned out to be useless. But you have nursed me so well. That's why this money I've saved I'm giving to you. Think of this as a gift from a father."

"Big House Baba, what use do I have for your bag of jewelry after I've had to shed my honor, which is the greatest wealth a woman can ever have? Sabitari is sinful, is a whore, but she's not greedy, Baba. Give your wealth to your son and daughter-in-law. They are your rightful heirs." Sabitari's eyes had become wet, and she returned home without accepting the bag.

The old man did not want to leave his wealth to his uncaring family, so he died with the bag of jewelry on his chest. The next day, the villagers who had gathered to take his corpse away saw that the bag was intact. Ramdev's son picked it up and found gold necklaces, gold earrings, silver anklets, a necklace of silver coins, and gold coins: nearly fifty or sixty thousand *rupees*' worth of jewelry. The son thought to himself, May God bless you, Sabitari. Didn't you feel greedy for this wealth?

Yesterday, Nanakau Pathak arrived in the city from the village and told me, "Sabitari *chhinar* is dead. Very generous and kind she was.

She gave us many things, made us obligated to her for many things. We hated her, and she loved us dearly. She managed Sukai's household, served him completely. She served the whole village. She showered her fiery youth on the entire village. She was a river, a flooding river that reaches every home, creates havoc in the village, and leaves behind a soft, alluvial soil in which all the people flourish."

Who was Sabitari *bhauji*? A morally loose woman? A goddess who served the village by bringing it hope for prosperity? A village-wife who satisfied the villagers' needs? I don't know. But she served the village with her mind and her body, and for that she received her name: *chhinar*.

LETTER FROM KATHMANDU

Isabel Hilton

Isabel Hilton is a London-based writer and broadcaster. She is founder and editor of *Chinadialogue*, an independent, non-profit organization based in London, Beijing and San Francisco. She has reported from China, South Asia, Latin America, Africa, the Middle East and Europe and has written and presented several documentaries for BBC radio and television. Before founding *Chinadialogue* she was a writer and/or editor for a number of newspapers, including *The Sunday Times*, the *Independent* and the *Guardian*. She has authored and co-authored several books and holds honorary doctorates from Bradford and Stirling Universities.

ROYAL BLOOD

The Crown Prince was in love. Is that what drove him to kill the King and Queen and seven others?

On the evening of Jestha 19 in the year 2058 by the Nepalese calendar – June 1, 2001, as that day was known by the rest of the world Dr. Upendra Devkota was operating on a patient in his private clinic in Kathmandu, unaware that, a few miles away, King Birendra of Nepal and fourteen members of his family had been shot. Devkota is the country's leading neurosurgeon, and an expert on head injuries; his day job is a badly paid position at the large, overcrowded Bir Hospital, and, like most Nepalese doctors, he supplements it with private practice. Devkota, who is forty-six years old and speaks a precise, fluent English (he was trained in Glasgow, at the Institute of Neurological Sciences, and in London, at the National Hospital for Neurology and Neurosurgery), told me that he had completed the surgery – a neck operation – and had sat down to discuss the case with a family member of the patient when a deputy surgeon burst into the room and told the relative to leave. The deputy is normally soft spoken and polite, and the breach of etiquette was startling: the message he delivered brought Devkota to his feet. There had been a disaster, the deputy said. The Crown Prince of Nepal, Dipendra, had been injured by a bullet. Moments later, an aide-de-camp to the royal family appeared on orders to find and fetch Devkota.

The doctor told his deputy to call the members of his surgical team and put them on emergency standby. Devkota knew only that the Crown Prince had a bullet wound, but the fact that they had summoned him meant the wound was in the head. He was driven off in an Army jeep at reckless speed, its red lights flashing. (It had already hit two vehicles on its way to Devkota's clinic.) "I thought I was going to have a head injury myself," he said.

The jeep entered the gates of the military hospital, which was crowded with armed soldiers and vehicles. The trauma resuscitation unit was on the ground floor. There was a body on every one of the gurneys, and more casualties lay on the floor. The junior Army doctor on duty that evening was working furiously to resuscitate a patient. Other specialists had been rounded up and were just arriving. A switchboard operator was phoning for blood donors.

Devkota was shown a man who was bleeding from both ears and whose arms and face were paper white. "I just glanced at him – an older man wearing a pale kurta and pajamas and a Sai Baba locket. The tube was in and they were bagging him" – pumping air into his lungs. "I felt the pulse and was told that they had been bagging him for fifteen minutes. He was lifeless, I said, and rushed on."

The royal physician, Khagendra Shrestha, met Devkota and showed him a stretcher on the floor covered by a sheet. Shrestha pulled it back, and Devkota recognized Qyeen Aishwarya. He knelt down and put his hands around her head, and it started coming to pieces. The skull had been blown apart. Shrestha was in a state of panic. "The entire royal family," he said, "has been shot."

The King's youngest son, Nirajan, was dead from more than thirty bullet wounds. Shruti, the King's daughter, was in critical condition;

her heart was scarcely beating. There were more casualties – eight members of the royal family were to die that night – but Devkota still hadn't seen the Crown Prince, who was on the floor above, in the operating theatre. As the two doctors headed for the stairs, they passed the first patient again. Shrestha identified him. "His Majesty the King," he said.

"I hadn't recognized him," Devkota told me, even though he'd met the King several times. "I felt deeply depressed. I took his pulse and paid my last respects. Then I had to rush on."

Devkota changed into surgical greens. A tube had been inserted into the Crown Prince's mouth, and a team was pumping air into his lungs. A bullet had gone in one temple and out the other, and brain tissue and blood were oozing from the wound. Devkota ordered blood and tested the Prince according to the Glasgow Coma Scale, which runs from fifteen (normal) to three (vegetative). Dipendra scored four: dilated pupils, pain perception, some neurological response. Devkota knew he could neither move the patient nor delay. As he waited for the blood to arrive he phoned his wife. Something terrible had happened, he told her, and almost everybody in the royal family was dead. She should lock the doors and let nobody in. Devkota was in a state of barely suppressed terror. He had no idea what had happened, but three possibilities kept recurring: there had been an Army coup; Maoists had broken into the palace; or there had been some kind of coup involving the Indian secret service. Any one of these possibilities, he knew, would be a catastrophe for Nepal. Whichever it was, he reasoned, the chances were that those responsible were there at the hospital, perhaps among the armed men downstairs. Would they let him try to save the Crown Prince if they had just tried to kill him? He feared for himself and his family.

There were no other injuries to his patient, but there was heavy internal bleeding; there would be brain damage. Devkota cleaned up the wound, insuring that no metal fragments remained inside, and he then removed the damaged tissue. A plastic surgeon closed the exit wound.

Downstairs, people kept arriving. Prema Singh, a relative of the King's by marriage, was met in the parking lot by another distraught member of the royal family. "Dipendra has shot everybody," the sobbing woman said.

The Crown Prince? This was inconceivable. "What rubbish you're talking," Singh snapped.

Inside, Singh found the Queen Mother sitting in an anteroom with the King's aunt, who was weeping. "My baby's gone," the aunt told Singh. "With my own hands I said goodbye." The Prime Minister, Girija Prasad Koirala, was in the crowded corridor with Prince Paras, the King's twenty-seven-year-old nephew. Paras was unharmed and was trying to telephone his father, Prince Gyanendra, the brother of the now dead King. Gyanendra was at the royal retreat, in Pokhara, a hundred and twenty miles away. It was raining, and a helicopter had been sent to get him, but the weather had forced it to turn back.

A brain scan of the Crown Prince confirmed bleeding into the ventricles of his brain. He was taken to intensive care, and his head was elevated. He was sedated and given drugs to reduce the swelling. A surgical team was preparing to operate on Gyanendra's wife, and another to operate on the King's youngest brother, Dhirendra, who was badly wounded in the chest. One of the King's sisters was waiting to have two fingers amputated. A cousin and the King's son-in-law had already been moved upstairs to the operating theatre.

By then Devkota had left the theatre and joined a group of doctors in an anteroom. He got a glass of water. He hadn't eaten since lunch and was in a state of nervous exhaustion. It was only then that he heard the first account of what had happened. It was, bizarrely, a relief. "I had been through hours of agony, wondering who had done this. Then one of the doctors said that the rumor was that it had happened at a private event and that the Crown Prince, the man I'd operated on, had done it."

Devkota waited at the hospital until dawn, when it was suggested that he get some rest and return at ten in the morning. But, just as he was about to leave, word came that Prince Gyanendra had at last been brought in by helicopter. Gyanendra was the only member of the royal family in a position to take control. Devkota watched him inspect the casualties wordlessly, his face serious and distressed.

Gyanendra led a group of high officials up to the hospital library and closed the door. Rumors of what had happened were spreading in a ripple of telephone calls that rapidly widened across Kathmandu. By morning, CNN and the BBC were broadcasting the first news – that the Nepalese royal family had been killed at the Palace and that Crown Prince Dipendra was believed to be responsible. There had been a dispute, they reported, over whom the Crown Prince was to marry. Crowds gathered at the gates of the royal palace and outside the National Election Commission, where the Royal Privy Council was holding an emergency meeting.

A successor had to be named before the King's death could be made public. Inside the hospital, palace officials were searching for a form of words. Constitutionally, the Crown Prince Dipendra, was next in line to the throne. But how could they declare King the man who had just killed the King? If Dipendra lived, he would have to be tried, but he would also be King. There was no provision in the Nepalese constitution for trying a king for anything, let alone murder.

Gyanendra sent for Devkota and asked him to describe the Crown Prince's condition. "I told him in clear terms that he was very unwell, and that the outlook was extremely dismal."

Three hours later, on the state radio channels, Keshar Jung Rayarnajhi, the chairman of the Royal Privy Council, read a brief statement in a tremulous voice. The King was dead, he said. "According to the grand traditions, we declare that His Majesty's eldest son, Crown Prince Dipendra Bir Bikram Shah Dev, will be the King of Nepal as of six o'clock in the evening 20 Jestha 2058." Since the new King was in the hospital and unable to carry out his duties, he continued, his uncle Prince Gyanendra was appointed regent. There was no further explanation.

An official thirteen-day mourning period was declared. Flags hung at half-mast, and the state machine, such as it was, shut down. Civil servants were ordered to refrain from eating salt for three days and to shave their heads. Thousands of ordinary citizens followed suit; barbers offered their services free. Kathmandu began to look like a city of off-duty monks. Shops closed, and the clubs and restaurants normally frequented by Kathmandu's wealthier young people were shuttered and empty. In the old quarter, the narrow, rutted streets were crowded with people shopping for food and the thin Nepalese newspapers that were sold from small piles on the damp pavement.

I was standing in one of these streets, looking at a high brick wall. Behind me an alley of small houses and rundown shops descended a slight slope, empty but for a dog that was giving close attention to its fleas. The undistinguished passageway had one extraordinary claim: a river of blood had once flowed here. The blood sealed the transfer of power from the Shahs to the Ranas, the two most powerful families in the country.

The Shahs had ruled Nepal since their warrior ancestor Prithwi Narayan Shah had conquered a scattering of rival princely states across the Himalayas and united them, in 1769. He was a legendary and merciless soldier, fierce enough to keep the British East India Company, which was already extending its power across India, from direct conquest of Nepal. He left his descendants a territory that would ultimately stretch from Mt Everest, on the border with Tibet, to the malarial plains that rolled into India in the south, and which contained dozens of different ethnic and caste groups and more than a hundred languages and dialects.

The high brick wall I was looking at had belonged to the courtyard of the royal barracks – or the Kot – the place where the Shahs had lost their power. The place was still a barracks, as it had been on September 15, 1846, a date that, until June 1, 2001, had been reckoned the most notorious in Nepal's history.

The kingdom had been in chaos for months as court factions fought for control and the junior queen was ascendant. That night, she summoned all the high officers to the Kot, determined to avenge the assassination of a favorite. The assassin, Jang Bahadur Kunwar, a ruthlessly ambitious son of a military family, arrived first, accompanied by six brothers and three regiments of soldiers, who waited outside. In the past, Jang Bahadur had not hesitated to kill for advancement, but that night the killing was on a scale that earned him a place in history. In the confusion of the acrimonious meeting, weapons were drawn and shots were fired; Jang Bahadur's soldiers forced their way into the barracks courtyard. Twenty-five nobles were cut down, along with an unknown number of soldiers and retainers. When the King, Rajendra Shah, arrived at the courtyard, he was so unmanned by the screams and the sight of blood running beneath the gate that he fled back to his palace. He died the next year.

The Shahs continued to occupy the throne, but Jang Bahadur Kunwar was now the country's supreme de-facto power. He purged the kingdom of his rivals and distributed the top jobs to members of his family. To consolidate his position, he drew up an apocryphal genealogy that conveniently demonstrated his descent from a royal house, the Ranas, a powerful family that had been Indian princes in the fourteenth century. He adopted the Rana name, and, with his newly raised caste status, his family became acceptable to Indian royalty. At first, the "Ranas" were barred from marrying members of the Nepalese royal family, but by 1854 the ban had been lifted. Henceforth, Jang Bahadur's descendants controlled the Shahs politically and were impossible to separate from them dynastically.

For more than a hundred years, the Ranas ruled Nepal as hereditary Prime Ministers, building up immense personal fortunes while eighty-five per cent of their subjects made a meagre living through subsistence farming. There was no distinction between state revenues and the Rana private purse. Giant palaces were built in a Western neoclassical style. The largest, the Singha Durbar, had more than a thousand rooms, organized around thirteen courtyards, plus a theatre, a huge galleried hall (which now serves as the parliament chamber), and a Versailles-inspired hall of mirrors. From its deep balcony, the Ranas acknowledged the crowds that had been summoned to gather in the wide avenue below.

But under the Ranas' rule the country stagnated. By the time their power was broken, in 1951, Nepal was among the poorest lands on earth. Two-thirds of the children died in infancy, and the average life expectancy was thirty-five years. Only two per cent of the adult population was literate. In the entire nation there were sixty miles of railway, only a few miles of paved roads, and no electricity outside the Kathmandu Valley. Nepal was isolated and unchanged, locked in a medieval past. And the Ranas, despite their splendor, could never escape the sordid associations of the founding act of their power: the Kot massacre. And now, in the official silence that followed June 1, 2001, it was easy to believe that another murderous struggle for power had occurred.

Old stories took on new life as people tried to comprehend the incomprehensible. King Birendra, it was pointed out, was the eleventh generation of kings. As everybody knew, a curse had been pronounced on the first Shah king of Nepal by one of his defeated enemies, who had promised to serve faithfully for eleven generations, and then reappear within the family and destroy it in an act of vengeance. A curse seemed no less credible than some of the other stories. King Birendra and his son Dipendra had both been popular; Gyanendra and his son Paras were not. The previous August, half a million people had petitioned the King to punish Paras after he killed a popular musician in a drunk-driving incident. Gyanendra's absence from the murder scene was interpreted as foreknowledge. Paras's presence was equally suspicious – he was one of the few unscathed – and it gave strength to the theory of a power struggle. That the popular and apparently dutiful Crown Prince Dipendra had shot his whole family because he wasn't allowed to marry the woman he loved seemed the least likely possibility of all.

On Saturday, June 2nd, twenty-one hours after the killings, a funeral procession set off from the military hospital to the Pashupatinath Temple, bearing the bodies of the eight dead – Dipendra's parents, his sister, his brother, his uncle, and three of his aunts. The procession was headed by a mounted guard of honor, followed by a police band playing sombre music, and then the King's body on an open bier, wrapped in saffron cloth. The Queen was next, in a covered palanquin, then the bodies of her son and daughter. Half a million people lined the route. As the cortege passed, they wept, threw flowers, and shouted, with affecting futility, "Long live King Birendra."

Beneath the temple, on the banks of the Bagmati River, the royal ghats, the platforms where the bodies would be cremated, were piled high with wood. It was nearly ten o'clock, and dark, when the fires were lit. As the smoke rose from King Birendra's funeral pyre, the first heavy drops of an approaching monsoon began to fall.

The next morning, Prince Gyanendra issued his own statement, trying to disguise the horror of Dipendra's last act. "According to a report of the incident received by us," he said, "an automatic weapon went off suddenly, seriously injuring His Majesty King Birendra Bir Bikram Shah Dev, Her Majesty Qyeen Aishwarya Rajya Laxmi Devi Shah, His Royal Highness Crown Prince Dipendra Bir Bikram Shah Dev, His Royal Highness Prince Nirajan Bir Bikram Shah, and other royal family members and relatives." As an explanation, it was worse than silence.

Fearful of what might happen next, people formed lines outside the few functioning shops in order to stockpile kerosene and cooking gas.

By Sunday afternoon, Dipendra's condition had worsened. Devkota informed Gyanendra that the Prince had no chance of survival. What did he want to do? Gyanendra consulted the Queen Mother. Dipendra's life support, he told Devkota, was not to be switched off unless his heart stopped. It stopped at three-forty the following morning. Dipendra had been King for less than forty-eight hours.

Gyanendra was now King of Nepal, the third king in four days. The enthronement ceremony was conducted in a misty rain within the walls of Hanuman Dhoka, the Shahs' first royal palace. Gyanendra looked profoundly depressed. There was still no credible official explanation of the events that had placed him on the throne. He rode back in an open chariot drawn by six white horses. As the procession passed, an unusually silent crowd watched. There was little clapping. In one spot, hecklers jeered, "Death to Gyanendra!" When the chariot disappeared into the palace, crowds gathered just outside the gates, shouting "Gyanendra the murderer!" and throwing stones at the palace walls. The police responded with tear gas.

The new King was known as a less sympathetic leader than his brother – a hard-nosed businessman – and his image wasn't helped by his son Paras, with his heavy-drinking swagger and his readiness to draw a gun. That evening, the new King addressed his subjects in a brief television broadcast. Now he promised the truth. He appointed a three-man commission – the Chief Justice, the Speaker of the House, and the leader of the Unified Marxist Leninists, the main opposition party to investigate the events at the palace and report their findings within three days. The leader of the opposition party resigned the next day. To add to the confusion, a Maoist rebel leader published an article in a local newspaper lamenting the death of King Birendra and accusing Gyanendra and sinister foreign forces of being behind the massacre. The newspaper's editor and two of its directors were arrested on suspicion of sedition. For those in search of an explanation, it was further evidence that the truth was being suppressed.

A curfew was announced: anyone in violation would receive one clear warning before he was shot. The streets had emptied by that afternoon, when Dipendra's body was driven on an Army truck to the same sacred site where his victims had been cremated, two days earlier. That night, two protesters were shot.

On the night of the killings, a hostile crowd had gathered outside the family home of Devyani Rana, the woman who had been linked to the Crown Prince. There are hardly any photographs of her. She had never courted publicity, ruled few people outside her social circle would have recognized the woman who might have become the Queen of Nepal. After June 1st, her name was known everywhere.

The heavy gates of her home remained shut. Devyani was said to have left for Moscow, where her family had business interests. She was also said to have fled to the family home in Delhi. (Her presence in India was indirectly confirmed when her brief statement for the inquiry was delivered to the Nepalese Ambassador in Delhi.) There were rumors that she was pregnant, that the couple had been married in a secret ceremony. A relative said she'd been ill.

I called the house in Delhi, one of several there that belonged to Devyani's Indian relatives. There was no answer. Later, I drove around Delhi, testing the resolve of the guards on several of the family's large properties (one consumed an entire city block). The guards insisted that nobody was there.

"I saw her father at the funeral," an elderly politician told me. "We were at the military hospital, and the bodies were in the open air. The place was full of flies. He was so downcast, almost fallen. He's a respectable gentleman, educated at Oxford. He knew me and how close to the palace I was, how intense the pain was. He gave me his arm. I felt he was barely containing himself. He must be overwhelmed, thinking about his daughter's future."

Few people outside Devyani's intimate circle had known the details of her relationship with the Crown Prince, although the fact that they were a couple – and that the royal family opposed it – had been the subject of gossip. But the mystery at the root of the Prince's desperate act, and the reason that the royal family had objected so stubbornly, was not explained. According to Prabakhar Rana, a business partner of the recently enthroned King Gyanendra, "Devyani is attractive, well educated, and well brought up. She does have a filthy temper, like all

Rana girls, but I was very fond of her." As a Rana, Devyani was a member of the family that had married into the royal house assiduously for a hundred and fifty years. She was also the granddaughter, on her mother's side, of an Indian maharaja.

"Why did they not let them marry?" Prabakhar Rana said. "Her father is a politician – ambitious but not popular. Perhaps the late King felt he was a liability."

It was one theory; there were many others. There had been hints of a family feud – Devyani was said to be in some way the wrong sort of Rana. Rabi Shumshere Rana, uncle to both the late King Birendra and his Queen, a diminutive former general in his seventies (who, like many family elders, has a passion for lineage expressed in long recitations of the family tree), explained Devyani's ancestry – after several digressions involving collateral sub-branches and a few asides on the progeny of junior wives. Devyani was descended from Dhir Shumsher, the brother of Jang Bahadur, the perpetrator of the Kot massacre. As it happened, the Queen was also descended from Dhir Shumsher, but from a different branch. "The Qieen," Rabi said, "had in mind a different bride for her son, one who was from the same line." He shrugged. "I don't see the issue, but the late Queen was a very powerful character. If she made a decision, it couldn't be changed."

Rabi's generation had submitted without question to arranged marriages; for them, the issue was straightforward: it was the duty of a son or a daughter to obey. "I saw my wife only once," he said. "In the palace. The second time I saw her, we were betrothed. The third time was our wedding. In marriage," he added, "love comes afterwards."

Glancing reprovingly at my skirt, he said, "My granddaughter comes before me dressed like that." He smiled. "I cannot scold her. It is the way things are. Going to restaurants, travelling – that's the modern thing to do.. But in my time we went to friends' houses or on picnics. After television came, people began to imitate Western hooligans."

Some thought it was a matter of caste. Under the Ranas, Nepal was a nation of rigid social hierarchies reinforced by a Hindu caste system that had penetrated every ethnic group. Strict Brahman families still avoid eating in restaurants for fear of being served food prepared by socially unclean hands.

"You don't see untouchables here in Kathmandu," Arzoo Rana Deuba, the wife of a former Prime Minister, told me. "But go out into the countryside. The other day in my husband's constituency, some Dalit women were served tea by a Brahman boy. They were terrified. They thought they would go to hell." There had also been suggestions that Devyani's maharaja grandfather was not quite of the first rank of royalty, even though her family is one of the richest in India: it was said to have possessed a swath of northern India the size of France before being unburdened of it by the British. In fact, Devyani's mother had observed that her daughter would have a hard time adjusting to life in a family of such modest means as the Shahs. Surely even the royal house of Nepal could hardly view marriage with the granddaughter of such a maharaja as a social step down.

"For the royal family," Arzoo Deuha said, "blood is the only basis of their position. They didn't want to jeopardize it."

The rules, I was told by Prema Singh, who herself had married into the royal family, are that the Queen of Nepal must he Hindu and of pure blood for five generations. "It means regular marriage," she said. "A senior wife. One of Devyani's ancestors on her mother's side was not quite a senior wife." It was whispered that Devyani was descended from a concubine. "The royal family minded about lineage," Singh added. "After all, what's the difference between them and commoners if they marry just anybody?"

Was that what it came down to – a late rush of dynastic panic, a defense against the modern world and its different ideas of legitimacy? Had the royal family destroyed itself by insisting on the irreducible meaning of royalty?

Devyani's life, too, was riven by conflicting demands of modernity and tradition. She was educated but not employed. On the one hand, she enjoyed the privileges of wealth – shopping trips to Delhi and London, servants to fetch anything she required; on the other, she was subject to the restrictions of Kathmandu's oppressive upper-class society: a life, for marriageable young women, of carefully screened events, extended family obligations, visits to the gym, dress codes, and the strict rules that governed with whom, and how, she could socialize.

The relationship was said to have begun in the greater freedom of

England, seven or eight years earlier, when Dipendra and Devyani met at the home of a mutual family connection. It had continued through contrived meetings abroad and more circumspect assignations in Kathmandu. Lately, though, Devyani and Dipendra's behavior had grown more reckless.

In a severe lapse of protocol the couple had been seen increasingly around town. The proprietor of the Fire & Ice Italian restaurant, a few hundred yards from the royal palace, had shown me the couple's favorite table. They were such regular customers, she said, that she had been searching for a gift for the Prince's upcoming thirtieth birthday.

Prema Singh had witnessed the couple's public displays. At a party in May, she had mentioned to the Crown Prince that her daughter was engaged and in love. "I, too, am in love," Dipendra said. At the Golf Ball, he and Devyani had sat at separate tables and talked on their cellphones.

Devyani had clandestinely visited the Prince in his quarters at the palace. And they had contrived to meet secretly at the Sydney Olympic Games, a trip that suggested a degree of intimacy that in itself would have ruined Devyani's marriage prospects. To an onlooker like Maya Rana, Prabakhar's daughter, the couple was heading for trouble.

"Dipendra was acting as though the King didn't exist," she said. "This is a feudal society. For a royal courtship, the family comes to your house to ask for your daughter, then guards are posted outside the house. You only meet under strict supervision. Devyani knows the rules."

The most scandalous episode occurred at a party this year at the Hyatt Hotel. The couple had stayed behind until very late, and had danced together. Then the Prince kissed Devyani in public – in the parking lot. It was Rabi Shumshere Rana, the diminutive general who told me of this episode. The recollection of it still rendered him indignant. "In front of three hundred drivers," he said. "No Nepali Prince does something like that. The King doesn't even wave. He never acknowledges the presence of other people. It's impossible to imagine."

Despite Dipendra's apparent devotion to Devyani, he had other girlfriends. The situation, Maya said, had begun to weigh on Devyani, who was afraid that she was going to be the laughing stock of Kathmandu.

She had stopped travelling. "She wanted to be with people who kept telling her that it would all work out," Maya said. "People were beginning to say that if it didn't happen she was finished."

The day of the massacre, Maya saw Devyani at the gym.

"It was about five o'clock. We had a few jokes. But she was uptight on the subject. I said 'What's happening?' and she snapped, 'Nothing's happening. What should be happening?' She still didn't know what the Crown Prince would do."

Dipendra was nearly thirty, Devyani two years older – another strike against her, according to Rana elders. Both were past the conventional age of marriage in their social circle. Local newspapers had begun to comment on the Crown Prince's not marrying. The situation had reached the point where the King and Queen had told the Prince that if he insisted on making Devyani his wife he would have to forfeit the crown. Nirajan, Dipendra's younger brother, was soon to be married – with his parents' approval – and it was known that he was being considered for the succession. "It wasn't that the family had told Dipendra he couldn't marry her," Prema Singh said. "They were not unreasonable people. It was just that he couldn't be King."

There had been a warning of the impending disaster, but it had not been understood: although the royal astrologer had predicted a catastrophe in June, it was assumed to be an earthquake. The royal family, like most Nepali families, took no decisions without first consulting an astrologer (although, when told that the astrologer had predicted that Paras would one day be King, the Queen Mother laughed). Even in the confusion that followed the massacre, the royal astrologer had been asked to choose the auspicious moment for Gyanendra's enthronement.

I made my way to Patan, just south of the Bagmati River, to see the royal astrologer. Patan had once been the seat of a line of Malia kings, who were conquered by the Shahs. Less than half a mile from the ancient Durbar Square, which is crowded with temples and shrines, I found the astrologer's house. I crossed a tiny yard and came to a low doorway. It was pitch black inside. In the corner was a steep wooden ladder, which led to a small, low-ceilinged room, where the royal astrologer sat cross-legged before a low table. A group of clients sat before him in respectful consultation as a young assistant carefully filled in details on an astrological chart.

The astrologer showed no surprise at my arrival. I wondered, frivolously, if he had known I was coming. He nodded and directed me to a cushioned bench and returned to his clients. After some minutes, he rose and joined me. He gave me his card: "Prof Dr. M. R. Joshi Ph.D. (Urban study and planning), Royal Astrologer and Geo-Astro Consultant." He gazed at a small window in the corner and described for me his training – long years of Sanskrit and mathematics, of geography and astro-science, with travels to the observatories in Greenwich and Mexico, a degree from the university at Varanasi in India – which had prepared him for his duties at court. These included recording the exact moment of birth of members of the royal family, choosing a child's name according to the position of the heaven, and determining the precise time to celebrate the rites of passage, which were all observed with the solemnity due state occasions.

I asked if the Prince's astrological chart had given any hint of what was to come.

The astrologer shifted slightly, as though pained by the vulgarity of the question. The room fell silent as the clerk and the clients listened intently, eager for the celestial explanation of recent events.

"It was a good chart," the astrologer said. "Of course, not every planet is good for everyone. Jupiter, Saturn, and the sun are in Taurus, according to our Eastern astrology, and Taurus is not friendly. There's a tug-of-war with the sun. The radiation is irregular and creates disturbances." He paused. "This is a very difficult subject," he added, giving me a firm look. Then he continued, steering gracefully toward past successes. "We predicted World War II. And the exact date of Saddam Hussein's war."

Had he no inkling of what Dipendra was going to do?

He had heard about the massacre, the astrologer said, just like any other citizen: a friend phoned and told him. He was summoned to the palace for the death rituals. The astrologer admitted that he had been surprised. "But I drew no conclusions," he said.

Was there anything unusual about Dipendra, I persisted. Any clue at all?

The astrologer could not remember. The chart was usually burned with the body, and the ashes thrown into the river. He did remember the expensive and elaborate chart of the Prince's great grandfather King Tribhuvan, the astrologer said, brightening. He'd seen it as a child. It had been edged with gold and was so large that it required four men to carry it. Then the astrologer was suddenly melancholy. There was little opportunity these days, it seemed, for calculation on such an epic scale. "If only there was time. . . . I love to calculate charts, but there is no time."

There was a living to be earned, however. The astrologer sighed and returned to the more modest requirements of his waiting clients.

As the Prince grew up, the traditions of highborn semi-divine males still informed his education. As a teenager, he was taken on a hunting expedition in the royal game park to kill his first tiger, though the days of abundant tigers were over. He had been a scout, under the supervision of his great-uncle Rabi Shumshere Rana, and a guru to the royal family took charge of his education in ritual and spiritual matters. The formalities of royalty, and its many rules, were constantly reinforced by his parents.

The senior members of the family had perfected an unblinking stare, disdaining to acknowledge the presence of lesser mortals. They were iconic and aloof. They were there to be displayed to their subjects, not to see them. (In the mid-eighties, after some consultation about the habits of Queen Elizabeth II, Queen Aishwarya persuaded her husband that she should occasionally be permitted to smile in public. Her first smile was the talk of Nepal.)

But the Prince's generation was starting to enjoy growing social freedom. His father had studied abroad and had negotiated his own truce with Western modernity. For his sons, the King chose an experimental school in Budhanilkantha, a suburb of Kathmandu, that had been set up, with the help of the British government, to provide a modern education for bright Nepali children of any background. To avoid discrimination against lower-caste boys, the English headmaster had proposed a radical system in which each boy would be known not by his family name but by his first name and a number. No discussion of family status was allowed. In Nepalese terms, it was a social experiment of an advanced order.

Everybody knew, of course, who the Crown Prince was, and they also knew his cousin Paras, who attended the same school. The Crown Prince, the principal told me, was a cooperative and hardworking student. Paras, I later learned, was made to leave the school early, after returning drunk from a weekend at home and driving his car around the campus at high speed. With some embarrassment, the school was forced to suspend him.

I looked at the school yearbook for 1986, Dipendra's final year. There he is, frozen in grainy black-and-white, a slender, good-looking boy, grinning in the front row of the football team, dressed in a toga for the school production of "Julius Caesar," and, again, in the formal class portraits, as No. 832 Dipendra. The caption reads, "Enjoys football and golf, shooting and scouting. His first aim is to serve his country in the best way for the common good."

In an earlier generation, Dipendra might then have been confined to the palace and the hunting park, his friends and acquaintances screened for suitability. Instead, on leaving school he went abroad. After a summer of coaching by his tutors – John Tyson, his English headmaster, found him intelligent but thought he was lonely in the palace ("I remember thinking that the only friend he had there was his dog," he said) the Crown Prince continued his education at Eton.

He returned to Nepal and took up his post in the Army, where he flew helicopters and honed his shooting skills. He had always loved guns and was allowed to "test" new weapons and recommend purchases to the King. He kept an M-16, a twelve-bore shotgun, and a small pistol in a gun cabinet in his room.

At Tribhuvan University, in Kathmandu, he took a degree in geography and was working on a doctorate, but opinions of his intellectual abilities varied from "above average" to "mediocre." So did opinions of his character. In public, he appeared affable, approachable, and dutiful; he could work a crowd. When he met the Nepalese team at the South Asian Federation Games two years ago, he shook hands and mixed with the athletes, in an act of unprecedented informality. But some who met him socially saw him as a spoiled member of Kathmandu's jeunesse doree – rich, arrogant, and willful, a young man who had been drinking since the age of fifteen, and who had no scruples about using his position to rescue his beloved cousin Paras from the police station after a violent incident; someone who had fitted a silencer to a gun so that he could blast away at cats and crows on the palace grounds without disturbing his parents.

I talked to Dipendra's friends and acquaintances, looking for anything that would shed light on his transformation from respectful son to mass murderer. Nothing I was told explained what he had done, beyond several accounts of a streak of insanity in the family and the hazards of inbreeding. One professor showed me a chart he'd drawn that purported to illustrate that the Crown Prince was the direct recipient of the genetic inheritance of several of the madder members of the family. I puzzled over how this squared with the same professor's description of Dipendra as an intelligent and rational man. But we were all guessing.

I had begun to feel that cognitive dissonance was a Nepalese national characteristic. Day after day, the newspapers were filled with black-ruled photographs of the royal family, displayed along with the condolences of local business firms, with no mention of the circumstances of the deaths. Tributes to Dipendra were published that omitted the fact that he had killed his family. "Hearty felicitations" on the accession of King Gyanendra appeared that made no reference to the gruesome prelude to his enthronement. There was a sense of waiting, but nobody seemed sure for what. Foreign residents talked of leaving. Parliament was closed, and of the government there was no public trace. As I travelled around the city, there was still talk of an attack – from India or the Maoists. The sense of helpless drift created apprehension of further catastrophe. Anything seemed possible except perhaps the story that Dipendra had shot his family in a rage over its refusal to let him marry the woman he loved. It was the one thing that, in the absence of plausible alternatives, I was increasingly convinced was true.

The monsoon rain had settled in and a heavy, humid morning gave way to a sudden afternoon downpour, which sent people scattering for shelter as street traders hastily threw plastic sheets over their goods. Outside the high south gate of the royal palace, formal state portraits of the late King and Queen had been propped up against the railings, and incense perfumed the warm, moist air. The palace, a glum modern structure, reminded me of the Beijing railway station: a gray tower set on an uninspired red brick building.

Under the Ranas, the Shah kings had been virtual prisoners in their palaces, revered as the incarnation of the god Vishnu but serving only as a decorative stamp to legitimatize the rule of their rivals. Then Birendra's grandfather King Tribhuvan orchestrated the overthrow of the Rana prime minister, with the support of a democracy movement inspired by the end of the British Raj, in India, four years earlier. There were even elections in 1959, won by the Nepali Congress Party; the following year, Tribhuvan's son King Mallendra jailed the leaders and banned political parties.

But by then the outside world had begun to arrive. At first, there were only a few diplomats and adventurers, but in the seventies the hippies hit town, drawn by the low cost of almost everything. Overland to Kathmandu became the pilgrimage route of the counterculture. They settled on a run-down street, rapidly nicknamed Freak Street, near the city's ancient temples, and cultivated a mind-altering ethic of drugs and mysticism. Thirty years later, the street is a jumble of cheap lodgings, drug dealers, and tourist shops. Most of the founding freaks are long departed, although a few of them have gone into the trekking business. But the door they pushed open admitted other foreigners – the tourists and the aid agencies, who challenged old habits by example and by design. The result is a bizarre reality, a dissonant collage of medieval traditions and the modern world. In the streets of the capital, the sixteenth century seems to exist in a chaotic patchwork with the twenty-first. My taxi-driver, fighting his way through the choking traffic of Kathmandu, carefully circumnavigated the somnolent cows who had parked their sacred rumps in the very center of a narrow street. At impromptu shrines to the dead royal family, people were praying and burning incense. Semi-naked holy men mingled with teenagers in tight jeans who teetered in platform shoes along the lethally uneven pavement. I passed a jumble of crudely painted signs advertising Internet providers, computer courses, and classes in English on my way to houses occupied by people whose status derived from their place in a society that, for all its changes, is still essentially backward-looking and jealous of its privileges.

This almost modern Nepal had a dark side, illustrated by the story of Padam Thakurathi. Thakurathi is a former journalist and editor. Throughout the nineteen-eighties, his publications were regularly closed down, and he was frequently jailed for his activities, a misfortune that gave him an unanticipated scoop one day when a fellow prisoner identified the King's brother Dhirendra (one of the casualties of the night of June 1st) as a key figure in Nepal's drug trade. Thakurathi went on to publish the story, without explicitly naming the royal family "Those people," he told me, "were agents of the Mafia in Nepal. The royal baggage was never searched, so it was easy for them to take whatever they wanted out of the country – temple idols, antiques, heroin, and marijuana."

Thakurathi had been a disillusioned member of the Panchayat system, a cosmetic parliament that had been set up in the sixties by King Mahendra after he banned political parties. "It wasn't working," Thakurathi said. "And I realized that people had to stop blindly following the royal family. So I started publishing stories about what went on inside the palace." The stories provoked the royal family, and there were efforts to close down his newspapers; for instance, his compositors were all arrested, and he had to scour Kathmandu for replacements and pay them overtime to get the paper out. Then he received a phone call from an aide to the King's brother, offering him any sum of money if he would stop publishing. ("I was really encouraged! I knew I must be right.") When Thakurathi planned to print a story linking the palace to a scandal involving heroin smuggled through the Nepalese team at the Los Angeles Olympics, the decision was made to silence him for good. Late one night, his wife was awakened by a sudden noise. When she switched on the light, she saw blood gushing from her husband's head. A gunman had cut through the screen of their single-story house and shot him in his sleep. An ugly scar now runs across Thakurathi's shaved head, ending in a deep indentation over his sightless right eye.

Political leaders, too, were repeatedly exiled or jailed in their long battle for democracy. There were student strikes in the seventies, bomb attacks in the mid eighties, and a steadily mounting toll of arrests.

Finally in 1990, rage against the monarchy broke out in mass protests in Kathmandu.

As revolutions go, it was brief and relatively bloodless. During it, the young Prince Dipendra faxed his father from Eton, urging him to accept the constitutional monarchy. After two months of protests, thousands of injuries, and some fifty deaths, the King gave in.

The era of absolute rule under contract with the gods was over. From now on, the Nepalese royal house would be subject to the doubt that undermines constitutional monarchy everywhere: what, in a democratic age, gives them their power, position, and privilege? For the Shahs, the final answer was blood "pure blood," as defined by ever stricter and more archaic rules.

In the short term, though, political retreat saved the monarchy. The sins of the Shahs were forgotten as the quarrelsome politicians who now took over displayed a capacity for greed and corruption that exceeded anything the monarchy had ever done. There have been ten governments in the past ten years, and out of the splintering parties of the left an armed insurgency erupted in 1996, led by self-styled Maoist intellectuals who took Peru's Shining Path as their inspiration. By early this year, their influence extended over nearly a third of the country. The government was paralyzed for months as the opposition tried to force the resignation of Prime Minister Koirala, an unpopular man widely accused of corruption. (During the King's funeral procession, mourners hurled stones at the Prime Minister's black Mercedes, shattering the windows and denting both sides.) In the week before the massacre, strikes had left much of the country without transport, and fermenting piles of rubbish built up in the potholed streets of Kathmandu.

The unassuming King Birendra had come to seem like the only man who could command the affection of his frustrated and disillusioned people. "Even I," the businessman Prabakhar Rana said, "looked on the King as our last hope. I went to sleep saying, at least we have the King."

On the eleventh day of mourning, a katto ceremony is held, a practice that insures that a dead person's soul will find peace and not disturb the living. It requires an act of sacrifice by a Brahman, a holy man who takes on the burden of the dead man's soul by eating an unclean meal. He is then given money and an elephant and is driven from the Kathmandu Valley. King Birendra's ceremony, on June 11th, had been marred by an unfortunate incident. As the elephant was on its way to the capital, a woman had run between its legs, honoring a local superstition that this would help her conceive a son. The startled beast picked her up with its trunk and threw her to the ground, killing her instantly. But if the portent for Birendra's katto ceremony were bad, the omens for Dipendra's, held two days later, were worse.

First, there was trouble finding a Brahman who was willing to lose caste for Dipendra. The man who was finally persuaded to take on the role, Devi Prasad Acharya, looked nervous and unhappy. He sat cross-legged, under an awning, surrounded by objects representing Dipendra's possessions. There was an implausible collection of furniture: a sofa and two armchairs, a few stools, a television set, and some bedding. A photograph of Dipendra gazed out from its silver frame, as though he were surprised to see his personal effects on display. Acharya seemed reluctant to touch the meal. Flies were buzzing around an uncooked goat's leg. There were piles of fruit and vegetables. Finally, he swallowed a few mouthfuls, then retired behind a screen to dress in his mock royal costume.

He mounted the waiting elephant, which set off down the path to the river, followed by a solemn procession of dignitaries and a less decorous swarm of cameramen.

Suddenly the elephant trumpeted and turned back up the path, sending politicians and press scrambling for safety. The mahout hung on to its ear and managed to swing the beast around, but, again, it turned to lumber dangerously back toward the temple. The third time, with a second mahout clinging to its tail and its decorative canopy slipping, so that it looked like a dowager who has had too much to drink, the recalcitrant beast was coaxed into the river's brown, fast-flowing current.

A few days later, I found Acharya. He lived with his wife and son in a dark brick building near the Pashupatinath Temple, where the royal family had been cremated. I sat outside on a low stool, and Acharya sat opposite me, his legs crossed, his breath coming in gasps. A group of curious children gathered round to stare. He wore a vest, and around his neck hung a gold chain that had once belonged to Dipendra.

The elephant had rebelled, he said, because he had been cheated. He had held out for a house, but they hadn't given him one. Now, he said, the landlord was asking him to leave, because, since the katto ceremony he was unclean.

The landlord smiled apologetically. "It's true," he said. "My family is religious and we cannot keep him here now." Dipendra's restless spirit was causing unease, it seemed, even after death.

The day after Dipendra's katto ceremony, the word spread that the official report on the massacre would be released that night, two weeks after the killings. In the parliamentary compound, I joined reporters and television crews who fought their way into a room that was clearly too small. A collection of weapons lay on a table in the center of the room. The report's two authors took their places, and the speaker of the parliament began to summarize their conclusions.

He read the statement in Nepali and in English, then stepped forward to show the evidence. He picked up the guns, one by one, as television crews elbowed each other aside for shots of him posing, smiling, with the guns that had killed the royal family. He picked up an M-16 assault rifle and pointed it playfully at the press. Beside me, a Nepalese journalist groaned and covered his eyes at this leap from tragedy to farce.

A camouflage jacket and trousers belonging to Dipendra were pulled out of a black plastic bag and displayed, like the skin of an animal that had been shot. He held up a pair of gloves and black leather boots. Over the din, journalists were shouting questions. The speaker declined to answer. "The report will be posted on the Internet," he said.

If the report was intended to convince the public of the official story, it was not an overwhelming success. Despite its length and the evidence, it did not attempt to answer the central question: what was it that had triggered Dipendra's murderous attack?

The Crown Prince's day had apparently been normal. He had spent the morning in his office and had lunched with his parents. That afternoon, he visited the Satdobato sports complex to check on the preparations for the upcoming national games, and then rejoined his parents to attend a formal tea party at the home of a guru. They returned to the palace – a family dinner was scheduled for later that evening – and the Prince went off to play a game of billiards, his aide arranging the balls for him. The palace billiard room had a bar and a CD player, and the young set often met there. It was connected by a deep veranda to a sitting room where the Queen Mother liked to spend these evenings. Nearby was the dining room, where the buffet would be laid out. The evenings included only close family, and the aides waited discreetly in a side office; even the servants withdrew, leaving the guests to help themselves to drinks.

At 7:15 p.m. the Prince's aide ordered some wine and poured Dipendra a single shot of Famous Grouse. Then, leaving the Prince to his billiard game, he went to arrange parking for the guests, who would be arriving shortly.

The day before, an aide had telephoned Rabi Shumshere Rana, the King and Queen's uncle, to invite him, as usual, for seven-thirty. Rabi did not wear his watch to these functions, he told me, because the King was so forgetful about dinnertime. "Sometimes it could be eleven o'clock before we ate, even midnight. If I wore a watch, I would get nervous." He remembers, though, that he arrived promptly and that only one other guest was there, Maheshwar Kumar Singh, an uncle of the King by marriage. Rabi is one of the few people I met who has no doubt that the Crown Prince murdered his family. Rabi was standing a foot away from Dipendra when he shot the King.

Dipendra, dressed in the traditional informal costume of kurta and pajamas, offered Rabi a drink. Rabi chose a White Horse Scotch. Other guests arrived, and Dipendra continued to dispense drinks. Then, unnoticed by Rabi, Dipendra and his aide went off by car to fetch his grandmother from her residence, a short distance away.

When the Queen Mother was installed in her sitting room, Dipendra and the guests paid their respects; the protocol was that nobody should drink without first toasting her health. Rabi sat down with the old woman, while the younger members of the family gathered at the far end of the room to await the arrival of the King and Queen. The King arrived last, from his office, at eight-thirty.

According to Dipendra's phone records, he called Devyani on his cell phone at 8:12 p.m. – apparently from the billiard room. They spoke for one minute and nineteen seconds. At eight-nineteen, Dipendra called one of his aides and asked him to bring some "special" cigarettes, described in the report as a mixture of hashish and an unnamed black substance. Dipendra had been smoking such mixtures for at least a year, even at public events.

According to Rabi, most of the guests were in the Queen Mother's sitting room. The Prince had returned to the billiard room along with Paras and Nirajan, his younger brother. Although there had been no discussion of his marriage, Dipendra had told Paras that both his mother and grandmother opposed it, and he planned to discuss it with his father on Sunday. Then, bizarrely, according to some accounts, Dipendra appeared to fall down drunk and was carried to his room and left there to recover.

Dipendra sounded drunk when Devyani called back, a while later. This time, they spoke for more than four minutes. In her taped evidence to the committee, Devyani said that she was worried enough by his slurred speech to call one of his aides, Raj Kumar Karki. Karki was at home preparing for a trip to the United States and told Devyani that he was off duty. A few minutes later, Devyani called back to insist. Still reluctant, Karki telephoned the aide on duty, whom Devyani had also telephoned, and who assured him that two servants had already been sent to check on the Prince.

They found Dipendra on the floor, struggling to undo the buttons on his kurta. They helped him undress, and he lurched to the bathroom, where they heard him retching. Reappearing a few minutes later, he sent the servants away and called Devyani again to reassure her. "I'm going to sleep now," he said. "Good night. We'll talk tomorrow."

But Dipendra did not go back to sleep. He got up and dressed in a camouflage shirt and trousers, black boots, an Army vest, a heavy leather ammunition belt, a military cap, and black leather gloves. Armed with an M-16 assault rifle, a 9-mm. Glock pistol, an MP-5K automatic submachine gun, and a twelve-bore shotgun, he left his apartment. His aide, seeing him leave, asked if he needed an emergency bag.

"It's not necessary now," Dipendra replied.

Rabi was still chatting with the Queen Mother. By the time he went to refresh his drink, most of the company had drifted back to the billiard room. The King was standing near the billiard table with a Coke, in conversation with his uncle Maheshwar Singh, his brother Dhirendra, and a brother-in-law. A group of women, including the Queen, were seated on a group of sofas near the billiard table.

"What's happening?" the King asked Rabi.

"No news," he replied.

Maheshwar Singh apologized for his wife's absence – she had an attack of gout. The King sympathized. Gout, he said, and high cholesterol ran in the family.

It was then that Rabi noticed a man in full-camouflage fatigues, wearing black boots and a cap. "He had come up behind me as I was looking at the King," he said. "It took me a minute to realize it was the Crown Prince. He was carrying a gun, one I hadn't seen before. It was no more than a foot long. It could have been a toy." Rabi said that he had raised his eyebrows in a gesture of inquiry. "I thought it was a joke," he explained. "He always liked to dress up and play jokes as a boy. He was a lighthearted man."

Dipendra smiled at Rabi and, with no change of expression, fired three shots into his father. Then he left the room.

Rabi could scarcely take in what he had seen. "The King had been shot in front of me. I was stunned. He didn't jerk or flinch. He just leaned over very slowly and began to sink. He was wearing a pale-yellow silk kurta, and a patch of blood began to seep through it. He looked surprised, and said to his son, 'What have you done?' I still half thought it was a joke."

Rabi shouted for a doctor. As it happened, there was one in the room, a young Army doctor, related by marriage to the royal family. He rushed over and the King sank into his arms. Maheshwar Singh held the King's head.

The Queen went outside to call for help. Rabi left the billiard room and ran across the veranda to take care of the Queen Mother. Mastering his panic, he entered the room. The Queen Mother had not heard the shots, and Rabi closed the heavy door behind him, trying to think of a pretext for locking it. But the key was not in the lock.

In the billiard room, the guests were still trying to register what had happened when Dipendra returned, his cap now pulled low over his eyes. From the doorway, he shot Gyanendra's wife, Komal. Then he shot his brother-in-law Kumar Gorakh. As the Prince advanced into the room, the King's brother Dhirendra tried to intercept him. "Baba," he remonstrated, "you have done enough." Wordlessly, the Prince shot him twice at point-blank range. The Prince then dropped the submachine gun and left the room. For a moment, there was silence – then pandemonium.

At the far end of the room, Paras had kept his head. He pushed the young women down behind a sofa, then shouted to Maheshwar Singh to get out of the line of fire. Maheshwar sprinted toward Paras and threw himself onto the floor beside the young princesses. The King's daughter, Shruti, dashed in the opposite direction, toward her father, but as she reached him she found her husband, Gorakh, lying wounded nearby. The Army doctor and the King's sister Shoba were still trying to stop the bleeding from the King's neck.

The King struggled to get up. He picked up the discarded gun, but his sister snatched it from him and threw it on the floor. Then Dipendra reappeared at the door, this time holding the M-16. Terrified, the doctor dashed for the safety of the sofa. The Prince approached the King and shot him again, at point-blank range, in the head. Then he shot and killed another uncle, the helpless Kumar Khadga, then his aunt Sharada. The light on the M-16 flashed on and off as he fired. He shot his sister, and as she fell on top of her wounded husband Dipendra shot his aunts Jayanti and Ketaki.

He turned toward the group that was cowering at the fur end of the room. Paras took a step toward him and shouted desperately, "What are you doing? What are you doing? Please go!" The Prince looked at him and hesitated. He did not open fire. He turned and left the billiard room, heading toward his own quarters.

The Queen Mother, meanwhile, unaware of the slaughter next door, had grown so irritated by Rabi's odd behavior that he felt obliged, at last, to tell her that the King had been shot. He told her to wait while he returned to the billiard room to see what was happening.

The King's aide-de-camp, on duty in a nearby office, as usual on these family occasions, had heard the gunfire, followed by the queen's shout for a doctor. He called for the guard and was moving, with military caution, toward the billiard room when he heard the second burst of shots. The room's glass door was locked, and he saw the royal family lying on the floor. The guards broke the door in, carried the King to a palace car, and raced to the hospital. By the time Rabi appeared, palace troops were frantically carrying the other casualties to cars.

There was no sign of the queen or her younger son, Nirajan. The last living witness to their fate was a kitchen boy who noticed them as they passed by. Prince Dipendra also went by, moving backward, a gun in each hand. The Queen was in pursuit, shouting at him. Then, from the dark garden, there was another burst of fire. Nirajan's body was found near the path to Dipendra's apartment. Dipendra discarded the M-16 and headed for his rooms, still followed, evidently, by the Queen. He climbed a few steps toward his bedroom, then turned and fired, killing his mother. He came back down the stairs, stepped over her body, returned to the path, and crossed a bridge. He was found by an aide, who had followed the sounds of his groans. He was lying by the bridge, shot through the head. His 9-mm. pistol had fallen from his hand into a pond.

There had been no further riots, despite a fear that the report would provoke them. Outside Kathmandu, though, there was another concern. On June 15th, the final day of state mourning, the Maoists attacked a police post in Nagar, in the west. Then, in a grim celebration on the eve of King Gyanendra's fifty-fourth birthday, in early July, they killed forty-one policemen.

I flew down to the Tarai, the flatlands near the Indian border. It wasn't under direct Maoist control, but the insurgents had a presence here, collecting "taxes" from businesses and aid agencies and occasionally showing their hand. I drove through paddy fields broken up by traces of a luxuriant jungle that had once covered the area. Now there was just a scattering of villages: crude mud-walled houses, thatched with rice straw. Barefoot children were filling plastic buckets at a pump. In a suffocating low brick schoolroom with a corrugated-metal roof, a woman was trying to teach an overcrowded class. She was not regularly employed, she explained. There were three salaried teachers, but they rarely appeared.

I asked the class if they knew what had happened to the King. They fidgeted on a crowded bench. A boy stood up. "Paras," he said. "It was the son of the King's brother who killed him."

An aid worker told me that, in rural villages like this, only one in five women could read, and very few managed to complete secondary school and earn the School Leaving Certificate that could free a child from the absolute poverty of the village, with its malaria and kalaazar fever and its perpetual edge of hunger. Among the unemployed, he said, the Maoists found willing recruits. "They ask them what they have got out of democracy."

Workers for an international aid agency in a neighboring district told me they pay a regular "tax" to the Maoists. When the charity was first approached and responded too slowly, a pair of masked men appeared and set fire to two vehicles. A nearby plywood factory was burned to the ground after the management declined to pay. Now the aid workers pay the taxes promptly, and the Maoists scrupulously issue receipts stamped with the heads of Marx, Lenin, and Mao.

The next day, I waited at an appointed meeting place for the Maoists. Two hours went by before they filed into the building: four small, thin dark men, who greeted me not with raised fists but with hands pressed together in the traditional Nepali greeting. They gave their names and their positions, one of them standing at attention as he spoke, like a child reciting the alphabet. Another wrote my questions down carefully in a small notebook.

"This is a people's war," said one who had introduced himself as Mohan Shishid. "The system now is a government for only ten per cent of the people, even though it is elected."

How long would the war take?

"Seven years, fifty years," Mohan said. I glanced at the others. Their eyes were fixed on the table where we sat. I asked them if the palace massacre had changed their strategy.

It had before the massacre, they had called for an interim government and for an all-party convention to draft a new constitution. I had heard of this plan, which had met with a lukewarm response from the elected government. But now there was a new situation.

"We don't believe Dipendra killed them," Mohan insisted. "It was Gyanendra and Paras, supported by external powers – the C.I.A in Delhi, working with the Indian secret service."

Why? I asked.

Because the Communist struggle was emerging in Southeast Asia and Birendra had been reluctant to deploy the army to stop it.

Our meeting broke off with the news that a police motorbike had been seen in the area. My visitors slipped out, one by one, and went their separate ways along the dirt road. The Maoists had vanished as quietly as they had appeared.

A short time later, in the Rolpa district, the Maoists captured seventy-one police officers. On July 19th, King Gyanendra ordered the Army in, a move his brother had always resisted.

The new King is rarely seen in public. The servants who had supplied Dipendra with drugs were dismissed, but the palace has done little to clear up the remaining mysteries. No one tested the Crown Prince's blood to determine what he had ingested on the night of the massacre. A month afterward, the general secretary of the Communist Party of Nepal (Unified Marxist-Leninist), the main opposition party, voiced a question shared by many of his countrymen: How, he asked, should the Nepali people view Dipendra, the fratricide, regicide, matricide, and suicide who had, nevertheless, briefly been their King? "Should he be honored," he asked, "or treated as a criminal?" It was a question to which neither the government nor the palace replied.

MASSACRE AT THE PALACE

Jonathan Gregson

Jonathan Gregson was born and raised in India. He read and taught history at Oxford and Queen's University in Canada before entering financial journalism. After working on the *Sunday Telegraph*'s city desk, he moved into travel writing, contributing regularly to the *Daily* and *Sunday Telegraph*, *Independent on Sunday* and *Time Out* and won the Travelex Travel Writers Award 2000. He is the author of *Kingdoms Beyond the Clouds*, *Bullet Up the Grand Trunk Road* and *Blood Against the Snow* as well as *Massacre at the Palace*.

THE FAMILY REUNION

The invitations to the usual Friday soirée at Tribhuvan Sadan had been sent out by the Palace Secretariat, as usual. Only members of the royal family and their in-laws were on the list. It was to be an informal family gathering: first drinks, and then a late buffet dinner at which everyone helped themselves. No ADCs or bodyguards would need to be present, since this was a strictly private occasion held in the safest cordon of the palace. Servants came only to bring in the food or refresh the ice as required. The king and queen, their three adult children, and some twenty other royal relations were expected.

There was nothing unusual. Such informal family reunions had been going on for nearly thirty years. The tradition was started by King Birendra himself, shortly after he ascended the throne. It was a good way, he thought, to keep the extended royal family together. The gatherings were usually held on the third Friday of the Nepalese month. In the Nepalese lunar calendar, the date fell on June 1.

The venue for the family gathering shifted around the palace complex according to who was host that evening. Sometimes it was held at Sri Sadan, the private apartments of the king and queen. At other times it was at the queen mother's residence. On June 1 it was the turn of the crown prince to play host, so the guests were invited to his private residence at Tribhuvan Sadan, the cluster of buildings that had grown around the hall where the king's grandfather used to receive guests.

Now the original hall was used mainly as a billiards room, though it had been enlarged into an L-shaped room with a bar area, a music center, and an adjacent sitting room. It opened up onto a veranda and gardens on one side. The crown prince's private apartments and bedchamber were just to the north, across a little bridge that spanned a stream leading to an ornamental pond. Other additions had been made to Tribhuvan Sadan over the years, obscuring the building's original plan but making it a comfortable enough spot for a family get-together.

For this evening, the six sofas in the billards room had thoughtfully been arranged in two semicircles – one at each end, so the elderly royals could sit and chat together apart from the more boisterous younger members of the family. When dinner was served, usually quite late in the evening, they would move to the dining room next door, where the food was already laid out. It was very informal. For the immediate members of the royal family, who as part of their "jobs" had to attend endless banquets and receptions, such cozy informality was a welcome relief. It was good to be able to talk without always having the servants around.

The only slight deviation from routine practice was that the invited guests had all been phoned personally by the crown prince's ADC to confirm they were attending. Usually, if anyone were to trouble to check on this, it would have been the queen's ADC and not the crown prince's. It was only a minor alteration to the customary form, not the kind of thing to think about twice.

The evening light was fading as the crown prince crossed the bridge from his personal apartments to the main part of Tribhuvan Sadan. He had showered and changed since returning from the tea party with the royal guru, and seemed to be in a much better mood. As host for the evening, it was incumbent upon him to be there well before any of the guests arrived. He was accompanied by his usual ADC, Major Gajendra Bohara. He went to the bar and poured himself a stiff whiskey. From the generous choice available he selected his favorite brand, The Famous Grouse.

Dipendra told his ADC to stay with him while he was waiting for the first guests to arrive. He moved down to the billiards table and had Major Bohara feed him balls so that he could practice some shots. Servants were setting the dinner places next door. The clock ticked on toward 7:30 p.m., when the guests were supposed to arrive.

The first to appear was Maheshwar Kumar Singh. It was his habit to arrive early. Maheshwar had been born into an Indian princely family and had married one of King Birendra's aunts. He had lived in Kathmandu for more than forty years and was a regular at the Friday night gatherings. A dapper figure in his Nepali cap and tight-fitting trousers, he bowed respectfully to the crown prince upon entering the room. Dipendra asked him what he would have to drink and poured out a whiskey with ice and water. At this point, the crown prince appeared to be "completely normal," smiling and making small talk.

Next to arrive was another of the king's uncles by marriage and a member of a great Nepali dynasty, the seventy-four-year-old Rabi Shamsher Rana. A retired general of the Royal Nepal Army, he too was a regular guest, though since his wife's death four years previously he had attended the family reunions alone. As acting bartender for the evening, the crown prince served him a large scotch. Rabi toyed with it as other guests arrived, for the tumbler had been filled to the brim, and he could no longer drink as he had in the old days. Dipendra asked Rabi whether he would like a game of billiards, to which the old general replied that he could not play properly because he had hurt his hand in an accident.

The queen appeared, wearing a red sari, just as the king's three sisters, Princesses Shanti, Sharada, and Shobha, arrived. Then Prince Nirajan wandered in with a CD in his hand. Princess Shruti was accompanied by her husband, Kumar Gorakh, but was without their two young daughters. There had been another party for the youngsters the previous week; this was for adult royals only. Besides, it was only a short distance to the palace from their family house in Kesar Mahal.

By now a stream of vehicles with assorted royal cousins and aunts aboard was entering by the palace's West Gate. Smartly uniformed guards snapped to attention and saluted as they drove first up a tree-lined avenue toward the main palace before turning left, past the back of the Secretariat buildings, to Tribhuvan Sadan. The royal guests were dropped off outside the ADC's office, from which it is but a short walk through a flower-filled garden to the veranda entrance to the billiards room. Cousin Paras arrived with his mother, Princess Komal, his sister Prerana, and his elegant Indian-born wife, Himani. He was escorting all the ladies this evening since his father, Prince Gyanendra, was out of town.

The king's other brother, Dhirendra, arrived along with his three daughters and his son-in-law, Captain Rajiv Shahi. Following his divorce, Dhirendra had lost his royal title and all the privileges that go with it. But plain Mr. Dhirendra Shah was back in favor with the king, who still considered his youngest brother very much a part of the royal family. Moreover, recently he had been on better terms with his former wife, Princess Prekshya, who had also been on the invitation list for that evening. But she was unable to attend.

Another royal divorcée, Mrs. Ketaki Chester, arrived, as did her mother, Princess Helen, and her physically tiny, immensely sharp-witted sister, Princess Jayanti. Princess Helen was there mainly to talk to her sister-in-law, the queen mother, and they were to spend almost the entire evening closeted together in a separate room.

The crown prince busied himself welcoming guests and dispensing drinks. The younger crowd sat at the end of the room farthest from the billiards table, where they could smoke without being noticed. Dipendra was a heavy smoker, but even though he was nearly thirty he dared not light up in the presence of the king or queen mother. It was contrary to protocol. If he was smoking when his father appeared he would immediately stub out the cigarette and have someone carry it away surreptitiously.

Dipendra joined the young set and started talking with Cousin Paras. As ever, the "marriage question" was in the air, and Dipendra told Paras he had been called in by his parents to discuss it. Paras did not mention it for the time being because it seemed obvious to him that the crown prince had been drinking. "What will you have?" asked Dipendra, still acting the host. Paras said he was thinking of just having a Coke, to which Dipendra replied, "You just want a Coke? I've been drinking whiskey."

Others present had begun to notice oddities in the crown prince's behavior. Dipendra was a hardened drinker, capable of downing a dozen whiskeys without his composure becoming ruffled. "He certainly wasn't drunk," commented Ketaki Chester. "Normally when he'd been drinking he just went quiet. This time he was putting on an act, bumping into tables and so on." Something abnormal was going on.

Paras asked the crown prince what had happened during the talk with his parents. "Oh, nothing," he replied. "We've been talking about the marriage. I talked with my mother and grand-mother, and they both said no. I will talk about it to His Majesty on Sunday."

Dipendra was closer to his cousin than to most of his immediate family. He admired Paras's recklessness and envied his "bad boy" reputation, while he had to play the "model prince." Paras had backed him in his decision to marry Devyani and remained Dipendra's closest confidant for discussions about his troubled marriage prospects.

Around eight o'clock Dipendra left his guests to drive around the other side of the main palace to Mahendra Manzil, the queen mother's residence. As host, it was his duty to greet his grandmother and escort her to the party. Whether anything was said between them concerning the marriage situation is not known, for Queen Mother Ratna has remained resolutely silent on the subject to this day. What was clear to everyone present was that when the crown prince returned to the party his mood had changed for the worse.

The queen mother went straight to the smaller room, known as Baitho Bathak, where she was accustomed to receive visitors. The older royals all trooped in to perform the ritual welcome on entering the queen mother's presence and then to pay their respects. Dipendra stayed behind in the billards room, pulled out his mobile phone, and called Devyani.

They talked for a little over a minute. The contents of their conversation remain Devyani's secret. It could well have been no more than small talk. They were in love, after all, and because they often could not see each other the two of them were in the habit of constantly chatting on their mobile phones. Devyani was preparing to go out to a party hosted by some wealthy Indian friends, Sanjay and Shilpa Dugar. If the crown prince could get away early after the family dinner party ended, it had been tentatively agreed they should meet afterward. But something said during their conversation appears to have upset Dipendra. His next call after Devyani was to his ADC, Gajendra Bohara. "Fetch my cigarettes," he commanded brusquely.

Similar orders had been received many times before, and Bohara asked a royal orderly called Ram Krishna KC to make up a packet of five of the prince's "specials," containing the usual hashish plus some mysterious black substance. ADC Bohara then proceeded to walk over to the billiards room. Rather than enter a room full of royals, he stopped at the east door and entrusted the cigarettes to Prince Paras. It seemed the right thing to do, since Paras was all too aware of the crown prince's smoking habits.

Only six minutes passed between Dipendra's ordering up the drugs and the next call. It was incoming, and it was from Devyani's personal landline. Dipendra did not accept the call, so it was transferred automatically to his ADC. Devyani said she was worried about the crown prince. His voice had sounded slurred. Could Bohara check out the situation? Curiously, she asked the ADC to look for him in his private rooms because he might not be feeling well.

Devyani was obviously very anxious about something. Once she had spoken to Bohara, she phoned another of Dipendra's regular ADCs, Raju Karki, on his home number. He was off duty and preparing to fly out on a trip to the United States for further military training. Devyani insisted he go immediately to the palace. Whatever she told him, it must have been persuasive. He dressed in his ADC's uniform and drove over to Narayanhiti at once.

Maybe she knew more than she was letting on. She was familiar with Dipendra's sudden mood swings and what he was like on drugs. But why ask the ADCs to look in his rooms? After all, he had just called her from the party.

At precisely the same time that Devyani was talking to Raju Karki, the atmosphere within the billards room became unsettlingly bizarre.

The crown prince began to fall about as though he were roaring drunk. He then slumped to the floor and appeared to have passed out. It was as out of character as it was embarrassing. Fortunately, most of the older family members were with the queen mother in her separate chamber. The king had not yet arrived but was expected at any minute. For the crown prince to be found unconscious would be a catastrophic breach of protocol, made worse by the fact that he was supposed to be hosting the evening.

Paras tried to revive Dipendra. "Not here, it's inappropriate," he tried to tell him. "The king has arrived." But it was no use. The crown prince appeared to be out cold. So four of the younger generation decided the best thing was to get him out of the billiards room immediately. They staggered under the weight of his unwieldy body, brother Nirajan and Captain Shahi taking an arm each while Cousin Paras held up his feet. Princess Shruti's husband, Kumar Gorakh, followed behind as this bizarre cortege lurched over the little bridge and up the steps leading to the crown prince's private apartments. They hauled him to his bed-chamber and placed him on a low divan. Switching off the lights, they left Dipendra to sleep it off and returned to the party in time to be present for the king's arrival, as was only proper.

King Birendra had been working late, as usual. This particular evening he had been closeted with his principal press secretary, Mohan Bahadur Panday, going over the details of a rare interview with a magazine editor. After years of self-imposed seclusion, Birendra was becoming more open with the press. As the discussion drew to a close, Panday asked and was granted permission to leave at about half past eight.

Rather than be driven around to Tribhuvan Sadan, Birendra chose to walk. Since his heart attack two and a half years earlier, the king had been advised to take more exercise. It was only five minutes' walk from his office, but even so he was accompanied by one of his ADCs, Colonel Sundar Pratap Rana. When he reached Tribhuvan Sadan, the king went straight to the small chamber where the queen mother was holding court, so that he could immediately pay his respects. Colonel Rana left him at the entrance, knowing, like the other ADCs, that this was a "family only" evening, then walked on to the ADCs' office. It was less than a minute away. Both he and the other officers on duty could easily be called, if needed.

The queen mother was surrounded by royal relations when the king walked in. They hurried to greet him, then everyone raised a toast to Queen Mother Ratna's health. She responded by suggesting that they replenish their glasses. In the world of palace etiquette, where things are said indirectly, this was a clear hint that she wanted a private conference. So most of the royal uncles and aunts departed, leaving only King Birendra, Queen Aishwarya, and Princess Helen with the queen mother. The four of them remained closeted in the private chamber for twenty minutes. What precisely they discussed is not known, though with three senior royal ladies present the subject of marriages – and not just Dipendra's, but plans for his brother, Nirajan, to marry a suitable Rana girl – may well have received their attention.

There are many reasons why Dipendra, intoxicated or not, should have wanted to absent himself while this kind of conference was going on. It was humiliating to be talked about in such a manner. Besides, he knew that all three royal ladies did not support his plans to marry Devyani. He did not need to hear echoes of their disapproval. It was preferable to absent himself entirely, even if it meant acting the drunken idiot.

The opinion of many who saw him falling about – that he was only acting rather than physically intoxicated – seems be borne out by what happened next. He had been left in his bedroom, apparently fast asleep on the divan, at a little after half past eight. He must have roused himself almost immediately, for just a few minutes later two servants sent by ADC Gajendra Bohara after he received the telephone call from Devyani found the crown prince trying to undress himself on the bedroom floor. Together they helped him, after which Dipendra went to the bathroom and apparently threw up. One of the servants believes he heard retching noises through the bathroom door. The crown prince then returned to his bedchamber and ordered the two servants out.

The next thing he did – just seven minutes after being deposited apparently unconscious on the divan – was to call Devyani again. Vomiting may have helped to clear his head, but it seemed to have been a remarkably swift recovery. She took the call on her mobile phone.

Her memories of what was said are confused: "He said he'd call tomorrow; then he said good night." Next, according to Devyani, he asked again about something he had already mentioned earlier, but then hung up before she could reply. She says she then called back, and Dipendra told her: "I am about to sleep. I'll call again in the morning."

Strangely, there is no record of that second call in the otherwise meticulous log kept by Nepal Telecom, only of an attempt to reach him from the land line of Devyani's friend, Debina Malla, which was automatically transferred to the palace switchboard, as is customary. Whoever was calling in hung up after one second. Obviously they wanted to talk to Dipendra and no one else.

In his last conversation with Devyani, the crown prince seems clearly to have intended to return to bed. In fact, he did the opposite. He dressed himself again, this time in military fatigues: camouflage vest, black socks, ill-matching camouflage combat jacket and trousers, his army boots, and a pair of black leather gloves. His next move was still more sinister. He assembled and checked his weaponry: the favorite 9 mm. Glock pistol; a stubby MP5K submachine gun; his preferred assault rifle, the Colt M-16; and a SPAS twelve-gauge pump-action shotgun, along with magazine pouches and webbing for carrying spare ammunition.

As Dipendra was about to leave his rooms, his faithful orderly, Ram Krishna, called out: "Shall the emergency bag be brought, sir?" The emergency bag contained weatherproof clothing, insect spray, a flashlight, spare batteries, and other items that might come in handy when the crown prince went trekking. Seeing his master dressed up in military gear and carrying guns, Ram Krishna quite reasonably assumed he was going on some overnight sortie outside the palace. "It's not necessary now," was Dipendra's curt response.

Once the king had ended his private conversation with his stepmother he rejoined the rest of the guests in the billiards room. The talk among the older men was about the army and whether it might be deployed against the Maoist guerrillas – all in a guarded, indirect manner, of course. The king, eschewing alcohol, was drinking a Coke on his doctor's advice, but he nonetheless sent for a cigar. It was one of the pleasures he still allowed himself occasionally.

One of the royal uncles, Rabi Shamsher Rana, engaged him in small talk. Another uncle, Maheshwar Kumar Singh, came up and apologized for his wife being unable to attend the party because of her arthritis. Birendra commented that many family members suffered from gout, uric acid, and high cholesterol.

He was still holding forth about the family's tendency to high cholesterol when something moved just beyond the French doors. At first, nobody noticed the "dark figure" dressed in camouflage fatigues, a peaked cap, black combat boots, and black leather gloves.

General Rabi claims he first recognized the crown prince and realized he was carrying at least two guns. "I thought he looked at me," the old general recalls, "and I think he smiled." Others describe Dipendra's face as expressionless throughout. Everyone present agrees that he never spoke a word.

"The king was standing by the billiards table," Ketaki remembers. "I was nearer the door than the others and saw Dipendra walk in." At first she thought he was playing some kind of practical joke. "Isn't he too old to be dressing up like this?" she asked her sister, Princess Jayanti.

Most of the people in the room thought Dipendra had come to show his father something. General Rabi saw the little MP5K submachine gun and assumed it was a replica or toy gun. At first King Birendra just stood motionless beside the billiards table, the glass of Coke still in his hand. Then he took a step toward his son. Without uttering a single word, Dipendra advanced with a gun in each hand and released three rounds at the king.

The retort of the submachine gun in such a confined space was deafening. Maheshwar, who was standing near the king, at first thought it had come from the TV. "It was very near my ears, and I thought my eardrums had burst. I blinked. I turned to see what was happening."

Others were better placed to observe as events moved rapidly on. "The gun rode up and some bullets went into the ceiling," says Ketaki. "It didn't seem that dramatic. There wasn't lots of ceiling coming down on us or anything."

"There was a burst of three shots," specified General Rabi Rana. He knew his firing drill: Bursts came in fives, in threes, or just single shots. But he had no idea how to react to the situation unfolding before his eyes.

"I just stood there watching. I knew he was a happy-go-lucky person, but this was no way to fool around. Then I saw the blood rushing out of the king's side. I screamed for an ambulance, but it seems no one heard."

During that first attack King Birendra was struck by two 9 mm. bullets from the stubby German-made submachine gun. For a few moments he remained standing, long enough to put down his glass very slowly. Looking toward his son, he said very quietly: "*Kay gardeko?*" – "What have you done?"

According to General Rabi, who was standing beside him, King Birendra started to collapse toward the left. Blood was already seeping out of a wound to his neck. The crown prince meanwhile retreated through the garden doors and out onto the veranda.

Still no one in the room moved. They could not believe what had just happened. "We did not think that he intended to kill," said the king's youngest sister, Princess Shobha. "We thought the gun had gone off by mistake."

Once Dipendra had returned outside, the wave of stunned silence that had engulfed the room evaporated. General Rabi and others rushed to assist the king. Dhirendra's son-in-law, Captain Ravi Shahi, was a trained army doctor. "His back!" he cried out, calling for assistance to support the king, who by then had collapsed on the floor and was bleeding profusely.

Suddenly there was total confusion. "People were in a complete panic about who or what was going on," Maheshwar testified. "I felt the queen had left. Perhaps she went outside? Maybe to the back? But she left. Then Princess Shanti began waving both her hands, wanting to know what had happened, and immediately went outside. Probably to call for help, what else? And as I recall, Princess Sharada also followed her."

Although King Birendra lay stricken, having taken two heavy-caliber bullets fired at point-blank range, he was still alive. Captain Shahi tried to staunch the flow of blood from the neck wound. "I am also hit in the stomach," murmured the king.

At that moment Dipendra strode back into the billiards room. Outside, on the veranda, he had swiftly rearmed. The Italian-made pump-action shotgun had been discarded. This time he carried the M-16 in his right hand, the machine pistol in his left.

He must have seen the group trying to help the king, heard his father's voice, and knew his mission was not accomplished yet. "If the crown prince had not returned at that precise moment," a palace secretary said later, "he might have thought the king was dead. Then things would have turned out very differently."

The crown prince had thrown down the submachine gun he had fired at the king. Possibly it had jammed, though later it was found to be in perfect working order. More probably he wanted someone else in the room to pick it up. That way their fingerprints would be left on the weapon used against the king, not his, since he taken care to wear gloves throughout. Or maybe through some twisted sense of personal honor, he wanted to give his victims a chance to strike back, to justify what was coming.

It was the wounded king who made a move to pick up the fallen submachine gun. But as he reached toward it, Princess Shobha stopped him. "I said, 'Leave this,' and snatched it. The magazine came out and I threw it away." It was a snap decision, no doubt based on her desire to prevent any more bloodshed. But it was one she has lived to regret. She had mistakenly thought that she was disposing of the only weapon in the room. As the magazine fell free and clattered to the floor, the last realistic chance of stopping the killing was thrown away.

Ketaki recalls how careful Dipendra was not to allow anyone to come around behind him. With hindsight, she sees the way in which this first phase of attack was executed as being "coldly calculated."

Dipendra had, after all, selected his prime target: his father, the king. With him out of the way, the crown prince would by the Royal Constitution of Nepal automatically be proclaimed king, whether he was a murderer or not. "The king is dead; long live the king" still applies in such cases, for the throne can never be left vacant. And if Dipendra had been declared king, then someone else could have been made a scapegoat for the royal murder. All the other family members, placed under house arrest, would be cowed into agreeing to the official version of events. And Dipendra would finally be in charge.

Certainly Dipendra's subsequent actions show he needed to be certain he had killed the king. Now armed with the M-16 assault rifle, he fired off a burst at his father, again at point-blank range.

The king's youngest brother, Dhirendra, was the first to make a move toward the crown prince. "Baba, you have done enough damage," he said. When his appeal to reason failed, Dhirendra tried to restrain his nephew physically. Dhirendra was a powerfully built man and had been trained in karate, but he was unarmed. Before he could get near enough he too was cut down by a burst of automatic fire through the chest.

Any warped logic or planning that might have explained Dipendra's actions so far seems to have been abandoned completely at this stage. Two others were caught in the fusillade that killed the King's brother. Kumar Khadga went down with bullet wounds to the chest that were to prove fatal. Princess Shruti's husband, Kumar Gorakh, was shot in the neck but survived. He recalls being targeted by the light on the M-16's telescopic sight. "When he held up the gun there was a flash. I thought, 'This is the end.' That was when I was hit."

Princess Shruti was rushing to her father's aid when she heard her husband mutter, "I also have been hit." She changed direction and tried to comfort her husband, cradling him in her arms. Sadly, that was enough to attract the gunman's attention. He fired again. Princess Shruti was wounded through the elbow and sustained internal injuries that would prove fatal.

Kumar Khadga had also fallen out in the open. His wife, Princess Sharada, went to him and lay over his body, sobbing, "What has happened to you, what has happened to you?" Blood spread across the floor.

A second time Dipendra retreated through the doors to the veranda. He was only outside a few seconds before advancing once more. Now he let off long bursts of gunfire, spraying the room indiscriminately. Three of his aunts, princesses Shanti, Sharada, and Jayanti, went down in the hail of bullets. Princess Sharada was trying to shield her husband with her own body. Princess Jayanti was trying to retrieve a mobile phone so that she could call the ADCs. That may have inflamed the gunman even further. He fired another burst into the fallen bodies. All of them sustained fatal injuries.

Ketaki was luckier, in some respects. She took one bullet through the lower arm and another that blew away the top of her shoulder, but she lived. "I didn't realize it at the time," she said, "but the blood had spurted all over my face and head. It must have looked like I had taken a bullet in the head, which is probably why I am still alive." Another of Dipendra's aunts, Princess Komal, had a bullet pass through her left lung. It missed her heart by centimeters; she was extremely fortunate to survive. As the wife of King Gyanendra, she is now Queen Komal of Nepal.

Most of those hit had been standing or lying out in the middle of the main hall, where there was no furniture to hide behind and any movement would immediately draw the gunman's attention. Another group had taken cover behind tables and a sofa at the far end of the sitting room. It was Paras who had urged them to take cover there, shouting to others still out in the open to duck and stay out of the line of fire.

Meanwhile, the killer was moving about the room. He approached the body of the king and kicked it around with his army boot, to make absolutely sure his father was dead. He did the same to his younger sister. Her wounded husband, Gorakh, recalls how methodically Dipendra "returned and picked out those who had been hurt, took aim and shot, took aim and shot." It was chilling. Ketaki saw him "swing the gun so casually and just shoot them again. It was deliberate. You could tell by the look in his eyes."

Then Dipendra walked over toward where most of the survivors lay huddling. Cousin Paras saw him standing by a tall chair right in front of them. "We fell in his direct gaze," says Paras, who began pleading for their lives. "What have you done, sir? . . . Please leave . . . What are you doing? . . . Only we are here . . . just us . . . Please go."

"Well, if he had hit all of us . . ." Paras left the ensuing bloodbath to the imagination. Besides himself, there were Maheshwar Kumar and General Rabi; his sister, Prerana; his wife, Himani; and three of Dhirendra's daughters. One of them, Princess Sitasma, was hiding behind the sofa. She had recently returned from being a student in Scotland, and only seconds before had narrowly escaped a bullet that went past her forehead. From her place of hiding she looked up to see her gun-toting cousin looming over them all. "Dipendra came, looked at us, and left," is how she put it.

For the gunman it was a bizarre exercise in absolute power, holding the lives of these people in his hands. But with a flick of the head, as though to signify, "You may live," he left the room. If he had decided to fire again at that group the eventual death count would have been doubled.

The king and twelve other family members lay dead or wounded inside the billiards room. But so far Queen Aishwarya and her younger son, Prince Nirajan, had been spared. Shortly after the firing started they had both gone outside. Ketaki remembers seeing the queen "marching out of the door" in pursuit of Dipendra. At the same time, the badly wounded Dhirendra said, "Either she'll disarm him or she'll get shot too." It was an all too accurate assessment.

"I called out to her twice," Ketaki recalls. "I said, 'No, don't go.'" She also saw Nirajan running after his mother. "It was the last I saw of them. Then I heard some shrieks." What exactly happened outside is not at all clear. None of the main protagonists lived to tell what really happened. Other witnesses saw or heard things only from a distance, and their accounts are confused and at times contradict each other.

The king's ADC on duty that night says he "heard gunshots and Her Majesty's, a woman's voice, saying 'Call the doctor.'" The Queen's ADC, who should have recognized her voice, is not so certain. "It could have been Shruti's or Her Majesty's voice," he testified. Neither of these senior ADCs moved from their office to investigate the firing. Instead, they both say they immediately tried to call the doctor. One used the ADC's office line; the other was on his mobile. Neither of them was successful.

The shooting inside the ballroom was all over in three to four minutes. During that critical period not one of the ADCs, whose office was less than 150 yards away, made it to the scene of the slaughter quickly enough to intervene. The junior ADC to the king, Captain Pawan Khatri, called up the military police on his radio set and then "ran forward." By the time he reached Tribhuvan Sadan the firing had stopped. He did see "a man in combat fatigues leave from the back door, on the garden side, with a gun whose light was still on."

Several palace servants, including kitchen boy Santa Bahadur Khadka, saw a "lady in a red sari" running through the garden. Queen Aishwarya was wearing a red sari that evening. He also saw the crown prince moving backward with guns in two hands. As he was moving backward, the woman in red was confronting him. "The two were not talking; they were running, shouting, screaming. I cannot say who was speaking. The women in the billiards room were [also] screaming."

Santa Bahadur Khadka may not recall what was said, but others within the palace that night apparently can. For besides the public report on the "palace incident," two other secret reports were drawn up on what actually happened that night – one for the king's principal secretary and the other for the head of palace security. Neither has been made public. Their contents are, however, known to senior palace officials.

It appears that after the shooting inside the billiards room had stopped, the gunman retreated across the gardens toward the crown prince's private apartments. Queen Aishwarya pursued him, followed by Prince Nirajan. She always had been a tough-minded woman, and now she was furious enough to confront the armed man in camouflage fatigues even if he had a loaded weapon in each hand. She just kept screaming at him – words including a Nepali phrase equivalent to "you filthy bastard." It was the ultimate act of confrontation. Perhaps she felt she was invulnerable, that her own son would never dare to touch her. If so, it was a serious misjudgment.

Two bursts of automatic fire were subsequently heard coming from the garden. It seems that Prince Nirajan was shot first. That view is supported from the position in which his body was discovered and the location of the spent cartridges, since no eyewitness to his death has come forward.

Nirajan may have been trying to protect his mother against his elder brother's fury. If so, it was a supremely brave thing to do, since Nirajan was unarmed. His own pistol, the same model 9 mm. Glock that his elder brother used, was later found inside the billiards room. It had not been fired once that night.

The twenty-two-year-old prince was shot nearly a dozen times and must have died instantly. He had two gaping bullet wounds to the head. He collapsed on the lawn in a pool of his own blood. His body was so riddled with bullets that when rescuers finally arrived they could scarcely lift it intact.

Only the queen still faced Dipendra. By now his father, sister, and brother all lay dead or dying. Only his mother lived on to challenge him.

Even now, in this eye of the storm, and after all the violence unleashed on those around her, Queen Aishwarya displayed a degree of self-confidence or recklessness that is hard to fathom. Rather than flee for her life into the surrounding darkness, the queen again approached the gunman. She ran across the garden and up the marbled steps leading to Dipendra's bedchamber, screaming as she went. The crown prince seems to have been backing off, or at least walking backward. Maybe her hunch was that he could not bring himself to shoot his own mother. Or maybe she was heading for Dipendra's rooms so that she could seize one of the other weapons he kept there, either to defend herself or kill the man who had murdered her husband and her two other children.

While the gunman continued to withdraw up the stairs that led to his bedchamber, she confronted him face to face. The queen had climbed seven steps when she must have realized what would happen next, for suddenly she turned around as though to flee. The gunman fired a long burst, hitting her from behind. Her skull was blown apart and most of her brains scattered over a wide area. Fragments of brain tissue, jawbone, and teeth, the red *tika* she had placed on her forehead, her ear-pins and broken red glass bangles were found in different places around where she fell. As with Nirajan, her body was also pumped full of bullets. Expert opinion confirms that she was shot from behind.

No one witnessed the crown prince killing his own mother. Nor did anyone actually see the final act of this tragedy. For this, Dipendra must have walked back toward the billiards room, crossing the small bridge over a stream feeding into the ornamental pond. Around this time somebody claims to have heard him shriek out "like a madman." The next thing they heard was a single shot. Having murdered all his immediate family, Dipendra apparently turned his gun on himself.

At that very last moment, maybe even he was scared. For the clinical efficiency displayed in the shooting of so many relatives was markedly absent in this attempted suicide. Did he lose his nerve? Or was it because, for some reason, he held the pistol in his left hand? That should not have made a great difference because, although Dipendra was right-handed, when it came to firing guns he was effectively ambidextrous.

A single bullet entered just behind his left ear and went right through the brain, leaving a massive exit wound slightly higher on the right side of his head. But it was not enough to kill Dipendra outright. He was found lying on the grass, groaning loudly, near the edge of the ornamental pond. There was a Buddha statue nearby.

Only slowly did the full extent of the carnage inside the billiards room become apparent. The bodies of the dead and wounded lay muddled together on the blood-soaked carpet, while those lucky enough to come through unscathed were still cowering in shock. The floor was a mess of scattered articles of clothing, much of it blood-smeared, along with broken spectacles and slippers and hastily discarded whiskey glasses. After all the noise of gunfire, there now followed an eerie silence.

"King Birendra was the only one who moved at all, making signals with his hands. All the others were quiet," said Ketaki, who by then had already lost a lot of blood. "Nobody was crying out for help," she explained, "because we knew help would come from somewhere. Then I heard Paras's voice."

The younger cousin with a bad reputation seems to have been the only person capable of doing anything. Ketaki says "Paras was very, very controlled. If anyone came out alive in that room, it is due to him."

After Dipendra had walked away into the gardens, in pursuit of or pursued by his mother and brother, Paras got up from behind the sofas and began moving around the scene of devastation. He remembers, "There were people on the floor. I approached Dhirendra to find out what happened. He said, 'Paras, my feet don't move, I can't move my feet, please move them.' I moved them a little, but he couldn't feel it." The badly wounded Dhirendra then said, "I can't see straight, look after your Aunt Ketaki." Paras says, "Then he told me to look for the children."

At that point Paras was still unaware that his own mother, Princess Komal, had fallen too. Then he saw her try to raise herself up and slump back down again because the dead Princess Shanti had collapsed on top of her. He helped his mother into an upright position, and she said, "I'm not well, I'm not well," all the while holding her bloodied forehead. "At first I thought she'd been shot in the forehead," he confessed. But on closer inspection there was no wound there. He soon ascertained that the blood was from Princess Shanti's wounds and not his mother's.

After that Paras ran to the queen mother, who had remained in her separate room throughout the massacre. He had heard more gunfire outside the billiards room and initially thought it came from the queen mother's private chamber. "I ran over there," he said, "but nothing had happened." So he briefly explained to his grandmother and Princess Helen that the king and many others had been shot, though sparing such elderly ladies all the details.

He next ran outside to find the ADCs, who had finally arrived. He explained to them, "There are dead people as well as wounded ones. Ignore the dead, but immediately rush the wounded to hospital." He ordered them to break down the glass panes in the French doors to permit easier evacuation.

In the event, the king was carried out first, although in Ketaki's opinion he was by then "definitely dead." But from there on Paras insisted that the rescuers evacuate the living wounded first, helping to get them into whatever vehicles were available and dispatching them to the hospital. Some, like Ketaki, were completely disoriented. She was losing blood fast from her shoulder wound, but still she insisted on finding her shoes because she was worried about cutting her feet on all the broken glass.

With the evacuation under way and more help arriving, Paras moved on to those still unaccounted for. "I told three people to go and look for the crown prince, the queen, and Nirajan," he says. The crown prince's ADC soon came running back to report that Dipendra had shot himself but was still alive. Both the queen and Nirajan were beyond hope. So Paras and ADC Gajendra Bohara loaded the two royal princes, Dipendra and Nirajan, into the same vehicle and drove them to hospital. It was a macabre load, killer and victim both propped up in the backseat together.

HIMALAYA

Michael Palin

Michael Palin is an English comedian, actor, writer, and television presenter. In addition to his numerous film and tele vision credits, he has also written several bestselling travel books, including *Around the World in 80 Days*.

My guide to the Nepali capital is Kunda Dixit, editor of the *Nepali Times*, an English weekly with a circulation of 8,000. It's crisply laid out and well designed and has a sharp, well-informed, provocative style. The most recent edition carries the latest World Terrorism Index, which shows that, despite the Maoists, Nepal still comes below the UK.

So I'm not entirely surprised to find that Kunda Dixit is an urbane, elegant figure with a shock of prematurely silver hair, dressed immaculately in a pale grey *labada* and knitted tunic. I am surprised to hear that his real love is flying and his fantasy is that, with a pilot suddenly taken ill, Kunda takes control, lands the plane perfectly and is asked to take over the national airline.

We meet up in Patan, once one of three independent kingdoms in the valley, and now almost a suburb of Kathmandu.

The jewel at the heart of Patan (pronounced Parton, as in Dolly) is Durbar Square, a dazzling collection of buildings dating back 350 to 500 years, to the days before Prithvi Naryan Shah, king of Ghorka, unified the kingdoms of the valley in 1768 and created modern Nepal. There are temples, palaces with golden gates, a huge bell suspended between two pillars and a lion on a column. Nepal was never colonized, so the architecture has no Western derivative and its distinctive fusion of Indian and Tibetan influences was created by the Newars, the people of the valley, and craftsmen of the highest order.

As we wander through the colonnades of the Krishna Mandir, a stone-built Hindu temple topped with a *shikhara*, the characteristically Indian, curvilinear spire, we can look across to the Royal Palace, in a completely different style, refined by the Newari architect Arniko in the 14th century. It has powerful horizontals of brick and timber with deep, overhanging eaves, projecting balconies cantilevered out over finely carved, timber supports, and, inside, an elegantly proportioned *chowk*, or courtyard.

Kunda tells me that the Kathmandu Valley, once a lake, is rich in fertile, alluvial soil. The kingdoms, grown fat from consistently good harvests, ploughed their surpluses into religion, festivals and fine buildings, competing with each other for the tallest tower or the biggest bell.

"They used to say there were more temples in Kathmandu than houses and more gods than people."

The buildings are not purely for show. A family arrives to do a *puja* at Krishna Mandir, unsettling a flock of pigeons, who create a sharp gust of wind as they take off, circle and descend en masse a few feet away.

The most dramatic building in the square is the five-storeyed pagoda of the Taleju Mandir, with a bronze stupa at its apex. The pagoda, a tapering succession of roofs symbolizing the various stages of enlightenment, was perfected here in Nepal, and it was Arniko who took the design to the Ming court at Peking.

One of the pleasures of meandering round Durbar Square is the immense amount of carved and sculpted detail. In the Royal Palace there are stone slabs called *shildayras* that carry historical records from the Lichavi period, 1,800 years ago. On the beams in the *chowks* are intricately worked and painted lotus flowers, dragons and swastikas, and the stone walls of Krishna's temple are adorned with athletic, erotic couplings.

"Krishna is the god of love," explains Kunda. "He's a young guy with a flute and girlfriends all over the world."

I'm rather envious.

"Our gods don't tend to have girlfriends. It's something we've rather missed out on."

The smallest of the old kingdoms was centred on Bhaktapur, seven miles east of Kathmandu. On our way out there we're waved past a police checkpoint set up since the Maoists recently brought their attacks to Kathmandu itself. They're searching all the buses that run out to the country areas in the east. According to Kunda, journeys that took 12 hours can now take 48.

Kunda's view is that the Maoists' recent change of tactics, targeting civilians in the capital, has lost them support.

"It's not that the Maoists are terribly brilliant or strong, just that successive governments have been weak and fractious and corrupt, and they (the Maoists) have tapped into that bedrock of neglect and apathy and frustration in the people. They've grown so fast precisely because everything else has been in such disarray."

With an estimated 10,000 to 15,000 rebels, with looted arms from the police and the army, how does he see the future?

There can, he is sure, be no military solution. There has to be compromise. The institution of monarchy is quite strong and Nepalis identify their country with it, but the King can no longer be an absolute ruler. He must be firm but fair. (Which seems to suggest he's neither.)

He points to achievements brought about by strong policies resolutely applied.

Forestry conservation has been a big success since local people were given their own areas of forest to administer, the hydroelectric programme, building of roads, water improvement projects. All give him hope.

"And," he concludes, "Nepal's press has never been freer."

We're turning into the bus park below the walls of Bhaktapur.

"The Prime Minister has been sacked, parliament is in limbo, but the press is free."

The day that started promisingly is growing grey and gloomy as, having paid our $10 fee to enter the city, we climb up the steps and in through a narrow, rose-brick gateway.

For Basil it's a nostalgic return. Much of Bertolucci's *Little Buddha*, on which he worked as both actor and stills photographer, was shot in Bhaktapur. Though smaller than Kathmandu or Patan, Bhaktapur, whose name means "city of devotees", once boasted 99 separate *chowks*. A powerful earthquake in 1934 did serious damage and now only five of these grand courtyards are left. That they are here at all is largely due to a German-sponsored reconstruction programme. The connection with Nepal seems a curious one, but it goes back a long way. A German Jesuit sent one of the Malla kings of Nepal a telescope as early as 1655. Hitler sent a later king a Mercedes.

As in Patan and, indeed, old Kathmandu itself, there is some glorious work in Bhaktapur. The Sun Dhoka (Golden Gateway) is an arched entrance surrounded by richly ornamented deities covered in gilded, embossed copper. The figures of the gods are still worshipped and I see young Nepalis touching them and then their foreheads as they pass. All over the temple area there are statues and carvings worn shiny by touch. We clamber up into a small, octagonal, carved timber gem called Chyasin Mandap, the Pavilion of the Eight Corners, an 18th-century original, meticulously restored around an earthquake-proof, steel shell. A much grander building stands nearby: Nyatapola, the tallest pagoda in Nepal. Five-tiered and standing 100 feet high, it somehow survived the 1934 earthquake quite unscathed. One might imagine this would increase its attraction for devotees, but when I climb up the long, steep staircase past sculpted ranks of temple guardians – wrestlers, elephants, lions, griffins – I find only dust and a group of street children. Apparently, this magnificent building is dedicated to an obscure Tantric goddess, Siddhi Lakshmi, who very few people have heard of, let alone worship. As the temples rely on rich patrons for their upkeep, Nyatapola remains neglected.

There is hope. Kunda is generally optimistic about the way the old city centres are looked after (all three are UNESCO sites). He's much less happy about the way modern development is going. The urban sprawl around Kathmandu is, he feels, destroying the identities of the three cities. They are becoming part of a Kathmandu conurbation, which is bad for Nepal. It increases the centralization of wealth and government in the valley, further alienating the country areas, and puts great pressure on limited resources. Water supply is becoming a major problem. The latest proposal is to bring water in direct from a glacier, 15 miles away. It will be the biggest engineering project in Nepal's history, and if it works it will only bring more people and more money to the central valley, further dividing the country. And it would not go unopposed. Only yesterday, Kunda reminds me, the Maoists destroyed a hydroelectric plant.

On our way back, the insalubrious suburbs, and the congested roads that take us through them, seem to bear out Kunda's darker prophecies, but life is not all gloom.

He tells the story of sitting next to Prince Charles (of whom he has a very high opinion) at a Nepali banquet. Halfway through the meal Charles upended a full portion of rice wine into his lap.

"Great embarrassment all round?"

"No, everything was fine." Kunda smiles at the recollection. "I told him that was the way we do our dry cleaning here."

FORGET KATHMANDU

Manjushree Thapa

Manjushree Thapa is a Nepali author, translator and editor. She grew up in Nepal, Canada and the United States and began writing after completing a BFA at the Rhode Island School of Design. She later graduated with a Masters in English from the University of Washington. Manjushree's essays and editorials have appeared in the *New York Times*, *London Review of Books*, *Newsweek* and other publications in the US, UK, Canada, India and Nepal. She has written several non-fiction titles including *Forget Kathmandu*, which was a finalist in the Lettre Ulysses award in 2006, *The Lives We Have Lost* and *A boy from Siklis*. Her novels include *The Tutor of History*, *Seasons of Flight* and *All of Us in Our Own Lives*. She lives in Toronto.

THE DIARY OF A BAFFLED BOURGEOIS

There came a time, at last, when it was no longer tenable for the Kathmandu bourgeois to deny the reality that democracy was failing. For me this came about eight months before the June 2001 massacre at the royal palace. It occurred to me that I did not like my ignorance about what was happening outside Kathmandu. I, a writer, a bourgeois with aspirations to being an intellectual, was perpetually lost, living in a mist of anxiety that would not clear. I was unhappy, and I was unhappy about being unhappy, for I knew that in the scheme of things I was immensely fortunate, and so should be happy.

Yet I found that every public disaster had the power to hollow me out. I was like a bad-politics junkie, and it felt as though bad politics were ruining my life. I kept up with what was happening in the country as much as any person, but watching the television news or reading the papers or listening to the radio left me feeling defeated – personally, intimately, as though tragedy had struck me or someone I loved.

There was no objective reason for this despair, because my own personal and professional life was quiet. I kept my contract with society. Like any proper bourgeois citizen I worked, I paid taxes, I contributed to causes that I believed in, I fulfilled my family duties, I communed with friends. I roughly functioned as I was supposed to. But for reasons I could not understand, my days were getting arduous. I kept seeing signs of calamity. Something bad would happen. I was not prepared for it.

My dread manifested itself as emotional malaise, a lagging in the heart. I would wake up, and before starting my work I would read the newspapers and feel fatigued before my day. I would scan some headline – the government-owned Royal Nepal Airlines Corporation had decided to lease a B-767 jet from Lauda Air. The mind is relentless – it fixates on details, it charts out scenarios, it mulls over implications. In leasing the Lauda Air jet, the RNAC was ignoring a directive by the Parliament's Public Accounts Committee. To lease the jet, the RNAC would have to offer a bank guarantee worth over a million US dollars, and an advance of one month's rent. Could the country afford this?

Why should that matter so much to me?

You're using everything as an excuse to be miserable, I would chide myself. But then I would pick up the papers and read something else, and my reason would dissipate. I began to believe, irrationally, that if something good happened in government all my troubles would go. If I could be sure that the country would not fall apart, I could get on with my life. I even thought: Maybe if G.P. Koirala resigns as prime minister I can be happy again. I knew this was ridiculous. But since 1990 G.P. Koirala had been prime minister four times, and the country had spent his leadership years in despair.

Didn't he know that the royalists were counting on democracy to fail? Conservatives said, "You call the Congress a party of democrats? It's the private den of the Koirala clan!" I was never an ardent supporter of the Congress, but like most Nepalis, I had expected much from the party. But it, like the UML, had proved wanting. Not only that, the future of the political parties also looked bleak. Not having studied at the local college campuses, I had no feeling for the Congress or UML student unions, and thought the politicization of students a bad thing: Young people should study. Yet it was true that the students had forced the referendum of 1980. Without student activism in 1990, there would have been no democracy. But today's student activists seemed to act robotically on their party leaders' orders, flooding the streets for every last power struggle, but never pressuring them to take seriously the scores of honest issues that meanwhile lay ignored.

Amid the pell-mell of the days, I sometimes found it so hard to keep my mood up that I wondered if I should get a pill that would make me cheerful. Sometimes on my errands I passed the house of a psychiatrist. I did not know him well, but exchanged greetings with his wife and children when we met on the street. The doctor was successful – he drove a car – and appeared amiable and informal. He met patients at a clinic in his house. I wondered if I should go there. His patients, coming out of his gates, were skeletal teenage girls with their families or husbands, or elderly men and women being led by the hand, or couples glancing nervously around as they got on their motorcycles. They looked like people with genuine problems. What was my business among them?

I decided instead to take up meditation, and was lucky to find a teacher who moved through Tibetan Buddhist rituals lightly, instructing students on techniques to control the mind. I read doggedly cheerful self-help books that had become available of late in Kathmandu's bookshops. I also joined a gym where all the machines functioned, and hot water was available even in winter (when Kathmandu's houses were all dry) and I began to feel that maybe I would be all right.

The problem was, my happiness tended to last only as long as I was meditating or on the treadmill. When I went back to my room and began to write a story, the anxiety would return. Perhaps this was the problem – writing was so interior; I was stuck inside myself, being of no use to society. I spent too many hours alone, uselessly, before a computer in a room that got no sun.

When I did go out on work or errands, I would see the middle-class youth of Kathmandu all looking strangely ebullient, as though they did not know that their country was in crisis. Young women were baring belly buttons and enhancing their height with platform shoes; young men styled their hair and wore body-hugging T-shirts. I was glad that they were not despairing, and wondered if I could be like them – not indifferent to the problems around me, but able to be blithe, nevertheless, on a day-to-day basis.

It was, I knew, pathetic to be disabled the way I was. I was not, myself, politically engaged. I had watched the People's Movement from the side, and to be honest would not die if democracy were to fail. People do live in dictatorships of all kinds – perhaps they do not live fully, but they do live. And if, say, the king were to effect a royal coup, would I go to jail to bring back democracy, spend five, seven, ten, even eighteen years for this cause? Probably not. I felt passionately that the past decade had fostered many important, positive changes, but I couldn't always say what these were.

And sometimes positive things felt negative. For instance, groups were forming everywhere to organize their interests. Strikes had become increasingly common. In December 2000, hotel employees started demanding a mandatory 10 per cent service charge. Hotel owners refused them, and the government was slow in helping to negotiate a deal, and so all of Kathmandu's hotels closed on 11 December, forcing tourists to move into tents, private houses and makeshift accommodations. Cancellations poured in as a result, and many trekking companies went under.

My work slowed down as the rest of Kathmandu slowed down. I wrote for hours every day, yet I always felt that I was falling behind or forgetting something important. It took a lot just to start writing after reading the morning papers. Maybe reading newspapers was the problem. They disturbed me. On 22 December, the Parliament's Public Accounts Committee summoned G.P. Koirala as part of its investigation into possible corruption in the Lauda Air jet lease, and I was wearied just to read the prime minister taking a high moral tone in response.

It felt like trouble was coming from every direction. On the day after Christmas, in the year 2000, violence erupted in Kathmandu.

Bollywood actor Hrithik Roshan had apparently said something derogatory about Nepal. Students affiliated with the left parties were marching to the Indian embassy with a letter of protest when, inexplicably, riots broke out, at the end of which four people were killed and 180 injured. It was bizarre. Who cared what an Indian actor thought of us? Not anyone I knew. Yet, when I went out that afternoon, the streets were littered with stones and rubber tyres burned at the junctions, befouling the air. Similar riots took place around the country. By day's end, the government had blocked transmission of Indian TV channels. The Nepal Motion Picture Association and the Film Artists Association of Nepal had condemned Hrithik Roshan. The Gopi Krishna cinema hall declared that it would never screen his movies. Scores of irate press releases flooded the newspaper offices.

When the situation calmed, reports eventually emerged that the monarchist coterie of the king's youngest brother, Dhirendra Shah, had incited much of the rioting, alongside the Maoists.

So it wasn't just negative thinking. Malevolent forces were indeed coalescing against democracy, and the people – caught up in their small lives – would be left watching as their rights vanished one by one. After the Hrithik Roshan riots, I no longer wanted to live in Nepal. There were more riots the next day, and people of Indian origin were attacked. Walking on the streets, I became very conscious of looking like a hill Nepali; I suddenly loathed my mainstream features. Five hundred demonstrators and 80 police were injured by day's end. A Nepali actor, who had once offered to shoot the prime minister if he got orders from Dhirendra Shah, was one of the rioters arrested. The government announced a ban on all Hrithik Roshan movies. Hrithik Roshan, for his part, denied that he had said anything bad about Nepal – and protested that in fact he loved his Nepali servants. Scores of press releases were issued against him that day as well.

The riots stopped after it was verified, the next day, that Hrithik Roshan really hadn't said anything against Nepalis. So what had these riots been about? Nobody knew.

It was like that. We never knew where to look for trouble, and once we sighted signs, we never knew how to interpret them. We wanted to see all the bright, good things that democracy had brought us, but in

Kathmandu the party leaders were forever bickering. Was this just a part of democratic culture, and was it right? On 28 December, 56 of the Congress party's 113 members of Parliament started an inter-party no-confidence motion against G.P. Koirala. The motion was led by the Congress's "rebel" faction head, Krishna Prasad Bhattarai. G.P. Koirala survived the motion, but only by making party members vote in an open ballot, without secrecy. Was this right?

The opposition parties were no better. Nine leftist parties, not including the UML, called for a two-day nationwide general strike. Was *this* democratic culture? General strikes, or bandhs, had become common by now. This one took place on 1 and 2 January 2001 – that was how we in Kathmandu started the new year, with no traffic on the streets and most shops and businesses closed. The tourism industry was hit hard by cancellations. Businesses were all beginning to flounder.

One day I thought: It is not fair to say that I blame bad politics for my unhappiness; my happiness actually *is* derailed by bad politics. I was keeping up with my meditation and exercise. I had even decided to take seriously to gardening, to tend to flowers. I also longed to visit my teacher at his monastery atop a hill on the outskirts of Kathmandu where the winds carried the fragrance of wild grasses and sunshine. Then suddenly it would all seem pointless: Any effort to make a life here would prove futile; the country was heading for all-out war.

In mid January, G.P. Koirala won the informal approval of the king to create an Armed Police Force to fight the Maoists. He said the Nepal Police had not been armed adequately, nor trained enough, to lead the counter-insurgency. Even so, their brutality during the Romeo and Kilo Sierra 2 operations had turned vast swathes of rhe countryside against "bourgeois" parliamentary democracy. Wouldn't a more lethal police body just spawn more antagonism? G.P. Koirala thought not. He also hoped that by creating an Armed Police Force he could avoid deploying the Royal Nepal Army, whose first loyalties – many felt – were to the king and only then to the country. If the army got involved, democracy would be lost.

It wasn't just I who was controlled by public events; many of my friends, too, were in the same state. We were always looking for signs.

Signs that our own lives – our nice, orderly lives – might eventually be compromised by all this trouble.

Around mid January, the Maoists issued the "Prachanda Path" – their guiding principles. Prachanda – who many still believed did not even exist – was now said to be heading the CPN (Maoist). Surely this couldn't bode well. Some friends called, their voices thin with panic. I knew we shouldn't be so fraught, but the world was going badly, and I felt we had to keep watch.

On 5 February, opposition parties demanded G.P. Koirala's resignation over the Lauda Air lease scandal, and over the government's inability to curb Maoist violence. Undeterred, G.P. Koirala formed a 37-member cabinet two days later. Five people had just died in a Maoist attack in Surkhet, west Nepal, in an ambush on the Chief Justice's convoy. The Chief Justice had survived only by chance. Immediately upon the formation of G.P. Koirala's cabinet, three people were reported killed in a clash between the police and the Maoists. Barely a week later, the Maoists exploded a bomb in Achham, west Nepal, killing two children and injuring 11 adults.

Life in Kathmandu was also growing chaotic. The Federation of Nepalese Transport Entrepreneurs organized a two-day strike of public buses and microbuses in response to student demands for a 50 per cent discount on fares, and a recent ban on vehicles more than 20 years old. The streets swarmed with people walking to work.

The day after the strike, 12 February, was the first day of the 19th session of Parliament, the winter "working" session in which bills got passed. There was always a buzz at the start of these sessions. They were what the 1990 People's Movement had been for, after all. Thirteen bills were pending from previous parliamentary sessions, and two new bills were to be introduced. One was a bill granting women limited rights to inheritance and abortion, and the other a bill to govern political parties. The women's rights bill, in particular, was immensely urgent. It had finally been tabled after years of delay, and though it granted only limited rights to women (women could inherit parental property but had to return it to their families upon marriage; only married women could obtain abortions, that too with the consent of their husbands), these limited rights were great improvements on the current laws.

But the session was to end without a single full day of work. On the first day, as the Speaker of the House Taranath Ranabhat struck the gavel, opening the session, a UML member of Parliament took the floor and launched on a tirade against G.P. Koirala. Another UML MP called for a boycott of Parliament. After two and a half hours of debate, all of the UML MPs marched out of the House, followed by those of all the other opposition parties, almost half the total strength of Parliament.

On the winter session's second day, as soon as the Speaker opened the meeting, MPs from every opposition party except for the Nepal Sadbhavana Party circled the rostrum, chanting slogans against Prime Minister G.P. Koirala. The chanting lasted six minutes, after which the Speaker adjourned the meeting.

The following day the same thing happened. Members of Parliament even exchanged fisticuffs.

The boycott of Parliament continued for days. Wasn't the UML discrediting democracy? Weren't all the parties doing so? On 16 February, G.P. Koirala met with the opposition parties in an effort to negotiate a way past the stalemate, but they continued to demand that he resign, and this he would not do. Three days later, a brawl erupted in Parliament as the minister for culture, tourism and civil aviation tried to present a government defence of the Lauda Air jet lease. As he headed to the rostrum, a UML member of Parliament pulled him back. The two exchanged blows, then others joined in the fracas and the meeting was adjourned.

The dysfunction of Parliament was making the Maoists look justified in criticizing "bourgeois" parliamentary democracy. The political parties were behaving irresponsibly. And the bourgeoisie was beginning to want to be saved by the king . . . An old pattern was repeating itself.

King-watching became an obsession all over again. On 26 February, King Birendra went on a state visit to China, and while members of Parliament wrangled, the media focused, with much adulation, on this visit. Would the king please step in to save the country? That was the undertone of the press coverage.

There were also reports at this time that the Royal Nepal Airlines Corporation had suffered a loss of 80 million rupees during the month and a half of Lauda Air service.

*

And then it was March. The weather got balmy, the sky seemed to lift, and all of Kathmandu was swept by winds and breezes. In between my writing hours, I remembered to take time to appreciate the small beauties of the world. How pretty, the gentians, pinks, roadflax, daisies and asters in the garden of my family home. I met friends more often, and I even, now and then, had fun. I scoured bookstores and tried to find international magazines to read so that I could gain a larger picture of the world. But the newspapers were hard to put down.

The parliamentary session of 1 March lasted for less than five minutes. There was a two-minute session four days later.

There were more sinister signs. In a single day, 34 Nepalis, mostly children, died of measles in Kalikot District. On the same day, the army was posted to the major custom points along the Indian and Chinese borders to check cross-border smuggling. According to the Federation of Nepalese Chambers of Commerce and Industry, goods worth 10 billion rupees were smuggled through the Indian border every year, and one billion rupees worth of goods through the Chinese border. The police and the government's revenue administration had been unable to check smuggling, and so the army had been called in to take over civilian duties.

Hotel employees were threatening another strike, again demanding a 10 per cent service charge. Unable to negotiate a deal with them, the government declared the hotel industry an essential service, banning its employees from going on strike.

As the days progressed the news got more and more disheartening. On 11 March, cadres of the UML and the CPN (Maoist) held joint mass rallies in Liwang, the capital of Rolpa District and the heartland of the Maoist insurgency. Had the mainstream left lost its cadres to the Maoists? Or were they two faces of the same coin? Twenty-four children died of an epidemic in Humla District on the same day. A report came out saying that there were 77,000 child labourers in Nepal. The editor of the Maoist affiliated newspaper *Janaadesh* was released from jail after a two-year incarceration, only to be arrested again. The lease of the Lauda Air jet was still under investigation by the Public Accounts Committee.

If things got bad enough, a strongman would step up, asking us to trade in our freedom for his efficiency. That was how democracy usually ended. King Birendra would effect a royal coup. Suddenly, everyone was saying he would take over. Many were saying he should.

Some people, of course, were able to see what they wanted to see and ignore what they didn't want to see, the way tourists who come to Nepal look at terraced fields and see their beauty but remain blind to the hard labour they extract from tillers. Some of my friends felt confident that democracy could not be defeated. The king just couldn't take over: democracy was too deeply rooted by now. Others just didn't care one way or the other. Some laughed as they heard that the Maoist leader of area no. 2, cell no. 10 of Kalikot District had ordered villagers to support the insurgency by killing dogs, because their barking alerted security forces to the Maoists' movement. "Anyone who defies this appeal will be severely punished by the people's government according to the people's decision," the Maoist newspaper reported.

April was a harrowing month, crowded with vague, unfocused anxieties. I slept heavily, and my dreaming was dense.

On 2 April, more than 500 Maoists armed with rifles, bombs and grenades attacked two police outposts in Rukum and Dolakha Districts, killing 35 policemen and abducting 24 more. Seven Maoists were also killed in battle. This was the single bloodiest incident since the insurgency started. In Kathmandu, bombs went off at the houses of a Congress member of Parliament and a former inspector general of police. The next day, Maoists looted arms and cash in several places.

The day after, Congress leaders ended Parliament's winter session. Not a single bill had been tabled; not a single full discussion had taken place. The final meeting of the session lasted two minutes. Though they had done nothing during the session, the members of Parliament were paid 6.2 million rupees, plus allowance and transport fares. This was the last session of Parliament the country was to have.

At about this time, a conspiracy theory that the palace was working in tandem with the Maoists gained ground. The 4 April newspaper reports had it that Maoist leaders Prachanda and Baburam Bhattarai had met a royalist member of the Upper House, Ramesh Nath Pandey.

Why was the palace meeting the Maoists? Was the palace's shadowy "underground gang" supporting the insurgency to eventually justify a royal coup in the name of counter-insurgency?

Yet if the royalists and the Maoists were succeeding in squeezing out democracy, it was because the party leaders were doing their bit to discredit themselves. On 4 April, again, the student wing of the splintered-off communist party, ML, called for a chakka jam, a shutdown of traffic. Two days later the same student group effected a nationwide general strike, and all schools, industries and businesses were forced shut. Meanwhile, a wave of panic was sweeping over the bourgeoisie. The Maoists were winning! On 8 April newspapers reported 80 people dead in the past six days of the insurgency and counter-insurgency. The police had started deserting their remote posts. On 9, 10 and 11 April, the Maoists held elections for the representatives of each of Rolpa District's 51 Village Development Committees, which they had renamed "Village People's Committees". They planned to form republican governments in their strongholds.

G.P. Koirala was bent on suppressing the Maoists by force. On 12 April, the king re-promulgated the Armed Police Force Ordinance. Three days later, the Maoists looted nine million rupees from a Jhapa District bank. The UML and the other left parties, meanwhile, continued trying to unseat the prime minister. At 9 a.m. on 16 April, leftist activists formed a human roadblock along Putali Sadak, the main road to Singha Durbar, to prevent the prime minister from reaching his office. It turned out he had entered Singha Durbar an hour earlier. Enraged, the leftist activists burned 12 government vehicles in a rampage.

Three days later, they held a mass rally demanding that G.P. Koirala step down.

G.P. Koirala had decided, by then, that even the Armed Police Force were not up to quelling the Maoist insurgency; the army had to be mobilized. On 18 April, he ordered the deployment of both the Armed Police Force and the Royal Nepal Army for the first phase of the Integrated Security and Development Programme, a newly developed "hearts and minds" operation targeted at Maoist strongholds. In so doing, G.P. Koirala came smack up against the army's resistance to civilian command. Two days later, the Chief of the Army Staff General Prajwal-la Sumshere Jung Bahadur Rana publicly asked all the major political parties to reach a national consensus on the deployment of the army. This was unheard of. Was he questioning the Defence Council's orders?

This unleashed a storm. Or yet another storm. Kathmandu was once again shaken by rumours of a royal coup. Even G.P. Koirala got skittish. He skipped Kathmandu without informing anyone, and went to his hometown Biratnagar, near the Indian border. Word had it that he wanted to be able to evade arrest should the army come for him, as they had decades earlier for his brother B.P. The UML and other left parties should have helped the prime minister to stare down the army; instead they announced another round of public protests against him. The UML General Secretary Madhav Kumar Nepal vowed to disrupt the next session of Parliament if G.P. Koirala had not resigned by then.

In the middle of all this, King Birendra received, from the Supreme Court, a bill that he had sent them for an opinion. The bench had unanimously found it in violation of the constitution. The bill had been passed on 26 July 2000 as the 6th amendment to the 1964 citizenship act. It allowed less xenophobic standards for establishing citizenship, and granted citizenship to men married to Nepali women (previously, only women married to Nepali men were allowed citizenship). It was the first bill that the king had not ratified immediately, as he was supposed to, but sent to the Supreme Court for an opinion. Now he ratified it, but with the Supreme Court's opinion attached. The king, too, was playing politics.

Meanwhile, 100 policemen had deserted their stations in remote outposts, and armed Maoists had staged an attack in Sunsari District in the east. There was always one thing or another, if it wasn't one thing it was another. On 26 April, the Centre for the Investigation of the Abuse of Authority ordered the arrests of a former executive chairman and a former board chairman of the Royal Nepal Airlines Corporation. A Congress party member, a former minister of tourism and civil aviation, was asked to hand in his passport. The Congress party immediately deemed the investigation to be politically biased.

The UML crowed. The same day, left parties carried out a chakka jam, in the evening rush hour, demanding G.P. Koirala's resignation. This was followed by a blackout. Over the weekend of the 28th and

29th, leftist activists patrolled the streets and stopped government vehicles, including the car being used by the Speaker of the House.

The prospect of a coup was looming large, but the political parties were too shortsighted to see it. April ended with the deployment of the army to Rukum, Rolpa, Jajarkor Salyan, Gorkha, Pyuthan and Kalikot Districts as the beginning of the Integrated Security and Development Programme. Army troops would reach the districts in two weeks to get the security situation under control. In the second phase of the programme, the army would be deployed to Kavrepalanchowk, Ramechhap, Lamjung, Dhading, Dolpa, Jumla, Sindhupalchowk, Sindhuli, Nuwakot, Dailekh Baglung, Myagdi, Tanahun and Achham Districts, where it would build infrastructure like roads and bridges. In the third phase, there would be long-term work to alleviate rural poverty. The Integrated Security and Development Programme seemed to be handing the development responsibility of the civilian government to the army. But the political parties were not concerned. They only wanted G.P. Koirala's resignation.

Despite all this, sometimes for brief periods I thought everything would be all right. I would attend a lecture by an articulate intellectual, and suddenly see some light. A journalist would report bravely on what was happening in rural Nepal. A civil rights activist would say something pithy. One or another Nepali would achieve international success, or someone very young would climb Mt Everest. One day I went to Kathmandu's zoo and saw that the animals were kept in conditions that were more or less humane. I watched a particularly effusive chimpanzee and felt my sense of normality restored.

But then my view would grow cloudy again. On 2 May, the Centre for the Investigation of the Abuse of Authority asked G.P. Koirala for clarification of his role in the Lauda Air jet deal. By this time, even his own party members wanted him to resign. But G.P. sent back a three-page letter challenging the Centre's jurisdiction to question what had been a cabinet decision. The head of the rebel faction within the Congress, Krishna Prasad Bhattarai, publicly demanded G.P.'s resignation. G.P. shot back: "Bhattarai's job is to ask for my resignation; mine is to refuse the same." Even the deputy prime minister and the foreign minister suggested that he resign, but at 78, G.P. wanted to keep holding on to power.

And I saw that terrible things would happen any day now, as the Congress leaders bickered among themselves – something nobody was prepared for – and everyone's lives would be given up to naked survival.

On 8 May, scores of members of a Maoist-affiliated student body, the All-Nepal National Federation of Student Unions (Revolutionary) – ANNFSU (Revolutionary) – attacked two "bourgeois" private schools in Kathmandu, destroying their computers and photocopy machines and setting the furniture on fire. Brandishing khukuris and iron rods, the assailants demanded that the schools lower their fees, and – because the schools' principals were of Indian origin – they chanted slogans against India. One million children all over the country stayed at home as the Public and Boarding Schools Organization decided to shut down all 8,000 of its member schools for three days in protest.

The news was, meanwhile, filled with the deployment of the army in the Maoist-affected districts. Gorkha District, home to the Shah kings, was also home to Maoist leader Baburam Bhattarai. It was, we now learned, to be a model district for the Integrated Security and Development Programme. The army would carry out 40 development projects here, constructing bridges and irrigation canals, implementing drinking water and electricity schemes, and supporting the collection, processing and distribution of herbs.

The Maoists carried on unhindered, skirting the army. On 13 May, three Maoists were killed in Surkhet District, two of them women. Five days later, the Maoists looted weapons in Kaski and Parbat Districts. On 19 May, the Maoists killed three policemen and injured 11 civilians in an attack in Okhaldhunga District, in the east. On the same day, their cadres held a mass rally in Bhawang village in Rolpa District, and announced the formation of their "People's Local Government" throughout the district. This took place just weeks before army troops were due to arrive there. The People's Local Government consisted of a 10-member committee, including members of the ethnic rights group Magarat Mukti Morcha, members of the Dalit rights group Dallit Mukri Morcha, local intelligentsia, women and Maoists area commanders. The Maoists vowed to form similar governments in Rukum, Salyan, Jajarkot Kalikot and Gorkha Districts, establishing a parallel government.

*

In Kathmandu, G.P. Koirala resigned as the general secretary of the Congress, only to appoint a relative. He also appointed two other relatives to the party's Central Working Committee.

Word had it that the Centre for the Investigation of the Abuse of Authority was going to announce any day now its findings on the Lauda Air jet deal. Before that could happen, though, the Public Accounts Committee of Parliament announced that it was charging both the Congress's and the UML's former ministers of tourism and civil aviation with corruption in another deal involving Royal Nepal Airlines Corporation's lease of a China Southwest Airlines jet. The UML suddenly lost steam; its leaders denounced this decision, though feebly. Days later, the Centre for the Investigatien of the Abuse of Authority announced that it was prosecuting 10 people in connection with the Lauda Air jet lease, including two foreign Lauda Air executives based in Italy and Austria. No mention was made of G.P. Koirala's culpability. I found myself wondering whether these prosecutions were politically motivated.

The UML rallied back and announced a three-day-long nationwide bandh from 27 to 29 May, demanding – what else – G.P. Koirala's resignation. No taxis or tempos or buses or cars ran for these three days, no shops or offices or businesses opened. So zealous were party activists in enforcing the shutdown that even the few vegetable vendors who defied other bandhs decided not to risk it this time.

During one-day bandhs, people generally cleaned their houses or caught up with chores. This time, though, they lost all will. They sat and watched Hindi movies and tele-serials. I did the same. On the first night I watched a ghost movie, though I didn't usually like those. I watched religious programmes the next morning, and a gleaming guru told me to keep Krishna in my heart. That day, two patients died in hospital because leftist activists had obstructed ambulances. On the third day, there was unrest throughout the country as people tried to defy the bandh. More than 600 people – and a line of cars – took out a rally in Kathmandu in protest. Most people, though, just sat home and watched soap operas, police shows, sitcoms, docu-dramas – anything that was on.

One day sometime after that, I got into a conversation with the manager of my gym about Upstairs, a jazz bar that the man frequented.

I had been meaning to go there for years, I said. I'm there every night after nine, he told me as he did his abs. He also talked about a resort not far from Kathmandu where he had done some bungee jumping: "It used to be the second highest jump in the world, but the highest closed down, so now this is the highest." Moving on to bench presses he said he had attended a fancy dress party at which two men had shown up in drag. "One really looked like a woman," he grinned.

So surprised was I by all the fun he was having that all I could say was, "Wow. That's great. That's cool." I did not begrudge him his fun; I knew, after all, that I would not feel any more lighthearted dressing up for parties, or jumping off bridges with my life on a rope, or even dropping by a bar to hear jazz. But the man's appetite for fun got me thinking.

Later, at Himalayan Java, a hip new cafe in Thamel, I looked at the young people of Kathmandu – a blithe, carefree generation – and found that I did resent them. The cafe was filled with people of my economic class – the Kathmandu bourgeoisie, who were unaffected, in any real sense, by the failure of democratic politics. They got on with their lives despite it all. Close to me sat a young woman in a halter top, bell bottoms and platform heels, a navel ring showing on her sleek stomach. Her face was frozen in a come-hither expression as she listened to the young man across her. He had gelled, spiked hair, and earrings, and sleek clothes offset by a big-buckled belt and bulky Doc Martens.

Why were these young people being so relentlessly hip? No, this was good. I sipped my iced mocha, thinking, here is a whole country writhing with youthful energy. There is an age, isn't there, at which one wants to smash all that is traditional, at which one wants to destroy the old and usher in the new? The youth were following the paths open to them. Those in Kathmandu were mimicking MTV VJs, and those in the villages were joining the Maoists. They were both, in their own ways, trying to force change.

Meanwhile, Amnesty International had begun to criticize the country's police for execution, torture and disappearances, and the Maoists for passing death sentences in their "People's Courts" and recruiting children into their ranks. Nepal could soon have one of the highest rates of human rights atrocities. Panicked, more and more of the bourgeoisie began hoping that the king would do something, anything, to restore order. Most of the royal family was unpopular, but about King Birendra Bir Bikram Shah the bourgeoisie had always been addle-headed. He was such a pleasant fellow. Because he now did so little as a constitutional monarch, he committed few mistakes. Because he controlled so few public funds, he was not tainted by money. Because he spoke so little, what he said sounded sage. He shone in comparison to the coarse, bungling party leaders of the day.

Eternal dynasty. The hows and whens of a royal coup became topics of endless conjecture in Kathmandu. All of us were convinced that it would happen. It almost seemed like there was a Panchayat propaganda hex on us. Our political parties would muddle endlessly, and the king would return to power, claiming that it was for our own good. We did not want a royal coup to happen. But we felt helpless to prevent it. And so all we did, when we heard a fresh round of rumours, was to hunker down and brace for the worst.

On 30 May, just as the Lauda Air jet lease hearings began at the Patan appellate court, the jet in question flew to Bangkok for routine repairs, never to return.

The next day, the Maoists set off a bomb at an offset press in Kathmandu, accusing the press of printing "obscene materials". No one could figure out exactly what printed material had angered them so much. Local UML leaders in faraway Musikot village, in Rukurn District, boycotted the chief district officer's all-party meeting on the army's Integrated Security and Development Programme. The country was in a shambles.

By now my interest in my work was petering out. It seemed to me that fiction couldn't keep up with our reality. Or I did not know how to make it. My friends were beginning to worry about their career prospects. Non-government organizations could no longer work in the villages without the fear of local Maoists turning against them. The cancellations in the tourism industry were affecting not just Kathmandu hotels and travel agencies, but also village inns and lodges. Businesses were closing. Artists were unable to find clients. The garment industry had declined in the last year, though the year before it had grown by 30 per cent. Eight people died of gastroenteritis in far-western Jajarkot on the last day of May.

As I walked through the Kathmandu streets late that afternoon, it occurred to me that all I ever did any more was worry. And if the way that Kathmandu's hip youth ignored their country's troubles helped nothing, neither did my anxious and burdened attitude. I thought: My life has become so aimless, so desultory, that I feel a compulsion to link it to larger, more compelling collective narratives. I am infusing my experience with an importance that is otherwise absent. I am trying to make my life interesting by linking it to bad politics. I had to do something to lift my mood. I might start by doing something small, I thought, something different to alter my days, or at least this day, or the next few hours. Perhaps being happy required nothing much: no marches or demonstrations, no political action, no grand gestures. Our lives are small, our problems are small, and maybe their solutions are also small.

On a whim I veered into a tandoori restaurant where my friends and I used to go when we were all feeling more upbeat about life. It wasn't the kind of place where women went alone – for a price the restaurant arranged girls. Most of the clients that day were male, though at a few tables couples were huddled over tea and snacks. I phoned a friend from there and said I'd come over with some food, and he said all right, so it was a date. I ordered a half tandoori chicken and naan, saag paneer and daal, and asked the waiter to home-pack it.

As I waited, my eyes fell on a couple at a corner table. The man was much older than his partner, who was another one of those image-conscious young women. She was wearing tight black pants and long, sharp heels. Her face was heavily made up. She could not have been more than 18. The man was in his 40s, the age when men bore of their wives. I wondered whether he was her lover or client.

As I looked on, something about the man struck me. The width of his back. He was wearing a chequered jacket, and was stooping slightly. I recognized the stoop. He had the same frizzy hair as the psychiatrist I had thought of visiting months ago. Most of his clients were young women who wore defeated expressions. This woman was not like that. She was the kind of woman that even insecure women warm to: bright, unapologetic about her youth, happy to claim her due. The man, leaning into her, wiped away a crumb on her lips. She laughed in a way that was meant to be both girlish and sexy.

When my home-pack order came, I paid and went outside, suddenly feeling confused. Evening was falling, and the first few cars had turned on their sidelights. My friend's street was blasted through with the sounds of car horns. The gap-toothed unevenness of the sidewalk frazzled me as I pushed through the crowds.

I did not enjoy dinner that night. My friend was going through a bad patch, and we talked awhile about the difficulty of finding work, and then we gossiped about common friends. We had dinner, then put on the television news. Once the headlines were over, my friend told me a joke that he'd heard that day.

"It's a little indecent," he said, slightly embarrassed. Then he went on. "There was a man on a crowded bus, and he was standing with his hands like this." He cupped both palms, and said, "No matter how much the bus jolted him around, the man wouldn't change the position of his hands." He smiled in anticipation of the joke. After a while, the people around began to notice this. Every time the bus stopped, all the passengers would reach for a railing or a chair back to hold onto, but this man would just balance himself with his legs, never changing the position of his hands.

Now one of the passengers on the bus was a policeman, who thought, this man is a Maoist. He's got explosives in his shirt, and the detonator is in his hands. Otherwise why would he keep from touching anything even when the bus turns?

So the policeman followed the man when he got off the bus. Even on the streets, the man kept his hands cupped. The policeman was sure he had found a Maoist. As they neared a police post, he arrested the man.

"But even after he was arrested, the man wouldn't stop cupping his hands. The police thought, This man is a hardened Maoist, we'll have to beat him into confessing. So they took him straight to the investigation cell. But before beating him, the inspector said, Now we're going to beat you, but you can avoid that if you just tell us why you're holding your hands like that."

My friend's face was flushed with glee. I was smiling along expectantly. Holding up cupped hands, my friend said, "And then the man said, Sir, this is the measurement of my wife's breasts. I was going to buy her a bra!"

My friend burst out laughing, and I also laughed, because it was silly, the man walking around with cupped hands. But my friend found it unusually funny. "It was just a man going to buy a bra!" he hooted, and began laughing so hard that he had to bend over to be able to breathe.

He was still bent over, his shoulders shaking, when I stopped laughing, and I looked at him, doubled up, convulsing, making a sound halfway between a sob and a squeal, and I realized that I hadn't seen him laugh this hard for a long time. He had been low for months on end now. When he lifted his head again he was still laughing, and his lips were stretched thin, his teeth were showing and his eyes were sparkling with tears. He looked like someone I didn't know. "A bra!" he sputtered and bent over once more.

I laughed, uncertainly, to keep him company, but I was also thinking – for my mind was merciless – why was he laughing so hard at a joke that wasn't that funny? How rare laughter had become in our lives.

For his sake I should have laughed longer, but my breath would not carry false emotion. My mirth died completely.

"A bra," my friend said again, weakly, then he finally sat up, and for a while we remained as we were, both facing the television, which was on sports news. My friend wiped away some tears and I smiled at him, but inside, I was pierced with sadness at the meagreness of happiness in our days.

I stayed on a while, as my friend made a few good-humoured remarks about the sports news. But the sadness inside me kept growing till I could no longer bear to stay on. "I'll go," I said, and I left him still watching the news.

Barely 24 hours after this, King Birendra Bir Bikram Shah and his entire family succumbed to the massacre at the royal palace.

FROM GODDESS TO MORTAL

Rashmila Shakya and Scott Berry

Rashmila Shakya was Royal Kumari from 1984–91. Having graduated with a Bachelor of Information Technology degree, she works for a private company as a software developer.

Scott Berry is an American author. His notable works include *A Stranger in Tibet*.

The Living Goddess Kumari is a Supreme Goddess... and She does not undergo any lessons or teaching. She also does not have any playmates. Her caretakers keep a watch on her day and night.

From, Siddhi B. Ranjitkar:
Kumari, the Virgin Goddess

Very little light comes in through the traditional, carved wooden windows of my bedroom in the morning. They face in towards the courtyard, so there is little sound either, even though the square outside by this time is full of the honking of early morning rickshaws, the swish of the long brooms of the sweepers, the bells of the temples and the chanting of priests. I hear only the vaguest echoes of all this, as I see only the palest reminder of the sun. But no one ever has to wake me up. I look forward to opening my eyes every morning and seeing all my dolls looking at me, for I have arranged them around my bed the night before.

Once I have greeted them, I make the long trip to my own bathroom, around a corner, up the steep stairs to the next floor, and down a passageway, where I find my red towel and red toothbrush. Already others are stirring, and I know that when I get back to my room Fufu, or "father's sister" (whom I think of as my mother, even though she really is my father's sister), or possibly one of her daughters Durga or Sita (usually Sita) will be there to help me dress and put up my hair. Dressing is something I can do well enough by myself as long as it is not a festival day, but I enjoy having my hair combed out and put up, even though it is pulled so tight that sometimes it hurts.

"Hold still, please Dyah Meiju," she warns as she pulls it up into a bun on the top of my head, and then puts a red ribbon around it. "Now for your *aajha*." She carefully applies kohl around my eyes, and then in two sweeping curves to above my ears. I will not be able to rub my eyes all day. With her right thumb she puts a red tika on my forehead between my eyes, and I am set up for the day.

By now it is breakfast time. I always enjoy breakfast because it is a meal I can share with others. Meals including cooked rice are considered special, so I must eat them alone on a raised platform in my own kitchen in the back of the palace. Since breakfast is only tea and deep-fried bread there is no restriction on where I have to be or whom I have to eat it with, and as a result it is an informal and enjoyable affair.

"Dyah Meiju, your teacher is here!" a woman's voice calls. That must mean it is 9 o'clock, for the teacher arrives from the school next door at that time. After finishing my tea, I go back to my room where he is waiting. The building is now astir with children getting ready to go to school.

"Dyah Meiju, the priest from the Taleju Temple has arrived," comes another voice. "It is time for *Nitya* Puja." This is always done around 9 a.m., but since the exact time is not important, sometimes – if the priest is late – my lesson can begin before the puja.

"Which one?" I call out.

"The young one." The one who gets on my nerves. The Acahju, or chief priest, is a dignified, elderly man who commands respect by his manner, so that there is no question of any nonsense with him. But the younger, stouter, priest, seems always to be irritated about something, and frequently loses his temper with everyone, except me of course.

I see one of my playmates hurrying by in her school uniform, and point to the stairway where the priest will leave his puja bag after taking out the items he will need. She smiles back in understanding. Not only does she have to do whatever I want her to do, but this is one of our favourite, often repeated, games. As soon as the priest is in the puja room with me, she will hide his bag.

I go into the room called the Singhasan, the one with the golden window looking out onto the street, and sit on my golden throne with seven nagas protecting me while the priest sits on the floor offering red powder, rice and flowers to my feet, and lighting small lamps, as he worships the human embodiment of the goddess Taleju for about fifteen minutes. This puja also includes the indistinct chanting of secret *mantras* and the performance of secret *mudras*, or hand gestures. Since not even I am allowed to know these, he covers his hands while performing the gestures. He will not offer me a tika, for he is allowed only to touch my feet. Only the women of the family are allowed to give me tika. Though the same ceremony is repeated every morning, and I no longer pay attention, I never get bored or fidgety, but simply sit there in my stony-faced way. I know that I am a goddess, that this is the way a goddess is treated and this is the way she behaves.

I know that I probably won't start my lesson now, for this is the time when worshippers usually come, and for the past week the same woman and her son have been here. The boy is about 6 or 7 years old, perhaps 2 or 3 years younger than I am, but he has still not begun to speak, and his mother has brought him every day in the hopes that I will be able to cure him. Most of my devotees have children with problems, particularly illnesses, so that I know I am important to children. I also have no doubt that I will be able to help him. Of course the mother does not ask me directly for what she wants, nor do I speak directly to her. Instead I remain seated on my golden throne while she pours a small amount of water from her left hand over my feet into her right hand then drinks it. She repeats this, but this time offers the water to the boy who also drinks it. In the distance I hear with satisfaction the priest fuming and shouting about thieves and missing puja bags, but I force myself to concentrate on the task at hand, for it is my duty to try to help the boy to speak.

Since it is a weekday, I hope that there will be no more worshippers so that I can finally begin my lesson. The teacher has only been coming for the last year, and every day our lesson is interrupted in this way, but I have discovered that learning can be fun, and I want to catch up with my playmates, all of whom go to the Nawa Adahrsa School next door in Basantapur Square. "One more worshipper this morning, Dyah Meiju," says Taba, the man whom I regard as my father.

Actually I am ready for this one because the family of the supplicant has paid for everything necessary for a *chemma*, or forgiveness puja and Taba has made all the arrangements, having first asked me if there was anything I would particularly like. A pale and ill-looking young man comes into the room with his family and looks at me hopefully. I know that I will be able to cure him if I want to, though since he is not a child, I am not particularly interested.

It seems he has unwittingly got himself into trouble with me. It is not the first time I have seen him, for he is a journalist who came to do a story about Kumari. It happens all the time and I always enjoy these visits because I get to hear yet again the stories about the Goddess Taleju and King Jayaprakesh Malla, or of Prithvi Narayan Shah dreaming of Kumari just before he conquered the Kathmandu valley. It is not that this young man actually wrote anything bad or untrue, but when the article appeared, his picture was inset above mine. Although I was entirely unaware of this, it was apparently enough of an insult to Taleju Bhawani as personified in me, that the poor man began vomiting blood. This puja is to ask my forgiveness so that he will be cured. No wonder he looks anxious. If I do not accept his puja, I can make things even worse for him. I have heard the story of an elderly priest who offered water to my predecessor, who stared hard at him before condescending to drink it. He died on the way home.

I am first offered chocolates and the red toy car I had requested. More importantly I am offered *sagun*, which consists of a boiled egg and a dried fish which are placed in my left hand, and a silver tumbler of *raksi*, the strong distilled spirit of the valley, which I hold in my right. Each of these items I touch to my lips to show that I accept the offering, to the visible relief of the young journalist. The *raksi* burns my lips pleasantly.

There was no question of my not accepting his puja. Though children are the only ones I really care about, I have no hostile feeling towards anyone, not even the irritable priest whom I enjoy tormenting, and am happy enough for him to be cured.

At last my long-delayed lesson can begin, though by now it is nearly 10 o'clock, the time when my teacher always leaves. I go back to my bedroom and sit opposite him on the floor with a small table between us. He is a very old man, tall and thin with thick, black-rimmed glasses that seem almost an extension of his black Nepali *topi*. Like the priest, he is dressed in the traditional Nepali *Daura Surwal*. He is not very energetic, or, it would seem, very interested in the lesson. But in a way I am lucky to have him at all for there is a belief that it can serve no purpose to attempt to teach a goddess, who by definition already knows everything. There is an even more discouraging legend that anyone who tries to teach a Kumari will die. But he does not seem afraid. In fact he hardly seems conscious.

"Not much time," he grumbles in Nepali in his thin, wheezy voice. My families (both of them) speak to me in our Newari language of the Kathmandu valley. Since I had started Kindergarten before becoming Kumari I had made a start in Nepali, as all school children do. The old man is a Nepali teacher, and this cannot help but be useful to me, but he is expected to teach me other subjects like English and Mathematics as well. "Would Dyah Meiju be so good as to multiply 17 times 14?" he asks.

"Two hundred and thirty-eight," I answer mechanically; hoping he will come up with something a little more interesting. His mathematics lessons consist of making me memorise the multiplication tables up to 22. My eldest sister Pramila, who visits me occasionally, but not often enough that I feel really close to her, says he should be giving me word problems, whatever they are.

"Yes, well that's good," he mumbles, sounding as if he is about to fall asleep. "Now, would Dyah Meiju kindly copy out these English words?"

I open my notebook and copy out a few words, taking special care to reproduce them exactly in all their elegance, for the letters are beautiful and exotic to me. "What do they mean?" I ask. He looks blank. "Are they really words? What do they sound like?"

"Time enough for that when Dyah Meiju has learned how to copy them. Mustn't try to run before we can walk." Even at nine years old,

I suspect that he will not tell me because he just does not know.

Outside in the distance, a school bell rings. "Time to go," he mutters struggling to his feet and forgetting to give me any homework. It hardly matters, for we will probably be interrupted again tomorrow.

My duties, such as they are have finished for the day, and I go in search of playmates. The house is large, made up of many long narrow rooms and passages much larger than the house where I spent my first three years, though I have no real memories of that. There are many children here, for Taba has two married sons and plenty of nieces and nephews. Enough of them are my own age that it should not be difficult to find someone to play with, and in fact until a year or two ago it never was. But in recent years they are all at the Nawa Adahrsa School, the one my teacher comes from.

Going from one long room to another, then down several passage-ways, and finding no one but my "big brothers" Gautam Dai and Ma-hendra Dai,[1] their wives and sisters, all of whom are much too old to play with, I decide to play with my dolls. I have a large collection. Some are dolls that have been bought in stores and have been offered to me by grateful devotees whose children I have cured, others are rag-dolls I make from bits of red cloth and discard when I am finished with them.

What should I do? Perhaps make a sari or a dress for one of them, or should I set them up in family groups? I decide on the latter and begin dragging them out of my room and setting them up in the side room that runs from the back to the Singhasan puja room, on the op-posite side of the courtyard from the kitchens. Soon I have a big pile, and then I begin sorting them out so that some can be eating, others cooking, others still sewing and gossiping. Most are girls, blonde and pale-skinned, though I do give them red tikas to make them seem more familiar. Their eyes shut when I lay them down. Sometimes one of the girls has to pretend to be a father doll, but there are plenty of babies, including one which never leaves its basket, and a couple of rag dolls. I bring out my little stove that another worshipper has given me, and all its miniature pots and pans. Everything works, and I have even learned how to light the little coal stove. Taba and Fufu have not been happy

---

[1] *Dai* is Nepal for elder brother.

about this, fearing that I might hurt myself, but seeing that I was careful, they have let me go ahead with it.

"The sun is in the right place. Perhaps Dyah Meiju would like to have her bath now." It is Sita, one of my "sisters" who usually helps me with my bath. Actually Dyah Meiju would rather play with her dolls just now, but I know that at this time of year, if I don't have my bath when the sun is shining in the window, it will be cold and unpleasant, so I reluctantly leave my dolls and follow Sita to my bathroom. The winter sun streams in the window which overlooks the back courtyard with its quacking ducks. No one but the family has access to this courtyard. It wouldn't do to have Kumari drying herself in the sun where she can be seen by just anyone.

The water in the bucket has been heated, and it feels pleasant as it is poured over me. I could manage my bath by myself, but no one has ever suggested this, and besides, I will need help with my hair and eye make-up when it is finished. It feels good afterwards to stand in the sun wrapped in my red towel until it is time to get dressed and go to lunch. This time, since I will be eating rice, I go and sit on my solitary platform in my own kitchen, while Fufu places a tray of *dal-bhat-tarkari* in front of me. This consists of hot cooked rice, potato curry, a mixed vegetable curry, and (what my eyes have searched for first) a spicy pickle made from tomatoes. "I'm glad to see that there is tomato *achar* today," I say a trifle haughtily and self-righteously.

"Oh yes, Dyah Meiju has no need to worry."

Last week I was served a lunch with no tomato achar, and refused to eat it until Fufu had gone out, bought tomatoes, and cooked them up into *achar*. I simply sat there until two o'clock when I finally got what I wanted. Dyah Meiju always gets what she wants.

The long afternoon stretches before me. My playmates are still in school, and I drift first to the front windows where I look out onto Durbar Square and the people passing by. There are rickshaw drivers hoping to get a foreign tourist, ragged, barelegged porters smoking a cigarette after carrying a heavy load, another staggering under the weight of a refrigerator strapped to his forehead. A Newari farmer carries vegetables in two baskets suspended from a carrying pole across his shoulders. Country women in colourful red saris are sitting on the steep steps of the Narayan Temple gossiping, while the occasional taxi blasts on its horn. Children my own age run around, some in blue or maroon school uniforms, others in rags. A little drama unfolds as a man on a motorbike almost knocks a man off a bicycle, but it all ends in smiles and laughter. A man with a tie and a briefcase, making his Nepali topi look incongruous, hurries across the space in front of my temple like his life depended on it. What can be so important? A woman I recognise is trying to sell little bags and necklaces to the groups of foreigners coming in my direction, and is using her little boy to get their sympathy.

My view is limited since I am not supposed to stick my head right out, but though I can see only the white Ghadi Bhaitak part of the Palace, where the King and his family wait for me on the first day of Indra Jatra, and three temples, it is really the people who interest me. Some are richer than me, most are not nearly so well off, but they all have something I do not have: they can all go where they want. I wonder, with no way at all of solving the puzzle, whether the ragged urchins playing tag have more interesting lives than mine. I try to imagine myself in their place, but it is just too hard.

I shrink back a little from the window so the foreigners will not be able to see me. In a few minutes, after the trinket lady finishes with them, I will probably have to show myself to them from the window in the back. My eyes go up to the window of another temple across the square where I see the lord Shiva with his arm around his wife Parvati. Like me they are looking out of a window and down at the square, but they are even more trapped, for as wooden images they cannot even leave their window. Then I hear one of the women of the house call, "Dyah Meiju, some foreign visitors."

It is not an order, for no one orders a goddess around, but I understand that because they will leave an offering on a small pillar in the courtyard, I have a duty to show myself at the window, just as I understand that I have a duty not to smile when I am there. Sometimes it is a bother, if I am playing with my dolls or dancing with the other children, but just now I don't mind. If I am not doing anything else and I like the looks of them, I might appear even if they have not left an offering.

Going back through the room where my dolls are still as I left them, I put on my serious Kumari face and step to the window. Sometimes the foreigners applaud, some of them do Namaste, and some just stand and stare. Sometimes I stay longer than others, depending on how curious I am. Where are they from, I wonder? Why are the women dressed so strangely? Is their hair that way naturally? Most of them, men and women, have cameras around their necks, but I know that if they point them at me I should step back. I wonder what country they are from, and wish I could just shout down and ask their Nepali guide. What is that country of theirs like? Would my teacher know if I asked him? Will I ever visit it? And what do they make of me? Don't they have goddesses in their own land? Wouldn't it be nice if I could just ask them whatever I wanted? Of all of them, the ones I like most are the ones I am told come from a country called Japan. They always applaud when I come to the window, and something in the way they look at me makes me think they understand me.

A little hesitantly, and without any real hope, I look down to one corner of the courtyard. No, as I expected they are not there. It has been about two years since I have seen them, two foreign girls a little older than me, dressed like Nepali girls in grubby *salwar khameez*. For a long time they came every day, sitting and looking up at me and smiling when I appeared for the tourists. Then one day when no one else was around, I called down to them that I had a ball, and why didn't we play? Of course they could not actually come in since they were not Hindu, but Taba, Gautam and Mahendra decided they could come to the bottom of the steps while I stood at the top and we could throw the ball back and forth. Sometimes they threw me sweets, and at others I would throw down some of my offerings. We could even talk since they spoke some Nepali.

But that was years ago. Just who they were or where they were from I never learned. Kids don't talk about things like that when they are playing ball and eating sweets. Will they ever come back?

Having seen enough of the palace square for the moment, once the foreigners have gone I wander into the kitchen used by my guardians. This is separate from my own, for everything of mine is used only by me, and food can only be prepared for me in my own special kitchen. The reason I like the family kitchen is because the window looks right out on to Nawa Adharsa School at right angles, and I am almost close enough to touch the children in the classrooms. I can almost tell what subject they are studying from what they are writing in their note-books. Of course not everyone is writing intently. Some, especially the boys, are misbehaving, throwing things at one another, or annoying the girls. Occasionally I hear the rough voice of a teacher, a teacher more energetic than mine, bringing them to order. It looks like fun. In fact at the moment, it looks a lot better than standing around waiting for everybody else to finish school.

I wonder if I can get away with feeding the fish without Gautam Dai noticing. I know he says it is bad for them, but everyone likes to eat, so why not fish? Hoping that he is in the little shop that he runs next to Kumari Che, I sneak to the back of the house where he has a nice aquarium full of colourful fish, but just as I am reaching for the food, I see that he has noticed me and has followed me. He must have come back for lunch. "Now, Dyah Meiju," he says, gently taking the box of fish food from my hand. "The fish have already been fed today, and you know that you might kill them if you give them too much. Let's go check on the birds."

He also likes to keep pigeons, and there are a lot of ducks as well. Knowing that I can eat duck eggs, but not chicken eggs, my devotees often offer baby ducks to be raised in one of the back rooms of the Kumari Che around the small back courtyard. I like the baby ducks, but lose interest in them as they grow up. For one thing, they smell bad. For another, one of my 32 perfections is to have a voice "as soft and clear as a duck's." Not very flattering. But there happens to be a fat puppy waddling around which I pick up and cuddle, somewhat to Gautam's consternation.

But I now hear the noise of children returning, and hurry up to the long, narrow rooms occupied by the family on the first floor to listen to the news of my playmates' day at school. They look a little uncomfortable as I join them, for when we are together, the word of the girl in red is law. "Go ahead," I tell them after they have all touched my feet. "Don't stop. I want to hear about your school." Normally I just sit and listen since I have nothing to contribute, as they talk about their lessons, complain about the naughty boys, and go on about who is friends with whom. I hear that a girl named Dilmaya got top marks on the English test, but a boy named Bikas was jealous, and he pulled her hair, so the teacher made him stand in the corner for the rest of the day. It is all a world away from mine, though the school is so close by. No one else seems to be learning the times tables up to 22. Maybe only goddesses do that. One day I will go to school, I'm sure, but just now it is very hard to imagine. Besides, when they talk about the short tempers of their teachers, sometimes I have my doubts.

Two girls, a little older than my playmates, come and join the group, though first they bow and touch my feet. My big sisters. Thin and rather intense, Pramila is already beginning to look like a young woman, and to act like one as well. Surmila, a year older than I am, is a lot more jolly and carefree. I ignore them. It is not that I don't like them, but I have never really figured out how they treat me with the deference and respect other outsiders do, or should we act like I have seen other sisters acting?

"Come sit with us, Dyah Meiju," suggests Surmila, the bolder of the two. I run away to my dolls.

The other children never come to play with me, but have to wait for me to come to them. Just now I want to be alone, so I take my little stove and go to my own kitchen where it is safe to light it, since I feel like making some snacks for my dolls. As the newspaper and wood chips light the charcoal and the stove heats up, I put on the tiny kettle and cut up a potato. This is something else that my guardians were not happy with at first, worrying that I might cut myself, but seeing that I was skilful enough not to do myself any harm, they gave in and let me have my own way. Eventually I wind up with something that is supposed to be tea and fried potatoes, which I serve to my dolls. It would be nice sometime to do this for real people, and to see them actually eat and hear them say what a clever cook I am, but of course I am not allowed to do anything for anyone else. After my dolls have finished with them, I usually give their snacks to the family, but am not sure what they do with them.

"Dyah Meiju, foreigners." I am busy feeding my dolls, and do not want to go, but I know it is my duty. It is no problem not smiling this time. I positively glower.

Afterwards I interrupt two of my playmates from a game of *karom* in one of the back rooms, and have them come and help me feed my dolls. Recently I have been spending a lot of time with my dolls, and

I know that my playmates are bored with them, but what is that to me? After a few minutes, they grow restless. "Would not Dyah Tata perhaps like to join in our *karom* game?" one suggests shyly. Only my playmates in the temple address me as "goddess sister". I am not in the mood for flipping disks of wood around a board and trying to get them into the holes in the corners, and I can force them to do whatever I want, but it is more pleasant playing with happy people, so I give in with the air of someone doing them a big favour.

"Tea time." My dolls have had their tea, and now it is my turn: *roti* or maybe fried potatoes and a sweet. Since cooked rice is not involved, I do not have to have my tea on my platform, and so I can sit around and talk with my playmates or whomever else I want to talk with.

After tea I find my mother waiting in the back room. Much more important as far as I am concerned, she has brought my little brother Sarbagya with her. He is now a fat toddler about two and a half years old, and before my mother even has time to touch my feet, I grab him and spin him around. He is my favourite of the family, by a long way, and while he is here I will not let go of him.

At last my mother, who is not much taller than I am, manages to get under him to touch my feet. Of course in a normal Newari family, a child bows down to touch his or her parents' feet, and this act of homage paid to me is something that makes it difficult for me to think of her as my mother. She then confuses me even more by ceasing to treat me as a goddess and chatting about my health (I am always fine) and about how my sisters are doing in school. Pramila is doing brilliantly as always, and is making everyone proud as the others try hard to emulate her. As with my sisters, I am not sure how to behave. The family always makes me feel terribly shy. Like my sisters, she wants me to sit beside her, and since she has brought my brother, I acquiesce, keeping him on my lap.

I enjoy her visits more since he was born. I used to be so shy with her that I found it easiest to just ignore her, though even as a small child I could see that I hurt her. For some reason, even when she was pregnant with my brother, I began to feel closer to her (though this did not happen when she was pregnant with my youngest sister Sunila just a year before) and once he was born we were both just crazy over him. For her it came as a tremendous relief after five girls to finally have a boy, and since the previous Kumari's mother had also had a son while she was in office, I got a lot of the credit.

Dinner, like lunch, is a solitary affair, but not particularly lonely. From my platform as I eat my *dal-bhat-tarkari* (and of course my tomato *achar*) I can not only hear the members of my family, my guardian family that is, chatting away and joking about events of the day, but I can see some of them as well. Their dining room is right next to mine, and I can even join in the conversation if I want.

After dinner I feel like company, but my playmates are doing their homework. I could make them form a little band and sing for me so I could dance, the way the star does in the Hindi and Nepali movies, but not wanting to chance the unhappy looks I get from both them and their parents when they cannot refuse, I go upstairs to where there is a large, glass-covered portrait of King Mahendra, King Birendra's father and predecessor. I use this as a mirror, and dance some of the numbers I have seen in Hindi and Nepali movies, imagining myself as the heroine. When I get bored with this I return to my dolls. They are still arranged in the long room opposite the kitchens, so I gather them all up in two or three trips and take them to my room. They will be my company when I curl up between my red sheets, and I arrange them so that whenever I wake up I will find them looking at me.

Everyone is tired now, and before bed-time we usually gather in the long first floor sitting room overlooking the courtyard to watch television. This is something new in our country, and everyone is quite fascinated by the pictures on the small screen. As the goddess, I get to sit right in front of the screen so that no one can block my view. I am so amazed that I hardly ever remember what I have seen except the dancers in the films. If I were not a goddess, sometimes I think I would like to be a dancer.

Before I go to bed I go to my bathroom and wash off my eye make-up. Then one of my "sisters" comes to take down my hair and help me out of my red dress and into my red pyjamas. I am not really supposed to add any personal touches to my room, but she overlooks the dolls.

It has been a day much like any other, though there are occasional variations. On the 10th day of some of the Nepali months one of a group of five priests called the Pancha Buddha perform a special puja with me called *Dasami* Puja. These are five priests of the Bajracharya caste representing the "Five Buddhas" that are seen everywhere in the Kathmandu Valley: particularly painted over doorways and on stupas, large and small. Each of them has his own colour and, when on a stupa, each faces one of the cardinal points, except for Vairochana who is usually considered to be at the centre (though on some of the larger stupas, like Suwayambunath, he faces just south of east). One of their human representations comes every morning to Kumari Che for a puja in a special room called the Agan Kota, but the only one that involves me is *Dasami* Puja. I can never differentiate between them, and think of all of them as "Guruju".[2]

On a Saturday, a holiday for everyone else, I will be busier with worshippers – there might be twenty or more – and there will be no shortage of playmates since there is no school that day. I have little to do during the day, everyone looks up to me, and hardly anyone ever tells me what I can and can't do. But sometimes I am lonely, and of course I am always looking forward to those 13 occasions during the year when I get to go outside my temple.

---

[2] Books and articles always say that they are involved in the Kumari selection process, but as far as I know, this is not true.

THE END OF THE WORLD

Sushma Joshi

Sushma Joshi is a writer and filmmaker based in Kathmandu, Nepal. *End of the World*, her book of short stories, was long-listed for the Frank O'Connor International Short Story Award in 2009. Her other published works include *The Prediction* and *Art Matters*. Her non-fiction reportage has appeared in *Utne Reader*, *Ms.* magazine, *Z Net*, *The Irrawaddy*, *Himal Southasian*, Bertelsmann *Future Challenges*, *The Kathmandu Post*, *Nation Weekly* magazine and other publications. In 2004, she was part of the staff at the *Nation Weekly* magazine (Kathmandu). Since 1997, Joshi has worked and consulted with international organizations working in social change and human rights, including the Harvard School of Public Health (Harvard University), UNDP, UNICEF, Integrated Center for Mountain Development (ICIMOD), Chemonics/USAID, and the Office of the High Commissioner for Human Rights (OHCHR).

AFTER THE FLOODS

Jethi died on one of those monsoon nights when the rains come with such force ordinary people give up any hope for salvation and wait for the end to come. Sometimes the rains just raise the heat and the sting of mosquitoes and bright green shoots of rice. At other times, they raise the wrath of the rivers that lie like somnolent snakes over winter, which are awakened by the monsoon to rage over the voluptuous folds of the Mahabharat hills in a heavenly tantrum of destruction.

For Jethi, the monsoon brought clouds with black undersides, streaked with innocent silver looks of eventuality. Then the clouds erupted into a storm that went on for three days, sweeping down through the river that swallowed her house, the firewood in her rafters, her children and with it, also herself.

Kamala was in Kathmandu when she heard the news. A stooped, weary man, wearing a patched waistcoat and carrying a dusty green army bag, arrived at her doorstep one morning. Kamala caught a glimpse of him through the marigold bushes. She had seen his face before, but she couldn't remember who he was. She ran to unlatch the gate.

"Are you Kamala from Seto-Khola?" he asked in a gruff voice, peering at her with penetrating eyes set under white bushy eyebrows. "Daughter of Habaldar Saila?"

"Yes, that's me." Kamala brought the palms of her hands together in a namaste. As soon as he spoke, she recognized him. How could she forget! It was the Old Man himself, Damar-Bahadur. Kamala had spent days climbing his trees and stealing his guavas.

He set down his ancient green Army bag, and extended his hand. Kamala looked down at the envelope he held out. A neat and cursive hand had written "Kamala" with a big flourish in the middle.

"Your grandson used to walk to school with me. Please come in." Kamala took the letter from him. The old man smiled, revealing missing teeth.

"And you and Jethi used to steal guavas from me," he said, arching his brows and looking at her with shrewd eyes. "Don't think I didn't know it was you and your sister. I saw you all the time climbing the trees."

"We were bad children," Kamala said, smiling. To her relief, the old man seemed to harbour no grudges. The old man had had a large number of guava trees on his land. He had, to their young eyes, appeared to be a rich man. "Here, please sit down on this mat. I'll get some tea." The old man lowered his body on the small concrete steps, unwrapped his waist-cloth and extracted his *beedi*. A puff of acrid smoke followed Kamala as she went back into the kitchen to make tea.

"And how is everybody in the village?" Kamala asked, setting down the hot tin glass. She had lived in Kathmandu since the flood nine years ago. Unlike Jethi, she had never gone back.

The old man did not reply. Kamala wondered if he had become senile, or if he was losing his hearing. "Everybody's well," he replied after a moment. He watched steam rise from the tea. He picked up the glass with caution, blew on the hot liquid, and took a long, leisurely slurp.

"Did you come to visit Maila Dai?" Kamala asked. Maila was his second son, a soldier in the Royal Nepal Army.

"I came down to visit Maila. Your brothers, those twins, they asked me to bring this letter to you. Had a tough time finding you too, with all these directions. But after all that walking, here you are." He spit a stray tea leaf from his mouth.

"Is there enough sugar?" Kanchi asked. She wanted to take away his tiredness, give him a drink that would make him feel at home.

"Enough," the old man replied. Kamala looked at his familiar profile. Life had taken its toll on him. Almost a decade had gone by since she saw him. Ten years later, he had a stoop in his shoulder and a thick nest of lines on his face. Wrinkles radiated in long arcs from the corner of his eyes into his leathery, brown cheeks. There was a look of sorrow in his eyes she could not remember.

"How were the crops this year?" Kamala had an intuition that he came carrying bad news.

"There were no rains last year, Bahini. This year, the rains carried away everything," the old man replied, sighing. He blinked, put down the glass that he was cupping with both hands, noisily blew his nose between two fingers, and flicked snot on the grass. He wiped his hands on the grass. Kamala felt dread gather in a tight knot inside her stomach. She could tell, without opening the letter, what it would say.

"I remember the floods. I was nine years old then." Kamala was stalling for time. She did not want the Old Man to tell her anything. She did not want to open the envelope.

The old man nodded, "I remember. We lost many people in that one. But people never learn. We should have planted the entire hillside with trees after that landslide, we knew those hills were fragile. Instead, there was cutting, and more cutting. Then the lumber people came, and they took half the hillside with them. Last year, there were no trees left."

Kamala remembered the day of the flood as if it was yesterday. She had spent the day with Jethi, her sister, stealing guavas from the Old Man.

"Kamala! Now! The Old Man has gone down the hill to get his hoe. Go now!" her sister's urgent voice sent her slithering up the trunk with gecko-like speed. Kamala swung on the branches like a monkey, shaking the fruit free for her sister to collect before the Old Man could wind his way up the curve of the hill again. Kamala was nine, thin and wiry. She ran around the hills with skinned knees and tangled brown hair, climbing trees as well as any of her five brothers. Jethi was fourteen, but she might as well still be a child, the way she behaved, leading her little brothers and sister on to childish pranks. The Old Man stood there, shaking his hands in impotent fury as he watched Kamala scamper down the tree, and run down the hill with the stolen treasure. Jethi and Kamala never let the guavas ripen. They didn't know what could happen to the fetal green fruit the next day: an entire season's worth could be wiped out in a day by the crows, or the hail, or the little boys down the hill.

The two girls looked at each other as they ate, and ate, all the raw possibilities out of the guavas. The slivers of astringent rind, the slippery, hard seeds, the pungent forbidden taste. The difficulty lay in knowing when to climb the tree to get the raw guavas before they were claimed by others. After that, the hardest thing was to extract the fragments of white seeds that sank like soft pebbles to their hiding places between the teeth.

Jethi and Kamala, after eating half the loot, hid the rest on their waistcloth, and rejoined the other children in the forest. The clouds gathered above them, thick and black. It had been raining hard for the past week. They sang as they chopped the firewood, thinking more rain meant a better harvest.

Jethi led the chorus, "*pani paryo, asina jharyo*." Because Jethi was Jethi and she couldn't resist, she made her voice as gruff and solemn as Dambar Bahadur until they were all laughing, even Dambar Bahadur's sons.

"You better watch out for Kamala, Didi. She was caught stealing guavas again," the women warned her mother as they stopped to fill their pots at the spring. Her mother, who was trying to bathe the twins at the small spring, clipped Kamala in the ear. "Aiya!" said Kamala, skipping out of the way. How come the women always saw her, not Jethi, committing these crimes? But unwilling to implicate her sister, she did not say a word.

The twins slipped in and out of her mother's hands with the slippery speed of naked seven-year-olds, screaming and beating their hands on their chests, soaking everyone in the process. "Jethi, you bathe these devils," her mother said, giving up in disgust. She stooped to squeeze the water out of the ends of her dhoti. "I have to help with the planting." The two sisters winked at each other as they felt the round fruit, wrapped securely in folds of cloth, pressing into their stomachs. That was the last time Kamala ever stole a guava.

That night, the rain erupted, beating down with a force beyond comprehension. It was the force that Kamala had always known was out there but was not prepared to meet with such suddenness. Who had woken her up that night in the confusion of warm bodies and anguished voices? All she could remember was the sudden panic, chaos, the hands pulling her from her bed towards the door. The sound of thunder and hail was deafening, but above it she could still hear her mother. "Kamli? Kamleeee!" her mother shrieked. "Wake up right now! We are going!"

"Ama!" Kamala wailed. Blinded by the rain, she stumbled up the muddy, narrow path. But the rain was lashing down and her mother was already far ahead in the distance, holding the twins' hands. "Walk carefully, Kamli. I know you are careful, Kamli. Be careful," her mother yelled out to her, her voice lashing in and out of the rain, until it sounded like: Kamli, careful, careful . . . and then she saw the mother shape disappearing around a bend in the hill.

Kamala gasped for breath. Her heart thudded like a stone inside her body as she ran to keep up with the shapes in front of her. The path was made treacherously slippery by the rain. A path that lay like a liquid red snake winding upwards towards the invisible sky, and downwards towards the pebbled, stony hardness of the riverbed. One slip of the foot, one loose root, one moment of indecision and her body could hurtle towards the crashing sounds and the white froth of the Seti river.

The rain was blinding. She felt the plants on either side of her, and she clutched at them, pulling herself up without seeing where she was going. Weeds, stinging nettles, brambles all pulled her up as she frantically clutched at them. She made her way up, the tears falling and blinding her as much as the rain, her breath in ragged gasps, her legs whipped and bloodied by the branches, instinctively following the shadow of her sister before her. She knew at the top of this steep wooded hill was a pine forest where her family was headed. At the moment, she could not imagine if she would get there.

The moment was so uprooted, blowing in the wind, whipped by the rain, freezing in the cold, that she almost wanted to give up and sit down on the path and let go of her grip. She saw herself washed away, like a leaf, down the hill into the frothing river, where the crest of waves, and the spirits hiding in them, would jump to pull her in. Then she would become a small fish swimming in the white foam. That is when the cry had been torn out of her, a thin wail: "Jethi!"

"*Aija*, Kamala. Come on!" Jethi yelled to her from inside the rain. She was scrambling up with all the wiry strength of her fourteen-year-old body. "It's only a bit farther away. Come on!"

So she climbed a bit more. Climbed, and climbed, until her legs started trembling with red-hot pain. "Jethi!" she cried again, in the sudden terror of knowing one is nine years old, and only a few feet ahead of death. "Jetttttttthiii!"

The voice of her older sister came down from the greyness above, with all the urgency of sisters who are caught in the conspiracy to steal raw fruit from the neighbour's tree. "Come on, come on. I see a guava tree over here. Come on, we can pick a few!!"

The voice of her sister floated out of the dream-like unreality of the rain. She was singing! "*Pani paryo, asina jharyo . . .*" Its raining, the hail is coming down.

Jethi sounded so solemn, imitating her Dambar Bahadur's gruff voice, her voice only occasionally fading in the rain, that Kamala gave a tired little giggle in between her sobs. Her sister could always make her laugh with her clowning, but now she just wanted to sit down and rest. As she started to look around for a rock to sit on, she saw the flash of her sister's head turning back.

> "*Gham pani, gham pani, syal ko biha, kookur janti, biralo bahun,*" Jethi's voice rang out.
> *Sun and rain, sun and rain,*
> *it's the fox's wedding.*

The dogs lead the procession,
the cat is the priest.

Jethi's voice was cheerful, as if she was on an adventure on a sunlit day, as she walked ahead with the sack of rice on her back.

"Jethi, I can't go any farther, you go ahead, I'll come meet you later," Kamala heard herself say, before she lay down in the blessed coolness of mud, and sighed. Her voice was instantly lost in the deafening sound of the rain. When she felt the hands of her sister on her body, she knew she had almost made it.

Kamala was told later than Jethi, abandoning the rice that she was carrying in her basket, put her sister inside it, carried her up for the rest of the way up the hill.

Their old grandmother, eighty years old and brittle as a winter branch, told them: "Go, all of you. I'm going back to take care of the *deuta*." She had walked back, slowly, towards the family shrine when Kamala's father picked her up and put her over his shoulders, carrying her up the hillside. She died, three days later, from the shock of the cold.

The rest of the family survived. They had been one of the few lucky families who had managed to get up on higher ground on time. Most of the people living below had been swept away before they could walk halfway up the hill.

It rained for the next five days, as if the rain was hell bent on washing them out from under the pine trees, where they ran for shelter. The rain was ferocious, and the pine trees swayed and creaked *oeeeee, ooeee*, mournfully, as if all the ghosts of the hillside had come to taunt them in their misery. Her father and uncles knew from the scramblings of their own childhood that there was an overhanging rock in the middle of the forest that would take a hundred years of rain to wash away, and that's where they stayed for the next fourteen days.

They ate nothing but mushrooms, scavenged from the ground, for two weeks. Just raw mushrooms, straight from the ground, like animals. She could still recall that humid-grey, earthy taste in her mouth when she thought about it.

At night, the big gaping scar in the hillside came alive with mournful cries. Sounds multiplied and echoed, and the family, stuck on top of the hill, almost went mad at night trying to sleep. Hundreds of people must have died in the flood, they knew. This meant that they were right next to the spirits of the dead who had never been properly cremated. They must be wandering, howling with rage and misery, in the chasm between the hilltop where they rested, and the base of the next hill, where their village used to be. Bir Masan, the keeper of cremation grounds, was out there somewhere, prowling through the dead bodies. Meeting him would bring death and destruction. Even meeting his shadow would make a person deathly sick. So Kamala's family huddled in a frightened cluster, listening to the echoes and whisperings, the muted screams and the forlorn crying of those who had been swept away.

The rain abated two weeks later. With the brightness of the blue sky had come the knowledge that half the terraced hillside that they had lived on for centuries had been washed away. There was a big jagged hole, as far as the eye could see, tearing like a scar across the surface where their village once used to be. The only thing that remained out of those hillsides full of corn, twenty-three houses, and the two hundred and sixteen people, was that big hole, mud and emptiness.

"We've lost all our land." Her eldest uncle had been the first one to say it. The others sat in silence around the fire, which they had finally managed to light out of the wet pine branches, studded with globs of resin. The smoke rose into the light blue of the early morning sky. "What are we going to do?"

"The women and children can go stay in their *maita*," Kamala's father suggested. The last time Kamala had visited her maternal grandmother, the old woman had fed her delicacy after delicacy, from fried goat liver to rice pudding, from sel doughnuts to fresh persimmons, all of which the old woman had set aside in anticipation of the visit of her daughter and two granddaughters. Kamala felt her mouth watering as she remembered the food. The old lady had been delighted to see her daughter's youngest girl for the first time. So much so that she had even given Kamala a pair of gold earrings, made of heavy gold, from her old, battered trunk, whispering to her not to show the other children because they might be jealous. The earrings, big ovals of solid gold, had never left her earlobes. "Yes, lets go!" Kamala said delightedly, when she heard her father suggesting another visit to her *mamaghar*.

"But we can't stay there for long, not with nine children," Kamala's mother reminded him. Her face was drawn with worry. Kamala, watching the fear in her mother's face, felt her momentary glee disappear. She felt the adults' worry press down on her.

"We can sell our gold," Kamala's aunt said in her soft, melodic voice. Her heavy gold bracelet clinked against the glass bangles as she raised her arm to show it. The only thing of value that they had been able to carry out of their homes was the heavy gold jewellery that lay on the body of the women – earrings, septum rings, nose-rings and bangles, attached to their bodies like permanent organs. "We don't have a lot, but if you sell it well, it will bring money."

"Perhaps we can buy a small plot of land with it," Kamala's eldest uncle said. "And we still have the pastureland." There was silence. Nobody said that the pastureland would hardly feed them like their farmland had done.

"All the cattle are gone," Kamala's mother, who did not shy away from unpleasant topics, reminded. The old people's mournful voices went on and on, talking all morning. This was not the funny conversations they had around the fire in their home – the cold, the rain, and the exhaustion had all taken a toll. Everybody sat there, huddled, with black circles around their eyes.

As they talked, her mother motioned to Kamala to come nearer. When Kamala sat down on her lap, her mother crushed some leaves in her hands and dribbled the herbs over the places where she had been stung by nettles. The dark red welts turned black, mixed with the green sap. Kamala felt her skin burn. She bit her lips to stop from crying out aloud. "You won't have a mark in two days," her mother assured her.

As Kamala sat on her lap, her mother unscrewed the earrings that her grandmother had given her from her ears. Kamala felt her ears lighten as the earrings were lifted. She felt naked, as if she were sitting in front of her family with no clothes on. Her lips trembled, and she felt the tears rolling down her cheeks. "Why are you crying? You're a big girl now," her mother scolded. Kamala, looked at her mother's face through a blur of tears, and saw that her mother was also crying.

Jethi, whose earrings had also been removed, wiped Kamala's face with her rough palm. "Come with me. I am going to show you something," Jethi whispered. Behind the pine forest was a huge meadow full of alpine flowers. As they ran across the grass, the sudden vastness of the space exhilarated Kamala, after the claustrophobic darkness that had surrounded the adults only a moment ago. When they came across a clump of small ferns, Jethi stopped.

"This is called a *rani sinka*," Jethi said, picking a lime green frond.

"Why?" said Kamala, sniffing, her breath still broken in uneven sobs.

"Because it is fit for a queen, that's why."

The fern had a shiny black stem, thin as a polished needle. "Will it hurt?"

"No. Give me the back of your hand."

As Kamala put out her hand, palm facing down, Jethi put the fern on it, and slapped hard. "*Aiya!*" said Kamala. Jethi removed the leaf to reveal the delicate design of the fern traced on the back of her hand in white powder. As Kamala looked at the design – exquisitely wrought in her hand down to the most minute detail – with awe, Jethi broke off a small section of the black stem, and inserted it through the hole in her earlobe. "This will keep your piercing open until we find you new earrings," Jethi said. Kamala put her hands up, felt the tiny twig where her earring used to be, and ripped it out of the lobe. "What are you doing!" Jethi said, vexed. Kamala slapped Jethi's hand away and stamped on the *rani sinka*, saying: "You wear those stupid sinka earrings! I want real ones!"

Kamala ran down the meadow and started to pick mushrooms. Jethi yelled: "You leave your earlobes empty, and your piercing will close up! Your ears will become stubby and ugly!"

Kamala ignored her and bent to pick up a large brown mushrooms. The floor was studded with all kinds, grey ones with long stems, white circles resting on stubby stems, bright red ones. Kamala had to learn fast which mushrooms were edible, which ones poisonous. "And don't you collect anything that will kill the entire family," Jethi shouted, as she saw her younger sister grabbing the mushrooms from the field. "I know better than you which ones to eat. I used to go and collect mushrooms with Mama," Kamala said haughtily. They picked in silence for a while, Kamala working one end of the field, and Jethi supervising her sister's work from a discreet distance. Soon, they had enough for the whole family.

Then, feeling like she had worked enough, Kamala dropped her pouch of mushrooms, and gave a hiccuping scream and ran up the hill. She had spied a goat grazing on the rocks. Kamala tried to grab the goat's tail. The goat, startled, sprang up the hillside and disappeared.

"Kamali!" Jethi said. "We could have eaten that animal, and now its gone!"

"Who was going to catch it? You?" mocked Kamala.

"You just come down from those rocks, and I am going to beat you for your insolence," Jethi threatened, waving a spindly stick. Jethi could scramble up the rocks as fast as her little sister. But on the night of the flood, she had caught a big splinter on her big toe in the rush to reach the hilltop, and she walked around with careful, measured steps since. Not heeding her sister's reprimand, Kamala turned her attention to dragonflies. It wasn't dragonfly season yet, but once in a while a bright blue one flew by.

"Don't scream and scare them, Kamali," said Jethi. "Here, stand still."

Kamala, mollifed, came closer. The dragonfly, a brilliant blue one, opened and closed its gauzy wings like a fan over a pink cluster of flowers. Then it settled on a big green leaf, sunning itself in a motionless daze, unaware of the two girls looking at it. Jethi's hand sneaked up to it. She clamped two tips of her fingers right over the top, swiftly, until the dragonfly was caught. It fluttered in her hands, rustling like paper. She brought it closer to Kamala so that she could take a look and see the two globular eyes. "See," said Jethi. "You have to sneak up on it and catch it when it is not looking." Like death, thought Kamala, as she felt her own fingers pressing down on the gauzy wings and felt the panicky flutter inside her palms.

"Gimme, gimme!" The twins, carrying switches of yellow alpine flowers, pounced on the two girls from their hiding place behind a rock. The twins had returned to their usual level of destructiveness after a few days of despondency. "I want it!" "No me!" In the scuffle the dragonfly lost a wing and fell down frantic and fluttering on the ground. "See what you have done, you fools!" said Jethi. "The dragonfly is going to die now, because it won't be able to fly." Both the twins got a punch over their heads from their elder sister, and were dragged down the hillside howling in protest. Kamala bent down and picked up the alpine flowers they had abandoned, then sat down on a flat rock, and looked at the fluttering dragonfly. A trickle of tears crept from underneath her eyelids, and she brushed it away. But the tears continued to come, and she cried briefly – for the dying dragonfly, for her lost earrings, and because the sores on her legs were starting to hurt her again.

A day later, Kamala's father, along with his brothers walked down the hill to the bazaar. The bazaar was full of people whose home had been swept away. People in muddy clothes clutched their few possessions: a cooking pot, a household deity, a red plastic box containing sindoor.

The shops, held together by branches and plastic tarpaulin, overflowed with sacks of rice in quantities never seen before. Sacks and sacks and sacks piled up towards the sky. Small brown, jute bags plump and splitting with rice. They walked around the bazaar, dazed by what they saw.

A small man with a fresh, bloody gash down his face, pointed to the white grains scattered on the ground. "What good fortune for these shopkeepers, huh, Dai. They got all this rice at dirt cheap rates from Kathmandu. It's sent by the government for the people affected by the flood."

They returned three days later, carrying sacks of rice on their backs. They were weary from walking. Her father had bought it on credit from the shopkeeper with whom he had a long-standing relationship, with the promise to pay it back within a year. He had put half of what remained of his land, the farmland he had on higher ground, as collateral.

Kamala's uncles, who had friends at the Bazaar, heard how the rice was sold by the relief workers, and how people in the district headquarters were stocking up, enough to last them for a year. This was the most rain to have fallen in the Mahabharat mountains in seventy years. A thousand, three hundred and thirty-six people have died, the government announced. Five lakh people were affected. This was the biggest flood, and for relief workers, the most lucrative.

"Wasn't that rice supposed to be distributed free to families affected by the flood?" the brothers asked, but the shopkeepers shook their heads and said: "Were they supposed to? We bought it with our own money." And all the bureaucrats and officials shook their heads in bafflement, pointing from the local politicians to the Home Ministry, from the Central District Officer to the Police, until at last there were so many people who were supposed to be responsible it became impossible to blame anybody. And nobody, of course, knew who was to blame.

Nine years later, Kamala continued to remember the flood each time the monsoon arrived. It was during the nights when the rain poured down, bringing no coolness to the heat, that Kamala found it hardest to fall asleep. Two weeks before the old man arrived at her door, a thunderstorm had taken place. Lightning, a flash of bright white electricity in the wet sky, had illuminated her room for a brief instant. Her body tensed in anticipation. The thunder, when it came, sounded like wooden houses collapsing in the rain.

She lay awake, sweat beading her upper lip, listening to the rain slam on the tin roof. She hated being under a tin roof. Then she remembered that the sounds, even under concrete roofs, had not gone away – the cyclical predictability of rain, cloud, water, and time culminating in an awesome moment that reminded her of the inevitability of death.

She closed her eyes, hoping that would drive away the sounds. Bright green spots slowly grew larger and larger, blossoming like shoots right inside the lids of her closed eyes. Her husband, Mani, was on her left. They had met and fallen in love two years ago. She was working as the baby-sitter for a wealthy business family. He was their security guard.

Mani had saved enough to put in an application for a visa to go to Korea. He had been accepted, and spent a year working in a packaging plant in Seoul. After his return, he carried a cellphone. He went to the STD-ISD booth every evening and made long-distance calls to his employers, with whom he spoke in Korean. He had worked in their factory, and they had liked him so much they had asked him to manage their Korean food restaurant, which they had started in Kathmandu. He had agreed, but with reluctance. Seoul was where his heart was. Sitting in the dusty restaurant in Thamel, he dreamt up elaborate entrepreneurial ventures for his future – an export-import business, a factory that would manufacture plastic, a packaging plant. He talked about how Kamala would accompany him to Korea once the baby could be put in a boarding school. Her son, now one and a half, had recently started to walk.

Kamala didn't want her husband to know how much the rain haunted her. She knew she was in Kathmandu, in the middle of a valley, and that there was no possibility of a flood. Her children would never wake up in the middle of the night, hear the roar of nature that has swelled to breaking point and then have to run up the hillside, leaving all possessions, all clothes, all firewood, all gods behind. They would never die, as Kamala almost did, trapped in a wooden house that collapsed under the weight of mud and debris brought along by a hillside denuded of trees, the soil as loose as if there was a giant anthill below.

The thunderstorm continued throughout the night. Kamala woke up in the middle of the night, and felt an excruciating pain in her head, as if she had been grinding her teeth so hard, and so long, the jaws had started to grind into the soft part of her brain. A piercing, needle-like pain throbbed near her ear. Blue dragonflies swarmed by her half-awakened consciousness, pushing her awake. She had dreamt that Jethi and her entire family were swept down the hillside in a deafening chaos of mud and timber. That's when she knew with certainty that Jethi was about to die.

It was impossible for Kamala to go back to the sleep. Midnight. Later. Even later. Time slipped by while Kamala lay there, pretending to sleep, hoping that her pretence would lull her to unconsciousness. She lay there, enmeshed in a bright haze of half dreams when she heard a mosquito whine, persistently, right next to her ear. She got out of bed and skirted the sleeping bodies, quietly switched on the light, inspected the round red mosquito bites, and then walked around the silent room.

Everywhere she went there was the presence of death, the smell of warm air and strange shapes of light showing the dusty crevices of night in a way that she had never seen before. Frightened of her own mortality, Kamala stood there, feeling the presence of Jethi who was sleeping in the village as if she was in front of her. Kamala had known then that her sister was dying. Those about to die have the power to touch people thousands of miles away in a way that is impossible for the living. Kamala understood this as if somebody had come and told her.

Kamala opened the front door and felt a blast of rain enter the room. The trees bent in the wind. She sat down by the doorway and felt the spray from the tin roof reaching her in a fine mist. The wind was gusting hard. A branch broke off and landed inches off her feet. The hair on her body stood on end from the cold wind.

Across the mossy courtyard, past the triangular brick borders, on the old brick wall, leaned a guava tree. As Kamala watched the rain beat on the leaves and slid off the wet trunk, she saw a single fruit fall. She walked out and towards the tree, her feet squelching on cold mud. The rain pelted on her with the solidity of hail. Rain slashing down her neck, she stooped and picked up the fruit. It felt like a talisman inside her closed fist.

Kamala limped back to the house. She was soaked, so she did not bother to run. She sat on the steps, her thin cotton blouse and sari clinging to her skin, and raised the guava to her mouth. Her teeth sunk into the hard green rind, through the astringent green rind to the white flesh, from the soft whiteness to the ochre crunchy seeds. She sat there, eating the fruit, breathing in the astringent smell, saying, under her breath, over and over again: *Hurry, hurry. Climb the guava tree.* Why had the universe spared her, but was now taking her sister?

She knew, even as she played this nine-year-old ritual in her mind, that she was fooling herself. This time, the tree was not going to offer its salvation.

Kamala returned to bed and lay down. She was shivering, but she did not change her clothes. She listened as the rain came splashing down, in miniature rivulets and streams, in tiny floods on the garden path. The cock from Sukumel Bajai's house crowed around four a.m. The earth exhaled the smell of wet earth. The smell of crushed leaf and bark floated into her room. By the time the sky lightened with the pale blue ink of dawn and the silence was broken by sparrows and temple-bells, she knew her ritual had failed. This time, the tree was not going to offer its salvation.

The Old Man laid down his empty tea glass with a sigh. He lit another *beedi*, and it glowed inside the tunnel he made with his fingers.

Jethi, he said, was a beautiful woman, too young to die. But die she did, on one of those monsoon nights when the rains come with such force ordinary people give up any hope for salvation and wait for the end to come. Sometimes the rains just raise the heat and sting of mosquitoes and bright green shoots of rice. At other times, they raise the wrath of rivers that lie like somnolent snakes over winter, and then are woken by the monsoon to wash away entire hillsides in a heavenly tantrum of destruction.

For Jethi, the monsoon brought clouds with black and silver undersides, the tears of the ocean borne on an unstoppable current from other continents, other places, foreshadowing death. Then it erupted into a storm that went on for three days, dumping silt and gravel of a disintegrating hillside into Sungdel village. The entire hillside slid down, a treacherous sludge of mud and debris, and swallowed her house, the firewood in her rafters, her children and with it, also herself.

The Old Man told her thirty-five houses, including a health-post, were swept away by the landslides. More than ninety houses were damaged. Forty-three people were dead, a hundred and fifty missing. But even in apocalyptic destruction, there are stories of miracles. The telecom tower in Udaypur had been destroyed by Maoists, and nobody knew about the flood until days later. When rescue workers arrived on the scene a week later, they found a miracle – two men alive in the debris. Everybody else in their village had been buried by the hill that slid down three hundred meters into the valley. Guided out by a capricious fate, those two had been left to live.

Jethi was not one of the lucky ones. She, with her youngest child tied to her back, had tried to hold on to the beam of the kitchen when she heard the water coming. They found her, three days later. The log, along with other detritus, had floated down and landed on the banks of a river further downstream. Jethi's hands were locked around the beam, as if she were holding on, even in death, to the spiritual centre of her dismembered home. The body was battered beyond recognition.

Then an ear-stud had caught one of the twins' eyes. The two boys, now sixteen, had been working in Diktel. They returned to the village when they heard about the flood. They couldn't find the area where their house had been. The entire village was covered over with a mountain of silt. They had dug through the area but didn't find any bodies. Then bodies had been recovered downstream, and they had gone down to see. They did not recognize their sister, but one of them saw the small ornament embedded in a corpse's ear. The tiny golden studs had been sent as a gift by Kamala for her sister's wedding a year ago. Brought over by her husband Mani from Korea, the studs were golden, with outstretched wings and bulbous eyes – two exquisite, machine crafted dragonflies.

BUDDHA'S ORPHANS

Samrat Upadhyay

Samrat Upadhyay is a Nepali author of fiction. He is Professor of Creative Writing and Director of Graduate Studies at Indiana University. Samrat was the first Nepali-born fiction author writing in English to be published in the West. His first book *Arresting God in Kathmandu*, a collection of short stories, won a Whiting Award for fiction in 2001. His first novel, *The Guru of Love* was a *New York Times* Notable Book of the Year in 2003. His other published works include *The Royal Ghosts* and *The City Son*. He lives in Bloomington, Indiana.

ELOPING

In Hetuda, Mohini waited by the window in a corner of the rest house, watching the traffic and the crowd in the street below, inhaling the smoke spewed by the buses that plied this dusty town on the way to the border city of Birgunj or back to Kathmandu. They'd arrived here at three o'clock in the afternoon on the day of her wedding. Every time Mohini thought about home, fear crawled up her skin. She saw Father's face, angry and bewildered, and mentally she offered him a fervent, tormented apology: Father, I didn't mean to. I had no choice.

She didn't want to dwell on what was happening at home, but hard as she tried, she couldn't help but picture Mother waking up in the morning and discovering Mohini's absence. Mother would think that Mohini had gone down to the courtyard for a bath or to the toilet. Humming, Mother would mentally check all the things she, along with a horde of women who'd soon show up, had to do this morning before the groom's party, escorted by a loud band, arrived around nine o'clock. Even when Mohini didn't come up after half an hour, Mother didn't make much of it. She'd meant to observe the courtyard from the balcony, but each time a hundred things – flowers for the ceremony, colored cloths the priest had demanded, sweets such as laddoos and pedas – had occupied her mind.

There had been some disagreement between the two families about the most propitious time for the wedding entourage to arrive at the bride's bouse. The bride's priest, after consulting several religious calendars and patros, came up with eleven o'clock. Bur the groom's priest had configured a time of nine a.m. as the most auspicious moment as dictated by the stars and the planets. "Amateur." he'd declared the bride's priest to be, and the bride's priest, the most humble of the two, had consulted his calendars and books again and scratched his head: the nine o'clock time his colleague had deduced showed the dark shadows of Mars in ascension, and everyone knew that Mars wreaked havoc on marriages, unless its corresponding position in the birth charts of both the bride and the groom neutralized its ill effects. The bride's priest consulted the groom's chart again. Mangal was safely ensconced in the fourth house, whereas in the bride's it sat in the fifth. "Impossible," the priest muttered to himself. But he was a young priest who had been forced to take over the family's occupation because his father had died abruptly, and he couldn't imagine going up against the elderly priest from the groom's side, someone who had known his father. Still, he meekly suggested to the bride's mother that perhaps the more venerable priest had miscalculated the influence of the planets. Mother rebuked him, saying that his dead father would probably have concurred with the groom's priest. "But, but, look here," the young priest stuttered, waving the patro at Mother.

She simply shoved him aside and said, "What difference does a couple of hours make? Devote your time to more important matters than quibbling over an hour here or there." It makes all the difference, the priest thought, but he didn't say more. Still, he had managed to plant a seed of doubt in Mother's mind. Her son had shacked up with the oil man's daughter without the benefit of astrological consultation, and she was sure that the stars, had their alignment been considered, would have directed her son to a different, less scandalous life. So Mother did pass on the priest's misgivings to the middlewoman who'd initially talked to Father about the alliance. The middlewoman scolded her, said the groom's priest was sought after by royalty and aristocrats, and how dare the young priest question his judgment! The matter was settled.

In her mind, Mohini saw the women from the surrounding houses barge into the living room, asking where the bride was so they could begin to style her hair and make her pretty. Father would already be down in the courtyard with the priest, making preparations for the big event, which, Mother would realize in a panic, was only a couple of hours away. "Can you shout at Mohini to finish up quickly and come up?" she yelled at her husband below. "She needs to start getting ready."

Father nodded. He was busy instructing some neighborhood boys who were setting up chairs for the guests. He shouted in the direction of the outhouse, urging his daughter to be done immediately. Then Father turned to help a boy string some colored papers across the length of the courtyard, and upstairs Mother rummaged for some gold and silver coins she'd need later.

"Has Mohini eloped? Where is she?" one of the women said, joking, and the rest guffawed; at the sound of their clamorous voices, Mother dropped a gold coin, which rolled across the floor, then slid under the large cupboard by the door. That's when Mother knew that something was amiss: she hadn't seen or heard Mohini all morning long. Asking the women to retrieve her coin Mother rushed down to the courtyard, perspiring. Without speaking to her husband, she made her way to the outhouse and softly called Mohini's name so as not to attract attention. When there was no answer she reached out and pulled the door, which swung open. The outhouse was empty.

She turned and ran back upstairs, ignoring Father, who called to her, asking why she was in such a hurry. There, one of the women was lying on the floor, her cheek flat against it, her thin arms groping for the coin under the cupboard. Mother reached Mohini's room, and out of desperation, she looked under the bed, wondering if the girl was hiding there because of wedding night jitters. She ran down again to the street, hoping that her daughter, on a whim, had sauntered to the corner shop to buy some spicy titaura. Mother looked left and right. By this time, her thumping up and down the stairs had aroused the suspicion of the women, who came to the window and asked her what the matter was. The more astute knew instantly the reason for Mother's desperate look and cried out, "She ran away, didn't she?"

A pedestrian who had stopped, attracted by the bright red cloth sign that announced AUSPICIOUS WEDDING, looked up at the women and shouted, "Who? The bride? She ran away?"

Everything exploded then. Father, who had been showing a boy how to tie the bamboo poles together for the wedding pyre, bellowed, "Who ran away?" He knew the answer before he'd completed his question. Letting go of the bamboo pole, he hurried upstairs and checked and rechecked every room, warning the women "Don't make a fuss. Mohini has probably just stepped out. Maybe she's hiding somewhere as a practical joke."

Less than an hour remained before the groom's arrival. Mother's small yellow suitcase with a broken hinge was missing, and its contents were found dumped in a corner of her bedroom. Father opened his safe and discovered that four hundred rupees had evaporated. "Your son probably has a hand in this," he said to Mother. "Send someone to that bastard's house immediately."

He glanced at the clock: half an hour left. Still enough time to salvage this, he thought, although his mind was getting slower by the minute. If Mohini had indeed sought shelter at her brother's house, he had enough time to drag her home. I'll tie her with ropes to the wedding pyre if I have to, he promised himself; I'll gag her with a piece of the priestly cloth. "Wait, I'll go myself." He warned the women in the room, "Not a peep to anyone. She's your daughter too, not only mine. If the groom's party arrives here before I do, distract them, act normal. If my nose is cut today, yours will be too." Not all the women were persuaded by this my-family-is-your family appeal. Some would be gleeful to witness the shaming of this family one more time, and now they pleasurably considered the likelihood that another scandal was about to strike the old man. But they did not show these feelings; their faces looked grave.

A small crowd, murmuring and gesticulating, had already collected below the AUSPICIOUS WEDDING sign. They fell silent as Father, dressed in his starchy wedding kurta suruwal, hurried in the direction of his son's house, scanning the street for the taxis that sometimes appeared on this side street. He couldn't find one, but that didn't stop him; he began jogging toward his destination. He prayed that no one from the groom's family would spot him in this state, his face flushed and frightened. Why had both his children chosen to bring such enormous pain to the family? He glanced up at the sky as if beseeching the gods, but saw only stealthy black clouds gathering. People said that a rainy-day wedding foretold great happiness for the couple; perhaps the swirling clouds did mean that his daughter was at her brother's house, simply afraid. In that case all he needed to do was coax and cajole her, use a sweet voice he vaguely remembered using when she was a child and climbed onto his lap, demanding stories.

Mohini loved – he remembered now – hearing him talk about the Giant Earthquake of 1934, which leveled the city and left thousands dead.

"Where were you, Father," Mohini asked, "when the earthquake struck?"

"I was in this room, right here," Father said. "It was a little bit past two in the afternoon. I was lying on the floor, dozing, when I heard a rumble, like something was boiling under the ground. I thought I was dreaming. But my whole body was shaking, so I sat up. You know that pomelo tree outside?"

Mohini nodded.

"It was slapping the side of the house – the whole tree swaying like a leaf. I stood, but the floor moved so much that I had to crouch. I cried for your mother, then remembered that she had gone to her parents' house." His wife had taken some leftover ghiu and chaku from the previous day's Maghe Sankrati festival to her aging parents.

"Father, were you worried about Mother?"

He had been more than worried. His in-laws' house was nearly a century old, with a roof that had already begun to crumble, and he couldn't see how it could survive any earthquake, let alone a monster this big. He could hear thunderous crashes as houses in the neighborhood collapsed. In his mind flashed a picture of his wife, buried under the rubble of his father-in-law's house. "A little," he told Mohini. "I didn't have time to think."

Even as his house rocked, he managed to stumble down the stairs, then was jettisoned into the street, where the ground moved back and forth like a sieve. All around him houses were collapsing, emitting booming sounds like cannon shots. Dust swirled, sideways and upward. Wails and cries penetrated the air. A young man crawled down the street on all fours.

Then the earth became still.

"And Mother was all right?" Mohini asked. "She didn't die?"

"Of course not, silly," he said, pinching her nose. "If she'd died, how would she be alive today to be your mother? Your mother, fortunately, had gone to the local dhara to fetch some water, so she was spared. But both her parents perished under the weight of the roof."

"Do people who die in earthquakes go to heaven?"

"Why wouldn't they? Of course they do. Besides, your grandparents were very religious people, so I'm sure they're sitting on God's lap at this very moment, just like you're sitting on mine."

"But people who kill themselves don't go to heaven."

"Where did you learn that?"

"Pradip Dai told me."

'And how does he know this? He's barely a few years older than you."

"He said people who kill themselves return to earth as ghosts and scare other people. He says that there's a ghost who lives under our stairs, a khyak, with no Flesh on his body, only bones."

Father laughed. "Your Pradip Dai is nothing but trouble."

"Pradip Dai says that at night, on the Rani Pokhari pond there are women kichkanni ghosts who float on water. He says their feet are strange, with their toes facing backward, their heels in the front. They prey on single men and suck their blood. Is that true, Father?"

"Nonsense," he said.

After a few moments, Mohini asked, "Father, do you love Mother?"

Her question had embarrassed him, for men didn't confess such love unless it was in the dark, at night in bed. He certainly hadn't felt the need to proclaim his love for Mohini's mother. They were husband and wife – didn't that say it all? But that afternoon of the earthquake, after the city stopped rocking and heaving, his heart had collapsed as he'd pictured his wife's body mangled under the weight of her parents' roof.

Driven by anxiety, he'd made his way across the city to her. Many houses had simply crumpled to the ground. Survivors walked around, injured, tottering, crying out for their loved ones. He could see, from across Rani Pokhari, that the beautiful Ghantaghar clock tower no longer rose to the sky. In the distance to the south, Dharahara's piercing top was absent; the monument had broken in half. As he moved into Asan and Indrachowk, he had to skirt or climb over mounds of rubble; he occasionally glimpsed a severed arm or a head among the debris. Once he spotted a face between the bricks, eyes staring, the mouth moving as though attempting to converse.

"The Tundikhel parade ground has ruptured," he heard someone say. In the Basantapur Durbar Square, the tops of several temples had been shaved off. The Kal Bhairav statue, with his glaring dark face, had remained more or less intact, and Father prayed in front of the fierce god, briefly, before heading on to Jaisideval, where he found his wife wailing, her childhood home in ruins, the pitcher full of water she'd fetched next to her on the ground. He'd put his arm around her, the first time in public, and asked her what was wrong. She'd buried her face in his chest, cried a bit, and said that she thought both her parents were dead.

Unable to answer his daughter's question directly; he'd ended up saying, "I love everyone in this family." He'd stroked Mohini's hair and whispered, "And I'll tell you a secret. I love you the most."

He tried to recall that voice as he pushed through the vegetable-buying crowd in Asan, but he couldn't. All he could hear was a preachy, judgmental voice that now began to castigate him, telling him how pathetic he looked running around, trying to find his daughter on the day of her wedding, with the groom's party, in full regalia, probably already en route to his house. Father felt like giving up; he wanted to crawl into a corner of the marketplace and weep. But he pressed on, pushed through the multitude until he reached his son's house, the very son he had expressly forbidden to attend Mohini's wedding.

"It'll create a bad impression," he'd said with pursed lips to Pradip when his son came over with his wife a few days earlier, on their first visit to the house since they got married. "You'll have to wait until the wedding is over. Then you can visit Mohini, but only after she returns here for a few days, not at her new home."

Pradip had glanced at Chanda, disappointed. "But she's my sister. Why can't I attend her wedding?"

"I can't stop you, but as a big brother, do you want anything to go wrong during Mohini's wedding? Do you realize how hard we've worked to secure this family, this groom, especially after the two of you" – he gave a small nod toward his son's wife, her presence, her validity as a new member of his family – "after you two . . . well. I'll leave that decision up to you."

Pradip looked pained, caught in a quandary. He turned to his wife, but she had her head down, too cowed by her father-in-law to say anything. Finally Pradip said, "Well, I so badly want to attend, but not at the risk of ruining things for my sister. I will visit her in her new home, though, in a few days, and you can't stop me." He addressed Mohini, who, throughout this exchange, had been quietly leaning against the wall. "Right bahini?"

As he neared Pradip's house, Father realized that he ought to have sensed something was wrong right then, for Mohini's face had paled when her brother mentioned visiting her at her new home. As he stood in front of his son's house, Father hesitated. Had Mohini done this out of spite? Had he been such a bad father? Had he been too strict? After all, it was not one child of his but both who had expressly defied his wishes and damaged the family name for generations to come. They had been good kids when they were young, and as a father he'd provided them with all they needed. So what went wrong?

Standing in the street, facing his son's second-floor window, Father was about to call Pradip when he became certain that Mohini wasn't inside. Fleetingly, he saw Pradip through the window, then his daughter-in-law, who, he had to admit, looked like a good, well-brought-up girl when he saw her a week ago. His son and his daughter-in-law appeared to be jostling in their room, laughing, mildly punching each other. Then Pradip turned his head and saw Father on the street, leaning against his cane, his face pale and stricken.

At first Pradip felt embarrassed at having Father witness the amorous scuffle between him and his wife; then it dawned on him that now was the time of his sister's wedding. He knew something was terribly,

terribly wrong. Yudhir came to his mind, suddenly, for his friend had, Pradip thought, been acting quite strange lately, casually plying him with questions about how he would feel if someone eloped with his sister, just as he'd eloped with Chanda.

"Why? Are you planning to elope with her, muji?" Pradip had said. "If you look at my sister with a crooked eye, I'll gouge it out, break your arms, and throw you into the Bagmati River."

Yudhir had failed to catch the joke and had become defensive. "What are you saying, yaar? Your sister is like my sister, isn't she? My question was more philosophical than anything." Pradip had thought that perhaps Yudhir had developed a small crush on Mohini; no surprise there, as she was beautiful, and no harm in a minor infatuation. But now, with Father outside his window, looking as if he was going to disintegrate like a poorly constructed doll, Pradip knew, instinctively, that his sister had vanished and that Yudhir was involved.

Pradip could imagine the two of them together, seated on a bus, shoulders touching, on the steep, winding road carved out of the sides of the hills that began at the western edge of the Kathmandu Valley. Their fingers occasionally inched toward each other, hidden from other passengers. Strained but hopeful smiles lingered on their lips. Yes, Pradip could see how it would be: he knew his sister, he knew his friend, and he knew their smiles. She must not have slept all night, waiting for the *ding-dong* of the grandfather clock to announce three in the morning. That's when she'd sit up, pull out the yellow suitcase from under her bed; she'd crammed it with a few of her clothes and some knickknacks. She wouldn't bother to change her crumpled dhoti, for she didn't want to waste any time, and the rustling of the clothes could wake up Mother in the corner. With the aid of the streetlamp, which threw some light into her room, she combed and knotted her hair, then tiptoed out. Her door creaked, as it always did. She nearly tripped over something Mother had laid on the balcony right outside her room, and she stopped momentarily, holding her breath. She didn't hear any movement inside, so she quickly went down the stairs with the nimbleness of a cat.

The bus ride was hair-raising. The driver was a wildly enthusiastic fellow who sang filmi songs half the way there, and he took risks with the dangerous curves that started as soon as the bus began to climb past Thankot.

She could tell that Yudhir was nervous, perhaps more than she was. He remained quiet as their bus nearly brushed against large trucks as the driver negotiated treacherous corners. Sometimes the bus's wheel came so close to the edge of the road that Mohini could look down a distance of hundreds of feet; it made her heart rise to her throat. Tribhuvan Rajpath was the country's first highway; it allowed people to come and go from the capital without having to walk for days. Because it was the only road out of the city, everyone called it By-Road.

The bus passed through clouds, and Mohini squeezed Yudhir's hand, to reassure him. "Once we get married and return in a couple of years, after earning some money, they'll accept us," she whispered, her head nestled against his shoulder. Gone was the confidence he had on the day when he challenged her to take this trip with him. Now he looked like a little boy, afraid of the punishment coming to him at the end of the day. As the bus droned on toward the south, climbing up and down the hills, white mountains shone to the north. Twice the bus had to stop because of landslides, which laborers in ragged clothes were clearing with shovels. Only a few years old, the highway sometimes closed down because of these landslides, at times for days. During these delays, the couple watched cargo being transported up and down the hills on ropeways.

The more their journey progressed, the more Yudhir avoided Mohini's eyes, and when he did look at her, he appeared frightened. When he smiled, the expression was so tentative, so forced, that she couldn't help but rub his chin with the back of her fingers and reassure him that everything would be okay that they were following the beats of their hearts, weren't they? But he didn't appear comforted, and strangely, his fears made her own anxieties more tolerable. "Scared?" she asked him.

His eyes were focused on the big windshield up front, which revealed rolling hills as far as the eye could see. "Just a bit worried, that's all," he said.

She knew that he lived with his uncle in the city; his parents remained back in the village. His uncle was a strict Brahmin and disapproved of his nephew's singing because most of the songs he sang were from films, which his uncle considered lewd and corrupt. His uncle wanted him to sing hymns and use his God-given talent solely for God's service, and since that wouldn't make a good career, had commanded him to pursue something else. "Sometimes I get so mad at the bastard," Yudhir had said to her in the Baghbazar hotel. "He is a good guardian, but he is stuck in the previous century. Do you know what he's like? If an untouchable person passes within five feet of him on the road, he'll head straight home to take a bath."

"I'm not an untouchable, but I am of a lower caste than you. What will he think of me?"

"Who cares what he thinks? He's not going to dictate my life for me."

As the bus wove in and out of the mountain clouds, and as the woman sitting behind them stuck her head out the window and began to retch, Mohini wondered if Yudhir too sometimes saw her with the eyes of his uncle. Then she dismissed this line of thinking and squeezed his hand.

She would have been right to wonder whether he had begun to view her differently. The moment they'd boarded the bus at five in the morning, guilt had begun to creep into Yudhir's chest, his throat; as they began their journey and the sun came up and the driver sped through the cramped roads of the hills, it had amplified until it consumed him. He was betraying a cherished belief of his uncle: caste purity. His uncle had given him more love and care than his own parents had. All right, so the man could be unreasonable and vexing, but he was still blood, and here was Yudhir, with this girl he hardly knew. She was sweet, yes, and he'd already tasted her juices, but what else did he know about her? Nothing. As her head rested on his shoulder and she murmured about plans for the future, he was already beginning to feel sick of her jasmine-scented hair oil, a smell he'd found intoxicating a few days ago. He stifled the urge to push her away and jolt her out of this stupid, stupid dream. I never promised to marry you, he told her in his mind. Already he'd begun cursing himself for this foolhardy move. Who was this girl? Nobody. He could have played with her for a while, taken her out to a movie or two, then moved on. He ought to have let her marry whomever she was about to marry, and within weeks she'd have adjusted to her husband and begun to feel happy with him. That's how things always worked. Rarely had he seen an arranged marriage, fixed by the couple's parents, fail, and rarely had he seen marriages born through silly romantic notions of love survive more than a few years. Our society, he theorized, channeling his uncle's voice, is simply not equipped to handle this thing called romantic love, even though our extravagant, melodramatic movies constantly lure us to it. For us, it's family, status, economic well-being, caste. A meeting of the minds trumps any meeting of the hearts!

Mohini fell asleep against his shoulder toward afternoon, as they began the descent to the lush vegetation of the lower hills. Beads of perspiration appeared above her upper lip, and every now and then she winced. Yudhir could sense the worries that arose in her dreams, and he felt sorry for her, for now he had begun to feel calm. He knew what he had to do, but he didn't know exactly when or how to do it. Once they began their train journey across the vast expanse of India on their way to Bombay, there would be numerous opportunities for him to simply slip way. He closed his eyes and saw himself stepping off the train onto the platform of a minor station somewhere, with the name of Sitapur or Rampur or Laxmanpur, in the searing heat of Bihar. "My throat is parched," he'd say. "Let me go find something to drink." And he'd simply go behind the small rectangular building that served as the train station and catch a rickshaw into town. He could even watch her from behind the station house: she would be at the compartment window, scanning the platform, her expression growing more anxious by the second, especially after the train whistle blew. Would she shout out his name? Would she too step off the train to find him, leaving their luggage on board? As the train jerked into motion, what thoughts would race through her head?

In the bus Yudhir closed his eyes, savoring her likely hysteria. Numerous strategies arose in his mind. As the bus stopped in the middle of nowhere and the driver stepped out for a trickle in the bushes, Yudhir knew that he could gently disengage himself from her right now and get off, in these lower hills with their numerous riverbed crossings, and hop on the next truck heading to the capital. What would she do then? She'd probably wake up about half an hour later and, not finding him next to her, at first think that he was chatting with a passenger up front. Still drowsy, she'd peel an orange, suck the juice, while her eyes roamed the interior of the bus, searching for him. When she realized he wasn't on board, she'd bolt to the front of the bus, lurching into passengers, and she'd yell at the driver that her man was missing. Negotiating a hairpin curve, the driver would say that it was impossible to turn back now.

She was softly snoring against his shoulder. The driver got back to his seat and started the bus. Yudhir would wait until Hetauda, then right after they stepped off the bus he'd tell her that he had to find a place to urinate, badly; then he'd vanish, catch the next bus to Kathmandu, or head to the border, watch a few movies in Raxaul or Muzaffarpur, and then return after a couple of days. His uncle would be angry at him for a day or two but so what? It was not as though he'd run away from a wedding his uncle had arranged for him! The thought made him laugh inwardly. The idiocy of this girl! What was she thinking when she decided to run away on her wedding day – of all days! – and ruin her family name forever? It was downright criminal. Her brother, Pradip, was another story; he was a man and his transgressions would be forgotten in a year or two. But not the daughter of the house. If Yudhir had a sister who'd behaved like Mohini, he'd flog her for what she'd done. This thought made him strangely happy – the idea of this girl being beaten by a man – if not him, then her father, or perhaps her husband. He could easily see his uncle beating this girl, if she were his daughter. The idea of punishing her physically for her monumental sin Yudhir found exciting, and to his surprise, he began to harden. He closed his eyes and pictured himself slapping her around a bit, then grabbing her roughly by the hair and kissing her fiercely on the lips, then asking her to take off her blouse and show him her breasts, which he'd then fondle. He'd command her to take off her sari and stand in front of him in only her petticoat. He'd tell her to begin rubbing herself down there, gently at first, then harder and harder, until she'd moan and ask him to come close. But he'd deny her request, say that she was a dirty girl and he wouldn't touch her in a million years. He was rock hard now, next to her on the bus, and he stealthily took her hand, placed it on his crotch, and rubbed it against his penis, picturing her with her pointed, delicate tits, her face pleading with desire. Abruptly he came, and then went limp. He lifted her hand and placed it back in her lap. His thighs were sticky now, and he was slightly disgusted with himself.

He could take her all the way to Bombay, he thought, begin a semblance of their life together in that giant, pulsating city. He could try for work in the film music industry, and she could get a job somewhere – as what, though? A girl from a respectable family, she couldn't possibly do housework. Could she get a job as a secretary? But she didn't know how to type and could speak only a smattering of English. Who would give her a job in that big city where, he imagined, everybody spoke perfect English? He would be the sole breadwinner, and she would be a burden, though he could tell that she'd work hard at home, making it spick-and-span for him, cooking him delicious meals every night. His optimism about becoming a singing sensation had dampened considerably since the morning. He was no longer sure that the path to stardom in Bombay would be easy. He knew he was talented, but how many young men like him all across India, were making the trip to Bombay right now, dreaming of breaking into the film music industry? The notion of battling hundreds of singers to reach the ears of a direcror or a producer tired him. He had a better chance, he thought, of winning the Bhagyodaya lottery.

"Foolhardy," he whispered to himself, and hearing his voice, she awoke and asked him where they were.

"I think Hetauda is close by. We can eat some snacks there and find a bus to Birgunj."

"I had such troubling dreams."

"They were only dreams," he said, smoothing her hair.

In Hetauda, they learned at the bus park that a big accident just up the road to Birgunj, near the toll station of Amlekhgunj, had obstructed traffic completely. Many Birgunj–Hetauda and Birgunj–Kathmandu buses had returned to Birgunj. "The road could be clear tonight, or tomorrow; we can't be sure," they were told. "Your best bet is to find a place to sleep here overnight, then try tomorrow. The government is sending some folks to help this evening."

And that's what they did. It was a two-story rest house in the main market, near the bus stop. Each floor had a large room with about a dozen cots, where the passengers slept. At the counter Yudhir looked at Mohini, who pulled fifteen rupees from her bag. An image of Father flashed through her mind, but she forced herself not to think about home right now.

As soon as they entered the rest house, because of anxiety or the dust in the air, Mohini began to cough viciously; Yudhir thumped her on the back, but still the coughing continued. He felt her forehead and said, "There's no fever." Her face was turning purple though, and he honestly became worried. He suggested that he go to buy some cough syrup because she seemed to have caught a cold – "a change of air and water, I'm sure" – and although she shook her head no, that he shouldn't bother, she continued to cough.

"You need some medicine," he said. "I'll be right back."

Downstairs he asked the rest-house owner where the medicine shop was.

It was less than a block away, around the corner, right next to the bus stop where they'd got off. He asked the compounder, who was seated inside on a stool, for a remedy for his wife's unrelenting cough, relishing how easily he called Mohini his wife, and how good it felt to say it. The compounder gave him the bottle, told him the dosage she needed. Yudhir stood outside the shop, holding the bottle in his hand, reading the label. Then he walked to the bus park. He asked around to see if a bus would be leaving for Kathmandu that evening. The drivers shook their heads. "Too dangerous," they said. A truck engine was revving up a few yards away. Yudhir walked toward the driver, who was a Sikh, wearing a large turban. In broken Hindi, Yudhir asked him whether he was going to Kathmandu. The Sikh caressed his mustache and said, "Come in, come in. I could use some company."

Yudhir hopped onto the high seat of the truck. In his mind he began forming excuses for his absence that would placate his uncle when Yudhir reached home early in the morning.

SNAKE LAKE

Jeff Greenwald

Jeff Greenwald is the author of five bestselling books, including *Shopping for Buddhas* and *The Size of the World*. His writing has appeared in many print and online publications including *The New York Times Magazine, National Geographic Adventure, Wired, Tricycle,* and *Salon.* He lives in Oakland, California.

When a Nepali mentions a naga, he or she isn't referring to a garden snake. The classic naga, a snake god, is the hooded cobra: the Arnold Schwarzenegger of the serpent world.

Nagas pop up everywhere in Hindu and Buddhist lore, savvy brokers between the spiritual and elemental worlds. Lord Vishnu, the great preserver of the Hindu trinity, dozes on the infinite coils of Ananta, a serpent-cumcouch, for eight months of the year (during the remaining four, he extricates humanity from its deadlier dilemmas). Shiva, the potent creator/destroyer, source of the Ganges, wears live cobras in his hair. Nagas are the wardens of the monsoon rains, and safeguard the Earth's trove of diamonds, jewels, and underground treasures. And it was Muchilinda Naga, a seven-hooded cobra, who sheltered the Buddha from the sun and rain during his seven weeks of meditation on the banks of the Anoma River.

Nowhere is the Asian respect for serpents more evident than in tantra. In these "secret teachings," snakes symbolize the deepest source of spiritual power. The kundalini lies coiled at our lowest psychic center: the root chakra, located between our legs at the base of our spine. Through specific meditations and practices – like measured breathing, sexual yoga, and the recitation of mantras – we invite that snake to dance. It climbs the spine, electrifying the six internal chakras. It reaches the *ajna* chakra, right between the eyes, then rises higher still, penetrating the cranium. There it illuminates the *sahasrara* chakra, the Lotus of a Thousand Petals, which hovers like a gnat above our skulls. When your kundalini hits that point, you know you've arrived. You embrace, with a single glance, all the manifestations of existence.

Once again, you've taken a bite of that big, juicy apple. And again, you have a snake to thank for it.

And what about Jordan? Maybe all he needed was a good snake dance: something to revitalize his long-dormant kundalini. I'd be home in less than a week – but I wondered if I might somehow convey, through telepathic alchemy, a real-time blessing from the Earth itself.

Ramana lay on a blanket inside the brick shed beside the shrine house, dozing beside his flea-ridden mongrel. I put my hand on the caretaker's shoulder and shook him gently. The dog growled, but hardly stirred. The shrine-keeper rose reluctantly.

"*Ramana . . . Malai naga puja garna manlaagchha.*"

He looked at me quizzically. What need had a Westerner for a snake puja? Aside from their mythic role in the monsoon, nagas were petitioned when ground was broken for a well, or a house, or when any new construction was about to begin. The offering was essentially a protection payoff, in hopes the local snakes would steer clear of the enterprise. Nonetheless Ramana nodded at my request, and ducked into the tiny brick building. A moment later he emerged, handing me a small brass flask filled with buffalo milk. He topped the rim with a nasturtium, muttering a brief prayer. I handed him a 20-rupee note and returned to my bench.

The mist was beginning to break. Shafts of light shot through the branches of a nearby eucalyptus tree and stenciled the green water. I couldn't see more than a foot down. How deep *was* this pool, anyway? What, or who, lived at the bottom?

Did I really want to know? It was a disturbing thought. As I peered over the pond's edge, I understood something. There is more to this snake thing than the idea of transformation. Snakes have another quality, as well: They abide in the depths. Black water is their domain, and we summon them out at our peril.

So what was Nag Pokhari, then? It wasn't the pathetic pool in front of me, covered with scum and algae. It wasn't the cartoon cobra with a goofy expression and forked tongue, peering archly from its capital. It wasn't the clogged jets ejaculating lamely from the reservoir's corners. It wasn't the benches, or the lotus, or the little temple by the entrance gate. It wasn't even the snakes themselves, assuming that any still lived here.

This domain of the nagas, this Snake Lake, was nothing less than a double-edged allegory for everything ecstatic and horrific about the prospect of liberation. The nagas and their domain are mythic metaphors, warning buoys on the unexplored waters of our psyches. Lacking sufficient wisdom, or the proper training, we plumb these depths with fear and awe: The transition from bondage to freedom, no matter how one approaches it, has a terrifying aspect. We are suddenly responsible for ourselves.

Our best shot, our *only* shot at liberation, lies within the liquid mystery of our own bodies. It's lurking in our depths, dozing in the silt, slithering between the smooth black fingers of the lotus roots, coiled between our legs. Until we plunge in, with a torch in one hand and a flute in the other, we'll never charm it awake.

Ramana watched with amusement as, with a halting prayer, I poured the offering onto the algae-rimed surface of Snake Lake.

KARNALI BLUES

Buddhisagar Chapain

Buddhisagar Chapain is a Nepali writer. He is best known for
his novel *Karnali Blues*.

Purnabahadur Bista!
Jagat Rawal!
Basudev Chaulagain!
Phulba Chaudhari!

Chandre ripped up some dub grass from the playing field, put it into
his mouth and pretended to chew. His face was turning blue, as if he
had been stung by a scorpion. Although the sun was hanging up in the
sky, I felt as if it was squatting on my forehead. Sweat drenched my face
as if I had been splashed with water.

Ninety-five students were spread out across the playing field, like
scraps of the question papers and answer booklets of the previous
examination. If anyone spoke I would die. From far away the sound of
the mill reached our ears: *tuktuk, tuktuk*.

Results day. At school the Sirs were reading out the results. Our
elder sisters' results were being read out in the classroom, the results of
classes below Grade 5 on the playing field. Karnabahadur Sir had taken
responsibility for announcing our results. Everyone wanted to hear his
name from Sir's mouth. Sir was turning the pages of the Lali Gurans exercise book and calling out the names. I was already semi-unconscious.

Oh Lord, may that exercise book never come to an end.

Sir shouted, "Aitabahadaur B.K!"

There, even his name has come. Aite jumped up and spun around.
He laughed like Shiva in the photo, standing on one leg: hehehe! He
was the biggest in our Class Three. Fourteen years old.

Sir was standing on a high bench. When he looked at the exercise
book he did so through strong glasses. After he said each name he
looked out over them. A white shirt, brown patterned pants, leather

shoes – Sir was always smartly dressed. There was always a muffler around his neck. That's why Sir was popular with everyone – he never beat us and he taught the class all three subjects. Lifting his eyes from the book he shouted –

Rambahadur Bogate!

Bogate too jumped up and ran towards the gate. Now ants began to run along the nerves in my brain. I felt as if my head was swelling and getting bigger and bigger, too big to support. I hung my heavy head low.

"We've failed, I reckon," said Chandre in a disconsolate voice. "Sir's book is nearly finished."

"We'll come at the end." I looked at Sir with great hope.

And then, Yuvaraj Gautam!

Yuvaraj wasn't there, so he didn't get up. Chandre's breathing whistled like a river. His lips trembled. He rolled his wet eyes at me and hiccoughed.

Sir shut the book, and I thought my breath would stop. All the students jumped up and danced and ran towards Sir, because Sir had pulled the red abir out of his pocket. They used to put abir on those who had passed. There were ten or twelve of us whose names had not come. I had failed. There now, there goes my blinky watch. I held back the sobs.

Sir was happily putting abir on the foreheads of the passes. The fails headed for the gate, hanging their heads. Chandre and I just sat where we were. Our sisters had passed. They would move up to study in Class Six. They came up to us, giggling. They both looked fresh in their sky blue shirts and dark blue skirts.

Parvati Didi bent down a little and asked "What happened?"

"Fail," I told her in a dead voice.

Suddenly Chandre burst into sobs. His body shook. Mamata Didi put her hand on his head and said, "Don't cry, my brother."

"Ba will beat me." Chandre wept uncontrollably.

"Don't cry, I won't let him beat you."

This affection made Chandre tremble even more.

"Study well next year," Parvati Didi said, "And you'll pass."

Holding our hands, our sisters got us up and made us walk. Three-Heads was standing near the gate with abir all over his forehead. Two boys were beside him. Three-Heads was chewing on a long stick of sugarcane. When he saw us he laughed mockingly, because there was no abir on our foreheads. Our sisters went out through the gate giggling and patting one another. We approached Three-Heads. That was the route we had to take. Three-Heads suddenly made as if to strike Chandre over the head with the sugarcane, whack! Chandre ducked to the right to save his head. All three of them laughed like demons on the radio, making the very school shake – hahaha.

"Passes eat sugarcane!" Three-Heads shouted at the top of his voice.

The two boys who were with him laughed, "And fails?"

"This here . . ." Three-Heads pointed at his private parts.

Chandre became tearful. He looked at Three-Heads from red eyes. I grabbed his arm and pulled him away, and he came along limping. Even when we were well past him, Three-Heads was still shouting.

Our sisters had gone on ahead without us because they were happy to have passed. Chandre and I were on our own. We didn't speak all the way home. Whenever we saw someone on the road we hid behind a tree. What would we say if they asked us if we'd passed?

We snuck down via the far bank of the Amauri Khola, in case they asked at the teashop too. Dusk had already fallen. The Amauri Khola was deserted. Chandre and I sat on the edge of the river. The breeze was cold – it was touching us inside, getting in through the torn armpits of our shirts and up through the gaps in our shorts. A little way off the yellow light of a lantern spilled out of the teashop. The murmur of people's voices reached us. The Sauji had recently begun to sell sealed bottles of raksi. People said the lights burned in the teashop until midnight!

Chandre was silent. He knew that tonight his father would thrash him. So he was refusing to go home. Even now his lips were trembling a little.

"Your father won't beat you, right?" Chandre looked at me.

I said nothing, I just lowered my head.

"Let's go," I said, catching hold of his hand.

He said nothing but slowly got up. We walked on, brushing off our shorts. Like dark stumps, we were returning home via the bank of the Amauri Khola at the time when the English news comes on the radio.

I was the stump in front, walking hurriedly, the other stump was Chandre, limping along.

"Come here," Ba called me as soon as he saw me.

I climbed up with a miserable face.

"You failed, didn't you? You didn't put your mind to it when it was time to study. Everyone passed, you failed."

The skin on my face tightened.

Ba stroked my hair. "I thought my son would study and become an important man, but you're on your way to being a cowherd."

My eyes filled with tears.

"You have saddened my heart, son."

I sobbed.

"All right, off you go. You'll pass next time." Ba pushed me gently away. "I'll bring you a watch next time."

I went down the stairs wiping my eyes.

"You've made us cry today." That was all Mother said.

"Study well from now on, you hear?" Sister looked at me, with the abir not washed very well from her face. "I'll teach you."

I cried all night. From time to time I thought of Chandre. His father must have beaten him badly. If only he had a father like mine – he didn't beat me, but he slapped my heart.

Next day, in the afternoon, Magarmama told us, "I had diarrhoea in the morning, and when I went outside there was a black shadow going towards the Amauri Khola. I was scared that it might be a ghost."

I knew that this was Chandre, because he said it was limping.

Chandre disappeared from the village that very morning.

His father searched all over for him. In Lamichane Basti, Tharu Gaon, Paharipur, everywhere. Ba said he even went to Katase and filed a report at the police post.

"Hey, did Chandre say anything to you?" Ba asked me on the third day of Chandre's disappearance, "Where might he have gone?"

"He used to say he'd go and see his brother," I told him, "Perhaps he's gone to Bombay."

"He didn't encourage you to go with him?"

I sat in silence. Ba's face darkened.

"Someone who runs away from home just for failing once is a

coward," said father, tossing a two rupee note toward me. "A son should not run away from home."

After Chandre ran away Ba was very frightened that I might run away too. Whenever he came back from Katase he would look for me immediately. By luck he would find me studying. After Chandre had gone I didn't go to the Amauri Khola for several days. After many days I met Bhagiram on the bridge near the Amauri Khola one Saturday afternoon. He set his fan down to one side and asked me, rubbing tobacco in his hand, "Where did that silly boy go?"

"Bombay."

"How could such a little boy get to Bombay?"

I couldn't forget Chandre for many days. Even in my dreams he seemed to be calling me. After a couple of weeks Ba went to Nepalganj for five days. He came home on the afternoon of the sixth day. Because it was Friday I had come home from school early and I was sleeping. I woke to the sound of his bicycle bell and ran downstairs, wiping the saliva from my cheek. Ba had brought a bunch of grapes, tucked into his waistband. His face was flushed. I went up to him shyly and touched my head to his feet.

"Be lucky," Ba said. "Is there no one at home?"

"She's gone to the shop to get some sugar."

"Go and get me some water, I'm parched!"

I hurried off and brought a pitcher of water for him. Ba drank it, making his adam's apple go up and down. Some water spilled down and wet his chest. Setting the pitcher down on the floor, he moved his hand towards his pocket. When it came out, there it was in his hand – a blinky watch.

"Come here." Ba took hold of my left wrist. In a second he attached the watch to my wrist. Ba asked, "What time is it then?"

"Thirty-five minutes and seventeen seconds past three" I said shyly.

"Go and study."

I ran off to the attic like a whirlwind.

At meal time that evening Ba told us that on his way back he was on the same bus as Lamichane Kancha. He told Ba that he had seen Chandre in a teashop in Nepalganj. He was washing tea glasses there. When he saw him he ran away limping.

"I don't know where he came from," the potbellied Sahuji shouted, "I gave him work but the little sod ran away again."

I couldn't sleep for a long time, thinking of Chandre. From time to time I pressed the button on the rim of the watch, and the watch lit up. When I was looking at the watch at 12:45:17 Ba woke up.

"How many more times are you going to look at your watch? Go to sleep now!" said Ba, yawning. Then he went back to sleep. I could hear the faint sound of his breathing.

Here in Matera there is no one as loving as my Ba.

NOTHING TO DECLARE

Rabi Thapa

Rabi Thapa is a writer and editor based in Kathmandu, Nepal. He is the author of the short story collection *Nothing to Declare* and the editor of the literary magazine *La.Lit* (*www. lalitmag.com*). Rabi's writing has appeared in *Outside On-line*, *Profil*, *Indian Quarterly*, *Himal Southasian*, *The Cricket Monthly*, *Live Mint*, *Mumbai Mirror*, *The Sunday Guardian*, *We Are Here* and *The National*. His short biography of Thamel, Kathmandu's famed tourist zone, is due to be published in November 2016, and he is now working on a book on Nepal's environment.

Nothing to declare. His father had grumbled about all the food his mother had packed into the suitcase – Nepali fruit drops, pastries and caramel rocks. "You know how they check everything these days. I'm sure you can buy all this in London anyway!" His mother had looked up from the suitcase wearily and shook her head. "No Raja, you don't get these things in London; Karki's son told me so. You can get those Indian sweets but not these. It's not the same! Think of how our son is going to enjoy them when he's over there . . ." She paused, her shoulders drooping of a sudden. Bikram, sensing his mother's sadness, broke in loudly: "Don't worry Mamu, I'll tell them it's Nepali Ayurvedic medicine – instant cure for homesickness! And if they give me hassle I'll just bribe them with some!"

Well, there hadn't even been any officials at customs. Everybody just rolled through with their trolleys. What kind of security was it?

The guy at passport control had given Bikram the onceover, though. Thank god his visa was in order. After all the trouble it had better be! But it didn't help to have a green passport. As soon as he'd seen it the official, who looked like an Indian, had asked him if he had any family in the UK. He did have an uncle in Reading but his friends in London had told him not to mention family. So he said no, he'd come to do a degree in computing at the University of Greenwich. The official had peered at him closely – he'd probably been pulled here by his own family in the first place, and look at him now – then stamped his passport. Clack! He was through.

Heathrow was really big and noisy. As soon as he wandered out the doors he felt as if he were being sucked into its chaos. He felt disoriented – all kinds of people milling about in all directions, bumping into each other and laughing and hugging and shouting. Where the hell was Raghav? He'd said he would be here to pick him up when had spoken to him before he left Nepal. Bikram manoeuvred his trolley over to where he saw some phone booths. But he didn't have any British money on him. There was a money-changing counter just past the phones.

"*Oi!* What're you doing, *mujhi?*"

Bikram wheeled around at the sound of his best friend's voice. Raghav stepped up to him grinning, all shaggy-haired like he'd never seen him before.

"So you got here finally! Welcome to the UK, *hai?* They didn't stop you at immigration then, seeing your thief's face?"

"You look like a terrorist from somewhere, look at this guy's hair, like a *jogi*. Your dad would skin you if he saw you!"

The two friends clapped each other on the back and laughed their way through the huzzbuzz of the terminal, oblivious to the crisscrossing of the world's peoples around them.

Less than half an hour later, they were out of Hounslow Central tube station in west London. Bikram grimaced as they bumped his suitcases along the pavement. "Hey, it's cold here man, is it always like this or what?" The autumn sky was bruised and heavy and a persistent wind snaked cold fingers around their necks.

Raghav smiled ruefully, drawing his jacket around him. "England, this is England. If the sun shines it's like a public holiday and people run around naked. You'll get used to it. You brought warm clothes like I said?" Bikram nodded, looking around the narrow street they were on.

London seemed distinctly ordinary. Identical low white houses with brown tiled roofs lined the street on both sides, fronted by raggedy

patches of grass and concrete. Cars were jammed into the short drive-
ways and parked on the street. Scarecrow trees stood disconsolate over
faded piles of leaves occasionally whipped up by the wind and scattered
over the pavement. They had passed a shop selling vegetables in boxes
right outside the station and all he'd seen around were blacks and
Indians. He'd even seen a poster for a Hindi movie on a wall. He supposed it was a poor area. What did they call them? Ghettos. "Hey, is this a
ghhheh-toe or what? Wherever I look I see *hapsis* and *dhotis*. The
kuires don't live here?"

Raghav laughed mirthlessly. "Why would they? They live in Notting
Hill, like in the movie. This is Zone 4 – it takes an hour by tube to get
to the centre."

"OK, so this is a 'remote area' then? Do we have Maoists here as
well? *Huh?*" Bikram sniggered and slapped his friend on the back.
Raghav started to speak but his words were swallowed up by a thunderous roar above them. Bikram stopped and looked up, slack-jawed.
A huge plane was lumbering past right above their heads, shredding
the doughy air with its screaming engines. "*Machikne*," he shouted.
"Where's that plane going?"

"You'll get used to that as well. You can see them lining up – six or
seven in a row – to land at Heathrow." They stopped in front of a house
that looked like all the others. "OK, here we are . . ."

A little while later, sitting around the small, plain living room with
cans of beer, Bikram felt as if he were back home – just like it was
when he used to ride over to Raghav's place for a smoke and a drink.
Of course Raghav didn't have this massive TV and sound system in his
room back in Kathmandu. His parents were a little on the stingy side;
it was a wonder they'd forked out the money to get him started here.
But the TV looked out of place in the humble dimensions of the space it
dominated, its sleek hi-tech contrasting with the off-white walls, frayed
carpet and worn, shapeless sofas.

"At least I'm independent now," Raghav declared, waving his free
hand around for emphasis. "Not that living in London you can save
anything working in a store. Whatever it is, it's better than just rotting
away in Kathmandu. Congratulations *hai*, you made it to the UK!" He
drained his beer and stood up. "You finished with that?"

Bikram nodded. "Yeah, give me one then. So, when are the other guys coming in? When did you say Suresh finished?"

Suresh was Raghav's cousin. Bikram had seen him often enough at Raghav's back in Kathmandu. "He should be back any minute, with the dope. We'll have a smoke, have some dinner, then head out for a bit of British disco. What d'you think? You haven't got *jetlyag* have you?"

Suresh worked at the Marriott in another neighbourhood. Raghav worked in a shoe store on the main street of Hounslow. Then there was Gaurav, a friend of Suresh's from Kathmandu. It wasn't a bad-sized house for four people, according to Raghav. They'd just moved from ten minutes away a month back, and they'd set aside a small room for Bikram: none of this rubbish about sleeping in corridors that he'd heard about while applying to come here. But of course he needed to find a job really soon. His part of the rent was two hundred and fifty pounds a month! That was more than 30,000 rupees. You could rent a whole house in Nepal for that!

Raghav returned with the beers, slumped into the sofa and started fiddling with the TV remote. "Hey, leave it on this song. Look at her ass, *mujhi!*" Bikram gulped his beer noisily as he stared at Jennifer Lopez shaking her way through a club scene. Great song. Great body. You never saw girls in Kathmandu like that. Though even that was changing.

"Good luck . . ." Raghav lighted a cigarette. "Don't know about J-Lo, but you might find a nice Indian chick tonight, if Srijana don't mind . . ."

Bikram pursed his lips.

"Just for one night, don't worry! Here the Indian girls are different, understand, they only look Indian, they act like they're *kuire*. Last week we went to this club, there were so many hot chicks there –" His mobile broke in with a tinny techno tune. "Wait a minute . . ." He went out into the hallway, talking and nodding.

He came back in. Bikram raised his eyebrows. "Who?"

"*Ey*, Suresh, he's just met this *hapsi* called Musti to get the G." Raghav chuckled as he sat back down.

"Musti? What kinda name is that?"

"Dunno . . . he's from Somalia, that hunger-death place. The day I got here last year I was going to the shops with Gaurav, and this *hapsi* just comes up to us and asks us if we want some, and gives Gaurav his number. So Gaurav calls him a week later and he's told to come to a pool place in Northfields, close to here. We get to the bar, it's all dark and smoky, and it's full of *hapsi!* You could barely see anything – just eyes, teeth and gold! And we only met this guy for five minutes the week before – the first *hapsi* I'd spoken to in my life, understand? I say to Gaurav: "*Oi*, which one is our *hapsi?*" He's dazed. "How should I know!" But we think, *mujhi*, let's have a look around at least. And Gaurav goes up to one of the *hapsis* playing pool and asks him, "Hey brother, you know where Musti is?" And he goes, "Musti? Hey, Musti!" And calls this other *hapsi* over, he looks just the same as everyone to us, and does the whole handshake thing." Raghav got up, ducking his head and gesticulating, as Bikram guffawed, delighted. "Here I am in my first week in England and I'm in a bar full of *hapsis* doing this hip-hop handshake with a drug dealer from Somalia.

"So we head back to his place. Musti wants to impress us with his stuff so he'll get regular custom, right? So I can see him rolling this heavy joint. He lights up and the joint is so strong he starts coughing straight away, you know, trying to keep it down but coughing all the same. And I can already see Gaurav turning to the wall to laugh and I've gotta keep this straight face and take the joint from Musti.

"We became his customers. Maybe his only customers! Soon as he picks up the phone he goes, "Hey man you want some?" And in five minutes he'll be outside the door. But it's good stuff. Suresh met him right now."

"How much d'you pay for it?"

"*Mujhi*, we pay twenty pounds for a small bag . . ." He cupped his fingers to indicate how much. "Normal London price. What to do?"

"Twenty pounds . . . 2600 rupees! *Mula*, we never had to pay in Nepal . . ." Bikram took refuge in his beer, shaking his head solemnly.

"Sure, but you never had to pay for *anything* in Nepal! We earn money here, but we spend it all – on food, rent, booze and dope."

Bikram frowned, discomfited. "I thought you sent money to your parents sometimes."

Raghav looked away. "*Hoina*, of course you save a little money. But you're on your own here. You make money yourself and you spend it on yourself. Everybody else, damn care." He eyed Bikram defiantly, adding, "Of course we help each other as well."

The doorbell rang and with a rattle of keys, Suresh and Gaurav strode into the living room. "Oho, Bikram! What's up?"

The grass was great. "*Jay Shambho*," Bikram had intoned as he'd fired up the joint. After a day and a half of dragging his suitcases around, senses peaked for gate signs, departure times and security checks, it was great to just chill out with his friends. Nepal suddenly felt far away – and perhaps not at all. Sure, his parents were thousands of kilometres away, and so was the dust of Nepal, but his own Nepal, smoking and drinking with friends, was right here. When Raghav hollered from the kitchen, "Hey boys! Come to eat rice!" he couldn't have asked for anything more. The heady spices of the chicken curry had been airing the house for the last half-hour and it had been all he could do to stop himself dunking his head into the saucepan, he was so hungry. He got up, crumpling his beer can, and converged on the kitchen with Suresh and Gaurav. Cursory politesses later – "Take, take, no no, come on, you're the chief guest, you take and then I'll take" – they all heaped their plates with steaming white basmati and ladled the rich gravy chicken, sienna red and pungent, on top. There was some bottled chilli pickle, and a curl of golden ghee to melt into the food. They sat down in front of the television, cross-legged, newspapers spread under their plates, and started trowelling handfuls of meat and rice into their mouths, only looking up to wet their eyes with the booty wiggling away on TV.

Bikram was tired, jetlagged he supposed, but he would make the most of this first night. Why not see what real clubbing was all about? He felt like he was on holiday.

"Come on guys, hurry up! Look at this singing *mujhi*, he's been doing his hair for an hour!"

Raghav sneered at Suresh, who was trying to check out his sideburns in the mirror from behind him.

"Well you gotta do it *yaar*, how d'you think I'm gonna get a girl if I look like I just dropped down from the hills? Here, where's the shoe polish?"

"What polish? Polish your cock, *mujhi*, and you might have a chance tonight!"

"*Hyaahh* . . . don't do this bad-luck talk man, just tell me where the polish is and we can go!"

It was almost ten when they jumped into Raghav's rickety Toyota, the four of them souped up and ready to get down. A riot of aftershaves rose from scrubbed and shaven faces, and Brylcreem and gel glinted blackly as they squirmed about and bickered. Between the strained booms and thuds of the cheap car stereo bursts of laughter spilled out on to the dank suburban streets greased with drizzle. As they left Hounslow behind and swung on to the motorway, the youths fell silent, perhaps feeling the joint they'd smoked just before they left. But it wasn't long before their chatter started up again. Raghav really wanted to get some action that night. He couldn't stop talking about it.

"Hey d'you remember last time, those girls we met? Maybe they'll be there tonight – the one I was sweet-talking . . ."

Suresh insinuated his rangy frame in between Raghav and Bikram and exclaimed harshly, "*Eh heh*, listen to this guy bullshitting; he sweet-talked her, he says. If you were so great then why'd she leave with that other guy at the end of the night, hm? Explain that to me, please!"

Bikram sniggered. "Yeah, meester, explain please . . ."

"Well lemme finish what I was saying, *machikne* . . ."

"Your talk is too much – action is louder than words, remember that. I'll show you how to talk to the ladies, don't worry, bro . . ." Gaurav spoke casually from the back seat, heavy gold necklace and silky black shirt glistening in the dark.

Suresh indicated Gaurav to Bikram, eyebrows scrunched up earnestly. "Yeah, brother, listen to the guru – before you came to the UK, we went to this place, he was dancing with two girls –"

"And buying drinks for both of them!"

"Yeah, then he comes and . . . what did you say to me then?"

Gaurav snorted. "Well, I had to decide which one to focus on! I didn't have enough money on me to keep buying both of them drinks . . . though how it would have been to give it to two girls –" He nodded to himself, momentarily distracted by the idea.

Bikram regarded Gaurav with new respect. "So what happened?"

"Well, they were just waiting for a guy to pick them up. When one started dancing with this *hapsi* I just steered the other girl away, getting a little closer, and then it was easy, I just got her in a corner and kissed her."

"And then?"

"Then she took me to her room *ni* – she was a student at a university in Windsor – all night *dey danadan*, bro!" He snapped the fingers of his right hand and slammed the palm down onto his clenched left hand several times by way of explanation.

Bikram snorted, shaking his head in wonder. "*Mujhi*. Hahahaha!"

They were off the motorway now and trundling through the narrow streets of Windsor, looking to park. Almost immediately, they managed to pip a BMW to a spot Raghav would have passed if Suresh hadn't yelled at him to stop.

The boys piled out of the car as the BMW roared past. The thick thunks of doors filled the street. They were headed to the pub next to Liquid for a few drinks first; it was too expensive to get drunk in the club. Nodding to the bouncers, they strutted in, heads turning casually to take in the crowd. Wetherspoon's was packed and buzzing with the ordinary excitement of another Thursday night. Gaggles of girls necked Bacardi Breezers, ogled by men strong-arming amber pints with reckless abandon. As a meeting point and watering hole for the two-hour window before the exodus to the club, the bar could not have been better placed.

Raghav pushed his way to the bar and leaned up on tiptoe. He was looking for Sushil, a Nepali who worked there. And there he was, calmly efficient as always, expressionlessly flitting from one tap to another. If the bar were left to the whites they'd get lynched by this thirsty mob in minutes. Sushil clocked him, smiled briefly and signalled him to wait.

The rest had clustered around a pillar in the middle of the brightly lit pub, smoking. Suresh was busy showing off his new phone to Bikram. "Look here . . . look at this video quality, not bad, eh? This one is more than ten minutes, with sound!"

Bikram stared earnestly at the tiny screen. "Hehe . . . what's he doing there?"

"Hahaha. I was just filming Raghav while waking him up – look at his face!" They burst into laughter.

Suresh explained, giggling. "You see this *mujhi* had just gone to sleep after coming back from work at one in the morning and we were trying to get him to come down and eat – see how pissed off he is!" Reliving the incident, they echoed and amplified the squeaks of laughter from the phone.

Gaurav stood aloof, nonchalantly leaning against the pillar. He'd already spotted a few girls he'd be looking out for in the club. "You guys don't have anything better to do," he spat out scornfully.

Suresh looked up, smiling. "What?"

Gaurav cocked his eyebrows in the direction of the girls. "Look there, bro – not bad *huh*?" Suresh drew himself up, squared his shoulders and stared at the girls, giggling away not fifteen feet from them. Two blondes and a brunette, all wearing sexy tops and short skirts. One of the blondes was a little plump but she had great tits, you could really get a good view.

"Look at that," breathed Suresh. And the buxom blonde caught his eye, wheeled around and wiggled her breasts at him before dissolving into giggles. Her friends were in hysterics.

"*Machikne,*" exclaimed Suresh and Gaurav at the same time, smiling goofily. Bikram's eyes widened. The brunette, who had a nice figure but rather plain face, waved at Gaurav. That was all he needed. Before the envious looks of his friends, he sauntered up to the girls and greeted each of them with exaggerated courtesy, laughing and talking. He exuded masculine confidence.

Raghav, returning from the bar, stopped short and followed the collective gaze. He started shaking with laughter, prompting Suresh to grab the pitcher of rum and coke he was carrying. "He's already started! *Oi*, Bikram, see what we told you? Learn from the guru!"

Bikram was, in fact, watching Gaurav intently. This could never happen in Nepal, he couldn't imagine it, not even in the hotel discos that the rich Rana and Shah kids went to, he was sure. With the people he knew and the way they were – it was almost like you had to marry the first girl you were seen holding hands with. Srijana's face seemed to shimmer in front of him; then Gaurav was back, smiling sardonically.

"Hey bro, give me some of that!" He grabbed a glass from Raghav and held it out to be filled.

"Well?" They looked at Gaurav expectantly. "What was all that talk about?"

"So you'll get to do them?"

Gaurav sipped at his drink and eyed the girls who were chattering away, not looking their way now. "The bitches!" he exhaled, jovially. "They wanted me to pay the cover charge for the one with the big tits, the one who said hello to Suresh."

Suresh grinned. "So what did you tell them?"

"Did you present your credit card to them, pin included?"

"Whores!" Gaurav sneered. "I said how about if I buy you a drink inside the club? And they said OK. The bitches were just trying to see how much they could get away with."

"No, you did the right thing – more chances if you pay for them inside the club." Suresh addressed Raghav, "Hey, how much did you pay for this?" Raghav looked supremely smug. "Don't worry guys, I got this *phree* . . . you know Sushil's there; he just filled it up and gave it to me. There must be a third of the bottle in there!" He held up the pitcher in triumph and they toasted each other enthusiastically. *Cheeyerrs!!!*

"That Sushil, *yaar,* he works like a robot – his hands are moving like a machine's, non-stop." Raghav imitated Sushil, deadpan. "Poor guy, he can't come with us because he needs to work at the airport at six in the morning!"

The club wasn't so busy for a Thursday night but a couple of hundred people were spread across three rooms of pounding house, hip-hop, and eighties music, and the boys were soon lost in a crush of bodies up against the bar in the main room. A vapid blue sheen enveloped everything and flashes of white and crimson glanced off bodies jerking and swaying to slick, bassy house. Gaurav grabbed his beer and went over to the edge of the dance floor, sizing up his prospects.

The unrelenting boom-clap-boom-clap, cheap horns, and silky vocals over deep, funky beats poured out of huge speakers set into the walls. A wall of music, chopped into sheets of noise by lights spinning in tandem. The dancers self-consciously circled each other, sucking on cigarettes and gulping beers. Bikram grabbed Gaurav's shoulder excitedly and pulled him around so he could see the girls from the pub on the far side of the floor. They were dancing together, waiting for something, it seemed. Gaurav's eyes lit up and he clapped Bikram on the back. Still dancing, he shimmied into the crowd. Bikram followed in his wake nervously, smoothing his hair back.

They made their way up to the girls, and Gaurav nodded to them and mouthed a hello. But they didn't even smile back. Unfazed, Gaurav started dancing next to the blonde with the big tits, so Bikram did the same with the brunette, grinning awkwardly. The girls continued dancing as if the boys weren't there. Bikram tried to catch the brunette's eye, but she was looking at nothing in particular, and seemed bored, her body jerking mechanically to the beat. After a few minutes, Gaurav put his arm around the blonde and pulled her to him. She just looked annoyed, shrugged him off and moved away. When the song ended, both girls walked off abruptly, leaving the two of them dancing together like idiots, pretending nothing had happened. Well, what could you do?

After a while, Suresh and Raghav came and joined them with fresh bottles of beer, and they all danced together, watching the girls not dancing with them, occasionally breaking away to go to the bar or the toilet. Gaurav disappeared for a bit, winking significantly, but soon returned looking sweaty and deflated, shouting over the music, "Today it looks like a Nepali disco here! Can't even talk to a girl without pissing off five of her bodyguards!"

Gradually, it ceased to matter. As the boys got drunker and drunker, they didn't stop eyeing the girls, but had lost hope of getting anywhere. They became more relaxed, laughed at each other's dance moves and consoled themselves, thinking: there's always a next time.

What bitches, Bikram muttered to himself as he approached the toilets. What was all that fuss about in the pub if they didn't even want to give a little? He passed a young couple in a corner; one of the guy's hands was on her tits, the other somewhere up her skirt. He had to force himself not to stop and just stare. He wondered what Srijana would think if she saw this place. If she saw him dancing with the girls here. Or trying to! But he was feeling good tonight. Drunk and high and happy. London, London. He had finally made it!

The toilets weren't busy. He was glad to see that the black who was there earlier, standing next to the sinks offering soap and paper towels for tips, wasn't around. Earlier, Raghav had waved away the towel the hapsi held out to him and simply wiped his hands on his trousers, but Bikram had innocently accepted a towel from the guy. So he'd had to tip the bastard as Raghav grinned, waiting by the door. What kind of job was that anyway, he thought as he urinated, aiming first left, then right, nodding to the muffled beats from the club.

The door swung open, the music suddenly became crisp, and was cut off again. Someone walked slowly past behind him. There were plenty of empty urinals, a whole row of them, but the man came and stood right next to him and started unzipping his trousers. Bloody kuire, Bikram thought as he continued to urinate. He glanced at his neighbour askance. Then he realized the man was staring at him he was looking at his cock! As Bikram jerked his head up in consternation the man – a big white guy with a tattoo of a serpent on his neck – shifted his gaze to Bikram's face, smiling broadly. A prickly sensation skittered up Bikram's scalp as he hurriedly looked away, finished and zipped up, not even bothering to shake himself dry. He half ran out of the toilets without once looking back, his heart pounding, sweating all over, and felt inexplicably relieved when he found the guys by the bar. They all laughed like maniacs, of course, when he told them what had happened. Raghav seemed to find it particularly funny. "You're a real hero from Nepal! You better stay with us now, that homo must be hunting for you!"

"Don't make so much noise about it," Bikram fumed, dragging deeply on a cigarette. "If it'd been you, you'd have stayed in the toilet, *hoina*?"

The night wore on. By the time the club started regurgitating its contents onto the pavement, the boys were all tired out. Gaurav looked surly, Suresh was quite drunk. Bikram was still a little shell-shocked. As they waited for Raghav to freshen up in the toilets, Gaurav told them about a girl he'd been chatting up in the eighties music room. "She was real pretty, you understand? I wish I had some pills, she wanted some, I would've given them to her free. Well not completely free, hehe . . ."

Suresh leered at Gaurav, disappointed. "Why didn't you invite her back to our place then, to smoke and have some fun? There's only four of us!"

Gaurav scowled. "Yeah, looked like she was going to come, the bitch – but she must have liked me to come and talk to me, not you!"

"*Mujhi,* you make too much noise . . . she came to you because you looked like Musti, that's why! Look at him! Meester Somalia!"

They all laughed and headed out of the club with Raghav, wet-faced and perky, feeling for his keys. As they drifted into the formless night, pushing past the hopeful taxi-drivers, you could hear Bikram exclaiming: "And I ran out of there so quick I didn't even have time to wash my hands!"

WANDERING SOULS, WONDERING FAMILIES

Weena Pun

Weena is a writer based in Kathmandu. A Stanford graduate, she has worked as an assistant editor at *Himal Southasian* and as a reporter for the *Kathmandu Post*. She has been finalising her first novel for years now, but is pretty sure the end is nigh. She is soon to begin an MFA in fiction at Cornell University.

O n 12 March 1988, the weather forecast for the Kathmandu Valley in the *Rising Nepal* read: "Partly cloudy with temporary thundershowers." No prediction of impending doom. There was just a note that the sun would set at 6:17 pm – two hours and 47 minutes after the final match of the Tribhuvan Challenge Shield Football Tournament was to begin at the Dashrath Stadium in the capital. Two minutes into the match, the Bangladeshi team, Mukti Joddha Sangsad, scored a goal against Nepal's Janakpur Cigarette Factory. Eighteen minutes later, a hailstorm brought the game to a halt.

Outside the stadium, blowing at 80 km per hour, the windstorm damaged phone lines and electricity wires, felled trees and sent corrugated iron flying off roofs. Before long, large pellets of hail began pelting the spectators, who rushed in panic, all at once, towards the southern gate, through which they had entered. But the accordion gate was open enough for only one person to squeeze through at a time, thus creating a bottleneck. In the ensuing stampede, 69 people were crushed to death. Two days later, the *Rising Nepal* announced a rise in the number of causalities by one, and printed out a list of the perished. In the last paragraph of the first column was my dad's name, misspelled with an additional "h".

For the next 23 years, this incident remained just that – a news item seldom mentioned in my family, never discussed. So firmly banished were the memories of both the stampede and my father that, when my mom recently learned about a lama who could summon *bai*s (wandering dead) and expressed her desire to talk to "Dad", we assumed she meant *her* dad. My sister even made a joke about granddad's notorious temper, suggesting that his soul would come back with a stick to strike us.

The fame of this necromancer had reached Mom through our house owner, who had travelled from Kathmandu to Pokhara, in western Nepal, to appease the wandering soul of his recently deceased first wife. Standing on our porch he recounted the trip, gushing about the lama's talent in seeing both the past and the future. As it turns out, death does not fling a person into nothingness; rather, it turns them into pestering souls needing constant attention from the living. So malevolent were these spirits that, if ignored or left unsatisfied, they would stand in the way of their kin's attempt at success. A believer in supernatural phenomena, Mom began to wonder whether Dad's unhappy soul could be behind her woes: my apparent financial failure, my sister's academic disinterest, and that elusive house to call her own. If we mollified his discomfort, would he also tell us, say, the date of my wedding? And since Mom was already going to be in Pokhara for work, would I then kindly join her there?

"No!" was my immediate response. How could the dead have answers to any uncertainty of the future? Not only was it ludicrous to think that the dead live – and live in *schadenfreude* – it was also downright creepy to think that someone might pretend to be Dad and that Mom would believe it. But then, slowly, curiosity took over. An image of a lama I had once seen in a picture stuck in my mind: a paunchy Buddhist monk sitting upright, high on a throne, his right foot on his left thigh, his robes splayed open on his lap, his eyes closed to some tantrik melody. I began to wonder whether, if Dad did speak via this lama, he would do so in a Magar accent, whether he would satisfy all the stereotypes of a Magar lad: insouciant, affable, *lende* – pigheaded.

I knew so little about Dad that this curiosity morphed into restlessness, into voyeuristic excitement until it gave way to uneasiness. I began to fear that my participation might be equivalent to mocking Mom's belief, or worse, trespassing on her intimate moments with Dad. Nevertheless, I agreed to accompany her.

FAITH

But first, a detour to Jorpati in the capital itself, to prepare myself for the encounter with the lama – to see whether I could look at "superstition" from a perspective other than one of condescension. A sister of one of Mom's close friends claimed to be possessed by Goddess Kali; believers called her Mata. Every Thursday and Saturday, from eight until noon, worshippers flocked to her, seeking reasons behind their miseries and assurances of future security. In her mid-30s, married and with a kid, she had been in the business, so to speak, for almost a decade.

Her small room on the ground floor sparkled with paraphernalia of Hindu worship: pictures of gods and goddesses, as well as Sathya Sai Baba; packets of unused incense; hands of bananas; pellucid veils; bells and flowers. Next to this altar she sat on a low chair while her devotees, mostly women and children, towed into the room, waited before her. When their turn came, these devotees, one at a time, would sit cross-legged in front of the Mata and spread out a mound of rice on a low table between them. Mata would then quietly light a few sticks of incense, stretch her back upright and close her eyes. After a few seconds of silence she would open her mouth, stick out her tongue and widen her eyes menacingly. Then, with her head lightly swaying side to side in an "X" motion, she would introduce herself to the devotee: *"Mahakali hun. Keka laagi daanki bolaani garis, e bhakta?"* (I am Goddess Kali. What did you call me for, O devotee?)

When I first saw this face, I could not help simpering with embarrassment. I had only known this woman as an aunt; to see her transform into a likeness of the mythical Kali was absurd. For one, her tongue was much shorter than Kali's famously elongated one. Further, she was plump and soft, nowhere near as fierce as Kali is assumed to be. But as one after another devotee bowed before her, opening up about their problems (mostly domestic and academic), my reaction shifted from that of a cynic to one more willing to listen in to the conversation, even a little humbled at faith.

One of the women complained to Mata that she hated coming home because the moment she stepped on the doorstep, an intense anger paralysed her. To this Mata replied, in a voice like a mother's rebuke, that the woman was seeking a happiness long disappeared. In order to feel better, she needed to allow in happiness in other forms as well. Although this piece of advice was peppered with ruminations on the alignment of different planets in different *yog*, and on conducting puja in and visits to different temples to realign them, it was effective. At the end of the session, when the woman received a pinch of blessed rice both as prasad and as a talisman, one could see relief radiating from her face. Faith had opened up bottled-up feelings and faith had, for now at least, drained them away.

I wanted desperately to believe that it was something like this, something as powerful as a sealed-up emotion, that was leading Mom to try to conjure Dad. If it was mere inquisitiveness about the future that was driving her, the Jorpati Mata could have easily quenched that longing. I did not want to believe in a malign, whiny monger image of my dad's soul, either. So, on further probing, Mom finally yielded: She said that she wanted to find out how Dad had died.

At first, this confession, this seeming morbid curiosity, sounded appalling, embarrassing and even offensive: no one stirs the dead to be entertained by the act of the individual's dying. Doubly embarrassing, however, was when bits of the facts surrounding the tragedy at the stadium slowly began to emerge in Pokhara. As I showed Mom the clippings from the *Rising Nepal*, especially the list, she looked at them in amazement – she had not realised that the incident was covered in the papers. Dad's passing away was made known to her by the police only a day after the incident, and by that time the police had already conducted the funeral rites. The last Mom saw of Dad was when, refusing to let her come to the stadium, he left with a neighbour's eight-year-old boy instead. As we traced the boy's name in the columns, Mom sat behind me, breathing heavily, perhaps due to the Pokhara heat, perhaps due to the list. Once we located the boy, towards the top of the second column, she said, "He must have died saving the kid."

ETERNITY

With this revelation, we headed towards Sundari bazaar in Pokhara. It was Saturday and only seven in the morning, but a crowd had already gathered in the courtyard of the lama's house. Twenty bags of rice, suggesting the number of dead to be raised for the day, neatly lined a low-raised platform on the deck. The long wait thus began, wiping away romanticised expectations one after the other.

At eight o'clock, the lama came out of the room from behind a beige curtain that hung on the doorway, and the first sobering surprise of the day hit me. The lama turned out to be, not a Buddhist monk, but a fleshy, energetic Brahmin woman, rather loud and rude, verging on disrespectful towards her guests. Standing on the doorstep, with her hands clasped in namaste and in a stern voice, she said to us gathered on the deck, "If your dead has not been dead for more than a year, go back; it cannot be aroused. Do not touch the bags of rice. Do not make a lot of noise. Turn off your mobile phones. Recording of the session is strictly prohibited." She would have made a better Kali.

As the day wore on, we soon realised that number 21, our number, was far away. Each invocation took about 20 minutes, sometimes half an hour. The first few were interesting to eavesdrop on. Sometimes a loud retching sound heralded the arrival of the spirit; sometimes this was indicated by a sob, a note of exasperation or a sick voice. When people demanded to know why a particular spirit was torturing them, the voice would sometimes grumble about infighting, or about the living wasting away its hard-earned money. A few times, though, the voice clearly rejected the charge of causing any malaise, singling out another individual as the perpetrator, the "witch", instead. Now and then the spirit would be nice – calming the crying relative by assuring that it would return to their dreams. But almost always, the spirit asked to be coaxed with sweets and regular puja.

As it became increasingly obvious that there was little more to the process of invocation, Mom and I started to look for other diversions. We began to wonder about the difference between a *bai* and *pitri* (any dead, despite its strong paternal connotation). We calculated the Mata's income per month at the rate of 320 rupees per invocation. A 20-year-old regaled us with his own journey to become a Mata – clearly, even men can become such. We listened to our grumbling tummies and, afterwards, to a famous radio personality, herself in line to see the Mata, interviewing others about Pokhara and Nepal Tourism Year 2011 – live. A story about a young man from nearby Damauli who had killed a couple after a Mata accused them of witchcraft did the rounds as well. But as the heat and hunger intensified, so did impatience.

At quarter past two in the afternoon, four people cheated their way in, saying they were of the same family, and took an hour to get out. There were still seven more people ahead of us, and time suddenly seemed to be passing by more quickly than we wanted. If the rumours were true that the Mata could not bring up the dead past five in the evening, we would have to wait until Thursday to arrange another session; for this Mata, like the Jorpati one, reserved the other days for prophesying. An awful sensation sank in as the clock marked 4:30, and then the Mata confirmed she would not see people past 5:30 – and there were still four more rice bags before us. Mom and I then started to pester the remaining people to be quick with their dead, and even gave a shot, in vain, at asking if we could go before them. "We came all the way from Kathmandu," we begged. "We cannot afford plane tickets or endure five-hour bus rides every time an appointment is botched."

The wait-and-see game ended at 5:10 when an old woman entered Mata's room with her son, and Mom, in her anxious state, followed her in. Seconds later, I joined in, with the 20-year-old soon-to-be Mata close on my heels. The room was more austere than the one in Jorpati, perhaps because the altar was behind a set of curtains. Here, the Mata sat on a cushion on the floor, against a wall adorned with bundles of peacock feathers. The clock on the wall read 5:20, evidently ten irritating minutes fast. Nonetheless, when the Mata did not shoo us out, calm returned.

I began to observe her, trying to pigeonhole her. A charlatan she was not, for no one can continue a charade for as long and as continuously as she carried on. A skilful healer who understood human relationships well, perhaps? Someone akin to a psychologist, or perhaps a social worker? But then, what to make of her telling this old woman that there was a witch in the family who was barring her son from professional success? Was she a home-wrecking bluffer? What went through her mind when, in a casual conversation, the 20-year-old confided that he too gets possessed by gods and spirits? Did she believe him? Whatever she was, she seemed to believe in herself, and so did her visitors believe in her.

FOREVER

As it turned out, the time limit was imposed not by the dead, but by Mata herself. Finally, a little past the deadline, Mom settled herself in front of the Mata, and I sat next to Mom.

"Name of the *pitri* and the *tithi* he died?" Mata asked, spreading the rice evenly on the plate.

Mom gave Dad's name and the date of his death as per the lunar calendar: Nawami.

The woman counted nine on her fingers and asked. "Who is this?

"Huh?" Mom was beginning to get nervous.

"How are you related to him?

"Husband."

The woman muttered mantras and asked Mom to light five incense sticks. "Did you bring your daughter?"

"Yes, the elder is here."

"Should have brought the younger one; he likes her more," Mata said. Her eyes were now closed. "Snuff the *dhoop* once I lie down."

She fell flat on her side while still murmuring mantras. A few seconds later, she shook her head, touched her belly as if in pain, and rose with her eyes still closed. Then, in a pained voice she asked why my sister had not come: *"Kanchhi aaena?"*

Mom began to cry. I fought back my own tears. In consolation, Dad shared that he was not a wandering soul anymore, but had found company with the gods in Pashupati temple in Kathmandu. He was thirsty, however, and in need of a pair of good shoes. He asked Mom whether she would offer him a glass of water later, and donate a pair of shoes to a baba. Mom continued to cry and, when she could, asked Dad about me and my sister. Dad told her to not worry about us, not even about marriage; we would turn out fine. Then, with eyes still closed, he reached across, held Mom's hand, and promised that once she had her own house, he would move in with her, forever.

Back outside, my eyes were still reacting to the dark interior. Suddenly, from beyond the overhead powerlines, from behind a hayrick, the arc of a rainbow shot high above the hills into the sky. The sight, seemingly so clichéd, challenged me to snigger, daring me to relapse into cynicism. But why denigrate beauty, and why keep a tally of the mistakes the Mata made? Why overlook that her Nepali acquired a Magar twang, with neutralised verbs, midway through the session? Why dismiss her reaching out to touch mom as a clever attempt to comfort her? Why raise questions, overanalyse and not relish the clear power at work here, the power of – empathy? Belief? A placebo? The important point, and the only point that mattered, was that love was alive, memories were strong, and Mom felt good.

THE GREATEST TIBETAN EVER BORN

Tsering Lama

Tsering is a New York-based Tibetan writer who was born and raised in Kathmandu. She has an MFA in writing from Columbia University where she was a TOMS Fellow, a Writing Fellow, and a Teaching Fellow. She has received grants and fellowships including The Canada Council for the Arts Professional Writers Grant and The Barbara Deming Memorial Fund for Women, as well as residencies from Catwalk, Omi International, Playa Summerlake, WildAcres, and The Lillian E. Smith Center. Tsering's work has appeared in *The Malahat Review*, *Grain Magazine*, *Vela Mag*, *La.Lit*, *Himal Southasian* and *Brave New Play Rites Anthology*. Tsering has taught as a Lecturer in Writing at Yeshiva University and a University Writing Fellow in the English Department at Columbia University. She is working on her first novel.

T hupten arrived at the Kathmandu airport, grabbed his duffel bag from the conveyor belt and walked right past the security check. There was a huddle of people waiting to put their bags into the scanner, and at the sight of him they gripped their rusty carts and shouted at the security guards, "*Oye! Ke ho esto?* Wake up, security!" But the skinny men didn't stand a chance at stopping Thupten. Instead, they just sat on their wooden stools, mouths agape as the strange longhaired man barrelled by with his duffel bag. Was he Chinese? Japanese? He didn't even look back! He just stomped by, right towards the sunny glass doors where a hundred greeters waited for loved ones, though Thupten knew none of them waited for him.

As he passed through the barricades, a dozen or so drivers swarmed around him, pulling at his shoulder straps and pointing him towards the parking lot. He settled on a wiry, flannel-shirted kid – 250 rupees. It was lower than the next price by a good deal but Thupten still couldn't believe he was paying so much. Ten years ago, with 100 rupees in your pocket you could have circled the whole city and bought a glass of bitter homemade *raksi* with change left over to flirt with passing girls.

Leaving the paved roads of the airport, the taxi burrowed into the mess of the city and the heat met Thupten with a vengeance. He wiped his face with his shirt that stank from the many hours of flight and shook his head. New sweat quickly formed on his forehead as the taxi was caught in a three-way jam involving a truck and a jeep trying to bully a rickshaw out of the way. Thupten's mouth was parched; he could now smell his own stench – something the airplanes' air conditioning had masked, and he could feel the exhaustion break through. This place . . . this place was paying him back for leaving years ago.

"Pull over here," Thupten said, seeing a row of stores. He went up to the counter of a shop bursting with goods. As he stared at the contents, he found he could remember some of them – Wai-wai and Rara noodles, Nabisco biscuits – but many seemed like new brands. He had not expected there to be new brands. He asked the storeowner for a bottle of water from the back of the fridge and then got back in the taxi, relieved for the first time to be heading home. But as he unscrewed the bottle's cap and arched his neck back to drink the cold water, the driver said, "It will be 400 rupees now, because we stopped."

Jiggy had been sitting on the roof terrace since breakfast, blasting tinny music from his cell phone and writing his thoughts in a notebook. The girls next door were also on their roof, gossiping, drying their hair in the sun and making eyes at him, just as he was making at them. At their request, shouted across the rooftops, he had put on Rihanna's "Umbrella", and raised the phone's volume as high as it could go. Jiggy put the cell phone on the stool beside him and got back to writing: "Wassup babes. U too gud for me. But I can't let U go, nah. Sho me a heart dat neva breaks. Sho me a eye dat neva tears. Sho me a skin dat neva cuts. Sho me a chance to luv U for real. Btw Ich liebe dich. Dat mean I luv U in German."

He was scribbling the draft of an e-mail to his American friend, Maria. She had come into his life a month ago at a karaoke bar in the city's tourist district. Jiggy's family had a small shop selling trinkets there, and in the evenings after he pulled down the shop's shutters, he and his friends passed through the crowded roads, going from one backpacker bar to the next to party with the foreigners. Maria, Maria, Maria – she had looked like a doll to him. With her yellow hair and small thin lips, she laughed heartily. The kind of laugh that invited others to join in. And she sucked in cigarette after cigarette, twirling them above her slender wrists as she sang along to the music. He had managed to get her e-mail address at the end of the night, gaining the courage to ask after she bought him and his friends some beer. Of course, all the guys wanted Maria – not only was she white, she was also not a desperately poor hippie. But Jiggy had just turned 17 a few days earlier, so they made way for him – with this tourist at least. She lived in Oregon, Maria did.

"Tru luv dun die. Tru luv dun have a happy ending. Coz tru luv dun have a ending at all . . ." Jiggy was mid-sentence when he heard a motorcycle pull up. Normally just the roar of motorcycles got him a little excited, but the sight of one coming to his squat little house, where the only wheels around were his rusting childhood bicycle, made him jump up from his stool and peer over. Had his father finally bought a motorcycle?

He saw a tough-looking man silence the bike and pull off his helmet. His ponytail fell on his shoulders, and Jiggy recognized him immediately: Thupten, the greatest Tibetan ever born in the Tashi Phuntsok Tibetan Refugee Camp – Jiggy's parents' old camp. He once played for the Tibetan national football team. One year, they had competed with other stateless teams such as Kurdistan and Northern Cyprus. Thupten had been on TV, running around in an official uniform – the first ever, for Tibet's first national team ever – carrying a Tibetan flag for the world to see. Since then, there would always be Red Label whisky for Thupten at the house of every relative. Even 12 years after he went to the West, Jiggy's family still spoke of him with fondness. And whenever something about America came up in conversation or was shown on TV, someone would invariably refer to Thupten. *Had he been caught in the big snowstorms shown on CNN? Were the flash floods happening in his area?*

Beyond this, Jiggy knew in his heart that Thupten was just special. He wasn't just a normal Tibetan. Something inside him was different.

He was a non-Tibetan in a Tibetan's body. Tibetans are good at waiting; at this, they are the champions. They will wait for their meat to dry until it becomes "edible"; they will wait for their barley wine to ferment; they will wait for the reincarnation of their great monks and, when they find them, they will wait until the monks are 18 before they can offer guidance once again. But that also means they wait patiently for handouts, for respect, for what is rightfully theirs. Not cousin Thupten. He was a self-made man and he wanted his share – now. Instead of pity, he inspired confidence. Fear instead of ambivalence. People said that Westerners had even asked him for help! And not a single person managed to fool him, though they did try, looking as he did like a plain old gullible Tibetan.

"Do they know who my grandfather was?" Thupten was saying as Jiggy came into the living room.

"Chocho!" Jiggy said, running barefoot down the stairs. His mother, aunt and father were seated in a semi-circle around the great Thupten.

"Jigdel?" Thupten leaned back abruptly in recognition, his voice quieting to a whisper. "Kunchoksum . . . now, I know I'm old . . ."

Was he joking? Jiggy could barely look him straight in the eyes, he looked so fierce. More fierce than Yamantaka, the Buddhist Terminator, the God of Death. More fierce than the rapper DMX, with his pitbulls and rippling muscles. "Thupten, my bro," he wanted to say, "U are definitely my fav cousin and imma stick wit U like P Diddy and Biggie Smalls TILL DA END. Or till U goes back to Canada. Or maybe U could take me wit U?" But before he could work up the courage to speak English to a real English speaker, his father interjected.

"So you were saying – what do you say to those white people in Canada?" Jiggy's father, Pasang, was beside Thupten, his nose literally two thumbs' distance from Thupten's cheek. *How embarrassing*, he thought. Jiggy's mother got up and went into the kitchen to make tea, while his aunt remained sitting glumly further down the sofa from Thupten at the blank TV screen. She had been watching some prayer recording on their TV all morning, which was why Jiggy had fled up to the roof in the first place.

"Pala, move aside!" Jiggy said, waving at his father, while he stood a respectful metre in front of his cousin, marveling at the excellent outfit Thupten was wearing: black boots, grey sweatpants and a puffy camouflage vest. *You could never find a vest like that around here*, he thought. *If only this country's shops were more like America, instead of being full of crap from China!* And Thupten's hair! It was long, halfway down to his elbows and tied in the back, thick as a branch.

Thupten unhooked the backpack strapped around his chest and flung it onto the sofa beside him. Jiggy's tiny aunt bounced in her seat. The pack had a military pattern too, just like his vest. He continued talking: "I say to them, 'Do you know who my grandfather was?' And of course, they don't. Because while they were picking their noses, Jampa Kalsang Phuntsokof Lithang in eastern Tibet was killing Chinese communists left and right. He was stockpiling guns from the CIA between barrels of rice wine. No one knows that about him – not even our camp folks, because he wasn't alive long in exile. And when the Americans abandoned us to make deals with China, he was the only one protecting our town."

Thupten paused dramatically to look around, then continued: "And do they know who my grandmother was? As a little girl, she pulled down the only tree in the valley and dragged it by its roots to the nearest monastery as an offering. She walked six hours to the *gompa* and the monks couldn't believe their eyes. She was a direct descendant of Genghis Khan. And my father's line met Jesus Christ – back before he was Christian, when he was wandering the Asian deserts looking for ideas! Who do you think gave him the most important rules in Christianity, the Ten Commandments? Straight out of Buddhist texts, just like rosaries. Have you ever noticed how the white people have the exact same number of beads in their rosaries as us?"

Jiggy looked at the rosary beads hanging limp in his aunt's fingers. He had never checked how many beads there were. He was an SLC graduate, had finished his Grade 10 exams. And though it took him three attempts before passing, he was relatively certain he had never learned about the CIA in Tibet or Genghis Khan screwing around in Tibet or even Jesus in Tibet. Obviously the Nepali teachers just did not teach such things – or, more likely, they had never done any real research like cousin Thupten.

Thupten turned to him and said, "That means, Jigdel, you have some Genghis blood running through your body, too. Don't forget that."

*

Genghis blood. Whenever Jiggy asked his mother what she remembered of Tibet, she always said that she remembered a lake beside their old house, hills to the side and plains all around. That was all. Then she'd tell him to eat his bitter *menzikhang* herbs, meant to curb the white patches recently popping up on his face. Fart flowers, *tukrimentok*, they called them, saying the patches came up because of his non-stop farting.

And his father was even more useless when it came to getting information about the past. He was younger than Jiggy's mother and was carried into exile as an infant. Jiggy's father's father was the only grandparent who survived the journey to Nepal. But he had drunk himself to death a couple of years ago, and Jiggy never even found out what he had done for a living in Tibet.

Jiggy's mother came in from the kitchen with a tray of tea and the expensive biscuits, Digestives, that she saved for guests. She stood beside Thupten and urged him to eat, holding the plate of biscuits to his chin until he finally rolled up his sleeves and took a piece. At this, his tattoos popped out like an exotic landscape.

"Tattoos!" Jiggy said, his big nose diving forward. "Are they real?"

"Oh, these?" Thupten asked, pushing up his sleeves up until they pinched his muscles. He revealed a Tibetan flag on one arm and *rangzen*, independence, written in thick black on the other. The family huddled around. Jiggy's father got off the sofa and stood directly in front of Thupten, bending at a near perfect 90-degree angle, while his mother and her sister oscillated between peering very closely and recoiling in dismay. Jiggy was now practically hovering over the magnificence painted over his cousin's dark brown arms.

Thupten slapped his arm with gusto. "You have to show who you are!" He slapped it once more. "Whenever I'm working at the food terminal, driving my forklift and such, and the supervisor or some other worker comes up to me, talking nonsense, trying to get the better of me, taking advantage of our Tibetan good nature, I always pull up my sleeves and say, 'Look. Here. I'm not just some country bumpkin. See this writing? It means freedom, independence. I'm Tibetan and I don't have a country anymore. I've never even been to my country but that's where I'll go someday, dead or alive. Yes right now, I'm just a guest in this country. But my people are in Tibet and they are waiting for me and I will return one day. So don't worry. That's where I belong.' That's what I tell them with my tattoos."

Jiggy looked at his parents damningly. If anyone asked, his mother always said that they were Sherpa, not Tibetan. She didn't want them to know that they were not ethnic Nepalis, that they were just guests living without papers, in a grey zone that the government tolerated but gave no way out of. Once a taxi driver tricked her into admitting that they were Tibetan. He kept saying things about Tibetans and she slipped and said, "No, we don't do that anymore." Fifty years they had lived in Nepal and still they could not just say they were Tibetan. "And, what do they say in return?" Jiggy's mother asked.

"What can they say, *ani*? They just know who I am after that."

Yangdol searched Thupten's aging face. She had known him since he was a toddler, obsessed only with playing football. Then, as he grew, he had made grand promises to make money and take her travelling around the world. *My favourite ani*, he'd called her. *Okay*, she always replied. But the West had embittered him. What had he thought, going so far just to say such things? Why had he not unburdened himself of the past instead? She would have left all of it, everything of Nepal and Tibet trailing behind as she flew away, like the white lines planes make in the sky. What would come from stamping yourself with needles and ink? Freedom. Return.

Pasang and she had gone as far from those early years as they could in this lifetime. They had survived and raised their siblings after their parents died. They had sold trinkets to tourists from their fanny packs and backpacks at first. Walking back and forth, resting along the way on perches and sidewalks for periods so they could go from morning to night. Now they had a store in the tourist district where she made and sold necklaces of imitation coral, imitation turquoise – imitations of what her mother had worn in Tibet.

"This arm," Thupten pointed at the bare shoulder, "will be my mother's. I want to write her name across it, after she recovers."

Yangdol looked at the others just as they looked down. A year ago Thupten's father had passed away, and a week ago his mother had fallen ill with pneumonia. Since Thupten's departure, his father had become the camp's gossip – wasting his days away on the shop stoops of the camp's main road, observing who went where and when. He had the sugar disease and the ailments of too much pride and purse strings that were too tight. His son regularly sent money home and his father hid the bills throughout the house. Under the mattresses, between clothes stacked in closets, under idols of deities in the prayer room, he tucked away the earnings of his son's toils. But just days after hiding the money, he would forget where he had put it. Still, he always bragged of his riches, and the entire camp talked with jealousy and derision of their home, dark and damp though full of unspent money in every nook.

Since leaving the camp to live in another part of the city, Yangdol rarely returned. It was suffocating to go back, and the taxi ride there was getting too expensive these days, taking over an hour along the cracked congested roads. But Thupten's mother would be the true loss if she did not survive. Only she could have prompted him to return.

"She's doing well though," he said with an uneasy smile. "The doctors say she can come back home tomorrow."

"That's because you're here now . . ." Jiggy said.

Everyone nodded in agreement. Thupten smiled. *Thank goodness,* thought Jiggy. *There would be good times ahead. Bring on the pool cue! Bring on the Carlsberg and chilly chicken! What good luck he had, that he was just the right age when Thupten came back. Finally, he was a man, old enough to experience his great cousin and not just in legend!* At night, at a smoky bar, on the back of a motorcycle, Jiggy's time had come and, however short, he was so ready for it, his palms itched.

"So what are you doing next?" he asked, then immediately worried that he had blown it.

Now his father would probably try to bring Thupten to play cards with the other old men behind the store. They would keep the beer and fried meat coming all day and night, and who could resist that? Jiggy's tongue stuck out of his mouth in anticipation. Why couldn't he have waited to ask his cousin his plans when they were alone?

"I have got to go meet a girl," Thupten said with a sparkle. "To go have a talk."

Jiggy bit his lip. *Free at last! Free at last! Thanks God Almighty I am free at last!* When his teacher had played an audio recording of Martin Luther King, Jr's speech in class, he had not clapped or cried like the other Tibetan students at those final words. But now he was so happy, he could feel the tears coming.

"Are you going to a bar with her? Have you tried the new one – The Factory? I could show you – you want me to show?"

"Maybe," Thupten said and turned to the rest. "She is the one my father had picked for me . . . a few years back."

Everyone gazed at him in disbelief. Thupten was nearly 39 years old and had ignored his father's wishes for his marriage for so long. Even Pasang and Yangdol had taken turns calling him in Toronto, urging him to marry a nice Tibetan girl.

"Shall I come with . . . ?" Jiggy asked.

"Just to see. Just to talk. There must be something about her. If my father liked her . . ." Thupten winked but could not finish the rest of his sentence. He looked at his relatives, so hopeful and expectant. Abruptly, he saw the taxi driver's terrified face again, the sweat on his neck, the rickety shell of the taxi. When the taxi had pulled up to Thupten's camp, he threw 250 rupees to the front seat and argued with the driver about the price hike. One thing lead to another and Thupten ended up holding the driver by his neck, threatening to break him like a chicken bone. Looking at his relatives now, he felt a sudden dread. He decided he could not stay any longer and bid them goodbye.

Pasang said something about playing cards, Ani Yangdol asked him to stay for lunch, her sister turned the VCR back on to play some video of praying monks, and young Jigdel followed him out the door. As he got on the motorcycle, Jigdel watched from the door. His face bore a large grin. His *tukrimentok*, his spiky hair, his desperation for life. Thupten wanted to tell him something – something to bring them both comfort, something about how life was full of possibilities:

"Maybe you can come to the West, try for a visa, borrow some money and fill a bank account with it so you look convincing as a visiting tourist to America. Then if you get through, never return, not for four or five years at least, if then. Work in a Chinese or Indian restaurant in New York City; they will pay you cash. Send the money home to your parents.

How they have suffered in this lifetime, suffering we will never know. And tell the lawyers and judges whatever you have to, whatever story of oppression you need to so they will let you stay. Work hard, work seven days a week if they let you, live in a one bedroom apartment in Jackson Heights with cockroaches and five other Tibetans who will always leave the apartment to work in places you never ask about. You will break each other's hearts every day when you see the exhaustion build and wear each other away. But they will be there to make you laugh and they will be a kind of family.

"And then if you are served papers to leave America, before you have even paid off the loans for the flights to America, then flee to Canada. Canada is the best country in the world. You won't experience why it is the best country in the world, but you will read about it in the magazines and newspapers; the surveys come out each year. They will take you in and you will start over and, one day, you will become a citizen if you tell the right lies, lies that are the truth, because in the end, in this lifetime, we Tibetans are mere beggars in this world. Good people will help you and you will fall in love with a girl somewhere along the way. She will love Tibet; she will love Buddhism. Her heart will break for your people and you will always hate her a little because of this. White people will like you – her family especially. They will invite you to stay at their house on holidays and weekends; they will let you sleep in her room and they will want you to call them 'mom' and 'dad' because they think you could never break their daughter's heart.

"You will tell your *ama* and *pala* about her and they will tell you that you are a fool. Ignore them; you are on the other side of the planet. Try to ignore them. You will hear of relatives' deaths, your uncle's, your best friend from high school; you will hear of new cousins entering this world; you will know of these things as sounds through a phone and you will try to grieve and celebrate but the emotions will not stretch so far, not such long distances, not after so long. Then you will hear the worst thing yet, the thing you cried about indulgently once as a child when you fathomed its possibility for the first time. Your father is dead. You will be in Montreal with your girl at the time, visiting the old stone cities that look like they were out of children's fairy tales. At the bar you will ask them for a beer but they will ignore you because you do not speak French. Your girl will be outside talking with old college friends, and you will try to find her so you can get a beer but you will not find her. The girl your father told you not to marry, not as long as he was alive. Never been so alone. You will slam your fist on the bar and say, "Monsur, one Heineken sil vu play!" Your finger pointing up. The bartender will look at you closely. You are on the verge of tears, a man with nothing to lose in a stony heaven. He will be kind enough to let you finish the beer before he kicks you out.

"Back in Toronto, you will work for two weeks straight, driving the forklift from four in the morning until four at night. Take that paycheck and beg for an advance from your boss and send all of it home to your mother. Tell her you cannot come home because of work; tell her you are doing well, eating plenty, and you will send more in a month. The Canadian girl will call you, she will e-mail; she will ask your friends about you; her father will even call you. But you will not answer. In your free hours, you leave your basement studio apartment. Each time, standing at your door, about to choose a place in the world to go, you are struck by the realization that you have no direction, nowhere to go. To a restaurant, to your mother's camp in Kathmandu, to that bar in Montreal. Nowhere is yours. The sad stupid shock at your door. And you realize, it will never leave you."

But instead of saying all this, Thupten put on his helmet and turned the key. At this, Jigdel pulled out his cell phone and turned up some song, loud. And as he drove away, his young cousin held the phone out so Thupten might hear.

THE ROYAL PROCESSION

Smriti Ravindra

Smriti Ravindra is a Nepali writer based in Mumbai, where she teaches English to high-school students. Her full length book, co-authored with Annie Zaidi, *A Bad Boy's Guide to a Good Indian Girl* was published by Zubaan, New Delhi, India in 2011. Her short stories have featured in several publications including *La.Lit, 42 Magazines, The Westerly Magazine*, and *Out of Print*. She is a regular contributor to a column in *The Kathmandu Post*.

O nly Preeti and Sachi had no fears. They sat at the edge of the gorge, the one that divided their neighbourhood from Chundevi, and dangled their feet into its abyss as though nothing could frighten them this morning – not the dark trees below their toes, nor the darker flowers. Between the gorge and the lane that rolled away from it, dipping and then rising into Ganesh Basti, lay a broad strip of land, soft and fat, woven and dappled with shamrocks. On mornings such as these women and men sat cross-legged upon the grass and planned weekends or talked politics. It was a perfect day for the royal procession that was soon to go down the Ringroad. The month was April and flowers were furious upon trees. The ground was green and marigolds grew accidentally along the lane, the flowers reappearing and disappearing as the path wickered amidst the houses and the fields. Wisps of clouds sailed the clean sky. The moon still floated, pale like china. There were people out on walks and some hinted at the possibility of democracy in Nepal in the distant future. Men agreed and disagreed, as discussions go, and others idled upon the meadow, but nobody, other than Preeti and Sachi, ventured too close to the gorge.

There were stories, not only of human ghosts, but of animal spirits trapped at the bottom, and of creatures, who, unable to crawl out into the sunlight, had morphed into unrecognizable beings.

The new school year had begun and the girls had their satchels with them. Sachi's was new and brightly orange, and though Preeti's was not, hers too was bulging with crisp textbooks and exercise copies still untainted by ink. The girls had decided to cover and label their books here and behind them, leaning on the shamrocks, was a roll of brown paper held together with a rubber band, a pair of scissors, a wad of cellophane sheets upon which the girls had placed a good-sized stone, and a band of Scotch-tape. In the gorge there were prehistoric animals and primaeval insects singing ancient songs but the girls were as oblivious to their antiquity as they were to the trees hissing like witches in the slight wind. They stared listlessly at the small wood that started where the gorge ended on the other side. And though they could not see Edna's mother, they knew she was walking up the lane towards them, holding her head and complaining to her husband about the morning sickness. Now that Sachi had started her periods, now that her breasts itched and were sore, everyone was pregnant. Now that it was not very cold, all the pregnant women were walking all day.

Sachi sighed. "Let's jump down and kill ourselves," she said.

"Let's," said Preeti.

And they sighed again and stared into the chasm. The gorge was bursting with morning glories and conefowers, and the bachelor buttons were intensely blue, like stars.

"Our frocks will get caught in the trees and we will be hanging like kites from the branches," said Sachi.

"All torn."

"Completely tattered."

"No point jumping."

Behind them the cellophane rattled in the wind, the Scotch-tape, standing on its side, rolled an inch forward, and Preeti's satchel, precariously balanced, fell on its back with a soft thump.

"Let's just cover the books," said Preeti.

So they crawled back onto the grass, took the books out of their bags, and stacked the textbooks into two piles. The taller one was

Sachi's because Sachi was in grade eight, two grades higher than Preeti. The girls had decided to be systematic this year. They would cover one of Sachi's books, then one of Preeti's, then one of Sachi's, then one of Preeti's. Whatever was left would be done the following week.

They mulled over the stacks, scarcely moving till Preeti shuffed her pile and placed her favourite book, *The History of Nepal*, on the very top. It had the prettiest cover, one she wanted to preserve better than the unlaminated, black-and-white covers of the others.

The History of Nepal had Prithvi Narayan Shah, Nepal's first Shah ruler, on the cover. He stood before the rectangular map of Nepal. In his left hand he held a sword, slanted to the ground. His right hand was raised and a ringed index finger pointed to the sky. He wore a crown frilled with emeralds and topped with the white plume of the bird of paradise. Behind him the throne, golden, thick and coiled upon itself, rose like fre. It was styled after the Shesh Nāg – the thousand-headed serpent upon which Lord Vishnu, the creator of cosmic destiny, reclined in the oceans of heaven.

"Let's cover this one first, please, please," Preeti said and the girls settled down to cutting brown paper to size, to pressing down the paper upon the book, to Scotch taping the flaps into place.

"If nobody marries us by the time we are twenty, let's marry each other," said Sachi.

"Yes," said Preeti and scotched a flap.

They continued to cut and fold, to cover and stick, but it was obvious that their hearts were not in the task. All week they had spoken of nothing but the royal procession and now that the morning was here Sachi was having her periods again.

"I am sick and tired of it," Sachi said.

"Me also," said Preeti.

Preeti was disappointed by Sachi's history book too. The cover was drab, showing not the glamour of monarchs and maps, but the monotony of national symbols – a cow, a rhododendron, a danfé, all in beige, and badly photographed. So finally, after finishing only two textbooks each, the girls slid back to the edge of the gorge and once again dangled their feet.

"But what if somebody does marry us?" asked Preeti, sucking on a tart candy. They swung their legs back and forth, their heels brushing against the small tufts of grass growing upon the walls of the gorge.

"Do you think Prince Nirajan will be in the car with His Majesty today?" Preeti asked. She hesitated a second before adding, "I think I am in love with Prince Nirajan." She looked at her friend but Sachi was gazing at the woods beyond the gorge. "I think it is all right to love Prince Nirajan. He is only fourteen, only three years older than I am."

"He is only one year older than me," Sachi said.

"That is not age difference enough," said Preeti. "There should at least be three years between husband and wife. Besides, Prince Nirajan looks too much like Rajiv. Last month I saw the Prince playing football on TV and I had to look a long time to make sure it was Prince Nirajan and not Rajiv. You cannot fall in love with Prince Nirajan. That will be like falling in love with Rajiv." Rajiv was Sachi's older brother.

Sachi pulled more candy out of her pocket and the girls sucked on the strips. When Preeti stretched back and lay on the ground there was a perfectly shaped cloud in the sky and a flock of swallows sweeping past it. "I could not fall in love with the Crown Prince," she said. "The Crown Prince is all ten years older than me. My parents will never agree to our match. Or maybe they will. What do you think? It is not a joke to be married to the Crown Prince. If I marry the Crown Prince I will be the next Queen of Nepal. That is no joke. It already makes me nervous, even though we will not be getting married for quite a few years."

"Of course," said Sachi.

They stared again, Preeti at the sky, Sachi straight ahead, and so when Edna's mother came close to them and yelled, they were startled.

"Do you want me to get sick right here?" Edna's mother yelled. "I have enough vomiting as it is with this endless morning sickness. Come right away, stupid girls. Just looking at you is making me dizzy. Do you want to fall into that hole, Miss Daredevils? Do you have no consideration for your mothers? Stupid girls." Sachi ignored her. Preeti rolled on to her stomach and tried braiding the shamrocks she had collected. "Right away or I will vomit in a second," yelled Edna's mother. "Why don't you go to the Ringroad and wait for the procession? You will miss it and pester everyone forever." Then Edna's mother turned around and took the lane back into Ganesh Basti. "I have had enough

395

SMRITI RAVINDRA

of this morning," she said, her head disappearing as the lane dipped down, then reappearing again with the marigolds.

The girls inched back to the grass and put away their books. They stuffed the brown paper into Preeti's satchel. They put the scissors into Sachi's. The Scotch-tape was a little further away and they forgot to pick it up. It stayed round and transparent on the ground. They rose, dusting their sleeves, dusting the grass-stained backs of their frocks.

"Should we leave our bags here? We could come back and finish," said Preeti.

"Thank you very much but no," said Sachi, rolling her eyes, so they wore their bags. Sachi pulled out two blocks of Fruitburst and the girls chewed on the gum as they made their way to the Ringroad.

They did not stay long upon the lane. Instead, they cut into the felds, balancing upon the dike. The fields were heavy, scented and deliberate with ripe panicles, and the air smelled of raw rice and raw leaves. The girls were similarly dressed in frocks with contrasting bodices and patterned slippers, but Preeti was untidy in her longish skirt and her flying hair, and Sachi was very neat. They were mindful upon the small, low walls. Sachi stepped accurately, Preeti tried to hop, but both were like tightrope walkers, aware of the dangers of falling into the waterlogged paddy.

"Does everyone have periods at thirteen?" Preeti asked.

Sachi plucked a grain and gnawed out a single seed of rice with her teeth. "You are too thin. Yours will probably come at fifteen."

"Oh," said Preeti.

"Does it hurt badly?"

"It is just very eww," said Sachi.

Then Edna's mother, who was still on the lane, saw them in the fields, half hidden by the thick paddy.

"Do you girls want to die today?" she yelled. "Get out of the fields. There are frogs there, and toads, and probably snakes."

"Pregnant women are tedious," Sachi said and the girls continued to walk, but from the corners of their eyes they could see Edna's mother waving her arms so they got out of the fields.

"I hope we see Princess Shruti," Preeti said, "even though I have heard mean things about her."

"What things?"

"When Princess Shruti was in St. Mary's School she forced her dorm-mates to drink a whole glass of water out of peanut shells. That is mean."

"That is not even possible," said Sachi. "That is just stupid rumours."

They walked quietly after that till they came to the Deep Dimples Video Store and Sachi started talking again. "Last week," she said, "I was on the terrace and I saw some guys on the other side, you know, where that dirty stream from the meat market gets into the gorge, and I was like eww, that is disgusting, you know? There were like six of them. I wasn't looking or anything, or even really thinking about them. They were pretty far off, you know, but I could see them. I guess I was kind of blank in the head, you know?"

"What about the boys?" Preeti asked.

They looked around for Edna's mother and cut through a small feld and emerged at the Ganesh Temple. They did their Namaskar without stopping or turning fully towards the god. "Nothing much," Sachi said. "They were there and I was watching them, just like that, just to have something to do while hanging the clothes out. Then these guys started going into the bushes, and I was like eww, why don't you just pee in the sewer? I mean, what is the point of going into the bushes if there is a river of pee flowing right in front of you? But then I noticed they weren't going into the bushes to pee."

"You could see all this from your terrace?" Preeti asked.

"Believe it or not, your wish," said Sachi.

"What happened then?"

"They were not peeing. They were plucking leaves," Sachi continued. "I was just watching them casually. The boys plucked leaves, crushed the leaves upon their palms and ate them, like tobacco. You know how it is? I figured I could see them from my terrace but they could not see me."

They stopped before Thapa Baje's house, the oldest slant-roofed house in the area, and looked at the bougainvillea arching over the main gate. Thapa Baje's house had the best flowers in Ganesh Basti. "Sure they could not see you," Preeti said. "Not clearly at least."

"Yeah," said Sachi, walking on. "Besides, they were a bunch of cheapsters and what did I care if they saw me or not?" She spat out her gum and pushed her hand into her pocket, fiddling for another piece.

"Must be doing drugs," Preeti said.

"Rajiv says there is poppy growing by that sewer. Isn't it disgusting to be eating anything by the sewer? I wouldn't eat anything from there, not for a million bucks."

"Yeah."

"You remember when Udip broke his arm and he said I pushed him?" Sachi asked.

Preeti nodded. "That was mean of him."

"Well, I did push him. He tried to kiss me so I pushed him and he fell and broke his arm. How stupid is that?"

"It's yuck," said Preeti.

They saw Edna's mother again, now sitting with her husband on a wall and watching one of the new houses being constructed. It seemed to the girls that there was always at least one house under construction in Ganesh Basti.

When Edna's mother saw the girls she called out to them. "Have you seen Edna?" she asked.

"No aunty," the girls said in unison and walked on.

They passed Sachi's Chinese-brick house with its green windows.

"He was there too, Udip, with the boys at the sewer," said Sachi.

"How do you know it was Udip. Weren't they very far away?"

"Oh," said Sachi, "I would recognize Udip if he was sitting on the moon," and she giggled.

"How can you see so much from your terrace? I can't see all that from mine."

"If you don't believe me I don't have to tell you," said Sachi. "Besides, your house is not tall enough."

They came to Edna's house after that. It was three storeyed and had English columns running through its length. Then, two houses later, it was Preeti's house and Preeti did not turn to look. She knew her house looked like a coop, like a poultry hole with its heavily grilled upper verandah and its rust-coloured parapet. She knew her house, one storeyed and fat-roofed, designed after the houses in the flatlands beyond the mountains, was old fashioned and shabby amongst the new, slant-roofed mansions being built in Ganesh Basti. Her house was like a gourd in a garden of roses, unattractive and plain. "Let them eat drugs by the sewer," she said. "What is it to you?"

"They were a bunch of goofers, that is what. So, I am watching and thinking that they can't see me. Then someone starts pointing at me and I think, oh, what does it matter? I must look so small from so far. So I keep spreading out the clothes. And you cannot even imagine what happened next. This one guy – his hair was all long and all, this guy, he pulls something out of his pocket and starts looking through it. I think it was a pair of binoculars."

"Oh?"

"Yup! These guys must be watching women through windows, movie style."

"Yuck!"

"I know," Sachi giggled. "It's totally eww, isn't it? Then they passed the binoculars around and I was so embarrassed about being in shorts. Thank god my shirt was a loose one. Whoever heard of binoculars being so readily available?"

Preeti had never seen real binoculars in her life. "Next time don't wear shorts then," she said.

"You are an idiot," Sachi said, still giggling. "They were so irritating I stuck my tongue out at them."

"What?"

"Yes. Then I gave them the finger." "What?"

"The middle finger, idiot. I gave them the middle finger, and they gave me theirs, and I gave both of mine back to them. Now," Sachi went on, hardly able to speak. "Now, every morning they sit around Deep Dimples Video Store and when I pass by they stick their tongues out at me and call me their morning glory. I hate it that I was wearing shorts."

Preeti stared at her friend and adjusted the weight of the satchel on her shoulders. "You are mad," she said.

And they were at the Ringroad.

The lane had been all brown, all dust, snaking through the neighbourhood, but the Ringroad was tar, briefly curving around Ganesh Basti like a deep gray carpet, graceful and attractive, the asphalt twinkling. On one side, bordering the neighbourhood, was the Greenbelt with tall and light green trees and soft violet mimosas. Here and there, within the Greenbelt, were kidney-shaped ponds choking with thick purple lilies and fat leaves so dark they were almost as black as the waters underneath. The girls had never seen what lay in those waters. If they went complaining to their mothers about lost balls, their mothers told them to play with something else. "That water is surely poisonous," they said.

The Ringroad was like a dream, quiet and without a single vehicle upon it. The air wrapped around the mimosas and came off fragrant. Policemen stood on both sides at regular intervals, lined upon the sandy sidewalks, some standing at ease and looking ahead, others working to direct traffic away from the street and into smaller, branching lanes.

Preeti wondered where the royal family was going to this morning. She had heard talks about India and about Pakistan, but she could not be sure. She was always a little afraid for the King when he travelled. It was a dangerous thing to be King. Being a King meant being blessed and being cursed, and she was afraid of the people, the gods, the animals, the temples, and everything else that seemed to rule a King, the way they did not rule her. She was not cursed. She could go where she pleased, when she pleased. But His Majesty and his family, they were cursed. They could not go into certain temples, could not anger certain gods, could not perform certain rites. If they ever went into the Budhanilkantha Temple, they would be bitten by the most poisonous snake in the world and would die before they could ask for water to soothe the fire in their throats. It terrified Preeti, this complete vulnerability in His Majesty.

"Let's go," said Sachi, and the girls started crossing the road.

A policeman blew his whistle at them. "Stay where you are," he said. "It does not look any prettier from there." He looked at Sachi and smiled.

Sachi rolled her eyes. "Men are just eww," she whispered to Preeti.

There were people gathered all along the sidewalks, waiting for the procession, and their noisy chatter had the policemen frowning and blowing their whistles at everyone. There were two mounted policemen on very tall horses, one on each side of the road, and the horses trotted rhythmically in place.

Preeti thought of Nepal and His Majesty as she thought of trees and their fruits, of skies and their birds, mountains and their clouds. She thought of His Majesty as moulded into the land, as Nepal herself. She adored the pictures hung upon the walls of houses, offices and shops, amidst oleographs and calendars of gods and goddesses, behind diyo lamps and incense sticks, reverentially garlanded with strings of marigolds and amaranths. The royal portrait in her school was in a circular frame, His and Her Majesties seated in deep chairs, His Majesty wearing the traditional daura-suruwal while Her Majesty sat serene in green chiffon and gold. Princess Shruti, the Crown Prince Dipendra, and Prince Nirajan stood behind their parents, their hands folded before them like members of a choir. The royal portrait in the school canteen showed His Majesty in an army outfit, sash across his chest, multiple badges and stars upon his shoulders. Her Majesty wore a sash too, and the badges, but her smile was gentle and she looked shy, like a little girl.

Preeti's favourite portrait was the one that came on TV before the programmes began. His and Her Majesty were fully majestic on the screen – silver cape, silver crowns topped with plumes of the bird of paradise, emeralds fringing the foreheads, heads so high up it made her dizzy. This was the portrait Preeti had bought off the sidewalk from a woman who also sold candies and dried fruits. Under this picture of His and Her Majesty was a quote: "The universe is woven and interwoven in Vishnu. From him is the world, and the world is in him."

It baffled Preeti that none of the walls in her own house had pictures of the royal family. She had asked her mother once and her mother had looked at her and said there was no reason to go banging nails upon the walls. "Look, nails everywhere. There is no need to crack the walls with more."

"Can't we Scotch-tape a picture to place?" she had asked.

"The glue will ruin the paint nice and proper, leave square marks upon it."

Preeti looked around. The paint was already ruined with age.

"We have all the gods on our walls," she pointed out, tilting her chin towards the many calendars hanging from nails.

"King Birendra is not god," her mother answered.

"He is. He is Lord Vishnu."

"Lord Vishnu," her mother said, emphasizing every word, "is a nuisance. He reclines and rests on his snake and the snake swims all day on the ocean and your Lord Vishnu gets properly blue with pneumonia and stiff with rheumatism. Poor Lakshmi has no other job than to massage his legs day in and day out. If he stopped sleeping on a snake and started doing something more useful, it would be much better, no? Chronic pneumonia and severe rheumatism, that is all it is."

Preeti stared at her mother, her mouth open. There were two Lord Vishnu calendars in the prayer room and one in the bedroom where this conversation was taking place.

Preeti had gone from her mother to her father. "Papa, why don't we hang His Majesty in our house?" she had asked.

"Because," he had answered, "because we don't hang politicians here, that is why." And he had laughed.

But Preeti did not care about her parents now. She had never seen His and Her Majesty in person, and the possibility, however remote, that she might today, made her doubly anxious. She held Sachi's hand and stared at the street, unaffected by the policemen treet-treeting their whistles and scolding.

"Aren't they handsome?" Sachi said, nudging Preeti. Preeti turned to look.

The policemen were handsome in their glowing, creaseless, light-blue uniforms. Navy blue caps hid half their faces and only their lips and their chins showed. The sky shone on their boots and their guns.

The policeman who had blown his whistle at them saw Preeti looking and said, "Heavy bag you are carrying."

"We have to have the books covered for class," Preeti said.

"Why don't you put it down? Nobody will steal it. There are policemen everywhere."

Sachi smiled and put her bag down but Preeti hesitated. No matter which frock she wore, Preeti felt shabby before a policeman.

"Put it down," the policeman coaxed and she removed the satchel from her back.

"When will it come, dāi?" Sachi asked.

"Any moment now, any moment. So keep it quiet and full of respect, won't you?"

The girls nodded. Preeti felt her heart fluttering in her head. Any moment now.

The Royal Palace started at Durbar Marg, the King's Way, and ended at Maharajgunj, the King's City, which meant the Royal Palace was two-and-a-half kilometres long. Just the numbers mystified Preeti. How could any palace be so long, and how could a family of just five people live in all of it? "His Majesty will have to take a car simply to get to the dining room," she said, talking aloud, and Sachi, who always understood everything right away, rolled her eyes. "Imagine him in his silk nightsuit, Sachi," Preeti went on, "driving his Rolls-Royce to breakfast. Of course, His Majesty does not drive his car himself, and there are many, many, many people living in the palace. His Majesty's breakfast is probably brought to him in his bedroom, probably in the Rolls-Royce too! But still, imagine, what must a King's Rolls Royce look like?"

"You are the insanest person in the world," Sachi said.

Preeti had read in one of the Casino Royale magazines at Sachi's house that His Majesty was the only person in Nepal to own a Rolls-Royce. She had sat on Sachi's bed and flipped the magazine from first page to the last, looking for an image of the car, but there had been none and Preeti had tried to imagine it all: the insides of the palace, the insides of His Majesty's car, the lives of the many, many, many people within these insides. It was the difficulty of the imagining, of trying to count the "many", that had confounded her – how many? A hundred? A thousand? She had imagined millions, but that would have meant the entire country!

"Do you think His Majesty will roll his window down and smile at us?" she asked Sachi now. "And maybe we will see Her Majesty too, no? It will be so sweet."

"His Majesty," said Sachi, "is probably in his palace right now, drinking whiskey. Daddy says His Majesty drinks whiskey without any soda." Sachi's father worked at the Casino Royale at the Yak & Yeti and had spoken with almost every member of the royal family.

"You are an ass," said Preeti.

"And you are obviously the most exciting person ever born, I suppose?"

"I don't want to stand with you," Preeti said. "And I don't want to be your friend. And I am only your friend out of pity. Edna thinks your legs are so long you look like a mosquito."

And Preeti picked up her bag and moved away. She walked towards a small crowd and as she walked she heard the far-off rumble of motorcycles. She felt the tickle of their vibration in her soles and she started to run. She ran so she could stand near the mounted policeman and his horse. She had never stood near a mounted policeman before and she laughed a little as she ran, her anger towards Sachi vanishing as suddenly as it had come. Everyone else seemed to be laughing too. The motorcycles were at the turn for the Ringroad and their growls were still diffused but Preeti could hear them getting closer and when she turned around she saw them coming at the turn, two at a time, and she threw her hands up and jumped, unable to contain herself.

A man before her said, "Oho!" and clapped his hands. Other people clapped too. Some whistled. One cried, "Āyo, āyo!" Another slapped his thighs. "Right here!" he said.

The policemen stamped their feet and from the "at-ease" transformed to "attention". They raised their hands in a smart salute and the sandy sidewalk clouded under their boots. Even the horses stood still. Preeti held her breath.

"He is a god," whispered a woman and held her son's hand. The son had long hair, almost touching his shoulders. He looked like someone who would take drugs by a sewer and Preeti felt her anger against Sachi return.

The motorcycles passed two by two before her and Preeti faced the road and shouted out the national anthem, gloriously crowning His Majesty, praying for more glory, more success, more land to befall him. She shouted out the tune, and all the while she kept an eye on the long-haired boy, all the while she dreamed of kicking him, of throwing him on the ground and breaking his arms the way Sachi had broken Udip's.

The boy pulled away from his mother and ran off into the crowd.

"These motorcycles are like no other motorcycles in all of the world!" he said. He kicked one leg and shouted "bhata-ta-ta-ta-tata", in imitation of the motorcycles. A few adults whacked him on his head for being a nuisance but he did not stop.

Preeti looked around for Sachi but she was nowhere.

The motorcycles really were like no other in the world. They were very big and very blue-black with red and blue lights blinking and dancing in circles on their heads. The riders, mysterious and unknowable under large, all enclosing helmets, had to bend low to hold the handlebars. Their hands were hidden in black leather gloves. They sat upon their vehicles like men from the future. They did not speed past and were surprisingly slow, as though they too were looking at the crowd as the crowd was looking at them, but they were not really looking either. The motorcycle men did not turn once towards the sidewalk. They never looked any way other than straight ahead. The engines roared like beasts upon the road.

Somebody caught Preeti's hand and she jumped up in surprise. "Oy," she cried when she saw it was Sachi.

"Hello," said Sachi, smiling.

"Want to race the motorcycles?" she giggled.

"No," said Preeti, and then, "I hate you." When she turned back to the road she had missed the last of the motorcycles that went past. "You just come and disturb me," she said.

Cars followed the motorcycles and Preeti shouted out. "The Rolls-Royce!" she cried. "There will be the Rolls-Royce."

A policeman turned around and shushed her. "Don't be so noisy," he said.

The cars were black but they looked blue under the sky. They had thin, silver antennae upon their hoods and they lulled the street with their soundless speed. The motorcycles had been so flamboyant – lights and sound and dark blue men in snow-white helmets – that the cars in their polished blackness, in their monotone, were dangerous and somewhat terrifying. The steel antennae shivered in the air and flashed like swords.

"Are you mad? His Majesty does not sit in any of these cars," Sachi said. "Men with long guns sit in these cars so if anyone tries to do fishy things they can shoot you right there. Dhickchiyaun!" she shot Preeti and Preeti glared in return.

"Why are you making gun sounds in the middle of a procession?" Preeti said.

The first four cars passed and more motorcycles came by. The pattern alternated. Motorcycles-cars-motorcycles-cars-motorcycles-cars-motorcycles.

"Nobody can know where His Majesty really is, stupid," Sachi went on. "He could be anywhere. He could have been in the very first car, and he could be in the last."

They talked softly, hardly above whispers, and Preeti felt the danger of speaking about royalty while standing so close to policemen.

The motorcycles varied and some were green and white, but the cars sliding by were identical, black with silver antennae.

"It is quite possible that His Majesty is not in any of these cars," Sachi said, keeping her voice low. "Daddy says that it is possible that His Majesty is not in the country at all, that he has disguised himself as such and such and taken the local transport to the airport. Anything is possible, my little candy. It is possible that there really is no His Majesty and the pictures and the movies, the speeches on the radio, all of this was invented because we cannot invent anything else and because we like interesting topics of conversation. Anything is possible, flowerbud."

"It is possible, dear cockroach, that you are mad and know nothing," Preeti said.

Sachi snorted. "I know everything, dear housefly. My daddy works in the casino and plays cards with His Majesty. I know everything."

"Well then, dear flea on a dog, if His Majesty plays in the casino with your daddy then he does exist."

"That too is possible, dear earthworm," Sachi said.

The long-haired boy came back to stand with his mother and Preeti glanced swiftly at Sachi. Sachi was looking at the road but Preeti felt the change in her friend. Sachi was different now. Her hair was longer, straighter. Her frock was shorter. Her skin was scented like wood.

More cars and more motorcycles passed before her and though Preeti refused to believe her friend's periods induced boredom, refused to be disheartened, she realized, rather quietly, that there was going to be no Rolls-Royce on display, that Sachi was right, that perhaps there was no His Majesty in the world, that even if there was, Preeti would, in all probability, never see him in person. He would not risk his life for her, would not roll his window down just to wave. She thought of the boys with their binoculars, and of Udip trying to kiss Sachi. She imagined him at the Deep Dimples Video Store, sitting with his friends on the staircase, slumped, sprawled, taking up almost half the narrow lane. She knew that one of the boys played the guitar, and another had long hair, and one of them looked like Rishi Kapoor when Rishi Kapoor was very young, and that when Sachi passed them she twirled around, like that girl in the Cadbury ad, and her dress few out and her polka-dotted panties showed, and she was their morning glory. She knew Sachi would not marry her. She would marry one of those boys. There wasn't enough age difference between her and Sachi. They were only two years apart and there needed to be at least three.

"We will never see His Majesty," she said finally.

The cars moved past, one after the other like a string of dreams, replicas of each other, and His Majesty did not roll his window down, and Preeti was a little disappointed in him for proving her right.

AFTERSHOCKS and

LET THE RAIN COME DOWN

Samyak Shertok

Samyak Shertok is a Nepali author. His honours include first place in both Writing Nepal: A Short Story Contest and the Vera Hinckley Mayhew Short Story Contest, honourable mentions for the Academy of American Poets Turner Prize and the Ethel Lowry Handley Poetry Prize, and a Northern Greece International Fellowship. His writing appears in *La.Lit*, *Papercuts*, *Inscape*, *The Kathmandu Post*, and several other publications.

AFTERSHOCKS

The Kathmandu sky sliced with unlive
wires. Highways broken like bread
or a body. The Vishnu Temple: a pile
of sandalwood beams & too many prayers.

After five hours of trying, when the call
finally goes through & I hear
my mother's voice, I learn
how to unash my lungs.
As I ran for the open field
I heard the house crack.
The line rattles. Is it her voice?

All day in Tempe, the sky is leaden
with the weight of spring.
The wind whips
the desert willows & Mexican blue palms.
A few drops of angled rain pelt
my window & then it stops.
Somewhere behind the bougainvillea,
Phoebe, tired of waiting for me to bring her food,
must be plotting a pigeon-ambush.

On Facebook, yet another picture:
the bust of a man in the ruins
of Kasthamandap. His breath
gnarled into the sal branches.
In this raw footage
shot from Swayambhunath:
How a city goes down & rises
in a pillar of ash.

Dear Himalayas, this morning I have nothing
to offer you. Not even a butter lamp
for your unwinged Garuda
or your one-thousand-year-old gods
now cursed to an exhale.
I sit at my desk & stare at the paper
white as the song of the earth
as it splits to womb so many Janakis.
Unable to find words, I write
& rewrite the silence.
My bones caw.
I tremble
until prayer becomes my body.

LET THE RAIN COME DOWN

Krishna wakes to the sound of the downpour rioting on the slate roof and the wind churning at the battered pine windows. A deep sleeper, he hasn't woke up at night in a long time, but tonight his eyes open as though from a *dog sleep*. Even in the dark, despite the torrent and the din, he can tell the roof is leaking where the shingles have either cracked or shifted in the wake of the relentless heat and commotion, allowing the rainwater to slip between the tiles. He can easily fetch two china bowls from the adjoining kitchen and place them on the floor to catch the falling raindrops but won't: last time it rained, his father had assured him he would replace the cracked tiles and make the roof watertight before the next drizzle, but even when the dark clouds had claimed the western sky and the quarry season was drawing to a close, he didn't exhibit the slightest interest in securing the new tiles needed for the repair. Does he even remember the promise he made to Krishna as he struggles to sleep the whole night because of the staccato sound of the drops hitting the ceramic? By morning when he wakes to boil water in a tea kettle on the wood stove, the rain will have dug deep into the mud floor and almost seeped into the pine joists underneath, and only then will he know he has to keep his word. Had Krishna's mother been around, she would have never let the rain drip into the house – not a drop.

Only when he pulls the homemade quilt over his cold collar bones and prepares to go back to sleep does he realize it's not the pelting or the wind that woke him – it's Bhishma, their dog, barking menacingly outside. Through the gaps between the howl and batter, he can hear his father coughing "*Huche! Huche!*" downstairs, a phrase he has come to depend on to impel Bhishma to chase away the monkeys feasting on the cornfield days before the harvest and the boys surreptitiously reaching for the pomegranates in the orchard with their tapering fingers.

Bhishma was his mother's gift to him for coming third in the seventh grade three years ago. She handed him a veiled wicker basket she herself had woven. When he removed the cotton cloth, it revealed a curled black Labrador pup, asleep, vulnerable.

"Name him."

"Me?"

"Well, he is yours now."

A month ago Krishna had read the abbreviated *Mahabharata* in his Social Studies class and in a throng of the demigods in the sweeping epic, Bhishma's vow of life-long celibacy so that his father could re-marry had stood out to him. It was not his "terrible vow" that im-pressed Krishna, however – it was his ultimate sacrifice for his father's rather narcissistic happiness.

"Bhishma. That's a lovely name!"

But when the pup whined incessantly, wasting away what energy he had been born with, Krishna regretted picking a name the lab looked unlikely to ever live up to. The mythical prince's courage to make a promise that would cost him his throne and eventually his life was per-haps too much for anyone to live up to, let alone a suckling pup. For the first two months, all Bhishma did was whimper and he never left the basket, hardly lapping up the corn soup or the buffalo milk.

Then one morning Krishna woke to find the bowl licked clean. At first he wondered if his father, finally giving up, had thrown away the food, but when he said no, Krishna was delirious. He cooked another meal for Bhishma right away, and within minutes of placing it by the basket, it was gone. In two months, Bhishma was porpoising around the yard, climbing onto his shins, and barking at him affectionately, his tail wagging all the while. And in three years, he had tripled his size and his whine had grown into a deep growl which scared the visitors and sent a dozen monkeys scurrying across the suspension bridge.

Propping his back against the pillow, Krishna gropes for the safety match on the makeshift headboard and strikes a stick, but the striking surface is damp and the brown cap crumbles before the head can catch the spark. He blows his warm breath onto the strip and with the fourth stick barely succeeds. Cupping the flame with his hand, he guides the teardrop flame to find the kerosene lamp and places the half-burned match on the wick until the lamp sputters to life. The burning light reveals a brass pitcher filled with stale water and his parents' grainy black-and-white photograph in an askew frame on either side of a Radha-Krishna bronze statue. He lifts the picture and wipes the glass with the edge of the sheet even though no dust has settled on it. This picture was taken a few months after he was conceived, his mother had told him, and although the photograph doesn't betray the slightest swell in her belly, he can see his life already pulsing through her pupils and fingertips, every part of her body conspiring to push nutrients into his tentative bones. Next to her is his father staring into the shutter too hard, and even though their elbows touch, the partition between them is unmistakable.

A week after receiving his mother's gift, Krishna woke to find his mother wasn't home. He trotted around the orchard hoping to find her pruning the dead twigs, but she was nowhere to be found. Back at home, he found his father slinging all clothes from the closet. The mattress had been upturned, quilt sprawled on the floor. All her saris, *pacchaura*s, and jewelry were gone, too – except for her *mangalsutra*. He almost asked his father what was going on, but the way his mother had taken everything but her wedding necklace told him everything there was to know. Bhishma was, in retrospect, his mother's parting gift. Had he known it then, he would never have accepted, but now the pup was the last tangible memory of his mother.

Carrying the lamp on his left hand, Krishna goes around the silo looming in the middle of the room, careful not to knock over the butter churner against the wall, and exits into the kitchen. Down the ladder, he descends a rung at a time. By the opposite wall of the main door at the foot of the ladder, when he reaches the back door to his father's bedroom, once their vibrant clothing store, he raises his hand instinctively but finds the door open. Lifting the lamp high forward, he can barely make out his father's silhouette wavering near the closed door that opens to the front yard. His father's right foot stamping on the hardwood floor and clapping of hands send a tremble toward him. Outside Bhishma continues to bark with the undiminished vigour and conviction.

Once it was clear his mother was not coming back, on several occasions he overheard the relatives and some of the villagers urging his father to remarry.

"Life is hard and long, *chhora*."

"Look at your boy. *Ram! Ram!* Who'll look after him?"

His father would nod and manage a saturnine smile, but as soon as they left he would go back to plucking the weeds or watering the roots in the orchard and pretend not to notice the women's blatant invitations to flirt.

His father continues to cough and clap, but what is he goading Bhishma for? At this time of the season the cornfield is only a shallow sea of saplings, and the monkeys know this as well as any farmer. Certainly no boys would brave the frigid dark for a bite of a raw pomegranate. He walks toward his father but stops a metre short from him. His father looks at him and then looks away.

"Go back to sleep."

The lamp reveals the profile of a face that has long succumbed to the grotesque twists of fate. As his father brings his hands together, the pallid fingers appear magnified. It's the same calloused hands that he feared the most when he and his mother returned after errands to collect debt from those who had not paid their dues by the deadline. His father was reluctant to sell cloth on credit, but in this part of the country no credit meant no business at all, especially when you faced stiff competition from the Newar shopkeeper by the suspension bridge who somehow managed to sell everything cheaper than they ever could. At least the villagers claimed so. But once the customers exploited his father's good faith to its limit, they would avoid his shop altogether, and his mother would have to go knock on their doors.

Krishna loved accompanying his mother on those trips, but it was not as much the affected hospitality of the villagers or his mother's company as it was the revelation of the disparity between him and rest of the village children that enthralled him in taking these long walks. He loved how clean and well-dressed he appeared in front of the children in tattered clothes tending to chickens and goats and the way they gawked at him made him feel like royalty. But when the sinking sun painted the skyline crimson and his mother showed no signs of returning home, Krishna would get worried. "Last time," she would say, but soon he learned that there would always be another last time. Unable to sleep in the houses with strange odours and singed ceilings, he missed the scent of pomegranate blossoms wafting into his window and felt sorry for his father for having to struggle with coaxing the kindling and stoking the fire.

Back at home, his father would be waiting for them at the threshold.

"How many times have I told you to not spend the night in some-one's house?"

"You think it's easy to pry money out of those clenched fists? Why don't you give it a try sometime?"

Unable to conjure up an argument or tame his temper, his father would then rely on his quick hands to get his point across, almost throwing his mother off-balance.

"Never take *chhora* with you again."

Since those years his father's hands might have become bony, but they still inflict the same terror on him.

Krishna rests the lamp on a shelf at a safe distance from his father. He hears Bhishma growl. Suddenly he realizes Bhishma has no cover from the rain – his kennel was never meant for monsoons. He reaches for the bolt of the front door, but his father grips his hands.

"Tiger. There's a tiger outside."

It takes him some time to register the information. In the past few months, a tiger had been tormenting a neighbouring village: first the Gurungs' goat went missing, then two lambs from the Thapas at the tail of the village, so they had formed an armed vigil group. Those who kept dogs clasped a hunting ring with sharp needles sticking out around their dogs' necks, hoping that would at least lengthen the tiger's assault and the growls would wake the house owners, if not the vigil group. There was no dearth of those, however, who doubted the effic-acy of the iron ring and opined that its heavy weight would only put the dogs at a disadvantage.

Krishna envisions a tiger on the front yard, strolling toward the pen by the buffalo shed where the goats must be bleating next to the fright-ened chicken coop. The only thing that stands between the tiger's canines and the goats' fragile necks is Bhishma, but now even Bhishma's growl is starting lose some intensity.

Bhishma recycles his barks and growls. The tiger makes no sound.

"We must do something."

"Yeah, sure."

"Scream out the window for help."

"It's raining. *Huche! Huche!* "

"The Vigil Group might hear us."

"In this wind?"

"We can't let Bhishma die."

"*Huche! Huche!* Go. Go."

"You're going to get him killed."

"He has the iron ring."

But the spiked ring is not going to help Bhishma topple the wild beast at least twice his size, just as his father's pantomime is not going to scare away the famished intruder that has already smelled its dinner. There's a hunting rifle that belonged to his grandfather somewhere in the house, but even his grandfather never went out with it. Most likely it is rusted and empty, and even if it's loaded, it would take a miracle for it to fire. He frantically goes through the shelves looking for something, and when he comes across a cotton rag, he stops – next to the rag on the shelf is Bhishma's ring. He fingers the pointed arrows and in doing so pricks his pinkie.

"The iron ring!"

His father doesn't look at him.

How could he? Dear God! How could anyone!

Now Bhishma's growls grow fiercer and shriller – and then that terrible cacophony of the scuffle takes over everything – even the rain. Bhishma issues a long interrupted cry of bark-growl-whimper. Krishna can hear the bodies wrestling, a body being picked up and tossed onto the floor, claws tearing into the flesh. Piercing cries of agony escape Bhishma's mouth. Oh God! No, no. Not Bhishma. Not like this.

Out the back door, underneath the ladder, he finds a desiccated branch from the firewood pile. After wrapping the rag around the branch and knotting its ends, he pours kerosene onto the wrapped end from the lamp and ignites it with the hissing flame. Carrying the torch aloft, he climbs the ladder, several rungs at a time. When he opens the window, he hears goats bleat and jump. The breaking of the bamboo rods of the pen reaches his ears too late. By the time he opens the other window which overlooks the shed, a goat squirms and suddenly grows silent.

"Tiger! Tiger! *Guhar! Guhar!*"

But even he can't hear his scream over the relentless pour. Beside the orchard, on the rippling field, the stripes of an animal sparkle in the cameo of the lightning. The downpour has abated to a drizzle and the wind has quieted down. He comes back to the window that overlooks the orchard and waves the torch. The yard is sodden and empty, the only sign of the tiger's visit is Bhishma's low squirming coming from the shed.

When he tries to unbolt the main door, his father holds the latch.

"Not yet."

"Let go of me!"

Krishna tries to wriggle his wrist free but can't. Next thing he knows he has swung the torch at his father, the flame almost catching his hair, which sends him collapsing onto the pile of firewood. Outside in the shed, Bhishma is a lump of nauseating flesh and broken bones, black blood trickling from the edges. Seeing him, Bhishma tries to lift his head but can only manage the slightest stir. He reaches for Bhishma's blood-smudged head and combs his hair. Bhishma looks at Krishna with his liquid eyes, wags his tail once, and then grows still.

The drizzle grows back to the downpour and the wind begins to shake the pomegranate trees.

"You let Bhishma die! You killed him."

"We have to go inside."

"Liar. Coward."

"Enough now."

"That's why she left you for that man."

His father raises his calloused hand but doesn't bring it down on his cheek. For the first time, Krishna feels neither fear nor the anger to retaliate. Instead he feels sick to his bones. Within days of his mother's disappearance, the news of her elopement with one of the debtors had reached every household. He looks straight at his father, and seeing his father's bloodshot eyes and palsied lashes feels sorry for what he has said. But before he can say anything, his father disappears into the house and emerges with the hunting rifle slung on his shoulder and boots laced to the shins. A few steps down the flagstone path, he stops but doesn't look back.

"If she really loved you, she would have never left."

Krishna notices something cracked and liquid in his father's voice tonight. As the footfalls start to fade, a wave of premonition and regret washes over him. When he turns around, his father is gone and all that remains is the impenetrable darkness.

Twenty years from now Krishna's wife, while picking the ripe pomegranates, will suddenly drop to the ground and never wake, leaving behind a three-year-old son. Then he will see his second wife, after having her own son and daughter, treat his eldest like an outcast, and will realize that his father didn't remarry not because he didn't find women nor because he caressed the false hope of his mother's return, but because he knew too much about stepmothers. Only then will he understand the sacrifice his father made for him and realize how he had mistaken his father's inability to express his feelings for his stoicism, and this moment will come to haunt him again and again as his son grows more gaunt and alienated with every passing day. This moment steeped in rain and darkness when his father gradually walks away from him toward the cornfield, fully knowing a man will be no match for a tiger, gun or no gun, when he could have run after him and said, "Papa, please. You are all I have now." For the rest of his life on rainy nights, he'll wake in the dark hours beside his mouth-breathing wife, Bhishma's whimpers and his father's "*Huche! Huche!*" ringing in his ears, and then unable to go back to sleep, he'll go upstairs and place his ear on his son's bedroom door hoping to catch the cadence of a stunted heart – but what he'll hear is something unintelligible like his father's hoarse coughs, the feelings all knotted and garbled at the throat, snarled clouds beyond the saving of even the rain.

PEP TALK

Muna Gurung

Muna Gurung splits her time between Kathmandu and New York City. Her fiction, non-fiction and translated works have appeared in *Words Without Borders, The Margins, No Tokens, Himal Southasian, VelaMag* and *La.Lit*. She received her MFA from Columbia University, where she was a teaching fellow. Muna currently directs a high school writing center in New York, where her students help her discover America through activities such as eating an entire packet of Sour Patch Kids while writing about the flavour blue. Muna also founded KathaSatha, an organisation that fosters a public writing and storytelling culture in Nepal.

Make some coffee, Arunn. Although, what you really want is a cup of milk tea, with cardamom, with cloves. Grind the organic coffee beans she bought in Nuwakot. Let the black liquid drip through the cloth of the clay cone into the cup. *This is the only way to drink coffee, really*, she used to say between cupfuls. Dump the second cup of coffee. Resist the urge to make things for two now. She never liked hers black anyway. You don't have sugar, you don't have milk, you're not a morning person. The cordless phone is low on battery. She doesn't live here anymore.

Forget the smell of her shampoo. The chemical sugar scent that lingered on her pillow, like the streaks of wet hair that arranged themselves on the bathroom tiles post shower when she forgot to pick them up. Forget how sometimes, when the faucets were dry, you two carried buckets of water into the bathroom. The first time you showered together, you thought it was an accident. She stepped out of her clothes to sit down on the low wooden stool. She loosened her hair and untangled her legs. You let out a soft *eh* as though you remembered something you'd long forgot, and gathered your towel and slippers to leave.

But she scooped a cupful of water and held it out to you. *We're made of the same things,* she said, *you should see the American women in the American locker rooms.* You hung your towel up on the door, took the cup from her hands, and poured the water over her head. You lathered places she couldn't reach as she listed secret sights from within an American locker room: a constellation of freckles threading the arms, shoulders and face, a passing brown lower back accented by an umlaut of dimples, faded pink nipples that look pasted or painted on, erratic black hair peeking from underarms, a warm bulge of belly shaded by a thin line of travelling hair, wrinkled thighs and necks creating folded patterns, an orange head of hair paired with orange wisps over delicate parts, and stubby dotted legs that slid on wet floors.

Remember the night she undressed you? Korean donors in suits had visited your work place, studied the profiles of students, pledged more money, and celebrated over chicken lollipops and large bowls of fruit punch. The insidious kick of the alcohol sent you stumbling home. She found you fiddling with the padlock on the chain gate. When she asked you if you were okay, you threw up. She dragged you up one flight of stairs, and leaned you against the doorframe of the bathroom as she took your clothes off. In that drunken blur, you remember thinking how you had never been naked in front of another woman. When you changed your clothes around others, you did what every girl in your hometown was taught to do: turn around, put your hands in your blouse, sling a new shirt over your head, slip your hands through the sleeves, and peel the first shirt off your back. But for the first time with sore clarity, you knew what you wanted. You wanted her to look at your body. The way you looked at hers. How her thighs held up by silver stretch-marks, widened and joined her hips, which rose and then dipped into her waist that circled up to touch her breasts as they fell away softly pulling down her birth-marked shoulders. But instead, she was fidgeting with the tap and calling you names: *Donkey brains! Donkey brains!* She drained out what felt like the largest cupful of brown water and rinsed you methodically. You were dried, tucked inside a thin dhaka shawl and left in front of the living room fan.

Don't think about that morning after, when you walked into her bedroom to apologise for your drunkenness. She stirred and turned around to face you. As she lifted her blanket to let you into her bed, your *I'm sorry* dropped gently on her pillow somewhere. Half asleep, she shook her head, draped an arm around your neck pulling you into a hug, as you felt her nipples soften against yours. *Shhh, let me sleep,* she said with breath like the insides of an old, worn plastic bottle. Winter had taught the two of you to huddle for warmth in the mornings but you had carried this ritual into the summer, and past the rains. Sometimes you slipped into her bed. Sometimes she floated into your room with her sun-dyed hair in a mess about her neck, her eyes barely open. You two laid in bed longer, especially on weekends when you felt no guilt about the day passing outside the window – her cousin in the office downstairs screaming on the phone *Forget Me Not Travels, Namaste,* the children playing marbles and fighting over discarded cycle tyres, the neighbour's chickens clacking and dodging city wheels, the pressure cookers whistling an indication of mid-day meals. Then, you two went to Rupa didi's store to buy a packet of milk, bread and vegetables for a late afternoon meal. She chopped and you cooked while tuning into English songs on the weekend FM stations.

Stop asking yourself how you got here. What if she hadn't seen you, a sixteen-year-old then, standing in school uniform waiting for glasses of sweet yogurt with raisins and pistachio at the lassi place in Assan? What if she hadn't been the only one to ask you how you liked the new school, the other students, and Kathmandu, as though she read your homesickness in the sweaty lines of your palms? What if she hadn't told you about the time she travelled with her father to your town? If she hadn't asked after your Kalpana didi who sold the best churpis that hung hardened on thick strings, yet melted milky in the mouth? What if, after that lassi day, you two hadn't spent the rest of high school sitting in the back rows of classes, giggling and tipping your chairs on two legs, your arms pushed against the walls, and your fingers locked? What if Sundays weren't days when she invited you over to her house, and you two walked up to the rooftop with bags of oranges, laid on your bellies, and did your homework until your elbows turned ashy and worn from resting on concrete? What if you hadn't spent all your pocket money calling her every evening from the phone at the knick-knack pasal outside the hostel? Pressing your lips so close to the receiver, as though you weren't going to see her jump right off that school bus at 7:15 the next morning. What if she hadn't left for America? What if you hadn't stayed in the city? What if you'd kept in touch? What if you hadn't seen her five years after high school – Americanised with her short hair and loose clothing – at a fundraiser party in Thamel, where you asked linen-clad tourists to sponsor an education? What if she hadn't recognised you? Hadn't asked you where you were living or told you about her father's death, or about taking over Forget Me Not, or about the empty family-owned apartment above the office in Lazimpat? What if, when you agreed to move in with her, she hadn't kissed your cheeks and nose and eyes so blindly and hugged you so tight you swore a part of her entered you? You felt like she never left in the first place.

Forget about the night you discovered that feeling lodged in your chest, in your breasts, that suddenly spread deep into your armpits. You felt its sharp yet vacuous presence grow as she told you about an American hiker, a man who had walked into Forget Me Not looking for an adventure. You initially dismissed it as nothing: another white man who wanted to learn Nepali for a minute, who had finally found his place in the world, and was now ready to open himself to a Nepali girl. But she wasn't any Nepali girl. In just the year you had lived with her, you watched her revolutionise her father's old travel agency by hiring only women staff and guides, and providing cheap eco-friendly trips. She had even appeared on the local women's magazine cover, as one of Nepal's "youngest social entrepreneurs"; her interview was so full of English words, you had a hard time sounding them out in Nepali letters. The feeling in your chest and breasts and armpits returned when you found out that her American hiker had done more than just inquire about a tour package. He had affected her in a strange way. One day, you found her stuffing her face with daal bhat and talking about foreign penises. *Did you know that a non-Nepali penis doesn't carry with it an extra cloak? The tip sticks out like a head. It wears a little cap. Like, like a mushroom.* Her commute home from her office below was now filled with laughter, as she spoke into the mobile phone in her renewed American accent. You had never imagined she would find a home in a random stranger. A home built on just one tiny hair of a fact that they had both read an obscure book written by yet another foreigner, a book about solitude of one hundred years.

Erase the memory of how the American, slowly and quickly became a part of the clanking of kitchen utensils. His cologne mixed with the smell of your chickpea potato curry, a dish she loved because she claimed *only Arunn could get the chickpeas to the right softness.* She used to be your garlic chopper, your dish-wiper, your green bean snapper, your can opener. But in what seemed like seconds, yet weeks and months, he had taken over parts of your role. He insisted on doing the dishes as she wiped and he said cans didn't need openers; they needed *a real man's muscles.* She laughed at his cocky jokes, as you stirred the chickpea curry to puree.

Clean up. Do things. Stuff the clothes she left behind in plastic bags, suck them skinny, and give them away. The other things that remind you of her, such as her toothless comb, her yellow plastic gun earrings, the hardened lentil gravy stain on the stove, three precious baby photos, her bathroom slippers, her pink nail clipper, the wooden stool, the smell of coffee in the apartment; pack the packables, eat the eatables, throw the throwables, give the giveables, keep the unkeepables. Like that memory of lining up for a warm samosa and milk tea in December, keep that.

Don't check the phone. She will call once she is completely settled in her new place. Somehow without anyone else's permission, you had imagined a home for the two of you. You had imagined yourself as an old lady on Saturday afternoons, squatting and scrubbing her back in the sun, counting her raisin-like moles. You had imagined carrying hot water bags into bed to soothe your aching backs. You had imagined learning how to knit socks for her so that she wouldn't slip around the house. But the American had other plans for her. You remember the moment she told you, teary eyed, about how exciting the journey had been. How ready she was to take the American seriously, their lives seriously. You remember asking her *should I leave too?* In that you meant, didn't it make plain simple sense that you would go wherever she went, that remember, you two were stitched that way? But she heard something else. She told you to *feel free to stay here,* that the place was empty anyway. But you know there is no space in this apartment for loss.

Forgive her for her language, her gestures, her love. Don't think back to her moving away party when she introduced you to the American's friends as her *girlfriend*, in English, and it validated your feelings for once. She spoke with you and around you as she recounted stories of how *we loved to sleep late into the day over weekends,* and how *we lived right next to the best samosa joint in town* and how *Arunn is the best masseuse* and how *her chicken curry, boneless, is simply to die for.* You noticed the way she jumped back and forth from present to past tense. But remind yourself to forget how she let your palm linger on the small of her back, and how when everyone had enough to drink, she pulled you to the sticky dance floor and swayed side to side guiding your arms to wrap around her waist, her right knee between your legs, her head on your chest, *we better find each other again*, she said.

Answer her call. She means it when she says she misses you. It was not her fault that she didn't feel the pain in your chest, your breasts, your armpits. The pain you never revealed to her. When you visit her some day, you will see that she has set her new living room in the same way she set yours. Extra cushions on the ground next to the sofa, the tables tall enough to slip legs under, the wind chimes made out of bangles singing near the windows, the baby aloe vera plant above the TV. You will find that she has lined the kitchen cabinets with newspapers, folded to fit perfectly. She will make tea with not enough milk and too much sugar. But you will drink it and tell her about how one of the students from your village is thinking of taking up taekwondo so that he can impress the girl he sees every morning at his bus stop. She will tell you how she misses Rupa didi's store. Then, concerned, she'll ask you if you've found a new roommate. You'll pretend to make a joke about how no one can ever replace her. She'll laugh and slap your knee.

Sleep, Arunn. Because ever since she left, you've spent your nights looking for her. You remember waking up to find yourself in the living room, standing in front of an empty sofa, because somehow your muscles didn't forget. They got used to you turning the TV off, nudging her awake, pulling her up by her arms onto her feet, walking her to bed as she muttered, *you're the best, Arunn*, then tucking her in, closing her door shut and walking away. Into your own room.

FLAMES AND FABLES

Prabhat Gautam

Prabhat Gautam was born and raised in Kathmandu and lives
in the United States. He started writing fiction as an under-
graduate student at Kenyon College, Ohio. When the earthquakes of 2015 happened in central Nepal, he was away from
Kathmandu and his parents. The opportunity to include *Flames
and Fables* in the anthology has been a chance to pay homage
to the city of Kathmandu, its present and past spaces, as well
as hope for a future that is better built, more prepared and
integral to Kathmandu's identity as a city of cities.

I*t was as if someone had fired a gun in the house, and all windows had been thrown open to get the smell of gun powder out
of the corners,* Rabin thought as he opened his eyes and looked
around the room washed with the sunlight streaming in through the
east and south windows. He hadn't heard gunshots in a while with
the city returning to its usual routine after the recent wave of curfews
and demonstrations.

He sat up on an upholstered bed, covered by a sheet with elaborate
dragon prints, monsters swirling and slithering on the cheap Chinese
fabric, swallowing their own feathery tails. Sitting on the edge of the
bed with his feet firmly planted on the grey carpeted floor, he looked
down at the sheet. It was blue, twisted and knotted because of his
nightmares, still damp with the perspiration that made his nightshirt
stick. *Blue Mimosa* was lying face down on the floor, a pagoda of read
and unread thoughts.

"Rabin, Rabindra," called a voice from outside the door. "Are you
awake yet?" He didn't answer. He disliked being interrupted in these
morning lulls. His coherence was a sluggish trail, while his reality remained hanging on a nail in some forgotten and empty room of his

dreams, beyond his reach.

"Do you want *dudhilo* tea or lemony? Rabin, answer me!" the voice demanded.

"Ama, I am awake. I am awake," he replied while staring at his ragged flat nails. He couldn't stop chewing them. The protective cuticles were peeled back to show the glistening pink of his flesh.

"I can come and cut the lemon, just put some water on the stove," he added, looking in the direction of the door. He thought of the tangy juices from the yellow fruit seeping into his cuticles, sending shocks of jittery pain up his spine. He stood up, his right hand trailed down and tugged at the elastic band of his briefs. He swung his upper body to the left and his head to the side, with crackles and pops.

"Your editor called about half an hour ago. He wants you to call him back on his mobile before you reach the office," Ama continued.

"What did he want this early in the day? Constant nagging and nothing else from this dead end job," exclaimed Rabin aloud, more to himself than his mother. The outburst weighed down with agitation and muffled by the door that separated mother from son, still pierced through. It travelled with a velocity straight to a specific place in the mother's heart, and set off dominos of her thoughts tumbling.

"How am I supposed to know that? Did I want you to be a *patrā-kar?*" Ama erupted. "There were so many opportunities that you squandered. We provided you with everything that you had asked for and yet, you dropped out of the engineering school. We had so many dreams for you, Rabin!" She slapped the door with her open palm. It made a loud and dull thud, the sound reverberating through the house.

"You are 26, Rabin! I don't understand why we still have to be your caretaker," she cried.

"Ama, I will be late for work if we start this now," he implored, looking out the open windows. Rabin had his mother's whetstone eyes and the square of his chin was neatly framed by the black hair of his goatee. Evelyn liked his goatee.

In the heat of afternoons, when they both sprawled on straw mattresses atop the sundeck of her rented apartment, Rabin would be in his shorts and Eve in her bathing suit, their bare soles looking skywards. Evelyn would roll over on her stomach and turn towards him. Her hands would reach to touch his cheeks. Her pale skin, covered from head to toe with sunscreen lotion and freckles, clashed against the deep brown of his body. The few feet high cemented walls of the balcony hardly hid them from the neighbors' prying eyes. Rabin would often catch the aunty from the house next door craning her neck while leaning off her rooftop. All that while, her pretense would be that she was counting the number of bitter gourds hanging on the climbers, which camouflaged her own bedroom windows.

"And oh, *she* called," Ama said. "*Evah-leen* wanted to chat with you at seven thirty *am*." It was without a doubt that Ama disapproved of Evelyn. In addition, this disapproval was collective, since Rabin's aunts and other relatives colluded with his mother to make sure that she heard an earful every time they saw Rabin and Evelyn together. "Don't go out and eat beef in Thamel with her again. Reeta aunty phoned and told me that she saw you going into a beef meat restaurant with an *angreji keti*. *Gori*, she is going to spoil you rotten!" she said with a heavy audible sigh.

"Rabin, what does *Gori* mean?" Evelyn asked while running her hands through his hair, glistening under the Saturday sun.

He looked into her sea-green eyes. Her cheeks were burning red and the golden nose ring trembled under her even breathing. She was fragrant from the shampoo, the one they had picked together in the humongous new department store around the corner.

"Don't be silly Evelyn, you know what *Gori* means," he replied with irritation. He didn't like these conversations. It had everything to do with their differences. Whenever he paid closer attention to how her skin folded around her body, she turned into something else in front of his eyes, – a porcelain doll with her toenails painted black and dark French bangs hanging over her eyes, unrecognizable and abstract. He wanted her to be more than what his imagination permitted, more than just a blur of stereotypes, popular images and fantasies. He didn't want her to disappear behind the faces of actresses, who he had gawked at for hours in those weekend screenings of Hollywood movies at the American Council.

Once when he was inside Evelyn, Maggie Gyllenhaal popped into his head. He didn't want it to be that way, it just happened. Maggie's face just came up and he couldn't help himself. For two weeks after that incident, he couldn't look Evelyn in the eye. Sometimes, the guilt was so unbearable that he couldn't even stand being in the same room as her.

"No, like I know what it means," she said, pursuing the topic stubbornly. "But I want to understand the connotations. Isn't fair skin one of the thirty-two prized features of a Hindu woman?"

"Oh, come up Eve! That's a pretty misogynist and ancient list, you know" he said, grinning. "The list also says that women need to have a waistline like that of a tiger and arms that look like an elephant's trunk. It does seem like your arm has a strong resemblance to a trunk, maybe that can help" said Rabin, grabbing her arm jokingly. "No Rabin, stop fooling around this. I am always going to remain an outsider to your family members," she said in a serious and abrupt tone, not responding to Rabin's efforts to make the conversation lighter. He noticed Evelyn's shoulders get tensed. "They are the damn harpooners and I am their white whale. They have made it their obsession to hunt me down, see me removed from your life." She punctuated herself by sitting upright; her hands now lay folded and tucked in the midst of her lap. She was a bundle of fragility and nervous anger in that moment, only nerves. Rabin leaned in closer to her.

"You don't need to bring *Herman Melville* into this and make this conversation so allegorical, Eve," he said, struggling to suppress the glee in his voice and trying to comfort her at the same time. Evelyn drew complex symbolic interpretations from almost everything that happened to her. "And are you honestly comparing yourself to a big albino whale?" He raised himself and grabbed her bare arms from behind. There it was, right under his fingertips, a tattoo on her arm brightly outlined in the clear noon light, swimming in black ink, the writhing blue body of *Moby Dick*.

"I mean, Hindus worship Vishnu, the god of whalers." Evelyn turned around to look at Rabindra's face quizzically.

Evelyn "Eve" Brough, native of Salem, Massachusetts, attended Boston College and got her B.A. in English. There, she picked up an obsession with *John Ashbery's* poems. She'd spend hours, cooped up and hidden in the stacks of the humanities library, poring over his poems, while missing lectures and not turning in her essays. It was on a whim that she decided to drop her post-college radio station job in Boston and work for an English newspaper halfway around the world. Richard, her ex-boyfriend, had been sharing stories from his recent adventures on the southern slopes of the Himalayas at the Philosopher's Bar in Cambridge. They were both leaning against a jukebox – *Son of a Preacher Man* was filling the room, mostly crowded with students from surrounding universities. After a while, the song stopped distracting Eve.

"Getting to Makalu base camp was the real adventure of my lifetime, Eve," Rick said loudly. "It was Kathmandu, which was just awful to get stuck in," he said, careful not to slur his words over the few liquor shots they had taken together. "Fucking claustrophobic man," he tried explaining. "Surrounded by these glowering hills all the time, missed the open salt water too much."

But that was the opposite of how Eve had been feeling. It was the open water and her hometown, which she had grown sick of. The harbor, her memories, friends and family, all of them crowded her mind, and jostled with her thoughts. She needed to get away. The sticky salt of sea on her skin and the fishy aftertaste hanging in her throat needed to be washed away with chilled air and cold water from a lost and lonely brook in the hillside. It didn't take more than two weeks for her to hear back from Abhi Sharma, editor of *The Himalayan Post*. The daily had agreed to hire her as one of their copy editors.

Rabin pushed the door open and stepped out into the hallway. The narrow passage was dimly lit by yellow light from a twenty-watt bulb, hanging naked from the ceiling. There was a calendar marked with the year 2056 plastered on the wall at the end of the corridor. Underneath it on a wooden stool was a maroon telephone set. Fifty-six years ahead of its Gregorian counterpart, the Hindu calendar had laminated pictures of Hindu deities on each flap, lounging and lording over offerings from the devotees. This month it was the elephant-headed Ganesh, with the unbelievable roundness of his gut, gluttonous appetite and broad expanse of his ear flaps. He sat on a plush purple cushion, guiltlessly eavesdropping on all conversations.

"Hello, Abhi-ji?" Rabin spoke into the mouthpiece. "It's Rabin. Was there something urgent that you wanted me to check on?" he asked.

"Rabin-ji, thanks for calling back," Abhi spoke from other side. "I wouldn't have disturbed you this early if it wasn't an important assignment."

"Of course, of course," he replied, rolling his eyes. This was the third morning call he had received from Abhi since the week started.

"I know that the political beat isn't your thing, but this is something interesting," Abhi said and waited for Rabin's response.

"Mhm?"

"A guy called me at home late last night. He said that he is a member of the politburo for the Maoist party," Abhi took a long swig of what could have been either tea or his morning peg of whiskey. "He is in Kathmandu for a couple of days. It's supposed to be an undercover visit. I want you to get an interview from him for this coming Monday's paper."

"Sure. Where and at what time I am supposed to meet him?" Rabin asked, suddenly excited at the prospect of meeting a Maoist rebel.

"I told him I would send my reporters to Athchowk at eleven-thirty. That's about two hours from now." He took another swill of his drink and smacked his lips. "This guy will be wearing a grey flannel shirt. Okay?"

Rabin jotted down the details on the Moleskine that Eve had given him. The frayed skin of his fingers grazed lightly on the ruled pages as he wrote in his curved hand.

"Got it, Abhi-ji," said Rabin, ready to end the call.

"By the way, why don't you ring up that American girl and take her with you! She needs to get out in the city and understand a few things about this damn revolution," Abhi added. He hung up without waiting for Rabin to respond.

Athchowk was a well-known intersection where eight roads converged. It belonged to the old part of Kathmandu, littered with narrow lanes and numerous courtyards. Houses built a few centuries ago still stood around the roundabout, while the families within them separated and scattered. Everything seemed to swell and breathe together towards the sky. At the center of the chowk was a stone pillar, on top of which there was a king's statue, kneeling on his left knee with his hands joined in prayer. On his right shoulder perched a golden bird, ready for flight.

"Rabin, remind me the story about that bird you had told me?" Eve asked, turning towards him. She was wearing one of her best sun dresses, with a light yellow silk scarf neatly tied around her head. The large flower prints on the fabric made her stand out even more. A bit outrageous for a supposedly clandestine meeting, Rabin had thought when he picked her up in the morning, but she was a marvelous distraction.

They had just arrived at the chowk. After his conversation with Abhi, Rabin had called up Eve to tell her about the assignment. She was glad that the editor had finally come around to throw something real her way. It was becoming tedious to be cooped up in the office all afternoon, correcting misplaced modifiers and educating Nepali English language reporters about subject-verb agreements.

She had been to Athchowk with Rabin once before. Their trip had been a part of a more usual routine that Eve and Rabin had established some weeks after meeting in the office. Once the newspaper had been put to bed, Rabin rode his scooter over to Eve's place. From there they would shoot off into the extending darkness of the evening. They would ride past books shops of *Putali Sahar*, climb through the steep hill of Ganaune *Pokhari* crowded with hoarding boards, and wind through clean residential neighborhoods of *Laxmipath* to speed past the blinking traffic lights near the *Narayanhiti* Museum. Kathmandu is a different chapter of a story during the night. Every now and then, Eve would lean in and whisper how much she loved being on the wheels with Rabin. She would place her hand near Rabin's heart and lost in the heady mixture of the scooter's speed, her chin on his shoulders and the warmth from her hand, Rabin's heart-beat would run ahead, skip and outpace the motor of his scooter.

One evening they had ended up in *Ason*, the medieval architectural core of Kathmandu, with its puzzling narrow lanes that snaked in and around for miles. They had been successfully lost for hours and didn't even bother to ask for directions. The scooter ran out of gas right about when they reached *Athchowk*. It was close to midnight and there wasn't much life out in the streets. Under the yellow glow of towering street lamps, they could see the sleeping bodies of beggars huddled under old jute bags, piled together with some mangy dogs near the pillar.

This afternoon, they were waiting a little further away, under temporary awnings made from bright blue plastic tarpaulins. At the base of the pillar sat several middle-aged women, the ends of their *sarees* covering their neatly combed hair drenched in mustard oil. One of them lighted up *Khukuri*, and passed around the smoke, while few others were chewing away at beetle nuts. In front of them were bamboo baskets full to the brim with bottle-green spinach, cilantro, radishes and mustard greens. There were pyramids of clementine and orange, the sticky pulp from heaps of jackfruit, gourds and melons coated the dusty ground. Ominous clouds were hovering in the sky; the hawker women uncovered their heads and stared patiently skywards.

One of them asked the other, "What do we do if it rains this afternoon?"

Her conversation partner, with her gaze fixed on the clouds and lips pursed downward with a frown said, "*Khai,* what to do? I have not sold a single thing today." A quiet audience to this conversation was the king's statue, sitting on top of the pillar for centuries and worshipping his city, with the bird as his only testament for a glorious prophecy.

"They say that on the day this golden swallow takes off from the king's shoulder," Rabin paused, "this city's people will be ready for self-rule."

"You mean, Nepali democracy version 3.0," Eve chimed in happily and expecting Rabin to acknowledge her wit and knowledge of Nepali history. "It's wild that some fifteenth-century authoritarian king of Nepal had thought of such a modern concept like self-rule," she added.

"Well, more like seventeenth century," Rabin corrected her. "You know, this country has always had its share of wise men and storytellers," Rabin spoke more to himself with self-conscious pride. "But none of that wisdom stays, except in fables and mute statues," he trailed off.

Just then they heard a commotion headed their way. The hawker women hastily started to collect their produce and run into the doors around the chowk, gateways to labyrinthine alleys and walkways. As they hoisted up the mats on which the vegetables had been piled, several melons and jackfruits rolled onto the ground. Some spilled out and fell off the bunched mats, to split open on the ground.

Eve could see flickering flames dancing several feet away. Many of those walking about stopped and stood. Everyone's eyes seemed to glaze over, not in fear but in a kind of unwavering expectation.

"Rabin, what on earth is going on?" Eve asked anxiously.

"Oh, it's the mid-afternoon *masāl julus*," he replied, his nervousness fixing him to the spot.

"Wait, is this *the* infamous procession I have heard about from every reporter at the office?" she asked.

The first *masāl julus* had happened in the summer of 2055. It started as a group of ten student youths, who wore black coveralls and blindfolded themselves. Each carried a burning torch in broad daylight and walked silently through Kathmandu's streets. The number of procession goers had gone up recently. No one knew where this group congregated and to where it finally dispersed. The photojournalists had tried their best to predict the site of the upcoming processions and had repeatedly failed at it. The black mass was ephemeral, as it never lasted more than ten minutes. This one heading towards Athchowk seemed substantial in size. There were about fifty men and women, their lips pursed together, leading one another silently through the streets. The naked soles of their feet padded over the dusty asphalt, and made sounds like when the snow falls on a quiet winter day. The flame under the blazing sun and their grave faces would startle just about anyone who saw them. Motorbikes, cycles, auto rickshaws and taxis had all parked themselves, quietly giving way to the procession.

Eve stood there overcome with fear as the blindfolded procession marched past her. Their flames threw translucent shadows on the ground and the heat from them smacked the bystanders on their faces. She turned towards Rabin but like hundreds of others who had lined up in the street to witness this ritual, he was spellbound. She on the other hand was just plain scared.

A bell tower struck the mid-hour reminder in the distance, and the quietly walking bodies tore the blind folds, their serene eyes staring ahead of them. And then, these bodies bolted into whatever alleyways they could jump into. The whites of their eyes, and orange flames hurled past Eve and Rabin in a blur, within seconds there was not a single torch in sight. The tension in Athchowk expanded and then dissolved. The traffic resumed itself with fury and silent spectators returned to their original pace, as if nothing out of the ordinary had just happened. It was at that moment when Rabin's face relaxed, that Evelyn understood what Rick had meant when he used the word "claustrophobic" to describe the city.

"Rabin, are you alright?" she asked, recovering from her own anxious thoughts and paying attention to his vivid face.

"Wasn't that something?"

"Yeah . . ."

"That was something . . ." he sighed and leaned against the closed metal shutter of a storefront.

"Yeah . . ."

CHAMOMILE

Byanjana Thapa

Byanjana Thapa was born in the south of Nepal, but brought up in Kathmandu, New York City and Geneva. She has loved English literature ever since she can remember, and has been writing since the age of ten. Her short story *Chamomile* was shortlisted for the Writing Nepal 2013 competition, and her poems have been published in many anthologies. Byanjana has a Bachelor's degree in Biology and is currently pursuing her Master's. She lives in Teaneck, New Jersey, and writes regularly on her blog *thewriterispresent.blogspot.com*.

Juhi was in town. It had been a decade since her last visit, and who knew when the next one would be? She wanted to see Shagun at any cost. They made hasty plans to meet at Hotel Annapurna, in the café that overlooked the pool. "One o'clock," Juhi had decided. She had a meeting afterwards. "So many years." *Fifteen, exactly*.

Shagun was running late. On a last-minute whim, her daughter Aditi had wanted to be taken to a school friend's house. The babysitter did not know where the baby's diapers were. The minutes slid by, pushed faster by the painful inching of Kathmandu traffic.

By the time she finally got out of the taxi and sprinted into the hotel, Juhi was already in the café overlooking the pool, cigarette in hand. *Of course. Like a chimney*, Shagun thought, patting down her frizzy fly-away strays before she walked towards the table. She tried sitting down. Juhi stood up immediately, and scooped her into a very tight hug, against which Shagun's neck craned uncomfortably. She breathed in heavy perfume. Floral notes. She remembered. *Femme. Hugo Boss, it must be*. She once had a penchant for perfumes.

They sat down. Juhi lit another cigarette, and offered one to Shagun. She refused politely.

"So," Juhi said between drags, "How have you been?"

"Good, busy," Shagun looked at Juhi's eyes, then at the table.

"Don't you have a daughter? How *is* your daughter?" *A smile, red lips stretched over white teeth. How are they not stained by that much smoking?*

"Good. She's seven years old. Aditi's her name. Very bright. A lot of trouble," Shagun spoke to the table top, reminding herself not to worry. Neel would pick their daughter up from her friend's house.

A lot of nodding, the smile still stretched taut. Juhi understood. "Ah. Children." She had a boy. He lived in England, with his father.

"His father is Eurasian," Juhi explained, tasting the word. *Eurasian.* She outlined it with the blood-red lips – enunciating. The old South Asian training in enunciation seeped through her new American twang. Shagun had gone through the same rigorous training. Each mispronounced or garbled word was met with a slap on the thigh. The sound awoke those dormant memories of the old school. Assembly lines she straightened out. The hormones oozing out of their skin into zits, hair, breasts. Behind the dilapidated buildings, business idea meetings: plans, anticipations. There they had stretched and widened. *So long ago.* She wondered whether they should talk about it. Frolic in old memories.

Instead, fillers –

"I also have a son now. He's just five months old."

"Really!" *Reaches out for her hand, briefly touching it before retracting.* "Good job."

"Yeah, thanks. It's definitely not the easiest job."

Another smile, another drag. "You work somewhere?" *Her eyes removed from the question, focused on some tomorrow.*

Shagun breezed through the answer. "No. I used to. I started at Nabil Bank. I mean, you know how I always wanted to start a business." Juhi nodded. "But there wasn't any money, and then, well Ma fell sick, and she wanted me to settle down. I got married, and you know having two kids – *whoo!* So hard to handle. Especially since Neel is never home. He can't help with the kids."

"Why not?" *The inquisitive eyebrow, furrowed.*

"Well, he works so hard, he has no time."

Lips pursed. "Really."

Like this, without the burning red lipstick, she suddenly looked like her old self. A hungry girl, she had been. Juhi had tried drugs and older men that she could attract. She had tried working hard at school. And yet satisfaction had always evaded her. *Is she still hungry?* She didn't look it. Sometime since those years of despondent youth, she had tried success, and had succeeded in getting it. There could no longer be a hunger. *Could there?*

"Are you hungry?" Shagun asked.

"Oh, no. Not at all. I had a little slice of apple pie, and some chamomile tea. Would you like a cup? Chamomile is very good for you. It has anti-stress, anti-inflammatory *and* detoxifying properties. It has flavonoids, too, which reduces the risk of stroke, diabetes. It's even supposed to –"

"I can't. Can't drink chamomile. I'm nursing still. Chamomile is not good for nursing mothers. Just a Sprite, and fish and chips. It used to be good here, and I'm a little hungry."

"What hogwash! I drank chamomile while nursing. And you? Drinking Sprite?" At the same time, to an approaching waiter: "A Sprite, please, and an order of fish and chips."

"Yes, I drink Sprite. Why?" Shagun said.

"You never used to! You hated carbonated drinks. Remember? All that sugar will give you diabetes!" *Mocking her now.*

"Soda helped the heartburn when I was pregnant. I still get it sometimes. So I had to start drinking it."

"You were such a pet. They loved you, didn't they, those teachers? Perfect grades, perfect manners. People pleaser."

"Hah!"

"And since when did you stop blabbering? Remember you *always* won the debate medals? And Rakshya always came in second. She hated you! All that gold, for talking! And now, look. Trying to be what? A one-word wonder?"

"Yeah, those medals," Shagun let out a small laugh. "They're gathering dust now. As for the talking, well, there is little talking to do, except opening my mouth to tell my daughter to stop whining!"

"Hah! Things do change!" *Another drag. The cigarette stub succumbs to the ashtray.*

"There was a time you wouldn't stop talking and wouldn't touch soda!"

There was a time. Of course, there was one. Those were the years of maybes. The years scribbled on their skins by their parents, whose ink seeped under the dermis and was imbibed by their very cells: the ink that wrote her completely off her course. The years of "I will never", *scratched*. "I will always", *scratched thrice, blotted out*. Not anymore.

No. Still.

The petroleum lines, now hers. The electric bills, now hers. The child. The children, now. The cycle. And her ideas, her potential?

She looked at Juhi, with her cool cigarettes, her sanitary removal from everything. The same Juhi, who once struggled with direction-less, chaotic questions, now had all the answers. She had to have the answers, because she had written a great many articles about them! She was an authority on women in corporations and science and at the same time, an authority on women who fetched well water and darned shoes. She had a business that promoted handicrafts by women in rural Nepal: she exported them to the United States. An old business idea, whispered behind a dilapidated building in *her* voice, Shagun's. She even remembered the day. One Tuesday lunch break, twelfth grade. On the same day she saw the bruise:

"Juhi! You have to stop seeing him! Isn't he thirty years old? Did he do this to you?" She poked at a sick, blue bruise on Juhi's arm.

"What do *you* care? He is the only one who wants me. What do *you* know about rejection? Tall and willowy. Aren't you going to be a hot-shot lawyer or some tycoon? That's what they say about you! You know what they say about me?"

The food and drink arrived, and as the conversation drew on, each sentence drew her further away. It was the way Juhi talked – the words that she wove like beads on a necklace in a perfectly aesthetic se-quence, a continuous progression of words. Words that could easily be drowned in the sound of a pressure cooker, and yet could pervade time. Her hands danced to these words, gesticulating about new ideas Sha-gun had never conceived; tracing the shapes of people and places that Shagun had never known. The life in her eyes: the spires of Viennese cathedrals, the sheer drop of the Grand Canyon. *An entire life lived, over a cup of chamomile tea.*

When she was done, there was an ocean between them. Shagun said nothing. *There was nothing.* In the foreground of the cigarette smoke, her fifteen years flashed and burned silently. Years hastily lived through, condensed into days and nights of nothings. It was these nothings that filled the void between them, that expanded in the hot summer air.

They both must have felt something die, for they shifted uneasily in their seats, not looking at each other. Juhi's phone rang, and she picked it up in relief.

"Yes, you can bring the car up. Bring the black sedan, it's for business. I will be out soon," she said, putting out her cigarette. She asked the waiter for the check. She turned to her now. *A smile of imminent departure.*

"Can I have one?"

Surprise. "A cigarette?"

"Yes."

"Why of course!" *Pushes the pack towards her, lighting it for her.*

"Remember the first time we tried smoking, outside Sahdev dāi's small gate, after school? We didn't even know how to light it! You coughed so hard!"

"Yes." *A strained smile. Her eyes evasive, counting over the day's remaining tasks.* "Yes. Those days . . . Listen, hon. I really have to leave. It's 3:30 and I have a meeting at 4:00 sharp, and the traffic is so bad here! How *do* you manage?"

"I manage."

"Well, I must absolutely leave, babe." She stood up and put down a five hundred-rupee note, batting down Shagun's protests over the bill. "It was so good to see you after so long!" *Hugs her.* "Give your children all my love. Should I drop you off anywhere?"

"Thank you, but I'll be fine. Give my love to your son."

"When I see him next!" *Walks away in long strides, laughing.*

Shagun gathered her things slowly, and walked outside. Juhi was gone. Hailing a taxi from the hotel would be expensive. A bus would take too long. She had to nurse the baby, he would be hungry. She decided to walk further down to hail a cab, but lost in thought, she kept on walking. Once at the Ganesh temple, her feet automatically led her through the habitual circumambulation; her mind was abuzz with the afternoon's heat and conversation. She walked the entire way back.

When she finally opened the gate to her house, she heard the noise of the TV. *They are home.* Her breasts, sore with hours of milk, leaked and throbbed painfully. She opened the main doors, and began to climb the stairs. She could hear the baby crying, calling for her. *Robbing away, with his tiny hands and his warm wants, all her maybes.* As this alien thought entered her she staggered under it, catching the stair-rails for support. *Had she?* She gasped for breath, and sat on the stone stairs for a while, clutching at her midriff, as though it would slip from her hands. She was having post-natal contractions. Cold pain pulsed through her. *Why? She had not drunk the chamomile.*

She sat still for several long moments until the contractions died away. The white noise from the TV was drowned by the buzz in her brain. Through the door's screen she watched the dying sun, not moving. Nothing moved except what moved inside her (something she did not fully understand): welling up from deep under, spilling out until her vision was blurred and her mind was confused by her body. It was an emptiness inside her, which hardened, knotted then broke, and it was everywhere. She cried for the warm bundle of flesh that could easily strip away everything with the curling and uncurling of a fist, and as she thought of this, her breasts leaked and the emptiness moved up against an old hunger. It tore her apart, and its blood tinged the sky red as dusk fell around her. *Soon, they will call. She will have to go back in.* When the mosquitoes descended, she finally got up. When she climbed the stairs, her hands and feet were stones. Alien were the sounds of the TV and the screams of the children, which magnified as she opened the door to their flat. The light in the hallway was off. She stepped in, her heart falling, and was swallowed by a new darkness.

THE LETTER

Rajani Thapa

Rajani Thapa is a Nepali writer based in London. Her writing appeared in the first issue of *La.Lit* in January 2013, to which she is also a contributing editor.

I'm writing another letter to V. Morning is breaking and I'm watching the square, gray-black intercom unit. When it's quiet I think I can hear Maisie's breathing. Nancy, the duty nurse, rolls her eyes. She listens when the monitor crackles and spews out Maisie's voices and screams. Unlike me, Nancy knows what to ignore and when to rush upstairs.

I'm a kind of saint to the residents of St. Michael's. I linger in their doorways to listen to their ramblings. My tiny adjustments to their meals seem to make all the difference. I'm young and unimportant. The nurses are stern and rushed. They're as set in their ways as the old people in their charge. I have to clean dentures, bedsores, and toilets, but this is almost the ideal job for me. When I do the night shift, I get about four hours of stare-at-the-wall time. There's nothing better than being awake, doing nothing. I read a book sometimes but it's hard to concentrate after everything you've been through during the night shift.

V and I have been writing letters to each other since we were children. Ever since he came to live with his grandparents in my neighbourhood in Maharajgunj. His grandfather was a tall, straight, and jovial military man. His grandmother was only ever seen peering out of a window in their house. People said she was crazy. A former servant of the family once told a story about how the old woman smashed up every plate in the house in a fit of rage. V kicked a ball was light and graceful, like he could float away. One day, the Major came to see my father about something and V came along. As the adults talked, he passed me a piece of paper on which he'd practised his signature – long squiggles in Nepali and in English. On the blank side of the paper, I practised my new signature and passed it back to him a few days later. There was a lot to write about over the years.

I can't concentrate on the letter. It's five o'clock; two hours until I have to start getting breakfast ready and three until the end of my shift. I set my pen down. The cat passes the doorway, long black tail flicking lazily. I involuntarily scratch my arm and feel a light tickle in my nose. The cat doesn't belong to St. Michael's but we have a few cans of food in the kitchen for it anyway.

I notice that my cursive handwriting gets unruly at the bottom of the page as my hand runs out of space. V's writing is rounded and precise. Unlike mine, it has hardly changed over the years save for a shift from blue to black ink. He started to make little cigarette burn designs on the paper when he took up smoking. The Major caught him once and put his own design on V's cheek. So everyone can see, he was told.

V and I became friends with Poonam when we were teenagers. She lived nearby and her parents were never home. We spent hours in her room smoking cigarettes and weed and drinking Khukuri Rum. But our real conversations were always by letter. Sometimes we even wrote them right in front of each other.

You're in front of me and your eyes are really red. I hope the Major doesn't come looking for you.

I get up to take a walk around before everyone wakes up. I take off my boots and walk down the corridor in my socks. The sun is coming through the skylights. Early mornings always make me think of Kathmandu. I wrote most of my letters then when I couldn't sleep.

I think of my mother's voice on the phone two days ago. She phoned to tell us that one of our cousins had to be rushed to the hospital with chest pains. It was early morning and her voice came out trembling through the speaker as my brother walked around it, gathering mobile phone, keys, and folders. When she said she was glad we were together at least, he paused for a split second before continuing to adjust his tie.

I think of the shadow of death creeping closer. First it was my grandfather's death a year and half ago. It was followed by my father's stroke and my aunt's breast cancer, now in remission but not forgotten. Then my uncle swerved on his motorcycle to avoid a stray dog. He recovered from his head injury but everyone says he isn't the same. I've begun to understand that every death builds and expands on all the other deaths before it.

I get to the kitchen and reach for the cat food on the counter. Immediately I feel the cat's arched body rubbing against my leg. I open the can and quickly dump the wet clumps into the bowl on the floor. I stifle a sneeze and walk into one of the rooms. I can hear loud breathing.

I saw V coming home one night on the back of someone's motorcycle. He stood outside the compound for a long time, his head leaning against the concrete pillar of the gate. When I went out to talk to him, he had a look on his face like he'd done the best bad thing in the world. He smelled faintly of vomit. His eyes were defiant. He told me he would write and walked inside.

I'm sitting on Janet's empty bed by the door. At seventy-two, she was the youngest here. Her bald head was always covered with a flowery scarf. After she died I asked Nancy who tied the scarf for Janet every morning. Nancy just rolled her eyes and asked me to pass her the triangular tablet counter for Irene's medicine.

I come to this room every couple of hours to help turn Irene and Maureen. I wonder what it's like to spend your days in bed, being turned over by other people. When it's with Nancy it's very quick. She's about a foot taller than me and grew up on a farm tossing bales of hay. We're supposed to use a slide sheet to gently manoeuvre the patients onto their sides, but Nancy just lifts them up.

I leave the room and walk back down the corridor and think I can hear the soft fall of rain. My anger at the London rain filled V with amusement. How can you be angry at the rain? In the still-dark living room, I can make out the house-shaped parakeet cages covered with towels. Jenny the 104-year-old, the oldest resident at St. Michael's, likes to sit here all day in her wheelchair. One of the nurses once wondered out loud, why can't we just cover them at night like the birds?

V started hanging out with a new group of friends last summer, a few months before I left Kathmandu for London. I went away for a couple of months, to visit my grandparents in our village. When I came back he looked thin and ill. He had dark circles under his eyes. I mentioned it to Poonam who just gave me a funny look and changed the subject. I noticed she started to avoid us.

I hear Bill muttering in his room as I walk back towards the staff room. "Just kill me," he'd said the first time I changed his catheter bag.

I glance at the staircase leading upstairs and wonder, for the millionth time, what happens if there is a fire in the night? With just me, a duty nurse, and all these people on the brink of death? Nancy says I have death on the brain. I worry too much for someone so young. But it's only since I've started working here. I want to ask V if he's started thinking like this too.

I'm finally free to leave at 8 a.m. The nursing home is full of voices and activity now. Nancy's already disappeared, probably gone off to her next job. I should go home to sleep but it has stopped raining for now and I decide to go see my friend in Whitechapel. Sometimes I still get mail there.

I find Alise inside, watching the news. She's from Latvia and used to work at St. Michael's but quit because it got too depressing for her. I visit her when I want company but don't necessarily want to talk. Or when my brain is like Maisie's monitor, spewing out crazy nonsense. She goes into her room and comes back holding three large, unlabelled bottles. Then she starts spraying recklessly in my direction.

"Hey? Does this smell like Eternity to you? Obsession?"

I duck and go and lie down on the sofa. Alise is now a perfume salesgirl. Her job is to persuade people that these are original designer perfumes, available at a fraction of the usual cost because of the plain bottles.

I think of my mother's phone call again. We were all rushing to get ready for work. After the news about my cousin, there was an aside about the Major's house getting burgled. Apparently the crazy old woman had a lot of gold and now it's all gone.

I mute the television and cover my eyes as Alise tells me about an imitation Wonderbra that she got from a Bulgarian friend.

I think of the last letter I had from V. It was about five months ago. He said that since I'd started working at St. Michael's, it was as if I'd caught a bug.

I said the world is full of sorrow and we are insignificant. He said the opposite was equally true.

I feel a light spray on my fingers. Alise is kneeling by the sofa and I notice, for the first time, the prominent joints of her fingers. I think of V's long, broad fingers and fat nails. I cover my face again and turn my back to her.

"Do you like this one? It's Obsession. Speaking of which, did you get a letter from your boyfriend yet?"

"Got one five months ago."

"*Five* months ago? What did it say?"

I hear her pacing around the room, spraying the cheap perfume everywhere. She's laughing hard as she does this. She comes and squeezes onto the sofa and puts her arm around me.

"And you've been writing to him, haven't you?"

"One of my friends in Nepal told me no one has seen him at all. She lives in the same neighbourhood. He's disappeared."

"*Disappeared?*"

Alise gets up and I hear her opening a drawer.

"I didn't even want to give you this. I hate how you're always waiting for his letter."

I take the envelope but I don't open it. I've come out in a cold sweat.

"Just show me that bra."

"But I didn't realise it had been that long. Don't you want to open it?"

"I'm done talking about him."

I hear her cackling laugh as she goes back into her room. When she comes out her shirt is unbuttoned and she is wearing a black push-up bra.

"Don't I look like Eva Herzigova?"

I nod absently.

"But seriously, shall I order you one of these?"

I sleep at Alise's all day and it's late by the time I get back on the DLR. The shortest way from the station to Wells Road is through a large field. My brother tells me not to take that route at night but I do anyway.

It's a bright night, the moonlight shining through gaps in the clouds. In the day, there are horses grazing here. Under the all-night downpour, the hard ground has come lushly, greenly alive, the wetness hovering above the grass in a fine mist. The pearly fragments of clouds seem very far away.

I walk along the diagonal slash pressed into the ground. There is a sprinkling of daisies on either side of the path. The white fence and the silhouettes of houses start coming into view.

I stop to take the envelope from my pocket and pull out his last letter.

The field is empty, the sky is empty, and the world is empty. I look at the blank sheet of paper for a moment and start walking again.

BATTLES OF THE NEW REPUBLIC

Prashant Jha

Prashant Jha is an author and journalist. A former columnist with *The Kathmandu Post* and Nepal correspondent for *The Hindu*, he is well-known as a keen observer of and comment-ator on Nepali political issues. *Battles of the New Republic – A Contemporary History of Nepal* is his first book.

BEING NEPALI

I t took me a while to realize that there was something different about us.

I used to study at the Modern Indian School in Kathmandu, and remember clinging to my mother, who taught English there, in the bus on my way to school.

In class and outside, we usually spoke in Hindi. India was the refer-ence point in most of our subjects and conversations. Mahatma Gandhi and the *Panchatantra* were as much a part of our consciousnesses as *The Jungle Book* and *Mahabharata* serials on Doordarshan; Independ-ence Day was 15 August and Children's Day was 14 November. The prayers we chanted during school assemblies were old Indian bhajans. Many of my classmates were Marwaris and Sikhs – making me in-finitely more familiar with Indian-origin ethnicities than the multiple surnames which punctuate the Nepali social landscape.

Life was comfortable, for there was a seamless linguistic and cultural homogeneity between school and home.

My parents spoke to each other, and to me, in English and in Hindi. I spoke to my brother in Maithili. My grandfather, Tatta as we called him, used to listen to both Nepali and Hindi news on the radio as we played with him in the evenings. Games meant cricket and Saturday afternoons were reserved for watching Hindi films on television. Aunts from Patna visited us during their summer holidays; in December, it was our turn to go to Delhi and spend the long winter holidays with our mausis. We occasionally made the eight-hour drive down to meet relatives in Rajbiraj which, we were told, was our hometown in southern Nepal.

I remember being conscious that Nepal and India were different countries; that they had different prime ministers; that Indian and Nepali news were broadcast in different languages; and that I was a Nepali, which meant that I was not an Indian like many of my cousins.

But the lines were too blurred, and I was too young, for these national distinctions to mean anything. It was as normal and happy a childhood as one could have.

There were some unnatural moments, however. When we used to go out to New Road to shop or Papa used to take us out for a meal, anyone speaking in Hindi was immediately hushed up. It is a memory that has stayed with me; there was something wrong about being ourselves, and speaking in the language that we felt most comfortable in, when others were around.

And then, in Class 5, when I was eight years old, my parents shifted me to a new school – Loyola.

The first day was a blur.

We were having lunch in the common mess. Two classmates who I had seen but not spoken to in the morning were sitting opposite me with their plates.

One of them asked where I was from.

Kathmandu.

He asked, "Jha pani Kathmandu ko huncha? [Can a Jha hail from Kathmandu?] He is Indian."

The other immediately chimed in, "Euta aru dhoti aayo. [One more dhoti has arrived.] The maade will get a friend now. Ha ha!"

I smiled weakly, not knowing what either dhoti or maade meant, and continued eating.

But there appeared to be a connection between being made fun of because of my surname, and being told that I was Indian. And I realized that there was a reason why my father asked us not to speak in Hindi.

It was important to run away from who you were, when confronted by outsiders, by normal people, by the "true" Nepalis.

In hindsight, there were possibly two reactions a child could have had to what was a bit of a scarring conversation – go into a shell, or try to be more "normal". And for some reason, perhaps due to the typical schoolkid instinct of recognizing where power resides in a classroom, I decided to do the latter.

So I hung out with the cool Kathmandu kids. I could not hide my poor Nepali, but fortunately the school had a speak-only-in-English rule which was quite strictly enforced. I joined the others in calling those with Indian-sounding surnames – Bararias, Agarwals, Mishras, Chowdhurys – dhotis, which I learnt was a generic, derogatory term to dismiss anyone "Indian", or maades, which was short for Marwaris. Cultural religious practices within my family were at odds with the other "Nepalis". On Dussehra, we turned vegetarian; they feasted on meat. At the end of the festival, the elders of the family blessed others with tika, which was a big event in the calendar; we did nothing of the sort. But I did not tell my new friends that and pretended that we did the same at home.

In a few years, I left to study in Delhi. And I felt far more at home than I did in school in Kathmandu, where I had not only constructed a divide between school friends and home, but also created a web of lies to sustain the fiction that I was as "Nepali" as any other student in the classroom.

But the problem did not disappear, and the first thing classmates in Delhi's Sardar Patel Vidyalaya asked was how I could be a Nepali – "You don't look like a Nepali at all." Or "Are you a Bahadur too? We have one who guards our apartment." A bit older by now, I had developed a somewhat more coherent response – you could be a Nepali without being a "Bahadur" or "looking" Nepali. In the common perception, Nepalis always have Mongoloid features.

It was only much later that I realized that I was not unique. I was privileged, for I came from an upper-middle-class, upper-caste family which sent me to Delhi to acquire a better education. My class allowed me to escape the handicaps that came with my identity, and access the best opportunities available.

All I had to suffer for my surname, for speaking in Hindi and Maithili, for being a "dhoti", for having relatives across in India, were a few taunts.

But for precisely the same reasons, millions of people in Nepal have had no access to power, have been subjects of systemic discrimination, have remained deprived of services, and have lived everyday with the burden of having to prove that they are, indeed, Nepali.

We are the Madhesis of Nepal.

THE MADHESI MUTINIES

Lahan can pass off as just another small decrepit town on the East–West Highway in Nepal's southern plains. But unlike the other anonymous bazaars that punctuate Nepal's arterial road, Lahan is central in the consciousnesses of the travellers who cross the Tarai.

Long-distance buses travelling from Kakarbitta – a town on Nepal's eastern border with Siliguri in West Bengal – to Kathmandu stop here so that passengers can refresh themselves; truck drivers halt here for the night; and ramshackle private buses from Janakpur to Biratnagar wait here the longest, with conductors screeching to attract the most passengers. A hospitality industry – from small dhabas serving daal-bhaat to "premium" hotels like Godhuli – has sprung up to cater to a diverse clientele.

But despite its small size – Lahan is all of one long road with a few small lanes branching off it – the town is more than just a passenger stopover.

Major government offices are located in Siraha bazaar, the district headquarters fifteen miles off the main highway to the south, right at the border with Bihar's Jainagar district. One of Nepal's best, the Sagarmatha Chowdhury Eye Hospital is on the main road. Most local journalists, and NGO representatives, use Lahan as a base to cover neighbouring districts like Saptari and Dhanusha. The landed classes of the nearby rural areas, professionals of Siraha origin, and workers from the region in Malaysia, India and the Gulf, who send money back home, all want to buy land or a house in Lahan.

Perhaps it is the constant movement of vehicles, and the mixed demography, with both people of hill and plains origin, which lends the town an unexpected energy, discernible in district politics if not in the stagnant economy. Influential locals meet every evening over paan and chai to exchange gossip – be it about the new government official who has just taken office, the big construction contracts in the pipeline, property disputes wrecking prominent local families, the newest caste-based power alliance, or the political machinations in the distant capital.

It was here, right in the middle of the highway town, that Ramesh Mahato was killed on 19 January 2007.

1

Three days earlier, 240 legislators – including eighty-three Maoists who had been nominated to an interim Parliament – had adopted a new interim Constitution.

For seven months, ever since the end of the second Janandolan, major parties, especially the Nepali Congress (NC) and the Maoists, had engaged in tough peace negotiations. At the end of November, an intricate Comprehensive Peace Agreement had been signed, formally marking the end of the war. In mid-December, the interim Constitution was negotiated, which declared that Nepal's "unitary structure would end".

Nepali politicians, mostly of hill origin, had spent all their time fighting each other, then fighting the king, and finally arriving at a multiparty alliance. Immersed in the divides between the monarchy, the parliamentary parties and the Maoists, and blind to the fact that it was six hill Brahmin – and a couple of Chhetri – men who were making all the decisions, they could not sense the simmering discontent on the ground – showing how disconnected all of them, including the Maoists, had become in the capital.

There was a backlash of unexpected ferocity from an unexpected quarter, challenging long-held notions of nationalism and putting Nepal firmly, and perhaps irreversibly, on the path to federalism.

Upendra Yadav – a schoolteacher turned mainstream Left politician turned Maoist sympathizer turned semi-underground regional leader – burnt a copy of the interim Constitution at Maitighar Mandala, an open green space in the middle of Kathmandu's power zone. In its vicinity lies the army road, home to the Nepal Army (NA) headquarters and its adjunct offices – the road was closed to the public after the military was deployed in the war against the Maoists. The Supreme Court and the Nepal Bar Association are a minute's walk away. And half a kilometre away is the Singha Durbar, the secretariat complex which is home to key ministries as well as the Parliament where the interim Constitution had been promulgated the night before.

Despite its proximity to state power, or because of it, the Mandala had emerged as the favourite site for protestors, from those organizing peace rallies to groups challenging the authorities. The democratic government post April 2006 usually deployed additional police, but treated protestors indulgently, perhaps because those running the government had themselves been on the streets till very recently.

But not this time.

Yadav, along with his supporters of the Madhesi Janadhikar Forum (MJF), then a cross-party forum, were immediately arrested, shoved into a van, and taken to Hanuman Dhoka – the capital's police hub familiar to most political activists, all of whom had spent a few nights locked up there at some point or the other in their careers.

Few people in Kathmandu knew either Yadav, or the MJF's, background.

The MJF's protests were not sudden. The Forum, as it came to be popularly known, had repeatedly warned of protests if the interim Constitution did not make a firm commitment to federalism. Madhesis – people who live largely, but not exclusively, in Nepal's southern plains; speak languages like Maithili, Urdu, Bhojpuri, Awadhi and Hindi; and maintain close linguistic, cultural, ethnic ties with people across the border in Bihar and Uttar Pradesh – felt a deep sense of resentment against the Nepali state, and the hill-centric political elite's discriminatory practices. They had historically seen regional autonomy in their own territory, the Tarai, as the only way of political empowerment.

The ambiguous phraseology in the interim Constitution about "ending the unitary structure", while remaining non-committal about the future state structure, was perceived as another way to concentrate all power in Kathmandu. Ironically, it was the Maoists who first pushed this demand, but they did not make it their central plank after coming over ground. The MJF also asked for greater political representation from the Tarai in Parliament and the future Constituent Assembly (CA) through an increase in electoral seats.

A month earlier, the only established party claiming to speak for Madhesi interests, the Sadbhavana Party, had made similar demands. A Sadbhavana minister was in government. Their strike in the western Tarai town of Nepalgunj opposing the interim Constitution had led to a riot-like situation between people of hill origin, backed by the local police, and Madhesi activists of plains origin in December 2006. This was perceived by Madhesis across the Tarai as yet another instance of the discrimination, the insensitivity and the racism of the state – compact discs containing videos of the "Nepalgunj riots" were being circulated across Tarai towns.

But the government did not pay heed, smug that these groups were too small to affect macro politics. The Maoists felt that disillusionment with the state would translate into support for them, little realizing that there was also widespread resentment against the former rebels for not having pushed the federal agenda enough. Powerful social groups in the Tarai, who had suffered during the insurgency, and other political rivals were instrumental in painting the Maoists as "betrayers" along with the "pahadi" state which was projected as an "oppressor for the past 240 years". In what was to be a costly political error, the Sadbhavana did not resign from the government or launch a mass movement.

No established political force was able to read the signal from the Tarai, no one could read the agitational mood that was building up. And this allowed the relatively anonymous Upendra Yadav to occupy the political vacuum and emerge as the face of Tarai politics, whose seeds had been planted more than five decades earlier.

2

In 1951, soon after the first democratic revolution against the clan-based Rana oligarchy, a Tarai leader, Vedanand Jha, disillusioned with the Nepali Congress (NC), had formed the Nepal Tarai Congress.

Its main demands included the use of Hindi as an official language, and autonomy for the Tarai. In the mid-1950s, when the then government decided to introduce Nepali as the sole official language of the country, there was resistance in the plains, even leading to clashes in Biratnagar in the eastern Tarai between groups supporting Nepali and Hindi. Those supporting Nepali were largely people of hill origin, pahadis, who were recent migrants to the Tarai; those demanding Hindi were people of plains origin, Madhesis, and Marwaris. The medium of instruction in educational institutions in the Tarai till then had been Hindi, with teachers from neighbouring areas of Bihar running schools. Locals feared that the imposition of Nepali would not only block the growth of their languages, but also disrupt livelihoods and reduce opportunities for growth.

But the ground was not yet ripe for ethnic identity- or language-driven politics. The big battle of the decade was for prajatantra, democracy, and the symbol of the democratic struggle was the B. P. Koirala-led NC. Structurally modelled on the Indian National Congress, the NC drew inspiration from the democratic and socialist guard of the Indian politics and gave space to leaders from diverse regions and ethnicities, including those of plains origin. Along with Kathmandu, it was the Taraibasis, the Tarai-dwellers, who were most active in the politics. The Koirala family itself was a pahadi family from Biratnagar, and the major battles against the Rana regime were fought in the Tarai towns.

Unlike royalist or communist parties, the NC was also the most inclusive in its symbols. Its leaders had spent a long time in exile in Banaras, Patna and Calcutta and were comfortable with the culture, lifestyle and habits of the Gangetic plain and North India. This helped the people in the Nepali plains relate to NC leaders at various levels – when they saw them wear dhotis, eat paan, speak in Hindi, or use familiar idioms, the pahadi-Taraibaasi divide became secondary. That many of these leaders had been associated with the Indian freedom struggle, and with political stalwarts across the border, gave them an additional aura.

All this meant that in the first elections of 1959, the Nepal Tarai Congress suffered a rout, and even Vedanand Jha lost his election deposit. The NC swept the polls nationwide, winning a two-thirds majority. In the Tarai, its image of a national, democratic and inclusive party, the co-option of the relatively influential upper-caste leaders of plains origin, and its appeal to the intermediate castes and the landless with a radical land-reform agenda helped. Identity and regional politics had lost out for now, both due to limited political mobilization around these issues but also because the NC had remained sensitive, at least symbolically, to the concerns of the people in the plains, it had treated them like citizens, and had won their confidence.

But the NC's efforts to build Nepali nationalism and the state in an inclusive, non-violent, liberal, gradual and democratic manner – which may or may not have succeeded – received a jolt almost immediately. The royalist project of aggressive nation-building, with faith in coercion, homogenization, integration and the construction of the "other", began in full earnest. Nationalism as propagated by Mahendra kept the land united, but it divided the people, apparent in the mutinies which were to rock Nepal four decades later.

King Mahendra took over in a royal coup in December 1960, sacking the elected government, dissolving the Parliament, and arresting all the top party leaders.

Mahendra's apologists built a case for autocracy. Their argument went along familiar lines – the monarch was concerned about keeping the "territorial unity" of the country intact. Nepal was among the "least developed"countries in the world. Literacy was in the single digits; geography had been unkind, with rough terrain and inaccessible mountains; the state had little money; and the country was just not ready for the populist aspirations a Westminster parliamentary democracy would have unleashed. A democracy "suited to the soil", akin to Ayub Khan- or Sukarno-style guided democracies in Pakistan and Indonesia, was more appropriate. An elaborate Panchayat system was designed, with layers of notionally representative bodies, culminating into a national Panchayat. But the bottom line was clear – the Palace was the source of all authority.

For the king, the biggest challenge in sustaining a relatively autonomous, autocratic regime was India.

The day after Mahendra's takeover, Jawaharlal Nehru called the move a "setback to democracy" in the Lok Sabha of the Indian Parliament. Recent accounts have suggested that Nehru knew of the coup in advance but did little to prevent it, for he shared an uneasy relationship with Bishweshwor Prasad Koirala and was happy to see him go. Senior Nepali lawyer Ganesh Raj Sharma, who was a close confidante of

B. P. Koirala, believes that Nehru knew that the king would dismiss the government but not that he would dissolve Parliament. This goes against the image of Nehru as a committed democrat, but the idea is plausible, for India's approach, in dealings with Nepal at the time, was imperial in nature. This is reflected quite clearly in the letters of "advice" Nehru wrote to Matrika Koirala, a Nepali prime minister during the 1950s and BP's elder half-brother – which have been made public now – and the actions of some of the earlier Indian ambassadors who behaved, in BP's words, as though they had been sent to run a district, not represent a foreign country.

But soon after the takeover, the government of India did provide a degree of support to NC dissidents who had escaped arrest and were based in India. Mahendra, his aides recall, felt that India would constantly try to weaken and topple him by using arashtra tatva, anti-national elements, which became synonymous with NC in the decades of Panchayat rule.

Mahendra got lucky, for China and India went to war.

As relations between Nepal's neighbours to the north and south deteriorated, he played what has come to be known as the "China card", subtly threatening the Indian establishment with the prospect of Nepal developing closer ties with Beijing, both politically and in terms of greater infrastructural connectivity. This would have left India vulnerable on another front. The policy of using the Himalayas as India's security frontier – as articulated by Nehru – would be in tatters, and Nepal would no longer remain a buffer state under the Indian arc of influence. Delhi quickly realized that it had to develop a more cordial working relationship with the Palace. Even if the king did not go all the way with China, the risks of antagonizing him entirely were too high. India snapped the support it was offering to Nepali democratic activists in exile; an armed movement launched by a section of the NC, using India as its base, fizzled out; and Mahendra found enough space and time to consolidate his regime.

But to do so, he had to deal with his biggest internal challenge, the Tarai, for two reasons. The plains were an NC stronghold, and had been the site of the struggle for democracy in the past. "Royalist nationalists" were insecure that activists for democracy, either on their own or prodded by India, could use the open border to destabilize the regime through actions in the plains. The short-lived armed movement after the coup, led by NC exiles, was concentrated in towns in the Tarai which reinforced the fear and led to the feeling that the plains must be controlled.

The other reason was the fact that the ruling elite just did not trust the Madhesis. They were seen as "migrants", "people of Indian origin" or "Indians", who had continued to maintain cultural practices and spoke languages which were distinct from the hill Nepalis. Their national loyalties were suspect, and the Palace felt that this was India's natural constituency which it could use to weaken the regime, or even to "break the country".

Besides being lucky, Mahendra was shrewd – perhaps the shrewdest leader Nepal has seen in modern times.

He constructed a narrative in which the monarchy was the symbol of the unity of the nation. And faith in the "glorious" history of the Shah dynasty, a common language (Nepali), a common religion (Hinduism), and a common dress (daura-saluwar) tied the country together. This definition of a "true Nepali" immediately privileged a certain group of people – the hill Bahuns and Chhetris – who fulfilled the above criteria. His suspicion of India as the biggest threat to "national unity" and "Indian-origin people" as swamping Nepali territory was visible in internal formulations as well, since Nepali citizenship required one to possess attributes which would distinctly set one apart from "Indians".

Like nationalisms of all hues, Mahendra's nationalism was fundamentally exclusionary. Muslims were second-class citizens since the state was officially Hindu. There was little chance that Dalits would be able to rise up and challenge the caste hierarchy given the manner in which the Hindu religion, with its entrenched hierarchies, had been given formal state sanction. The bulk of the indigenous people – Tharus, Magars, Tamangs, Gurungs, Newars, Limbus, Rais and others – were left outside the mainstream since many were neither Hindus, nor did they speak the Nepali language, and continued to maintain distinct cultural practices.

The Madhesis, too, were not true Nepalis since they could not speak the Nepali language, continued to wear dhotis which were reflective of a distinct culture and lifestyle, could not be trusted to support monarchy, and had "Indian attributes" given cross-border links and a shared culture.

Their exclusion happened not merely in theory, but in practice. An education policy, with the primary objective of perpetuating the royal regime and its version of nationalism, was introduced.

Nepali was the sole medium of instruction. Textbooks told children that Nepal was the creation of the Shah kings, conveniently glossing over the fact that the unification was seen as a conquest by most indigenous people who cherished their own tales of resistance, and that much of the Tarai's inclusion in Nepal was a result of arbitrary border demarcation after the Anglo-Nepal War of 1816.

The rulers were lauded for keeping the country independent even when India next door was colonized. Students were, of course, not told that Nepal had been humiliated in the 1816 war; the Rana rulers had accepted a subservient status to British India; Nepali Gorkhas, largely from ethnic communities, served as mercenary soldiers for the colonial army; and Nepali rulers had a slavish attitude to the British masters, reflected starkly in the way they rushed to their aid during the Sepoy Revolt of 1857. Nepali exceptionalism was based on Mount Everest and Lumbini, privileging spaces which merely happened to be in Nepal. And, along with pride, a sense of vulnerability was planted – Nepal was a landlocked country, external powers posed constant threats but the great king had successfully protected "national unity".

From a historical and political perspective, the Tarai found no mention at all in school curricula, except as a breadbasket. There was little a Madhesi could relate to when he was taught in classrooms – the language of instruction, the historical figures which were being mythologized, and the hill-centric cultural practices were all alien to him. But that was the aim, to make him more Nepali through pedagogy and force him to be ashamed of his own roots.

Discriminatory citizenship laws with impossible requirements to prove "descent" and to speak Nepali were framed, making it difficult for those of plains origin to acquire citizenship papers. This virtually disenfranchised them, since they could not buy land, access state services, or participate in politics. They had little choice but to be meek and pliant for survival. At the same time, people of "Nepali descent" – which could include Nepali speakers from Darjeeling and Sikkim in India, or Bhutan – were granted citizenship and encouraged to move to the Nepali hills and plains.

Mahendra also systematically built up on the trend that had first begun in the 1950s. With the clearing of forests and the eradication of malaria, people from the hills had slowly started moving down to the Tarai in large numbers. This was, to some extent, a natural process since the hills remained remote and the plains were seen as the path to progress and prosperity. But he made it state policy to encourage this migration, changing the demographic balance of the region and ensuring that it was not the Madhesis but hill-origin people who controlled local politics and economy. The Rana regime had distributed enormous tracts of land through the nineteenth and twentieth centuries in the Tarai to their loyalists, relatives and bureaucrats – all of hill origin. Through a flawed and selectively implemented Land Reforms Act, Mahendra did the same, giving land to recent settlers of hill origin while using the Act to make those influential landowners of the Tarai, who were potential dissenters, fall in line.

His suspicion of India and Madhesis was clear from the way in which the East-West Highway was constructed. An old postal road, Hulaki, connected the various Tarai towns, and was a mile off the Nepal-India border. Instead of upgrading that, the Palace made a conscious decision to construct the national highway several kilometres away from the border, even if that meant destroying extensive forest areas. The underlying fear was that building it next to the border, in Madhesi-populated areas, would give India enormous leverage. Instead, poor pahadi families from the hills were settled to the north and south of the new highway where small towns and economies sprung up. Lahan in the Siraha district, Dhalkebar in the Dhanusha district, Bardibas in the Mahottari district, Navalpur in the Sarlahi district, and Chandranighapur in the Rautahat district – all with a sizeable pahadi population – grew in importance at the time and became alternate political centres.

The country was also divided into zones where the Tarai, the hills, and the upper Himalayas were clubbed together vertically. So, for instance, the Sagarmatha zone had both the Everest Base Camp in the extreme north and Rajbiraj town – which shares a border with Bihar – in the same zonal unit, which made little administrative sense. Advocates of the model at the time used two arguments to justify the division – the optimum utilization of resources, especially river systems, and "national unity" which would result from the cohabiting of people of different regions. Madhesi activists have since claimed that this was a deliberate ploy to keep Madhesi-populated areas from developing a coherent regional identity. Either way, what is indisputable is that all the zones, and even the Tarai districts, were run by pahadi officials who viewed the Madhesis as outsiders.

Mahendra made room for the elites of all communities, including Madhesi castes, to be included in the Panchayat polity. If they were willing to accept the monarchy's legitimacy and hegemony, and become more "Nepali", a Jha, a Mishra or a Chaudhary could be accommodated in local power structures; be allowed to impose his writ and continue with his zamindari in localized areas; be given membership of the national Panchayat or bureaucracy and receive opportunities in the state-dependent economy.

My grandfather, Jogendra Jha, or Tatta, as we called him, was among those Madhesis who actively supported the monarchy. He was a trained doctor, but set up Nepal's first private construction firm. He indirectly dabbled in politics, financing leaders like Tulsi Giri, who was the first prime minister under the Panchayat system. Giri and Tatta had studied medicine together in Darbhanga, and Giri had encouraged my grandfather to migrate to Nepal after they completed their degrees. Bishwobandhu Thapa, who would serve as Giri's home minister, was a close family friend. Giri's and Thapa's children, and my father and aunts, grew up together.

Tatta had close links with political actors in Delhi, and often served as an intermediary between the royal regime and the Indian establishment as well as the Rashtriya Swayamsevak Sangh (RSS), which he had joined as a student at the Banaras Hindu University in the early 1940s. Before his death in 2001, he had often told me that he served as an intermediary between Mahendra and Pandit Nehru in the run-up to the royal coup in 1960. Nehru, he claimed, was in the loop about B. P. Koirala's dismissal.

On King Mahendra's request, Tatta co-produced Nepal's first private feature film, *Maitighar*. In the 1970s, he partnered with Mahendra's younger brother, Prince Basundhara, to set up Nepal's first private shipping company – a wildly ambitious project that fell flat, leaving him financially vulnerable. My grandmother would always remain furious at his overreach, but Tatta was a first-generation entrepreneur, a risk taker, and a survivor who knew how to navigate the power corridors of his times.

The point here is to highlight the fact that despite being a Madhesi, he was close to the establishment of the day. This indicated the slight opening that the system had for people of varied ethnic backgrounds. In return for loyalty, he got unprecedented access and opportunities – and we have benefited from those privileges. But he, and people like him, operating in the Tarai districts on a much smaller scale, were exceptions.

The larger pattern of how the Madhesis were to be dealt with was clear. Deprive them of citizenship and the rights that come with it; inculcate a deep suspicion about their "nationalism" among other population segments through organized propaganda; destroy their self-esteem by making them feel like outsiders in a land they consider their own; ensure that they have little political power; give control of areas where they are in the majority to state officials and people of hill origin; use their resources without granting representation; co-opt, bribe and coerce local upper-caste elites so that they maintain peace and order in a feudal, patronage-based economy; and locate the entire strategy in a broader context of a "foreign hand" which is out to attack "national integrity".

What you then get is an image that was common across the Tarai. A poor Madhesi villager visits a distant government office in the district headquarters, his hands folded, speaking subserviently to a pahadi official, struggling to stitch together a line in Nepali for the sahib who does not know the language of the area which he has been sent to administer, and pleads for citizenship, to become Nepali. And the only response he would receive: "Oye saale dhoti, go back to where you belong."

This was Mahendra's abiding gift to the Nepali nation.

THE LIVING GODDESS

Isabella Tree

Isabella Tree is an author and award-winning travel journalist. She was senior travel correspondent at the *Evening Standard* from 1993–1995. She has written several highly praised books including *The Bird Man: The Extraordinary Story of John Gould* and *Islands in the Clouds: Travels in the High-lands of New Guinea*, which was shortlisted for the Thomas Cook Travel Book Award. She writes regularly for the *Sunday Times, Evening Standard, Observer* and *Conde Nast Traveller* and her work has also appeared in *Reader's Digest: Today's Best Non-Fiction, Rough Guides Women Travel* and *The Best American Travel Writing*.

THE ROYAL ASTROLOGER

The royal astrologer lived in Patan, just south of the Bagmati. Hardly a move was made by the king or any other members of the royal family without consulting him. He advised them on auspicious dates for travel plans, diplomatic engagements, business meetings and every major personal decision in their lives. He was also a key figure in the selection process of the Kumari and determined auspicious times for all her rituals. If things went wrong, the royal astrologer was, alongside the tantric priests, first to be consulted. I hoped he would be able to shed some light on what had been going on in those fateful weeks leading up to the royal family massacre.

Patan is still often referred to by its older name – Lalitpur, City of Loveliness. Once, the two Malla cities of Lalitpur and Kathmandu would have been totally distinct but now, thanks to the continuous sprawl of buildings in between, Patan has become virtually a suburb of the capital. Its Durbar Square is barely three miles from the centre of Kathmandu.

Even now, however, Patan adheres to a gentler, kinder pace of life. Down labyrinthine backstreets, hidden courtyards echo with the sounds of hammers tapping against bronze, the rush of bellows and blowtorches, the insect whine of metal-grinders. Most of the original medieval layout survives. Elderly men in *topis* sit on resting platforms watching the world go by; women in saris wash their hair under *makara* spouts in sunken bathing-tanks; children chase each other around courtyard *chaityas*.

In Kathmandu, it was Mahendra Malla who had made his mark on the Durbar Square; here the temples and statues, pavilions and palace courtyards, devotional gongs and bells, sing the praises, first and foremost, of Siddhinarasimha Malla, Mahendra's great-grandson. Siddhinarasimha was the king who, according to legend, had recaptured the *mantra* of Taleju as it blazed across the heavens, having escaped the dying lips of his elder brother Lakshminarasimha incarcerated in the royal palace in Kathmandu. The Goddess's *mantra*, it is said, had given the young prince the power to defeat the notoriously hostile nobles of Patan and take the throne.

One of the first things Siddhinarasimha had done to secure his lineage in Patan was establish a temple to Taleju next to the royal palace, with a separate shrine for her in a courtyard he called Mul Chowk – a carbon copy of the system in the palace complexes in Bhaktapur and Kathmandu.

Siddhinarasimha's devotion to Taleju and his powers as a *siddha* were legendary. He would meditate for days on a stone platform in the palace courtyard of Sundari Chowk, sitting naked in the biting winds of winter and intensifying his austerity in summer by lighting fires all around him. And every morning the Rajarsi – Sage among Kings – as he was known, would walk across the water of the magnificent tank he had built in Taleju's honour in the palace gardens known as the Bhandarkhal, to pick lotuses for the Goddess.

While his private worship focused on his lineage Goddess, Siddhinarasimha was – like all Malla kings – conscientious in his patronage of the other gods. The stone *shikara* to Krishna at the entrance to Durbar Square was built by him; and at the far end, the magnificent Vishveshvara temple dedicated to Shiva, guarded by a pair of colossal stone elephants, was his doing too.

Siddhinarasimha, it is said, had vowed never to leave his people for the kingdom of heaven until the stone elephants of Vishveshvara temple had gone down to nearby Manidhara fountain to drink. He died, according to the chronicles, in 1710 at the grand old age of 104, his spirit living on in his beloved city, as the stone elephants, still firmly in their place, attested.

Walking through Patan's Durbar Square, meandering between temples, is far less stressful than negotiating the square in Kathmandu. Cars and motorbikes have been excluded from the area and pedestrians can take their fill of the temples without fear of being run down. On a clear day the snow peaks of Ganesh Himal power into the sky beyond the northern end. It is easy, strolling between the pagodas, to feel how a Malla city was intended to be – a bridge between heaven and earth.

The royal astrologer was up to his eyes in paperwork and consultations. His narrow house in the corner of a tiny courtyard, five minutes' walk beyond Durbar Square, was full to bursting. I joined the queue outside his door. Hill women in patterned tunics and full skirts, with heavy nose ornaments and ears dragged down with gold, squeezed up the narrow staircase; beside them, suited businessmen, sari-ed grandes dames with black handbags, and boys jangling motorbike keys. They had all come, bringing their birth-charts with them, for help with life's decisions and conundrums – what date to fix a wedding, whether to apply for a job in the Gulf, how to get a child to do better at school, what day to move house, what business to invest in, what time to set for a sacred-thread ceremony or first rice-feeding ritual, in what compass direction to start looking for a husband.

By the time I reached the front of the queue it was getting dark. The astrologer's office was a low-ceilinged room with pea-green walls, lit by a single strip-light. On one side several students in jeans – the astrologer's assistants – sat around a formica coffee table poring over heaps of scrolls, tapping at calculators, pulling battered reference books and curling papers down from pigeonholes on the wall.

The royal astrologer himself was on the other side of the room, nearest the window. He was sitting cross-legged on the floor behind a low desk, wrapped in a grey shawl with a brown woolly hat on his head, rocking from side to side like an irritable old elephant. His fingers were covered in chalk and chalky fingerprints covered his spectacles. There were birth-charts and blackboards, ink pots, exercise books and mathematical tables scattered all over his desk, and rupee notes floating about which he stuffed distractedly into a drawer as if trying to clear his mind. Behind him was a portrait of Ganesh, garlanded with Christmas tinsel, and faded photographs of himself and King Birendra with '70s sideburns.

He looked up as we sat down at last on the floor in front of him. "Ah! British lady," the ageing astrologer said, peering at me with interest through his spectacles. "I was speaking to the BBC on the telephone just the other day. They wanted to know if I had any new predictions." He flicked a hand towards the customers still waiting beyond the doorway. "But you see what my life is like. I have no time now for catastrophes and revolutions. Every minute is taken up with the flimflam of day-to-day."

He handed me his card – "Prof. Dr. M.R. Joshi PhD (Urban study and planning), Royal Astrologer and Geo-Astro Consultant".

"My family have been astrologers for thirty-two generations," he said. "I am eighty-two years old. I have spent seventy-six years at this desk and now I work harder than ever. I wake at 2 a.m., I see my first clients at 6 a.m. Sometimes I see my last clients at ten at night. I have no computer. All my calculations take a long time, the old way. I have barely time to sleep. It is not like in the past, when we had dozens of scribes and apprentices at our beck and call."

He gestured with the same dismissive flick towards his assistants. "They want to be astrologers but they don't have such good training. They have their minds filled with I don't know what. They don't know how much they have to study. They want quick answers."

He rattled off his own education, beginning at the age of six painting almanacs under his father; then sixteen years of Sanskrit, higher mathematics geochemistry, geophysics, geography and astra-science at university in Benares; followed by long sojourns abroad, studying at the Greenwich Observatory in London, poring over ancient charts in the Map Room of the British Museum, and then at universities in Mexico and the United States. But, like being a doctor, he said, no amount of training could beat experience.

"My father predicted the great earthquake of 1934 when I was a boy of fourteen," he said. "He worked it out two months before. He knew when it would happen so he told us to escape. We ran to Durbar Square. All these buildings collapsed. I rebuilt this house in clay with my own hands."

The old astrologer's life flashed by in a series of numerical computations.

"In 1942, when I was twenty years of age, my father and I predicted the end of the Second World War – our prime minister at the time wanted to know how long it would last. In 1991 I predicted the start of the Gulf War. It took thirty-five days to calculate the time of the first attacks."

Traditionally there were four royal astrologers who would cross-check their findings to make the most accurate predictions. Being the oldest, Mangal Raj Joshi was the most senior. Though the royal astrologers also had the country's interests to safeguard, their primary responsibility was to the king. They were invested with the vital task of drawing up horoscopes for members of the king's family. From their reading of the position of the heavens at the precise time of birth, it was the astrologers who would suggest the name of each royal child and who would inform the palace of the right moment for all the customary rites of passage. No state business, no foreign trips, meetings or receptions, no *pujas* or ceremonial duties were carried out by any members of the royal family without first consulting the astrologers. Horoscopes were drawn up, too, for important visiting dignitaries so the most auspicious days could be chosen for meetings and to give the king some indication of the characters he was dealing with.

"I have King George V's horoscope somewhere," said Mr Joshi with a twinkle in his eye.

"What about Queen Elizabeth II and Prince Charles?" I asked, trying to steer Mr Joshi closer to the present.

"I have theirs, too," he said.

"How did you find the details of their birth?"

"Ah, for people like the queen of England these events are always well documented. But nowadays it is easy to find out, even if someone is not famous when they are born. My students can get information from the

Internet. Recently we did charts to see who would win the American presidential election. I was able to tell the king the probable outcome."

"Were you right?"

"Fortunately," he grinned.

He unwound a scroll that was lying on his desk. The chart, known as a *chinna* in Nepali, or *jata* in Newari was made of shiny yellow paper, about six inches wide and two feet long, edged with decorative floral borders in red and green. It was covered in red and black letters or 'syllables' in Devanagiri script – black being the given letters of the known astrological formula; red, the added letters of that person's particular details, such as the exact time and location of birth, as recorded by the midwife; the name of the nearest shrine or temple to which they were born; their parents' star signs; number of siblings; the individual's name. This is the name the priest gives a baby at the time their *chinna* is drawn up and is often quite different from the familiar name used by friends and family. It is the official name used for all subsequent ritual purposes and *pujas*, including weddings and old-age ceremonies.

At the top of the chart was a figure of a deity in white; the bottom was divided into squares. There were wheels and geometric designs and tiny numerical figures all over it. I stared at it blankly as Mr Joshi prattled on about "lunar mansions" and "divisions" and "signs in the ascendant". It looked utterly incomprehensible.

I asked if this was what the king's birth-chart looked like. He couldn't show me that, he said – no one could see it except royal priests and astrologers; but royal birth-charts were always much more elaborate than anyone else's. The horoscopes of even the minor royals could be several metres long. In the past, royal birth-charts were truly magnificent things. Mr Joshi remembered seeing the horoscope of King Tribhuvan when he was a child. It was edged with gold and so large it had taken four men to carry it into the room.

"Nowadays, the palace is not willing to spend money on a horoscope like this," Mr Joshi said. "But without details – and without time to analyse – it is difficult to make accurate predictions."

"Were you able to make any predictions about this year?" I asked.

The royal astrologer shifted uncomfortably.

"This is a very difficult year," he said, "very inauspicious. Everyone knew there was going to be some disaster. We knew the six days around the cusp of May/June were going to be very bad for the king. But it was complicated . . . I thought there was going to be an earthquake. I told the newspapers that."

For decades seismologists had been warning that an earthquake in the Kathmandu Valley was long overdue. The astrologer was under considerable pressure to predict when this would be. In 2001 it seemed to have blinded him to other possibilities.

The world over, 2001 had been a year of exceptional turmoil, the astrologer explained. He cited the Gujarat earthquake that had killed 20,000 and left 600,000 people homeless in January, a spate of typhoons in Taiwan, tornadoes in the United States, floods in Bangladesh, earthquakes in El Salvador, numerous high-profile plane crashes and, of course, most recently, the terrorist attacks on the Twin Towers in New York on 11 September.

But it had also been a year of portent for King Birendra. A month or so before the massacre, Saturn had moved into Taurus – the sign it had last entered twenty-nine years ago. In the West this was known as a "Saturn return", an astrological phenomenon occurring at twenty-seven to twenty-nine or thirty-year intervals in a person's life, coinciding with the approximate time – twenty-nine and a half years – it takes Saturn to make one orbit around the sun. According to stargazers, a "Saturn return" has dramatic impact on a person's life, triggering a midlife crisis, perhaps, or a divorce or a volte-face in careers. It is the moment when a person crosses a major threshold, leaving behind one stage of their life and moving into the next. Birendra had been crowned on 31 January 1972, at the age of twenty-seven when Saturn was in Taurus. Twenty-nine years later, the return of Saturn into Taurus signified dramatic upheavals in the king's personal life, quite possibly jeopardizing his very position on the throne.

"What happens when there are bad planetary influences like this?" I asked. "Is there anything to be done to avoid them?"

"The planetary positions in the heavens and their effect on human beings are like the signals we receive through a radio or TV set," said Mr Joshi. "We have no influence over the programmes – but," he added with a wry smile, "we can use the remote control to change channels."

This was where the *dyas* came in. Worshipping a particular deity at a given time could ameliorate or even banish bad influences. It could change the course of fortune. Much of Mr Joshi's work was advising his clients on which *puja* to do, when, where and to which deity.

"Sometimes though, the influences are too strong to change," added Mr Joshi cautiously. Usually a family's *chinnas* are kept together in a jewellery box in the safekeeping of the eldest female member. But sometimes a horoscope is so powerful that it has to be kept in its own box, sometimes even in a separate room. If arguments break out within a family, it could be because opposing *chinnas* are kept too close together.

"What about Dipendra's horoscope?" I asked. "What was that like?"

"I drew Prince Dipendra's horoscope myself," he said. "It was not bad – it was quite good, in fact. Only the raj yoga – the rulership signs – were destructive. It did not look likely he was ever going to become king."

Another astrologer had interpreted this to mean that the prince's existence could prove destructive to his father's. Another read in it signs that were antipathetic to Dipendra's mother and had recommended, immediately after Dipendra's birth, that the baby crown prince be separated from Queen Aishwarya for a week in order to purify their relationship; but this was apparently not done.

"The birth-chart showed also complications with marriage," said Mr Joshi. "We advised King Birendra to delay his son's marriage until the prince was thirty-five. This seemed the safest way to proceed."

But it was precisely this delay that seemed to have triggered Dipendra's fury. The crown prince had been determined, according to his friends, to become officially engaged to the "love of his life" before his thirtieth birthday – 27 June 2001. His parents' refusal to grant him his wish had made him apoplectic. It was not just his age but his girlfriend that was the problem. Two years older than Dipendra, Devyani Rana was wealthy, beautiful and highly educated but she was also, according to the press, descended from the "wrong type" of Rana: the Chandra Shamsher Ranas – the Ranas who had been responsible for keeping the Shah dynasty prisoner for generations. Her father, Pashupati Shumsher Rana, was one of the most powerful men in the country. She was also the granddaughter, on her mother's side, of an

Indian maharaja: a provenance that would have provoked further opposition from Dipendra's dictatorial mother.

I wondered, though, if there hadn't been other objections to Devyani as the future queen. Had Mr Joshi seen Devyani's horoscope?

"It was not compatible with Dipendra's," he said solemnly.

Devyani's mother, Rani Usha, however, had been ardently in favour of the match. In the 1960s she had been rejected in her own bid to marry Birendra, then the crown prince. It seemed she was determined her daughter would succeed where she had failed. Rani Usha herself went, with her husband, to consult Mr Joshi.

"I told Devyani's parents – I said to them, 'No matter how many *pujas* you perform, your daughter will never marry the crown prince.' They refused to listen . . ." said Mr Joshi.

I began to sense something of the power play that was supposed to have arisen between the palace and Devyani's family. Rumour had it that Devyani's mother had commissioned two priests from Gwalior to travel to Nepal to perform a tantric *puja* to remove the obstacles to the match. Apparently they had arrived at the Yak & Yeti, one of Kathmandu's top hotels, in late May where they had aroused suspicion by asking how to procure certain *puja* materials such as parrots and snakes. The *puja* in question was thought to be that of Bagalamukhi, a fearsome weapon-wielding Hindu goddess. Devyani's mother had commissioned a painting of the goddess from a renowned *citraikar* in the previous weeks, sending it back repeatedly to the artist to add more arms and weapons. Officials at Narayanhiti Palace had been alerted and Queen Aishwarya was supposed to have commissioned a counter *puja* to block their efforts. Many people claimed this exonerated the crown prince. Dipendra had clearly not been the master of his own actions. He had merely been caught in the crossfire of tantric warfare. I remembered the account one of the survivors of the massacre had given reporters, describing the crown prince bursting into the room looking like the goddess Kali wielding countless weapons.

But the king himself should have been beyond the reach of such goings-on. According to what Yagyaman had told me, the king was inviolable as long as he had the blessing of the Kumari. The power of *shakti* surged within him. No amount of *pujas*, counter-magic or worship to other deities, tantric or otherwise, could penetrate the protective forces the Living Goddess generated around the king.

But the Kumari's powers are considered to be effective only as long as she remains pure and receives proper worship. The blotches that had appeared on the Living Goddess's face twenty-four days before the massacre indicated not only that something was rotten in the state of Nepal but that the Kumari herself had somehow lost her purity. She was no longer acting as an effective conduit between Taleju and the king.

I asked Mr Joshi why they hadn't changed Kumaris when this had happened, replacing the affected incumbent with a new one. Certainly, he said, the priests always have a Kumari in reserve – a Kumari-in-waiting – in anticipation of just such a misfortune. A little Shakya girl, with the right physical criteria and whose horoscope has already been checked against the king's, shadows the real one. Living at home with her family, this little girl, providing she remains healthy and pure, refrains from eating certain polluting foods and incurs no cuts or bruises or other blemishes, can be called upon to become Kumari in the event of a calamity befalling the incumbent. When she goes to school at the age of four or five, the priests identify another candidate. Hers is not an official position, Mr Joshi said; she is merely a standby in case of emergency.

At first, when ominous signs began to appear on the Kumari's body, spreading to her face, the priests did all they could to appease the Goddess and cure the Kumari of the complaint. They appealed to the palace for the king to send special offerings but none came. The monarch, they were told, was busy. Then, about twelve days later, Mr Joshi said, the unthinkable happened. The Kumari began to bleed. Her first menstruation had arrived without warning.

"Usually the Kumari is changed well in advance of her first menses, so there is never a gap between Kumaris," explained the astrologer. "But in this case it took everyone by surprise."

She has to be removed immediately, according to Newar custom, to a darkened room where she remains for twelve days while she undergoes the important Newar puberty rite of *bara tayegu*. Like ihi, *bara tayegu* is a rite of female empowerment involving the mock marriage of a Newar girl to a god – in this case the sun god, Surya. Its specific purpose is to eradicate the pollution traditionally associated with vaginal blood. As a result the dangers that orthodox Hindus attached to defloration, menstruation and childbirth are diffused and a Newar woman can go about her normal life much as usual during her menstrual period, cooking and eating with the rest of the family, and sleeping with her husband. The rite is especially important in the case of a Kumari, whose menstrual blood could otherwise be considered particularly dangerous.

Enthroning a substitute in a Kumari's place at short notice, however, is not a straightforward matter. It takes at least a fortnight to prepare a candidate Kumari for the powerful installation ritual. And this ritual – normally conducted on the eighth night of Dasain – has to be performed on another highly auspicious day.

The astrologer wobbled his head. "This is a black year, as I told you; there were very few auspicious days. We were waiting for the right time to change Kumaris."

"So, effectively," I said slowly, as the realization dawned, "there was no Living Goddess at the time of the massacre?"

"That is why these things came to pass," the astrologer confirmed. "Without the power of the Kumari, the king and all his dependants are exposed. They cannot be saved from the bad influences of the planets and the bad intentions of those who want to destroy them."

After the massacre the priests came to Mr Joshi to check that the horoscope of the reserve Kumari, which had originally been aligned with the birth-chart of Birendra, also agreed with that of the new king, Gyanendra. Fortunately, it did. On the next auspicious day, on 10 July 2001, forty days after the massacre, a new Kumari filled the vacant throne. The ship of state had been clawed back off the rocks and set afloat again. But whether it could survive the tempestuous seas that lay ahead would remain to be seen.

"A dark period on the Earth has passed," concluded Mr Joshi, restively adjusting his floor cushion. "Nepal must now find peace. But the signs are still not good. There are troubles to come."

I left the astrologer in a state of agitation, shuffling papers around his desk as though some vital document continued to elude him. A few persistent clients remained outside his door. The rest had given up and dispersed, disappearing into the night of inconstant stars.

THE VANISHING ACT

Prawin Adhikari

Prawin Adhikari lives in Kathmandu where he teaches and writes fiction and screenplays. He has translated *A Land of Our Own* by Suvash Darnal, and *Chapters*, a collection of short stories by Amod Bhattarai. He is an assistant editor at *La.Lit*.

THE BOY FROM BANAUTI

Grandfather would read one book here and another scroll there through the year, but only in November – after consulting his astrological chart – would he spread the contents of his father's old almirah in the palliative sun to drive the moisture and must out and to renew the mild poison in the hemlock that yellowed the pages. It was also the day of the year when we, the children of the extended family, were reminded of how much there is to learn, how much there is to inherit by way of words. Great-grandfather had collected or written with his own hand all of these obscure or pedestrian Sanskrit texts, boiling black angeri berries for the ink, sharpening nibs from bamboo and reed (because a quill, which originates in flesh, would have been profane), splitting bamboo to collect the thin film within to layer into paper. I hated the sight. It was a taunt, I knew it even then; I knew it was meant to burden the youngest boys in the family with guilt for not following the family trade, for packing their bags and going to an English-medium school instead of learning Sanskrit.

I hated that I was expected to learn, to memorize, to know. To remember details, causes and consequences, descriptions and explanations, names, genealogies, salutations and shortcuts to salvation. Examine the back of my head and you'll see scars from falling from heights, or objects falling on my head from heights: roofs, branches, low bluffs along

a stream, low walls, high walls. It is a miracle that I can remember anything at all. Yet, on such days in November, I was expected to kneel by
Grandfather's side and examine the past that my generation was meant
to inherit: prayers, puran, commentaries and poetry. On such days, my
schoolbag seemed extra heavy, doubly annoying.

"Come here," Grandfather called me on that particular day and made
me take off my shoes before I could kneel on the straw mat and yak-
hair blanket on which he sat. "Read this English," he said.

It was dated March, 1915. A dedication to Great-grandfather, in a
neat hand, written by the Chief Engineer, Allahabad Bridge, Allahabad,
on the title page of a handsomely produced copy of the *Amarkosh*,
a thesaurus of Sanskrit. Grandfather smiled. I couldn't tell what he
seemed more satisfied by: his father's adventures or his grandson's ability to read letters with a third-grade education. I hastily slipped on my
shoes, picked up my bag and walked away.

School was a mile away in the bazaar. A handful of us walked from
our neighbourhood in Panchayat Bhavan to the bazaar every day. It was
easier to walk along the highway, but Mother considered it too dangerous: each year, dozens died in motor accidents on the dirt shoulders of
the highway. She thought everything was designed to kill her youngest
child: trees, ponds, rivers, lorries and buses, wasps and hornets, berries,
foreigners. So we walked through paddies laid bare after the harvest,
dotted with stubble, dew-mulched and yielding underfoot. We jumped
nimbly over muddy irrigation ditches and raced between fodder trees
or houses along the way. Malla's steam-engine rice mill announced nine
o'clock with puffs of black smoke and a toot-toot-toot. That was our
signal to run to school, racing to be the first to cross the mill-yard, to
be the first to cross the highway to Gorkha, be the first to jump through
the gates at Sun Shine English Medium.

But on that day, I didn't want to run; I didn't want to reach the
school where each day I was punished during the morning assemblies
in the yard – for forgetting the national anthem when it was my turn
to lead the school, for nails hastily chewed down just before inspection,
for reading Surendra Mohan Pathak thrillers in Hindi or smuggling in
Nagraj comics for the boys who lived in the hostel. I didn't want to

face Mr Hansen from Goa, who taught social sciences and loved to pick on Rajendra, Bir Bahadur and me for not doing our homework. I ran ahead, slipped behind a hedge near my cousin Ishwor's house, and crouched to urinate as my friends walked past. They must have thought I had raced on, trying to breach the school gates before the nine-fifteen bell rang, before the principal's brother Amshu fetched his cane to whip the latecomers.

After rolling my socks into tidy balls to stuff into the shoes, stuffing the shoes into the school bag and burying the bag under banana-leaf mulch by the guava tree behind Ishwor's home, I sniffed the air and smiled to the sun. What a day! A clear sky, the sun mild on the skin, shades cold as they ought to be in November, and six whole hours languidly spread before me.

I wandered aimlessly, ducking to hide from elders who might know me or my parents or my teachers, stealing through kitchen gardens, crouching to watch buffalos tethered to stakes to soak in the sun, letting cactus thorns scratch the shin that itched, picking, sniffing at, and then flinging away, a dead bluebird. I wandered to escape rote and recital, to inspect closely how spit forces touch-me-nots to fold and to hide from the foliage long enough to fool it into unfolding, run a finger along the saw-edge of waxy pineapple leaves, pick beetles from cow-patties, squeeze between bamboos to squat on new shoots, eat wild kauso seeds and dig for fern roots, listen to the hoots of owls that perch on jackfruit trees and don't sleep, chase the howls of sly jackals that haunt the edge of the forest, forget lessons in arithmetic of yesterday, the past week, the entire year.

Ram Shah Madhyamik was quiet for the time of the morning. I marched right through the school grounds, in through the west gate, out through the east. None of the teachers who came to their doors tried to stop me. This wasn't my school, these weren't my tyrants. Here and now, I could walk unmolested by authority. What a world!

Then it was past the jalebi shop with the soot-faced boy, past Arjun's mother's hut, down the crumbling chalk-hill behind Koirala's Veterinary and Agriculture Shop that always smelled of poison, but on its board showed seeds and an egg and a hen and a cow all of the same size, life growing outwards, out to the downhill road to Gorkha, all the way to where the bridge across Marshyangdi stretched a full hundred metres, a crawl along the rails, spitting over the side, measuring the arc the wind made with the glob of spit before it became one with the river's foam, letting the river reel in my head, stepping back just in time to say, "Wah! Marshyangdi almost sucked me down!"

Daraundi met Marshyangdi by a corner stained with charcoal-strewn pits. Even during the day, even from afar, the corner had a strong, tidal pull, like being sucked into a separate world. The crippled babaji in the Shiva temple was awake, unusually early for him: it was common knowledge he dived to the depths of the rivers during the night to collect human bones, breaking the churned surface of the waters with his withered, shrivelled arm. He sat combing his long hair with his one good hand, fanning its oily grey length over one knee, out over the stone threshold of the small, squat temple. Like always, he called me with the shrivelled arm he normally kept in its wooden box, pointing up to the Sun God to whom he had offered the limb many years ago.

I ran down the chalky path to the river that curved along the base of the bluff with the Shiva temple. Daraundi carved pockets of still water or shallow pools where long beards of algae and clear pebbly floors alternated. If the sun lasted an entire day the shallow pools would become warmer than the snow-fed currents of the river. By my favourite wading spot was Pushpa, an equal delinquent, sitting on the reddest, smoothest rock. He wasn't wearing his uniform. When he saw me, he came bounding over rocks, leaping over the kids in the wading pool. We shook hands like men: Pushpa stark naked, me in my Friday uniform. He led me back to the rock where he was cooking his crayfish caught in the paddies by the river. Pushpa's catch was impressive: thirteen, plump, sun-roasted to a pink hue, soon curling to sniff their tails like dogs, soon crunchy and sweet. Pushpa leaped from rock to rock to the bush where his clothes sat under a stone, and I surveyed the world.

It was the usual crowd of truants. Shankar, Binod, Sujan, Kishor, Kumar, Omkaji, Amrit, Rupesh and Sudip Malla were diving and swimming. Sujan was only a year older than me, but he could swim clear across Marshyangdi during the floods, without getting a hair on his head wet, never once cutting his arms out of the river, jumping near Dadim Dhik near Ram Shah Madhyamik, floating all the way across as easily as if he were strolling through a wide meadow. I couldn't swim, and most of the boys were my uncles from my mother's side, an entire village of cousins and second cousins, who would gladly beat me up any excuse they found. Mother would take their side, too – she'd interrogate me on why I was wherever I happened to be apprehended by one of those thugs. So I sat on Pushpa's red rock until he called me to Hari-Hara.

Hari-Hara were two rocks, each the size of Bagaley Ba's smaller teashop near Narayan Malla's rice mill. Where they leaned into each other they made a short tunnel with a cold heart. Pushpa lit the cigarette he had brought for me. He pulled at it, puffed his cheeks out, and exhaled with a convulsive gathering of the chest and stomach. I took the cigarette. I didn't smoke it right away. I scratched the tip of my nose with my thumb, but didn't put the cigarette in my mouth. I spat through the gap in my teeth and rubbed the spit into the sand with the big toe. I whistled a little. I pulled at the cigarette and held my breath.

It felt like I had gathered all the dry leaves around the bamboo grove in Kunduley, all the brambles between Narighat and Khanikhola, all of last year's mustard stalks after harvest and lit a fire somewhere under my throat, above my stomach. My chest heaved; pellets of air hit my ears from the inside. Something like a snort or a giggle or a belch or a sneeze or a cry escaped from a corner of my mouth. I exhaled. The smoke had gone thin and black.

"Good!" I said as Pushpa puffed up his cheeks to keep the smoke captive. He opened his mouth, letting curlicues of smoke rise on their own. Pushpa pinched the cigarette, wrapped it in a syaula leaf and put it away. He made a whooping yell and jumped into the wading pool. Syankanchha and Rakesh and Keshav and Marichey and Gajaley's son waited for Pushpa to finish splashing around before dipping themselves up to the chin and thrashing with their legs.

I was still seeing tiny sparks of light – stars – just around my eyes, the part of life that is usually grey and invisible. Pushpa's stone felt too hot. I slid down the length of its smooth face, still wearing my uniform, and splashed into the pool. I slept in the water, looking up at the boys who came close to yell and laugh until another distraction took them away. I really could hold my breath: nothing seemed distinct, not even my hands, and any pebble held before my eyes seemed round and shiny and money-like. Riches. When I sat up, sputtering the little water that had gone in through the nose, gasping for air, I saw the boy from Banauti pointing, laughing at me.

Although he pointed at me, nobody else was looking. He laughed soundlessly, without a pip or a squeak. His head was shorn, perhaps because of the sores and scabs that mottled his scalp. He was related to me, if you drew a line that wormed six generations back and wormed forward again until it tied me to him. Properly, the boy from Banauti was an uncle from my father's side. His blind father sat outside their house to sell yogurt and walking sticks to people from Kathmandu trying to climb to Manakamana. His sister had thrown herself from the suspension bridge over Marshyangdi the day her friends told her that she had failed her SLC exams. Her friends had been joking, trying to scare her. She never got to know. The boy from Banauti now lived with Keshav's family, away from his blind father who still milked the buffaloes and polished walking sticks in his spare time, but also cried and cursed in angry fits, swinging his sickle and stick at anything that moved, until the foaming spit dried to salt and tore open the skin of his mouth.

"Why are you laughing?" I said. I knew why he laughed.

He thought I had done something funny.

"You're wet! Everything is wet!" he said.

"You're in the water. You're wet, too," I said.

"That is your school uniform," he said. "Your mother will be angry."

"And you don't even have a mother," I said. I plugged both ears with my fingers and plunged my head underwater. Small, slow bubbles through the nose. Continuous. Hold your breath until you are sitting upright. Wipe your face with your palms before exhaling. The boy from Banauti raised his head to look at me before concentrating on his hands. His lips and brows twitched.

"And your father is blind," I said. He didn't look up. I knew I would next tell him that his sister threw herself from the bridge. There was nothing else left to throw at him. Sujan was jumping on Kishor's shoulders, trying to keep him in the water, while Shankar was pulling Sujan's leg. The wading pool was still because everyone had chosen a rock each and was warming their ears to bring the water out. It is easy. Find a large, sun-cooked rock. Embrace it, facedown, with your ear glued to it. Close your eyes, and drift into warm, sticky dreams.

The boy from Banauti looked up. His chin quivered and the large, dirty-brown eyes turned wet and trembled. I sat by him. "What are you doing?" I asked.

"Nests," he said, "swallows' nests." He dug into the wet sand until water seeped from all sides into the rut. He dipped his palm, let the wetness run down to the fingertips and drip: solid, wet beads of sand. He arranged the beads, every drop placed with deliberation. Streets. Spires. Hedges. A temple with a dome that rose in two concentric spirals, like the domes in the books which Singapore Lahure kids brought to school. He stopped and pointed at my hands.

I scooped water and sand, but my beads fell in uneven sizes. The boy from Banauti laughed at first. I drew outlines on the sand for the layout of my village, patted down sand for the foundations, then started over. Now the boy from Banauti watched intently, added his own drops to augment, once using a crooked finger to scoop and transplant a bead to perfect effect, changing a hut to a sentry-box by piling up a pyramid of cannonballs on the roof. Then he started laughing. I laughed with him.

"Who works here?" He pointed to the newly finished sentry-box.

"I don't know," I said, "it is a sentry-box."

"I know what it is," he said. He was annoyed. "I said, Who works here?"

It is a stupid lump of stupid wet sand, I wanted to say. Everybody else was busy shouting or jumping. Pushpa and Sujan appeared by Hari-Hara. Sujan tried to blow smoke rings. Sujan could do anything a grown-up could. "I said, Who works here?" The boy from Banauti brought a finger too close to my sentry-box with the cannonballs on the roof.

You have to know. That is the whole point. Knowing. Exactly. Who, where, what, when. That is the point. Why. That is the point also. Otherwise you are just a stupid kid playing with wet sand. Just a stupid kid.

The boy from Banauti was raving now. I tried to imagine his blind father's rage. The last time we climbed to Manakamana, Mother had taken me to their home and had made me eat yogurt prepared by his father. The old man had insisted upon reading my fortune. His coarse fingers attentively hovered over the thin lines of my palms. He said good things. Then he cried. He said, "I wish my son had half the good fortune you have." He took my face in his hands, gingerly rubbed his hand over my forehead, said I had a wide forehead, one for fortune and fame.

The boy from Banauti knew – exactly who, where, what, when. Even the why. He was becoming more and more agitated. He had a name for each intersection of each neighbourhood, each face of the temple, the person sitting or absent from each window, everything being sold by each vendor in each derelict corner behind large warehouses. His was not a village, but a city, with a park where the king's younger son played with his vast army of retainers while the king did what? Hold jousts and chases to find an eligible prince for his daughter. Anybody speaking calmly would need a year to finish inventing and detailing everything the boy from Banauti knew and jabbered on and on about, but it took him less time than it took for me to work up a temper.

I kicked sand into his face. The stupid wet sand he had been play-ing with. I trampled down his vast city. I killed the sentry in my own sentry-box with the cannonballs on the roof. The sentry poked his head out of the tiny window, dull bayonet leading, trying to prop my foot up with a pin-prick. Then I kicked the double-spiralled temple to the face of the boy from Banauti. Although he sat there dumbstruck, his chin quivering, one hand on his throat to either stifle a scream or to bottle his breath, I knew he knew the where, when, who, how. I was the marauding why. I spread my arms wide, faced the sky and laughed maniacally.

I quickly picked one of Pushpa's shrivelled crayfish and chewed on it. Another. The boy from Banauti walked away. "I'll tell your mother," he said before disappearing behind a rock.

I left my clothes behind Pushpa's rock and admired my toes peeking out of the water. I slipped underwater and blew bubbles, holding each pearl of air at the cusp of my mouth, watching it pull its shape from within me, leave me to rush to burst against the sky. None of the boys had returned into the pool when I sat up to breathe. Back underwater, to the place where everything was indistinct and therefore looked like bright coins. Blue and black and beige and white pebbles like coins. There is a country somewhere in the middle of the Pacific, a place which *Yuva Manch Monthly* writes "Did you know?" facts about, where these pebbles are riches, precious as diamonds and malachite. Malachite. The World Cup is made of gold and malachite. Did you know?

Somebody grabbed my hair and lifted me out of the water. It was Binod, Shankar's twin.

"What did I do?" I screamed at him. He looked at me, puzzled, but didn't let go of my hair. I had to use my knees to stand. Pebbles and coarse sand scraped my kneecaps.

"Don't sit like that in the water, you ass," he said, "I thought you were drowning. That you'd drowned."

"I can hold my breath," I said. He grabbed me by the nape and threw me to the bank.

"Don't go back into the water," he said. Nobody else was around. He climbed Pushpa's rock. I climbed after him. One roasted crayfish fell into the river when my wet toes nudged it loose. A line of pale naked buttocks jumped from rock to rock, running downriver to where Daraundi met Marshyangdi. Babaji screamed from the temple, running from one corner to another, his atrophied hand still pointing to the gods.

"What happened?" I asked. Binod put a hand on my shoulder and rubbed the nape he had roughed but a moment ago.

Sujan and Shankar bobbed over Daraundi's water, racing fast towards Marshyangdi. Daraundi brought clear water, fed by glaciers, or mountain springs filtered through thousands of paddies, while Marshyangdi descended furiously, intent upon grinding together the rocks in her belly. Where Daraundi met Marshyangdi, Daraundi recoiled. Sujan was thrown back by that recoil. Shankar dived into the seam, came up for air thirty paces downstream. Everybody else ran along the river, shouting, screaming. A line of people stood on the suspension bridge and pointed this way and that, made noises that didn't carry to where we stood. My toe slipped an inch and I lurched slightly; Binod caught me by my arm and steadied me on the rock without taking his eyes off Sujan and Shankar.

"What is his name?" Binod asked. Whose? "The boy. You were making swallows' nests with him. The boy from Banauti."

"He is my relative," I said. I didn't know his name.

"He fell," Binod said.

Sujan and Shankar could be seen, diving, coming to the surface, riding the white water of the rivers to propel them to whirlpools that swallowed bodies. Amrit and Omkaji shouted to Sujan and Shankar. Sujan dived once more, but Shankar came to the bank. He floated on his back in a corner, one hand grabbing the rock behind him. Sujan finally climbed out of the water, but stranded himself between two granite ledges with water on either side. He crawled to a narrow bar of sand and hid his face in his hands.

Pushpa climbed his rock, teetered with one hand on my shoulder. He brushed off the remaining crayfish into the river.

"What was his name?" Binod asked Pushpa, who shook his head.

"We should have asked," Binod said sombrely. He put his hand on my shoulder and rubbed my neck. "Go home," he said. "Go home, but don't talk about this. Don't mention you were here."

Pushpa and I buttoned our shirts in silence. I hadn't yet learned how to tie shoelaces quickly. It took me a while. Up the hill, in the temple, Babaji was locking his arm into a wooden box suspended from the roof. "Go home," he said perfunctorily. Pushpa threw away what remained of the cigarette, still wrapped in the syaula leaf. I wanted to stand on the edge of the bluff and read the rivers in both directions, as far as my eyes could see. Who knows when the boy from Banauti will call for help, I thought. But it felt like it had been a very long day. The most recent minutes were interminable, like the yarn on my mute uncle Madhav's dhaka loom, looping around something not very far, anchored to the weight inside, and each thread returning, over and over, to the same place, just a slightly different spot.

Pilgrims on the suspension bridge continued to peer into the current long after it made any sense for them to. What a day! Not even noon yet, the sun still mild and pale, and a boy disappeared even as dozens of people watched. Six generations ago, there had been a man who worked in the jungles along these very rivers, tended to his cows, gathered fodder and firewood, read fortune for a small fee. From him came hundreds, including Grandfather who sunned his yellowed pages of scriptures while his distant cousin groped blindly at the air in Banauti for his son's return; from the first astrologer came the sister who jumped into the river, and from him came I: truant, delinquent, ignorant. I knew nothing of those who had passed before me. There was one who could have known, who could have conjured their faces and voices through an act of will and invention, but the river took him before I could ask his name, before I could ask him how his mother had died, or if he remembered her at all. And it made me melancholy to understand that I didn't know enough about the boy from Banauti, or about myself.

CANDY

Nayan Raj Pandey

Nayan Raj Pandey is the author of a short story collection, *Chocolate,* and three novels: *Ghamkiri, Loo* and *Ullar.*

After leaving the Pajero at the district headquarters, the personal assistant and I headed out on foot. A village road. Dirt and dust. A horrid stench. Shit and dung. Why had the villages become so filthy?

I was walking to my village. People always complain that we leaders forget our villages after winning the elections. I was returning to silence that complaint. This was the first time I was returning to the village after winning the elections and leaving for the capital. I felt as though I were in an entirely new place. I had some candy in my pockets. I was going to hand it out to children.

"Minister-jyu, it looks like we've lost our way."

"Oh, you're right." I was unnerved when the personal assistant pointed this out to me. "The main road branches off at Sallaghari. But we're at Dharmapur," I said, wiping the sweat from my forehead.

"Minister-jyu, let's do this: let's follow that trail over there to Sallaghari. That looks like a shortcut."

The personal assistant seemed to have a feel for the village. I followed his advice and took the other trail. I had no desire to go to Dharmapur anyway. That was where I got the fewest votes. A total of three hundred.

"Those traitors gobbled up sixty thousand rupees!" I silently cursed the residents of Dharmapur and made a pledge: "I won't pass a budget for this village."

I had made this pledge to myself, and yet, as though overhearing my thoughts, the personal assistant said, "'Yes, hajur, we shouldn't pass a budget for this village."

*

I grew vexed again. Once again, we had gone past Sallaghari. We had reached Chitrapur now.

"You fool, we can't go into this village. They'll beat us up."

As soon as I said this, the personal assistant began to tremble. "We might get ambushed. Let's go back to Sallaghari, Sir." He looked as though he might wet his pants.

We took the road to Sallaghari. Spotting strangers on the road, a few children began to follow us. I took some candy from my pocket and gave it to them.

It turned out that the main road branched off at Bansghari, not Sallaghari. I had gotten them mixed up.

The Chairman of the Sallaghari Village Development Committee rubbed his hands together when he saw me and said, "Minister-jyu, now that you're here, have some tea before heading off." It was the first time since leaving the capital that I'd seen anyone rub their hands. It lightened my heart.

"What are the problems in this village?" I asked the Chairman.

"There's a huge problem with drinking water," came the reply.

"Be patient, Chairman-jyu, don't worry. In five years I'll wash this whole village in water," I assured the man, but to myself said, "You'll get nothing," and handed out some candy there as well.

Afterward, I scolded the personal assistant, "Is this any way to conduct yourself? Leading us in the wrong direction?"

"Sir, it's my first time here. I don't know the way. I thought you'd know the way. You were born and raised here. You won the election from here."

This was embarrassing. "All right, never mind. Now let's take that road over there. We'll get to my village that way." When we reached Bansghari, I said proudly to the personal assistant, "See? This is Bansghari."

But upon entering the village I realised it was Dandagaun.

I now understood the problem with being a minister. A minister can't ask directions to his own village. I decided that the next time I'd bring a map to my village. I told the personal assistant about this plan.

He was delighted by it. We walked on, but we couldn't find the way. If I had a map I wouldn't get lost. My plan about the map now struck me as highly prescient and relevant.

"You launched the democratic revolution of the 1990s from this very village," an elderly man recalled when we arrived at a different village. I found this information tantalizing. I almost said, '"Oh, really?" I had forgotten all about this but couldn't really say so. My problem was even more acute now. This hadn't turned out to be my village either. There was only one consolation: all of these villages fell in my constituency.

"Take out your pen," I ordered the personal assistant. I made him list the names of all the villages we had visited.

The personal assistant was ecstatic: "Minister-jyu, you've visited all these villages on foot. This will make for incredible news, Sir."

Such was my foresight.

The road widened as we walked on. I believed we were finally nearing my birthplace. But once again we arrived at another village.

The relentless sun made me longingly recall air conditioning. I remembered the Pajero. I recalled my room in the Ministry. I began to worry that the assistant minister would hire all of his own people in my absence. I was also gripped by the fear that he would rake in all the commissions himself.

I asked the personal assistant: "Which is greater? The village or the nation?"

With great emotion, he replied, "The nation."

"In that case let's return to the capital."

"Yes, hajur. It's better to return to the nation than to waste all this time looking for a village."

I turned around.

On the way we met another group of children. I handed them the rest of the candy.

The candy was finished and the road to the village had come to an end.

THREE SPRINGS

Jemima Diki Sherpa

Jemima Diki Sherpa is a freelance writer, interpreter, and community organiser from Thame Valley in Solukhumbu, Nepal.

When there are gatherings in our valley, the women sit with the women and the men sit with the men, and the children tear about evading adult arms that reach out to obstruct their fun. The men form a long line on low benches along the front wall of the house, patriarchs sitting at the end closest to the fireplace with the wide-legged weariness of ageing masculinity; down through the established householders with their roars of laughter, past the young fathers bouncing sticky toddlers on their laps, through the self-conscious new and prospective grooms, to the awkward youths who cram together and snicker and mutter and jostle each other.

Everyone wears down jackets.

In such a line as this, a gambler would have good odds that any man, picked at random, has stood atop of Everest; chances better still that he has been partway up the mountain a dozen times only to return to Base Camp, collect another load, and head off to cross the treacherous icefall again. What elsewhere is extraordinary – the raw material that can be spun into charitable foundations, movie rights, pub boasts and motivational speaking tours – is quotidian in the villages of Thame Valley. Even our monks shed their deep red robes in spring and come back snow-burnt, the marks of sun goggles etched pale across their cheekbones and their lips chapped flaking white with bleeding crimson cracks.

When I finished high school and left Kathmandu for university in New Zealand, I was conditioned for the reactions my last name would elicit. "They ask how many kilos you can carry," says every Sherpa who has ever travelled abroad. But I was caught by a more common response: "Shuuurpa," in the muted antipodean accent, "Seriously? That's AWESOME!"

It is something to behold, the open-hearted enthusiasm that the Sherpa name elicits in the western mind. It is (as every random company that has capitalized on it well knows) the branding motherlode – stimulating a vague positive association founded on six-odd decades of mountaineering mythbuilding. I wondered what deep, subconscious connections, what snippets of information, what flashes of imagery were being evoked.

"Awesome" how? I came to ask myself. More importantly, "awesome" for whom? Uncharitably, I imagined them imagining themselves as conquering heroes, assisted by a legion of Sherpa faithful ready – and cheerful – to lay down sweat and lives in service for arduous, but ultimately noble and glorious, personal successes. Still, it is undeniable that, in "post"-colonial democracies where ethnic minorities carry the burden of insidious and vicious prejudices at every turn, Sherpas are fortunate. Everyone loves us, everyone trusts us, and everyone wants their own collectable one of us. Internet listsicles call us "badass" and we have a very large, very coveted piece of real estate in our back yard. It is a stereotype, sure, but a positive one.

Any vague hopes my new acquaintances may have had of me self-lessly and singlehandedly lugging their furniture up stairs on moving days were swiftly dashed. I lived life some, and then meandered my way home more than half a decade later. Village-born though I was, and potato farmers and yak herders though my grandparents may have been, despite the yearly trips to the Khumbu homeland I am a Kathmandu city girl. Like post-arts degree twenty somethings the world over, I was adrift. With equal parts defeat, hope, terror, self-congratulation and wildly under-informed plans and good intentions, I arrived "home" to live in Thamo, elevation: 3550 metres, population: maybe fifty people on a good day.

Village life. This should be amusing.

That was Spring 2012, on the first of the Nepali year. It seemed a fitting day for a new chapter.

Two weeks later, a first cousin died on Everest.

Family circumstances were such that I hadn't seen him since we were both infants. My father and another cousin walked to Tengboche to attend the funeral. Grimfaced, they returned. He had a wife and a three-month old baby, and the then-standard five lakh (roughly US$5000) payout for fatalities would not extend far past the death rites.

Morbidly, perhaps, I read a surprisingly long article on his death. His safety harness had not been clipped in; veteran western (and only western) climbers quoted by the half-dozen on the topic of Namgya's death. Overconfidence, the implication was, even though the quote hedged, "I wouldn't say it's because they are overconfident". Strong Sherpa competitive spirit, intra-village rivalries. "A bit complacent." Sometimes novices just plain forget. "These guys just pretty much dance across the ladders."

This was my first adult experience of the endless, repeating nature of death talk during the spring season. So-and-so, from village such-and-such, his cousin – no, married to her sister, my aunt's – it happened like this. He was such a good person. They say he fell into a crevasse. Om mani padme hum.

And then: "These boys, they go too fast. They hurry to get more work."

For a lifetime of mountaineering talk, I'd always tuned out. Nuptse and Lhotse get mixed up in my head, and I can never remember the elevations of things, or how many acclimatisation nights there are before a summit, and every climbing company has a name that sounds the same – Adventure something, Mountain something.

But here was how it connected to life, to the cousin I barely knew, to other relatives I knew better who were still on the mountain. As a young high altitude expedition worker, the more you carry, the more you are paid. There is a per kilogram equation for payment, and there is value, both in hard cash and in securing future work, in proving you are good. If you prove you're good, you get hired next season, possibly recruited by one of the better companies, climbing literally up the mountain and figuratively up the ranks. The best way to do all this is to move fast and carry a lot. And the best way to do that is to dance, possibly unclipped, across the icefall ladders.

And yet. This one potential factor, this one whisper of motivation, the veteran mountaineers did not make mention of when the article posed the question: "Why did Namgya skip a seemingly simple, and potentially life-saving step?"

So it must have been that Sherpa competitive spirit.

Spring finishes. The potatoes have been planted. The summer fog rolls in, and Thamserku disappears into the mist for days on end. Summer finishes. In autumn I prove I am an exceedingly incompetent dilettante potato harvester. I have better luck interviewing people for an academic study; in a Namche coffee shop, I approach a foreign climbing guide. He pretends to be cagey and worried about his name getting out there. I read him the consent form. Anonymity. You'll really just be a data point, I say curtly, and he looks a bit crushed. He rambles and makes grand pronouncements on how things should be run if anyone was thinking properly. Question 8.1, how satisfied are you in your job. Very satisfied. Question 8.4, do you have plans besides guiding in the future. Maybe write a book about my experiences, he says. The Nepali guides I've asked repeat: Khai, tyeti bela nai bichar garnu parcha. Or Ke garne, aru bikalpa nai chaina. Question 8.3, ajai kati barsa samma yo guiding kaam garnu huncha hola. Aba jati barsa samma jiu le saath dincha bhanumn na, bahini.

Autumn finishes, and the winds grow colder. Mid-December we descend to Kathmandu. We aren't the only ones; people have trickled down from all the mountain areas, flowing into a river that swirls and swirls clockwise around Boudha in the winter sun.

Spring again, and a friend from university arrives with her boyfriend. I introduce them to khukuri rum, and the next day of collecting tickets and packing for the mountains aches by for all of us. The air in Lukla is crisp, and we set off, arriving home the next day. I open up the house, and it is eerily undisturbed despite my aunt's visits. They have plenty of time and a trip to Gokyo won't fill it all, so for days we sit around and read books and make coffee and listen to Kiwi reggae.

I'm bringing in some laundry when my cellphone rings. It's a friend from Kathmandu who works for an international news bureau – there's been a fight, have you heard, who do you know at Base Camp.

The internet has gone mad. Links upon links, hundreds of comments, this one said, then he said, then he said, accusations, counter accusations, updates, debates, threats, tantrums, analysis, They, Us. I read and I read.

Two aunts and a woman I don't know are weeding a field below ours. I go down and sit with them, and they break for tea out of a thermos and a huge pot of boiled potatoes, peeled with grit-stained hands and dipped in salt and chilli powder from a plastic bag. Did you hear about some fight? I ask, and they haven't. But an icefall doctor has died, originally from down in Solu, but married to so-and-so in her village, two daughters, nyingje . . .

My friends and I leave for Gokyo. I carry a pack of cards and along the trail I teach them how to play Callbreak, nabbing guides and porters to come and be our fourth player. Only a couple of hands in at tiny lodge in Dole, the game is somehow taken over by trekking guides and I am left keeping score. It becomes a high stakes game of champions – expert card counters with perfect dramatics. "On a king of hearts, and my . . . three of spades. La kha ta" Uproar. The round finishes, and as the cards are shuffled some go out to take a leak. I ask – hey, this fight. The foreigners are pissed off apparently, have you heard . . . ? Nothing, but – the icefall doctor, I was in Lukla once and we stayed in the same place for two days, such a nice guy, good experience, but . . .

We reach Gokyo and the lodge owner, an aunt of a cousin, lets me use the internet for free. The catch is I have to go to the unheated outside room, a maze of satellite phone wiring and solar batteries, where a creaking PC is connected via LAN cable to the router. I can see my breath.

Unread messages, most on the latest in the brawl circus. So-and-so's "expert" opinion that Sherpas are, as a culture, fundamentally incapable of violence; so-and-so's equally "expert" opinion that the jig is up, they've always been spoiled brutes. And then that phrase: The Sherpa Mob. I snort with laughter, and make Sherpa Mobster jokes on Twitter until the cold creeps up to my thighs from the concrete floor and my fingers begin to seize.

I go inside the dining room to warm up. Husband-of-aunt-of-cousin has heard something about an argument but no details, khai, someone must have done something to set someone off. But did you hear, Mingma, the icefall doctor, was it two daughters or three . . .

The next day my friends and I trudge for what seems to be an eternity up the glacier to Gokyo's fifth lake. It's the best view of Everest, the lodge owners have assured us – better than from Kalapatthar. When it finally comes into view, Cho Oyu looms to our left as we face eastward – and there it is. Barren black rock, a rather bland dented triangle compared to the beautiful, dramatic ridges that surround it.

All of this, for that.

I see my friends off, and make my way back to Namche. I'm in a lodge kitchen, eating popcorn and listening to four men I don't know, one with wind and sunburn scabs so bad along his cheeks that it looks like reptilian scales. They're fresh down from the climbing season and drinking cans of beer. I think of asking them about the fight, but one begins to talk about how a foreign climber – a woman, not his client – came upon a corpse on the mountain and began wailing and crying and wouldn't move. I had to grab her and shake her, he says, I had to yell at her – if you stop you will die, we'll all die right here, that one's gone already, let it go . . .

The conversation moves on. Spring finishes. The summer fog rolls in, and our elderly neighbors move their livestock up to the high pastures. They come down occasionally, bringing treats of fresh milk or yoghurt or soft young cheese. Without their animals to feed our scraps to, I spend a lot of time reading about composting techniques. I have a month's work with a group of foreign students. A young Sherpa academic is with us for the first part of the journey. We stop for the night at her aunt's lodge. Her aunt rents horse rides to tourists. "She's saving any money she gets from that for an iPhone," she tells me, and we laugh. Later, as a moth flutters above the bed, I wonder what Namgyal might have been saving for. An iPhone costs what an iPhone costs, and so does a future for a baby daughter.

The group moves on, often the only foreigners on the trails in the summer mists. In one village we invite the women's savings and credit group to talk to them. A member laughs when she tells me how much they save each week. Their group savings really wouldn't go far up here, where inflation rises steeply every year. "Being in Sherpa culture has become too expensive in Khumbu," she says.

The students leave. I stay on, then later try to fly out from Lukla and get stuck in the fog for eight days before the plane arrives. In Kathmandu, the monsoon rains cease and summer finishes. I return in the autumn.

It is strange, trying to recall the last time you saw someone who lived, with such comforting regularity, at the periphery of your own life. My mind stubbornly insists that on the last day when my father and I were walking down towards Kathmandu for the winter, Au Tshiri called for us to come in for a cup of tea. But I know this may just be a trick of the brain, a composite of every other time he made that same invitation. In my memory, he's spinning a thread of yak wool through a spindle that dangles from his fingers, but again this may just be echoes from every other time I saw him, leaning in a sunny spot somewhere beside his house with the nasturtiums that grow up the front on strings that guide them, calling out to me, "When did you come? Where is your father?"

I try now to remember when in the last two years he began building the extension on his home, a retirement plan – a tea shop and bakery. But when exactly, spring or summer or autumn it was that we got that sack of rice as a contribution to the build and my aunt went down to help with something – digging a trench for a cable, perhaps? It eludes me. It seemed as long as I could remember there had been the chipping of rocks, the digging of foundations, the laying of stone, the smell of fresh cement as I walk past, observing now a window has gone in, a wall is up, the roof . . . until my father and I stopped in on him one time as we passed – from where? The everyday things you don't make note of – and it was finished, neatly painted, and he was inside making a tray of lamps for an offering. I'll make tea he said, this can wait – no, no, we replied, we'll come back another time.

It is spring again, and this year I am still in Kathmandu. The heat is stifling; I had forgotten what this time of year is like here. And then, on Friday, the news comes in, the body counts, four, no six, no ten . . . I call my father. I'm ok, he says in his measured, understated way, but things here are not good. Four from our Thame valley, he says, I heard someone from Khumjung, and two from Pangboche. Au Tshiri went as well.

For a moment, I think I have misunderstood.

On Monday the cremations happen. It was a good day, says my father, very clear and none of the wind or rain that can make a cremation difficult. His sons were both there. The most auspicious spot was on the slope with the waterfall, you know the one. From there we could see the smoke from another cremation happening down-valley in Phurte. I guess another one was happening up-valley too, but not for the one in Yullajhung, they didn't find his body . . .

A cowardly part of me is glad I am here in Kathmandu with only the hum of the neighbor's generator in my ears, not there, not listening to that conversation multiplied many-fold – so and so, from such and such a village, and so and so, from such and such a village, and so and so, such a nice man, with daughters and sons and wives and fathers, the brother of this one and the cousin of such and such, and the details, repeated over and over, that will break your heart – this was his last season, he said, or he had to go to pay off the debts from his brother's operation, or his leg had only just healed from his last climbing accident two years ago, or his mother had a bad premonition and begged him not to go. . . .

I picture next year, at gatherings around Khumbu, when the women sit with the women and the men sit with the men, when the children dart about and pull faces at each other from behind their parent's backs, and the cups of tea are poured and served first to the patriarchs, then to the householders, down the young fathers and husbands. In each line there will be gaps, like missing teeth – if remaining teeth could all shuffle forward, the way that the adolescents, now a little less awkward than last year, will move a little closer to the fire to fill the spaces of the ones that are missing.

THE BULLET AND THE BALLOT BOX

Aditya Adhikari

Aditya Adhikari is a journalist who has written widely on Nepali politics. Based in Kathmandu, he wrote a regular column for the *Kathmandu Post* between 2008 and 2012.

TWO REGIMES

The international media flocked to Nepal to cover the royal massacre in 2001 and discovered a raging insurgency. From then on, a steady flow of journalists came to explore what they perceived to be an exotic, anachronistic rebellion. By late 2004, reports in both the domestic and foreign press often stated that around 70 per cent of Nepal's countryside was under insurgent control. This was perfectly adequate shorthand: the Maoists were present and possessed influence in almost every part of the country. But the degree of their control varied considerably across districts. Their power was not absolute even in their strongholds, namely the hills and mountains of the mid- and far-western regions. Even within districts that were almost entirely controlled by the rebels, the state maintained a presence in the capitals. The Maoists did wield power in other areas, such as the hills in the eastern region, but their ability to exercise control over the population was more limited, given the frequent incursions of state security forces into those areas.

Nonetheless, the Maoists had successfully established a formidable parallel regime, and both sides strove to make territories under their sway impermeable to their enemy. The army barricaded sensitive installations and imposed curfews at dusk. In Musikot, the headquarters of Rukum, for instance government offices and schools were surrounded with barbed wire and mines.[1] Visitors from Maoist-controlled villages were treated with suspicion and often harshly interrogated. Officials in Bajura district's capital taunted villagers who came to collect government-provided rations: "You join Maoist marches and then presume we will give you rice?"[2] Travelling beyond the district capitals was also difficult, as people had to pass through multiple checkpoints where they had to explain the reasons for their travel. A trader in Baglung complained that his business had almost collapsed: "We need to get special permission from the local administration to supply dry food, batteries and other goods [to the villages.]"[3]

Meanwhile, Maoists posted sentries in their base areas to guard against incursions by the army. Outsiders who wished to enter these areas required prior permission from the rebels. Local residents, on the other hand, were discouraged from leaving their villages as they could leak sensitive information to the state security forces. And if too many people left the villages, who were the Maoists to indoctrinate or depend on for their needs? Villagers were hence required to obtain travel documents from the rebels if they wished to travel to the cities. If they wished to travel to India or the Gulf states for employment, they had to acquire a travel document *and* pay a tax. In some cases, travel was forbidden altogether. These measures were not always effective. Large numbers of people evaded the rebels and fled Nepal's villages during the years of the conflict, to seek work and shelter in the cities or in India. On occasion, therefore, the Maoists took more drastic measures to deter movement. In Kalikot district, for instance, they destroyed a bridge over the Karnali River, thus cutting off fifteen VDCs from the outside world.[4]

AMONG THE BELIEVERS

Some joined the Maoists out of compulsion or desperation, as when security forces killed their family members and they had nowhere else

[1] Kishore Nepal, *Under the Shadow of Violence*, Kathmandu: Centre for Professional Journalism Studies, 2005, p. 96.
[2] Ibid., 109.
[3] Ibid., p. 36.
[4] Sushil Sharma, *Napurine Ghauharu* (*Wounds that Cannot be Healed*), Surkhet: Manavadhikar Janautthan Kendra Nepal, 2008 (2065 v.s.), p. 45.

to turn for protection. Some were coerced into joining the party; while some of them came to believe in the rebels' worldview, others fled at the first opportunity.[5] Then, among the thousands of young people who joined the party during the war, there were also those who saw the movement as an escape from their circumscribed social lives and opportunities. The Maoists offered them an avenue for personal advancement and a medium for expressing their rage against society.

Devi Prasad Dhakal of Sindhupalchok exemplified the latter category. Born into straitened circumstances, he was sent to Kathmandu to work as a domestic servant at the age of seven. It was only two years later, when he went back to his village, that he began primary school. Later education posed its own challenges. The secondary school in which he enrolled was over an hour's walk from his house. He was always late for school, as he could leave home only after collecting fodder for the cattle and worshipping the family gods. This bred in him resentment towards his father and a hatred of religious rituals. He took to stealing grain from home and selling it for pocket money. In the absence of a supportive, encouraging environment, he failed his SLC examination. This foreclosed opportunities for going elsewhere, and he remained in his village, helping his brothers till their small plot of land.[6]

But Dhakal wanted more from life than his peasant ancestors. He grew increasingly bitter towards his family and their ways and thirsty for adventure and independence. In late 1998, he ran away to Pokhara, the second-largest city in Nepal's hill region. After a period of sleeping on the streets, he found a job as a busboy and dishwasher at a restaurant in the city's bustling tourist area. There he came under the influence of a college student who secretly supported the Maoists. Dhakal was a willing protégé; he felt he had finally found a way to enlarge his narrow existence. Politics had always attracted him. As a schoolboy he had heard that the communists stood up for the poor, and this had led him to become involved in the UML's student wing despite his family's

---

[5] See Human Rights Watch, "Children in the Ranks: The Maoists' Use of Child Soldiers in Nepal", vol. 19, no. 2(C), February 2007.

[6] "Rabindra", Devi Prasad Dhakal, *Ujyalo: Gajuri Byarek Breksammako Atmabrittanta (Light: My Story up to the Gajuri Barrack Break)*, Kathmandu: Jhilko Prakashan, 2011 (2068 v.s.).

disapproval. More recently, he had experienced the brutality of power first-hand. During one of his first nights in Pokhara, when he was sleeping on the street with some child beggars, a group of policemen had accosted them, beaten them up and taken all their money. Later, the son of a prominent Nepali Congress politician had shown up with a group of friends at the restaurant where Devi Prasad worked. They were rude and noisy, and Dhakal muttered that the politician's son looked like an animal fit for a zoo. Someone in the group overheard him, and they called the police. Dhakal was again beaten and locked up for the night. He thus became a convert to the idea of violence against authority.

Dhakal was initially tasked with distributing pamphlets, putting up posters at night and taking food and other items to rebels in jail. Gradually his responsibilities increased, and on 31 July 2000, he quit his restaurant job and went underground as a full-time Maoist activist.

Thus Devi Prasad Dhakal became one among many who left their families and homes to join a secretive, hierarchical and tightly knit group whose members were constantly on the move. They had to flee from villages when they heard that state security forces were approaching. Those assigned to the Maoist military had to trek through difficult terrain in the hills and mountains, often under cover of darkness, to reach the site of planned attacks. Those assigned political duties had to travel from village to village taking the party's ideology to the population. They had to walk long distances to deliver messages for their leaders, meet their counterparts from across the country and establish party committees in new areas.

The hardships were severe. They often had to go hungry and sleep in the open. Then there was the ever-present fear of injury, torture or death at the hands of the security forces. Many who joined the rebels in an initial surge of enthusiasm soon fled back home, despite the possibility of reprisals.[7] But for many others, it was the first time they had become part of a collectivity with a fixed goal, and this offered a kind

---

[7] During a visit to Jumla district during 2005, the journalist Sushil Sharma met a group of schoolchildren who had been attracted by Maoist propaganda and joined the party. Unable to bear the hardships, they had soon returned home. But the local Maoists threatened the school authorities with consequences if they allowed the children to re-enroll, and urged them to rejoin the party. Sharma, *Napurine Ghauharu*, pp. 56–63.

of fulfilment and liberation. The party satisfied their desire for power and tamed their discontent and restlessness, and it was easy to find camaraderie and companionship among fellow rebels who often came from similar backgrounds.

They were taught to see themselves as exemplars of a new *janabadi* culture in the making, a culture that would encompass the entire nation when the party took power and established a Maoist New Democracy (*Naya Janabad*). *Janabad* is the term for democracy commonly used by Nepal's communists, and as such emphasizes socio-economic rather than political equality. (In contrast, the words *prajatantra*, and later, *loktantra*, have been used to describe political systems that prioritize the values of liberal democracy.) The adjective *janabadi* is usually translated as "democratic" although "proletarian" better conveys its meaning.

The Maoists defined their *janabadi* culture in opposition to the dominant culture of the countryside, which they viewed as being caste-ridden and superstitious. Their activists were encouraged to deliberately transgress traditional norms. They often ate beef, for example, breaking the powerful Hindu taboo. The *janabadi* culture also opposed the "bourgeois" culture of Nepal's urban middle class, where individualism reigned and Hindi films and images of Western consumerism shaped desires. Maoist activists were taught to embrace fierce collectivism and reject inwardness. As the Maoist leader Jayapuri Gharti wrote in a letter to a junior activist, "You have been fulfilling your role but I feel that is not enough . . . You seem rather introverted. You should open up and participate more actively in debates and discussions. You should break out of the world's social formalities and expand your relationships."[8]

These activists mostly came from rural backgrounds, and during the war they travelled extensively through villages across the country. Meanwhile the state security forces maintained a strong presence in urban areas, whose large populations were mostly unsympathetic to the Maoist cause. Whenever rebels from rural areas visited the cities, they would find themselves lost and isolated. An activist assigned to Kathmandu wrote to a fellow comrade in another region during a

---

[8] Mohit Shrestha, *Jyudo Sapana* (*Living Dreams*), Kathmandu: Akhil Nepal Janasanskritik Mahasangh, Kendriya Samiti, 2009 (2065 v.s.), p. 120.

particularly trying moment: "I hope you have been informed about the situation in the valley. The army has captured all of our responsible comrades. Only a few of us remain. We are not in touch with any of the responsible senior comrades. What should we do? What shouldn't we do? We are in great confusion."[9] This was after the collapse of the second cease-fire when the army had virtually decimated the Maoist organization in the city.

In such moments of strain and hardship, the young Maoist activists would have found ideological succour in what their leaders had taught them and the books they had read. To instil *janabadi* values in their cadres, the leadership encouraged them to read the revolutionary fiction that had inspired them in their own youth. The Nepali translation of the slim Chinese novel *Bright Red Star* was especially popular among the younger Maoist activists.[10] Those who found themselves alienated in the city might have identified with Tung-Tzu, the protagonist of *Bright Red Star*.

The story begins in the 1930s. Tung-Tzu's father goes to join the Chinese revolutionaries, and then a local landowner kills his mother. He spends part of his childhood among communist guerrillas (who are depicted as universally trustworthy, brave and willing to sacrifice their lives for the cause of their country's liberation). But for reasons of safety, he is later sent to work at a rice shop in the city. Tung-Tzu has to conceal his identity, loses touch with the party comrades, and is treated harshly by his employer.

The rice shop owner is an avaricious, unscrupulous man who sells rice mixed with stones. Even when the whole city is starving, he hoards grain, hoping to sell it at a more lucrative time. Tung-Tzu witnesses how the shopkeeper bribes the police, and soon learns that the shopkeeper

---

[9] Lekhnath Neupane, *Chitthima Janayuddha* (*The People's War in Letters*), Kathmandu: Vivek Sirjanshil Prakashan, 2008 (2065 v.s.), p. 55.

[10] Li Xintian, *Chamkilo Rato Tara* (*Bright Red Star*) [1974], translated by Sitaram Tamang, Kathmandu: Pragati Pustak Sadan, 2003 (2060 v.s.). In her study on youth participation in the Maoist rebellion, Ina V. Zharkevich notes how the majority of her informants mentioned this novel as their favourite book. She further writes that newcomers to the Maoist military camps in Kathmandu were each given a copy of the novel, which, along with an English–Nepali dictionary and Sun Tzu's *The Art of War*, was considered essential reading for PLA fighters. Ina Zharkevich, "A New Way of Being Young in Nepal: The Idea of Maoist Youth and Dreams of a New Man," *Studies in Nepali History of Society* 14, No. 1 (2009), p. 86.

is also on good terms with the landowner who killed his mother and was complicit with Japanese imperialists. I began to understand clearly, Tung-Tzu says, "that the oppressive local landowner, the profiteering shopkeeper of the city, the police captain, the forces of the White Army and the Japanese imperialists all belonged to the same group."

These words must have resonated with the Nepali Maoist activist who had landed in the city. Like Tung-Tzu, he would have seen all the hostile aspects of society as branches of a single oppressive power. He would have likened himself to the young Chinese revolutionary in the novel, and gained a stronger faith in the Maoist cause. Seeing how Tung-Tzu eventually return to the guerrillas, avenges his mother's murder, and participates in the Communist capture of Beijing, he might have thought, as his superiors insisted, that a Maoist victory was historically inevitable.

An article by the activist Khil Bahadur Bhandari echoes Tung-Tzu's feelings about the city/country divide. While spending two nights in the town of Hetauda amid fears of being captured by the army, he wrote:

People in the city live an extremely confined life. "They are status-quoist and opportunists. They lack empathy; they don't care whether other people live or die. They are only concerned with their own happiness . . . But people in the villages are not status-quoists and opportunists. One person's suffering draws on everyone's empathy. A new ideology and new power have taken the villages by storm, and they are far ahead of the cities in the [political] movement.

GOPAL KIRATI

Gopal Kirati was one of the Janajati leaders whom the Maoists won over to their side after persistent efforts. He was born into the Khambu community in 1955, in the mountain district of Solukhumbu in eastern Nepal. His memoir offers a familiar leftist narrative of rural oppression and victimhood during the Panchayat regime. Kirati recalls how his family suffered under the *pradhan pancha* (local chief) in his village. He was in his early teens when his father died, and his mother had to sell their family land, livestock, jewellery and their prized radio set to pay off their loans to the *pradhan pancha*. Kirati quit school after seventh grade and worked as a porter for six years, carrying loads for tourists trekking through Nepal's mountains. Despite the hardships, Kirati enjoyed travelling and observing the various peoples and cultures across the country.

Like many others who would later join the Maoists, Gopal Kirati was initiated into the communist movement by a relative. Hari Narayan Thulung, his brother-in-law, was a schoolteacher affiliated with one of the communist factions. In 1983, when the twenty-eight-year-old Kirati was considering joining the British Army, Thulung tried to dissuade him by giving him a copy of *Seema*, a play by the popular leftist poet-musician Rayan. The play depicted the sufferings of Nepalis recruited into the British army. It had a shattering effect on Kirati. He recalled that after reading the play, he said to his brother-in-law: "We are indeed a wretched lot. I must do something with my life. What should I do if I don't join a foreign army?" Hari Narayan replied, "We have to launch a revolution in the name of the country and the people."[11]

However, in succeeding years, Kirati's attraction to communism was superseded by his growing empathy for the ethnic struggle. While staying in Kathmandu during his travels, he became involved with various organizations working to preserve and promote Kirati culture. Kirati made friends with fellow Janajatis who worked as labourers in the tourist and carpet industries. He helped organize celebrations during important Kirati festivals such as Yokwa, Chasok and Sakewa. He told his friends Kirati folk tales that he had heard from his mother as a child, the same stories he used to tell his childhood friends back in the village. "Looking back," Gopal wrote years later, "I feel that it was through telling stories that I started to become a leader."[12]

Gopal Kirati participated in the 1990 movement for democracy, but refused to support any of the major parties. Along with some friends, he published and distributed pamphlets which, while supporting the cause of democracy, prioritized ethnic claims. "There should be democracy, not Brahminism (*Bahunbad hoina, prajatantra hunuparchha*)," was their message. "Ethnic rights should be guaranteed, the state

---

[11] Ogura, 'Realities and Images of Nepal's Maoists after the Attack on Beni' (n/p. revised version, unpublished).

[12] Mao, 'On Protracted War'.

should be made secular." On 6 April Kirati took part in demonstrations in Durbar Marg, the street in front of the royal palace. He was badly beaten by the police and had to get eight stitches on his head. He was still in hospital when he heard the news that the king had agreed to dismantle the Panchayat system and restore multi-party democracy. The news caused widespread jubilation, but Kirati was unmoved. By now he firmly believed that violent struggle alone could bring about a real social transformation: "I believed that a new political system could only be established through the sacrifice of thousands of martyrs."[13]

Like many other ethnic activists, Kirati started his own organization, the Khambuwan National Front (KNF), soon after the establishment of parliamentary democracy. The KNF aimed to forge a more militant ethos than other ethnic organizations. "The 1990 constitution enabled the oppressed nationalities to rise up," wrote Kirati, "but it did not give them their rights."[14] As the constitution did not allow formation of parties along ethnic lines, the particular grievances of ethnic groups remained unaddressed. This, according to Kirati, was what led him to choose the path of armed struggle.

The Maoists' declaration of People's War in 1996 emboldened Gopal Kirati. He issued a public statement indicating "qualified support" for the Maoists. On 22 July 1997, the KNF carried out bomb attacks in three locations in Bhojpur and Solukhumbu districts. In each location the target of the attack was a Sanskrit school – a potent symbol of upper caste culture and tradition. Kirati had launched his struggle for ethnic autonomy.

Kirati's statement came at a time when few people openly supported the Maoists. It attracted the attention of Maoist leaders, even though his organization was relatively obscure. Thinking that an alliance with Kirati could gain them support in the east, the Maoists sent Suresh Ale Magar to meet him. Later, Baburam Bhattarai invited him to Gorakhpur, a town in North India.[15] In April 1998, following negotiations, the two publicly declared that they had formed an alliance.

---

[13] Ibid.

[14] Dhaneshwar Pokhrel, *Beni Morchako Smriti: Shabdachitra* (*Memories of the Beni Front*), Kathmandu: Akhil Nepal Lekhak Sangh, 2010 (2067 v.s.), p. 3.

[15] Interview with senior Maoist leader, January 2013.

But the alliance fell apart after seven months. Kirati denounced the Maoists and resumed his armed struggle independently. The Maoists managed to placate him, only to antagonize him again. This became the pattern of their relationship. As both sides were caught in the perils of war against the state and had few allies, each would periodically reach out to the other. Before long, quarrels would erupt and Kirati would announce that he had parted ways with the Maoists.[16]

The friction arose partly because the Maoists sought not only to cultivate Kirati but also to educate him. In a May 1998 piece about the Khambuwan National Front, Bhattarai praised Kirati's writing for expressing rage against ethnic oppression and commitment to armed struggle. The KNF's desire to ally with the Maoists was commendable, he said, but Kirati seemed guided more by passion than reason. "Revolutionaries need both intellect and emotion," Bhattarai wrote. "Although emotions dominate in the early phase, intellect must eventually take precedence over emotions."[17]

In Bhattarai's view, the KNF's singular focus on ethnicity was misguided. Kirati had not understood that ethnic groups had evolved with the development of productive forces, he wrote. There are no inherent differences between the various ethnic groups. Rather, the characteristics of each ethnic group were determined by their position in the changing relations of production. Because the KNF had not grasped this properly, its members perceived the upper castes of the hills as their sole enemy and main obstacle to their liberation. Their demand for autonomy hearkened back to the tribalism of a bygone era, when the country was divided into many tiny principalities. But a return to the days of self-contained and self-governing ethnic units was no longer possible or desirable. The KNF's struggle should be directed not merely against the upper castes, but rather against the 'feudal thought and behaviour' within all caste and ethnic groups.[18] KNF members should develop class consciousness and ally with the poor and oppressed from all groups.

---

[16] For details see Dambar Krishna Shrestha 'Ethnic Autonomy in the East', in *People in the People's War*, Kathmandu: Himal Books, 2004, p. 17–40.

[17] Bhattarai, 'Khambu Sangharshako Rooprekhabare Kehi Tippani (Some Comments on the Form of the Khambu Struggle)', pp. 202–6 in *Nepali Krantika Aadharharu*, p. 202.

[18] Ibid., p. 205.

Although he was not in principle opposed to these Maoist beliefs, Gopal Kirati was deeply suspicious of them. Through the 1970s
and 1980s, communist leaders who would later form the UML had
preached the doctrine of the primacy of class in the eastern hills. Kirati
supporters were told that their traditions were retrogressive, and urged
to break from them. But after the UML transformed into a parliamentary party, its predominantly upper-caste leaders had abandoned their
Kirati cadre. "The UML reduced Marxism, which emphasizes the need
to fight against all kinds of injustice including ethnic oppression, to the
trite slogan of class liberation," wrote Kirati. "Today it has degenerated
into a party of Brahminical counter-revolutionaries."[19] Kirati believed
that by emphasizing class and undermining the importance of ethnicity,
the upper-caste communist leaders had deliberately tried to perpetuate
their dominance over the marginalized ethnic groups.

As part of their effort to discipline and educate Gopal Kirati, the
Maoists tried to merge the Khambuwan National Front into their own
organization. In October 2001, following negotiations, the KNF was
officially merged with the Maoist-affiliated Limbuwan Liberation Front
to form the Kirat National Front. Kirati proposed that he should lead
a separate armed force, but the Maoist leaders rejected the idea. They
believed that Khambuwan cadre were undisciplined and needlessly
violent in their dealings with the population, and had to be tamed.
They also insisted that a centralized military structure was necessary
for the success of the armed struggle. They demanded that KNF cadre
be merged into the People's Liberation Army. Kirati and his supporters,
chafing at what they perceived to be Maoist high-handedness, once
again severed ties with the Maoists. On some occasions, the cadres of
the two organizations beat up and even killed one another.

Eventually, however, Kirati was won over. On 15 July 2003, his
organization permanently merged with the Maoists. It had become
clear that he would not be able to wage armed struggle independently.
His organization remained small and negligible, while the Maoists
had become immensely powerful. They commanded substantial influence even in the eastern hills. Moreover, by now Kirati was convinced

---

[19] Kirati, *Sarvahara Netritvako Saval*, p. 128.

that the Maoists were genuinely committed to ethnic demands, even though their top leaders were predominantly upper-caste. On several occasions Maoist chairman Prachanda met Kirati privately to convince him of the Maoists' positive intentions. Kirati was given membership in the Maoist central committee and the United Revolutionary People's Council (URPC), the Maoists' parallel government.

The degree to which Kirati had internalized the Maoist point of view was manifest in a speech he made in Khotang district in January 2004. The occasion was a mass meeting where the Maoists declared the establishment of the Kirat Autonomous Region People's Government and appointed him as its head. In the past, said Gopal Kirati, the struggle of the Kirati people had been of a purely ethnic nature. But as Kiratis had now achieved leadership of the parallel government under Maoist leadership, they should not seek to dominate the members of the other castes and ethnicities who lived in the region. Otherwise they would be no different from the feudal rulers. Rather, class should now take precedence over ethnic claims. The Maoists would work to ensure that the *jana sarkars* represented all the caste and ethnic groups in the region. Those who did not accept this policy would be guilty of ethnic chauvinism.[20]

---

[20] Ibid., p. 170.

KATHMANDU

Thomas Bell

Thomas Bell is a British journalist and author. He studied at Oxford and the Courtauld Institute of Art before moving to Kathmandu to cover the civil war in Nepal for the *Daily Telegraph* and *The Economist*. He was later Southeast Asia correspondent for the *Daily Telegraph*. He lives in Kathmandu with his family.

In Asia old objects are not generally considered beautiful for their age, which is a peculiarly Western taste. New things are preferred, so ancient wooden carvings are periodically touched up with colourful enamel paints. The fabric of the temples is layered, as they are renewed with fresh donations. When temples are rebuilt after an earthquake, which occur on average about once a century, old pieces of carved timber might be reused even as the structure is altered and worn out parts replaced. In this way these holy buildings are both old and new. Rather, like other things in nature, such as a whirlpool, a forest, or a coral reef, they are constantly occurring in the same place. It is possible, up to a point, to look at the whole city as just such an eternal system.

When Sundar Man Shrestha was a teenager in the early 1960s his mother used to wake up screaming because in her sleep she was being strangled by a witch. "Every night she screamed and it was a real problem for us," he emphasized. He hung one of his brother's nappies at the door, hoping that might keep the witch away, but it didn't work.

Waking one morning he found a large cat in the house, peeping at his sleeping mother through a gap in a door. "It was a big cat, this big, and I said 'Cat, you are a witch. I am going to kill you'." The cat was trapped in a room, backed into a corner. "I kicked it and it went back on its legs like this, it put its front paws out in front, and it disappeared.

The image faded."

After that the bad dreams stopped, but there were other hauntings. During the spirit-infested season that follows the horse festival, in the spring month of Chaitra, it used to be necessary to eat more garlic, just to keep the ghosts away. Old people remember a large one that would block the passage into Nag Bahal, one of Patan's biggest squares, and refuse to let anyone pass. Around the corner, at the fountain by the Kumbeshwor temple, the slapping sound of a woman washing clothes was sometimes heard after midnight. If she caught you before you fled the square, you would die. And near the bridge between Patan and Kathmandu there was a rankebhoot – a "lamp ghost", which may only have been the light of phosphorescent gasses escaping from the rice fields. The children who lived down there enjoyed watching travellers running in the evening, to be within the safety of the city before night fell. It wasn't only the rankebhoot that frightened them. The kitchkandi under the bridge posed an even greater hazard.

"These things have been disappearing since electricity came," said Sundar Man. "Before, people used to terrify each other with stories."

"They've all gone. They were all scared," agreed his mother-in-law, Dhana Laksmi. She wore a hat and a hearing aid. Her eyes twinkled and she had one tooth left on top at the front. She poked it forward coquettishly to show when she was teasing. I wanted her to be my informant on the traditions of the city and I returned to her for advice frequently. She considered me pitifully ignorant of the realities of nature. Now she looked at me with concern. Did this interest in ghosts mean I was having trouble with them?

The only ghost Dhana Laksmi ever saw was in the yard outside her house, when she went to sweep before dawn one morning, decades ago. It looked like an old woman but it was smaller than a living person. When she asked it what it wanted it left without speaking to her. After that she never stepped out until first light. "You'd be afraid too, if you saw it," she pointed out.

The ghosts hadn't disappeared altogether. Kitchkandis are spectres that stalk beneath bridges, in the disguise of a beautiful woman. If she seduces a man then he will die, but he has a chance because her identity is betrayed by her feet, which point backwards. To keep kitchkandis at bay some taxi drivers hang a charm of women's bangles from their rear view mirror. I asked them if they were afraid, and the young men mostly laughed, but one driver offered a subtle view. Since the fields around the city had been covered with housing there were fewer ghosts than there used to be, he said. However, although he wasn't a Newar himself, he believed that the old spirits still haunt those areas where many Newars live.

Sometimes when the electricity returns after a power cut, even if the lights, the kettle and the fan don't immediately come on, something almost imperceptible changes and you realize that the power is back. Everyone lives surrounded by wires, buried in their own walls and in the houses all around them. When a man and a boy came to install cable television they brought the line from a tangle on a pole somewhere, through a low passage and over a rooftop, looped it from the corner of one building to the next and arrived at my bedroom window, adding another strand to the complicated web of the city's wiring.

The air is a living vehicle of radio, text messages and wireless internet. The ground is scored and raised by a network of poorly repaired trenches, where extra pipes have been added to the water mains until the pressure is so low that, during the few hours a week when the water flows, people use pumps to get it out of the pipe and into the tanks beneath their houses. The ancient, buried conduits that supply the fountains are little understood. Sometimes a spout that had been dry for decades would flow again after an earthquake, before the depredations upon the aquifers and the deeper foundations of modern developments made half of them permanently derelict. Wells, tanker deliveries, rubber hoses and the copper jars carried on the hips of women complete the city's water system.

Another infrastructure, no less recognized and more slowly changing, runs through the old parts of the city. A grandmother spirit, who can be nasty, inflicting severe stomach cramps or worse if she is not properly invoked, resides at junctions in the chwasa stones. People bring objects that present a magical threat to their household to the chwasa: the clothes of the dead, a baby's umbilical cord, or the ashes of a torch that has been used in an exorcism.

Nasahdya, the god of sound, is represented by an empty space; a triangular hole in a wall that opens his passage through the buildings, because he can only travel in straight lines. Every neighbourhood has its guardians; its own full set of those gods (Nasahdya, Ganesh, Durga, Bhairab . . .) that daily life requires. Apart from the empty space of Nasahdya, these guardians are uncarved, natural stones, which have never been moved from the place where the earth divulged them. They form a network of gods and goddesses, spirits and ancestors that underpins the city, its genii loci.

Many courtyards have another stone somewhere, which is Lukmahdya, the Hidden Shiva. The old lady Dhana Laksmi told me Lukmahdya's story on his feast day, wrinkling her nose and poking her tooth at me. The god entered the city after he'd given a demon the power to turn people into ash and, realizing that he needed somewhere to hide, he chose the garbage of the courtyards for his camouflage. "You know that small yard?" she said. "That's where we used to throw our rubbish. That's where he is." Even heaps of reeking trash were holy, if they were in the right place. Even the dogs in the street and the crows on the roof were gods, and had their annual festivals.

[I saw in Patan] a large number of destroyed houses, as the natives rarely repair a house: rather, anyone who regards himself as a man of distinction constructs himself a new house and lets that of his father decay.[1]

–Prince Waldemar of Prussia (visited in 1845)

Hirakaji's son Sunil pointed out a house to me while we were walking together, a low brick building with tiny windows filled by wooden grilles, where as a boy he once paid a few rupees to watch a pornographic film. The same house had belonged to Gayahbajye, who was a famous priest and a powerful magician. His powers were so great that he transported gods from different parts of the Valley and placed them in the temples near his home. A room inside has been left empty since he vanished while meditating there hundreds of years ago.

The low wooden door was opened by a woman who introduced

---

[1] Kaevrne, Pat (transl). 1979. 'The Visit of Prince Waldemar of Prussia to Nepal in February and March 1845'. *Kailash* 7(1). p. 39.

herself as Gayahbajye's daughter-in-law, by which she meant that she was married to his remote descendent. The lady was an amateur painter and she had decorated the small low rooms with her own watercolours, of birds and local monuments. She showed me the special room, with an electric lamp through a hole in the kitchen wall. It was dark, with a pile of timber in it. Some priests, and officials from the government's Department of Archaeology, had come to investigate the mystery, she said, but when they started digging the room began to fill with water and they abandoned the attempt. She spoke as if it was yesterday, but this happened fifty years ago, before she was born. Every morning she worshiped the wall outside with poinsettia flowers and rice.

Gayahbajye's house stood in a square of fine old buildings, until old houses on two sides were replaced with new ones in the early 1990s. Enclosing the square to the south was the imposing fifteenth-century shrine of a secret god, open only to initiates of Gayahbajye's lineage, until part of it was demolished in 1996. In 1997 half of Gayahbajye's house was torn down too.[2] Kathmandu people do not find the old houses picturesque. Sometimes a magnificent carved window, centuries old, is cut in half when a brother – inheriting his part of the ancestral property – rebuilds his side in brightly painted concrete. There is no charm in inertia; living in a small dark house in the shadow of your brother's lofty statement, your wife jealous of your brother's wife. In this way the city is constantly renewed by the ambition of pious family men.

The prayer for consecrating a new house begins:

"Oh well-born son! Any man in Nepal, whether he be a philanthropist or not, should build a house as follows: assemble carpenters and brick makers and other incarnations of Bisvakarma as necessary. Then, choosing an auspicious time, prepare and bake bricks. Have the auspiciously ordained foundation laying ceremony . . . Then build a magnificent house with the proper auspicious marks and proportions. If a man does this, I call him great."[3]

---

[2] Niels Gutschow. 'Urban Patterns in Patan', in *The Sulima Pagoda* pp. 81–86.
[3] 'Prayers Read at the Consecration of a House', published in Slusser, *Nepal Mandala*, pp. 420–21.

The family priest will determine whether or not a proposed building site is auspicious or is, for example, already occupied by naga serpents. An astrologer will determine whether the venture is a wise investment, and the best time to start work.

Dhana Laksmi told me the story of a shopkeeper in Mangal Bazar, called Hem Narayan. He was advised that if he built where he intended then the nagas who lived there would have no outlet, and would bang their heads on his foundation. He took a cavalier attitude.

"If the nagas bang their heads who will suffer?" he asked.

"The oldest man in the family."

"What about the kids, will they be affected?"

"No," he was assured. "The kids will be fine."

"I might as well, then," the old man reasoned. "I'm going to die soon anyway."

The foundation was laid but before the first storey was complete he and his brother fell ill. When the fever subsided, twenty-one days later, they found themselves preposterously stooped. Their heads bobbed in front of their shoulders like tortoises'. Their caste was Mahaju and people knew them from then on as the leaning Mahajus.

For as long as the streets and courtyards have lain where they do now a house has been about eighteen feet from front to back, with a wall in the middle, dictated by the nine-foot span of the floor beams. Wealthy families and kings built four blocks at one time to create a courtyard. For the rest that was achieved more gradually, until a space was enclosed by four houses and an extended family enjoyed their privacy and security within. This courtyard is a chowk, where children play, clothes are washed, grain is dried, men gamble at cards and the family eats feasts. The chowks are the basic unit of the old quarters. The height of the roofs' ridge beams, where they met each other end to end or at right angles, was roughly the same. The skyline was a hand-knitted pattern of clay-tiled slopes, with the pagoda-roofs of the temples rising above them.

O client, many lucky signs must be present and many rules of proportion must be observed when a house is built . . . First the smoke of the brick kiln goes up to heaven and the 330 million gods smell it and ask where it came from; the king of the gods, Indra, tells them that it is the smell of smoke made on earth by an ambitious man who is firing bricks to build a house to stay in; and the gods, hearing him, immediately give their blessing: "Fortunate and upright man! May this house be well favoured; may it be durable; may it be without flaw; may it be a dwelling place of Laksmi; may the builder live long; may his heart's desire be fulfilled!"[4]

To stop the rain from washing away the mud between the bricks Kathmandu's builders invented a wedge-shaped brick, which covers the joints and gives the most prestigious buildings a smooth burnished lustre. These walls are prone to bulging under their own weight so a wooden frame is made to stiffen them, like the steel inside reinforced concrete but much more expensive. Where the timbers show on the surface they are decorated with carved serpents and the heads of animals.

The foundations are not deep so, in time, uneven settlement will cause the walls to crack. And, because the stones of the foundation do not rise above ground level, the base of the walls will be exposed to surface water making the ground floor damp. At every stage of the construction, as the door jambs and lintels, window frames, floors, ridge beam and roof tiles are put in place, a puja is done and red and yellow powder is smeared on the unfinished building. In this way the gods run through the house like the wiring. There will be a few small gaps in the brickwork where the bamboo scaffolding was fixed. They will be overlooked when the builders leave and sparrows will nest there. No nails are used anywhere in the structure. If water seeps in and rots the pegs that hold the frame together an empty house can be ruined in a few monsoons.

The ground floor is a shop, storeroom or workshop. The sleeping and living quarters are in the middle and the purest and most private places, the kitchen and the puja room, are nearest to heaven.

O well-born, may the merit of your good deed help you to attain the four goals of life, the seven kinds of well-being, the eight kinds of property, and rid you of the eight terrors . . . may you have good fortune and happiness in all ten directions and at all three times.

4 Prayer for consecrating a house, reproduced in Slusser, *Nepal Mandala*, pp. 420–421.

Good luck to the whole world!

In the old parts of the city, when people refer to a house they often mean the site it stands on, and every structure that has ever stood on that site. It is a continuous family institution, of which the fabric (like the people in it) is continually replaced. When someone breaks down the beautiful old brick and timber house his ancestor made, and builds for his family in their ancient place a new concrete home (ugly inside and out, and cold in the winter) the new structure retains the centuries-old shape of the plot and the hierarchy between the storeys above it. Before he starts to build he digs a hole, does a puja in it, and fills it in. Then he digs the foundation.

Hirakaji and all of his neighbours, who were descended from the same ancestor, had each rebuilt their share of the ancestral site in concrete. The old house, before it was divided by inheritance, must have been large, with a passage through the centre into the chowk behind. One afternoon I was working at my desk, and I suppose I was unable to concentrate, because I wandered onto the roof to look out over the rooftops and the pinnacle of the Mahabuddha temple, and someone bolted the door from the inside. I was stuck up there, until a neighbour appeared on his roof. I stepped over the low wall and followed him down his stairs. The upper floors of his house were dark, the walls were unplastered and the windows were unglazed. We passed through rooms piled with the clay moulds of statues, and down unlit stairs, until we emerged not on the other side of the passage, as I expected, but into the chowk behind. The history of the family had made a labyrinth inside that group of buildings.

At its most local levels, of the neighbourhood, or the individual house, Kathmandu is ordered by religious concepts, either around holy stones, or divinely sanctioned carpentry and bricklaying techniques. The same is also true of the city as a whole.

In the sacred diagrams called mandala the principal god or goddess is worshipped in the centre, surrounded by a retinue of related deities, representing the different aspects of the governing spirit's nature, and their relationship to the power at the centre.[5] A mandala is something

---

[5] 'A mandala is an arrangement of deities conceived of in sets (of four, eight, sixty-four or more) laid out along the axes of the cardinal points around a centre.' David Gell-

like an icon, which channels the power of the god it depicts, and therefore something like a prayer or a spell. I also read that each ancient city is a giant mandala, a diagram of the order of the universe, with the king's palace at the centre, surrounded at the margins by the temples of the Eight Mother Goddesses, by the twelve sacred bathing places and the eight cremation grounds.[6]

So I went to see a Buddhist priest of the Vajracharya caste – a gubaju – because they are the ones with the power and the responsibility to master and mediate this side of life to the laity. I had a whole sheet of typed questions: What does the city's mandala mean? Does it belong to a particular god? What's the meaning of the festival of Mataya? (I thought the tortuous route of that day-long procession might hold some secret.) Can one also think of a single house as a mandala? Would it be possible to draw a map of the city, which wasn't a map of chowks or streets but a map of gods? I was fascinated by the idea that the city had a secret design, but I couldn't understand what the nature or meaning of such a scheme could be, so I didn't know what to ask him.

The gubaju lived in an upstairs room by the bus park at Lagankhel. The passage to his narrow stair was stacked with boxes of the same crockery and thermos flasks as were for sale on the pavement outside. The walls of his room were almost entirely covered by pictures of gods, and tableaux of traditional life, which seemed to have been cut from magazines or calendars. Especially prominent were several large pictures of himself in his robes, adopting special postures, with a bright sunburst inserted behind his head by the photo studio. On the windowsill there were two white doves in an iron cage. It was a bright fresh autumn day and the gubaju had his windows open. On my recording of the interview there is a constant hubbub of the bus conductors and market traders outside.

The gubaju was in his eighties, sitting cross-legged on the floor. He rifled through heaps of paper and handed me photocopied scraps: a mandala of the goddess Durga with a Sanskrit text beneath; a Newari

ner, *Monk, Householder and Tantric Priest.* p. 190.

[6] 'A mandala is a circle, a mystic diagram of varied form, and in ancient Indian usage signified an administrative unit or country. From at least the sixth century ad., in conjunction with the word 'Nepal' it signified to the Nepalese the Kathmandu Valley and surrounding territory.' Mary Shepherd Slusser, *Nepal Mandala*. p. vii.

text he'd composed himself on the faults of modern society, and the rituals that would correct them; a list of forty-nine holy places of the Valley that he had visited and their holy days; and a history of his most illustrious ancestor, a tantric who performed magic acts. He chuckled and pulled his legs tighter around himself as he talked. I asked him about the city's mandala.

"In ancient times," the gubaju said, "the Kathmandu Valley was a lake and at that time it was a golden age. In the Age of Treta, the bodhisatva Manjushree cut the mountain and let the water flow out. Only then people started settling here."

That much I knew. I asked him about the mandala again and he said, "It is like a mandala. The centre is Gujeshwori. In whichever direction you go from there, east, west or whichever, is 7 kos [14 miles]. People celebrate the day Manjushree cut the mountain on the tenth day of the waning moon of Mangshir." He took out his charts and showed me.

I pressed him again. "Actually, we don't talk in detail about the mandala," he admitted. "It includes everything, birds, animals, human beings, everything, but we're not allowed to explain it. The first god that was created was Gujeshwori, who is both male and female and began creating the other creatures. All the other creatures came out of Gujeshwori." I was following him more or less. I knew that at Gujeshwori there is a hole in the ground, fringed with stone petals, which is related to female power somehow. It does stand somewhere near the centre of the Valley. And I wasn't surprised by his secretiveness, because I had read that gubajus reveal the real truth of their religion only to the initiated, and there would be no question of my ever receiving it.

We were interrupted by a woman who had come with her two children to consult him as a healer or magician. The children, she complained, were not doing well at school. He prescribed some rituals. She touched her head to his feet, and she paid him with a small plastic bag of what seemed to be flour. After they'd gone I tried another tack and asked him about the Eight Mother Goddesses, whose temples are in a ring around the city.

"The Eight Mothers are outside the city, not inside," he said. "We can explain it up to the Eight Mothers, but the mandala inside the circle of the Eight Mothers we cannot explain. Eight is a very significant number. They are for protecting people against disease, fire, water and so on. These goddesses are located in the eight directions."

He talked about many things. I tried to hold him to what I saw as the point, and to work through my list of questions, but I may as well have been asking "How many hamburgers make a Wednesday?" for all the sense my questions seemed to make to the gubaju. I drew a diagram of concentric circles like I'd seen in a book, representing the location of the most important buildings in the centre of the city and the lowest on the outskirts, and I asked him about it.[7]

"In the past," he said, "when you are in high rank you go nearer to the centre and if you are poor and of low rank you have to move out of the city. The king, the palace, is in the centre and near the palace are the higher-ranked people."

"Maybe it was to do with land prices?" I said.

He ignored it. "In the centre are located the gods and goddesses. In the next yoni come . . . how to explain it? . . . they are just like spirits. Then comes the human yoni. Then comes the demon yoni, then the animal yoni. The furthest place is Narka. Narka is hell. Altogether there are six yonis," he said, noticing that I had sketched only five. The gubaju spread out a different mandala on the floor between us. "This is simplified," he assured me. "A small number of gods are depicted – there are sixty-four gods here. The deeper you go the more gods there are.

"I don't know about Kathmandu but I know in detail about the Patan area," he said. "I have a dispute with the priests of Kathmandu. They say I don't know about the things of Kathmandu, but when we have debates about religion I have defeated them many times, because I have done research on this mandala which they have not done."

I left when the old man had talked for as long as he wanted to, and at the time I was disappointed I hadn't received a clearer explanation, perhaps resembling some kind of map. Now it seems he gave as clear an account as I could have hoped for. And for what it was worth I already had a book with a translation of the liturgy that gubajus use, describing the Valley's mandala. So if he wouldn't discuss it with me, or

---

[7] Gellner. *Monk, Householder and Tantric Priest*, p. 48. 406 notes.

if I couldn't understand his explanations, I could get some impression. When a gubaju begins a ritual he recites in Sanskrit:

> OM, now in the period of the Attained One, Lion of the Sakyas [i.e. the Buddha] . . . in the Kali world era . . . in the Himalayas . . . in the land of Nepal . . . flowing with the four great rivers . . . adorned with the twelve holy bathing places . . . surrounded by the mountains . . . the Eight Mothers, the Eight Bhairavas . . . on the south bank of the Bagmati . . . in the city of Lalitapattana [i.e. Patan], in the kingdom of Aryavalokitesvara [i.e. the red god Bungadya, who came down my street in his giant cart] . . .[8]

Working from the inside out, it would go something like this: in the centre is the Buddhist god Cakrasamvara, surrounded by four goddesses and the four Kings of the Directions. Then there are three circles of lotuses, thunderbolts and flames. In life, the king's palace sits in the centre. He is not exactly a god, but anyone can incarnate aspects of the divine and in the king's case he incarnates aspects of the loftier lords in heaven. His palace is surrounded by the temples of the greatest Hindu gods. They receive pure, vegetarian, non-alcoholic offerings from Brahmin priests. Courtier families and priests live near the palace and the various other castes live among one another throughout the city. Each caste has its own affinities to different gods, according to its nature and occupation. In the middle ranks of the caste system, for example, Jyapu men (of the farming caste) have an affinity with Bhairab, Shiva in his wrathful aspect, who is also associated with beer. Jyapu women have an affinity with Hariti, the Buddhist goddess of smallpox, who has power over young children, so they act as midwives.

On the city's outskirts, the low castes, by performing unclean tasks such as butchery or drum making, or conducting death rituals, absorb pollution on behalf of the community, allowing the high castes to stay pure. The edges of the mandala, or the areas beyond the ordered life of the city, are the land of the dead. Butchers are permitted to live just inside the gates but the lowest, most impure people, the Pode sweepers'

[8] 'Adya mahadana' ('And now the great gift') cited by David Gellner, Monk, Householder and Tantric Priest. p. 191.

caste, who shovel shit, must live outside, where the demons and the witches also live, and where the ghosts are most numerous among the rice fields. They are the receptacles of all the bad omens, of all the pollution, degradation and filth of the city, and their affinities are with the lower and more dreadful spirits. The cremation grounds are near their homes, each associated with a Mother Goddess to whom the Pode act as priests. The goddesses receive blood sacrifices and offerings of alcohol. Just as the Brahmin priests of the high gods are themselves high and pure, so the untouchables can have great and frightening powers, like the blood-drinking divinities to whom they minister.

In the wilds around the edge of the mandala there is a ring of skulls. The mandala is more than a map of the city. It is a social and political ideology, a description of the order of the universe, which is repeated in a well-ordered city here on earth.

POEMS

Itisha Giri

Itisha Giri is a Nepali writer based in Kathmandu. Her poems have been published in *La.Lit* and she works freelance as an editor.

I HAVE CREATED

I have created –
a country for you where your fractured self
lives by multiple names –
and no pen can pin you down to be the one that
belongs to someone else.

I have created –
a land for you that is yours
to dig deep for roots
that give life to the blood
running through the many layers of you.

I have created –
a town for you where you can walk
hand in hand, coupled together
in your fits of desire.

I have created –
a womb where your tiny apparitions
float on their backs until you flip them over–
into your salty embrace and
you both come up for air.

BUILDING HOUSES

Drive a stake through the heart of the city,
squeeze a square outwards –
thrusts a spike upwards
and own what lies beneath.
Bury the land's history, its muffled screams,
with layers of concrete,
uproot the trees that line your claim
and replace them with steel grilles
tied together with plastic tendrils.
Lays the bricks –
one on top of the other
one floor at a time, upwards
and then stare down at me.
Hammer those nails of lead,
first into the door hinges,
and then into my head,
every thud, thud, thud,
a cerebral point you make
of desires that have turned into needs –
as I feel my insides rattle,
on your cement conveyor belts.

WHEN I HAVE A DAUGHTER

When I have a daughter,
I will pinch her every day so her skin turns to rhino hide –
so she feels no pain when cornered by a stranger's hand at play.

When I have a daughter,
I will lash her with my tongue –
so she is ready for it when someone else calls her names.

When I have a daughter,
I will cover her room with a thousand, wide-open cutout eyes –
so she is used to someone else's stare.

When I have a daughter,
I will teach her to disappear into thin air, like a ninja –
so she is never in the wrong place, at the wrong time.

When I have a daughter,
I will teach her of lust and of pleasure –
so she never feels any shame.

When I have a daughter,
I will bathe her in milk tinged with acid every day,
so when someone decides to attack her,
like a snake charmer, she is immune to the venom and its decay.

ZEBRA CROSSING

I don't care for zebra crossings,
nobody does, in a poor country.
Everybody just wants to cross,
whenever and wherever.
Everybody wants to get to the other side,
of all that needs to be left behind.

Things were different when I was small,
I cared for the Scouts and their badges,
I cared so much that one day, the whole day,
in my pleated skirt and my feathered hat,
I asked people,
to use the zebra crossing.

HOME

On the streets of Brick Lane
with a sting in my eyes
and a spring in my step
I smelled fevered hay
smoked under the sun of *Bastipur*.

In the shop on Drummond Street,
my grandma's kitchen unravelled itself.
The tiny corner in *Muzaffarpur*,
where eggplants the size of my thumb
played touch and go with mustard seeds.

The officer's quarter in *Begusarai*
next to the canal, turned to Camden in my mind
as in front of me
the red water snakes glided along,
keeping time like the N29.

In a courtyard in Spain,
under the shadow of the *Caracoles*
a lemon tree interrupted
the spread of concrete under my feet,
and I was once again in *Bastipur* where
a blood-splattered goat
flapped around headless as I squinted away its pain.

These places from my past,
are now difficult to tell apart.
When I'm asked to pick one as my own,
or choose one to be the truth I know,
I hide inside the hardened shell on my back,
made from a wet paste of my crushed bones,
and like a snail,
I feel
at last, at home.

CRACKED EARTH

Niranjan Kunwar

Niranjan Kunwar is a Nepali author, educator and assistant editor at *La.it*. He returned to Nepal in 2013 after living in the United States, mainly in New York City where he completed a Masters in Childhood Education. Niranjan worked as a teacher in two different private schools in Manhattan. He now works as an independent Education Consultant in Kathmandu and enjoys participating in meaningful projects that involve collaboration with other educators, teachers and students, as well as writing. After the April 25 Nepal earthquake, Niranjan joined hands with a few friends and coordinated relief missions for six weeks from a bed and breakfast in Sanepa called The Yellow House. *Cracked Earth* was written during this time and first published by *lalitmag.com* on May 10, two days before the second quake. Apart from *La.Lit*, his writing has appeared in *Himal Southasian*, *The Kathmandu Post*, *The Huffington Post*, *Record Nepal* and *ECS Media*.

The Saturday evening a week after the earthquake was stunning. I happened to walk out of the Yellow House in Sanepa right after sunset, during that short period when the sky was still glowing with various hues of copper-red while clusters of houses beyond the Ring Road were starting to shimmer, getting ready for night. Standing by the roadside, I gazed at the distance for a few moments. An orange halo surrounded Kirtipur; its outer edges seamlessly faded and dissolved into the rapidly darkening sky. A bit later, while eating *bara* with friends at a restaurant's front yard, I noticed the moon – almost full, radiating lucid, white light – a strange juxtaposition to the calamity that had befallen us.

The calm, quiet beauty was unsettling.

After dinner, I took a taxi to the flat I was renting near Patan Dhoka.

I had not slept there since the quake, living instead out of a backpack, stuffed with an assortment of things – laptop, chargers, pajamas, T-shirts, granola bars, toothpaste, three sets of underwear and socks, a notebook, a water bottle and an umbrella. The times I sneaked in to change clothes and shower, I was scared. The crows in the garden squawked, perhaps warning us of another catastrophe. The tremors and the jolts have been continuous.

On that moonlit Saturday night, I walked up to the third floor, realizing that the fear had evaporated. Perhaps because an engineer had inspected the building earlier that day. So I permitted myself to return to normalcy. Would things ever be normal again though?

As I pulled dirty clothes out of the backpack, my mind automatically ran through the week – where I'd slept, who I'd met. What exactly had happened?

The night of the quake, that other Saturday, seemed endless. The aftershocks kept coming. A friend had put together some pasta and noodles. But I had no appetite.

Sunday – sleeping with my family in the living room – provided comfort.

I walked a lot on Monday. All the way from Baneshwar, through Sankhamul, and up the alleys of Patan. I paused briefly in front of the gray debris of the Radha Krishna temple in Swotha and walked over to the Durbar Square. Locals were barring onlookers from entering, so I briskly made my way through narrow alleys to my flat.

For a while, it was difficult to figure out where to go, what to do. I made some coffee while the phone charged. The crows were particularly noisy. Donating blood seemed like a good idea. So I strode towards Patan hospital, went to the lab, lay down and watched a small plastic bag gradually fill with my dark red blood. A couple of hours later, I met friends at the Yellow House to start an earthquake relief initiative. In the evening, I tagged along with old friends to their place in Khumaltar. I slept well that night.

The rest of the week was exhausting. We stationed ourselves at the Yellow House from eight to eight and mobilized volunteers to go to Kathmandu's outskirts on relief missions. The nights were blurry, sleep punctuated by fitful moments of wakefulness.

I can't account for Thursday night. Where had I slept? It had to be one of three places, but my mind was a blank. In any case, it didn't matter. I'm one of the lucky ones. That's one thing I have been telling myself a lot these past few days. One thing that has been clear.

Yes, I'm one of the lucky ones, part of the crew who are still living, left to witness. "The dead had it easy," a villager in Sindhupalchowk told a friend. "I thought I was gone too," this guy had said. "But, here I am, still living."

Yes, we are the lucky ones. We are the survivors, shaken but determined to rise. We are also the privileged ones. No one, not a single person in my circle has even been injured. It was only on Friday night that I heard about an acquaintance who had been trapped under the rubble in Patan Durbar Square and is now recovering in a hospital. A few friends, living in high-rises, will have to find new apartments. But they will manage. The suffering after the earthquake is directly related to class and wealth. The rich are mostly fine; the poor are either dead or devastated.

So what do the living do? What do we do? What did you do during the days after the quake? I know that some of us surrounded ourselves with friends, had meetings, made haphazard plans, tried to figure out what the government was doing, how soon the aid would arrive. We tried to figure out who was doing what.

The government was initially absent. When it emerged, it sent out mixed messages. Soon, what everyone knew became validated by its response. The Nepali government neither has the capacity nor the mechanisms to cope with a disaster of this scale. Worse, it didn't even have the imagination to plan and respond. They say power corrupts. But it became clear that the powerful are also less empathetic. No one is surprised.

I still believe that we are all doing what we can. Some people are brave and generous, some are lazy and stupid. What makes matters complicated, in times of crisis, is when stupid people act brave and smart ones get lazy. This is only one of many challenges that Nepal is facing now.

But some have good instincts. They think fast and quick, knowing that the able and capable ought to help the needy. I saw plenty of great examples this week. Young, dazed boys and girls from Kathmandu gathered at the Yellow House. Unprecedented numbers went out to Kavre and Nuwakot, to Sindhupalchowk and Gorkha. The earthquake has, ever so slightly, softened hard-hearted city dwellers.

Over eighty percent of houses demolished in one district? What does that even look like? What are they doing? How are they living? The young and old from Kathmandu are going out in droves, in cars, jeeps, buses, trucks and motorbikes. The folks from the city have been going to the villages.

For my part, I have not gone outside the valley yet. I have not even ventured to the old neighborhoods of Kathmandu to see the destruction. Walking through Old Patan was enough for me. But I have decided to commit my energy to volunteering for an indefinite period of time. We all do what we can. I am not going to worry about the rest. This past week has shown that every day is different. We all now know, more deeply than before, that anything can happen to anyone, anytime. We all know what it feels like when the ground shakes.

On Saturday night, in an attempt to attain normalcy, I sat at the balcony the way I used to before the quake. The view was intact. The neighbor's buildings and garden looked exactly the way they did before. One of the trees was in full spring bloom. The red flowers adorning her made her look like a young bride. The sky was clear. The temperature was mild. There was a cool, gentle breeze. This time, I wasn't all that unsettled. I felt a deep sense of gratitude for the bright red flowers and the quiet, beautiful night.

It was time to go inside and scroll through the newsfeed. I had avoided that all week. But I was curious for more information.

Within an hour, I turned into a voyeur. I watched one YouTube video after another; googled American and Indian news channels. We are all aware of the perplexing relationship between violence and entertainment. That video of a building collapsing in Bhaktapur – I watched it twice. Although saddened and shocked, I kept clicking. The unlucky ones got it bad. The screams, the fear, the dead bodies. Half-broken faces on hospital beds. Entire neighborhoods in ruins; numerous villages decimated.

Conflicting emotions, something we all have to manage. When the quake struck, even when I was under the table, listening to the rattles, feeling the banging and the thuds, I felt strong and vulnerable at the same time. One moment I thought, this is it. This is what we had been afraid of. I will get through this. And the next moment, I was worrying about my life, worrying whether the building would withstand the quake.

When we finally came out, when we looked at each other in disbelief, people holding on to friends and strangers, our faces were etched by the earthquake. That etching, that mixture of shock and fear, evolved over the hours, as more news came. When we heard of Dharahara, about Basantapur, about people dead or trapped in the rubble, our faces became canvases, outlined with thick black markers of sorrow. Grayblue brushstrokes have been improvised on our faces over the weeks, brushstrokes of confusion, of pain, of utter loss, but also of solidarity. We look at each other for signs, for clues, for something. We know that we have been marked deeply. It is not just Nepal, not just Kathmandu Valley that was struck. Each one of us, each one of us living in this country, away from this country, travelers who have passed through over the decades, people who have admired our architecture and written books about our people, each one of us, I know, during this past week and the days after, have felt, to varying degrees, a bleak, dull ache.

But we have time. We will have time to figure out what has happened, where we want to go from here. No one knows what's ahead – how the next few weeks, months and years will unfold.

A week after the earthquake, our volunteers checked in with each other. We had dived into this mission without a fully thought-out plan. When we started, it felt like there was nothing else we could be doing, should be doing. We responded to phone calls all week long, telling other volunteers to take leadership, form groups, get resources, go out, do anything they could. That was the nature of the crisis. It was not just beyond comprehension, it was beyond our means. But a week later, we found a natural closure to one chapter. It felt like we could take a breath, take care of ourselves and move on to another phase. We would continue our efforts, we decided, but perhaps with a more realistic scope. On that note, we cracked a few jokes and drank beer. Laughter helped. It felt like a perfect ending to earthquake week.

In my bedroom, I kept reading. The US Army was deploying 500 troops and aircraft to help with aid mobilization. A lot of people seemed to be doing something. We will need to pick up the pieces, but we also need to figure out what exactly we want to do with our days and weeks. Life moves inevitably ahead, a friend wrote earlier in the week. It may be helpful to step out of chaos and try to achieve some clarity. Our Facebook pages are loaded with earthquake news, photos, stories, catharsis, suggestions. Let's try to take a little break. Frantic friends from abroad, your funds have helped and we will do what we can. Try to enjoy your short spring.

I decided to close down my computer and get some sleep, a bit unsure whether I would really sleep deeply or for eight straight hours. Sure enough, my sleep broke around 4 a.m. I could feel the bed gently vibrating again. I thought the fear had evaporated. But I was wrong. Some of it had trickled inside me, reaching depths that was untouched before, just like the impending monsoon will. The rains will fall down heavy and hard, exploring fresh new paths inside our cracked earth.

RAM VHAROSH IS SEARCHING FOR HIS FACE

Shrawan Mukarung

Shrawan Mukarung is a Nepali poet and musician. He has published two collections of his poetry, the first of which was entitled *While Searching for the Country*. Mukarung is famous for his poems, such as *Bise Nagarchi Ko Bayan* and is an acclaimed Nepali writer of the new generation. He received a Moti Award from the National Youth Service in 2003.

A day in the twenty-first century
standing before the plain mirror of democracy
Ram Vharosh was suddenly devastated.

Where had Darwin's fourth face gone?
Where was the man from Earth?
In the long and deceitful journey through Time
somewhere, the face had fallen off.
Ram Vharosh was devastated.
His twin eyes afire with rage –
search the streets for his lost face.

Perhaps it is possible to find
in the distance between home and school
the lost hair-clip of a girl-child
studying in a primary school in the hills;
it is possible to find
at a rest-house, with the police, in a hospital

– or dead in a dark basement –
an elderly man lost in the vast city.
In this remote countryside swallowed by frost-wave
where does one search for a face?
But, Ram Vharosh, agitated –
marches on – in search of his lost face.

In the valleys of the Madhesh
his many urgent steps
are melting under the intense heat of his sweat
The fields and their soil where he has toiled
and his thick-clotted blood in the water
the well of his tears
make marshes from the still ponds of his struggles
The hearts that flutter repeatedly in these trees
are his –
The endless spread of the horizon of dreams
and the expansive civilization
are his –
But, no, nowhere is his lost face
In this moist countryside, like in a cursed land
the golden ears of harvest-ready paddy
sway and swagger like a new Choudhary
Mustard flowers in their ripe abundance
smile like new-minted zamindars
Far, in the distance –
Who is that, going away in a bullock cart?
Who is it?
He searched, but, no – the face isn't there
From sun up till sun down
only the bullock cart keeps rolling away, receding.

A fine day in the twenty first century
standing before the plain mirror of democracy
Ram Vharosh was suddenly devastated.

Where did I drop my face?
A face can be lost in the struggle against malaria –
he is trying to enter the thick jungles of history
A face can be lost while fighting against a flood –
He wants to interrogate the sources of
rivers and streams of the present

While subserviently massaging the flesh
of the masters, the face can drop to their backs –
He needs to talk to the masters.
While he diligently polishes shoes
the face can fall to the people's feet –
He needs to talk to the people.
Standing before the plain mirror of democracy
Ram Vharosh is searching for his lost face.

Astonishing!
They who have lived many lives as Kamaiyas
don't have their faces anymore!
Astonishing!
They who have lived many lives as Kamalaris
don't have their faces anymore!
Astonishing!
They who have lived many lives as Badinis
don't have their faces anymore!
What miracle is this?
Where have they disappeared –
the faces of my loved ones?
Ram Vharosh was astonished.

At the foothills of the Everest
are the footprints of his dense suffering
Everywhere there are
haliyas, coolies,
Everywhere there are
living metaphors for the anxious epochs

spent as serfs
But his face is nowhere –
and, he searches still for that lost face.

A day in the twenty-first century
as he stood before the plain mirror of democracy
suddenly, reflected on the mirror
he saw a faceless million more –
a million other Ram Vharosh
And, Ram Vharosh burned with agitation!

He touched the colors of Phagu
but didn't find his face in any of the colors
He drank in the colors of Maghi
but didn't find his face in any festive song
Trampling over the pride
of the mountains that touched the skies
close by –
With his pair of eyes afire with rage
Ram Vharosh –
agitated before the plain mirror of democracy –
stood before me, and said –

'O, Poet!
I've discarded your favorite poet
I've broken your favorite poet's busts
Like a scarecrow
who propped up your poet before me?
O, Poet!
The day when your poet was propped up
was the day when I lost my face
O, Poet! O, New Poet!!
Search for my lost pace in your poems
Search for it today! Search for it right now!
And I will keep your statue in my heart.'

A day in the twenty-first century
Ram Vharosh,
standing before the plain mirror of democracy
suddenly became a man!
I, the new poet –
standing behind the plain mirror of democracy –
suddenly became a statue.

THE KABHRA TREE AT THE CHAUTARI

Swopnil Smriti

Swopnil Smriti is a poet from Panchthar in eastern Nepal

Grandson – A long time ago
here was a giant Kabhra tree.

(*After resting her load of taro leaves*
Grandma started weaving the yarns of her tale)

Three long, long ropes couldn't encircle it's trunk
No mad raging storm could shake it
Neither could floods or landslides take it with them:
that giant, that Kabhra tree –
It was the *mainam* of the village life, they say
It was the *murumutsiling* of the power of the settlements

At its crown, like a bridge suspended between sky and ground
the moon would rise;
Under its shadows the farmhands measured the days
When it shed its leaves, it was Udhauli
When it grew new leaves, it was Ubhauli
They say – the ancient civilization of the locals
was all in the heart of that Kabhra tree!

Its branches spread in ten directions –
the biggest branch pointing to Phaktanglung Himal
the tangle of roots spread in seventeen directions

the thickest root turning towards Chotlung
Hand in hand, round and round, singing, Ha . . . Ha . . .
Matching step to lockstep, adorned in chyabrung,
– jumping, frolicking –
Greatest celebrations of love, under the Kabhra tree!
Grandson!
The tangle of that Kabhra's roots was fragrant with the scent of
an ancient communism
And the tops of that Kabhra was the Shangri-La empire of singing
cranes!

But, listen – Grandson!
In the Bikram Sambat year so and so – a long time ago –
And by a long time, I mean – a very, very long time ago –
Your grandfather's grandfather's grandfather saw in his dream
– *Loom! Loom! Kādyang! Kūdūngdūng . . . dūng . . . dūng . . .*
Haryākk!
A nightmare – a thunderbolt splitting the Kabhra tree!
But, when he awoke, he saw in a fork on the tree
the three-leaf sapling of a Pīpal, springing from wild-cat turd . . .

(*The breeze blows through the chautari – siririririri . . . ririri . . .*
riri . . . ri,
We – grandmother and grandson – are lost in the world of tales
Have I – as I listened to a story about a Kavra tree – turned into
one?
What did happen thereafter, Grandma? Go on!)

Ask what all didn't happen!
The Pīpal bore its roots into the Kavra
And to the Kavra came a slow death
The Pīpal grew bigger and bigger
Until one day –
the Kavra became just a hollow heart and flaky bark
Within it, the Pīpal stood with the uncontainable vitality of youth

But, even as the Pīpal trampled the Kavra under it and danced in
the breeze
the progeny of the old Kavra mistook it for a new Kavra
Listen, now – Once the old Kavra fell, they say –
the heads of young men and women also fell
the children became lifeless, like well-stitched dolls
the Mūndhūm dharma of the wise old fell –
The hearts fell and the country fell
Misery alone found birth in the village
Hunger and thirst alone found new incarnations
Once the Pīpal trampled the Kavra under it, they say –
they say that is when the culture of oppression and exploitation
began
When the yellow leaves of the Pīpal spread wide
they say this round chautari was built under it
With a grand ritual-fire and human sacrifice
And with each morning, an offering of blood
That is when it all started – they say, Grandson –
the history of envy and grudge . . .
when in the Kavra tree started the history of the Pīpal
hatred was born in the people
rage was born
war was born
. . . .
Grandson!

(*After taking a deep breath*
Grandma let her tale rest for a bit!)

The story is longer that the Tamor river
It is time to feed the hogs – let's go home!

(*It was my turn to carry the load.*
Before me, leaning on her cane, Grandma continued her story.)

Grandson! On that chautari
so many despots out for conquest
have stopped to rest
They tied their horses to Pīpal roots
and whistled their deathly calls . . .

. . . .

Grandson! On that round chautari –
no matter how long we sit to rest
we remain just as tired! . . .

. . . .

Grandson! That is the very branch
from where your great-grandfather was hanged and lanced
That is the shiny rock where
– your great-grandmother, then with child –
was picked and thrashed, picked and thrashed
until her belly tore open . . .

THE DEEPER CATASTROPHE

Shradha Ghale

Shradha Ghale is a Nepali writer and editor who lives in Kathmandu. Her writings have appeared in *The Kathmandu Post*, *Record Nepal*, *Nepali Times*, and the Indian online magazine *The Wire*. Over the past year she has been leading relief and rebuilding efforts targeted toward marginalised communities in the earthquake-affected districts of Nepal.

I first travelled to Rasuwa district some ten years ago. Just a day's drive north of Kathmandu, yet it seemed a different world altogether. High, rocky mountains and pine forests instead of gentle foothills and valleys, mani walls, chortens and Buddhist prayer flags instead of Hindu shrines and temples; elderly people who spoke their own language and greeted me with a 'tashi delek' instead of a 'namaste'; Tamang women dressed in angdung and syade and men who spoke Nepali with an accent that would invite ridicule in Kathmandu. Everything I encountered along those trails seemed new and unfamiliar, far removed from what I, with my middle class upbringing and education, had been taught to imagine as 'Nepal'. And yet this, too, was Nepal.

In this less familiar Nepal, in the upper regions of Rasuwa district lies Gre, a village that is part of Gatlang village development committee (VDC). All 166 houses in the village were destroyed when a 7.8 magnitude earthquake struck on 25 April 2015. Two people were killed. Dozens more would have died had the entire village not been gathered outside to watch an excavator pushing boulders down a ledge, a sight that offers much entertainment to people in Nepal's hill villages.

Lakpa Tamang, a 46-year-old muleteer, was not among the lucky survivors. He was with his mule in Langtang when a quake-triggered avalanche buried him along with hundreds of others, including many foreigners trekking in the region. A few weeks after the earthquake, I met Lakpa's wife Pasang Bhuti when I arrived in Gre as part of a volunteer relief group. Like everyone else, Pasang's family was living under a sheet of tarpaulin and surviving on meagre rations provided by a monastery. She only spoke Tamang, her mother tongue, and barely understood Nepali. So her young neighbour, a tenth-grade student at a school in Syafru Besi, served as our interpreter. Pasang was as traumatized by her husband's death as by the prospect of having to rear four children all by herself. The wages Lakpa earned as a muleteer were her family's main source of income. The crop they grew on their tiny piece of land was not enough to feed them for the full year.

During our conversation, Pasang asked me at least three times if I could take her youngest child, a three-year-old girl, to Kathmandu. She wanted me to place her under the care of an organization that could provide her a good education. "Kathmandu is far, you won't get to see your daughter often. Are you sure you want to send her away?" I asked. "Yes," she said, "I am helpless here. I cannot support her in any way." Next I learned that Pasang's older daughter, aged 9, had already been taken to Kathmandu by some organization. Neither Pasang nor her sons or neighbours knew its name. I was alarmed. There had been reports of child traffickers entering quake-affected villages in the guise of saviours. How could she risk sending her daughter with an organization about which she knew nothing?

"Sadly, parents here are willing to take risks," said Dawa Norching, who had been helping us with our relief work in the village. "The last thing they want is for their children's lives to resemble their own. They see no future for them in the village."

To get to Gre village from Kathmandu, we first drive for nine hours on blacktopped road and stay overnight in Syafru Besi, a starting point of the Langtang trek. Next morning we drive uphill for two hours on rough road, and then walk for about an hour. In terms of physical distance, Gre is far, but not very far, from the capital. Yet you can't but describe it as a "remote village", a term that denotes, in my mind at least, not just the physical distance from Kathmandu but also the degree of poverty and deprivation enforced by Kathmandu. It is one of those places where a Kathmandu dweller might travel as a well-meaning tourist, admiring the beauty of rural landscape, lamenting the condition of people who live there, and turning every observation into a lesson to be shared with her kind. (As it happens, there are many "remote villages" even within and right outside the Kathmandu valley, in places like South Lalitpur, Bhaktapur and Kavre.)

Most people in Gre are subsistence farmers who grow just enough crop to make ends meet. They have to walk for 2–3 hours to reach the nearest health facility. There is one school that provides education up to eighth grade. According to Dawa, the quality of education is dismal, language being one of the main problems. The few teachers employed at the school do not speak Tamang. Teaching takes place in Nepali, a language the local children can barely grasp. As a result they have to repeat the same grade for several years. Students who complete eighth grade usually try to continue school in Syafru Besi, but eventually drop out as they cannot keep up with their peers. This leaves them with little hope and low self-esteem. "If the school was any good," said Dawa, "maybe I wouldn't have dropped out after seventh grade to become a driver." He thought for a moment and added, "But maybe I would have. There was no money at home."

Things were more or less the same in the next village, Gatlang, which has the same name as the VDC of which it is a part. All the houses had been flattened by the quake. Seven people had lost their lives. For weeks after the earthquake, no relief could reach the village as landslides had blocked the roads. Now the road was open but people had yet to receive adequate help. Some locals complained that their village had been severely neglected compared to Langtang, which had received much attention in national and international media not only because it suffered terrible devastation, but also because it happened to be a popular trekking destination. "Our people have no connections in Kathmandu or abroad," lamented Ashok Tamang, who grew up in Gatlang. "Everyone is poor and illiterate. We have produced no role models. Can you imagine, not a single student who sat for the SLC board exam passed this year."

The villagers chatted with us and fed us potatoes boiled in their makeshift kitchens before lining up to collect the relief supplies. We distributed cooking pots and some water supply pipes, essentials they lacked even in the best of times, and for which they would have queued up even if there had been no earthquake. Their weathered hands and faces spoke of years of unrelenting hardship and deprivation. They had suffered the impact of a catastrophe far deeper than a sudden tremor of the earth: a history of systematic exclusion and exploitation.

Few other communities suffered as directly at the hands of Nepal's ruling class as the Tamang people from the villages now ravaged by the earthquake. For centuries after the creation of the modern Nepali state in 1769, the Tamang were virtually enslaved by Kathmandu's high-caste rulers. In their valuable study of the Tamang of central Nepal, David Holmberg and Kathryn March have shown how the Tamang people in present-day Rasuwa, Nuwakot and Dhading – some of the districts worst affected by the quake – were compelled to work as lab-ourers for the ruling elite during the Rana regime (1846–1950). The Tamang, classified as "enslaveable alcohol drinkers" in the 1854 civil code, had to collect fodder for royal herding operations; walk for sev-eral days to carry dairy products to Kathmandu; work at royal fruit plantations around Trishuli; grind charcoal at the gunpowder factory in Nuwakot; produce paper for the administration; and serve as porters for the military and civil administrations as and when needed. Not only were these workers unpaid, they even had to carry their own rations. Meanwhile, they were forbidden from collecting firewood for them-selves or grazing their cattle on land controlled by the royal herding operation. If a Tamang family's cow strayed into the royal pasture, the high-caste authorities would beat the owner, not the 'sacred' cow.

Further, high-caste people who migrated into the Tamang heart-land used deceit and unscrupulous lending practices to dispossess the indigenous Tamang of fertile fields. As Holmberg and March write, "Almost all Tamang have direct experience – if not in their own lives in the lives of their kin – of the appropriation of land through the manip-ulation of writing related to land."[1] The descendants of Ranas continue to own large tracts of land in Rasuwa. Locals still remember the late

---

[1] David Holmberg and Kathryn March with Suryaman Tamang, "Local Production/ Local Knowledge: Forced Labour from Below", *Studies in Nepali History and Society*, Vol. 4, No. 1, June 1999, pp. 5–64.

Sachit Shamsher Jung Bahadur Rana, former army chief and advisor to the king, as the wealthy owner of the apple orchards in Gatlang. Another Rana family is said to own vast stretches of land in Dandagaun.

The end of Rana rule did not mean an end to the oppression of the Tamang. Acts of resistance by the Tamang were met with violent state repression. In 1959, when the Tamang of the aforementioned areas rebelled against exploitative Brahmin moneylenders in their villages, King Mahendra's troops swept into the area to reassert order. Many were arrested and beaten; others were summarily executed.[2] Over the past half century, Nepal has witnessed three major waves of democracy, including an armed communist movement, but the situation of the Tamang has changed little.

The Tamang community of Yarsa was among those exploited and forced into poverty. Yarsa VDC, which lies on the eastern side of the Trishuli River, was an area in which the Ranas ran their herding operation. Until a few years ago, Yarsa was inaccessible by road. A rough gravel road now connects the VDC to the highway, but due to lack of public transport, locals still have to trek long distances to get to the nearest health facility or market. Throughout the bumpy four-hour ride from Syaubari through Yarsa, we did not come across a single vehicle; only locals bent double under the loads on their backs. The earthquake and aftershocks had left parts of Yarsa extremely vulnerable to landslides. The entire community of Ghormu village had been displaced. Many cracked and unstable hillsides were likely come down in the monsoon rain. Villagers who came to collect relief supplies had to walk, sometimes for up to five hours, past such dangerous hillsides.

Denied basic rights and opportunities in their country, most young people of Yarsa have no choice but to seek employment abroad. A large number of young women from Yarsa are working as domestic help in Kuwait and Lebanon. Men mostly work as labour migrants in Malaysia.

"The factory job was tough, but at least I was earning something," said Gore Ghale, a father of four small children. After years of trying his luck, Gore finally found a job last year in an iron factory in Malaysia. He took a loan at thirty-six percent interest from a neighbour

---

[2] David Holmberg. "Violence, Non-violence, Sacrifice, Rebellion, and the State", *Studies in Nepali History and Society*, Vol. 11, No. 1, June 2006, pp. 35–64.

to bear the cost of travel, recruitment agency fees and initial expenses at his destination. But a month after he started working, he sustained a serious head injury on the job and had to be hospitalized for three weeks. After a long recovery process, Gore finally resumed work and was beginning to hope for a better life for his family when he heard about the earthquake. He rushed back home in a state of panic and anxiety. All the houses in the village including his had been destroyed. Nine people had lost their lives, including his wife, who was buried by a quake-triggered landslide when she was collecting firewood in the forest. Dazed and distraught, Gore was now living under a tarpaulin sheet with his children. If he returned to Malaysia, there would be no one to look after his children; his youngest was only three years old. If he stayed back, he would neither be able to support them nor pay off his loans. "If only," he said, hesitant to make a direct request, "if only someone would help send my kids to a good school."

Ashok Tamang, who had been helping us with relief work, was the most educated member of his community in Gatlang. He was, in his own words, "I.A.-failed, meaning, he passed the tenth grade board exam but could not make it through twelfth grade. He was among those who had been working round the clock to bring relief into his home area – coordinating with relief organizations and groups, preparing lists of households, assessing people's needs, mediating potential conflicts, orienting Kathmandu visitors with local social and political dynamics, and ensuring that relief is distributed in an organized and equitable manner. But he did not have a stable source of income. He had tried his luck at various organizations that ran development projects in Rasuwa, but to no avail. He lived in the village, spoke the local language, knew his people and was deeply committed to improving their lives, but was not "qualified" enough to work in organizations that boasted of their "bottom-up" approach. If he got very lucky, he would be hired as a local "social mobilizer" for a few months. A stable, full-time job perennially remained a distant goal.

In every affected village I visited, I met young people like Ashok who had played an indispensable role in ensuring their communities' survival in the aftermath of the earthquake. Youth who had been working in extremely challenging conditions, despite personal losses, amid immense physical risks, without any material reward. They have intimate knowledge of their place and people and tremendous potential to bring change in their villages. But they have little formal education, cannot speak English, and have no access to networks of power in Kathmandu. This leaves them with very few avenues of personal development. Those fortunate enough to get an NGO job are usually at the bottom of the aid system's hierarchy, a mere "local" with no authority to shape the organization's programmes and policies.

One way such youth might hope to expand their network and gain access to power is by becoming a member of a political party. Most of the local volunteers I met on the ground were members of one of the major political parties. We realized only later that the young people who had been helping us reach the most vulnerable populations of Rasuwa were all members of the Unified Communist Party of Nepal (Maoist). They had kept silent about their affiliation for two reasons. First, most of them had thrown themselves into rescue and relief work out of genuine concern for their community, not out of a desire to raise their party's profile. Second, they knew we belonged to the class of people who consider themselves to be above narrow political interests, and so they assumed we would be squeamish about associating with the rank-and-file members of a political party.

The "locals" are understandably wary of displeasing visitors from Kathmandu. Even the most naïve among us are in a position to question, correct, interrogate or repudiate them according to our assumptions. Stressing the importance of localised radicalism, historian David Ludden has observed how every nation has an imperial history and retains "imperial inequalities" between its elites at the centre and people at the periphery.[3] Such inequalities become evident even during a casual interaction between, say, a Kathmandu-based development professional and "field staff". Those from the "centre" will assess, evaluate and decide while the latter will listen, oblige, call them "sir" or "madam", and earn ten times less. These inequalities, so entrenched in Nepal's development aid world, were reenacted during relief work in the quake-affected

---

[3] David Ludden, "Where is the Revolution?: Towards a Post-National Politics of Social Justice", *The Mahesh Chandra Lecture*, Social Science Baha, 2008.

villages. While Kathmandu dwellers saw their relief trips as noble and intrepid missions to disaster zones, for most people in the affected villages, coming to others' aid was almost like reflex action. In the face of such catastrophe, helping their community was the only thing to do. No photos of them handing out bags of rice and tarpaulin sheets on social media, no fulsome praise for being disaster heroes. An implicit assumption was that youth like Ashok were just doing their duty while youth from Kathmandu, like myself, were venturing out of our comfort zones in a spirit of magnanimity.

After exploring various ways to support Pasang Bhuti's daughter, I found a safe and trusted children's home in Kathmandu with an excellent track record. The home usually took children who had lost both parents, but this time they were willing to make an exception. On learning that Pasang's daughter might be able to go to school in Kathmandu, several more parents sent me similar requests from the village. I could not help them. In fact, despite all my efforts, I could not even bring Pasang's daughter to Kathmandu. The local volunteers spent weeks gathering required paperwork from Pasang's family and the ward administration office. But just when we thought everything was ready, the District Child Welfare Board refused to issue a permit for the child to leave the village, citing cases of rampant child trafficking. Another child we had identified for admission to the orphanage was Asmita Chepang from Dhading district. Her house was completely destroyed by the quake. Her father died many years ago and her mother had left the family and married someone else. Asmita's sole guardian was her ailing grandmother, who sold cucumber slices to passengers on the highway and was desperate to find a sponsor for her grandchild. But due to travel restrictions imposed by the government, Asmita could not leave the village.

There was no question that the government had to make every effort to prevent trafficking of vulnerable children. But were blanket restrictions an adequate solution? What would happen to those children after they were protected from the hands of traffickers? Had the government done anything to safeguard their future, or to ensure that mothers were not desperate enough to give their children away? Far from it. Four months had passed since the earthquake struck. Nearly 5000 schools in the affected districts had been completely destroyed. Amid all the noise about 'reconstruction', the government had not even started building temporary classrooms in many remote areas.

One example was Alampu VDC in Dolakha district, epicentre of the 7.3 magnitude earthquake that struck two weeks after April's massive quake. Alampu's population is almost entirely Thami, an indigenous ethnic group that has historically suffered from problems common to many indigenous communities – economic deprivation, illiteracy, cultural discrimination, appropriation of land by high-caste groups, heavy debt, and alcoholism. Men in the village mostly work as migrant labourers in Malaysia and the Gulf countries. The women are left to shoulder all the household responsibilities and the burden of debt.

The quake had destroyed all 685 houses in Alampu as well as the three public schools and the micro hydro station that supplied electricity to the village. To collect relief, villagers had to walk down to Babare, spend the night crammed together under a tarpaulin sheet, and then trek back next day along precipitous trails with loads of supplies on their backs. It was a long, perilous journey. The tremors had formed deep cracks in the hills, and in several places, survivors returning with relief had been wounded or killed in landslides. Those carrying corrugated iron sheets for roofing had sustained serious injuries when the sharp-edged sheets slid down their backs and cut their legs. On 4 July 2015, a woman who was returning with roofing sheets to build a temporary shelter fell ill on the road and died soon after reaching home. Her husband, a wageworker, has been mentally unstable since and her seven children have been left in the lurch.

Four months after the earthquake, children of Alampu still had no idea when classes would resume. The micro hydro plant lay broken and people were living in darkness. The government, which had been amassing billions of dollars from foreign donors for post-quake reconstruction, had virtually no presence in Alampu. The VDC secretary lived in the district capital Charikot and had little clue about what went on in the village. The chief district officer, a Brahmin man now replaced by another Brahmin man, was known to be irresponsible and apathetic. According to Bikesh Thami, a local of Alampu and president of Thami Youth Association of Nepal, almost all the relief that came into the village was provided by non-governmental organizations and volunteer groups. Bikesh and his friends were now hustling around in Kathmandu in search of private donors willing to help rebuild vital infrastructure: schools, toilets, the micro hydro plant and drinking water reservoir. Needless to say, rebuilding such essential public facilities should have been the government's top priority. "But we can't rely on this government," said Bikesh. "I know they have collected lots of money for reconstruction, but who knows when it'll reach the victims."

For the poor and marginalized survivors, it is a battle even to be recognized as victims. They have little information or access to government bodies, which are dominated by high-caste men. They cannot forcefully articulate their needs in Nepali or navigate the bureaucratic maze. Many are still struggling to obtain the "earthquake victim identity card" without which they will not get relief or compensation from the government. In Bhorle VDC of Rasuwa district, at least 23 families who became homeless after the disaster had yet to be officially recognized as victims even four months after the earthquake. They had not even received the small cash grant that the government had pledged for building temporary shelters. Meanwhile two temporary residents of Rasuwa with houses in other districts had each obtained a victim identity card that entitled them to full compensation. One was section officer at the district development committee (DDC) and the other secretary of Dhaibung VDC. Similarly a technical assistant at the Bhorle VDC office was known to have arranged a victim identity card for his son-in-law who lived in Kathmandu. The identity card was issued from an area in Dhaibung where the officer's wife was chairperson of the Ward Citizens' Forum. What was more, his nephew was a computer operator at the DDC office. It was not a mere coincidence that the well-placed individuals in that advantageous network all belonged to the high-caste group. This in a district where more than 80 percent of the population is Tamang.

A large body of disaster literature has amply shown that vulnerability is closely linked to race, class and ethnic inequalities. Unsurprisingly, more than 60 percent of the earthquake victims in Nepal were from marginalized ethnic groups.[4] Although obvious to anyone travelling in the affected districts, this observation was not made openly in the days following the earthquake. A different narrative had taken hold at the time. For instance, at a meeting of former bureaucrats held soon after the earthquake, one speaker stressed that Nepalis were helping their fellow citizens "out of a feeling of humanity, irrespective of caste or ethnicity". This, he said, had discredited those who claim that our society suffers from caste and ethnic problems. The high-caste bureaucrat saw no irony in the fact that he was making that statement in a room full of former bureaucrats, all of whom belonged to his caste.

Many others would voice similar sentiments in the coming weeks. "The crisis has united us all"; "The youth have shown we are first and foremost Nepalis"; "A new civil society is in the making"; "We will rise and rebuild the nation". There was no dearth of commentaries applauding the resilience of the Nepali people. For some time the chaos bred heady optimism among the least affected. While the relief initiatives of Kathmandu's young volunteers were undoubtedly necessary and commendable, the self-congratulatory optimism also allowed many to preempt any questions about the deeper causes of the tragedy. The disaster was seen as entirely natural and inevitable, shorn of its social and political meaning. It was only after the initial excitement subsided that we started pointing out some fundamental features of the catastrophe. Kathmandu had not been "flattened" as some reports in the international media suggested. Districts outside the capital had suffered much more. Both in and outside Kathmandu, the hardest hit were the poor who could not afford strong houses. More women died than men. Dalits were among the worst hit in areas with mixed populations. An overwhelming majority of the victims belonged to the Tamang community.

A week after the earthquake, we raised some funds from friends and family and made our first relief trip to Sindhupalchowk, the district that suffered massive destruction and the highest number of casualties. On arriving at our destination in Badegaun VDC, we realized that the population in the village was predominantly Brahmin and Chhetri, with a few Dalits who lived in a separate settlement. All of the 165 houses in

---

[4] 'The Tamang Epicentre'. *Nepali Times*. Issue No. 776, 10–16 July 2015.

the village had been destroyed. At least 19 people were killed, mostly women (two of whom were pregnant) and children. There were parents who had lost their children, a man who had lost his wife who was almost due to give birth, and others whose elderly parents were killed. Families huddled under the open sky next to their collapsed houses. Their livestock had been buried and there was a stench of death in the air. The body of a ten-year-old Dalit girl had yet to be recovered, and her father's hands were bruised from digging through rubble for days.

Naturally, in the face of such indiscriminate suffering, the last thing on our minds was the caste or ethnic identity of the victims. It did not occur to us that the chain of contacts that had led us to the village, as well as the locals who were coordinating the distribution were all Brahmin men. Educated and articulate men dedicated to their community; it was thanks to them that the distribution went so smoothly. No tensions arose; everyone seemed satisfied. Relieved, we were on our way back when we ran into some angry locals from a village further up. They were all Tamang. They had seen our supplies trucks and were hoping to get some of the rations. "No one has brought us anything," they complained. "These Brahmins are clever and know how to get relief. We heard the government is sending them food supplies. If this goes on, we'll have no option but to seize the supplies."

After we returned to Kathmandu, we received a number of calls requesting support for Sindhupalchowk, each from a high-caste person. This was somewhat disconcerting. More than 3500 people had lost their lives in that district; nearly half of them belonged to the Tamang community. How could we ensure that our support reached the most vulnerable communities – those who lived higher up in the hills, far from the road and the gaze of media, without access to information, support networks, or connections in Kathmandu? We had to be more rigorous in our search, less willing to take things at face value.

In the following weeks, we visited several affected communities that have always been far removed from access to power and resources. Dalits of Rakathum, Ramechhap, who were hesitant to come down to the distribution point because crossing the river on a rafting boat would cost them 50 rupees each way; landless Dalits of Kafalsanghara, Nuwakot, who were already struggling for daily survival and burdened with loans taken from high-caste families when the quake destroyed their huts; Majhi families of Sukhajot, Ramechhap, whose traditional livelihood, i.e. fishing, is increasingly threatened by anti-poor conservation policies; Tamang families of Thuman and Chilime VDCs in Rasuwa, who would walk for 3–4 hours each way in the scorching sun to collect rations that would barely last them two weeks; Tamang people of Haku, Rasuwa, whose entire village was swept away by a landslide and who were now being shunted from one temporary camp to another because private landowners could only allow them on their land for so long. In short, people whose vulnerability to disaster is inextricably linked to decades of exclusion and whose path to recovery is going to be painfully slow and difficult.

"Relief worth millions of rupees is sitting at Kathmandu airport while our people are hungry, homeless and sick," said Prem Tamang, a member of the constituent assembly (CA) between 2008 and 2012. "But we can't bring those supplies to our villages unless home minister Bamdev Gautam is sufficiently appeased." A small, soft-spoken young man with incredible drive and an unfaltering commitment to his people, Prem had been leading relief efforts in the most hard-to-reach areas of his home district Rasuwa. The government's inept response to the disaster did not surprise him. After all, most of the authorities coordinating rescue and relief could not even understand the accent of the local people, let alone their problems.

14 out of the 18 VDCs in Rasuwa are principally inhabited by the Tamang; three have mixed populations; and in one, the population is predominantly Gurung. But the current CA member representing Rasuwa, the newly appointed chief district officer, and the outgoing one are all Brahmin men.

Things were never different. Even if a Tamang reaches a decision-making post against all odds, he has to struggle to fit in a system dominated by high-caste men. Kulman Ghising, former managing director of Chilime Hydropower Company, is one example. The 22 Megawatt Chilime hydropower project supplies electricity to the national grid and is based in Chilime VDC, Rasuwa. One of the few Tamangs to reach the top position in the company, Kulman had played a key role in ensuring that the local community had 10 percent of shares in the hydropower project. During his tenure he had also created employment opportunities for the locals and initiated socioeconomic development activities in the project areas. He was thus a well-liked and respected figure among the locals of Rasuwa. But immediately after the November 2013 election to the constituent assembly, the newly elected CA member from Rasuwa and other Brahmin political leaders are known to have lobbied the energy minister and home minister to remove Kulman from the post. He was sacked soon after, in July 2014. Locals of Rasuwa, members of the Nepal Electricity Authority's trade union, and members of different political parties launched massive protests demanding Kulman's reinstatement, but in vain. The government cited the end of his tenure as a reason for his dismissal. But Prem and other locals assert that he was removed to serve the vested interests of the water mafia, commission agents and powerful shareholders, who had long felt threatened by his sympathetic relationship with the indigenous locals of Rasuwa.

"Why do you think the Tamang are so poor despite living in an area so rich in natural resources?" Prem asked. "Development mostly comes to us in the form of extraction. The Chilime hydro project makes a profit of hundreds of millions of rupees each year. This year the project made a profit of 850 million rupees, but less than 3 percent of that amount was allocated for the district. The profit is made at the cost of local resources and environment. So how do you justify the local community receiving such a negligible fraction?"

Another example he cited was Langtang National Park, which was declared a protected area in the 1970s by the former royal elite. Indigenous locals within the park area have suffered enormously since the park was established, especially during the first two decades. Their daily livelihood practices – collecting forest resources, grazing and swidden agriculture – were criminalized in the name of conservation. Wild animals from the park destroyed their crops and threatened their survival but they could neither hurt the animals nor seek redress from park authorities. They were routinely harassed, arrested and fined. Despite the creation of a buffer zone in 1998, the heavily militarized park area continues to arouse resentment among locals. Forest use is still severely restricted.

Local participation in park management amounts to tokenism. And the unequal power relations between the park authorities and the indigenous population remain unchanged.

Excluded and impoverished for too long, the Tamang cannot even benefit from the developments now taking place around them. For instance, the Rasuwagadhi transit route opened in 2014 to boost cross border trade between Nepal and China. Locals of Rasuwa can even obtain a special permit to travel across the Tibetan border to Kyirong bazaar. But it is outsiders who have gained the most from this opening, not the indigenous Tamang, who lack the social and economic means to start a profitable business. Many of them serve as porters for high-caste and Newar businessmen, carrying their merchandise for wages.

The development ventures in Rasuwa have thus largely failed to improve the lives of the indigenous population. Due to poverty, illiteracy and lack of access to state institutions, the Tamang cannot compete with outsiders in benefiting from these "enclave developments", to use anthropologist Ben Campbell's phrase. As Campbell has shown, the steady institutional growth of Dhunche, the district capital, has in many ways further weakened the economic potential of Tamang villagers, subjecting their small-scale enterprises to new regulations and criminalizing their traditional livelihood practices, such as making homebrew alcohol, cutting timber and fuelwood, and slaughtering female buffaloes.[5] Further, he writes: "If any unity of reason is to be found in these diverse developments it is perhaps most evident in the multiple roles of the military at the periphery."[6] The police and army check posts along the Pasang Lhamu highway, the army base at Dhunche, army patrol squads in Langtang National Park, the army base at Rasuwagadhi – the Nepali state may be apathetic to the needs of indigenous people but it can deploy enough armed troops to make them behave.

"That is precisely why we have been demanding federalism that recognizes our identity," said Prem. And he is not alone in expressing this demand. For the past decade, marginalized groups in Nepal have

[5] Ben Campbell, "Heavy Loads of Tamang Identity" in *Nationalism and Ethnicity in Nepal,* eds. David N. Gellner et al. Vajra Publications, 2008, p. 220.
[6] Ben Campbell. *Living Between Juniper and Palm: Nature, Culture and Power in the Himalayas,* Oxford University Press, p. 183.

been campaigning for the establishment of a federal system that grants them greater control over governance in their home areas. While federalism may not be a panacea for the embedded structural inequalities, they argue that only a federal state structure will loosen Kathmandu's stranglehold on the rest of the country and give the marginalized populations a chance to improve their economic, political and cultural life. If Rasuwa were part of a federal province with a degree of autonomy, the indigenous population would have much stronger chances of using the resources in their territory – land, river and forests – to develop their villages, create job opportunities and boost the local economy. Their children could get an education that respects their language and culture rather than one that instills shame and feelings of inadequacy. The Tamang could join local government bodies and get involved in making decisions that vitally affect their lives. They would not have to wait for Kathmandu's approval even to build a short stretch of road in their village. And in times of disaster, relief and reconstruction aid could be sent directly to the affected province instead of being stuck or stolen in Kathmandu.

Sadly, there is no sign that this vision will become reality anytime soon. The ruling parties had agreed to establish a federal system back in 2007 owing to pressure created by the decade-long Maoist rebellion and various campaigns by marginalized groups. The process of drafting a new constitution began in 2008 but dragged on for years, with high-caste political leaders gradually wresting control of it. The earthquake presented a perfect opportunity for the ruling parties to assert their will over the citizens, who seemed too traumatized and vulnerable to offer much resistance. As I write this, they are trying to ram through a new constitution that will reverse even the few gains made during the last two decades. They have agreed on a political map that delineates provincial boundaries in a way that further entrenches the power of the traditional elite. Protests have erupted across the country and the government has resorted to violence, killing several people and injuring many more. In the latest incident, six policemen were killed in west Nepal when Tharu protesters demanding a federal province turned aggressive. The Tharu are among the most disadvantaged indigenous groups in Nepal. Exploited for generations as bonded labourers, they were systematically targeted for torture, killing, rape and enforced disappearance by the state during the civil war.[7] Those opposed to Tharu demands are now burning Tharu homes, shops and radio station in retaliation. Any hopes that a new and just society might be built on the ruins of this historic disaster lie shattered, though it seems unlikely that the marginalized people will give up the fight.

---

[7] "Conflict-related Disappearances in Bardiya District", United Nations Office of the High Commissioner for Human Rights. December 2008.

POEMS 1976–2015

Wayne Amtzis

Wayne Amtzis is a photographer and writer from New York. He studied at Syracuse University and UC Berkeley before completing a Masters in creative writing at San Francisco State University. Wayne has lived and worked in Asia since 1976 and his writing has been published internationally and in Nepali translation. He has written, edited and translated several titles including *Sandcastle City/Quicksand Nation*, *Days in the Life*, *Two Sisters* and *Flatline Witness*. He lives in Kathmandu, where he teaches meditation under the guidance of Tsoknyi Rinpoche.

URNS

As he molds wet clay into water jugs
the potter spins a tire
levered into a sunken mound
at his doorstep. Beside him, his wife,
her hands weathered, purposeful,
shapes spouts, lips and handles.
Urns as wide round as a woman with child
stand in a circle radiating
out from the crouched, intent couple.
From among these, their offspring,
you choose an orphan with delicate neck.
And I another, ample and full bodied,
for storing water we will haul
from the village well. That first morning in the farmhouse
below Kopan monastery, spider-necklaces
slung across the path glistened,
draping us in a moist scented light.
The urn we set in a dark corner, ¾ full,

with a clay pot of yogurt
or a jug of fresh milk cooling within.
The orphan we later carried,
each in turn, in the crook of our arms,
along the paddy ridges,
through and around bamboo groves
back to the city. The all seeing
clear blue eyes of the Boudhanath stupa
taking us in on that moonlit
parting night

1976

WHERE PATHS CROSS

Between glint of sun and stiff-banked shadow
women quarry and haul stone. Busted rocks slung in a basket,
heads bent forward, bare feet muddied by the path,
the last and least stooped
stops to beg from those off the bus at road's end.
While the late-risen moon
sets in the west, unheeded, she follows her sisters
porting stone and baskets of wood
to the towns below. As the trail snakes lower
shedding its moods – at a mountain quarry
trees worshipped with blood;
in fields all around paddy hangs heavy with gold;
all along the way, footsteps steadfast and sure,
bamboo sways in the wind.

On the valley floor, behind a medieval town
where fields die for a cash crop of bricks
and gray towers spew smoke,
barefoot bare-chested younger brother
bears with heavy bar two bright-lipped brass urns,
well water so deep we hear each full-fathomed gasp.

Down the valley-rim road, blinding in its reach,
a deluxe bus slides by.
Those who rose to catch the sun over Everest
return from what cannot be seen
to pass what can. Back-bent men move in unison.
Wooden mallets break open the earth.

1978

RITE OF WAY

Up from Durga's Mandir,
past pigs scratching themselves on stone-faced idols,
Kathmandu rises out of a dying river.
Apartments overlook temples fallen prey to pigeons and rats.
Where footpaths and alleys stumble and sprawl,
at the foot of the full-bellied elephant god, Ganesh,
a supplicant lies submerged,
breathing mantra through a shroud of sand.
Afloat, on the raft of his ribs,
a flurry of butter-lamps rise and fall to a harmonium's
wind-sprung song. Beyond the derelict Kastamandap temple
at the city center crossroads, a trio of flute, drum and voice
celebrate an unearthing. Nudging by,
a battered old Chevy veers into the crater
where a dug-up idol lies exposed.
Pedestrians push past, oblivious to the rite interrupted
and the one taking place. Above the chasm, a tire spins,
but the feted god lies unmoved.
Confused and wary,
the out-of-place traveler leans on his horn.

1981

NOT YET THIRTEEN

Slung over shoulders, wooden signboards
shout ROMANOV VODKA. Sporting Romanov Vodka T-shirts
five young men file and weave through Kathmandu's moving
throng
A youth in jeans stops mid-street to watch them pass
Notched on his imitation leather belt
the letters: T, E, X, A, S announce a destination and life
he's keen to pursue. Straight ahead
against a wall, a pock-faced boy
kneels on the sidewalk, last in a long row of men
squatting on makeshift stools ready to polish shoes
In the stale shadows of a government building
where people line up to pay bills or make inquiries,
two young girls coil against a gate
selling cigarettes to those waiting inside
and to those passing. The oldest,
not yet thirteen, the other, maybe nine
As they lean on each other,
the youngest laughs when the Romanov Vodka boys pass
Not-yet-thirteen has forgotten how to smile
Her eyes downcast
Hidden like the darkest of moons.

1993

AT FIRST TREMOR

The slender white tower no longer dominates the square
Noodle & beer-spangled signs swim above buildings
ready to collapse at first tremor.
Anchored by rocks, headlines trip us up
Relying on rumor, steadied and assured, we pass
unscathed through the course
set on the path – of piled clothes & towels
– of men shining shoes. Where roads slightly askew

slow down the flow of man and beast,
a market meanders. In shifting sunlight,
propped up by hand & shoulder
torn shirts, bare feet, each as poor as the other,
men and boys wait for work
Trrp trrm trrp trrm A stove sputters
Its fumes laced into a murky pool of tea & milk *Hissstrrmm*
hissstrrrm Nuggets collide in a roiling sea of oil
Like punctured tires, crisp misshapen hoops of dough
pile up. No one is buying *Hissstrrmm trrp trrm* . . .
Along a traceless path, farther in,
a sunken square shaded by a Bodhi tree
Smooth stone beneath bare feet.
Where bathers lean, a stone-dragon spumes
Beyond, and below civilized spur,
mud hovels rise from the garbage-banked river
claiming this city as theirs. In dust-clogged knots of sunlight,
where a man roasts peanuts,
and another dips wool into a vat of dye
a woman combs long black flowing hair
Washed & oiled, wet & free. Below,
where river once flowed, in a sea of refuse, pigs sleep
Shifting on one foot, arms apace,
a man spits out words he knows will wake them.
In that same riverbed,
midst an indifferent audience of buffaloes & pigs,
a circle of men closes in. With women among them,
a circle of men listen and rise

1995

SAND CASTLE CITY/ QUICKSAND NATION

("on the banks of the river, naked children are building houses of
sand" Sarubhakta)
Dank cries, interrupted prayer,

even the self-arisen stupa, Swayamhbu, in the Form of Light,
sinks in on itself, though resplendent,
ashamed. In the rank Kathmandu dawn
as the city-in-play aspires,
a nation-on-hold conspires. *Aspire. Conspire.*
How the currents cross!
Where hollow spires rise from makeshift foundations,
sandcastle banners lure all comers. *Get in! Get out!*
before quickening sands gulp you down.
Let storied sandman dollars float you away
– to the promised land, to the glorious Gulf, go.
Or better yet, grab a khukuri-pass to London
or a lottery ticket to ride to Queens and beyond.
From rock-scrabbled trails, with far-flung stride
to a subway straddled walk-up,
like a hawk from locked-down boarded-up villages,
glide. Then California dreaming
bide your time, safe and far from gut-wrenching tides
that turn here every day.
Sandcastle dreamer, quicksand schemer,
take a farewell glance all around
at what's been done, not done, undone –
the gone paddy, the multi-tiered warrens are no mirage.
The city's swamped in garbage, its rivers, crawls of stench.
As the tide sweeps out, Swayamhbu, its gilded light
cloaked in eye-stinging haze, sinks in on itself . . .
In incensed dawn, at every corner,
smoke coils from tires burning
and night after day, the coming age,
in the Form of Might
readies itself, fierce and unyielding,
as its devotees gather, torches in hand.

2005

NIGHT CLOSES IN

Night closes in with its breath taking grip
Night that walks in the guise of day
Light footed across the rubble morning comes
as if rising from the dead. That which came and came again
leveled a world. In that sudden tolling,
what great works were interrupted?
The beating of a heart A heart! Nine thousand hearts!
The mirrors that temper vanity lie shattered,
and multiply. See how they run
– to pixel the pain – to instant message grief
Hands set to the unremitting tasks ahead
are deeply stitched with glass, with shards of light.

For 2 days I was healthy, in touch with the earth.
All it takes to make me whole, I realized
as I turned in place: is a 7.8 shot and a 6.7 chaser.
Now the earth stills and I'm left spinning,
a partner without a dance. Eyes no longer widen
with a survivor's camaraderie and a tale in the offering
But shrink with hurt mourning the lost.
A hawk still glides. My gaze cannot pretend:
The city below, rubbled all around
is not the same. The town below is not the same
The villages below are not. And will never be.
That which came and came again
leveled a world. That which leveled a world
leveled our souls. "My village is dead"
"My village . . .
No light rises from the rubble.

2015

THE CLOUD SPAWNED SEA

Clogged and rift-threaded through cracked-heeled earth,
trespassed trails run to sky, to cloud spawned sea.
Knuckled under, no gods remain
embedded in the ruptured creviced Himals
In the disinherited valley below
no drunk-dragged chariot can haul them back.
All heave . . . thrust keened, muscle vented
to reach through prayer shouldered molder and rot
to the heaven hived core, voices
rose on city-wide wings. Two days into the 12 year cycle,
the red god's chariot[1] stands stymied,
a footnote to the gloom, inauspicious: history's tell. The *Bungamati* temple: a pile of rubble.
Like a match lit in a sunken cave
this day's quake-spied dawn
swallows its fire. The valley, a star sapphire
set in busted stone
Slipped in haste from a finger of its stunned devotees.

2015

THE STOMACH SUFFERS FROM LACK

The stomach suffers immensely
It suffers from lack. The spine bent and hobbled with hurt,
the spine that held up the stairs
and resisted the shifting walls, the spine
carries us forward, stiffened, but not broken
The hands, palms dark and swollen,
knuckles split, fretted with blood
broke our fall and drag us still from the rubble
The soles of the feet with so many years
ground into it. And the heels

---

[1] Rato Machendranath. Every 12 years the rain god is carried in his chariot from Bungamati to Lalitpur

that steady us, ridged like the bark of a tree,
Soles and heels, with the legs tireless
and drained, that sprang us free, rock us now
here where we crouch. Head in our hands,
lips broken like the earth beneath the stream
that long ago fled, and the teeth,
so few, gapped like houses that stood along the ridge,
jailors, holding back the cry
that overtakes us: the heart suffers from loss,
it suffers severely. The tongue, furtive,
caked with the stench of its own saliva, wanting
to . . . wanting to speak, and the eyes,
those darlings of life, weary from never closing,
the eyes link and sustain us
as we look to each other, and without turning
away, as we look within, lifting us,
lifting us . . .

2015

CITY ON HIS BACK

Nepal's the one
who barefoot bent and weary
waits, who barely moves,
but leans he must,
against the weight, against the road.
Nepal's the one
who at your beck and call
heaves the city on his back,
who swallows sweat, breathes fumes,
whose breath's gone,
who puts off death by drawing from the end
in days, in pennies gained,
who asks why one man crouches
and one man sprawls,

why one man hauls the city on his back,
and another rides, that city rising all around.
Nepal's the one against the wall,
whose blood's thin, whose chest caves in,
who being who he is, can't go on . . .
Goes on

2015

EXTENDED COPYRIGHT

Ed Douglas: *Chomolungma Sings the Blues*
© Ed Douglas 1997, 2001. First published in the UK by Constable and Company Ltd, 1997. Paperback edition published by Robinson, an imprint of Constable and Robinson, 2001. This excerpt reprinted by permission of Little, Brown.

Jon Krakauer: *Into Thin Air*
© Jon Krakauer 1997, 2000. First published in the UK in 1997 by Macmillan. This edition published in 2011 by Pan Books, an imprint of Pan Macmillan. This excerpt reprinted by permission of Penguin Random House and Pan Macmillan.

Khagendra Sangroula: *Music of the Fireflies*
© Khagendra Sangroula and Prawin Adhikari, 2015. Translated by Prawin Adhikari. Printed by permission of the author and translator.

Manjushree Thapa: *The Tutor of History*
© Manjushree Thapa, 2001. Published by Penguin India, 2001. This excerpt reproduced by permission of Penguin India and Aleph Book Company.

Maya Thakuri: *Trap*
From *Secret Places: New Writing from Nepal*. Edited by Frank Stewart, Samrat Upadhyay and Manjushree Thapa. © University of Hawaii Press, 2001. Published by Manoa Journal, University of Hawaii Press. Translated by Manjushree Thapa. Reprinted by permission of the translator and editors, and by permission of The Printhouse.

Dhruba Sapkota: *The Scream*
From *Secret Places: New Writing from Nepal*. Edited by Frank Stewart, Samrat Upadhyay and Manjushree Thapa. © University of